DUN & BRADSTREET

GUIDE TO
$YOUR INVESTMENTS$®: 1994

NANCY DUNNAN

HarperPerennial
A Division of HarperCollins*Publishers*

Dedication: To Doctors Jay Cooper, Mark Persky and Alan Steinfeld of the N.Y. University Medical Center, for their extraordinary expertise and kindness.

Grateful acknowledgment is made for permission to reprint:

"Calculating Growth Rates" table from *Security Analysis,* Fourth Edition, by Benjamin Graham et al. Copyright © 1962 by McGraw-Hill, Inc. Reprinted by permission of McGraw-Hill, Inc.

Material from *Donoghue's Moneyletter*, *Donoghue's Money Fund Report*, and *The Treasury Manager* reprinted by permission of The Donoghue Organization, Inc., Holliston, MA 01746.

"Top Performers" table reprinted by permission of *The Hulbert Financial Digest*, 643 South Carolina Avenue SE, Washington, DC 20003.

"Dun & Bradstreet" is a registered trademark of The Dun & Bradstreet Corporation and is used under license. The title *$Your Investments$*® is a registered trademark of HarperCollins Publishers, Inc.

Designer: Gayle Jaeger

ISSN   73-18050
ISBN   0-06-271539-9
ISBN   0-06-273120-3 (pbk.)

CONTENTS

Acknowledgments

ONE   GETTING STARTED ON YOUR INVESTMENT PORTFOLIO   1

      Introduction   1
1   Special Advice for 1994   6
2   Building Your Own Investment Pyramid   14
3   Finding Safe Places for Your Money: Banks, Money Market Funds, CDs, and
      Credit Unions   23
4   Protecting All Your Investments   39
5   Moving from Saver to Investor   51
6   Investing with Mutual Funds   69
7   Using Closed-End Funds   94

      THE INVESTOR'S ALMANAC   100–107
      Antique Fishing Lures   102
      Stickley Furniture   103
      Oriental Rugs   105

TWO   WHEN THE BEARS ARE OUT OF THE CAVE   109

8   Bond Basics: How Corporate Bonds Work   110
9   U.S. Treasuries: Bills, Notes, Bonds, and EE's   121
10   Convertibles: Income Plus Appreciation   130
11   Municipal Bonds: Last of the Tax Shelters   135
12   Nontraditional Bonds: Maes, Junk, and Zeros   143

THREE   WHEN THE BULLS ARE RUNNING   155

13   Stocks: Common and Preferred   156
14   Over-the-Counter Stocks   176
15   Utilities   180
16   Options   185
17   Stock Rights and Warrants   195
18   New Issues   201

FOUR   HIGH RISK FOR HIGH RETURNS   205

19   Foreign Stocks, Bonds, CDs, and Currencies   206
20   Commodities   218

21   Precious Metals   224
22   Financial Futures and Market Indexes   227
23   Splits, Spin-offs, Small-Caps, Spiders, and Stock Buy-Backs   233

FIVE   YOU AND YOUR ACCOUNT   241

24   Finding the Best Professional Help   242
25   Managing Your Brokerage Account   255

SIX   FINANCING YOUR LIFE-STYLE   271

26   Housing   272
27   Family Finances   280
28   Retirement Living   288
29   Social Security, Retirement, and Pension Plans   292
30   Insurance and Annuities   308

SEVEN   TAXES AND YOUR INVESTMENTS   319

31   Dealing with Your Taxes   320
32   Alphabetical Directory of Your Investments and Their Tax Status   326

EIGHT   YOUR CUSTOMIZED PORTFOLIO   337

What To Invest In . . .
   If You're Just Out of School   338
   If You're Newly Married or Living with a Significant Other   339
   If You Have a Family   341
   If You're an Empty Nester   342
   If You're Retired or About to Be   343
   If You Have or Are Starting a Small Business   344
   Protecting Your Portfolio During Hard Times   346

APPENDIX   INVESTMENT ANALYSIS AND INFORMATION SOURCES   349

A: Managing and Investing Your Money with a Computer   350
B: Behind the Scenes: How to Read Annual Reports   353
C: Balance Sheets Made Simple   357
D: Using Technical Indicators   369
E: Where, What, When: Exchanges, Indexes, and Indicators   382

Glossary: Wall Street Jargon Made Simple   388
Index   393
Index of Securities   402
Mutual Funds   405

ACKNOWLEDGMENTS

American Automobile Association, St. Louis, MO: Jeffrey L. Pack
American Stock Exchange, New York, NY: Judy Chuisano
Bankcard Holders of America, Herndon, VA: Gerry Detweiler
Burnham Securities Inc., New York, NY: Jay J. Pack
Dow Theory Forecasts, Hammond, IN: Charles B. Carlson
Dow Theory Letters, La Jolla, CA: Richard Russell
F.D.I.C., Chicago, IL: John S. Stevens
Federal Reserve Bank, New York, NY: Bart R. Sotnick
Investment Company Institute, Washington, DC: Betty Hart
KPMG Peat Marwick, New York, NY: Thomas Hakala
Mount & Nadler, Inc., New York, NY: Hedda Nadler
NASDAQ, New York, NY: Joan Ward
National Association of Investment Clubs, Royal Oak, MI: Ken Janke
New York Stock Exchange, New York, NY
Standard & Poor's Corp., New York, NY: Arnold Kaufman, Jon Diat
Thomas Heller, Tax consultant, New York, NY
Wertheim Schroder & Co., New York, NY: John Murray

Special thanks to:
    Robert Wilson, HarperCollins Publishers
    Marcy Ross
    Joseph Spieler

GETTING STARTED ON YOUR INVESTMENT PORTFOLIO

INTRODUCTION

Sophie Tucker put it well when she said, "I've been rich and I've been poor, and believe me, rich is better." You too can start on the road to riches or increase the riches you already have during 1994 by heeding the suggestions/advice in this year's edition of *Dun & Bradstreet Guide To $Your Investments$® 1994.* It doesn't matter whether you have $5,000, $50,000 or $550,000. At all three levels and those in between there are many investment choices, so many in fact you may have difficulty deciding where to put your money. That is what this section, Part One, will help you sort out. It will simplify what can otherwise be a tough decision-making process. Gathering and understanding the information needed to make those decisions is your first step in building up your riches and becoming at ease in the financial world.

BEGINNING INVESTORS

Please start by reading *all* of Part One, "Getting Started on Your Investment Portfolio." Here you will find information on basic, time-tested smart choices, as well as on:

- How to pick a money market fund
- How to get the best deal at your bank
- The advantages of a credit union
- When to move into mutual funds, and which ones
- How to protect and insure your money

SEASONED INVESTORS

Begin by reading Chapter One, which contains new and timely advice on:

- Alternatives to CDs and money market funds
- Your taxes under President Clinton
- Special investments for 1994
- The NAFTA impact

Then move on to the "Investors Almanac" and Part Two to size up the risks and rewards of more sophisticated investments.

WHAT YOU CAN DO
TO IMPROVE YOUR
FINANCIAL LIFE

1   *Be aware.* Take time to learn how to handle your money. It is a fact
    that a stock market crash, a recession, high unemployment, or generally
    hard times are at one time or another part of our lives. Therefore, to
    put your trust in time or your spouse or parents, or even the corporation
    you work for, to take care of your present and future financial needs is
    childlike and unrealistic. Although many regulatory agencies, as well
    as the Securities and Exchange Commission, the stock exchanges, and
    the Federal Reserve Board, make every effort toward maintaining an
    orderly market and stable economy, you too should take certain steps
    to protect yourself in this fully globalized investing world. To choose to
    remain uninvolved or ignorant about the stock market, the direction of
    the economy, and the workings of the entire financial world is not only
    to court disaster but to invite financial loss.

2   *Be informed.* The two best defenses you have against trouble are
    relatively simple: The first is *information,* and the second is
    diversification. After taking time to learn how the economy, individual
    companies, the banks, interest rates, the dollar, and inflation affect your
    investments, you may still lose money some of the time, but you will
    win far more often if you are both diversified and informed.

YOUR FINANCIAL LIBRARY

Read one of these publications each week. They are arranged by
approximate level of sophistication, beginning with the most elementary.
Subscriptions are available for each one.
- *USA Today*
- Your local newspaper
- *Bottom Line Personal*
- *U.S. News & World Report*
- *Better Investing* (National Association of Investment Clubs)
- *Consumer Reports*
- *Money*
- *Your Money*
- Standard & Poor's *The Outlook*
- *New York Times*
- *Investors Daily*
- *Wall Street Journal*
- *Business Week*
- *Barron's*
- *Value Line*

Begin by reading at least one intelligent financial publication each week. Select one that matches your level of sophistication. Carry it with you (see the box on page 2). Watch the market news on CNN, CNBC, or PBS television or listen to broadcasts on public radio. Know what's happening in this country and abroad.

3   Then, *diversify*—among types of investments and risk levels. Check your holdings against the investment pyramid on page 19. Make certain you have dollars invested in several levels.

HOW TO PICK WINNERS

There was a time when all an investor had to do was pick attractive stocks or bonds. Now you're faced with a bewildering variety of choices, often involving hefty commissions. It's important to determine if they are speculations or investments. To boost your success ratio:

- **Don't become involved with special "opportunities"** until you've developed a balanced portfolio. Stay away from futures, indexes, most new issues, and other complicated investments. These are dominated by the professionals, who have more skill, knowledge, and money than most individuals—and even they get hurt.
- **Don't follow the crowd.** The majority opinion is often wrong. Every major market advance has begun when pessimism was loudest and prices lowest.
- **Don't dash in and out of the market.** You'll find your profits are eaten up by commissions.
- **Don't be in a hurry to invest your money.** If you miss one opportunity, there will be another just as good and possibly better along soon.
- **Don't fall in love with your investments.** There is always a time to be in a stock, a bond, a money market account, and a CD and a time to be out. Remember, with few exceptions most investments become overpriced, and no tree ever grows to the sky.

HOW TO CALCULATE THE EFFECT OF INFLATION

YEARS FROM NOW	4%	5%	6%	7%	8%
5	1.22	1.28	1.34	1.40	1.47
10	1.48	1.63	1.79	1.97	2.16
15	1.80	2.08	2.40	2.76	3.17
20	2.19	2.65	3.21	3.87	4.66
25	2.67	3.39	4.29	5.43	6.85
30	3.24	4.32	5.74	7.61	10.06

SOURCE: Reprinted with permission from *Encyclopedia of Banking and Financial Tables,* copyright © 1980, 1986, Warren, Gorham & Lamont, Inc., Boston, Mass. All rights reserved.

THE POWER OF COMPOUND INTEREST

A REGULAR INVESTMENT OF $100 PER YEAR, INVESTED AT:	WILL, COMPOUNDED ANNUALLY AT THE END OF EACH YEAR, GROW TO THIS SUM AFTER THIS NUMBER OF YEARS:							
	5	10	15	20	25	30	35	40
6%	$564	$1,318	$2,328	$3,679	$5,486	$7,906	$11,143	$15,476
8	587	1,449	2,715	4,576	7,311	11,328	17,232	25,906
10	611	1,594	3,177	5,727	9,835	16,449	27,102	44,259
12	635	1,755	3,728	7,205	13,333	24,133	43,166	76,709
14	661	1,934	4,384	9,102	18,187	35,679	69,357	134,202
16	688	2,132	5,166	11,538	24,921	53,031	112,071	236,076

To get the corresponding total for any other annually invested amount (A), multiply the dollar total given above for the yield and the number of years by $\frac{A}{100}$. Example: You plan to invest $75 per month, $900 a year. What capital sum will that provide after 35 years, at 12% compounded annually? Check where the lines cross for 12% and 35 years: $43,166 × $\frac{900}{100}$ = $388,494. Note: The totals will be greater if: (1) the deposits are made at the beginning of the year; (2) compounding is more frequent.

SOURCE: Reprinted with permission from *Encyclopedia of Banking and Financial Tables,* copyright © 1980, 1986, Warren, Gorham & Lamont, Inc., Boston, Mass. All rights reserved.

THE MAGIC OF COM-POUNDING

In view of our renewed emphasis on safe investing during troubled times, one point that's worth repeating is the positive impact of compounding, or earning income on income, by prompt reinvestment of all interest, dividends, and realized capital gains. As shown in the accompanying tables, savings can mount at an astonishing rate over the years.

➤ THE RULE OF 72 For a quick calculation on how long it takes to double your money, use *the rule of 72:* divide 72 by the yield. Thus, at 9%, it will take 8 years; at 10% about 7 years; at 12%, 6 years to double your money.

LISTENING TO THE PROS

John Kenneth Galbraith, in his book *The Great Crash,* reminds us that John D. Rockefeller told the press after the crash of October 29, 1929, "Believing that fundamental conditions of the country are sound, my son and I have for some days been purchasing sound common stocks." To this Eddie Cantor replied, "Sure, who else had any money left?"

After reading the *Dun & Bradstreet Guide to $Your Investments$®* and becoming an informed investor, you too will be able to decide if you wish to follow Rockefeller's notion or side with Mark Twain, who said, "October. This is one of the peculiarly dangerous months to speculate in stocks. The others are July, January, September, April, November, May, March, June, December, August, and February."

If not all your investment decisions turn out to be spectacular, and no one's ever are, and if at the same time you have adequately diversified, the worst scenario will still leave you upright and in good shape. But then, cut your losses. As Warren Buffett, the chairman of Berkshire Hathaway, Inc., said in one of his annual reports, "Should you find yourself in a chronically leaking boat, energy devoted to changing vessels is likely to be more productive than energy devoted to patching leaks."

Personally, I like Mae West's attitude best: "Too much of a good thing can be wonderful." May 1994 be a wonderful year for you and your investments.

1

SPECIAL ADVICE FOR 1994

"The safest way to double your money is to fold it over once and put it in your pocket."

There's some debate about which great wit first offered this advice (most say it was Frank McKinney Hubbard who worked on the *Indianapolis News* in the 1930s, where as Kim Hubbard, he wrote and illustrated stories about the rustic philosopher Abe Martin), but there's no debate over the fact that it's not easy to double your money. However, there are some things you can do to increase your wealth during 1994 in addition to folding over any spare bills you have on hand.

AN INVESTOR'S ROADMAP FOR 1994

Although it's impossible to predict just what will happen in the financial world during 1994, there are six possibilities that seem to me to deserve serious consideration—that taxes will go up (read our words), that the U.S. stock market will hover near its highs, that parts of Europe will enjoy economic recovery, that the North American Free Trade Accord (NAFTA) in some form will become reality, that Clinton will aim to keep interest rates low, and that we will all grow older. These six observations lend themselves to unique investing possibilities for 1994, and with some old-fashioned thoughtfulness and research, you just may be able to make money on them. Add your own particular spin to the following.

THE 1993 TAX ACT

The new tax law is now a fact, and you must look now for ways to cut back on the amount you will owe the IRS. Here are five moves you can make today to protect your investment portfolio.

1 *Income Taxes.* The top income tax rate rose from 31% to 36% for couples with taxable income after deductions, of $140,000, $115,000 for singles, $127,000 for head of household and $70,000 for married filing separately. And, there will be a 10% surcharge on people making $250,000 or more, putting them in the 39.6% bracket.

➤ ACTION STEP Invest to reduce taxable income, using municipal bonds, municipal mutual funds and unit investment trusts. Rising tax rates means their yields are worth more to you on an after-tax basis (see Chapter 11). Also consider stock in *John Nuveen Co.* which is the leading packager of stock-exchanged listed closed-end municipal bond funds. Its business could thrive as more Americans, socked with higher taxes, turn to its product. Two other stocks which could benefit in a similar way are *AMBAC Inc.* and *MBIA Inc.* Both companies insure municipal bonds.

2 *Social Security Taxes.* Starting in 1994, as much as 85% of some senior citizen's social security benefits will be taxed, up from the current 50%.

➤ ACTION STEP Fund your retirement plans as fully as possible—that includes participating in as many tax-deferred savings plans possible—IRA, 401(k), Keogh, SEP, etc. (see Chapter 29).

3 *Retirement Plans.* Social Security benefits eventually will be curtailed and more and more companies, due to the rising cost of doing business, will be forced to reduce retirement benefits or even drop defined benefits plans. This means you'll have to fund much more of your own retirement savings.

➤ ACTION STEP Look into tax-deferred variable annuities, such as *Fidelity Retirement, Scudder Horizon Plan* and *Vanguard National Home;* minimum investments are $2,500, $2,500 and $5,000 respectively (see Chapter 30).

4 *Pension Distributions.* Starting in 1993, lump-sum distributions from company retirement plans, made to your by check, became subject to a 20% withholding, even if you make a tax-free rollover of the money into an IRA. To make the rollover without incurring taxes, you must deposit the full amount of your plan's payout in an IRA within 60 days, even though 20% of it has been withheld and paid to the IRS. That means you have to come up with 20% of the rollover yourself— out of your pocket.

➤ ACTION STEP Don't have the plan distribute the money to you. Instead, have the plan's trustee make a direct transfer of the money to your IRA. If the payout of funds never goes through you, the withholding does not apply.

5 *Capital Gains.* Congress did not raise the capital gains tax. The current rate is 28% which seems mild compared with the new top income tax rates of 36% and 39.6%.

➤ ACTION STEP Consider taking advantage of the spread between income tax rates and capital gains rates by investing in growth stocks. These tend to have low or no dividends but pay off in capital gains when you sell. Look to real estate also. It can generate gains which are not taxed until you sell. Consider residential rental property which will bring in income to cover expenses and at the same time offer some tax breaks. (see Chapters 26, 31 and 32).

IS THE STOCK MARKET TOO HIGH?

With the market's valuation historically high as we go to press, it's a good time to focus on stocks that are less volatile than the market as a whole. One way to do this is to select those with a low beta. Beta is a statistical measure of volatility. A beta of 1.00 indicates that, over a certain time period, the stock moves in step with the overall market as measured by the Standard & Poor's 500 Index. If the beta is over 1.0 then the stock moves more than the total market, although in the same direction. For example, a beta of 1.4 means that the stock can be expected to rise or fall 40% more than the general market. Stocks with betas below 1.0 tend to make less dramatic moves than the S&P 500.

These 13 stocks all have had betas of 0.75 or lower for the last several years. You can expect them to fall less than most stocks should there be a market correction or decline. All are rated A— or above by S&P. In addition to this list, check utility stocks—they too typically have low betas (see Chapter 13).

COMING RECOVERY IN EUROPE

With interest rates heading down in some countries, with a rising standard of living in many, coupled with a more organized and functioning European Community, we can expect a gradually improving European stock market. Chapter 19 offers many specific investment suggestions, but here are two additional ideas. Since it is extremely difficult to know when a foreign market (or our own market, for that matter) is at the bottom, dollar cost average into a mutual fund. Two no-load funds that have 50% of their assets in European stocks are *Harbor International* and *Vanguard's Equity Fund: International Portfolio.* Also consider purchasing closed-end funds when they sell at a discount, such as the *France Growth Fund* or *Growth Fund of Spain.* Both trade on the NYSE.

THE NORTH AMERICAN FREE TRADE ACCORD

Political posturing aside, some form of NAFTA will become part of our economic lives. These U.S. stocks, whose profits will benefit from freer trade between nations, are also solid choices for long-term growth. Read the annual report and current *Value Line* analysis for each one before purchasing shares. (For specific Mexican stocks, see Chapter 19.)

A BAKER'S DOZEN LOW BETA STOCKS

COMPANY	SYMBOL	PRICE/JULY 1993
Alexander & Baldwin	ALEX	$24
Block (H&R)	HRB	35
Bruno's, Inc.	BRNO	10
Eaton Vance	EAVN	34
Flowers Industries	FLO	17
Luby's Cafeterias	LUB	23
Old Kent Financial	OKEN	33
Quaker Oats	OAT	65
Ralston Purina	RAL	39
Raytheon Co.	RTN	60
Smucker (JM)	SJM (A)	22
Valspar Corp.	VAL	36
Worthington Industries	WTHG	29

- *Burlington Northern.* (NYSE:BNI; $55) This railroad company will benefit from any increase in shipment of goods and the fact that its headquarters are in Fort Worth, Texas, not too far from the Mexican border, is an obvious plus.
- *Donnelley (R.R.) & Sons.* (NYSE:DNY; $30) This printing company has acquired a large Mexican printing firm, Laboratorio Lito Color, and is doubling the size of its San Juan del Rio operations.
- *Gerber Products.* (NYSE:GEB; $24) As the leading producer of baby foods in Mexico, a country with a high birth rate, the firm is well positioned.
- *Keystone International.* (NYSE:KII; $26) This manufacturer of values and flow-control products derives over half its sales from foreign operations and already has a firmly established Mexican business.
- *Kimberly-Clark.* (NYSE:KMB; $47) Owns about 40% of Kimberly-Clark de Mexico, one of Mexico's leading companies. It could see substantial earnings gains as the country's standard of living improves.
- *Rubbermaid.* (NYSE:RBD; $30) The firm acquired CIPSA, the number one plastics and rubber housewares company in Mexico. Like Kimberly-Clark, it will benefit from a rising standard of living among Mexicans.
- *Southwestern Bell.* (NYSE:SBC; $40) Its 10% ownership of Telefonos de Mexico, the Mexican telephone company, puts SBC in the right place at the right time: as more Mexicans earn substantial incomes, one of their first purchases will be a telephone.

CASHING IN ON THE GRAYING BABY BOOMERS

During the past 50 years, the number of Americans over the age of 50 has just about doubled, to 63 million. Demographers predict that in another 30 years, that figure will nearly double again. This trend has created interesting investment possibilities.

➤ HEALTH CARE As we grow older, our need for health-care products and services such as pharmaceuticals, surgical supplies and special housing rises. These stocks could outperform the market. Prices are as of July 1993.

- *Abbott Laboratories.* (NYSE:ABT; $26) This diversified health care firm has a strong position in nutritional products, hospital supplies and diagnostic products including AIDS testing.
- *Biomagnetic Technologies.* (OTC:BTIX; $4) Has developed an FDA-approved diagnostic system for finding abnormal electrical activity in the brain.
- *Beverly Enterprises.* (NYSE:BEV; $11) Operates nursing homes and retirement living centers with a subspecialty in treatment of those with Alzheimer's disease.
- *Biomet Inc.* (OTC:BMET; $10) Manufactures and markets surgical implants and orthopedic support devices.
- *Bristol-Myers Squibb Co.* (NYSE:BMY; $57) The world's second largest pharmaceutical company with impressive overseas-derived profits.
- *Foundation Health Corp.* (NYSE:FH; $35) Provides managed health

care services to some 1.1 million people through HMO and government contracts.

- *Manor Care.* (NYSE:MNR; $20) A leader in the nursing home and lodging industry.

➤ SUNBELT ENERGY Because so many older people retire or live part-time in the south, energy consumption there is up. These public utility companies could benefit from this trend.

- *Florida Progress Corp.* (NYSE:FPC; $35, 5.5% yield) Serves 1.1 million customers.
- *SCANA Corp.* (NYSE:SCG; $49, 5.6% yield) Holding company for South Carolina electric and gas service; has about 2.2 million customers.
- *TECO Energy.* (NYSE:TE; $49, 3.9% yield) Holding company for Tampa Electric; has 461,000 customers.

GETTING OUT OF THE LOW INTEREST RATE TRAP

Most of us never think of bank CDs as risky investments. After all, they are insured and offer guaranteed rates. Yet today's rates on CDs and bank money market accounts are so low that they do indeed present a certain kind of risk—reduced earning power. And, with higher taxes around the corner, returns will be further reduced.

Conservative investors, retirees and many others dissatisfied with these paltry yields face a common problem: what to do when CDs come due. Great numbers have been leaping into mutual funds, or into individual stocks and bonds to earn higher returns, often without understanding what they are investing in and how much risk is involved.

Before turning to mutual funds and/or the market, you should understand two concepts:

1 The higher the yield, the greater the risk.
2 Yield and total return are not the same thing.

The first point is self-explanatory, but let's take time to fully understand the second. The yield on traditional savings accounts and CDs refers to a level of interest paid on your principal and that does not fluctuate in value. Yet when investing in a mutual fund, other than a money market fund, you are purchasing shares in a fund at the fund's net asset value. This NAV will rise or fall as market conditions change, so when you go to sell your shares, they may be worth more or less than what you paid for them. To determine the total return of a mutual fund, you must take into consideration **both the income earned and the gains or losses in the fund's net asset value.**

Now let's look at some relatively low risk alternatives to CDs, bearing in mind that none of them offer the double digit rates of the past.

1 *Money-market funds.* Although these pay just about the same as bank CDs, they have a clear advantage: their portfolios are invested for an average maturity of 30 to 90 days. This means that when interest rates begin to climb again, money funds rates will also move up. Rates

on bank CDs will not rise as quickly because banks pay whatever they want and will not pay higher rates unless necessary.

➤ ACTION STEP Switch to a top-yielding fund; several continually pay almost one percentage point above the average rate. That makes the difference between breaking even after taking taxes and inflation into consideration, or losing money.

The *United Services Government Securities Savings Fund* (1-800-873-8637) is a good choice for those who pay high state and local taxes because the income earned is exempt from these taxes. (The fund invests only in U.S. government or government-backed obligations.) The three states where investors don't get this tax break are Maine, New Hampshire and Pennsylvania.

For other top-yielding money market funds, see box on page 31.

2   *HH Savings Bonds.* These government-backed bonds have a guaranteed minimum yield of 4%, paid out once you've held the bonds six months. The interest is distributed twice a year. You can redeem HH bonds at any time, but you forfeit some interest if you do so in the midst of a six-month period. Interest is exempt from state and local taxes.

You can't buy HH bonds. You must first buy EE bonds, hold them for at least six months, and then exchange them for the HH bonds. Your bank can do this for you. There's a $15,000 limit on how much you can invest into EE bonds each year. During the six months while you're holding the EE bonds, you'll earn a small amount of interest. Interest on both bonds is electronically deposited into your bank account every six months.

More about EE and HH bonds in Chapter 9.

3   *Short-term bond funds.* These fixed-income mutual funds hold bonds that mature in one to three years. Because your money is tied up for this time period, their yields are generally 1 to 1½% higher than yields on money market funds. When rates do rise, the fund manager can sell some of the older, low-rate bonds at little loss and immediately replenish them with the new higher yielding one.

➤ ACTION STEP Get the prospectus for *Scudder Short Term Bond Fund,* 1-800-225-2470. Its yield in the spring of 1993 was 7.61% when the average one-year CD was yielding 2.91%. The fund's average annual returns for one-year was 9.21% and for five years, 10.94%.

4   *Tax-free bond funds.* If your income puts you in or above the 28% tax bracket look to tax-free municipal bond funds. The stated rate of return may seem low, but you could actually make more money than if you purchase a higher-yielding taxable fund and then pay federal, state and local taxes on that income.

➤ ACTION STEP Consider *Vanguard Muni Bond Limited Term* (1-800-635-1511) whose yield in the spring of 1993 was 3.76% which is the equivalent of 5.22% if you're in the 28% tax bracket, or 5.45% if you're in the 31% bracket.

If you're willing to take on more risk, consider an intermediate term muni fund for a higher tax-free yield. *Vanguard Muni Bond Intermediate Term* was yielding 5%, which is equal to 6.94% in the 28% tax bracket and 7.25% in the 31% bracket.

For more on municipal bonds and bond funds, see Chapter 11.

5 *Treasuries.* These government securities, which range from 13-week T-bills to 20- or 30-year bonds, are issued by the U.S. Treasury to finance the federal debt. They are among the safest of investments since they are backed by the government. While the yield on a one-year T-bill is about the same as on a one-year bank CD, the income you earn is exempt from state and local taxes. So, if you live in a high-tax state such as New York, California or Minnesota, the tax advantage is critical. And, because you can buy Treasuries directly from the Federal Reserve banks, you do not have to pay a brokerage commission.

$HINT: Boost your yield on Treasuries by setting up a laddered portfolio— that means buying different maturities ranging from one-year bills to two-year notes to four-year notes to 10-year bonds. Then as the different securities mature in different years, reinvest the proceeds in another Treasury issue with a higher yield—if rates have risen. (If rates have fallen, you'll still be ahead because you will have locked up your money at the old higher yields.)

For more on Treasuries, see Chapter 8.

6 *Index funds.* One way to protect your money which you will read about continually in this book is through diversification. To do this and get a decent yield you can buy shares in a fund that actually invests in other funds.

➤ ACTION STEP Look into the *T. Rowe Price Spectrum Income* (1-800-638-5660) that invests in seven other funds offered by the T. Rowe Price family—ranging from money market to junk bond and high dividend stock funds. The spring 1993 yield was 6.3%. Its total return in 1991 was 8.1% and in 1992, 7.8%. The seven funds it invests in are: Equity Income, International Bond, High Yield Bond, New Income, GNMA Fund, Short Term Bond and Prime Reserve, a money market fund.

Another choice: *Blanchard Flexible Income Fund* (1-800-829-3863) that invests in U.S. government and investment grade bonds, but has about 30% of its portfolio in higher risk junk bonds and 40% in international bonds.

☐CAUTION: Although the fund has been yielding about 8%, it is only a year old and has not posted a long-term track record.

7 *Corporate bonds.* Although Treasuries are safer since they are backed by the government, corporate bonds offer higher yields. There are a number of A-rated corporates with yields ranging from 7% to 10%. Locking in yields when rates on other types of investments are much lower is always a smart move. Confine purchases to bonds listed on the New York or American exchanges so price quotes can readily be checked and so you can find a market should you wish to sell. One particularly sound category to consider: Bonds issued by public utility

companies. The overall creditworthiness of utility bonds is typically high because they provide a needed service in an almost monopolistic setting.

➤ ACTION STEP   Consider these utility bonds, rated A or better:

- Central Power & Light
- Indiana Bell Telephone
- Southern Indiana Gas & Electric
- Virginia Electric & Power

➤ ACTION STEP   Consider these corporate bonds and notes, rated A or better:

- Becton, Dickinson
- General Electric
- Shell Oil
- Warner-Lambert

8   *High yield stocks.* Electric and gas utility stocks traditionally pay high yields. For suggested issues, see Chapter 15.

§ HINT: Purchase shares through a discount broker to save on commissions; once you have made your initial purchase, sign up for the company's dividend reinvestment plan, if it has one. See page 263 for more on this way to buy stocks and avoid commissions.

Other high yielding stocks rated 1 by *Value Line* for safety:

- *1838 Bond Debenture*   7.6% yield
- *Royal Dutch Petroleum*   5.2%
- *Eli Lilly*   5.1%
- *New Plan Realty Trust*   5.6%
- *Bristol-Myers Squibb*   5.1%
- *Texaco Inc.*   5.1%

9   *Closed-end bond funds.* Many investors shy away from these funds, which actually trade as stocks on the various stock exchanges, because they don't understand how they work. (See Chapter 7 for details on closed-end bonds funds.) Ignoring them, however, means ignoring a good investment opportunity because many of them, especially those that invest in U.S. and foreign debt, are relatively high in safety and have solid yields.

- *Putnam Intermediate Government Income Trust.* (NYSE:PGT; $8½; yielding 6.8%)
- *Dreyfus Strategic Government Income Fund.* (NYSE:DSI; $11½; yielding 8.3%)
- *Dreyfus Closed-end Strategic Municipal Bond Fund.* (NYSE:DSM; $10½; yielding 6.7%) This stock has the distinct advantage that the interest earned is free from federal income tax.

2

BUILDING YOUR OWN INVESTMENT PYRAMID

One of the questions I am asked most frequently is, "How do I get started investing? I just don't know where to begin." It's a very valid question. Before the proliferation of financial products and computerized communication, the answer was relatively easy. Investment choices were limited, and only a few basic concepts governed the ways in which you could make (or lose) money. The basic choices available for most individuals were stocks, bonds, the bank, and then later, one mutual fund. Those limitations, however, are no longer true.

We now face many changes in the financial world—a bewildering array of old and new investment products, including SPIDERS and LEAPS— and we are also being introduced to many ways to buy foreign stocks, bonds, mutual funds, and currencies.

Of course, some old familiar themes are still with us: Inflation and interest rates are still low, especially by historic standards, and the impact of the banking crisis and the recession have not gone away. But even old familiar things are changing: the government reduced the rate on EE Savings bonds and changed ways in which interest rates on these bonds are computed.

In fact, the world of finance is changing so rapidly that unless you are up to date and well informed, you'll be left in the dust. That is why *$Your Investments$* can make the difference between a well-informed decision and pure guesswork. This guide helps you determine if you're better off buying a bank CD or a Treasury bill, making a play in commodity futures or a high yield bond, using your broker's research, or following the technical charts.

Whether you are a new investor or a sophisticated money manager who has weathered numerous bull and bear cycles, this vital reference book brings you more data on the familiar vehicles of Wall Street, introduces you to new products, and offers you the best in smart money-making strategies that are followed by the professional investment community.

This chapter focuses on the INVESTMENT PYRAMID—a visual way to see how much risk accompanies various investments and when it is appropriate to add each one to your portfolio.

BECOMING A SAVVY INVESTOR

Before you plunge into your pocket and buy 100 shares of a reportedly "hot stock" or set up a personally tailored investment program with a stockbroker or financial planner, it's wise to take a few moments to decide your answers to three key questions:

1 What do I want to derive from such a move or investment?
2 How much can I sensibly afford to invest?
3 What are my major financial goals?

Random purchases of stocks, bonds, and mutual funds may initially seem rewarding, but they are unlikely to fulfill your long-range goals. To get the most out of your investment dollar, the answers to these three questions and some background preparation are essential. The four homework assignments below can produce large benefits in the long run, enabling you to make better investment decisions whether you make them on your own or with professional guidance.

KNOW THY WORTH

Before making any type of investment expenditure, whether it's buying a stock, a bond, or a house, you must know your net worth. This is one of the first questions most stockbrokers, money managers, and bank mortgage officers ask. If, like most people, you're uncertain of the precise answer, don't panic. Figuring out your net worth is easy. All you need is a free evening, a calculator, your checkbook, bills, and a record of your income. Then follow these two easy steps:

1 Add up the value of everything you own (your assets).
2 Subtract the total of all you owe (your liabilities).

The amount left over is your net worth. You can use the worksheet on the following page as a guide for arriving at the correct amount. When figuring your assets, list the amount they will bring in today's market, which could be more or less than you paid for them originally. Assets include cash on hand, your checking and savings account balances, the cash value of any insurance policies, personal property (car, boat, jewelry, real estate, investments), and any vested interest in a pension or retirement plan. Your liabilities include money you owe, charge account debts, mortgages, auto payments, education or other loans, and any taxes due.

KNOW WHERE THY WORTH IS GOING: BUDGETING

Some form of budgeting should be part of your overall investment plan. It's not only a good way of knowing how much you're spending and on what, but it is also a sensible means of setting aside money for investing, our primary concern in this book. If you need help in establishing a budget for investing, use the worksheet on page 16. In order to budget dollars for investing, try setting aside a certain dollar amount on a regular basis, even if it's not an impressively large number. Mark it immediately for "savings/ investing." Ideally you should try to save 5% to 10% of your annual income; if you make more than $70,000 a year, aim for 15%. Don't talk yourself out of budgeting for investing simply because it is a nuisance to keep track of what you spend. You'll be convinced of the wisdom of saving and the advantages of compound interest if you take a look at the table below, which shows what happens to $1,000 over twenty years when you put it

---

FINDING YOUR NET WORTH

ASSETS as of _____ (date)		LIABILITIES as of _____ (date)	
Cash on hand	$_____	Unpaid bills	
Cash in checking accounts	_____	Charge accounts	$_____
Savings accounts, money market fund	_____	Taxes, property taxes, and quarterly	
Life insurance, cash value	_____	income taxes	_____
Annuities	_____	Insurance premiums	_____
Retirement funds		Rent or monthly mortgage payment	_____
IRA or Keogh	_____	Utilities	_____
401(k) plan	_____	Balance due on:	
Vested interest in pension or		Mortgage	_____
profit-sharing plan	_____	Automobile loans	_____
U.S. savings bonds, current value	_____	Personal loans	_____
Investments		Installment loans	_____
Market value of stocks, bonds,		Total liabilities $_____	
mutual fund shares, etc.	_____		
Real estate, market value of real			
property minus mortgage	_____		
Property			
Automobile	_____		
Furniture	_____		
Jewelry, furs	_____		
Sports and hobby equipment	_____	Assets $_____	
Equity interest in your business	_____	Minus liabilities _____	
Total assets $_____		Your net worth $_____	

---

in an investment yielding 5¼% and the income earned is reinvested or compounded.

KNOW THY GOALS AND PRIORITIES

After you've accumulated money to invest, your next homework assignment is to decide what you want to accomplish by investing. If you were to take a trip to Europe or travel by car across the country, you would bring along a good road map. This should also be the case with investing, only the road map would consist of financial, not geographic, destinations. When you travel

---

WHAT HAPPENS TO A $1,000 INVESTMENT AT 5¼%

FREQUENCY OF COMPOUNDING	1 YEAR	5 YEARS	10 YEARS	20 YEARS
Continuous	$1,054.67	$1,304.93	$1,702.83	$2,899.63
Daily	1,054.67	1,304.90	1,702.76	2,899.41
Quarterly	1,053.54	1,297.96	1,684.70	2,838.20
Semiannually	1,053.19	1,295.78	1,679.05	2,819.21
Annually	1,052.50	1,291.55	1,668.10	2,782.54

through Italy, you decide what towns, cathedrals, or monuments you want most to visit; how long it will take you to get from one to the next; and approximately what it will cost. The same procedure should be applied to your financial journey through life. Your highlights or destination points may include some of these:

- Building a nest egg for emergencies
- Establishing an investment portfolio
- Reducing taxes
- Preparing for retirement
- Paying for a college education
- Buying a house, car, or boat
- Traveling or taking a cruise
- Investing in art or antiques
- Adding on a room or installing a swimming pool
- Setting up your own business

Goal setting, you will discover, enables you to take firm control of your financial life, especially if you actually write your goals down. The process of listing goals on paper, perhaps awkward at first, forces you to focus on how you handle money and how you feel about risk versus safety. Divide your goals into two sections: immediate goals (those that can be accomplished in a year or less) and long-range goals.

If you're single, your immediate goals could be:

- Obtain a graduate degree
- Join a health club
- Save for summer vacation
  Longer-term goals:
- Buy a car
- Set up a brokerage account or buy shares in a mutual fund
- Purchase a co-op or condo with a friend
  If you're married and raising a family, the goals might shift to include:
- Setting up educational funds for children
- Building a growth portfolio
  Singles and marrieds closer to retirement tend to seek other goals:
- Shift bulk of portfolio to safe, income-producing vehicles
- Increase contribution to retirement plan
- Find appropriate short-term tax shelters
- Set up a consulting business; incorporate

Regardless of your age or income, individual goals make it easier and more meaningful to stick to a budget and to save for investing. Putting aside that 5% to 15% every month for an investment program suddenly has a very tangible purpose—one that you personally decided on.

BUILDING YOUR INVESTMENT PYRAMID

Once you know why you want to invest, you are ready to think about your investments as part of a pyramid in which each level builds on the earlier ones. This approach to investing offers a carefully designed, diversified system that provides for financial growth and protection regardless of your age, marital status, income, or level of financial sophistication. As you can see by looking at the illustration, you begin your financial program on the pyramid at Level 1. It is the lowest in terms of risk and the highest in safety. As your net worth grows, you automatically move up to the next level, increasing both the amount of risk involved and the potential for financial gain.

Level 1 covers life's basic financial requirements and includes:

- An emergency nest egg consisting of cash or cash equivalents such as savings account, CDs, money market funds
- Health, life, and disability insurance
- A solid retirement plan, including an IRA, Keogh, or 401(k)

Before leaving this level, you will have saved enough cash or cash equivalents to cover a minimum of three to nine months' worth of living

---

YOUR CASH FLOW

WHERE IT COMES FROM		WHERE IT GOES	
INCOME	ANNUAL AMOUNT	EXPENSES	ANNUAL AMOUNT
Take-home pay	$_____	Income taxes	$_____
Bonus and commissions	_____	Mortgage or rent	_____
Interest	_____	Property taxes	_____
Dividends	_____	Utilities	_____
Rent	_____	Automobile	
Pensions	_____	maintenance	_____
Social Security	_____	Commuting or other	
Annuities	_____	transportation	_____
Tax refunds	_____	Insurance	
Other	_____	Homeowner's or	
Total	$_____	renter's	_____
		Life	_____
		Disability	_____
		Child care	_____
		Education	_____
		Food	_____
		Clothing	_____
		Household	
		miscellaneous	_____
		Home improvements	_____
		Entertainment	_____
		Vacations, travel	_____
		Books, magazines, club	
		dues	_____
		Contributions to	
		charities or	
		organizations	_____
		Total	$_____
		Surplus or deficit	$_____

expenses. This minimum is your emergency reserve, and when you've achieved this goal, you're financially solid enough to advance to Level 2.

Level 2 is devoted entirely to safe income-producing investments such as corporate or municipal bonds; Treasury securities; longer-term CDs; zero coupon bonds; and real estate (your primary residence)—all of which are described in this book.

Although safety is key at this step, the liquidity factor emphasized in Level 1 is now traded off for a higher return or yield. And because some of these items, notably zero coupon bonds and CDs, are timed to mature at a definite date, they provide ideal means to meet staggering college tuition bills and retirement costs.

Money to buy real estate is also included, not only because it gives you a place to live, but also because historically real estate has appreciated significantly in value. At the same time, it offers tax benefits in the form of deductions for mortgage interest payments and real estate taxes.

Level 3 involves investing for growth. At this point you can afford to be more adventuresome, more risk-oriented, and less conservative; and this book shows you how to turn away from liquidity and assured income and toward growth and blue chip stocks, conservative mutual funds, convertible bonds, and rentable property. If you find you're interested in the

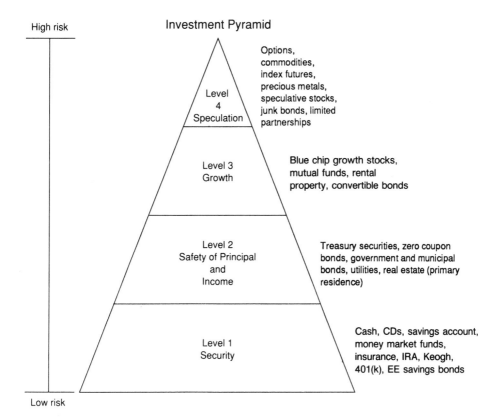

Investment Pyramid

High risk

Level 4 Speculation — Options, commodities, index futures, precious metals, speculative stocks, junk bonds, limited partnerships

Level 3 Growth — Blue chip growth stocks, mutual funds, rental property, convertible bonds

Level 2 Safety of Principal and Income — Treasury securities, zero coupon bonds, government and municipal bonds, utilities, real estate (primary residence)

Level 1 Security — Cash, CDs, savings account, money market funds, insurance, IRA, Keogh, 401(k), EE savings bonds

Low risk

HINTS FOR THE BEGINNING INVESTOR

- Don't think you're going to get rich immediately. It takes time and wisdom to become a winning investor.
- Don't start to invest in stocks or bonds until you've saved the equivalent of at least nine months of living expenses in a money market fund or other liquid investment.
- Know if you are investing for *income* or *growth*. Many people never figure this out and are disappointed in their returns.
- Then pick a stock, bond, or mutual fund that matches your goal to generate immediate income or long-term appreciation.
- Start by investing only in stocks or bonds of leading companies. They have proven track records, a lot of research on them is available, and there will always be a buyer if you should wish to sell.
- Buy a stock *only* if you can state a reason why it will appreciate in price or pay high dividends; merely feeling good about an issue is not a solid enough reason to justify purchase.
- Don't churn your own account so that commissions eat up any profits. Even if the average commission is only 5%, your stock will have to move up at least 10% to be even.
- Spread out your risks. Every company has the potential to be a loser some of the time.
- Decide on the maximum amount that you're willing to lose and stick to it.
- When you lose, if you do, try to determine why your security went down.
- Read about investing and investments regularly.

FINANCIAL RESOLUTIONS FOR 1994

I resolve to:
- Pay myself every month—to make savings the first bill paid after my mortgage or rent
- Set up a realistic, automatic savings plan
- Live within my income
- Organize my financial papers
- Review or write my will
- Subscribe to a financial publication . . . and read it
- Be an informed investor, not a speculator
- Spend half an hour each day listening to or reading about financial matters
- Invest only in things I understand and learn about those I don't

stock market, this is the ideal time to join an investment club and learn by doing so.

Level 4, the pinnacle of the pyramid, is given over to the riskiest investments, which may or may not yield spectacular returns. These include speculative stocks, stocks in new companies, takeover candidates, options, commodities, index futures, gold and precious metals, junk bonds, and limited partnerships, all vehicles discussed in detail in the following chapters.

AVOIDING FOUR COMMON INVESTMENT MISTAKES

You may think that only novices make investment mistakes—not true. Here are four traps into which the pros as well as new investors often fall, along with practical solutions for each. Page references are to further material on the topic within this book.

1 *Chasing yields.* With CD and money market fund rates at all-time
   lows, it's easy to go after high yields, forgetting that with higher
   yields come higher risks. There's also danger in stretching out
   maturities of bonds, notes, and CDs sold by stockbrokers in order to
   get higher yields, because when interest rates start to rise, these
   investments drop in value. If you have to sell before maturity, you
   could lose money.

   Solutions: 1) Stagger bond and CD maturities so you continually have money coming in for re-investment should rates go up. 2) Put only one-quarter of your income portfolio in risky, high-yield bonds or bond mutual funds. (See Chapter 12.)

2 *Failing to diversify.* It's easy to keep doing what works and overlook
   the importance of dividing your portfolio into different investments—
   ones that work in different ways so you are protected when interest
   rates move up or down or when the market is bullish or bearish.

   Solutions: Divide your money between these categories: a) money funds, CDs, and Treasury bills; b) domestic stocks; c) foreign stocks; d) domestic bonds; e) international bonds; and f) real estate. Then, within each category, you can diversify even further. With stocks, into blue chips, small-caps, utilities, growth stocks, and some new issues.

   Within the bond category, you can further divide your investments into different maturities (ranging from short- to long-term); into tax-free municipals, and into different risk levels: government bonds, AAA-rated corporate bonds, and higher risk junk bonds. (See Chapters 9 and 12.)

3 *Not taking advantage of dollar cost averaging.* Most investors either
   put too much or too little into stocks or mutual funds at one time.

   Solution: Instead, invest a set amount on a regular basis, say once a month, to smooth out market fluctuations. You'll generally wind up making purchases at a lower cost per share than if you bought all at once. (See pages 263–264.)

4 *Hanging onto a losing investment.* Too often we are taken with a

stock or other investment, so that it's hard to admit we made a mistake.

Solution: Set a percentage loss figure and stick to it. Write it down in your investment book or on your computer disk. When you sell, note why the investment turned out to be a loser so you can avoid repeating your error.

3

FINDING SAFE PLACES FOR YOUR MONEY:
Banks, Money Market Funds, CDs,
and Credit Unions

Throughout your investment life there will be many times when varying portions of your assets should be kept liquid—that is, readily available. The traditional savings account simply won't do anymore; the interest rate is far too low. Fortunately, you have several other options: 1) interest-bearing checking accounts (sometimes called NOW accounts); 2) bank money market deposit accounts; 3) bank certificates of deposits (CDs); 4) money market mutual funds; 5) U.S. savings bonds; and 6) U.S. Treasuries. (The latter two are discussed in Chapter 9.) All are appropriate for sure income and preservation of capital, as illustrated on Level I of "Your Investment Pyramid" (page 19). The table below will help you compare the current yields for each one (as we went to press) as well as their average minimum dollar requirements and for how long you either can or may wish to have your money invested in each one. I don't by any means suggest you put all your money in these safe havens—their yields are too low—but you should certainly earmark about one-quarter of your assets for this Level I category. Investors—amateurs and pros—have come to realize that the stock market is indeed unpredictable, and diversification is not just mumbojumbo from the mouths of conservative financial advisers and writers such as myself; it is indeed the basis of protecting one's investments in economic climates of all kinds.

§ HINT: Know the difference between interest rate and yield. Interest rate is the annual return without compounding. The effective yield reflects compounding—daily, monthly, quarterly, annually. Compare bank *yields* if you plan to leave your earned interest in the bank. Compare interest *rates* if you are taking out your earned interest.

AT YOUR BANK

In late 1992, new Federal Insurance Deposit Corporation (F.D.I.C.) rules put limits on the interest rates weaker banks can give customers, while at the same time permitting well-capitalized banks to determine their own interest rates. So, undercapitalized banks and savings and loans can no longer pay extremely high rates; however, it pays to shop around, because rates, fees, products, and services continue to vary from bank to bank. Although it's time-consuming, it can mean as much as ½% to 1½% difference in the interest your money will earn. All things being equal, however, there's something to be said for having all or most of your banking business at one institution. Called "relationship banking," it may mean you can get higher interest on your savings, lower fees on your checking, and better terms on

SAFE HAVENS

INVESTMENT	YIELD	AVERAGE MINIMUM INVESTMENT
1 to 3 Months		
Money market mutual funds	2.69%	$1,000
Bank money market accounts	2.45	1,000
Super NOW bank accounts	2.23	2,500
Short-term CDs	2.81	500
3-month Treasury bills	3.05	10,000 initial; 5,000 thereafter
Passbook savings account	2.50	50
Credit union sharedraft	3.00	50
3 Months or Longer		
12-month CD	3.09	500
1-year Treasury bills	3.40	10,000 initial; 5,000 thereafter
7-year Treasury notes	5.56	5,000 (1- to 4-year maturities)
		1,000 (4- to 10-year maturities)
10-year Treasury bonds	5.97	1,000
EE savings bonds	4.00	25

(As of July 1993.)

your loans. That's because when all your banking is lumped together, you become a more important customer. But find out first.

Passbook Savings. Fewer and fewer banks offer the old-fashioned passbook savings account to new customers. Most have replaced it with a statement account, which provides a monthly or quarterly computerized update of your savings transactions. The minimum balance requirements ranges from $1 to $100; in large cities, sometimes even more. Most savings accounts pay only between 2% and 3%. Your total yield will be based on (1) the starting date of calculation, set by the bank (sometimes this is the day of deposit, but often it's the first business day of the suceeding month) and (2) on the method of compounding. Obviously, the faster your money is reinvested the more it will earn. Your savings will earn more when interest is compounded daily than when it is compounded annually.

Which Checking Account? You obviously want to find not only the safest bank, but the one with the lowest fees and the highest interest rates. Which checking account may be determined by how much you can leave on deposit every month. If you can only leave a small amount in the account every month, then you probably will qualify only for a noninterest bearing checking account and you'll pay per-check charges and possibly maintenance fees. If, however, you can keep more on deposit, you'll be able

---

FINDING YOUR TRUE YIELD

To find out which NOW account offers the best deal, use this simple formula:

1 Take the minimum deposit and multiply it by the interest rate:

$$\$2,500 \times 6\% = \$150$$

2 Then multiply the monthly service fee by 12 and subtract the total from your annual interest income:

$$\$4 \times 12 = \$48$$

$$\$150 - \$48 = \$102$$

3 $\$102 \div \$2,500 = 4.1\%$. This is your true yield.

---

to have a NOW account (negotiable order of withdrawal) and earn interest. With a NOW account, however, if you fall below the minimum balance set by the bank, you will no longer earn interest and in some cases be subject to additional charges. A recent survey by the Consumer Federation of America revealed that a NOW account cost depositors an average $111 a year in fees and charges, after interest income. Fees for a NOW account range from $5 per month and 15 cents per check to $12 to $20 and 25 cents. Rates, too, vary, with the average (in July 1993) being about 2%.

Geography may determine whether or not you qualify for a NOW account. In smaller cities and towns, required balances tend to be lower: $250 to $1,000. Major city banks often require $2,500. If you are a member of a credit union or can join one, open a sharedraft account: Over 85% of credit unions offering this type of checking account do not have service fees. Dividends (the credit union equivalent of interest) on sharedrafts vary, too, but in many cases are higher than interest on NOW accounts. (See Chapter 3 for more on Credit Unions.)

$ HINT: Be certain you understand how your bank uses the word "daily." Daily interest does not mean that the bank compounds interest daily. It means that the interest is compounded quarterly or semiannually based on the average of your daily balance.

☐ CAUTION: Unless you have a very small amount to save or are opening an account for a child, avoid savings accounts; better interest rates are available through the accounts described in the rest of this chapter. To get the most out of your bank:

1 Ask for overdraft checking privileges, that is, a permanent line of credit that prevents you from bouncing a check. The bank will automatically cover your check even if you don't have enough money in the account—for up to a predetermined dollar amount. You will have to pay back the loan plus interest.

2 Once you have more than $2,500 in your NOW account (or whatever

the minimum balance required is), move the excess into a money market deposit account at the bank or to a money market mutual fund—whichever has better rates.

3   Don't buy bank-printed checks. You can save money by ordering checks from Checks in the Mail (1-800-733-4443) or Current, Inc. (1-800-426-0822).

BANK MONEY MARKET DEPOSIT ACCOUNTS

The counterpart of a money market mutual fund at a bank is a money market deposit account. They pay relatively competitive interest rates, offer liquidity, and, like all bank accounts including savings and NOWs, are insured up to $100,000 by the F.D.I.C., or, at a savings and loan, by the F.S.L.I.C. They tend to pay slightly lower yields than money market mutual funds and Treasury bills. The rates change periodically with changes in overall short-term rates, which is also true of money market mutual funds. The minimum to open ranges from $1,00 to $5,000.

These accounts also offer convenience—most banks let you write checks on them for any dollar amount, although they limit the number of checks you can write to third parties (anyone but yourself)—typically to three checks per month to a third party and three preauthorized transactions (as might occur when you arrange in advance to pay a specific bill such as a mortgage payment.) You may withdraw cash in person generally as often as you like. On the other hand, money market mutual funds let you write as many checks as you like, but you must write them for a minimum amount—$250 or $500 usually.

Yields and penalties for falling below the required minimum vary from bank to bank. So, find out if your bank avoids paying interest on a money market deposit account if the balance drops below a certain minimum.

CERTIFICATES OF DEPOSIT (CDs)

CDs, also known as time certificates of deposit, are safe, reliable savings instruments available at most every local bank. The certificate indicates that you have deposited a sum of money for a specified period of time (six months, one year, etc.), at a specified rate of interest. The fact that they're insured up to $100,000 has made them popular with savers seeking a high level of safety.

Banks are free to set their own minimum amounts, but they tend to range from $500 to $5,000 and more. Those that are $100,000 or over are called "jumbo CDs" and pay a slightly higher yield.

Although CD rates, terms, and dollar amounts vary from bank to bank, the following are generally available:

- 7- to 31-day CD with interest rate tied to that of a 13-week T-bill
- 91-day CD with interest rate tied to that of a 13-week T-bill
- 6-month CD with interest rate about ¼% above T-bill rate for the previous 4-week period
- 30-month CD with rate about 1% higher than that of shorter-maturities

HOW COMPOUNDING AFFECTS RETURNS ON A $1,000 CD OVER A
1-YEAR PERIOD

RATE	DAILY	MONTHLY	QUARTERLY	ANNUALLY
5%	$1,051.27	$1,051.16	$1,050.95	$1,050.00
6	1,061.83	1,061.69	1,061.37	1,060.00
7	1,072.50	1,072.28	1,071.86	1,070.00
8	1,083.28	1,083.00	1,082.44	1,080.00

SOURCE: Carteret Savings Bank, Morristown, NJ.

Determining how long to tie up your money is not always easy. If you've invested in a 3-year CD and interest rates rise, you'll be stuck with the old lower rate. On the other hand, if rates fall, you'll be glad to have locked in the high yield. In general, if rates are falling, buy longer-term CDs, and if they are rising, keep the maturities short.

You should also ask the bank how you will find out when your CD is due. The bank should either send you a reminder or call you a few weeks beforehand so you can decide whether to withdraw your certificate or roll it over into a new CD.

$ HINT: To maximize your return, buy a CD in which the interest is not actually paid out until maturity. This gives you the benefit of compounded interest.

Bank CD ads are often confusing, with two rates given: the fixed rate and the yield. You'll note that the yield figure is always higher, but to earn it, you must leave your CD at the bank for one full year at the same fixed rate. For example, if your bank advertises a fixed rate of 4.5% and a yield of 4.75% and you purchase a 6-month CD and take it out at maturity, you will earn only the 4.5% rate. On the other hand, if you purchase a one-year CD and leave it in for the full twelve months, you will earn the compounded 4.75% rate.

Remember, too, that if you take out your CD before it matures, you will be penalized; however, early withdrawal penalties are usually waived in three instances:

- If the owner dies or is found to be mentally incompetent
- If the CD is in a Keogh or IRA retirement plan and the depositor is over 59½ years old
- If the bank offers penalty-free early withdrawals

$ HINT: Before you buy a long-term CD, check out the Treasury note interest rate, especially if you're in the 28% tax bracket. T-note interest is exempt from state and local taxes; interest on CDs is not.

UNIQUE CDs
To remain competitive with money market mutual funds and other banks, some institutions market CDs with added imunitives. For

BANK CDs VS. T-BILLS

If you can afford to invest $10,000, compare the 6-month money market certificates with Treasury bills. In most cases (especially in states where income is taxed), the T-bills will be a better deal. Here's the calculation:

1 Since T-bills are sold at a discount, use this formula:

$$D = \frac{L}{360} \times SY$$

D = discount per $100 face value
L = life span of security
360 = number of days in financial year
SY = stated yield

With a 180-day T-bill and a 9% yield:

$$D = \frac{180}{360} = .5 \qquad .5 \times 9 = 4.5$$

Subtract the 4.50 ($450) from $10,000 to get $9,550 cost.

2 The true yield of the T-bill is more, because T-bill trading uses a 360-day year, but your money works 365 days and the stated yield is based on the cost.

$$TY = \frac{D}{C} \times \frac{365}{L}$$

TY = true yield
D = discount
C = cost
L = life span of security

With that 180-day T-bill, a yield of 9%, and a cost of $9,550, the true yield is 9.56%.

$$TY = \frac{450}{9550} \times \frac{365}{180}$$

$$4.71 \times 2.03 = 9.56\%$$

3 Interest on T-bills is exempt from state and local income taxes. Interest on the certificate is fully taxable.

4 If the certificate is cashed in early, there's a penalty. With T-bills, there's an active aftermarket, so you will get more than you invested since the sales price includes accumulated interest—unless there's a sharp rise in interest rates.

example, there are adjustable-rate CDs, in which the interest rate fluctuates weekly along with the average T-bill rate or some other stated rate. Other banks have "designer CDs," in which you set your own maturity date so you can time it to come due when your child goes off to college, when you retire, or when you will need a lump sum of money. There are also CDs with yields tied to the Standard & Poor 500 Stock Index, to the price of gold, even to the cost of college tuition.

➤ BUMP-UP. Bump-up CDs give you one or two opportunities to get higher returns when the issuing bank raises its CD rates after you purchased yours.

```
CDs WITH A TWIST

BANK                                      SPECIAL FEATURE
American Charter, Omaha, NE               Rises with interest rates
  (1-402-390-5000)                          every 6 months
College Savings Bank, Princeton, NJ      Rises with college tuition
  (1-800-888-2723)
Northeast Savings Bank, Hartford, CT     One-year tax advantage
  (1-203-280-1110)
Wells Fargo Bank, San Francisco, CA      Continual deposits;
  (1-415-396-3188)                         expandable CDs
```

➤ STEP-UP. The rates on step-up CDs, also called "rate builders," move up at a set pace at a predetermined time, say every 3, 5, or 12 months. Check the initial rate carefully: many step-up CDs start about 1% lower than the going rate.

§ HINT: If you have $50,000 to $100,000 to invest in a CD, negotiate your rate. Banks may pay between ¼% and 1% more on large CDs.

Before rushing out to buy one of the atypical CDs, find out precisely how the yield is calculated, whether it is tiered (the larger your deposit, the greater the interest rate), if it is automatically renewed upon maturity, and if so, whether at the same rate or a new one.

ZERO CDs

Some brokerage firms offer zero coupon CDs in a variety of maturities. This type of CD does not pay interest on a regular basis. Instead, it is sold at a discount from face value. The interest accrues annually until the CD matures. You must report the income for tax purposes each year as it accrues.

§ HINT: Zero CDs are more volatile in price than regular CDs, so plan to hold them until maturity.

JUNK CDs

During 1990, some banks started pushing a new type of investment popularly known as junk CDs.

☐ CAUTION: They're actually subordinated notes and are *not* insured by the F.D.I.C. or F.S.L.I.C. Although they have high yields—3 percentage points above Treasuries—they are not high enough to compensate for the fact that they are uninsured and that there's almost no secondary market. In addition, banks can call many of these notes prior to maturity. Denominations are as little as $1,000.

WHAT IS THE TRUE RATE?

Bank CD ads are often very confusing, with two rates given: fixed rate and yield. The yield figure is always higher, but to earn it, you must have your CD at the bank for one full year at the same annual rate. For example, if your bank advertises a fixed rate

---

FOUR WAYS TO MAKE MORE MONEY AT YOUR BANK

- *Stagger your maturities.* Mix your CD maturity dates, say, for 6 months, 12 months, and 15 months. If interest rates rise, you can reinvest CDs that mature at the new rate. If rates fall, your longer-term CDs will be earning the old, higher rate.
- *Invest your CD interest.* Ask your bank to invest your CD interest automatically in a money market deposit account. You'll earn interest on your interest yet have access to the money without incurring a withdrawal penalty.
- *Snowball a CD.* If your bank offers higher rates on larger CDs, it may pay to roll over several small CDs into one big one. Select a target date, say 1 month after your longest-term CD matures. When you renew your smaller CDs, have them mature on that date. Then all your CDs will mature on the same day and you can reinvest in one large CD with a high rate.
- *Establish your own interest-bearing checking account.* Instead of depositing your paycheck into your checking account, put it in your money market deposit account. Several times during the month, transfer money to cover your checks. You will earn money market rates and be less tempted to spend without thinking about it first.

---

of 6.5% and a yield of 6.75%, and you buy a 6-month CD and take it out at maturity, you will earn only the 6.5% fixed rate.

$ HINT: Roll over your 6-month CD so that it is on deposit the full year in order to earn the effective annual yield. In most institutions, the original yield is applicable even if the yield falls.

BROKERED CDs

Buying a CD through your stockbroker is often a better deal than buying it through a bank, because yields tend to be higher. That's because brokers have access to CDs from banks across the nation and are not limited to just one institution. Merrill Lynch, for example, can tap 160 banks, which gives investors more choices in terms of maturity, yield, and risk factor. And since brokered CDs are still bank CDs, they are insured up to $100,000.

Stockbrokers usually do not charge fees for CDs because they receive their commission from the issuing bank. Brokered CDs are also more liquid than their bank counterparts because they can be sold by your broker in a "secondary market." And there's no penalty for selling prior to maturity as there is with a bank CD.

However, the value of CDs, just like bonds, rises and falls in direct relationship to interest rates: if interest rates rise, the price of your CD will fall and you'll receive less than face value if you sell. If interest rates fall, you may be able to sell your brokered CD at a premium because it's worth

BROKERED CDs

FIRM	MINIMUM
A. G. Edwards (1-800-999-4448)	$1,000
Fidelity (1-800-544-8666)	5,000
Edward D. Jones (1-314-851-2000)	5,000
Merrill Lynch* (any local office)	1,000
Piper Jaffray & Hopwood (1-612-342-6000)	1,000
Prudential-Bache (local office)	1,000
Charles Schwab (1-800-435-4000)	5,000
Quick & Reilly (1-800-221-5220)	10,000
Quick & Reilly (1-800-522-8712 in NY)	

* Merrill Lynch's CDs are rated by Standard & Poor's.
(Data current May 1993.)

more, since its rate is higher than that being paid on newly issued certificates.

☐CAUTION: CDs purchased from a broker seldom pay compounded interest. The broker typically puts each interest payment into a money market fund that is part of your account at the firm. The interest is often lower than that being paid on your CD. Check with the broker first, so you understand exactly how your interest will be handled.

$ HINT: Some brokers sell CDs of troubled S&Ls in order to get higher yields. Make sure the CD you're buying is from a federally insured institution. The broker must tell you the name of the bank.

OUT-OF-STATE CDs

If you're seduced by ads for higher yields at out-of-state banks, remember that the grass isn't always greener. Proceed with caution and steer clear of troubled banks and S&Ls. Even though your money is insured up to $100,000, if the institution is closed,

MONEY MARKET FUNDS WITH COMPETITIVE YIELDS

Alger Fund	1-800-992-3863
Dreyfus Liquid Assets	1-800-645-6561
Dreyfus Worldwide Dollar Fund	1-800-645-6561
Evergreen Fund	1-800-235-0064
Fidelity Spartan	1-800-544-8888
Flex-Fund	1-800-325-FLEX
Vanguard Prime Portfolio	1-800-662-7447

☐CAUTION: Fidelity Spartan charges $2 per check if there's less than $50,000 in the account.

there may be a delay in getting your money out, and there have even been cases where high yields have been reduced.

$ HINT: Robert Heady, publisher of *100 Highest Yields,* a newsletter ranking federally insured banking institutions, suggests purchasing CDs only from banks whose net worth exceeds 5% of assets and have recorded a profit for the previous two quarters.

To find the nation's best CDs, check Heady's newsletter, *100 Highest Yields,* P.O. Box 088888, North Palm Beach, FL 33408; 1-800-327-7717; 8 issues $34; 52 issues, $98; and the Friday issues of the *Wall Street Journal,* which lists the top-yielding CDs for 1-, 2-, 3-, and 6-month and for 1-, 2-,

---

THE PLUSES OF MONEY MARKET FUNDS

- *Daily income.* Dividends are credited to your account each day, which means that your money is always working for you.
- *Liquidity.* There is no minimum investment period, and there are no early withdrawal penalties. Money can be withdrawn quickly by telephone, mail, wire, or check.
- *Stability of principal.* Most money market funds have a constant share price of $1. This makes it easy to determine the value of your investment at any time. Earnings are also paid in shares, so the value of a share never increases above $1. For example, if your interest in a money market mutual fund averaged 8% and you invested $1,000, at the end of 1 year you would have 1,080 shares worth $1,080.
- *No fees or commissions.* When you buy shares, all your money goes to work immediately.
- *Small minimum investment.* Some funds require as little as $500 initial investment; most minimums are between $1,000 and $2,000. In general, funds do not require shareholders to maintain the minimum investment as an average balance.
- *Safety.* Your money is used to buy prime debt of well-rated corporations or the U.S. government and its agencies. If you choose a fund that invests only in U.S. government securities, your yield will be ½% or so lower, but you can count on Uncle Sam's guarantee. Money market funds bought through your stockbroker are protected by the SIPC. This is because shares of money market funds are in fact securities (not cash). When held by a SIPC member in a customer's securities account, they are protected by the SIPC against the brokerage firm's failure but *not* against declines in the value of the securities (or shares) themselves. (See pages 46–47 for details on SIPC.)
- *Checkwriting.* Most funds offer this service free, although some require that checks written be for at least $250 or $500.
- *Continual high yields.* If rates drop, you will receive the higher interest rate for about a month afterward until the high-yielding securities are redeemed. With a bank, the yield changes more frequently, usually on a weekly basis.

and 5-year maturities. Several personal finance magazines, such as *Money* and *Your Money,* run lists of high-yielding CDs and bank money market deposit accounts.

MONEY MARKET MUTUAL FUNDS

These funds are pooled investments sold by mutual funds, insurance companies, and brokerage firms. They take your cash and invest in something called the money market—a term that describes the way in which the government, banks, corporations, and securities dealers borrow and lend money for short time periods. Money market mutual funds invest in such short-term financial instruments as Treasury bills and notes (government IOUs), CDs (bank IOUs), and commercial paper (corporate IOUs). Many also invest in repurchase agreements, bankers' acceptances, federal agency securities, Eurodollar CDs, and Yankeedollar CDs.

Money market funds are an excellent parking place for your money while trying to decide where to invest. They are not a true investment except when rates are high. Their rates are almost always slightly higher than the bank equivalent, a money market deposit account.

To buy shares in a money market fund, you simply call the fund directly or your stockbroker. You can get your money out at any time, either by writing a check (the fund provides the checks) or by wire.

You can find a list of money market funds in the financial pages of most newspapers and several financial magazines list those with the highest yields. Or see the boxes on pages 31 and 34 for suggestions.

THE MONEY MARKET: WHAT IT IS

Contrary to popular belief, the money market does not exist in the heart of Wall Street, or in London, Brussels, or even Washington, D.C. Nor is it housed in an impressive Greek revival building. The money market runs throughout the country and is made up of large corporations, banks, the federal government, and even local governments.

When any of these institutions need cash for a short period of time,

---

MAJOR USES OF MONEY MARKET FUNDS

- As a nest egg
- As a place to accumulate cash for a large expenditure, such as a house, a car, taxes, or a vacation
- As a temporary place to deposit large amounts of cash received from the sale of a stock or a property, an inheritance, an IRA rollover, etc.
- As a parking place until you find a desirable stock, bond, or other investment
- As a resting place for funds when switching from one mutual fund to another within a family of funds

WHAT THE MONEY MARKET MUTUAL FUNDS BUY

- *Bankers acceptances:* drafts issued and sold by banks with a promise to pay upon maturity, generally within no more than 180 days
- *Certificates of deposit:* large-denomination CDs sold by banks for money deposited for a minimum time period (14 days, 91 days, etc.)
- *Commercial paper:* unsecured IOUs issued by large institutions and corporations to the public to finance day-to-day operations, usually in amounts of $100,000 for up to 91 days
- *Eurodollar CDs:* dollar-denominated certificates of deposit sold by foreign branches of U.S. banks or by foreign banks; payable outside the United States, the minimum is generally $1 million, with maturities of 14 days or more
- *Government-agency obligations:* short-term securities issued by U.S. government agencies
- *Repurchase agreements ("repos"):* short-term buy/sell deals involving any money market instrument in which there is an agreement that the security will be resold to the seller on an agreed-on date, often the next day. The money market fund holds the security as collateral and charges interest for the loan. Repos are usually issued as a means for commercial banks and U.S. government securities dealers to raise temporary funds.
- U.S. Treasury bills and notes

ULTRASAFE MONEY MARKET FUNDS

	YIELD
Mutual Funds Specializing in U.S. Treasury Securities	
Capital Preservation Fund (1-800-321-8321)	2.61%
Fidelity Government Reserves (1-800-544-8888)	2.47
Fidelity U.S. Treasury Money Market (1-800-544-8888)	2.64
Vanguard U.S. Treasury Money Market Portfolio (1-800-662-7447)	2.82
Tax-free Money Market Funds	
Calvert Tax-free Reserves (1-800-368-2748)	2.33
Dreyfus Tax-exempt Money Market (1-800-645-6561)	1.96
Franklin Tax-exempt Money Fund (1-800-342-5236)	2.28
Lexington Tax-free Money Market (1-800-526-0056)	2.25
USAA Tax-exempt Money Market (1-800-531-8181)	2.25
High-Income States: Triple Tax-exempt	
Fidelity Massachusetts Tax-free MM Portfolio* (1-800-544-8888)	1.55
Prudential-Bache New York Money Market Fund (call local office)	1.80
Seligman California Money Market Fund (1-800-221-2783)	4.93

* Double-exempt.
(Yields as of July 1993.)

they borrow it from this seemingly elusive money market by issuing money market instruments. For example, the U.S. government borrows through Treasury bills, large corporations through commercial paper, and banks via jumbo CDs.

These instruments are purchased by other large corporations, banks, and extremely wealthy investors. The instruments pay high interest rates because the dollar amounts involved are so large, the maturity lengths are so short (1 year or less), and the borrowers are well known and considered excellent risks. These money market instruments, not stocks and bonds, constitute a money market mutual fund's portfolio.

BANK DEPOSIT ACCOUNTS VS. MONEY MARKET FUNDS

Competition between money market funds and bank deposit accounts is reflected in the extra services they advertise, such as free checking, discounts on brokerage services, no-fee credit cards and debit cards, extended lines of credit, and direct deposit of pension and dividend checks. Both institutions are vying for your dollars.

The key benefits of a bank account are these:

- Easy access at a number of local offices.
- Instant interest, as new deposits are credited immediately. With money market mutual funds, it takes a couple of days for the mail to get through and up to 5 days or more for the check to clear.
- Instant credit, as local merchants will accept checks drawn against your bank account but may balk at cashing one from a mutual fund's bank, especially if it is an out-of-state bank.

On the other hand, money market mutual funds are required to pay out all their earnings after expenses to shareholders and tend to pay higher rates than banks. Banks are required to pay only the rate that they decide on and advertise. The more competitive the banking atmosphere, of course, the higher the interest rate will be.

➤ SELECTING THE RIGHT MONEY MARKET FUND Although there are several hundred money market mutual funds, they fall into four basic categories. Knowing which one is best for meeting your investment goals will help narrow the search.

- *General funds.* Available from your stockbroker or directly from the fund itself, by calling its toll-free number, general funds invest in nongovernment money market securities.
- *Government-only funds.* Also available directly or from a broker, government-only funds limit their investments to U.S. government or federal agency securities. Because their portfolios are backed by the "full faith and credit" of the U.S. government, they are regarded as less risky; consequently, they have lower yields than general funds.
- *Tax-free funds.* Available directly or from a broker, tax-free funds restrict their portfolios to short-term tax-exempt municipal bonds. Their income is free from federal tax but not necessarily from state and local taxes. These are generally advisable only for investors in the

28% tax bracket. Their yields are, of course, much lower, sometimes about half those of a regular money market fund.

Even though their yields are lower, tax-free money market funds are more appealing, now that other ways of sheltering income are limited by the 1986 Tax Reform Act.

- *Triple tax-exempt money funds.* Designed for residents of high-income-tax states, such as New York, California, Massachusetts, and Connecticut, these invest in short-term tax-exempt municipals and are free from federal, state, and local taxes for residents of the states and localities that issue them.

By shopping around you will find that some funds have higher yields than others (see the table on page 34). At various times the yield discrepancy has been as much as 3% to 3½% on taxable funds. But the current yield is not the only factor to consider; look also at the 12-month yield and the character of the fund's holdings.

➤ MATURITY The risk factor—even though it's quite minimal with money market funds—rises with the portfolio's maturity. By law, any money market fund that says it keeps its net asset value at $1 per share is required to limit its average portfolio maturity to 90 days. If you're a conservative investor, select a fund with maturities of 90 days or less. If you're willing to assume more risk, you may get a slightly higher yield.

➤ QUALITY Lower-quality portfolios lead to higher yields but also higher risk.

➤ EXPENSES Money market funds take an annual management charge, called the *expense ratio,* from the investor's assets. These fees range from about 0.48% to 0.80%.

Funds that have the highest yields are often those with fewest expenses deducted from the portfolio's earnings. According to *Donoghue's Money Fund Report,* expense charges generate nearly two-thirds of the discrepancy in yields. You can actually boost your returns by switching to a fund with lower expenses. Among the funds whose expenses have been low for a number of years are Vanguard and Kemper. Some funds actually waive fees. According to Sheldon Jacobs, editor of *No-Load Fund Investor* newsletter, Dreyfus Worldwide Dollar, the Flex-Fund, and Fidelity Spartan have guaranteed fee waivers seemingly for an indefinite time.

💲HINT: The average money fund's expense ratio as a percentage of assets is about 0.75%. Therefore, a fund earning 10% gives a yield to investors of 9.25%.

WHEN INTEREST RATES CHANGE

Now that you've been introduced to three of the key "safe havens" for your money—bank money market deposit accounts, money market mutual funds, and CDs—it's time to understand what to do when interest rates change and how to track such changes.

The best indicator of trends in CD and money market account rates is something called the federal funds rate—the rate banks charge each other for overnight loans. If a bank must pay more itself to borrow money, it

---

TAKE ADVANTAGE OF INTEREST RATE CHANGES

1 When rates are low: buy short-term CDs.
2 When rates begin to rise: put more money into your money market account so you can ride up with the rates.
3 When rates are high: lock in yields with long-term CDs. Move money out of money market accounts into higher-yielding CDs.
4 When rates are falling: immediately lock in with a CD before they fall further.
5 When rates are low: invest over the short term and add to your money market account so that your cash will be available for reinvesting when rates begin to rise.

---

will try to raise more money to pay for this increased cost by offering higher yields to potential depositors. The federal fund rate is listed in the financial pages of major newspapers.

To determine what action to take when interest rates move up or down, read the box below.

CREDIT UNIONS

A credit union is a cooperative, not-for-profit financial institution organized to provide checking, savings, loans, and other financial services for members. Membership is limited to those having a common bond—occupation, association, etc.—and to groups within a community or neighborhood. Many credit unions allow members to remain members even if they move away or change jobs.

Credit unions are member owned and controlled, with each member having an equal vote and the opportunity to serve on the board of directors. The board, elected by the membership, sets dividend and interest rates. Board members are volunteers, except for the treasurer, and they may not receive payment for their services.

Credit unions are either state or federally chartered. State-chartered unions are supervised by a state regulatory agency. Federally chartered ones are supervised by the National Credit Union Administration, an independent agency in the executive branch of the federal government. Member share accounts are insured up to $100,000 per account by the National Credit Union Share Insurance Fund.

There are approximately 13,890 credit unions representing more than $241.9 billion in assets and over 64.5 million individual member-owners.

Credit union CDs, sharedraft accounts (interest-bearing checking accounts), and money market deposit accounts pay extremely competitive rates, often ½% higher than banks. Loans may be ½% lower. Credit unions can afford to undercut their competitors because they are nonprofit corporations, don't pay taxes, and are essentially volunteer directed.

Credit unions are also available for students. The Credit Union National Association Foundation, Inc., offers a training manual for student credit unions entitled *Handbook for College Student Credit Unions.*

$ HINT: To find a credit union near you, call the Credit Union National Association's special help number, 1-800-358-5710.

FOR FURTHER INFORMATION

For material on loans, savings and protecting your money, contact:

Credit Union National Association
P.O. Box 431
Madison, WI 57301

For information on how to pick a bank, with specific details on banks in the greater New York City area, read:

Jeff Blyskal, "Finding the Best Bank for Your Dollar," *New York* magazine, December 7, 1992.

4

PROTECTING ALL YOUR INVESTMENTS

The recent wave of failures and mergers of financial institutions has caused even the most trusting investors and savers to question how safe their securities and cash are in the nation's banks, savings and loans, mutual funds, brokerage firms, and insurance companies—and rightly so.

AT YOUR BANK

Over the past several years, more banks and savings and loan associations have been liquidated or merged than at any time since the Great Depression. The number of commercial and savings banks on the F.D.I.C.'s trouble list now numbers about 900. The troubled banks hold nearly $400 billion— more than 10% of the banking industry's total assets.

THE FACTS

Most of the country's commercial banks are insured by the Federal Deposit Insurance Corporation (F.D.I.C.), an independent government agency. To be eligible for membership in the F.D.I.C., a bank must meet certain standards and be regularly examined by both federal and state agencies. Member banks pay insurance fees, which are in turn invested in federal government securities. This constitutes the F.D.I.C.'s Bank Insurance Fund. In addition, the F.D.I.C. may borrow several billion dollars from the U.S. Treasury if it needs to.

Most savings and loan associations (also known as thrifts), which prior to August 9, 1989, were insured by the Federal Savings & Loan Insurance Corporation (F.S.L.I.C.), are now insured by the FDIC through the new Savings Association Insurance Fund (SAIF). Some savings and loan associations are insured by state insurance, and a very few are privately insured. A handful of savings and loan associations have absolutely no insurance at all.

Most credit unions (95%) are insured by the National Credit Union Administration (N.C.U.A.); others, by state agencies.

The F.D.I.C. and N.C.U.A. are backed by the federal government, and money insured by them is considered safe since the government would presumably come to their rescue. Banks that are insured by a state or privately, however, do *not* have the backing of the federal government.

WHAT YOU CAN DO

The solution is not to tuck your money under the mattress but to bank only at federally insured institutions. And know the facts about insurance.

GOVERNMENT PROTECTION

FEDERAL DEPOSIT INSURANCE CORPORATION BANK INSURANCE FUND
- Insures depositors for up to $100,000
- Consumer hotline: 1-800-934-3342
- Address for more information on evaluating your bank: 550 17th Street NW, Washington, DC 20429

SAVINGS ASSOCIATION INSURANCE FUND
- Insures depositors for up to $100,000
- Consumer affairs: 1-800-934-3342
- Address for more information on evaluating your S&L: 550 17th Street NW, Washington, DC 20429

NATIONAL CREDIT UNION SHARE INSURANCE FUND
- Insures depositors for up to $100,000
- Telephone: 1-202-682-9640
- Address for more information on your credit union: 1776 G Street NW, Washington, DC 20456

RULES FOR EXISTING ACCOUNTS:

- Contrary to popular opinion, or wishful thinking, the government doesn't insure $100,000 per account. Instead, it insures $100,000 per person at any one bank or savings and loan in any one right and capacity. If you have several savings accounts, even at different branches of the same institution, and they are all in the same name, they are lumped together for insurance coverage. In other words, if you have four accounts in the same name in one institution, you are insured only for a total of $100,000, not $400,000.

- The $100,000 figure applies to both principal and interest. So, if you have $98,000 in an account and you then earn $5,000 in interest, your account will be insured for $100,000, leaving $3,000 uninsured.

- If you have money in a checking account, a savings account, and a CD at one bank, in your name, you do not get $100,000 of insurance for each account—you only get a total coverage of $100,000. And, changing your name on different accounts, by using a middle initial, for example, will not change your coverage.

- If you are married, you can get coverage for more than one account: You and your spouse can each have an individual savings account. You may also have one joint account. In addition, you can set up two trust accounts, known as revocable testamentary accounts, one in trust for your spouse, the other being your spouse in trust for you. This type of account pays the balance to the beneficiary upon the death of the trustee. And you could each have an IRA account. That's a total of seven accounts. With $100,000 in each, all $700,000 would be insured even though it's all in the same bank.

☐ CAUTION: If you left that $700,000 in one single account, $600,000 of it
would NOT be insured.

■ Some other types of testamentary accounts are insured separately if
the beneficiary or beneficiaries are "qualified" as kinship—a child,
stepchild, grandchild, step-grandchild or spouse. An account in trust
for a parent, niece or friend is treated as another account in your
name and does NOT get separate coverage. Note that these types of
accounts are insured to $100,000 per qualifying beneficiary. Thus, an
account in trust for your three children is insured to $300,000.

■ Joint accounts are insured separately from individual accounts, but
with certain limitations—you are insured for up to $100,000 on the
money you have in all joint accounts at any one bank. If, for instance
you have $100,000 in three joint accounts at the same bank—one
with your wife and one with each of your two daughters—your share
of each would be $50,000, or half, for a total of $150,000. Of that
only $100,000 will be insured.

■ The F.D.I.C. treats all joint accounts owned by the same combination
of people at the same bank as being one account. So, if you and your
spouse have a joint checking and a joint savings account, the two
together are insured for up to $100,000. And don't try reversing the
order of your names or using your Social Security number on one and
your spouse's on another—it doesn't work.

$ HINT: If you have a loan or home equity line of credit at your bank,
check its financial condition (see ways to obtain reports below). If
your bank should fail, you could lose access to your credit line—a real
problem if you need the money.

Remember, too, that changes in your life can affect your F.D.I.C.
coverage. For example, death could convert your joint account to an
individual account and thus put you over the $100,000 limit. Or, your
interest accrual or a large cash payment, say from the sale of a home,
insurance proceeds, inheritance, or a lump sum pension distribution, could
likewise toss your balance above the insurance limit.

CHOOSE ONLY INSURED PRODUCTS

Banks offer both insured and uninsured products. If you
are uncertain about a particular product, ask the bank
to give you written assurance regarding its coverage.
Products that are typically insured include: checking
accounts, savings accounts, NOW accounts, Christmas club accounts, certificates of deposit, money market deposit accounts, and trust fund accounts.

Banking products that are NOT typically insured include: annuities,
mutual funds, life insurance, stocks, bonds, government securities (Treasury
bills, bonds, notes), repurchase agreements, and commercial paper, which
includes shares of the bank's stock.

IF YOUR BANK FAILS

Some F.D.I.C. rulings have been changed and additional
modifications are expected. Before the recent amendments
were adopted, the F.D.I.C. sought to transfer all a failed bank's or thrift's

deposits to a new buyer. Now, however, the corporation transfers large deposits only when such transactions are the least costly method of resolution of the bank or thrift to the BIF or SAIF fund.

☐CAUTION: If a federally insured institution fails, regulators will liquidate the assets, and insured depositors will be paid usually in 5 business days. If you have money in excess of the $100,000 insured limit, however, you will have a pro rata stake for that portion in excess of $100,000, along with other creditors, and you may or may not get that portion of your money back.

BANK CHECKUP

You can protect your money by taking these steps: Get an overview of the financial condition of your bank, savings & loan or credit union. For fees ranging from $10 to $35 you can get various reports on the financial health of your bank from these two private rating companies:

Veribank, Inc.
P.O. Box 461
Wakefield, MA 01880
1-617-245-8370; 1-800-442-2657

Bauer Financial Reports
Box 145510
Coral Gables, FL 33114-5510
1-800-388-6686

Charges $10 for the first report; $2 for the second.

HOW TO TELL IF YOUR BANK IS IN TROUBLE

Experts give this advice regarding a bank's financial health:

- *Step one.* Get a copy of your bank's annual report and financial statements.
- *Step two.* Request and read the "Report of Condition" on your bank (not available for branches, only main banks). It will tell you how much the bank is making, what its loan portfolio is made up of, and what percentage of loans is nonperforming. The F.D.I.C. will bill you $6. Do not send cash. Order from:

F.D.I.C.
M.I.S.B. Disclosure Group, Room F-518
550 17th Street NW
Washington, DC 20429
1-202-898-7112; 1-800-934-3342

- *Step three.* Once you have gathered these documents, here's what to look for:
- Excessively rapid growth of commercial loans indicates a bank that

hasn't enough expert people to check credit ratings and make loan assessments.

- Unusually high loan portfolio yields indicate that the bank may be making risky loans.
- Increased reliance on funds outside the bank's natural market suggests lack of client support and a pulling out of outsiders at the first sign of trouble.
- How solid is the bank's loan portfolio? Determine by comparing nonperforming assets (loans that are 90+ days overdue or are no longer accruing interest) to total loans, the F.D.I.C. bank standard being 1%.
- Could the bank handle a run? Look for a loan-deposit ratio of no more than 70% and a minimum of 5% in cash or short-term investments.
- *Step four.* Watch the stock. If your bank is publicly traded, follow its price. A big drop can signal trouble. Bank of New England's price, which was a little over $9/share at the beginning of 1990, dropped to under $1 just before it was taken over by regulators.
- *Step five.* Look at lending activity. The bank's loan portfolio should be diversified and not largely concentrated in real estate and/or foreign debt.
- *Step six.* Get ratings. Banks should be willing to tell you how their securities are rated by Moody's Investors Service and Standard & Poor's Corp., two independent rating services.

HELP FROM REGULATORS

If you're having a problem with your bank, call one of the regulatory authorities listed below. They are surprisingly accessible, often more so than your local bank official. If you need to file a written complaint, include a brief statement describing the problem and a list of the steps you've taken to try to resolve it. Include your bank account number and copies of all documents.

Ask the customer service department which regulator oversees your bank—they are legally obligated to tell you.

FDIC
Office of Consumer Affairs
550 17th Street NW
Washington, DC 20429
1-800-934-3342

Federal Reserve Board
Consumer & Community Affairs
Mail Stop 198
20th and C Streets NW
Washington, DC 20551
1-202-452-3946

Office of Thrift Supervision
Consumer Affairs Division
1700 G Street NW
Washington, DC 20552
1-202-906-6237 or
1-800-842-6929

U.S. Comptroller of the Currency
Compliance Management
Mail Stop 642-C
490 L'Enfant Plaza SW
Washington, DC 20219
1-202-622-2000

- *Step seven.* Give your bank this test:
- Does the bank have enough equity? This determines whether it has a cash cushion to cover big losses. The bank's total assets and its total equity, also known as shareholder's equity, are on the statement of condition in the annual report. Divide assets into equity and express the result as a percentage. Beware if equity is below 5% of assets.
- Does the bank have too many "problem" loans? Problem loans or notes are those that are 3 months or longer past due or that are unlikely to ever be paid—these are noted in the section called "past due and nonaccrual loans." Look at the bank's loan-loss reserve balance; this is money on hand to cover problem loans. If problem loans are greater than loan-loss reserves, the bank could be headed toward insolvency.
- Check the bank's profitability. If its net income—listed in the call report—is positive, it's okay. If it's negative, then the bank is losing money, and you should divide the latest year's loss by the months of red ink. The result is the average monthly loss rate. Then divide the bank's equity by the average monthly loss rate to find out how long the bank can keep losing money at the current rate before it runs out of equity.

IF YOUR BANK OR SAVINGS & LOAN FAILS Should the unthinkable happen and a federally insured bank or savings & loan fail, the Savings Association Insurance Fund (SAIF) will either liquidate the institution's assets to pay off depositors or transfer assets to a healthy institution. You may have to wait, but you will receive your principal and interest, up to $100,000.

In most cases, in fact, a solvent institution takes over the failed institution's assets and liabilities. For example, the April 1990 collapse of Seamen's Bank for Savings in New York, the largest bank failure of the year, was estimated to cost the F.D.I.C. $2.8 billion. Seamen's 13 branches, valued at $2.1 billion, were sold to Chase Manhattan Bank for $5 million.

☐CAUTION: When accounts of a failed institution are transferred, the new management can lower the interest rate being paid on CDs or increase the rate you pay on a home-equity loan or other credit line. However, you must be given prior notice and time to make penalty-free switches to another institution that has more favorable rates. If bank officials won't let you know whether they are honoring your existing terms, take it as a warning and begin looking for a new bank or savings & loan.

If you have a loan, the loan cannot be called in by the new bank under any conditions not spelled out by the original loan agreement. Check your agreement for loopholes.

IN A MUTUAL FUND

Since the 1987 stock market crash, questions that were once unthinkable— Could a mutual fund close down? Could it cancel the investor's right to redeem shares? Could it run out of cash to meet shareholders' demand?— are unthinkable no longer.

The mutual fund industry is governed by the Investment Company Act of 1940—but that doesn't guarantee total protection. Here are the facts:

➤ BANKRUPTCY The assets of a mutual fund belong to the shareholders, and all securities are held in trust by a third party. A fund's directors can theoretically ask shareholders to allow the fund to close down if assets have dwindled away and it is no longer profitable to operate, for example, but to date this has not happened.

It's far more likely that a troubled fund will merge into a larger, healthier one; this often happens when a bank, S&L, or brokerage firm goes bankrupt. However, a very small fund that is poorly managed might be unable to attract a merger candidate.

If a fund were to liquidate, the shareholders' fortunes would depend on market conditions and the quality of the fund's holdings. The S.E.C. would oversee the sale and subsequent distribution of assets. A small fund with large holdings of thinly traded securities or little cash on hand could be in for losses if the market were down.

➤ SUSPENSION OF TRADING Trading can be suspended only in national emergencies—closing of the New York Stock Exchange, presidential assassination, war, etc. However, even under these circumstances, you still have the right to place a redemption order—and such an order would lock in the price at the end of the day.

➤ CASH RESERVES The fund managers hold cash and Treasury securities in their reserves, plus proceeds from security sales. Funds also have bank credit available to them: they can borrow $1 for every $3 of assets. Yet a heavily invested fund, when faced with a barrage of redemption requests, might have to sell stocks even when it would prefer not to.

$ HINT: Invest only in a fund that has at least 10% or more in cash reserves.

➤ PROTECTING YOURSELF IN THE FUTURE (1) Find out if your fund has an office locally; if so, keep some of your money there, so you can have access to it in person. (2) Prepare the fund's official redemption form or letter, and be prepared to send it by Express Mail if the telephone systems are overloaded.

$ HINT: It doesn't matter what time of day you put in your mutual fund buy or sell order; as long as it's in before 4 P.M., you're guaranteed the closing share price that day. Phones are busiest in the morning.

IN A MONEY MARKET FUND

All investors want to know how safe their money market fund or account is. It's very safe. But every investment has some degree of risk. Money market funds have an excellent safety record, primarily because they invest in short-term securities of the government, large institutions, and corporations. However, on April 12, 1990, Mortgage and Realty Trust declared bankruptcy, affecting $150 million in outstanding commercial paper. About half that paper was owned by a number of money market funds, including T. Rowe Price and Alliance.

In each case, the parent companies of the affected funds bought back the defaulted paper, thus preventing any losses to investors. That event underscored a fact that had largely been ignored—that money market funds, while very safe, are not totally risk free.

The basic principle to keep in mind is: The shorter the maturity of an investment, the lower the risk.

Short portfolio maturities keep a fund's risk level to a minimum, because a bank or corporation whose securities are sold in the money markets is not very likely to default in such a short time. In addition, securities that mature so quickly seldom fluctuate in value. A money market mutual fund's securities must mature in 1 year or less, and no one individual security may make up more than 5% of a fund's assets.

$ HINT: The average maturity is about 40 days. You can check maturities in the financial section of your newspaper.

For the ultimate in safety, select a fund that invests only in Treasury issues (see list on page 34). These are backed by the full faith and credit of the U.S. government. They are called "government" or "Treasury-only" funds. The yields are about 1% lower than nongovernment money market funds.

Several other factors contribute to the superior safety of money funds: (1) Money fund managers continually analyze and compile ratings of the strength of the issuers of money market instruments. Whenever an issuer's credit rating declines, the name is deleted from the acceptable list. (2) The SEC regulates the funds, requiring annual independent audits, detailed data in the fund's prospectus, and making other disclosure requirements. Money market funds must have:

- Ninety-five percent of their assets in the highest-grade commercial paper. The other 5% can be held in second-tier paper, such as A-2 or P-2, but no more than 1% of this can come from the same issuer.
- No more than 5% of a fund's total assets can be invested in the securities of a single issuer, except for those of the U.S. government.
- The average maturity of a fund's portfolio can be no more than 90 days, down from the previous requirement of 120 days.

☐ CAUTION: If your account is with a bank that has F.D.I.C. or a savings and loan that has F.S.L.I.C., it is insured up to $100,000 per account name. Money market mutual funds with your stockbroker are protected by S.I.P.C. Money market mutual funds purchased directly from the fund are not insured unless the fund itself indicates that they are. Be sure to ask.

$ HINT: Invest in a large money market fund, one with at least $1 billion in assets. It's more likely to protect shareholders than a small fund.

AT A BROKERAGE FIRM

The Securities Investor Protection Corporation is a $691 million fund supported by nearly 8,100 member brokerage firms. It also has a $1 billion credit line with the government that can be activated only by the SEC. The

S.I.P.C. is neither a government agency nor a regulatory agency. Rather, it is funded through assessment of dealer members. All brokers and dealers registered with the SEC and national stock exchanges must contribute. If a member brokerage firm fails, the S.I.P.C. appoints a trustee to liquidate the firm and perhaps transfer customer accounts to another broker. (If the firm is small, the S.I.P.C. may decide to cover losses from its funds immediately.)

If it has the securities on hand, the liquidating firm will send the securities registered in customers' names directly to them. If it does not have enough securities to meet all customer claims, the customers will receive them on a pro rata basis, and any remaining claims will be settled in cash. However, this ties up your money for several months.

If the brokerage house in liquidation does not have enough securities or funds to settle all claims, the rest will be met by the S.I.P.C.—up to $500,000 per customer, including $100,000 for any cash held in the brokerage account.

The S.I.P.C. covers only cash and securities, that is, stocks, bonds, CDs, notes, and warrants on securities. Commodities and commodity options are *not* covered. Shares in money market mutual funds *are* covered by the S.I.P.C.

$ HINT: Extend your coverage by opening a second account as a joint account with your spouse, as a trustee for a child, or as a business account. Each account receives full protection—$500,000.

Keep in mind that the S.I.P.C. covers losses due to the failure of the firm, not losses because investments turned out to be of poor quality or because securities fell in price. And many brokerage firms carry additional insurance, about which you can ask your broker. In the past 21 years, S.I.P.C. has liquidated about 228 firms, more than half in their first 4 years.

Burned by the poor performance of the stock market in 1987 and the American investors' subsequent flight to safety, brokerage firms and sponsors of various investment products have added a new enticing feature to their advertisements, touting them as "guaranteed" or "insured." The idea, of course, is to make high-risk investments appear safe. Many of these guarantees have questionable value and are being investigated by the SEC. Ask your broker or financial planner these questions when you're faced with what appears to be a come-on:

- How much of my money is being invested in the primary product? Where will the rest be invested?
- How long is the guarantee or insurance good for?
- Am I protected against market loss?
- If the project or investment fails, who is responsible for covering the losses?
- Who backs the insurance or guarantee?

IN A PENSION PLAN

Think of pension plans like any other investment—one that requires safeguarding.

- Defined benefit plans promise a set amount upon retirement, usually a percentage of earnings multiplied by the number of years you worked at the company. Most are insured by the Pension Benefit Guaranty Corporation, "an F.D.I.C.-like agency that will pay each employee up to about $28,000 a year if the company fails.

☐CAUTION: A company can terminate a fully funded pension plan at any time and pay benefits in a lump sum or buy annuities from insurance companies to take over monthly benefit payments. When that happens you have lost your protection.

- Defined contribution plans, which include 401(k)s, profit sharing plans, and employee stock option plans, include more than 80% of all private pensions. The amount contributed to the plan by you and by your employer is typically a percentage of your pay or the company's profits.

☐CAUTION: You are not guaranteed a specific amount upon retirement. You get the contributions plus any earnings. And, this type of plan is not insured by the Pension Benefit Guaranty Corporation.

About one-third of the money in defined contribution plans is invested in a Guaranteed Investment Contract (GIC), which, like bank CDs, pay a guaranteed interest rate for a set time. GICs are sold by insurance companies; if you do not live in one of the states that insures these plans, your money is backed by the insurer only. If the insurance company is in bad shape, then so is the GIC it sells.

🅂HINT: Ask your company's plan administrator for a copy of Form 5500, the financial report the plan is required to file with the Labor Department. For help in understanding the form and your retirement plan in general, send $6 to Pension Publications, 918 16th Street NW, Washington, D.C. 20006 for a copy of "Protecting Your Pension Money."

If your pension money is invested with an insurance company, read that section in this chapter for safety tips.

AT AN INSURANCE COMPANY

In recent years, several life insurance giants became insolvent. Heavy investments in junk bonds brought Executive Life Insurance Company to its knees and Mutual Benefit Life Insurance was seized by New Jersey regulators, making it the largest insurance failure in the nation's history.

Consumers have less protection when life insurers fail than they do when banks tumble. Insurance companies are regulated by state commissioners, not by federal authorities, and there is no national fund to cover losses. Instead, when an insurer fails, state regulators collect assessments from other insurers operating in the same state to pay off policyholders. Rules regarding who is eligible for reimbursement vary from state to state.

Until policies can be transferred to another company or some other arrangements are made, insurers typically lose access to the cash value of their contracts, sometimes for periods of a year or more. It is possible that, in the final analysis, they may get less than the contract's full value.

$ HINT: Call your state insurance commission to make certain you would be covered under the state guaranty system if your insurer became insolvent. Some state plans cover contract holders of companies headquartered in that state regardless of where they live; others guarantee only their own residents and only if they are insured by companies licensed in that state.

You should also check the four independent services that rate the financial conditions of insurance companies: A.M. Best, Moody's Standard & Poor's, and Duff & Phelps.

PROTECTING YOURSELF AGAINST NEW SCAMS

A surprising number of intelligent people are taken in by scam artists, who seem to know just how to swindle money out of investors and savers alike. The best of the scam artists tie their pitch to current events, thereby improving their credibility and creating a sense of urgency. They do best among the elderly, who tend to be more passive (or kindly) when it comes to dealing with strangers.

As the American public becomes increasingly tired of telephone solicitations, scam artists are switching to other means, primarily church groups, professional societies, and group help organizations. Some have even managed to infiltrate organizations that help families of AIDs victims. Once the swindler has made (or says he has) a substantial amount of money for one member, he then tries, often with success, to work the whole group.

According to Barry Guthary, president of the North American Securities Administrators Association, cold callers are enticing investors to replace CDs with higher-yielding investments at much greater risk, even when there are penalties for early withdrawal of the certificates. The majority of the victims are people on fixed incomes. An "Investor Alert," published by N.A.S.A.A. and the Council of Better Business Bureaus, warns that banks, in an effort to keep depositors' money, are offering investments, mutual funds, and annuities that may not be covered by federal deposit insurance.

$ HINT: To protect yourself, never give a cold caller your credit number, your bank account number, your Social Security number, or write him a check.

IF YOU ARE ELDERLY OR HAVE ELDERLY FRIENDS YOU SHOULD KNOW THAT:

- Con artists study obituaries, notices of probate proceedings, and real estate transactions to find elderly victims.
- Con artists know that the elderly often have substantial savings or proceeds from pension and insurance policies.

- Widowed men and women often lack experience in managing finances if their spouse took care of such matters.
- The elderly are often home alone with no one to ask them to think twice about an impulsive investment.
- Elderly people tend to be less suspicious of strangers and more willing to talk to them, even to invite them into their homes.
- Today's elderly grew up thinking a handshake was the right way to make a business deal.

FOR FURTHER INFORMATION

For information about the SIPC and what it covers:

SIPC
805 15th Street NW, Suite 800
Washington, DC 20005
1-202-371-8300

If you have a complaint or a question about your bank, write to the Consumer Services Division of your State Banking Commission or Department in your state capital. If you live in New York, write to:

Consumer Services Division
New York State Banking Department
2 Rector Street
New York, NY 10006
1-212-618-6445

For information about a brokerage firm and its insurance:

Office of Consumer Affairs
Securities & Exchange Commission
450 Fifth Street NW
Washington, DC 20549
1-202-272-7440

For the booklet "How to Get Safety Information from Your Financial Institution," send $2 to:

Weiss Research
2200 North Florida Mango Road
West Palm Beach, FL 33409
1-800-289-9222

It includes postcard questionnaires you can send to your bank, savings & loan, insurance company, or stockbroker, along with simple instructions on how to interpret the answers.

5

MOVING FROM SAVER TO INVESTOR

TRUE GRIT

Now that you have set aside money in several safe places where it is earning well above the savings account rate, you are ready to stretch your wings and move into the arena of the true investor. Incidentally, before you leap from saver to investor, you should have a minimum of 6 months' worth of living expenses in one of the safe havens discussed in the previous chapters. That means if you need $4,000 per month to operate comfortably, set aside $24,000 in a combination of CDs, Treasuries, and money funds. Then if you are hit with a financial emergency, such as losing your job or getting a serious illness, you will have immediate liquid resources to draw upon.

$ HINT: If you feel your job may be in jeopardy, set aside at least 9 months of expenses—it's taking longer for people to find new jobs in these hard times.

Moving from saver to investor is a step many people, especially those with a conservative bent, find difficult to take. Some, in fact, never manage to make the move at all. Although there's nothing inherently wrong with leaving your money in a safe haven, during inflationary periods you may actually lose money, and during a bull market, even a moderate one, you'll be on the sidelines. And, for those facing high taxes, these safe investments are not truly safe at all, for instead of reducing your federal income tax bite, they add to it.

Of course, no investment is for all seasons. Review the tables on pages 60–61 to help you determine which vehicles are best during various economic periods. Keep in mind that the greater the risk you take, the greater the potential return.

MUTUAL FUNDS VS. INDIVIDUAL SECURITIES

One of the first key decisions you will have to make as you move from saver to investor is whether to select your own stocks and bonds or to buy shares in a mutual fund. Mutual funds, in which professional portfolio managers make all the buy and sell decisions, are described in Chapter 6. There are more mutual funds than stocks trading on the New York Stock Exchange. By reading the chapters on mutual funds, stocks, and bonds, you can arrive at portfolio conclusions that suit your investing temperament and income level.

If you are interested in stocks, a good place to begin is in your own backyard. Investigate your local utility company or a corporation headquar-

MOVING FROM SAVER TO INVESTOR

INVESTMENT	WHERE TO FIND	FACTS TO KNOW
Savings account	Bank, credit union	What is the interest rate? How often is it compounded? Is it federally insured?
Money market deposit account	Bank, credit union	What is the interest rate? How often does it change? Are there withdrawal penalties/limitations?
Certificate of deposit (CD)	Bank, credit union	How much money will I have at maturity? Can I roll it over at the same or a higher rate? Are there withdrawal penalties?
Brokered CD	Stockbroker	Will my interest compound? If I sell my CD back to you before maturity, will I lose money? Is the originating bank sound?
Money market mutual fund	Brokerage firm, mutual fund	What is the yield? What is the fund's average maturity?
EE savings bonds	Bank, Federal Reserve, Bureau of Public Debt	What is the current rate? When do the bonds mature?
Treasury issues	Bank, Federal Reserve, Bureau of Public Debt	What is the current rate? If I redeem early will I lose money? Is there a fee?
Stocks	Brokerage firm, investment club	What is the commission? Is there a dividend? What is the *Value Line* rating?
Bonds	Brokerage firm	What is the commission? Can the bond be called? What is the yield? What is the rating?
Mutual funds	Mutual fund, brokerage firm	What is the total return for 6 months, 1 and 5 years? Are there fees?

tered in your area. Call for the annual report and ask a local broker for additional research information. Another easy way to dip into the market is by purchasing shares in the company you work for or one whose products or services you use and like. If you are wedded to your Reeboks or if you love Kellogg cereals, you might like to start down the investor's path by purchasing stocks in those companies.

HOW TO SET UP A MONEY-MAKING PORTFOLIO

The world of finance is complex, competitive, subject to economic and political pressures, and dominated by shrewd, powerful people who control billions of dollars. For most Americans who can save only a few thousand dollars a year, making money in such an arena sounds difficult, if not impossible.

Yet everyone can be a successful investor if he or she takes time to set specific objectives, to learn the facts, to adhere to proven profitable rules, to be patient, and, most important, to use common sense. Sometimes success comes quickly, but over the long term, making money requires careful planning and conscientious management.

You may feel that the index arbitrageurs, institutional managers, huge fund managers, and program traders control the game. To a large extent they do—yet market crashes take them down too, in many cases more than the smaller individual investors who don't panic and don't sell out at overwhelming losses.

If you proceed with caution and gather sound information, you have one major advantage over the big guns: You care more about your money than any stockbroker, fund manager, or financial adviser ever will.

PREVENTIVE PORTFOLIO MANAGE-MENT

If you are averse to risk or want to reduce your risk quotient, here are seven easy preventive techniques that will enable you to maintain a healthy portfolio and weather any future declines in the market.

- *Diversify.* To some extent you can protect yourself from market swings by owning a mixture of stocks, bonds, precious metals, real estate, and other investments, because seldom does everything decline at the same time.
- *Buy for the long haul.* If you plan in general to hold your stocks 1 to 3 years, day-to-day and month-to-month fluctuations can largely be ignored.
- *Select investments on the basis of quality.* Take advantage of low-priced high-quality stocks. Ignore rumors and study the fundamentals.
- *Include high-yield investments.* Common stocks with high dividends, preferred stock, high-yielding bonds, and closed-end bond funds all help cushion dips in the market.
- *Investigate convertibles.* Their yields are higher than the underlying stock of the same company, and should the stock fall in price, the convertible (CV) will fall less.

- *Use dollar cost averaging.* With both mutual funds and stocks, this approach enables you to buy more shares at lower prices and fewer shares at higher prices, as well as to ignore short-term market gyrations. (See page 263 for more on dollar cost averaging.)
- *Don't buy on margin.* You will be able to hold your stock through all kinds of weather if you buy for cash. With a margin account, you are subject to margin calls from your broker. (For more information on margin accounts, see Chapter 25.)

How you manage your money is largely determined by your personality, your specific financial goals, and your tolerance for risk. In the broad sense, your choices are (1) between sleeping well and lying awake worrying, (2) between managing your money and letting someone else do it, and (3) between income and growth. For most people, the first choice is the most important: Don't make investments that keep you awake at night—money by itself is never as important as peace of mind. It's absolutely impossible to be a successful investor when you're fearful!

WHAT TYPE ARE YOU?

Investors fall into three broad categories: *conservative, aggressive,* and *speculative.* By and large, your portfolio should reflect some of each, the emphasis shifting with market conditions, how much money you have, your age, and family responsibilities.

➤ CONSERVATIVE The conservative investor seeks safety and income and aims to preserve capital. In most cases, conservative investors look at an investment's yield and pay little heed to the impact of taxes and inflation on their money.

Investment choices are (1) fixed assets such as CDs and short-term Treasury bills, notes, or bonds and (2) solid, income-producing stocks such as utilities and real estate investment trusts.

☐CAUTION: Avoid taking the path of least resistance—that of being an ultraconservative investor who stashes large amounts of money in savings accounts or money market funds or, even worse, buys stocks and holds them until forced to sell because of the need for cash or money to live on.

The conservative approach provides peace of mind, but it's very poor protection against inflation and low interest rates. If, for instance, the cost of living rises 4% a year, and your conservative investments don't keep pace, you will actually lose. With a 4% rise, the real purchasing power of every $1,000 is cut to $822 in 5 years and to $703 in 10 years.

Conservative investments should, of course, constitute a portion of everyone's portfolio, but they are most appropriate for people who are retired or soon to be, are on fixed incomes, or earn low to modest salaries.

➤ AGGRESSIVE The aggressive investor is more comfortable moving money about and is interested in total return; that is, income plus price appreciation. Such an investor does not hesitate to sell in order to take profits.

Although some of this investor's money is in conservative holdings, the bulk is spread between quality growth stocks, corporate and municipal bonds, convertibles, and real estate.

The aggressive investor is likely to have substantial income, be at least a decade away from retirement, and not need investment income for day-to-day living.

➤ SPECULATIVE Speculative investors may not always be gambling Las Vegas-style, but they often try to outwit the market and the pros. As long as speculators research their choices carefully and use only money they can afford to lose, they may very well make money—lots of it. However, they are just as likely to lose everything unless they force themselves to sell when their investments attain specific levels.

Speculative investors favor takeover candidates, junk bonds, precious metals, and leveraged real estate. Such investors should be well off, with steadily increasing sources of income.

For additional suggestions on equating your appetite for risk with your investment choices, see the PYRAMID on page 19.

FINDING MONEY TO INVEST

Saving is essential for achieving your personal economic goals, security, and a carefree life when it comes to money. But it is not enough to set aside money sporadically. You must save regularly.

$ HINT: After paying your rent or mortgage, make your first monthly check out to yourself; earmark it for investments or your IRA, Keogh, or money market account. Then begin paying your bills!

Other painless sources of money to invest:

- Dividend checks
- Gifts
- Bonuses
- A raise
- Tips
- Automatic payroll deduction plan
- Inheritance
- Free-lance activities
- Company savings plans
- Tax refunds

Much of the information you need to analyze the wide range of investments and develop your own personal strategy is readily available from annual reports, investment services, and financial newspapers and magazines. Investment newsletters are also helpful.

Most portfolios consist of stocks, bonds, U.S. Treasury obligations, real estate, precious metals, and limited partnerships. No one portfolio should consist of only one type of investment—diversification is one of the best lines of defense against losses. We will introduce the various types of stocks, bonds, and other securities in the following chapters.

SPOTTING ECONOMIC TRENDS

To build and maintain a profitable portfolio, you must develop a sense of the country's economic strength or weakness. By following these key short-term market indicators, all of which are reported in the media, you can take the pulse of the nation. (More market indicators are described in Appendix.)

- *Capacity utilization.* Measures the activity of U.S. manufacturers and the percentage rate at which factories are operating. A healthy rate is about 85%. When it drops, unemployment is high.
- *Consumer price index.* Also known as the cost-of-living index (COLA), it measures price changes for goods and services. Its components include housing, food, transportation, clothing, medical care, and electricity.
- *Gross domestic product.* The GDP measures the total value of all goods and services produced and sold in the United States over a particular time period. It tells whether the U.S. economy is expanding or contracting. Less than 2% is regarded as slow growth; over 5% is a boom. When the GDP declines two quarters in a row, it indicates that a recession has begun.
- *Index of leading economic indicators.* This index represents 11 components of economic growth, ranging from stock prices to housing permits. If it falls for 3 or 4 consecutive months, an economic downturn is likely.
- *New car sales.* Consumer buying trends are reflected in this purchase pattern, reported every 10 days. Keep track over a minimum of 2 months.
- *Retail sales.* Compare monthly sales with those of the previous month, 6 months, and 1 year.
- *Department store sales.* These reflect both regional and seasonal trends but can be an accurate indicator if they confirm other trends.
- *Housing starts.* Any improvement indicates optimistic consumer attitudes and, quite often, lower interest rates.
- *Unemployment.* This statistic reflects the overall status of the country's economy. Watch it regularly.
- *Federal funds rate.* This figure, which fluctuates daily, tracks the interest rate banks charge each other overnight.
- *Prime rate.* Interest rate banks charge their most creditworthy customers. Follow at least 3 months.
- *Broker loan rate.* Interest rate for brokers borrowing money from banks.

$HINT: For more information on how to use economic trends, read: *Market Movers*, by Nancy Dunnan and Jay Pack (NY: Time-Warner Books, 1993).

KNOWING WHEN TO BUY LONG MATURITIES

Interest rates are constantly moving up and down. Rate changes impact directly on the appeal of certain investment choices that are popular with conservative investors such as Treasury bills and notes, money market funds, and CDs. When rates peak, and start to head down, high yields are suddenly history. When that happens, you want to be locked in, not only to profit from high rates but also to benefit from rising bond prices that always accompany falling rates. On the other hand, when rates are low you want to be in short maturities so you can reinvest as rates rise. Use the box on page 64 as a guideline for timing your investments with changing rates.

There's no magic formula for knowing when to purchase long-term bonds, CDs, or Treasuries, but these four common indicators provide an accurate view of interest rate trends:

- *Money market maturities.* The average maturity on money market funds reveals the direction the fund managers think rates will take. This figure, available from the funds and also reported in many newspapers, tells the maturity of Treasury bills, CDs, and other short-term securities in a fund's portfolio. Short maturities allow fund managers to capture high rates more immediately and also indicate that they think rates will climb even higher. Rates tend to turn downward when maturities reach 39 or 40 days.
- *Gold prices.* The price of gold is traditionally an indication of the direction of inflation. Rising metal prices mean rising inflation, which in turns signals rising interest rates.
- *Prime rate.* A drop in prime usually occurs after other short-term rates have fallen, indicating that banks anticipate the downward spiral to continue. When prime drops, investors should lock in high yields.
- *Yield curve.* This illustrates the relationship between short- and long-term interest rates (see page 129). Usually long-term rates are higher than short-term rates to reward investors for tying up their money for many years. When short-term rates are higher, the yield curve is "inverted." An inverted yield curve generally indicates that interest rates have not peaked.

DOS FOR SUCCESSFUL INVESTING

DO investigate BEFORE you invest. Do not buy on impulse, hunch, or rumor. Make all investments according to your goals for income and/or growth. Take nothing for granted. Get the facts lest the lack of facts gets you.

DO limit your purchases until your forecast is confirmed. When you feel you have latched onto a winner, buy half the amount of shares you have money for even if it means buying less than a round lot. You may lose a few points' profit by waiting, but you will also minimize your losses. Watch the action in the marketplace, and when your judgment appears accurate, buy the other half of your position.

DO focus on the downside risk. An important aspect of buying stocks is not how much you can make but how much you can lose. If a stock's dividend, asset value, or price history clearly indicates a limited downside risk, it's probably a good investment.

DO buy only stocks quoted regularly in the *Wall Street Journal, The New York Times,* or *Barron's.* You want a ready market that will attract other investors when you sell.

DO investigate AFTER you invest. There is no such thing as a permanent investment. (Even IBM has bounced up and down over the years.) This caveat applies especially to small companies that show great promise at the outset but all too soon fall by the wayside.

DO watch trends: of the economy, of the stock market, of industry groups, and of the stocks in which you are interested. Stock market leaders change almost monthly, so what was favorable in January may be sliding in June.

DO set realistic goals and target prices when you make the original commitment. Roughly, these should be 35% to 50% higher than your cost, and the time frame should be 24 to 36 months. Once in a while, a stock will zoom up fast, but investments usually move up slowly and steadily, with interim dips, to new highs.

DO diversify, but carefully. As a rule of thumb, a $100,000 portfolio should have no more than 10 securities, with no more than 20% in any one company or industry. However, you can put as little as 5% of your assets in special high-risk investments. Above $100,000, add one new security for each additional $10,000.

DO stay flexible. This will let you make the most profitable use of your money during any specific period. When yields on bonds, CDs, money market funds, and Treasuries are 8% or more, move part of your savings into these areas. When the yield drops, take your profits and invest the proceeds in quality common stocks where the chances of appreciation are greater.

DO keep a list of 10 "future" investments. Review them periodically to determine whether any offer greater prospects for faster rewards than the holdings you now have. This list should include stocks, convertibles, bonds, and, when appropriate, limited partnerships. Don't switch as long as your original investments are profitable and appear to have reasonable prospects of reaching your goals.

DO watch market timing, and never be in a hurry to spend your money. If you miss one opportunity, there will be another soon.

- *When trading is active,* buy at the market price. If you're dealing with a stock that is beginning to attract attention, you may save a point or two by waiting for a temporary dip. But if you are convinced that this is a wise investment, make your move, even if there is a decline later.
- *When trading is slow,* place your order at a set price and be willing to wait a while.

DO be patient. Never flit from one stock to another. This will make your broker rich, but it will cut your potential profits and, unless you are very wise and very lucky, will not increase your capital. Four trades a year, at an average cost of 1% of stock value, equals 4% of income. (You may save a few dollars by using a discount broker.)

In normal markets, it takes a quality stock 2 to 3 years to move from undervaluation to overvaluation. Always remember that by definition, investments are long-term commitments and rarely create millionaires overnight.

DO upgrade your portfolio periodically. Review all holdings quarterly and plan to sell at least one security every 6 months. Replace the weakest securities with those on your "futures" list. Be slow to sell winners, because this will leave you with less profitable holdings. On the average, a successful portfolio will be turned over every 5 years, about 20% annually.

DO average up when you choose well. Buy more shares as the price of the stock rises.

DO set selling prices, preferably stop-loss orders at 15% to 20% below your cost or the recent high. This is discussed in greater detail in Chapter 25, but it is a key factor in successful investing. It is just as important to keep losses low as to keep profits high. At times, this can be a tough decision, so action should be taken only after you have learned the real reason for the price decline. If the company runs into temporary difficulties, don't panic. But if research concludes that profits will be below projections, it's usually smart to sell now. You can always buy back later.

DO stand by your investment rules. Once in a while, it will pay to make exceptions, but in successful investing, rules should seldom be broken.

DON'TS FOR SUCCESSFUL INVESTING

DON'T invest in a vacuum. You must have a systematic, sensible, long-range plan for your personal, business, and retirement savings. Wise planning is easy, enjoyable, and rewarding. Lack of planning leads to mistakes that can be more costly than spending the time to understand the fundamentals of investing.

DON'T be overly conservative. This means limiting the portion of your savings allocated to fixed asset or income investments, such as money market accounts, CDs, preferred stocks, and Treasuries. These are safe, but they rarely grow in value. Most of these holdings should be viewed as temporary parking places while you wait for more rewarding opportunities, or as a segment of your total portfolio.

DON'T be overly optimistic or pessimistic about the market or the securities that you own. Even the best corporations falter now and then: Their growth slows or their markets change. Smart professionals recognize when this occurs and also when the stock price soars to an unrealistic level. When any stock becomes clearly overvalued by your standards, sell or set stop-loss orders.

DON'T be lured by the "greater fool theory": that the price will keep rising because someone else will be foolish enough to pay far more than the stock is worth. When you have a pleasant profit, cash in.

REVIEW YOUR PORTFOLIO WHEN . . .

- there's a significant move up or down in the stock market.
- prime and other bank interest rates change.
- a new tax law is passed.
- the dollar becomes substantially stronger or weaker in the international market.
- there's been a major scientific breakthrough.
- regulatory agencies adopt a new policy.
- the inflation rate changes.
- there's a change in political leadership.
- foreign-trade restrictions are put into effect.
- a new international trade agreement is reached.
- new rules are passed on margin accounts.
- war begins or ends.
- the economy changes from boom times to recessionary times, or vice versa.
- bond interest rates change.
- there's a shortage in a key commodity or energy source.

DON'T rush to buy bargains, regardless of the pressure from your adviser or broker. When a stock is at a low price, there is usually a reason. It may not appear to be logical, but major investors are either skeptical or uncomfortable. They will not start buying until their peers do so. Once you spot a bargain, wait until the price and volume start to rise, and then proceed cautiously, buying in small lots even if it costs more money.

DON'T average down. A stock that appears to be a good buy at 20 is seldom more attractive at 15. When there's a serious decline in your current favorite, either your research is inaccurate or your access to the latest information is inadequate. Ask your broker to check with the research department. If you are wrong and keep buying as the price declines, you'll only compound your mistake.

DON'T assume that a quality rating will continue. With cost squeezes, foreign competition, governmental regulations and edicts, and fast-changing financial and market conditions, even stable corporations can become less attractive in a few months.

DON'T heed rumors. Wall Street is a center of gossip, hopes, and fears, but a rumor is *never* a sound reason for investment decisions. By the time you hear or read it, the professionals have made their move.

DON'T forget that a stock does not care who owns it. The price per volume of the trading of its shares is the result of forces far stronger and wealthier than you are or probably ever will be.

DON'T look back. There's no way that you can reverse your decision. If your judgment was wrong, there's nothing that you can do about it except learn from it.

> ## ... AND THEN TAKE THESE STEPS:
>
> - Buy more stock of a proven company when the market falls and prune out losers when it rises.
> - As rates move up, lock in higher yields in CDs and longer-term bonds; as rates fall, start short term—under 2 years—and look to stocks.
> - Determine your new tax bracket and talk to your accountant about ways to cut taxes.
> - When the dollar is stronger, go to Europe on vacation; when it weakens, buy foreign currencies.
> - Select one or two stocks within the industry to buy.
> - Look for investments that will benefit, such as environmental mutual funds, waste and hazardous waste removal stocks, engineering companies, and water purification stocks.
> - If inflation increases, interest rates will rise, so turn to money market funds and high-yielding CDs. If inflation decreases, stocks will do well.
> - Read the newspaper to determine the current administration's priorities—military buildup or reduction; concern about education, the environment, or health care; protection of the rich—and position on taxes. Invest in areas where there's likely to be increased spending.
> - Reduce holdings in companies or mutual funds heavily dependent on foreign sales.
> - Look for corporations already operating or prepared to operate in that country.
> - Call your broker to discuss implications for your account.
> - If war starts, buy military stocks or investigate which commodities may be in short supply, depending on location of the conflict—copper, gold, wheat, oil. If war ends, decrease military holdings.
> - If the economy is booming, take profits. If a recession starts, build up cash reserves and buy stocks at their lows.
> - If rates go up, buy longer-term bonds. If rates decline, keep shorter term.

REDUCING FEES: A PAINLESS WAY TO BOOST YOUR RETURNS

By reducing your investing costs, you can painlessly raise the returns you make on stocks, bonds, mutual funds, and other investments. The impact of these fees and other charges on your profits can be impressive.

There are three basic types of investing costs: (1) sales commissions, which you pay when you buy stocks, bonds, and load mutual funds; (2) mutual fund expenses; and (3) the spread: the difference between the ask price at which dealers sell a security to the public and the bid price at which they buy it back. Spreads are particularly heavy in purchasing zero coupon bonds, municipals, and over-the-counter stocks.

U.S. TREASURIES

Banks and brokerage firms charge sales commissions for buying and selling Treasury securities, which range from $25 to $50+ for up to $10,000 worth of securities. Ask before you buy.

$ HINT: Avoid commissions by purchasing direct from the Treasury through its Treasury Direct system. For a free brochure call your Federal Reserve Bank. (See page 123.)

MONEY MARKET FUNDS

These mutual funds are sold without any sales charge or commission; however, their management expenses can take a bite out of your yield. (See page 31 for a list of money funds with the highest yields.)

$ HINT: Call several funds or read their prospectuses to find a fund with an expense ratio below 0.6%. But remember, an extremely low expense ratio often means that management is absorbing some of the costs to push up the fund's yield and attract customers. This is often the case with new funds. Once the fund has new investors, it may raise expense charges.

MUTUAL FUNDS

Funds sold by brokers, called load funds, charge front-end loads or fees of as much as 8.5%. Many funds have back-end loads of up to 1.5%, which go into effect when you sell your shares. Still others have 12b-1 fees—an annual fee of up to 1.25% to cover marketing costs to bring in new shareholders. These 12b-1 fees are on top of annual management fees, which range from 0.3% to 1.5%. (Management fees are highest for international stock funds, which must be actively managed.)

The SEC passed a ruling in the spring of 1988 that all sales charges and fees must be listed in the fund's prospectus accompanied by a table showing their precise effect on a $1,000 investment after 1, 3, 5, and 10 years.

$ HINT: Select no-load funds; check the fund's expenses for the year.

STOCKS

The lower the number of stocks you buy and sell, the wider the spread. With actively traded stocks, which includes most blue chips, the spread is typically narrow—say 12¢ per share. Yet a thinly traded stock that sells over the counter (OTC) could have an ask price of $5 and a bid price of just $4.50. Another point to keep in mind with OTC stocks: if you buy from the market maker (a broker/dealer firm that keeps the stock in its inventory), then you pay only the spread. On the other hand, if you buy through a broker who must in turn get the shares from a market maker, you wind up paying the spread plus the broker's commission.

If you buy less than 100 shares of any stock (100 shares being a round lot), you pay an odd lot charge, typically 12½¢ per share.

$ HINT: Buy in round lots; buy OTC stocks from the market maker, listed in the "pink sheets" directory available from most brokers. (See page 177 for more on pink sheet listings.)

DISCOUNTERS
You can cut sales commissions by buying through discount brokerage firms, although you have to give up the research and personal feeding and care you get from a full service firm. Yet you'll save as much as 50% to 80%. (See Chapter 24 for more on discount firms.)

Discounters also relieve you of another fairly new expense: annual fees for customers who do not actively trade their accounts. The leader of this charge, Merrill Lynch, charges $30 a year for accounts that generate less than $100 a year in commissions. Other firms have similar charges.

BUY STOCKS DIRECTLY

A handful of companies let investors buy their shares directly, thus bypassing a stockbroker. To find out, call the company's Investor Relations division. Among those that do are Central Vermont Public Service, Citizens First Bancorp, Exxon, Procter & Gamble, and Texaco. You can also purchase stock directly from a number of public utility companies if you live in an area serviced by them. These include Carolina Power & Light, Cleveland Electric Illuminating Co., Duke Power, Hawaiian Electric Industries, Minnesota Power & Light, Philadelphia Suburban, San Diego Gas & Electric, and Wisconsin Energy.

And yet another way to reduce your cost of buying stocks is to have your dividends automatically reinvested in additional shares. (See page 263 for full details.)

MUNICIPAL BONDS
Spreads, which are built into the bond's price, are higher for odd lot purchases. With munis, an odd lot is less than $25,000. If you buy a municipal bond in the secondary or aftermarket from a broker who does not have it in inventory, your yield is further reduced by about an eighth of a percentage point to cover the broker's costs in getting the bonds from another dealer.

$ HINT: Buy actively traded bonds, and new issues in particular. Spreads are typically 0.75%, compared to as much as 4% to 5% for odd lots. Try to pick bonds from your broker's inventory.

ZERO COUPON BONDS
The pricing of zeros tends to be confusing, and hefty spreads are not uncommon. Some brokers have been known to charge as much as 5%.

$ HINT: Shop among several brokers, asking how much you must invest per $1,000 face value for the particular zero you want. Then ask what the effective yield to maturity is. Buy from the broker with the lowest price and the highest yield.

INVESTMENT CLUBS

If you're skittish about picking your own stocks or nervous about working with a stockbroker, you can circumvent these problems by purchasing

WHEN INVESTMENTS PERFORM BEST

INVESTMENT	ADD TO YOUR PORTFOLIO	RISK LEVEL
Growth stocks	When economy is growing at above average rate When interest rates are stable	Medium to high
Blue chip stocks	During slow to moderate growth periods When interest rates are falling	Medium
Utility stocks	When interest rates are falling When energy costs are falling	Low to medium
Long-term bonds	When interest rates are falling	Low to medium
Short-term notes and bills	When interest rates are stable or falling	Low
Money market funds and CDs	When interest rates are rising	Low

stocks through an investment club, a team approach that is used by thousands of Americans.

An investment club is a group of individuals, often neighbors, co-workers, or friends, who meet once a month, contribute a set dollar amount, and invest the common pool in stocks. Every member is responsible for doing research on individual stocks on a rotating basis. They then report their findings to the club, and members debate the risks and rewards of each stock and finally take a vote on which ones to buy.

Much of the guidance for clubs comes from the National Association of Investors Corporation (NAIC), a nonprofit organization operated by and for the benefit of member clubs. This association, which has been the force behind the investment club movement in the United States since the 1950s, has about 150,000 individual and 7,600 club members. Membership is $30 for clubs plus $10 for each club member and $32 for nonmember individuals. The association offers detailed information on how to start a club, how to analyze stocks, and how to keep records.

Clubs and individual members of NAIC can also dispense with brokerage commissions by participating in NAIC's "Low-Cost Investment Plan." Under this program, clubs can buy as little as one share directly from about 90 major participating companies, such as Disney, Kellogg, McDonald's, Mobil, and Quaker Oats, for a one-time charge of $5 per firm. Most of these corporations do not charge a commission, although some have a nominal

JOIN AN INVESTMENT CLUB

If you'd like to start building a portfolio of stocks, but feel uncertain about making your own selections, join an investment club in your area. By pooling your money with that of 15 to 20 other people and sharing research, you can comfortably begin to develop investment savvy.

Kenneth S. Janke, president of the National Association of Investors Corporation, says the following three guiding principles followed by clubs enable them to frequently outperform the S&P 500:

1   Invest a fixed amount regularly to eliminate the guesswork of trying to time the market.
2   Reinvest earnings to take advantage of the magic of compounding.
3   Invest in stocks growing faster than the economy.
For details on joining a club, contact:

National Association of Investors Corp.
1515 East Eleven Mile Road
Royal Oak, MI 48067
1-313-543-0612

fee ($3 to $5) for each transaction to cover their expenses. All of these companies also have dividend reinvestment programs, so instead of taking dividends in cash, the club or individual members automatically reinvest the dividends in additional shares of the company's stocks.

According to a recent NAIC survey, 61.9% of its clubs bettered the Standard & Poor's 500's total return over a ten-year period.

KEEPING GOOD RECORDS

Most of us realize that good records are essentially for cutting tax bills, but proper documentation of investments can also improve profits and make estate planning less onerous. By keeping track of investments' performance, you can weed out those that are poor performers or no longer meeting your financial goals. Records are also critical to your family's financial security should you become ill or die. Here's a look at the documents you need to keep:

- *Stocks.* Keep all confirmation slips of trades plus the most recent quarterly dividend reinvestment statements and year-end dividend reinvestment statements. When you sell you can minimize taxes by selling the high-cost shares first. Give your broker the purchase date and cost of the shares you want to sell. Follow this up with a written note in case you need it for the IRS. Documentation of stock transactions should be kept for 6 years.
- *Bonds.* The same record-keeping rules that apply to stocks also apply to bonds. In other words, keep the confirmation slips if you are buying a bond for which you have to pay some accrued interest to the

---

RECORD-KEEPING TERMS

- *Cost basis.* The original price of an investment.
- *FIFO.* A way to calculate the cost basis of an asset that is part of a larger holding purchased at various prices. With first in, first out, securities are sold in the order in which they were bought.
- *Dividend reinvestment.* Automatic investment of cash dividends in additional stocks or mutual fund shares.
- *Accrued interest.* The portion of interest on a bond due for the time period between the last interest payment and the sale date. The buyer pays the seller this dollar amount in addition to the purchase price.

---

seller at the time of purchase. For example, if the last interest payment was 2 months ago and the next one is 4 months in the future, you must pay the seller the 2 months' interest due him or her, since you will be receiving the full payment. This amount returned to the seller can be subtracted from your taxable income. This amount should be noted on your confirmation slip.

- *Mutual funds.* With mutual funds, as with stocks and bonds, you must pay taxes on any price appreciation when you sell your shares. Therefore, when you buy shares in a mutual fund, save the confirmation slip indicating the number of shares you bought and what you paid for them.

Certain funds pay interest or dividends. In addition, you may get distributions of capital gains from the sale of investments held in the fund's portfolio. Taxes are due on these payouts in the year in which you receive them. Should you reinvest this money in more fund shares, save the statements recording this reinvestment transaction. Otherwise you may forget to include these distributions as part of your "cost basis" when you sell. Some firms send out cumulative statements, in which case you need to save only the December one, which lists all transactions for the year.

If you decide to sell only some of your shares, your records will help you decide which ones to unload. The IRS assumes that you are selling the first shares you purchased *unless* you specify to the contrary. This is called "first in, first out" (FIFO), and can be unnecessarily costly if you have regularly purchased shares in a fund that has continually increased in value.

There are two other options besides FIFO: the identifiable-cost and average-cost approaches. With the identifiable-cost approach, you specify to the fund that you are selling a certain number of shares purchased on a particular date or dates. With a rising fund, this approach enables you to sell the most costly shares—those purchased most recently—and postpone taxes on the cheaper shares purchased

WAYS TO EARN INTEREST

Part of your money should be put to work earning more money. Here are ways to do just that. (Data as of July 1993.)

INVESTMENT	RISK LEVEL	YIELD
Bank money market account	Low	2.45%
Money market mutual fund	Low	2.69
Certificate of deposit (6 month)	Low	2.81
Certificate of deposit (1 year)	Low	2.98
Certificate of deposit (5 year)	Low	4.78
Treasury bill (3 months)	Low	3.40
Treasury bill (1 year)	Low	3.48
Savings bonds	Low	4.00
Treasury note (5 years)	Low	4.99
Treasury bond (10 year)	Low	5.75
Ginnie Mae certificate	Low to medium	6.60
Utility stocks	Medium	7.00
Utility bonds (A-rated)	Medium	7.40
Corporate bonds (a-rated)	Medium	7.45
Utility bonds (BBB-rated)	Medium	7.65
Preferred stocks (Utility)	Medium	7.78
Preferred stocks (Junk bonds)	High	10.00

earlier. If you sell by phone, send the mutual fund a letter confirming this fact. Keep a copy of your letter plus the transaction statements for 6 years.

With the average-cost method, you find the total cost of all shares ever purchased, including reinvestments, and divide by the number of shares you own to arrive at the cost per share. Then, multiply this by the number of shares you plan to sell to find your total tax cost. This method must be entered on tax Schedule D when you report the sale, and you must use the same method for future sales.

FOR FURTHER INFORMATION

NEWSLETTERS
Call or write for sample issues if you are interested in receiving continual data on the funds.

Income & Safety
Institute for Econometric Research
3471 North Federal Highway
Fort Lauderdale, FL 33306
1-800-327-6720; 1-305-563-9000
Monthly; $49 per year
Covers money market funds, Ginnie Maes, and tax-free bonds.

100 Highest Yields
P.O. Box 088888
North Palm Beach, FL 33408
1-800-327-7717; 1-407-627-7330

Monthly; 8 issues for $34; 52 issues for $98

PAMPHLETS

Money Market Mutual Funds
Publications Division
Investment Company Institute
1600 M Street NW, Suite 600
Washington, DC 20036
1-202-293-7700

25¢; explains how money market funds are regulated.

Why Save and Invest at Your Credit Union
National Credit Union Association, Inc.
P.O. Box 431
Madison, WI 53701
1-608-231-4000

Free; explains benefits of using a credit union.

New York Stock Exchange Investors Information Kit. Contains:
- *Capital Market Book*
- *Understanding Stocks and Bonds*
- *Understanding Financial Statements*
- *Getting Help When You Invest*
- *Glossary*
- *Margin Trading Guide*

$12; prepay by check or money order. Send to:

New York Stock Exchange
P.O. Box 5020
Farmingdale, NY 11736
1-516-454-1800

RECORD KEEPING

The Standard Homefile
$19.95 + $3.50 shipping from:

Financial Advantage
3444-101 Elliott Center Drive
Elliott City, MD 210432-4153
1-800-695-3453

Includes plastic-coated file dividers and a helpful 48-page handbook.

6

INVESTING WITH MUTUAL FUNDS

Although there's no one ideal investment for everyone, mutual funds come closest for many of us. A mutual fund is an investment company in which an investor's dollars are pooled with those of thousands of others; the combined total is invested by a professional manager in various securities—primarily in stocks, bonds, government securities, foreign currencies, and options—or in different combinations of these vehicles. Because you can buy shares in a fund for minimums ranging from several hundred to several thousand dollars, funds give all investors, even those without deep pockets, access to the entire market. And once you buy shares you can add to your account with as little as $100 or $500.

Funds also offer a wide range of investment objectives and philosophies—from conservative to middle of the road to extremely aggressive, so there is a fund to match every conceivable investment goal.

TWELVE ADVANTAGES OF MUTUAL FUNDS

Funds have a number of key advantages of owning individual stocks or bonds, especially for those with less than $30,000.

1 DIVERSIFICATION Unless you have at least $30,000, it is almost impossible to have a properly diversified portfolio. Mutual funds, on the other hand, with 30, 40, even 100 securities in their portfolios, provide excellent diversification.

2 PROFESSIONAL MANAGEMENT Mutual fund managers are professionals with experience and a wealth of research to assist them in managing their portfolios. If their fund's performance falters in comparison with those of its peers, the fund manager may be replaced.

3 SWITCHING PRIVILEGES When a management company, such as T. Rowe Price, Fidelity, or Vanguard, sponsors more than one type of fund (and most do), you may switch from one fund to another within this so called family, as the market changes or as your goals change. Most funds offer free switching, although some impose nominal fees.

$ HINT: Select a fund that permits the portfolio manager to shift out of stocks and into U.S. Treasury bills, jumbo CDs, and other higher yielding cash instruments if it looks like the stock market may decline. This gives you added protection when the market or interest rates change direction.

4 ACCOUNT PAPERWORK Mutual funds handle the details of all transactions efficiently, mail dividend checks promptly, provide

accurate year-end summaries for income tax purposes, and are always ready to answer questions on their toll-free phone lines.

5 SAVINGS AND CHECKING Many funds will set up an automatic monthly savings plan, wiring money from your bank into the fund. If your employer has a direct deposit payroll program you can have part or all of your payroll check automatically invested in certain funds. U.S. government checks, federal salary, and veterans' benefits can also be automatically invested. More and more funds are offering to sweep dividends and capital gains earned in one fund into another fund within the same family. Money market funds and some bond funds have check-writing privileges. However, unlike bank checking accounts, there's usually a $250 or $500 per check minimum, and you may be allowed only to write a limited number of checks per month.

6 DOLLAR COST AVERAGING This involves regularly investing a set dollar amount in a fund—say, $150 to $500 per month. Many funds will automatically transfer money from your bank account into the fund every month. For example, you put $100 into a mutual fund every month. The shares fluctuate in price between $5 and $10. The first month you buy 10 shares at $10 each for a total of $100. The second month, because the market dropped, the shares are selling at $5 each, so you buy 20 shares at $5 and so on. At the end of 4 months you have acquired 60 shares for your $400 at an average cost of $6.67 per share (400 ÷ 60). (*Note:* during this same period, the average price per share was $7.50.)

$HINT: For a free brochure on "Dollar Cost Averaging," contact: T. Rowe Price, 100 East Pratt Street, Baltimore, MD 21202; 1-800-638-5660.

7 IRAs Most funds permit investors to open IRAs with considerably smaller dollar amounts than they require for their regular funds. This is a smart way to invest in a fund whose minimum otherwise is too high.

8 TELEPHONE TRADING Most funds sold directly to the public allow you to buy, sell, or switch fund shares over the telephone.

9 DISTRIBUTION OR REINVESTMENT OF INCOME Mutual funds distribute money to investors in two ways: income dividends and capital gains distributions. *Income dividends* represent the interest and/or dividends earned by the fund's portfolio holdings, minus the fund's expenses. *Capital gains distributions* represent a fund's net realized capital gains—when there are profits in excess or losses on the sale of any of the portfolio securities. Both income dividends and capital gains distributions can usually be reinvested in the fund automatically, usually at no cost.

A summary of the distributions made to each shareholder annually, called a Form 1099, is sent to the shareholder and to the IRS.

☐CAUTION: Automatic reinvestment may not always be in your best interest. Mutual funds pay their largest distributions when the stock market is relatively high. Instead of reinvesting at the high level, you may do better to take the cash and wait for the market to decline. Then your cash will buy more shares.

10 BENEFICIARY DESIGNATION You can name your beneficiary by means of a trust agreement so that your investment goes directly to your designated heir when you die, with none of the delays and expenses of probate. Consult your lawyer, because some states prohibit this transfer.

11 REGULAR INCOME CHECKS You can set up monthly or quarterly income in several ways: a) by buying shares in several funds, each with different dividend payout months; b) by arranging for regular quarterly dividends to be paid out; or c) by arranging to redeem automatically the dollar value of the number of shares you specify. There's usually a $50 or $100 minimum per month. The fund will mail a check to you monthly, quarterly, or annually.

12 INFORMATION AND SERVICE Almost all investment companies provide toll-free numbers. Call to learn about prices, minimum investments, charges, and types of other funds available for switching. You can also ask for forms for setting up automatic withdrawals and for switching into other funds.

SYSTEMATIC WITHDRAWAL PLANS (SWPs)

SWPs, long a favorite with retired people, are also ideal for making mortgage payments, paying insurance premiums, or other regular commitments. SWPs are an alternative to traditional written or telephone requests for withdrawal of your money from a mutual fund. Under an SWP, the fund periodically redeems the dollar value or percentage you request. Payment is made by check to you, to a third party, or to your bank account.

The amount required to maintain an SWP varies with each fund, but typical SWPs require a $5,000 or $10,000 minimum opening balance and a minimum $50 per month withdrawal. You can withdraw money monthly, bimonthly, or quarterly. Some funds permit you to withdraw only on the same day each month; others permit withdrawals on any day.

SWPs offer several advantages:

- Steady stream of controlled income prevents overspending.
- Paperwork is reduced.
- Plan eliminates telephoned withdrawal requests.

And some disadvantages:

- You may draw out more money than you need or than you earn on the principal.
- May lead to apathetic attitude about saving.

Funds offer one or more of four types of withdrawals: (1) straight dollar amounts, (2) a fixed number of shares, (3) a fixed percentage, and (4) a declining balance based on your life expectancy.

$ HINT: If you don't wish to tap your principal, remove your money at a lower rate than the fund's increase in net asset value.

Keep in mind that withdrawing a regular dollar amount is in effect

---

USES FOR SWPs

- To pay your mortgage
- As a monthly living allowance for college students
- As income while on maternity leave
- For retirement
- To provide care for someone in a nursing home
- To meet insurance premiums
- As income while on sabbatical
- For alimony or child support payments

---

reverse dollar cost averaging. In dollar cost averaging (see page 70), you invest an equal dollar amount every month and in this way buy more fund shares for the same amount when the market is down and fewer shares when it's up. In a fixed-amount withdrawal plan, you are forced to redeem more shares when the market is down to meet the set dollar amount and to sell fewer shares when the market is up.

If you use a percentage plan, the number of shares you need to sell in a down market will tend to be less.

$HINT: Another way to withdraw money regularly is to keep your dividends and capital gains distributions from stock and bond funds instead of reinvesting them. This way, you won't need to sell shares. If your dividends and capital gains distributions add up to more money than you need, reinvest the excess in a money market fund.

Remember, too, that the day you pick to redeem your shares is not the day you'll receive your check. Ask the fund how soon checks are mailed out, and ask your bank how long it will take for checks to clear.

□CAUTION: Each withdrawal of funds is a taxable event, usually because of capital gains. Keep records of your withdrawals to simplify year-end tax calculations.

HOW FUNDS WORK

All mutual funds operate along the same lines. They sell shares to the public at net asset value (NAV) price. (NAV per share equals the total assets of the fund divided by the outstanding shares minus liabilities.) The money received is then pooled and used to buy various types of securities. So when you buy into a fund, you are really buying shares in an investment company, but the assets of this company consist not of a plant or equipment but of stocks, bonds, and cash instruments. The price of your shares rises and falls every day with the total value of the securities in the fund's portfolio.

As the owner of mutual fund shares, you receive periodic payments, provided your fund does well. Of course, if the fund has a poor year, you

---

THREE WINNING FUNDS

Balanced or total return stock funds that seek both dividends and capital gains have outdistanced the average equity fund in recent months.

- Wellington (1-800-662-7447)*   8.11% return
- Fidelity Balanced (1-800-544-8888)   14.33% return
- Lindner Dividend (1-314-727-5305)   10.24% return

    (*A Vanguard fund)
    (Return figures: Jan–June 1993)

---

stand to lose money; that is, your NAV will fall. Most funds pay dividends every quarter and capital gains distributions annually. Capital gains distributions result when a fund sells some of its securities at a profit. You may elect to have your earnings reinvested automatically in additional fund shares, usually at no cost.

➤ OPEN VS. CLOSED Funds are either open- or closed-ended. In an *open-end fund,* shares are continually available to the public at NAV. The fund's shares are always increasing or decreasing in number depending on sales to the public.

A *closed-end fund* has fixed capitalization and makes one initial issue of shares. After that it trades as a stock on the major stock exchanges or over the counter. In other words, it closes its doors to new investors, and shares can be purchased only by buying the stock. Prices are determined by supply and demand: When buyers are plentiful, the price of the stock rises, and vice versa. Depending on market conditions, the price will be above or below NAV. When a closed-end fund is selling at a discount from NAV, the investor has an opportunity to see profits from price appreciation. (See Chapter 7 for more on closed-end funds.)

HOW TO SELECT MUTUAL FUNDS

There are thousands of mutual funds available, so how do you go about finding those that are right for you? The first and most important factor is to know *why* you are investing, just as with any investment. Are you seeking growth, income, or a tax-free return? Only after you have clarified this decision should you go about selecting a fund. Here are some other factors to keep in mind when picking a fund.

➤ MANAGEMENT'S SUCCESS This is measured by the fund's ability to make money. There are three ways to study a fund's success: 1) follow its share price or net asset value (NAV); 2) track its yield, the amount of income it pays out; and 3) look at its total return; this figure takes into consideration share price changes and then adds in the results of reinvesting income or dividends, plus any capital gains or losses after expenses. (Capital gains and losses result from the sale of securities by the fund's portfolio manager.) Although all three figures are important, the third—the total return figure—is the only overall indicator of how well a fund is doing because it shows the total profit generated by the fund. (**NOTE**: A capital gains payment serves to reduce the fund's NAV because the fund pays out money that prior to payout counted toward the value of the entire portfolio.) The total return figure is also the best one to use when comparing one fund with another, or one type of fund with another type of fund.

The total return figure over one, three, and five years, as well as from the beginning of the year to date, is given in financial publications and from the funds directly.

$HINT: Keep in mind that in a growth fund, the yield figure is not terribly
important because the stocks in the fund were selected for their
potential price appreciation, not for their dividends income. In fact,
the stocks may not even pay dividends. What is important in a
growth fund is whether the share price has been rising steadily for
several years. On the other hand, in an income or bond fund, the
yield is important because you selected the fund for income.

Study the total return figures for several years, in both up and down markets. Excellent funds have never been first in any one year, but have done better than the market in good periods and have lost less in bear markets. One of the best guides is the annual *Forbes* magazine report in late August. This issue rates funds on the basis of performance in both rising and falling markets. To get a high score, the fund must perform consistently in relation to other funds, in both up and down periods. Adjustments are made to prevent exceptional performance (good or bad) in any one period from having undue influence on the fund's average performance.

Other popular periodicals such as *Money, Your Money,* and *Kiplinger's Personal Finance* track fund performance in every issue. *Morningstar,* a weekly reference service, updates mutual funds and their performance; it is the most thorough in coverage. (See "For Further Information" at the end of this chapter for details.)

➤ FEES Fees and other costs are an important consideration in selecting a mutual fund—the more of your money that goes to the fund the less you have making a profit. For example, if you put a $1,000 into a fund with an 8.5% commission or sales load, you will be purchasing only $915 worth of shares.

The law requires all funds to list their fees at the beginning of the prospectus and it must give an easy-to-understand illustration in actual dollars of how much the fees are.

▪ *No-load funds.* These funds do not charge a sales fee, known as a load
(or burden). Most are sold directly by the fund through advertising.
Money market mutual funds, even those sold by stockbrokers and
banks, are virtually all no-load. However, there are some theoretically
no-load funds that actually have low loads—2% to 3%.

▪ *Load funds.* These are sold by stockbrokers, financial planners, or
brokerage divisions of banks, who charge a commission every time

you buy new shares. The legal limit is 8.5% of the amount invested. This amount is deducted from the amount of your initial investment. Thus, on a $10,000 purchase, the dollars that go to work for you are reduced by the 8.5% load to $9,150 ($10,000 − $850).

$ HINT: There is no evidence that load funds perform better than no-loads, so if you don't need help in selecting a fund, go with a no-load and save the fee. And, if you plan to invest for 1 year or less, always select a no-load. One year is seldom long enough to make up an 8.5% sales fee.

■ *Back-end loads* (also called redemption fees). Some funds charge this fee when you sell your shares, thus reducing your profit or making your loss even greater. They are levied against the net asset value.

■ *Deferred loads* (also called contingent deferred sales fees). These are deducted from your original investment if you sell shares before a specified time passes after buying them. They may be based on a sliding scale, often 6% the first year, moving down to 0% in year.

■ *12b-1 fees* (also called hidden loads). These are named after the SEC regulation that authorized them in 1980. It allows the fund to deduct the costs of advertising and marketing directly from the fund's assets. They typically range from .25% to .30%, but can be as high as 1.25%.

■ *Reinvestment loads.* These take a small amount out of the interest, dividends, and capital gains that are reinvested in your account. The maximum is 7.25% of the total investment. For example, if you receive a capital gains distribution of $100 and you automatically reinvest these gains, the fund can retain $7.25 as a selling fee and reinvest only $92.75 in new fund shares.

■ *Management fee.* Every fund, load and no-load, charges a management fee to pay the adviser who manages the portfolio. The typical management fee is ½% to 1% of the fund's assets. It may be a flat rate or a sliding scale that gets smaller as the fund's portfolio gets larger.

➤ TURNOVER This shows the dollar amount of stocks or other holdings sold in relation to total assets. Thus, if a fund had assets of $100 million and sold $75 million in stocks in one year, the turnover would be 75%. This is considered high for a blue chip stock fund and may indicate the manager is either speculating for short-term profits or not making successful choices. A high turnover rate also means the fund will be paying high commission costs and that you'll have higher capital gains distributions, which are taxed in the year distributed. For example, T. Rowe Price Growth fund, which contains primarily high quality stocks, has had a turnover rate that fluctuated from 30% to 51% over the last five years, while its Intermediate US Treasury fund, which holds Treasuries of 3 to 7 year maturities, had a turnover ranging from 175% to 195%.

$ HINT: Two excellent sources for studying turnover rates are *Morningstar* and *The Individual Investor's Guide to No-Load Mutual Funds.* (See "For Further Information" at the end of this chapter.)

➤ SIZE The larger the assets of a mutual fund, the smaller the amount

---

YIELD VERSUS TOTAL RETURN

It is important to know the difference between yield and total return when evaluating a fund.
- *Yield.* This is the income per share paid to the shareholder. It is derived from dividends and interest and is expressed as a percentage of the current offering price per share.
- *Total return.* This measures the per-share change in the total value of a fund, from the beginning of the year to any given date. Total return is derived from dividend and interest income, capital gains distributions, and any unrealized capital gains or losses.

---

each investor pays for administration. However, stay away from funds whose assets have been under $50 million for over 5 years. If a fund hasn't grown, its performance must have been so poor that new shares could not be widely sold.

➤ EXPENSES Some funds, like some people, are more frugal than others. The best measure of a fund's cost is its expense ratio. Expressed as a percentage of the fund's assets, it includes management and 12b-1 fees, but not sales loads or redemption fees. Obviously, the higher the expense ratio, the less the fund has to pay its shareholders out of earnings. In general, common stock funds have higher expense ratios than bond funds; likewise, smaller funds have higher ratios than larger funds; international funds and precious metals funds have higher ratios than domestic funds. Fixed income and index funds have the lowest. The average expense ratio for common stock funds is 1.5%; for bond funds, 1.0%. It's wise to avoid funds with expense ratios over 1.5%.

➤ VOLATILITY The relative volatility inherent in a mutual fund is measured by its beta. You can use this figure to compare the fund's volatility with that of the stock market as a whole. (The market's beta is always 1.0 and a money market fund's beta is always 0.) If your mutual fund has a beta

---

LOW-COST FUND FAMILIES

FUND	EXPENSE RATIO
Vanguard	0.45%
Dreyfus	0.71
Federated	0.73
Merrill Lynch	0.74
USAA	0.78
T. Rowe Price	0.92

of 1.0, it will move with the market. In other words, if the market is up 5%, the fund will be up on average 5%. A mutual fund with a beta of 1.5 is 50% more volatile than the market, so if the market is up 10%, the fund will be up on average 50% more, or 15%.

The beta essentially compares the risk of the fund with the risk of the overall market. It is helpful in selecting a stock fund; less so for a bond fund. Bond funds respond to changes in interest rates, not the market. If you are selecting a bond fund, you should check the ratings given the bonds by Standard & Poor's and Moody's as well as the maturity of the portfolio, rather than its beta.

HOW TO BUY FUND SHARES

You can buy shares in no-load funds directly from the funds themselves. You'll find their toll-free numbers as well as performance figures for many listed in several financial magazines, including *Money, Your Money,* and *Kiplinger's Personal Finance Magazine.* Simply call the number and request the prospectus of the fund in which you're interested. Many no-load mutual fund companies have offices in cities throughout the country where you may stop in and pick up prospectuses and general literature.

THE PROSPECTUS

You must read the prospectus before investing in a fund. Although it may appear formidable at first glance, a half-hour with this step-by-step guide will crystallize the entire process and enlighten you about the fund. Here's what to look for:

- What the fund's investment objectives are. These will be spelled out at the beginning.
- A risk factor statement.
- What strategies will be used to meet the fund's stated goals.
- The degree of diversification. How many issues does it hold?
- What is the portfolio turnover? A low rate, below 75%, reflects a long-term holding philosophy, whereas a high rate indicates an aggressive strategy.
- Fees and expenses. Check in particular the cost of redeeming shares, which should not exceed 1% per year.
- Rules for switching within a family of funds and fees, if any.
- Restrictions. Will the fund sell securities short, act as an underwriter, engage in selling commodities or real estate? What percentage of total assets is invested in any one security? Be wary of a fund that is not adequately diversified.
- How much the fund has gained or lost over 1, 5, and 10 years.

$ HINT: Whenever you see a mutual fund with a telephone number listed in this book, it is a no-load (or low-load) fund and can be purchased by calling the fund.

To buy shares in a load fund you must contact a stockbroker or other commissioned sales person. Banks and some discount brokerage firms also sell load funds.

Load and no-load funds and their net asset values are also listed in the financial pages of major newspapers. *Barron's* has one of the most complete listings.

Closed-end fund, which trade as stocks and have a limited number of shares available, are sold by stockbrokers. The next chapter is devoted exclusively to closed-end funds.

SIX TIPS FOR BUYING FUNDS

1   You will earn less over time in a load fund than in a no-load fund if both produce identical returns. That's because the sales load cuts the size of your initial investment.
2   A fund with a front-end load is preferable to a fund with a redemption fee if you are investing for growth. That's because the front-end load or fee will be based on a smaller dollar amount, assuming that the fund does indeed produce capital gains.
3   A back-end load is usually preferable to a front-end load if you are investing for income. That's because more of your initial investment dollars will have time to earn interest.
4   Look for a stock fund that has doubled investors' money within five years—i.e., a 100% total return figure for five years.
5   Look for a bond fund that has a five-year return of around 50%.
6   When you buy, set a stop-loss figure, say 10% or 15% below current NAV. That way you'll keep your losses small, even if you misjudged the fund or market trends. (See page 257 for more on stop loss orders.)

➤ HOW TO READ FUND QUOTES   You will find a listing of mutual funds in the financial pages of the newspaper (see the accompanying example). Funds are listed under the sponsor's name, such as Vanguard or Fidelity. The first column is the name of the fund, then the NAV, or "Bid" as it may be called. (The NAV is the price at which fund shareholders sold their shares the previous day.) The next column, "Offer Price," is the price paid by new investors the previous day. When the offer price is higher than the NAV there is a load: The difference between the NAV and the offer price is the sales commission. Funds with "NL" in the offer column are no-loads. A small "r" next to a fund's name indicates that a redemption charge may apply. Funds do not always have an "r" when they should, according to a study done recently by the American Association of Individual Investors. (Redemption fees are also called back-end loads.) The "p" denotes that a

HOW MUTUAL FUND SHARES ARE QUOTED

	NAV	OFFER PRICE	NAV CHANGE
Dreyfus Funds			
Cap V p	12.35	12.93	+.12
Index	17.21	NL	−.14
Interm	13.93	NL	−.02
Levge	17.63	18.46	−.14

p—distribution costs apply
NAV—net asset value
NL—no-load

fund charges a fee from assets for marketing and distribution costs, also known as a 12b-1 plan.

$HINT: When a distribution is made to shareholders, the NAV is reduced by the amount of the distribution per share. So, buy shares just after a distribution to save paying tax on the distributed amount. Call the fund to get exact dates.

Keep in mind that the NAV column states the price the fund will pay to buy back its shares; but from your viewpoint, it's the price at which your shares can be sold. The offer price is the price you will have to pay to buy shares in the fund.

$HINT: Don't panic if a fund's quoted price doesn't change much over the year. You may buy shares at $10 per share and find them the same a year later. That's because 90% of income and capital gains have been distributed to shareholders. Instead, judge the fund's total performance (capital appreciation plus dividend income) as a percentage gain or loss. The figure is available by calling the fund.

TYPES OF FUNDS

Mutual funds come in all sizes, shapes, and combinations. It is extremely important that you match your personal investment objectives with those of the fund. The accompanying list summarizes the broad objectives and should be read carefully in order to familiarize yourself with the various terms or bits of jargon the funds use to describe what they do with your money.

Keep in mind that there are scores of other mutual funds,many of which are described in chapters relating to specific types of securities. Before you commit any money to a fund, do your homework and make certain you understand exactly what you are investing in.

TYPES OF MUTUAL FUNDS

FUND	OBJECTIVE
Aggressive growth funds	Seek maximum capital gains, not current income. May invest in new companies, trouble firms. Use techniques such as option writing to boost returns. Highly risky.
Balanced funds	Aim to conserve principal, generate current income, and provide long-term growth. Have portfolio mix of bonds, preferred stocks, and common stocks.
Corporate bond funds	Seek high level of income. Buy corporate bonds, some U.S. Treasury bonds or bonds issued by federal agencies.
Flexible portfolio funds	May be 100% in stocks or bonds or money market instruments. Have the greatest portfolio flexibility of all funds.
Ginnie Mae funds (GNMAs)	Invest in mortgage-backed securities. Must keep majority of portfolio in these securities.
Global bond funds	Invest in debt of companies and countries throughout the world, including the United States.
Global equity funds	Invest in securities traded worldwide, including the United States.
Growth funds	Invest in common stock of well-established companies. Capital gains, not income, is primary objective.
Growth and income funds	Invest in common stock of dividend-paying companies. Combine long-term capital gains and steady stream of income.
High-yield bond funds	Keep two-thirds of portfolio in lower-rated corporate bonds (junk bonds) to achieve high income.
Income bond funds	Invest at all times in corporate and government bonds for income.
Income equity funds	Invest in companies with good dividend-paying records.
Income mixed funds	Seek high current income by investing in equities and debt instruments.
Index funds	Buy stocks to match an index such as the S&P 500.
International funds	Invest in equity securities of companies located outside the United States.
Long-term municipal bond funds	Invest in bonds issued by states and municipalities. In most cases, income earned is not taxed by the federal government.
Money market mutual funds	Invest in short-term securities sold in the money market. Safe, relatively high yields.
Option/income funds	Seek high current return by investing in dividend-paying stocks on which call options are traded.
Precious metals/gold funds	Keep two-thirds of portfolio in securities associated with gold, silver, platinum, and other precious metals.

TYPES OF MUTUAL FUNDS (*Cont.*)

FUND	OBJECTIVE
Sector funds	Concentrate holdings in a single industry or country.
Short-term municipal bonds	Invest in municipals with short maturities; also known as tax-exempt money market funds.
Single-state municipal bond funds	Portfolios contain issues of only one state so that income is free of both federal and state taxes.
Socially conscious funds	Avoid investments in corporations known to pollute, to have poor records in hiring minorities, and to be involved in the military, tobacco, and liquor industries.
U.S. government income funds	Invest in a variety of government securities, including U.S. Treasury bonds, mortgage-backed securities, and government notes.

HOW MANY FUNDS SHOULD YOU OWN?

With over 3,800 funds, it's not easy to decide which ones to own or how many. Although there is no magical "right" number, common sense suggests somewhere between three and ten not including a money market fund—ten being the maximum most people can track on a regular basis. Of course, it also depends upon how much money you have to invest. If you have $5,000 saved in addition to your emergency nestegg, then one or two is appropriate. In the long run, your goal is to cover different aspects of the market and thus protect your investments from wide economic and industry swings. Aim to pick funds that will do well at different points in the economic cycle.

BUYING ON MARGIN

If you're an aggressive trader, you can buy mutual funds on margin. You must pay 50% of the total cost of your transaction up front. The rest you borrow from your broker. Before doing so, see pages 267–268 on how a margin account works, and beware of the pitfalls.

Among the brokerage firms offering mutual fund shares on margin are these:
- Charles Schwab & Co. (1-800-435-4000)
- Jack White & Co. (1-800-233-3411)
- Quick & Reilly (1-800-221-5220; 1-800-522-8712 in NY)

BUILDING A BASIC MUTUAL FUND PORTFOLIO

DOLLARS TO INVEST	NUMBER OF FUNDS	TYPE
$4,000 or less	one	Money market fund
$4,000 to $5,000	two	+ a government income fund
$5,000 to $10,000	three	+ a balanced fund
$10,000 to $20,000	four	+ a growth and income fund
$20,000 to $30,000	five	+ a high quality corporate bond fund
$30,000 to $40,000	six	+ a tax-exempt municipal bond fund
$40,000 to $50,000	seven	+ an aggressive growth fund
$50,000 to $60,000	eight	+ an index fund
$60,000 to $70,000	nine	+ a small cap stock fund
$70,000 to $80,000	ten	+ a sector fund
$80,000 to $100,000	eleven	+ an international stock or bond fund

$ HINT: Begin by picking a fund that is already diversified, such as *Vanguard Star* or *T. Rowe Price Spectrum Growth.* Both hold a mix of other funds within their own mutual fund family.

A PORTFOLIO OF MUTUAL FUNDS

Above you will find information on how many funds you should consider owning, based on how much you have to invest, your financial goals (whether you want income, growth, or tax-free returns), and how much risk you wish to assume. The principles behind building a mutual fund portfolio is similar to the general financial guidelines outlined with the INVESTMENT PYRAMID in Chapter 2; that is, the first funds you purchase should be less risky than those you buy as you accumulate more wealth. We have suggested four specific funds to fit into the categories on page 84, with one exception, specific money market funds (as listed in Chapter 3). The funds are either no-load or low-load and are available directly from the sponsor. They are arranged in the same category order as we suggest you buy them, starting with a government income fund and ending up with an international or global fund.

$ HINT: Although these funds have generally turned in superior performances over the last three to five years, you should call for current total return figures before purchasing shares. As we've noted before, no investment is forever.

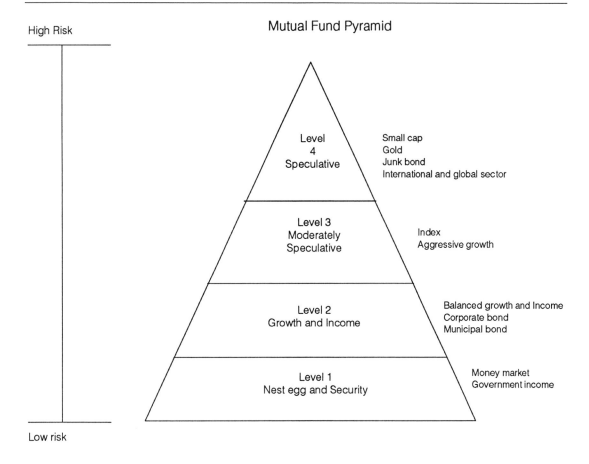

High Risk

Low risk

Mutual Fund Pyramid

Level 4 Speculative — Small cap / Gold / Junk bond / International and global sector

Level 3 Moderately Speculative — Index / Aggressive growth

Level 2 Growth and Income — Balanced growth and Income / Corporate bond / Municipal bond

Level 1 Nest egg and Security — Money market / Government income

TYPES OF MUTUAL FUNDS

GOVERNMENT INCOME FUNDS

Benham Treasury Note	1-800-472-3389	⎫
Dreyfus U.S. Gov't Intermediate	1-800-782-6620	⎬ Level 1
Fidelity Spartan Gov't Income	1-800-544-8888	⎭
Rushmore US Government Intermediate	1-800-622-1386	

BALANCED FUNDS

CGM Mutual	1-800-345-4048
Twentieth Century Balanced	1-800-345-2021
Value Line Income	1-800-223-0818
Vanguard Wellington	1-800-662-7447

GROWTH AND INCOME FUNDS

Berger One Hundred & One	1-800-333-1001
Dodge & Cox Stock	1-415-434-0311
Fidelity Growth & Income	1-800-544-8888
Safeco Growth	1-800-426-6730

TYPES OF MUTUAL FUNDS (*Cont.*)

HIGH QUALITY CORPORATE BOND FUNDS

Benham Target Maturities	1-800-472-3389	Level 2
Scudder Short Term Bond	1-800-225-2470	
SteinRoe International Bond	1-800-338-2550	
Vanguard Investment Grade	1-800-662-7447	

TAX-EXEMPT MUNICIPAL BOND FUNDS

General Muni Bond (Dreyfus)	1-800-645-6561
Safeco Muni Bond	1-800-426-6730
Scudder High Yield Tax-Free	1-800-225-2470
Vanguard High-Yield Muni	1-800-662-7447

AGGRESSIVE GROWTH FUNDS

Berger One Hundred	1-800-333-1001	
CGM Capital Development	1-800-345-4048	
Kaufman	1-212-344-2661	
20th Century Ultra	1-800-345-2021	

INDEX FUNDS

Level 3

Fidelity Market Index	1-800-544-8888
Peoples MidCap Index	1-800-645-6561
Schwab-1000	1-800-435-4000
Vanguard Index Trust Extended Market	1-800-662-7447

SMALL CAPITALIZATION STOCK FUNDS

Columbia Special	1-800-547-1707
Evergreen	1-800-235-0064
Founders Frontier	1-800-525-2440
Janus Venture	1-800-525-8983

SECTOR FUNDS

Fidelity: Technology	1-800-544-8888	
Neuberger & Berman Selected Sectors	1-800-877-9700	
T. Rowe Price New American Growth	1-800-638-5660	
Vanguard Energy	1-800-662-7447	

INTERNATIONAL STOCK FUNDS

Level 4

Harbor International	1-800-422-1050
Ivy International	1-800-235-3322
Lexington Worldwide Emerging Markets	1-800-526-0056
Scudder Global	1-800-225-2470

INTERNATIONAL BOND FUNDS

Fidelity Global Bond	1-800-544-8888
Freedom Global Income	1-800-225-6258
Scudder International Bond	1-800-225-2470
T. Rowe Price International Bond	1-800-638-5660

SECTOR FUNDS

If you're confident about what industry or industries will do well during 1994 and 1995, consider a sector fund, one that invests in a single industry. Keep in mind, however, that although such funds offer greater profit potential than broader-based funds, they're also far riskier. This risk factor is reflected in their great price volatility.

☐ CAUTION:

- Stocks in a given group tend to fall in unison.
- Most sector funds stay fully invested or nearly so even when their industry has a slide. They are less likely to switch portfolios into Treasuries or cash equivalents. Select a fund that's part of a family of funds so you can switch out when your industry turns sour.
- It's difficult to use past performance to predict future performance in this group.
- Read one or two of the newsletters listed at the end of this chapter, plus *Value Line Investment Survey* and Standard & Poor's *Outlook* to keep up to date on industry developments.

$ HINT: Limit your investment in sector funds to 10%. Since they focus on one economic area, you'll reduce your chances for loss if that particular sector experiences a downturn.

INVESTING IN GOOD CAUSES

Earth Day, held in April, heightens the country's awareness of the urgent need to save our environment, specifically, the importance of developing better methods of energy conservation, waste management, and pollution control. Wall Street offers ways to invest in the emerging business of environmental housecleaning.

➤ SOCIALLY RESPONSIBLE MUTUAL FUNDS Socially responsible investing is not a new phenomenon. Several such mutual funds have been around for years, but they're now getting more attention. The goals of these funds range from avoiding firms that deal in liquor, tobacco, or military weapons

---

TYPES OF SECTOR FUNDS

Agriculture	International
Chemicals	Leisure
Computers	Precious metals/gold
Defense/aerospace	Real estate
Energy	Service
Environment	Socially responsible
Financial services	Technology
Foreign countries	Transportation
Health care	Utilities

LEADING STOCK FUNDS

These six funds have consistently performed above the average equity fund regardless of market conditions.

FUND	TELEPHONE
Fidelity Contrafund	1-800-544-8888
IDEX	1-800-624-4339
AIM Constellation	1-800-347-1919
IDS New Dimensions	1-800-328-8300
AIM Weingarten	1-800-347-1919

to championing the environment. Others look for companies that are involved in community development and low-income housing projects.

The granddaddy of socially responsible investing, *The Pax World Fund* of Portsmouth, New Hampshire, is a balanced stock and bond fund that was started in 1971. The fund, which has $487 million in assets, will not buy companies in the liquor, tobacco, or gambling industries, and it emphasizes health care and education stocks. For the 12 months that ended in 1992, it was up 2.66%.

The Dreyfus Third Century, started a year later in 1972, is a much larger fund with $510 million in assets. It invests in companies that protect or improve the environment, that make careful use of our natural resources,

SOCIALLY RESPONSIBLE EQUITY FUNDS

FUND	TELEPHONE	TOTAL RETURN/ JAN-JUNE 1993
Calvert Social Investment	1-800-368-2748	−2.35%
Dreyfus Third Century	1-800-645-6561	−0.12
Parnassus Fund	1-800-999-3505	+5.71
Pax World Fund	1-800-767-1729	−0.77
Pioneer Fund (stocks)		+6.32
Pioneer II (stocks)		+6.58
Pioneer III (stocks)	1-800-225-6292	+5.29
Pioneer Bond Fund		+7.67
Pioneer Muni Bond Fund		+6.25
Pioneer U.S. Government Trust		+6.42

SOCIALLY RESPONSIBLE MONEY MARKET FUNDS

FUND	TELEPHONE	YIELD AS OF JULY 1993
Calvert Money Market Fund	1-800-368-2748	2.52%
Pioneer Cash Reserves		2.41
Pioneer U.S. Government	1-800-225-6292	2.58
Pioneer Tax-Free Money Fund		1.74
Working Assets Money Fund	1-800-533-3863	2.13

and that are involved in occupational health and safety and consumer protection. All companies must be equal opportunity employers. Dreyfus will, however, invest in firms with military sales. For the 10-year period through March 31, the fund chalked up an annual return rate of 12.75%.

The Parnassus Fund in San Francisco was named for a sacred Greek mountain overlooking the oracle at Delphi. It follows a contrarian philosophy, investing only in stocks that are out of favor with the investment community. Among the factors used in building its portfolio: Companies must produce a product or service of high quality, be sensitive to the communities where it operates, and treat its employees fairly and well.

The Calvert Social Investment Fund invests in companies that make quality products and environmentally responsible goods. They must be equal opportunity employers, promote women and minorities, and provide safe workplaces. The fund will not buy companies primarily engaged in the production of nuclear energy or weapons systems, or those doing business in South Africa.

The 18 funds operated by *The Pioneer Group* rule out investments in liquor, tobacco, gambling, or firearms.

➤ SOCIALLY RESPONSIBLE MONEY MARKET FUNDS In addition to these stock funds, there are several socially responsible money market funds for those who want a parking place for their cash. The largest, *Working Assets Money Fund,* was started in 1983 with $100,000 by a group of 8 Bay Area people interested in educating the public on social issues. It invests in money market instruments that help finance housing, small businesses, family farms, higher education, and certain types of energy.

INDEX FUNDS

These funds buy the same securities that make up an index and therefore their performance mirrors that of the index, such as the S&P 500, the Small Cap Index, or the S&P 100. They offer a way for individuals to participate in the long-term growth of the overall stock market, at a relative low cost. There are more than 70 index-linked funds. Because they are designed to closely match the performance of major market yardsticks, they have several unique advantages:

1 During bull markets they provide full market participation.
2 Because their portfolio turnover is low and they don't require large research staffs, most have low operating costs, thereby boosting your returns. (These funds sell shares only when a stock is deleted from an index or when net redemptions force stock sales.) The average equity fund has an expense ratio of about 1.4% versus a little under 1% for index funds.
3 With low portfolio turnover, capital gains tend to be less than for actively managed funds. Therefore, taxes on such gains are deferred for the most part until the fund shares are sold.
4 These funds provide excellent diversification and you know exactly what stocks you're invested in at all times.

```
┌─────────────────────────────────────────────────────────────┐
│                                                               │
│   INDEX FUNDS                                                 │
│   ▬▬▬▬▬▬▬▬▬                                                   │
│                                                               │
│   FUND                        INDEX TRACKED  TELEPHONE        │
│   Dean Witter Value-Added Equity   S&P 500   1-800-869-3863   │
│   Fidelity Market Index            S&P 500   1-800-544-8888   │
│   Peoples Index (Dreyfus)          S&P 500   1-800-645-6561   │
│   Peoples MidCap Index             S&P MidCap 1-800-645-6561  │
│   Schwab-1000*                     Schwab-1000 1-800-435-4000 │
│   Vanguard Index Trust 500         S&P 500   1-800-662-7447   │
│   Vanguard Index Trust Extended                               │
│     Mkt                            Wilshire 4500 1-800-662-7447│
│                                                               │
│      * Index of 1,000 largest publicly traded U.S. companies. │
│                                                               │
└─────────────────────────────────────────────────────────────┘
```

FUND	INDEX TRACKED	TELEPHONE
Dean Witter Value-Added Equity	S&P 500	1-800-869-3863
Fidelity Market Index	S&P 500	1-800-544-8888
Peoples Index (Dreyfus)	S&P 500	1-800-645-6561
Peoples MidCap Index	S&P MidCap	1-800-645-6561
Schwab-1000*	Schwab-1000	1-800-435-4000
Vanguard Index Trust 500	S&P 500	1-800-662-7447
Vanguard Index Trust Extended Mkt	Wilshire 4500	1-800-662-7447

* Index of 1,000 largest publicly traded U.S. companies.

The oldest of these funds, and the largest, is the Vanguard Index Trust 500 Portfolio. This no-load fund has 250,000 shareholders and some $5.3 billion in assets. It owns almost all the stocks in the S&P 500 in proportion to their market capitalization. Over the last ten-year period, the fund has returned about 18% annually, outpacing the average growth and income funds whose average annual return for the same period was 15%.

TAXES AND MUTUAL FUNDS

Each time you touch your mutual fund shares there are tax implications that must be reported to the IRS, including these:

- When you switch from one fund to another within a family, the IRS considers this a sale in one fund and a purchase in another. You must report your profit or loss.
- When your fund earns dividends and taxable interest and passes them on to you, you must pay taxes on this distribution.
- When your dividends are automatically reinvested in more shares, you must report this as dividend income.
- When there are capital gains distributions, these must also be reported.

For further information, read IRS booklet No. 564, "Mutual Fund Distributions," and contact T. Rowe Price for a free copy of "Calculating Taxes on Mutual Funds," 100 East Pratt Street, Baltimore, MD 21202; 1-800-638-5660.

$ HINT: If you buy shares in a fund just prior to its annual earnings distribution, you will be taxed on this distribution even though the value of your new shares drops to reflect this distribution. Buy just after distribution.

When you sell mutual fund shares, there are two ways to pay taxes on them: FIFO (first in, first out) and specific identification. Unless you notify the fund otherwise, it will assume you are selling the first (and generally the least expensive) shares you bought. This is the FIFO method. However, this method generally incurs more taxes. For that reason, some investors use the specific identification method, but it involves a lot of paperwork. You must write to the fund and tell it to sell specific shares, listing the dates and amounts of purchase. You pay taxes only on the minimum amount of profit.

An alternative, where the shares were left in the custody of a custodian or agent and the shares held in the account were purchased at different prices, is to elect one of two "average basis" methods—"double category" or "single category."

Under the "double category" method, all shares held in the account are divided into two categories: (1) those held short-term (one year or less) and (2) those held long-term (more than one year). The average basis in each category is the total adjusted basis of all shares in the category divided by the number of shares in the same category. The category from which shares are sold may be specified to the custodian or agent who must confirm in writing that such specification was made, otherwise the IRS will consider shares sold came first from the long-term category.

Under "single category," all shares in an account are considered part of a single category and the average basis is the total adjusted basis of all shares divided by the number of shares in the account. Shares purchased first are considered sold first. In either case, you must specify on your tax return that an average basis method has been used, specifying which method—double or single category—was used.

TAX-FREE FUNDS

Should you be in a tax-free mutual fund? To compute how much you need to earn on a taxable investment to equal a tax-free one, use the following formula:

$$\frac{\text{tax-exempt yield}}{\text{1 minus your tax bracket}} = \text{equivalent yield of a taxable investment}$$

For example, if you're in the 28% tax bracket and a tax-exempt bond is yielding 10%, you would have to receive a yield of 13.8% on a taxable investment to be equivalent:

$$\frac{.10}{1 - .28} = .138$$

In the 31% bracket, a tax-exempt bond yielding 7% is the equivalent of a 10.14% yield on a taxable investment:

$$\frac{.07}{1 - .31} = .1014 = 10.14\%$$

$ HINT: In all states, dividends from U.S. Treasury money funds or bond funds are also tax-free, even though you have to pay federal tax on them. And you may be eligible for a foreign tax credit if you own a mutual fund that invests in stocks or securities of foreign corporations. Watch for an indication on your 1099-DIV form of foreign tax paid on your behalf.

WHEN TO SELL YOUR MUTUAL FUND

A fund is not forever. Just as you revise your stock portfolio, you should do the same with mutual funds. They should be evaluated periodically and weeded out, for no fund is perfect for your needs forever. Unquestionably the toughest decision you will face is knowing when to sell. Here are some objective signals for selling and/or switching funds:

- If the portfolio manager quits
- If the fund's performance ranks in the bottom third of funds of its type for over a year
- If the fund lags the market averages, such as the S&P 500
- If the stock market shifts dramatically. Equity funds generally suffer during bear markets. Switch from stock to money market funds at the beginning of a bear market. As a bull market begins, move into conservative blue chip funds. As the bull begins to roar, put more dollars into aggressive growth funds.
- If interest rates rise. Bond funds tend to be hurt when interest rates move up. Sell bond fund shares when rates start to decline, but buy bond funds with longer maturities when rates seem to be at or near their peak in order to lock in the new higher yields.

WHEN A MUTUAL FUND MANAGER LEAVES

Just when you've found a fund that's making money, the portfolio manager suddenly leaves to run another fund. Do you stay or follow him to his new home? Generally you're all right to stay put, at least for 6 months, during which time you can see how the new manager is performing. This is particularly true if switching means paying high redemption fees. If it's a money market fund or an index fund, the manager has relatively little to do with performance so there's no need to change. However, consider following the manager to his or her new fund after 6 to 12 months if:

1 its investment goals match yours;
2 your current fund, under the new manager, is underperforming in its category 6 to 12 months after the changeover;
3 the new manager revises the fund's strategies so it no longer fits your needs—it becomes too conservative or too aggressive, for example.

FOR FURTHER INFORMATION

GENERAL DIRECTORIES

*Individual Investor's Guide to No-Load
   Mutual Funds*
American Association of Individual Investors
625 North Michigan Avenue

Chicago, IL 60611
1-312-280-0170

An annual guide with evaluative data on 500 no-load funds; $24.95.

Donoghue's Mutual Fund Almanac
IBC Donoghue Organization
P.O. Box 91004
Ashland, MA 01721
1-508-429-5930 (in MA); 1-800-343-5413

Annual with data on more than 2,400 funds; $39.95 + $3 shipping.

The Handbook for No-Load Fund Investors
P.O. Box 318
Irvington, NY 10533
1-914-693-7420; 1-800-252-2042

An annual directory with useful ideas on how to pick a no-load fund; performance data on 1,300 funds; $49.

The Investor's Guide to Low-Cost Mutual Funds
Mutual Fund Education Alliance
1900 Erie Street
1-816-471-1454
Kansas City, MO 64116

Performance figures, assets, turnover rates on 325+ funds; updated every January and July; a bargain at $5.

Mutual Fund Fact Book
Publications Division
Investment Company Institute
1600 M Street NW, Suite 600
Washington, DC 20036
1-202-293-7700
$15

BOOKS AND PAMPHLETS

Warren Boroson, *Keys to Investing in Mutual Funds* (Hauppauge, NY: Barron's Educational Publishing, Inc., 1992), $4.95.

Sheldon Jacobs, *How to Pick the Best No-Load Mutual Funds for Solid Growth and Safety* (Homewood, IL: Business One Irwin, 1992), $18.

The pamphlets below are free from:

Publications Division
Investment Company Institute
1600 M Street NW, Suite 600
Washington, DC 20036
1-202-293-7700

A Close Look at Closed-End Funds
What Is a Mutual Fund?
Discipline: Dollar Cost Averaging

Mutual Fund Values
Morningstar Inc.
53 West Jackson Blvd.
Chicago, IL 60604
1-800-876-5005

Like *ValueLine:* covers 1,240 funds in detail; updated every other week; $395/year; 3-month trial, $55.

NEWSLETTERS

The No-Load Fund Investor
P.O. Box 318
Irvington, NY 10533
1-800-252-2042

A monthly analysis of the no-load funds; $105.

No-Load Fund X
DAL Investment Co.
235 Montgomery Street, Suite 662
San Francisco, CA 94104
1-415-986-7979; 1-800-323-1510

Monthly; lists top performers by investment goals; $75.

Mutual Fund Forecaster
3471 North Federal Highway
Fort Lauderdale, FL 33306
1-305-563-9000; 1-800-327-6720

Monthly; ranks funds by risk and profit potential; $100.

Sector Fund Newsletter
P.O. Box 270048
San Diego, CA 92198
1-619-748-0805

Monthly; tracks the sector funds; $117: 3-month trial, $27.

For sampling of newsletters:
Select Information Exchange
244 West 54th Street
New York, NY 10019
1-212-247-7123

SIE is a financial publications subscription agency providing a group of trial subscriptions to various investment newsletters. One trial group comprises 20 different mutual fund services for $11.95.

The Clean Yield Newsletter
Box 1880
Greensboro Bend, VT 05842
1-802-533-7178
Monthly; $95/year

Written for concerned individual investors and financial professionals, this stock market newsletter profiles 2 stocks per month and updates 8 others. It screens companies for their environmental practices and weapons production and presents a monthly model stock portfolio.

The Social Investment Forum
430 First Avenue North
Suite 290
Minneapolis, MN 55401
1-612-333-8338

Associated membership in this nonprofit coalition of individuals and investment professionals that promotes ethical investing is $65. Membership includes the *Forum Guide*, which provides information on stockbrokers, financial planners, mutual funds, money managers, newsletters, and organizations involved in ethical investing, plus the group's newsletter. The *Forum Guide* may be purchased separately for $45.

7 USING CLOSED-END FUNDS

Many investors shy away from closed-end funds because they simply don't understand how they work. Yet overlooking these hybrid creatures—part mutual fund, part stock—can mean missing a good investment opportunity. Many offer investors the opportunity to buy their portfolio assets at a discount.

Closed-end funds, also called Publicly Traded Investment Companies, are similar in some ways to open-end mutual funds, described in the previous chapter. Both are investment companies that take money from thousands of investors and assemble portfolios of stocks, bonds, convertibles, and other securities to meet the fund's stated investment goal, and then issue shares to the public. Both use professionals to manage their portfolios.

However, the similarities end there. There are key differences. Open-end mutual funds continually issue new shares as people invest their money and they buy back their shares when investors sell. Not so with a closed-end fund. These funds raise their initial capital by issuing a fixed number of shares in a process similar to selling a new stock issue. After this initial offering the fund is closed, hence its name. It does not issue new shares (unless it has a secondary offering later) nor does it redeem shares.

From this point on, the fund's shares trade in the secondary market on one of the stock exchanges or over the counter as regular stocks. That is why they are sometimes called "publicly traded" funds. Shares cannot be purchased directly from the fund itself. Instead, you must buy and sell them through a stockbroker and you pay a commission, just as you do when trading common and preferred stocks.

UNDERSTANDING DISCOUNTS AND PREMIUMS

The relationship between a closed-end fund's market value and its net asset value (NAV) is quite different from that of an open-end mutual fund. Each closed-end fund has a NAV and, like a mutual fund, it changes daily depending on the market value of the stocks and bonds in its portfolio. When you sell shares in an open-end mutual fund, you receive the net asset value per share, minus any redemption fees. But the NAV is not used to determine the market price of the fund's shares; i.e., its price on an exchange or over the counter. Because they are traded on the exchanges, their shares fluctuate in price based upon demand, just as with any stock. And this price moves independently of the portfolio value. When buyers of the fund outnumber sellers, the price rises, and when sellers outnumber buyers, the price declines. The result: the price of a closed-end fund's shares may sell at a premium to (above) or at a discount (below) from its net asset value (NAV), depending upon investor interest in the fund. (The NAV is the market value of the fund's portfolio divided by the total number of shares outstanding, minus any liabilities.) For example, if a fund has a NAV per share of $15, based on the current market value of its portfolio, but is priced at $12, it is selling at a 20% discount. Or to look at it another way, when a share of a closed-end fund is selling at a 20% discount, every $12 invested in a share puts $15 in assets to work for you.

The NAV for each closed-end fund and its stock price plus whether its selling at a premium or a discount from NAV (expressed as a percentage) are listed in the financial press (see box below).

You'll find that most newly issued closed-end funds trade at a premium to NAV, reflecting the start-up costs of the fund. That's because a portion of your investment, often 7% to 8% goes toward paying underwriting expenses and commissions to brokers who sold the fund at the initial offering. For example, if you pay $10 per share to buy at the initial offering, approximately $9.30 would go toward actual investments.

$ HINT: Generally avoid buying shares at the initial offering. Wait until the share price drops below NAV in the secondary market.

TYPES OF CLOSED-END FUNDS

There are several types of closed-end funds:

- *Closed-end stock funds.* These invest in common and preferred stocks. Some specialize in a given sector, such as health care or energy. (Examples: Gabelli Equity, Blue Chip Value, Cypress.)
- *Closed-end bond funds.* These invest in a range of bonds, including high quality corporates, low-rated or junk bonds. Some invest only in U.S. government bonds, in municipal bonds, or bonds of foreign governments. As with any fixed-income investment, the price of closed-end bond funds move in the opposite direction from interest rates. (Examples: 1838 Bond-Debenture, ACM Government Opportunity, Nuveen NY Muni, First Australian Prime Income.)
- *Closed-end convertible bond funds.* These have portfolios consisting of bonds that can be converted into common stock. Convertibles offer relatively high yields in comparison to some other investments and they also have a potential for capital gains. (See Chapter 10 for more on convertibles). (Example: Lincoln National Convertible.)
- *Closed-end single country funds.* These specialize in stocks of a given country or geographical area. (Examples: The New Germany Fund, the Asia Pacific Fund, or the Irish Investment Fund.)
- *Closed-end dual purpose funds.* These funds have two classes of shares. The income shares are entitled to all of the dividends paid out or interest earned. The capital shares receive all the capital gains. Dual-purpose funds usually end 10 to 15 years after being launched.

When they are terminated, income shares are redeemed at a specific price. Owners of capital shares divide up the fund's remaining assets, either by liquidating the fund or by converting it to an open-end status and permitting investors to sell their shares at NAV. The closer the ending date, the more likely the fund's discount will disappear. If you are a long-term investor and buy at a discount and hold your shares until the termination date, you will make a nice profit. (Examples: Quest for Value Capital Shares, Quest for Value Income Shares, Hampton Utilities Capital Shares.)

BUYING A CLOSED-END FUND

You should go about selecting a closed-end fund just as you would any other investment: determine your investment goal and the amount of risk you wish to take and then find a fund that meets your requirements.

Unlike open-end mutual funds, most closed-end funds issue a prospectus *only* when they are launched or on the rare occasion when they issue new shares. You can learn about a closed-end fund's investment objectives, services, extent of portfolio turnover, the proportion of a fund's shares owned by officers and directors and other facts from the fund's reports to shareholders. Funds will supply copies upon request. As a shareholder, you will receive an annual report.

Be certain to study the fund's performance record and its expense ratio. The average expense ratio for open-end stock funds is 1.3%, so avoid fund's with ratios much higher than this with the exception of single country funds, whose expenses run higher than average.

☐CAUTION: Closed-end bonds funds can use their capital to maintain their dividends (and investor interest), even when it's not earning enough to cover the payouts. The dividend will probably be cut, eventually.

When buying a fund you should also be aware of the discounts and premiums to NAV. The rule of thumb is, all other things being equal, avoid selling at a premium to NAV and aim to buy when the fund's price is at a discount to NAV. Funds tend to trade at a premium when the portfolio contains issues of foreign companies located in countries that have a promising outlook for growth. (See Chapter 19 for more on single country closed-end funds.)

It's important to keep in mind that the discount or premium is primarily a function of investor sentiment, rather than changes in the fund's underlying portfolio value.

YOUR RETURN

There are three basic kinds of return for investors in closed-end funds:

- *Dividend income.* Funds receive interest and dividend income from the securities in their portfolios. This income, minus fund operating costs, is distributed to shareholders as dividends.
- *Capital gains distributions.* Most funds buy and sell portfolio securities throughout the year. If a net gain is realized from these sales, most funds pay all or most of this money to shareholders as a capital gains distribution.

GOVERNMENT CLOSED-END BOND FUNDS

- ACM Government Income Fund NYSE:ACG Price: $11⅜ Yield: 8.3%
    Portfolio consists primarily of U.S. government and agency debt and some foreign government debt. Managed by Alliance Capital of New York.
- Putnam Intermediate Government Income Trust NYSE:PGT Price: $8½ Yield: 8.4%
    Has most assets in U.S. government securities, some in debt of foreign governments, and cash. (Prices as of May 1993).

- *Capital gains.* If you sell shares in the fund for more than you paid for them, you then make your own capital gain through the sale.

SHAREHOLDER SERVICES

Services vary from fund to fund. Some of them offer:
- *Automatic reinvestment* of dividends and/or capital gains distribution. By reinvesting, you automatically buy more shares, which adds to your original investment and allows even larger holdings to earn still more.
- *Cash investment* plans let you invest a specified dollar amount in the fund at various intervals.
- *Cash withdrawal* plans let you receive a specific amount from the fund at certain intervals. Payments come from selling shares only if dividend income and capital gains distributions become insufficient.

FOLLOWING CLOSED-END
FUND PRICES

By checking the daily prices of closed-end funds in the stock listings of most daily newspapers, you can get still more information, including the fund's high and low prices for the past 52 weeks; dividend payments made in the past year; the volume of sales for the previous day; and the change that price represents from one day earlier. (NOTE: Even publicly traded funds that invest in bonds are included in some stock tables). *Barron's* lists net asset values, discounts and premiums in each weekly issue. The *Wall Street Journal* does the same for stock funds on Mondays and bond funds on Wednesdays.

$ HINT: *Value Line Investment Survey* reports on about 40 closed-end funds among the many companies it follows. For extra protection, you may wish to confine your purchases to those given high rankings for safety and timeliness by its analysts. *Value Line* is available at most libraries and brokerage firms.

CHECKING CLOSED-END FUND PRICES

The *Wall Street Journal* has two categories for closed-end funds. One is called "publicly traded funds" and the other "closed-end bond funds."

EQUITY FUNDS

FUND NAME	STOCK EXCHANGE	N.A. VALUE	STOCK PRICE	% DIFF.
• Diversified Common Stock Funds				
Adams Express	NYSE	$20.38	$21	+3.0
Blue Chip Value	NYSE	7.72	8	+3.6
Zweig Fund	NYSE	10.95	12¾	+16.4
• Specialized Equity and Convertible Funds				
American Capital Conv	NYSE	24.12	22	−8.8
Austria Fund	NYSE	7.94	8	+0.8
Duff & Phelps Utility	NYSE	10.23	11⅛	+8.7
Petrol & Resources	NYSE	30.79	28½	−7.4

CLOSED-END BOND FUNDS

FUND NAME	STOCK EXCHANGE	N.A. VALUE	STOCK PRICE	% DIFF.
• Bond Funds				
1838 Bond Debenture	NYSE	22.07	24½	+11.0
MFS Special Value	NYSE	15.49	16⅛	+4.1
Global Income Plus	NYSE	9.64	9½	−1.5
Dreyfus NY Muni Income	AMEX	10.38	10¾	+3.6
Nuveen CA Muni Value	NYSE	10.64	11½	+8.1

SOURCE: Wall Street Journal, May 1993.

Explanation:
 1st column: The names of the funds.
 2nd column: The exchange on which the fund is traded.
 3rd column: Net asset value per share—the market worth, at the end of the prior week's trading, of the fund's total assets (securities, cash, and any accrued income), after deducting liabilities and then dividing by the number of shares outstanding.
 4th column: The market price of the stock for the final transaction of the previous week.
 5th column: The plus or minus figure indicates the percentage premium (+) or discount (−) above or below the fund's net asset value per share at which the shares are selling.

WHEN TO SELL YOUR SHARES

As with all your investments, you should determine a selling point when you make your initial purchase. But before you achieve that profit, two conditions may appear, indicating that you should sell your shares:

■   If the market is at a high. Traditionally, closed-end fund premiums and discounts reach their best levels when the market tops, not when it bottoms.

■ If new, similar funds are brought to market. For example, in
   November 1989, the Berlin Wall fell and the existing Germany Fund,
   which had been around a long time, catapulted to an 80% premium in
   two months. Then, during the first quarter of 1990, three new
   Germany funds were launched and by the end of April, all four funds
   were selling at discounts and their underlying NAVs had also declined.

FOR FURTHER
INFORMATION

Investor's Guide to Closed-End Funds
Thomas J. Herzfeld Advisors
Box 161465
Miami, FL 33116
1-305-271-1900
$325/year or $60 for 2-month trial
Monthly

Also publishes: *The Annual Encyclopedia of Closed-End Funds,* which has
one page each on 395 funds; $70 for the 1993-1994 edition.

Wiesenberger's Investment Companies
CDA/Wiesenberger
1355 Piccard Drive
Rockville, MD 20850
1-800-232-2285

An annual guide evaluating closed-end funds, mutual funds, unit investment
trusts, and variable annuities; $295 + $19.95 shipping.

THE INVESTOR'S ALMANAC

Do you love to rummage through flea markets and antique shops and visit auctions? Or perhaps you're looking for an exciting, less traditional way to spend your bonus, small inheritance, or profit from sale of a stock.

There are endless numbers of "offbeat" investment choices if you are willing to be experimental. The Investor's Almanac highlights three of the most timely such choices. These do not come with a guarantee that you'll make a huge killing, but you certainly will have fun learning about a new field, and, of course, you may see a solid return on your investment over the long term.

Before you invest in any one of the three Investor's Almanac selections, spend some time doing background preparation. A suggested reading list is provided. If you know experts in these areas, ask them for advice and additional suggestions. In terms of collectibles in general:

- **Buy only what you like.** If later on the value should fall or if you decide to sell only part of your collection and keep this particular item, you should be left with something you cherish.

- **Focus on something.** Random collecting tends to be less valuable over the years. Decide on an art form or category. Then try to specialize in an artist, period, craftsman, or country. Unrelated individual pieces have less marketability than a cohesive collection.

- **Set aside a limited dollar amount.** You can revise this amount annually. Don't take all your money out of your money market fund or sell your Exxon stock to move into exotic investments. If you should suddenly need cash when everything you have is tied up in baseball cards, farmland, or estate jewelry, you

will be forced to sell, and if at the time prices are low, you will have made a poor investment decision. It's always best to diversify.

- **Buy in your price range.** If your resources are modest to start with, begin small. As circumstances and finances improve, you can always go after more elaborate and expensive items. It is unwise to take a second mortgage to make your first purchase.

HOW TO PROTECT YOURSELF

Many collectibles, including the model trains, furniture, and marbles described on the following pages, are found at antique shops, galleries, through dealers, and at shows and flea markets. When you buy from these sources, you have enough time to study each object. But when making a bid at an auction, the gavel swings fast and decisions must be made almost instantly. In this pressurized atmosphere, keep these points in mind to protect yourself from "auction fever" and buy the right thing at the right price.

➤ DO YOUR HOMEWORK Study up on the item. Know the price range.

➤ READ THE CATALOG Purchase the catalog in advance of the auction. It will give dollar estimates as well as a description of the items for sale. During the auction, write down what each item sold for and use these figures as price guidelines in the future.

➤ ATTEND THE PREVIEW Study the lots on display and make notes in the catalog regarding their size, age, condition, etc. Take a pen, pad of paper, small flashlight, magnifying glass, and a tape measure with you. At the preview open drawers, look for cracks, plug in lamps, look for identifying marks, signatures, initials, etc.

➤ MAKE A LIST OF THE ITEMS YOU REALLY WANT A list will help you avoid auction fever and buying everything in sight.

Then, at the auction:

- After registering, you will be given a number and something to bid with, most likely a paddle.

- Next, find out what the incremental dollar amounts are. Some auctioneers move up by $10; others by $100. Ask, or check in the catalog.

- If you don't want your bidding noticed, sit either near the front, a little to the side so you can see others bidding, or in the back rows.

- Listen to the bidding terminology. "Silver looking" is NOT the same as "sterling silver." Wait to place a bid after you have become at ease with the auctioneer's patter. Know if you are bidding by the piece or by the lot.

- Get a feel for the timing of the auction. The most important items are generally brought out toward the middle of the sale, when the crowd is largest and has been "warmed up." After the major items have been sold, the crowd may thin out, leaving less competition for the remaining items. This is an excellent time to bid, provided, of course, the items you're interested in have not been auctioned off.

- Never be the first to bid on an item you want. Auctioneers often set an arbitrary opening price which may turn out to be artificially high. If so, it will drop in price if there are no bidders. Watch who else is bidding. You certainly want to avoid bidding against yourself. Bid as you sense the price rising or when it's near the top.

DECIPHERING AUCTION CATALOGS

Auction catalogs are excellent resources and should be read carefully. Often they are available well in advance of the auction, giving you time to comparison shop and study various subject areas. Catalogs spell out:

1 *Terms of the sale,* including deposit requirements, method of payment, how to place absentee bids, buyer's fees or premiums, and when and how purchased items should be picked up.

2 *Policy on reserves.* Although all items are sold to the highest bidder, in practice it may be somewhat different. Some lots have a "reserve" or minimum price. If a lot does not actually bring this price, it can be withdrawn. Some auction houses use an "R" to designate that a lot has a reserve price.

3 *Descriptive statements.* These are usually given to aid the bidder if the piece is by a well-known artist, craftsman, or designer. Be aware of such phrases as "attributed to" and "in the school of," which indicate that the experts are not absolutely certain that the work is indeed by a certain person.

4 *Descriptive information.* Catalogs often tell the style, patterns, colors, ounces, measurements. The term "style" may signal a reproduction. For example, a Queen Anne table means the piece is from the chronological period of Queen Anne; on the other hand, a Queen Anne Style chair means it is a reproduction of that style and may have been made yesterday.

5 *Guarantees or warranties.* Catalogs are not perfect. Neither are experts and appraisers. If you purchase an item described as silver and it turns out to be silver plate, or mahogany that is really walnut, you may have a claim against the auction house.

6 *Presale estimates.* Estimates represent the auctioneer's opinion based on the current market. If you're interested in an item and it seems way above your price limit, don't despair. The estimate may be too high or interested people may not show up at the auction—any number of circumstances can reduce that sale price.

GETTING AN APPRAISAL

To get an official evaluation or appraisal of your collectible you need to hire an appraiser. An appraisal, which is a statement of an accurate and realistic value of a possession made by a knowledgeable person, can be used for establishing an item's worth, either for insurance coverage or to determine the price to ask when selling. Appraisals are also required by the IRS when something of value is donated to a charity and you wish to declare a deduction.

An official appraisal must be written, dated, and signed. It should also indicate whether the appraisal is the fair market value (used for selling the item, dividing an estate, or donating it to charity), or replacement value (for insurance reimbursement). The object appraised should be described in as much detail as possible and the number of pieces being appraised should be made clear. For example, if the value given is for a pair of vases, a set of 12 water goblets, etc., these numbers should be given.

Before hiring an appraiser, ask what he or she charges and for an estimate regarding how long it will take. Some charge a flat fee; others an hourly rate.

$ HINT: Never hire an appraiser who asks to be paid a percentage of the dollar value of the appraisal.

LEADING U.S. AUCTION HOUSES

Christie's
  502 Park Avenue
  New York, NY 10022
Sotheby's
  1334 York Avenue
  New York, NY 10021
Phillips
  405 East 79th Street
  New York, NY 10021
C. G. Sloan & Co.
  919 E Street, N.W.
  Washington, DC 20004
Richard W. Skinner, Inc.
  585 Boylston Street
  Boston, MA 02116
DuMouchelle's
  409 Jefferson Avenue
  Detroit, MI 48226
Garth's Auctions
  2690 Stratford Road
  Delaware, OH 43015

Although there are no licensing or educational requirements for becoming an appraiser, you can find a reliable one through the International Society of Appraisers. This group grants membership to appraisers who have 5 years of experience. Recommendations from a bank's trust department, a lawyer, or a museum or gallery are also suggested.

FOR FURTHER INFORMATION

International Society of Appraisers
485 West Berkley
Hoffman Estates, IL 60194
1-708-882-0706
American Society of Appraisers
Box 17265
Washington, DC 20041
1-703-478-2228

ANTIQUE FISHING LURES

These little contraptions, which attract a fish's bite by imitating the motion of prey, are becoming collector's items. Prices have been on the rise ever since the press began covering George Bush's fishing trips, and this relatively new field offers good investment opportunities. The most famous lure of all, the 135-year-old Haskell Minnow, brought $22,000 at an auction. There are only about 30 of these silver-plated minnow lures with brass finds and tail in existence. They were patented in 1859 by Riley Haskell, a gunsmith from Painesville, OH.

Lures fall into two general categories: metal lures, called spoons or spinners, and wooden lures. Metal lures, the older of the two types, were made before the Civil War, while wooden ones came along about 1890.

In the 1980s an expensive lure cost only $30 and many were just $5 to $10 each. Today a good quality collectible lure generally start around $100.

However, not every old lure is worth collecting. According to the National Fishing Lure Collectors Club, about 90 percent of them are not distinctive enough to qualify. Look for mint condition, age, and rarity; otherwise, you haven't got a collector's item. Unusual color, glass-bead eyes, and hand-painted gills push up values.

The best places to look for lures are at flea markets, garage sales, swap meets, old boathouses, long-forgotten tackle boxes, or the back rooms of sporting stores. A handful of dealers specialize in lures as do some country auction houses, especially in Maine, New Hampshire, Massachusetts, New York, Michigan, and Pennsylvania. But as with any investment, don't bite at the first offer; gather information first.

Like with any antique, age, condition, and rarity are the primary determinants of value. Those listed as MIB (mint in the box) are most valuable—many of the boxes were nicely designed.

➤ METAL LURES A Vermont fisherman, Julio T. Buel, got the first lure patent in 1852. It's said that he dropped a kitchen spoon in the water and saw a big trout swallow it, but this may be a fishy story. Nevertheless, Buel built a successful factory in Whitehall, NY, where he turned out serpentine shaped metal lures. Spoons and spinners made by other producers that are also prized include: Archer Wakeman, Harry Comstock, and the two New York state makers, Julio T. Buel and W.D. Chapman.

➤ WOODEN LURES Often carved from cedar, the best of these lures (or plugs as they are also called) are brightly or imaginatively painted, with gill marks done in a color to help them stand out. The earliest had black-painted eyes; later, glass eyes, sometimes imported from Germany, were added.

Wooden lures are said to be the invention of Jim Heddon, a beekeeper from Dowagiac, MI. His earliest plugs were wooden frogs. He used the heads of ladies' hat pins for eyes. In 1901 he and his family founded the James Heddon's Sons. The company published a catalog every year from 1903 to 1953, which provided accurate records for collectors, each one documenting all the models and color variations the company produced, along with annual dates.

Other key makers of wooden lures to look for are: Shakespeare, Creek Chub, Pflueger, and South Bend.

➤ HOW TO SPECIALIZE
- Collect those with a sense of whimsy: barebreasted Mermaids, those shaped like beer bottles, or Creek Chub Beetles (made only in Indiana), which look like ladybugs.
- Specialize by material (metal or wood).
- Specialize by maker, or by state of origin (Michigan and New York being the two with the most makers).
- Focus on the animal: minnows, frogs, muskrats, and baby ducks.
- Collect by quary for which they were intended: salmon plugs, muskie plugs, miniatures one inch or less in length, intended to use with a fly rod.
- Collect by color.
- Specialize in homemade lures carved by old-time fisherman and guides. They have a wonderful charm, very much like American folk art.
- Collect lures made by smaller companies: Paw Paw, Moonlight Bait Co., Keeling, and Eger; these were small companies that produced a fairly full line. Others made only a single bait: the Immell Bait Co. made the Chippewa bait; Michigan Life-Like made the Michigan Life-Like Minnow.

FOR FURTHER INFORMATION

To learn more, join:

The National Fishing Lure Collectors Club
P.O. Box 0184
Chicago, IL 60690
313-842-2589

Membership is $25/year and includes a quarterly newsletter with announcements of forthcoming shows, auctions, and swapmeets along with classified ads.

BOOKS
Carl F. Luckey, *Identification and Value Guide to Old Fishing Lures and Tackle* (Florence, Alabama: Books Americana, 1991).

STICKLEY FURNITURE

The Arts and Crafts Movement, which flourished in this country from 1900 to 1920, is an umbrella term for everything from Adirondack rustic to mission-style furnishings. The movement was the craftsmen's protest against what they regarded as fussy, silly, Victorian furniture and design. In contrast, Arts and Crafts furniture, especially the mission style, is characterized by its sturdy, linear designs and lack of decoration.

Most pieces have straight lines and are made of solid oak with no veneers, merely stained a warm brown. The wooden joints were intentionally left visible, as part of the overall style.

Gustav Stickley (1858–1942), the acknowledged leader of the movement, began producing handmade pieces of furniture at his company, the Craftsman Shops, in Eastwood, New York, starting in 1898. His two brothers, Lee and John George, ran the L. and J.G. Stickley Company in Fayettesville, New York. Gustav's handmade pieces, produced until about 1916, are recognizable by their clean, unadorned lines and use of heavy oak.

Despite their durability, these sturdy pieces eventually fell out of vogue. By the 1960s they could be found in used-furniture shops with price tags often below $100. Then quite surprisingly, in the 1980s, Stickley furniture was suddenly fashionable again, with Barbra Streisand paying a record $363,000 for a 1902 sideboard at a Christie's celebrity auction in 1988. At this same auction, Peter Wiles, Gustav's grandson, who had inherited many originals, had put up 21 pieces for sale—couches, chairs, clocks, and sideboards. They brought a total of $858,000, almost three times the estimate. Other celebrities, including Jack Nicholson, Richard Gere, and Steven Spielberg, also bid up prices.

The owners of the Stickley plant, Aminy and Alfred Audi, were in the audience that memorable evening. The next day they decided to capture the renewed interest in Stickley by making fine quality reproductions, using the same materials and workmanship as Gustav. As their repros came on the market, prices for the originals fell. Even the major collectors stopped buying, because the originals had soared so in price.

➤ INVESTING TODAY Because of the 1980s price corrections, original Stickleys are now selling at far more reasonable prices: a dining table that once went for $40,000 recently, sold for only $7,000; a Morris chair, once worth $18,000, commands about $8,000. Some smaller items can be found for $5,000. Curiously, however, as the prices of the antiques fell, enthusiasm for the Stickley reproductions has increased. A repro of a 1910 tall case clock, for instance, sells for $4,600, while the original recently brought $18,000 at an auction. A reproduction of the sideboard Ms. Streisand bought sells for $10,000.

$ HINT: The reproductions are keeping the furniture popular and in the public's eye. There are, of course, a limited number of originals, which means their prices will eventually rise again.

You can tell the repros from the originals in two ways:

1 The originals used the best oak and have fine finishes; the reproductions do not.
2 Most of the originals are labeled or branded with Gustav's name and shopmark—a small joiner's compass with the words "Als ik kan" in the middle. (Flemish for "To the best of my ability.") The repros do not have this mark.

FOR FURTHER INFORMATION

Visit:

Craftsman Farm Foundation
2352 Route 10 West
(Box 5)
Morris Plains, NJ 07950
1-201-540-1165

This is Gustav Stickley's home and museum, located about one hour from New York City. Call first; open only several days a week.

The Virginia Museum of Fine Arts
2800 Grove Avenue
Richmond, VA 23221
804-367-0888

The St. Louis Art Museum
One Fine Arts Drive
St. Louis, MO 63110
1-314-746-4599

Both museums have several original pieces on exhibit at any one time, plus reference material on the Arts and Crafts Movement.

Study the reproductions:

The original Stickley designs and the name are now owned by Aminy and Alfred Audi. Contact the company for information on showrooms open to the public.

L. & J. G. Stickley, Inc.
One Stickley Drive
Manlius, NY 13104
1-315-682-5500

BOOKS AND CATALOGS

David Cathers, *Furniture of the Arts and Crafts Movement* (New York: New American Library, 1988).

John Crosby Freeman, *The Forgotten Rebel: Gustov Stickley and his Craftsman Mission Furniture* (Watkins Glen, NY: Century House, 1966).

Robert Judson Clark, *The Arts and Crafts Movement in America 1876–1916* (Princeton, NJ: Princeton University Press, 1972).

Mary Ann Smith, *Gustav Stickley: The Craftsman* (Dover Publications, 1983).

Stickley Catalogs. Reissued by Dover Publications, 1991–1993.

Gustav Stickley, *His Craft* (Morris Plains, NJ: Craftsman Farm Foundation, 1991).

ORIENTAL RUGS

Although many antique Oriental rugs cost almost as much as a new car, they have the distinct advantage of lasting longer and appreciating more in value. And, you don't have to spend as much as you would for a Lexus or Jaguar. Only a handful of experts compete for the rarest rugs, leaving a plentiful supply of good quality, beautiful rugs, within reach of many investor's budgets. In fact, prices now are considerably less than they were in the late 1970s, when collectibles were tauted as being inflation-resistant, and less than they were in the 1980s, when spending money was "in" among many well-heeled Americans. When the stock market collapsed in 1987, prices for Oriental rugs fell almost as rapidly.

Today, however, a renewed interest in rugs is just beginning to push prices up again, making this a good time to invest or expand your collection. Adding to slowly increasing price tags is the fact that Iran, heir to the rugmaking traditions of the ancient Persians, has lost its leading place in the market: when the reign of the Ayatollah Khomenini began, many rugweavers fled the country and others left their looms to make money in the more lucrative oil fields. As the production and export of new Persian rugs began to decline, the value of the limited supply of older, antique rugs rose. As production

in Iran dropped, other rug weaving countries took over: China, India, Pakistan, and Rumania. Even these newer, handmade rugs are expected to rise in value in time because the ongoing decline of nomadic life is destroying the weaving tradition.

Although Oriental rugs have been popular in this country only relatively recently, they've been around a long time. Some experts believe the first ones were made in the fifth century B.C. The practice of rugmaking spread throughout the Middle East by nomadic tribes who raised sheep. The first rugs were flat, with no pile and no designs. By the sixteenth century, Europeans began to import Oriental carpets from Persia, India, Afghanistan, and China. Initially, they were used for wall hangings, but eventually they made their way down to the floor. Rugs made in Persia from the sixteenth to the early eighteenth century are considered the finest and are extremely valuable.

Throughout the rug belt, which stretches from Rumania to China, carpets are still made the same way for centuries: meticulously knotting thousands of strands of wool yarn, which form the pile, into a base of cotton or wool cords. Some are woven without pile and look more like tapestries. In India these are called *dhurries;* elsewhere in the rug belt they are called *kilims.* A finely produced 9' by 12' Oriental rug takes three weavers three to six months to make.

➤ GETTING STARTED The first step in buying an Oriental rug is to look at a good many of them by visiting reliable dealers. Study their inventories. Ask if you can take a rug home for a trial period or to another dealer for appraisal. If the answer is no, or even a reluctant yes, take your business elsewhere. A reliable dealer will also identify a rug by country of origin as well as type and give you a written receipt identifying its origin and approximate age.

You can also learn a great deal by attending auctions—but don't bid on your first visit. Often there are experts on hand who can answer questions, and auction catalogs provide useful information. Before you bid or buy you must know how to tell the difference between a machine-made and a handmade rug and decide whether you want an antique (over 100 years old) or a less expensive semi-antique (50 to 100 years old).

105

Among the other points to check before investing:

- *Knots.* Check if the rug was made with double knots or single knots. Most Persian rugs use double knots to tie the pile into the flat rug. Double knots are regarded as a sign of quality and they are stronger. A finely woven *Isfahan* has about 400 knots per square inch or more. A museum-quality silk rug might have 900 knots per square inch. A good quality Chinese carpet has 54 knots per square inch.

$ HINT: To estimate the number of knots, count the threads in one inch of fringe and divide by two, since each knot covers two threads in the foundation and square the result.

- *Shape.* Most handmade Oriental carpets tend to be slightly crooked.
- *Fringe.* Older rugs have more value if the fringes at the ends and the selvages (the side edges) are original, even if not in perfect condition.
- *The quality of the wool.* The best comes from young sheep—in fact, from the chest of the sheep. Rugs made from this wool are soft, not harsh and somewhat higher in price. Avoid dry wool as it wears out more quickly and sometimes doesn't hold the dye well.
- *Silk.* A silk rug is more fragile than those made of wool, but if antique or semi-antique, it can be very valuable. **TIP:** Avoid modern silk rugs that do not appreciate.
- *Weaver.* The weaver's personality should appear somewhere, perhaps in a symbol or signature. (Machine-made rugs are perfectly designed and do not have such personal touches.)
- *Dyes.* Antique rugs were made with natural dyes. Although chemical dyes never develop the antique patina of natural dyes, they are easier to use and have become almost universal in rugmaking since World War I.

$ HINT: Antique and semi-antique rugs are sometimes painted with dyes to cover up worn areas. Wet a white handkerchief and rub it over the spot. If color comes off, the rug has been touched up, entitling you to a discount at the very least.

☐ CAUTION: The large Persian area rugs, a favorite of many decorators, cost more but are less prized by the experts because they were made for export to the West.

➤ INVESTING TIPS FOR NOVICES If you're a beginning collector, you might want to focus on smaller tribal or village rugs, which are generally less expensive than big Persian carpets. Among the best picks are Middle Eastern *kilims*, also known as flatweaves because they do not have the rows of knotted wool that create pile. Many have unusual abstract designs and serve well as wall hangings. Although the most prized are Turkish carpets dating from the nineteenth century and earlier, you can find handsome Indian *dhurries* in the $1,000 to $5,000 range. Woven saddlebags and cradle coverings, which are smaller in size, may even be less. After you've become experienced you can consider moving up to a Sarouk or Kashan rug for $2,500 to $5,000.

An old Turkish *kilim* should feel soft and have a mellow patina, a rich feeling. If the colors are harsh, it's probably relatively new.

☐ CAUTION: Most of the Oriental rugs sold by the large department and carpet stores are machine-made. Check carefully before purchasing. A hand-knotted rug will have little flaws or variations in the design, while machine products appear perfect. And stay away from "one day only" rug auctions held in hotels. There's no guarantee that the carpet is antique, handmade, etc.

Once you have your rug, you should wash it every four years and have it moth-proofed. Rotate it regularly to prevent heavily traffic areas from wearing it out.

FOR FURTHER INFORMATION

Visit:

The Textile Museum
2320 S Street N.W.
Washington, DC 20008
1-202-667-0441

This museum has one of the finest rug collections in this country. The museum has learning seminars open to the public and sponsors educational trips for members to visit outstanding private and public collections and exhibits throughout the world.

Call:

The Oriental Rug Retailers of America
458 East Paces Ferry Road NE
Atlanta, GA 30305
1-614-294-3352

The association will provide, free of charge, the names of several member retailers in your area.

BOOKS

Jon Thompson, *Oriental Carpets* (New York: E.P. Dutton, 1988).

An excellent introduction, with a section for buyers and sellers with good practical advice.

Walter A. Hawley, *Oriental Rugs—Antique and Modern* (New York: Dover, 1970).

A standard reference work with excellent illustrations.

Joyce Ware, *Official Price Guide, Oriental Rugs* (House of Collectibles, 1991).

CONFERENCES

The American Conference on Oriental Rugs meets every other year. For details on the February 1994 conference in Chicago, call 1-312-474-9277.

WHEN THE BEARS ARE OUT OF THE CAVE

Most people initially feel more at ease with bonds than stocks, perhaps because they know bonds provide fixed income, during any kind of market. Yet bonds in recent years have become almost as volatile as stocks. So, even if you have always looked upon bonds as your safe investment, take time to read Part Two and update your position. You'll learn about the safest bonds (those issued by the government) as well as the riskiest (junk or high-yield bonds). In between there is information on how to evaluate bonds, use the rating services, read the quotes in the newspaper, and get call protection.

Part Two covers these broad categories:

- Corporate bonds
- Bond mutual funds
- U.S. Treasury issues
- Savings bonds
- Convertibles
- Municipal bonds
- Junk bonds
- Ginnie Maes and Ginnie Mae funds
- Zero coupon bonds
- CMOs

8

BOND BASICS:
How Corporate Bonds Work

If you want to protect your principal and also set up a steady stream of income, bonds, rather than stocks, are the answer. Most investors buy bonds for their income because they generally generate greater returns than CDs, money market funds, and stock dividends. They have another key advantage: as long as you hold bonds until maturity, you know exactly how much money you will get back—typically $1,000 per bond—and precisely when you will get it.

Bonds also offer greater security than most common stocks since the issuer must pay interest on its bonds before it pays dividends on its common or preferred stock. By contrast, a corporation can and often does cut back or eliminate the dividend on its common stock.

Bonds are issued by corporations, by the U.S. government and its agencies, and by states, municipalities, and their agencies. The latter group, also called "munis," are discussed in Chapter 11; high-yield or junk bonds appear in Chapter 12; and Treasuries, or government issues, in Chapter 9. This chapter is devoted to corporate bonds and corporate bond funds.

HOW BONDS WORK

Bonds, unlike stocks, are debt. They can best be described as IOUs, or as contracts to pay back money. In other words, when you buy a bond, you become a lender, loaning money to the issuer. In return the issuer owes you the dollar amount shown on the face of the bond plus interest. (You may actually get a bond certificate to put in your safe deposit box, although increasingly bond ownership is recorded in the form of book entry. This means the issuer maintains a record of bond buyers' names but does not send them certificates.)

The interest rate, officially called the *coupon rate,* is fixed—that means the issuer pays no more and no less for the entire life of the bond. Bondholders receive their interest payments on a regular schedule, generally every six months. The amount you get back when the bond matures is called the *face value* or *par*—typically $1,000, although sometimes $5,000.

Bonds mature anywhere up to 40 years, although those that mature in 1 to 10 years are known as notes. Those that mature in 5 to 10 years are called intermediate-term bonds; those issued for over 10 years are called long-term bonds.

Many investors mistakenly think of bonds as being stable in price, almost stodgy. This is simply not true. When bonds are first issued by a corporation or the government, they are sold at face value or par, but immediately afterward they move up and down in price, trading in what is called the *secondary market.* If they are selling at above par—above $1,000—they are said to be at a *premium.* If they are trading below par, at a *discount.* The reason they move in price is in response to changes in interest rates, as explained in greater detail below. The formula is easy to remember:

- When interest rates move down, bond prices move up.
- When interest rates move up, bond prices move down.
- The further away the bond's maturity date, the more volatile its price.

This price fluctuation actually offers you another way to make money with bonds in addition to earning a fixed rate of interest, and that is by selling your bonds at a higher price than you paid.

NOTE: You'll find that in the financial pages of newspapers, the prices for bonds are quoted on the basis of $100, so always add a zero to the price—a bond quoted at $108 is really selling at $1080.

FIVE KEY REASONS TO BUY BONDS

➤ DIVERSIFICATION When stock prices are depressed, bond prices tend to be high and therefore are a viable alternative to stocks.

➤ CURRENT INCOME Annual interest payments must be made to bondholders at the stated rate unless the company files for bankruptcy or undergoes a restructuring of its debt. Therefore, your steady stream of income is guaranteed in all but the worst situations. And, if the company restructures its debt, it will issue new securities in exchange for existing bonds.

➤ CAPITAL GAINS If you buy a bond at a discount (below $1,000 or par) and sell it for more than you paid, you'll have a profit.

➤ SENIORITY Interest on corporate bonds must be paid before dividends on common and preferred stocks of the same company, again protecting your income.

➤ SAFETY Ratings are available on corporate bonds that help determine how safe they are as an investment. Both Moody's and Standard & Poor's, independent rating services, rate the financial solidness of corporation's and their bonds on a continuing basis.

UNDERSTANDING BOND YIELDS

In order to be successful with bonds, it's necessary to understand on bond yields and price fluctuations work. Like stocks, bonds move up and down in price, their market value changing any number of times a day in reaction to interest rate movements. This is because bonds have a fixed rate of interest, and the only way the market can accommodate the changes in overall interest rates is by changing the price of bonds. For example: If you buy a bond at par ($1,000) and it has a coupon rate (the annual rate paid to bondholders) of 10%, you will receive $100 each year in interest payments. Now let's say that interest rates move up and the corporation that issued your bond needs to raise more money. The new bonds it issues must pay a higher interest rate in order to attract investors, otherwise no one will buy them. The new rate may be 10.5%. Now, the corporation's older bonds—the ones you own—will fall in price, perhaps to $960, in order to compensate

for the fact that their yield of 10% is less appealing than the new 10.5% rate. The older bonds are now selling at a discount.

What if interest rates fall? Exactly the opposite occurs: the corporation will be able to issue new bonds paying a lower rate of interest and the older bonds, the ones you own, will rise in price, immediately becoming more desirable, due to their higher coupon rate. They now will sell at a premium.

Here's an example of how bond prices move with interest rate changes, supplied by the Vanguard Group. If you own a 30-year bond that yields 8%:

If the yield...	The price will...
• rises to 9%	• fall 10%
• rises to 10%	• fall 19%
• falls to 7%	• rise 12%
• falls to 6%	• rise 28%

When dealing with bonds, you'll come upon five different types of yields:

➤ COUPON YIELD This is the interest rate stated on the face of the bond: 6.75%, 7%, etc. It is determined by the issuing corporation and lt depends on the prevailing cost of money at the time the bond is issued.

➤ CURRENT YIELD ON THE PURCHASE PRICE This is the annual interest payment based on the bond's current market price. It is higher than the coupon yield if you buy the bond below par and lower if you buy the bond above par. For example, an 8% coupon bond selling below par at $900 has a current yield of 8.9%. (Take the annual interest payment, which is $80, divide it by the current bond price ($900) and multiply by 100.)

➤ YIELD TO MATURITY This is the current yield and the gain or loss you will get if you hold the bond to maturity.

Since maturities vary and the current yield measures only today's return, the bond market relies on the yield to maturity (YTM). This is the total return, comprising both interest and gain in price. Put another way, it is the rate of return on a bond when held to maturity. It includes the appreciation to par from the current market price when bought at a discount or depreciation when bought at a premium. To approximate the YTM for a discount bond:

1 Subtract the current bond price from its face value.

2 Divide the resulting figure by the number of years to maturity.

3 Add the total annual interest payments.

4 Add the current price to the face amount and divide by 2.

5 Divide the result of step 3 by the result of step 4.

Example: A $1,000 7% coupon bond due in 10 years is selling at 72 ($720). The current yield is 9.7% ($70 ÷ $720). The YTM is about 11.4%.

$$1,000 - 720 = 280$$

$$280 \div 10 = 28$$

$$28 + 70 = 98$$

$$720 + 1,000 = 1,720 \div 2 = 860$$

$$98 \div 860 = 11.4\%$$

The YTM is the yardstick used by professionals, because it sets the market value of the debt security. But to amateurs, the spread—between the current and redemption prices—is what counts, because this appreciation will be added to your income. You get a competitive return while you wait—usually over 8 years, because with shorter lives, the current yield is modest: for example, AT&T 5½, 97 at 88. That's a current yield of 6.3%, but each year there will be an additional $24 price appreciation per

$1,000 bond *if* the bond is held to maturity in 1994.

➤ DISCOUNT YIELD This is the percentage from par or face value, adjusted to an annual basis, at which a discount bond sells. It is used for short-term obligations maturing in less than 1 year, primarily Treasury bills.

It is roughly the opposite of YTM. If a 1-year T-bill sells at a 6% yield, its cost is 94 ($940). The discount yield is 6 divided by 94, or 6.38%.

➤ YIELD TO CALL This is the same as yield to maturity except it is based on the assumption that the bond will be redeemed by the issuer at the call date.

$ HINT: Yield to maturity and yield to call are not listed in the newspaper. Your broker can give it to you or you can find it in Standard & Poor's *Bond Guide*, available at many libraries.

THE BOND PROSPECTUS

In addition to using the S&P and Moody ratings and your stockbroker's research, you can evaluate bonds on your own by looking at the bond's prospectus. This document details the issue's financial features, the means of payment, what the money raised will be used for, and what analysts think about the issuer's creditworthiness.

The two key points to look for are:

- *The amount of debt the company has already issued.* Heavy debt means that much of the money raised by this issue could go toward interest payments on the company's debt.

- *The bondholder's claim on the company's cash flow.* Is it a first claim or subordinated? You want one with first claim. Often the employee pension plan has a higher claim on revenues than bondholders should there be a default. Note, too, whether the pension plan is funded or unfunded; if a large part is unfunded, discuss the appropriateness of the investment with your broker.

HOW BONDS ARE RATED

GENERAL DESCRIPTION	MOODY'S	STANDARD & POOR'S
Best quality	Aaa	AAA
High quality	Aa	AA
Upper medium	A	A
Medium	Baa	BBB
Speculative	Ba	BB
Low grade	B	B
Poor to default	Caa	CCC
Highly speculative, default	Ca	CC
Lowest grade	C	C
In default	—	D

Ratings may also have + or − sign to show relative standings in class. Bonds at BBB level and above are considered investment grade.

NINE THINGS TO CONSIDER WHEN BUYING BONDS

There are a number of factors to keep in mind when selecting corporate bonds for your portfolio. A bond's value depends first and foremost on the credit quality of the issuing corporation. Bonds of a solid successful corporation are certainly a better investment than bonds of a weaker firm. The following guidelines will help boost the safety level of your investment:

- The bond's quality rating. Bond issuers are rated by independent research services. They analyze the financial strength of the corporation, project future prospects and determine how well the corporation is prepared to cover both interest and principal payments. The two top services, Moody's Investors Service and Standard & Poor's, tend to reach the same conclusions about each bond.

  Watch, too, for changes in bond ratings. When a bond is upgraded, its market price will probably rise and the yield dip a bit. Downgrading of a bond signals possible trouble and so the value of the bond will decline. (Downgraded bonds are called "fallen angels" on Wall Street.) However, if the rating is not too low, and you are not adverse to risk, you can sometimes make money purchasing a "fallen angel" you believe will be eventually upgraded, either as the economy improves or as the corporation makes changes that puts it on a more solid financial footing. **NOTE**: Slight rating shifts are not terribly important as long as the rating is A or better.

  And remember, the lower the rating, the higher the yield a bond must pay in order to attract investors. That's why very high yielding bonds are called "junk bonds."

- The interest rate, or coupon rate. This is the fixed dollar amount you will be receiving. You want a competitive rate.
- The maturity date. This is the date when you will be paid the face value of the bond. Pick maturity dates that meet your needs, say to pay college tuition or fund your retirement. Remember that by staggering your maturity dates, you will have a stream of income coming due that can be reinvested if interest rates go up. On the other hand, if rates fall, you will have locked in the higher yields.
- The current yield. This is the coupon rate divided by the current market price of the bond.
- The yield to maturity. This combines the current yield with the price you paid for the bond if that price was more or less than the face value.
- The yield to call. This gives you the yield, assuming the bond will be called in or redeemed before maturity date. (Calls are explained below.)
- The bond's backing or collateral. Bonds are categorized as either *secured bonds* or *debentures*. Secured bonds are backed by the corporation's plant, equipment, or other assets. If the collateral is real estate, the bonds are called mortgage bonds; if the collateral is equipment, they are called equipment certificates. If the corporation defaults on its bond payments, these assets can be sold to pay off the bondholders.

  Debenture bonds are far riskier in that they are unsecured, backed only by the overall ability of the corporation to meet its bills and other obligations. If the company declares bankruptcy, debentures cannot be paid off until secured bondholders are paid.

- Poison put provisions. These guarantee that bondholders in a company that is taken over can redeem their bonds at par. Poison puts accomplish two things: they protect investors and discourage unwanted takeovers. (This was more important during the 1980s when there were a rash of corporate takeovers.)
- Special Terms. Most bonds issued by the federal government and corporations carry

---

HOW TO MEASURE BOND QUALITY

A handy formula for determining investment-grade bonds is the number of times total annual interest charges are covered by pretax earnings for a period of 5 years.

	BEFORE FEDERAL INCOME TAXES	AFTER FEDERAL INCOME TAXES
Industrial bonds	5×	3×
Public utility	3×	2×

CHANGES IN BOND RATINGS

UP:	Embassy Suites
	B+ to BB−
	Chrysler Corp.
	BB to BB+
DOWN:	Rohr Industries
	BB− to B
	Sears Roebuck
	A to BB+

SOURCE: Standard & Poor's, May 1993.

---

a fixed coupon as well as a fixed date of maturity. But there are occasionally serial bonds in which a portion of the issue will be paid off periodically. Usually, the earlier the redemption date, the lower the interest rate, by ¼% to ½% or so. These can be useful if you have a target date for need of money. Serial bonds are widely used with tax-exempt issues, and CMOs, which are discussed in Chapter 12.

SHORT VERSUS LONG-TERM MATURITIES

Keep these points in mind when deciding what maturity bond to buy:
- The shorter the maturity rate, generally the lower the yield, but:
- The shorter the maturity, the less the bond is affected by interest rate changes and inflation.
- The longer the maturity the higher the yield.
- The longer the maturity the more likely the bond will be redeemed or called early; and then you will be paid off but will be

forced to reinvest this money at lower rates.
- To get the highest yields, invest for the shortest time possible while rates are rising. When rates have peaked, sell and buy longer-term bonds to lock in those high yields.
- You can protect yourself against price declines to some extent by purchasing high-grade bonds at a discount—that is, below face value. This is especially true if their maturity is not far away.
- Rather than having all your bonds come due at the same time, own a spread of bonds to come due every year or so. That way you'll periodically receive cash, which you can reinvest to keep the cycle going. Spreading out maturities also tends to average out the effects of price changes.
- If you have less than $50,000 to invest, diversify through a bond mutual fund or unit investment trust, which will also help reduce your risk.

Unlike most stocks, many bonds have thin markets, trading only now and then. That means that quotes for these issues may not be listed in the newspaper. The trading transactions of bonds that you should consider owning are listed in financial publications: daily in major newspapers, weekly in *Barron's* and other specialized publications.

The table below shows a listing for an AA-rated AT&T bond with a coupon of 7⅛% and a 2002 maturity date. The high price was 101⅞ and the low 101⅛, with the last sale at 101⅜, down 1/4 from the last sale of the previous day. Altogether 1,468 $1,000 bonds changed hands.

Each bond pays $71.25 in annual interest, so the current yield is 7.0%. In the year 2002 each bond will be redeemed at 100 ($1,000) for a loss of $13.75 per bond. The yield to maturity

---

HOW TO READ CORPORATE BOND LISTINGS

STANDARD & POOR'S RATING*	ISSUE	CURRENT YIELD	SALES ($1,000s)	HIGH	LOW	CLOSE	CHANGE**
AA	AT&T 7⅛, 2002	7.0%	1468	101⅞	101⅛	101⅜	−¼

* The rating is not shown in the press.
** From previous day.

is competitive with that of new issues. (NOTE: If you purchased the bonds when issued at par ($1,000) and held them to maturity, there would be no loss. The loss here of $13.75/bond applies to those who purchased the bonds when they were selling at a premium (around 101), that is, above par.)

When reading a bond listing in the newspaper, keep in mind that:

- Although bonds are issued at par ($1,000), in the financial pages of newspapers they're quoted on the basis of $100, so always add a zero to the price; for example, a bond quoted at $108 is really selling at $1,080.
- "Current yield" is the annual yield you will receive if you buy the bond at that day's price. If it's selling at a discount from par (the issue price), the price given in the "Last" column will be under 100. If the bond is selling at a premium or above par, the price will be above 100.
- "Sales" stands for the number of $1,000 bonds traded that day. (Bonds are usually priced at issue time at $1,000 each.)
- The small "s" that sometimes follows the interest rate means "space" and is used to separate the interest rate from the next group of numbers—the year in which the bond matures.
- The letters "cv" indicate that the issue is a convertible bond and can be exchanged for a fixed number of shares of common stock of the issuer.
- The letters "zr" before the maturity date indicate that the issue is a zero coupon bond.

SPECIAL TYPES OF BONDS

The variety of bonds is almost endless, far too great to cover in a general investment guide such as this. Some of the more interesting ones are described below; foreign bonds are discussed in Chapter 19. The leading sources for in-depth bond research are given under "For Further Information" at the end of this chapter.

➤ DEEP-DISCOUNT BONDS This type of bond sells at a price substantially below par ($1,000), which means that the bond buyer receives not only the coupon rate but also the dollar appreciation to par at maturity. Some deep-discount bonds are initially offered at discounts; others

drop in price because of credit uncertainties or changes in interest rates. These bonds can be extremely profitable, but those selling at a discount in the secondary market because their credit rating has deteriorated are highly speculative.

Example: Western Digital, 9%, due 2014, 83, for a yield to maturity of 11%.

➤ EQUIPMENT CERTIFICATES This classical type of bond is issued by airlines, railroads, and shipping companies to finance the purchase of new equipment. The certificate gives bondholders first right to the airplane, railroad car, etc., in the event that the interest and principal are not paid, thereby providing the investor with an added element of security.

Example: Seaboard Coastline Railroad Equipment Trust, 11⅜%, due 1995, 112.

➤ FLOATING-RATE NOTES These are notes on which the interest rate changes periodically, often as frequently as every 6 months. The rate is tied to a money market index such as T-bills. This variable interest rate enables investors to participate in rising interest rates, but it is far less appealing when rates are falling. Floating-rate notes, which usually have a 5-year maturity, tend to pay lower yields than fixed-rate notes with the same maturity.

Example: Citicorp Floating Rate Notes, 6.5%, due 1998, 99¼.

➤ FLOWER BONDS Flower bonds, issued between 1953 and 1963 at rates that today are no longer competitive, now are available *only* in the secondary market. They were designed to pay estate taxes after the death of the bondholder. The bonds today sell at a deep discount. You'll have to ask your broker for quotes.

The appeal of flower bonds is that they are valued at full face value at any time even prior to maturity provided they are used to pay estate taxes. To qualify, the bonds must have been purchased by the deceased; they cannot be purchased by the estate and used retroactively. If the portfolio of the deceased, for instance, contains $50,000 worth of par face value flower bonds, they will pay $50,000 worth of estate taxes, *even* if the market price at the time of death is only $25,000.

Note: Consult your accountant prior to purchasing flower bonds in the secondary market.

➤ OPTIONAL MATURITY These bonds can be redeemed by the investor at specified times, frequently after the first 5 years.

➤ YANKEE BONDS These dollar-denominated bonds are issued in the United States by foreign governments, banks, and institutions. When market conditions are better here than abroad, these bonds tend to pay higher interest than other bonds of comparable credit quality.

Example: Kingdom of Sweden, 8⅛%, due 1996, AAA-rated, NYSE, selling at 102.

➤ CREDIT CARD SECURITIES A relatively new type of bond, these are backed by credit card debt. In May 1990, Citicorp issued a record $1.4 billion of credit card debt. Investors are almost entirely institutions, not individuals. Most credit card securities are rated AAA.

UNDERSTANDING RISKS

As with all securities, there are some disadvantages to bonds, especially when purchased at par, which is the usual price when a bond is first sold to investors.

➤ LIMITED APPRECIATION Bond values move in the opposite direction to interest rates: up when interest rates fall and down when rates rise. The recent rises and falls in interest rates have sent bond prices moving like yo-yos, so the bond market is no longer the safe harbor it once was. If you buy a bond today and interest rates fall, you'll make a profit if you sell. However, if rates climb back up, you'll lose if you have to sell your bond before maturity.

➤ EROSION BY INFLATION Since bonds have set interest rates and pay back the principal at a future date, they do not offer a hedge against inflation.

➤ CORPORATE REVERSES Corporate financial woes can hurt bonds. Two prime examples: Chrysler and Navistar. Stick with high-rated companies, A or above (see table to right for bond ratings).

➤ FIXED RATE OF RETURN Stockholders have an opportunity to enjoy increased dividends, but bondholders do not receive interest rate increases unless they hold special floating-interest notes.

➤ CALLS Most corporate bonds are sold with a "call" feature that allows the issuer to redeem the bond before maturity. The conditions of a call are set when the bonds are first sold to the public. Bonds are not usually called in if the current rate of interest is the same as the bond's coupon rate or higher.

However, if interest rates fall below the bond's coupon rate, it is likely to be called in, because the issuer can now borrow the money elsewhere at a lower rate. When this happens, you lose your steady stream of income. You can protect yourself from early calls by purchasing bonds with "call protection," a feature that guarantees the issue will not be called in for a specific number of years, often 10. The call protection date is listed in the prospectus and in both Moody's and Standard & Poor's bond guides, available at your library or any brokerage firm.

➤ DIFFICULTY REINVESTING INTEREST Unless you buy zero coupon bonds or shares in a bond mutual fund, automatic reinvestment of interest is seldom available, as with stock dividend reinvestment plans. Therefore, you must find ways to reinvest your coupon payments as you receive them. One partial solution is, instead of depositing interest checks in a low-yielding savings or NOW account, to add to your shares of a low risk bond fund. Or, accumulate enough money to buy zeros.

➤ LIMITED MARKETABILITY With taxable bonds, there are two major markets: (1) the New York Stock Exchange, where a relatively small number of debt issues of major corporations are traded with daily quotations, and (2) the over-the-counter market, dominated by bond dealers who handle U.S. government bills, notes, and bonds; debt of smaller companies; and special offerings and packages via bid and asked prices.

With small lots (under 25 bonds), the prices can fluctuate widely from day to day or even during a given trading day. The spreads between the offers by the buyer and seller normally run from ⅜% to ½% in strong markets, up to 3% in weak markets, and even more with little-known issues.

$ HINT: Unless you have special knowledge, buy only bonds or debt issues whose trading is reported in the financial press.

GET CALL PROTECTION

To attract investors for long-term commitments, corporations usually include call protection when they issue new bonds.

When a bond is called, the issuer exercises a right (which will appear in the prospectus) to retire the bond, or call it in, before the date of

---

PICKING THE RIGHT BOND OR NOTE

If you want to invest $10,000 in bonds for 10 years, you have these choices:
- A 6-month T-bill that will be rolled over at each maturity.
- A 2- to 3-year Treasury note that at maturity will be turned into a 7- to 8-year note at a somewhat more rewarding yield *if* interest rates go up.
- A 10-year bond to be held to redemption. This would be best if you expect interest rates to decline or stay about the same.
- A 15- to 20-year bond to be sold at the end of 10 years, best if you expect rates to fall, but the longer the maturity, the greater the risk if rates climb.

---

maturity. This right to call gives the issuing corporation the ability to respond to changing interest rates. If, for example, a corporation issued bonds with an 11½% rate when rates were high and then rates dropped to 7%, it would be to the issuer's advantage to call in the old bonds and issue new ones at the lower prevailing rate. In fact, it is often so advantageous that a corporation is willing to pay a premium over par to call its bonds.

There are three types of call provisions you should know about:
- *Freely callable:* Issuer can retire the bond at any time; therefore, it has no call protection.
- *Noncallable:* Bond cannot be called until date of maturity.
- *Deferred call:* Bond cannot be called until after a stated number of years, usually 5 to 10.

The call price is the price the issuer must pay to retire the bond. It's based on the par value plus a premium, which in theory often works out to be equal to 1 year's interest at the earliest call date. For example, an 8% bond would theoretically have an initial call of $1,080—the $80 being the premium. However, there are many variations. For example, the call price can be specified, or it can be based on

a declining scale, with greater premiums given for calling in during the earlier years.

REFUNDING PROVISIONS

This feature permits a company to call in or redeem its old, high coupon rate debt in order to reduce its interest expenses by issuing new bonds at a lower interest rate. Some bonds offer refunding protection. The new bonds will pay a lower interest rate, a negative for the investor.

A call on a bond is nearly always bad news for the investor. That's because issuers seldom call a bond when interest rates are rising and when getting your money out would enable you to reinvest at the higher rates. On the contrary, bonds are generally called when rates are declining and you would prefer to lock in your higher yield by keeping the bond. So try to purchase bonds with call protection. Check the prospectus or ask your broker.

In effect, call protection guarantees a minimum period of investment income at the stated coupon rate.

Example: Viacom International, 10¼% debentures, due 2001, are noncallable to maturity. This means that an investor who buys these bonds in 1994 can look forward to 7 years of receiving a 10¼% coupon.

If you pay any premium above par in buying these bonds, you must understand that

---

CALL ALERT

Your broker should advise you about the call status of any bond; otherwise, be certain to ask. Calls are also listed in the bond's prospectus and in Standard & Poor's and Moody's bond guides, available from your broker or at your library. Here's how it looks in the bond dealer's guides or on quote sheets:

Corporate bond: "NC" means noncallable for life.

Government bond: "8½ May 1994–99" means the bond matures in May 1999, but is callable in 1994.

this premium reduces your overall yield to the call date (see "Yield to Maturity," page 111).

SINKING FUND PROVISIONS

Often a corporation borrows millions of dollars in any one bond issue, so quite obviously that amount of money must be available when the bond matures and the bondholders are paid back the full face value. In order to retire a portion of that enormous debt, some issuers buy back part of it, leaving less to be paid off at one time in a lump sum. In the process they shrink the debt. The money used to do this repurchasing is called a sinking fund. When a corporation sets up a sinking fund, it means that it must make periodic predetermined cash payments to the custodial account set up for this purpose.

With a sinking fund, the corporation pays less total interest. With a 25-year issue set up to buy back 3.75% of the debt annually, for example, 75% of the bonds will be retired before maturity. This means that the average life of the bonds will be about 17 years, not the 25 years anticipated by the investor.

A sinking fund adds a margin of safety for investors: The periodic purchases provide price support and enhance the probability of repayment when the bond matures. But it also narrows the time span of the bond, so that there will be

---

DEBT FOR EQUITY

A variation on the sinking fund is **defeasance,** which is used by corporations to discharge debts without actually paying them off prior to maturity. The company arranges for a broker to buy a portion of the outstanding bond issues for a fee. The broker then (1) exchanges the bonds for a new issue of corporate stock with a market value equal to that of the bonds and (2) sells the shares at a profit. The corporate balance sheet is improved without harming operations or prospects.

---

less total income for the long-term investor. Sinking funds benefit the corporation more than the bondholder.

☐ CAUTION: Watch out for call provisions on high-coupon utility bonds. An example is the case of Niagara Mohawk Power 10.20% of 2005. These are callable from March 1, 1993, at a price of 103.27. Ask your broker to check the prospectus or call the company's investor relations division to inquire about possible call dates before buying any utility bond.

SWAPPING BONDS FOR TAX PURPOSES

To the serious (and affluent) investor, swapping bonds can be profitable: A loss can reduce taxes; a higher yield can boost income; a wise switch can raise quality and extend the maturity of the debt.

Example: Investor X owns 25 ABC Bonds, 9%, due in 1996—at par ($25,000). They drop in price to 85 (25M × $850 = $21,250). He gets an annual income of $2,250 with a 10.6% annual yield (9 ÷ 85 = 10.6).

Seeking a tax loss, he sells them, for a $3,750 loss ($25,000 − $21,250 = $3,750). This loss can be used against any capital gains he may have. If he has no capital gains, he is limited to a $3,000 capital loss against ordinary income.

THE SINKING FUND

A sinking fund specifies how certain bonds will be paid off over time. If a bond has a sinking fund, the company must redeem a certain number of bonds annually before maturity to reduce its debt.

- *Advantage:* Bondholders get their principal back earlier than the maturity date.
- *Disadvantage:* If the coupon rate is high, bondholders will not want to retire the bond early.

If your bond is called in, you will be notified by mail and in the newspaper. You *must* take your money, because interest will cease at the specified time.

He then buys 25 XYZ 10¾s, due 2013, at 82 and thus replaces his bonds with a better-quality investment while establishing a tax loss.

If you have a sizable loss in bonds, consider swapping if the results are beneficial and help you to meet your investment objectives.

BOND MUTUAL FUNDS

If you have a small amount to invest or simply don't wish to select your own bonds, you can buy bonds through a mutual fund or closed-end fund.

Mutual fund shares can be purchased for as little as $250 to $1,000, with smaller increments thereafter. Most funds encourage automatic reinvestment of interest for compounding—something that individuals rarely do on their own.

The yields may be a bit less than those available from direct investments, but you get diversification, convenience, and the opportunity to switch to other funds (bond, stock, or money market) under the same sponsor.

- *Evaluate the portfolio.* For safety, choose funds with the most A- or better-rated holdings. For good income, look for those with lower-quality issues (but not too low). The highest yields are available from junk

CLOSED-END BOND FUNDS

FUND	YIELD	PRICE	SYMBOL
High Yield Income	10.9%	$8	HYI
MFS Gov't. Markets	9.8	7⅜	MGF
Putnam Master Inc. Trust	8.8	9	PMT
First Boston Income	9.8	9	FBF
ACM Gov't. Income	8.3	11⅝	ACG
John Hancock Inc. Sec.	7.5	17	JHS
Ft. Dearborn Inc.	7.1	17¼	FTD

SOURCE: Standard and Poor's, *Stock Guide,* May 1993.

bonds—but they are also highest in risk, as explained in Chapter 12.
- *Check the performance.* Follow performance over at least 5 years, long enough to include both bad and good years for debt securities.
- *Look for frequent distributions.* A mutual fund that pays monthly ensures a steady cash flow. If this is reinvested, compounding will be at a more rewarding rate. Buy right before the distribution declaration date.

Open-end bond funds, called mutual funds, continually issue new shares to sell to investors.

PROS AND CONS OF CLOSED-END BOND FUNDS

PROS
↑ Closed-end funds do not have to sell off their portfolios when the market declines as open-end funds must do in order to meet redemption demand by investors.
↑ The managers tend to have greater flexibility in portfolio composition. A fund selling at a discount is sometimes a take-over candidate.

CONS
↓ Funds react very quickly to interest rate changes: When rates rise, bond prices fall, and vice versa.
↓ Many funds buy lower-quality bonds to boost yields and to compete with older funds that sell at a discount.

THREE WAYS TO MAKE MONEY IN BONDS

- *Recognize a bull market in bonds.* It usually takes place before a recession when interest rates begin to drop because the demand for credit is easing up.
- *Recognize when to sell.* Sell just before an inflationary spell when interest rates climb because the demand for money is up.
- *Understand event risk.* Bonds tend to lose their value if their issuer is taken over or if the company is restructured. Buy only those new bonds that have protective provisions.

They are available directly from the fund or through your stockbroker. (See Chapter 6.)

Closed-end bond funds do not issue new shares or units after their initial offering. Instead they trade on one of the exchanges or over the counter. The capitalization of this type of fund is fixed at the outset, and investors must buy shares either at the initial offering or later in the secondary market or aftermarket. This means that the price of a closed-end fund is determined by two variables: (1) the public's demand for its shares and (2) the value of its portfolio. Therefore, such funds sell either at a premium or at a discount from the portfolio's net asset value. Like their open-end cousins, closed-end funds are professionally managed, contain a wide variety of bonds, and make monthly distributions. (See Chapter 7 for more on closed-end bond funds.)

$ HINT: New funds often have high sales fees, as much as 7%—which is part of the offering price. So wait and buy in the secondary market, where you'll pay only your broker's commission. Select a fund selling at a discount.

Closed-end bond funds are listed each Wednesday in the *Wall Street Journal.*

FOR FURTHER INFORMATION

BOOKS AND PAMPHLETS

Marcia Stigum and Frank J. Fabozzi, *The Dow Jones–Irwin Guide to Bond and Money Market Investments* (Homewood, IL: Dow Jones–Irwin, 1987).

NEWSLETTERS AND NEWSPAPERS

The Bond Buyer
One State Street Plaza
New York, NY 10004
1-212-943-8200
Published daily; $1,897/year; $15 per copy; two-week trial, free

Investor's Guide to Closed End Funds
Thomas J. Herzfeld, Editor
P.O. Box 161465
Miami, FL 33116
1-305-271-1900
Monthly; $60 for 2-month trial; $325/year

9 | U.S. TREASURIES: BILLS, NOTES, BONDS, AND EE'S

There are no safer securities than U.S. Treasury obligations, which are backed by the full faith and credit of the U.S. government. So, if you're looking for a risk-free investment, invest in the federal government. Uncle Sam is continually borrowing money, and he has an excellent reputation for paying back his debts.

In addition to safety and affordability, Treasuries provide interest that is exempt from state and local income taxes—a plus for anyone, but especially those who live in high-tax states. And if interest rates fall, you can sell your Treasury for more than you paid.

Treasuries are also easy to unload because of the enormous size of the government bond market. In fact, the Treasury market is the world's largest securities field, with average trading volume in excess of $100 billion annually.

So, are there any disadvantages? Yes. If interest rates rise after your purchase, the value of that Treasury will fall because new issues will pay a higher annual interest; to make up for that, buyers will pay only a discounted price for the older issues. Of course, if you hold your Treasuries until maturity, you're guaranteed to get the full face value.

☐ CAUTION: The government also has the right to call its bonds prior to maturity, as it did in 1991, although this very rarely happens.

Another disadvantage is the rates are lower than on corporate bonds with comparable maturities—but then, corporates are also a riskier investment.

BUYING NEW TREASURIES

Buying Treasuries is not difficult. You can, of course, buy them from a broker, but you'll pay a minimum commission ranging from $25 to $100, which lowers your yield. Since fees vary, call several full-service and discount brokers.

$ HINT: Even though you pay a fee or commission, it's convenient to use a broker, especially if you sell your Treasuries before maturity.

You can sidestep the commission by buying them yourself at one of the 36 Federal Reserve Banks or branches, or by mail.

Just follow these 8 steps:

- *Step 1.* Contact your Federal Reserve Bank for a tender form and information on how to purchase Treasury securities through the Treasury Direct System (see list on page 123). You can also pick up the tender forms in person or by writing to: U.S. Treasury, Division of Consumer Services, Washington, DC 20239-0001.

- *Step 2.* Fill out the form for opening a Treasury Direct account and for entering a noncompetitive bid. Note that you must fill in your bank's routing number if you wish to have payments made directly to your bank account. This number is printed on your checks.

Although the Treasury prefers that you submit the official tender form, you may actually submit a tender by letter. If you do, be sure to type or print the following information and then sign the letter in dark ink: a) the face amount of the securities you wish to purchase; b) the maturity; c) whether you are submitting a noncompetitive or competitive bid (specify yield when making a competitive bid); d) your name and mailing address; e) your Social Security number (if the securities are being purchased in two names, you must supply the Social Security number of the first-named purchaser); f) your telephone number during business hours; g) your

121

A POTPOURRI OF RATES

INVESTMENT	YIELD/ RATE
6-month CD	2.81%
1-year CD	3.09
Money market mutual fund	2.69
Money market deposit account	2.45
1-year Treasury bill	3.40
7-year Treasury note	5.56
10-year U.S. government bond	5.97
30-year U.S. government bond	6.66
AA-rated 10-year corporate bond	7.50
A-rated 20-year corporate bond	8.01
High-yield (junk) corporate bond	10.00
Ginnie Mae certificate	7.00
Federal Home Loan Agency notes	7.50

(As of July 1993)

Treasury Direct Account number, if you have one.

If you do not yet have a Treasury Direct Account, then include: h) your Direct Deposit information—the name of the financial institution and its routing number, your account name, number, and type (checking or savings account). You will also need to include a W-9 certificate or a signed statement by the first-named owner certifying, under penalty of perjury, that you are not subjected to backup withholding tax. (Call 1-800-TAX-FORM to order the W-9, or pick up one at your bank.)

■ *Step 3.* Mail the tender and payment to your Federal Reserve Bank or its branch. Print or type in large letters on the front of the envelope: TENDER FOR TREASURY SECURITIES.

■ *Step 4.* If you bid in person, your noncompetitive tender must be in by noon the day of the auction. If you're bidding by mail, your tender must be postmarked by midnight the day before the auction and received by the Federal Reserve Bank or branch by the issue date to be accepted for that auction. A cashier's check is necessary for T-bills, but a personal check is acceptable for notes and bonds. Checks are made payable to the Federal Reserve Bank of (CITY). All checks must have the name and Social Security number of the purchaser on the face of the check. Endorsed checks are not accepted. If you're paying in person you can use cash. You may also use Treasury securities maturing on or before the issue date of the new T-bills.

■ *Step 5.* Auction results are announced by the Treasury in the late afternoon of the auction day. Many Federal Reserve Banks have 24-hour recorded messages giving the results as well. (Auctions are not open to the public.)

■ *Step 6.* The government will set up a Treasury Direct Account, called a Master Record, when you submit your first tender form. You may review your Account at any Federal Reserve Bank or branch, or request that a Statement of Account be mailed to you. It consists of name, address, phone number, Treasury Direct Account number, tax information, and payment instructions. It also provides detailed information on all your Treasury securities maintained in the account. Whenever a change is made to the account information, such as when you receive interest payments or when money is received upon maturity of a security, you will receive a copy of the updated record. (T-notes and bonds pay interest twice a year. T-bill interest, which is slightly more complicated, is described below.)

■ *Step 7.* Through the direct deposit payment method, interest, discount, and principal payments are electronically deposited into your account at the bank you designated on the tender form.

■ *Step 8.* You can also specify that interest and principal payments be automatically deposited into your bank account; and, that the Treasury roll proceeds over into future auctions. However, unlike a mutual fund investment, in which all interest, dividends, and capital gains can be reinvested in more fund shares, the Treasury rollover involves only your original investment.

$HINT: Buying Treasuries directly at auction works best for those who plan to keep them until they mature. You can sell Treasuries on the secondary market, but only through a broker or bank, which again entails paying a commission.

If you are already holding Treasuries in your bank or brokerage account and wish to transfer them to the Treasury Direct system, submit New Account Request Form PD 5182, available from a Federal Reserve Bank.

THE FEDERAL RESERVE BANKS AND BRANCHES

- ATLANTA. Securities Service Dept., 104 Marietta St., NW, Atlanta, GA 30303; 1-404-521-8653
- BALTIMORE. Box 1378, 502 South Sharp St., Baltimore, MD 21203; 1-410-576-3300
- BIRMINGHAM. Box 830447, 1801 Fifth Ave., Birmingham, AL 35283; 1-205-731-8708
- BOSTON. Box 2076, 600 Atlantic Ave., Boston, MA 02106; 1-617-973-3810
- BUFFALO. Box 961, 160 Delaware Ave., Buffalo, NY 14240; 1-716-849-5000
- CHARLOTTE. Box 30248, 530 East Trade St., Charlotte, NC 28230; 1-704-358-2100
- CHICAGO. Box 834, 230 South LaSalle St., Chicago, IL 60690; 1-312-322-5369
- CINCINNATI. Box 999, 150 East Fourth St., Cincinnati, OH 45201; 1-513-721-4787
- CLEVELAND. Box 6387, 1455 East Sixth St., Cleveland, OH 44101; 1-216-579-2490
- DALLAS. Securities Dept., Box 655906, 2200 North Pearl St., Dallas, TX 75265; 1-214-922-6770
- DENVER. Box 5228, 1020 16th St., Denver, CO 80217; 1-303-572-2473
- DETROIT. Box 1059, 160 West Fort St., Detroit, MI 48231; 1-313-964-6157
- EL PASO. Box 100, 301 East Main St., El Paso, TX 79999; 1-915-544-4730
- HOUSTON. Box 2578, 1701 San Jacinto St., Houston, TX 77252; 1-713-659-4433
- JACKSONVILLE. Box 2499, 800 West Water St., Jacksonville, FL 32231; 1-904-632-1190
- KANSAS CITY. Box 419440, 925 Grand Ave., Kansas City, MO 64141; 1-816-881-2409
- LITTLE ROCK. Box 1261, 325 West Capital Ave., Little Rock, AK 72203; 1-501-324-8272
- LOS ANGELES. Box 2077, Terminal Annex, 950 South Grand Ave., Los Angeles, CA 90051; 1-213-624-7398
- LOUISVILLE. Box 32710, 410 South Fifth St., Louisville, KY 40232; 1-502-568-9236
- MEMPHIS. Box 407, 200 North Mid-America Mall, Memphis, TN 38101; 1-901-523-7171
- MIAMI. Box 520847, 9100 N.W. 36th St., Miami, FL 33152; 1-305-471-6497
- MINNEAPOLIS. 250 Marquette Ave., Minneapolis, MN 55480; 1-612-340-2075
- NASHVILLE. 301 Eighth Ave. North, Nashville, TN 37203; 1-615-251-7100
- NEW ORLEANS. Box 61630, 525 St. Charles Ave., New Orleans, LA 70161; 1-504-593-3200
- NEW YORK. Federal Reserve P.O. Station, 33 Liberty St., New York, NY 10045; 1-212-720-6619
- OKLAHOMA CITY. Box 25129, 226 Dean A. McGee Ave., Oklahoma City, OK 73125; 1-405-270-8652
- OMAHA. 2201 Farnam St., Omaha, NB 68102; 1-402-221-5633
- PHILADELPHIA. Box 90, 100 North Sixth St., Philadelphia, PA 19105; 1-215-574-6680
- PITTSBURGH. Box 867, 717 Grant St., Pittsburgh, PA 15230; 1-412-261-7802
- PORTLAND. Box 3436, 915 S.W. Stark St., Portland, OR 97208; 1-503-221-5932
- RICHMOND. Box 27622, 701 East Byrd St., Richmond, VA 23261; 1-804-697-8000
- SALT LAKE CITY. Box 30780, 120 South State St., Salt Lake City, UT 84130; 1-801-322-7900
- SAN ANTONIO. Box 1471, 126 East Nueva St., San Antonio, TX 78295; 1-210-978-1303
- SAN FRANCISCO. Box 7702, 101 Market St., San Francisco, CA 94120; 1-415-974-2330
- SEATTLE. Securities Services Dept. Box 3567, Terminal Annex, 1015 Second Ave., Seattle, WA 98124; 1-206-343-3605
- ST. LOUIS. Box 14915, 411 Locust St., St. Louis, MO 63178; 1-314-444-8703

TREASURY BILLS

Treasury bills mature in 3 months, 6 months, or 1 year. T-bills, as they are often called, are issued in minimum denominations of $10,000, with $5,000 increments. New issues are sold at a discount from face value and are redeemed at full face value upon maturity. If, for example, you buy a T-bill through the Treasury Direct System, you write a check for $10,000. Shortly after the auction you are refunded by mail or electronic deposit into your account—the "discount" that is equal to the interest rate determined at the auction. Let's say the discount or interest rate is 4%: you'll get a check for $400. When the T-bill matures, the Treasury will pay you $10,000, the full face value. Because they are guaranteed by the full faith and credit of the U.S. government, investors have no risk of default. In fact, if the federal government goes into bankruptcy, it won't matter what types of investments you have!

T-bills constitute the largest part of the government's financing. They are sold by the Treasury at regular auctions where competitive bidding by major institutions and bond dealers takes place. Auctions are held weekly for 3- and 6-month maturities, monthly for 1-year bills. (Occasionally the government issues a 9-month T-bill.) The yields at these auctions are watched very carefully as indications of interest rate trends. Floating-rate loans, variable-rate mortgages, and numerous other investments tie their rates to T-bills.

➤ FIGURING YIELDS Because T-bills are sold at auction at a discount from face value, there is no stated interest rate. You can determine their yield by using the formula in this box:

DETERMINING THE YIELD ON A 1-YEAR T-BILL

$$\frac{\text{Face value} - \text{price}}{\text{price}} = \text{``annual interest rate''}$$

$$\frac{10,000 - 9,100}{9,100} = \frac{900}{9,100} = 9.9\%$$

Thus a 1-year 9.9% bill will be purchased for $9,100 and redeemed 12 months later at full face value, or $10,000. This gain of $900 is interest and subject to federal income tax but is exempt from state and local taxes.

➤ TO DEFER INCOME WITH T-BILLS Since Treasury bills are sold at a discount price—that is, at less than face value—and are redeemed at maturity at full face value, they do not pay an annual interest. Therefore, in the following example, you would not have to pay taxes until your T-bill matured in 1995. This is to your advantage if you expect your income to be lower in 1992.

Example: You buy a $10,000 1-year bill in February 1994 for $9,380. Your real yield is 6.6% ($10,000 − $9,380 ÷ $9,380). When you cash in the bill in February 1995, you will receive $620 on a cash investment of only $9,380.

$HINT: Use T-bills as a short-term parking place for money received in a lump sum, say from the sale of a house or yacht, as a bonus, or from a royalty check. Think of them as interest-bearing cash.

TREASURY NOTES

These intermediate-term securities mature in 2 to 10 years. They are issued in $1,000 and $5,000 denominations. The $1,000 minimum is usually available only on notes of 4 to 10 years. Notes maturing in 2 to 3 years are issued in $5,000 denominations. The interest rate is fixed and determined by the coupon rate as specified on the note. It is calculated on the basis of a 365-day year. Interest earned is paid semiannually and is exempt from state and local taxes. Two-year notes are issued monthly; 3-year notes, quarterly; and 4- to 10-year notes, also quarterly.

T-notes are growing in popularity with investors, primarily because they are more affordable than T-bills (which have hefty $10,000 minimums), but also because their longer maturities usually give investors a higher yield. Another plus is the fact that they are not callable, so you are guaranteed a steady stream of income until maturity.

TREASURY BONDS

These long-term debt obligations are also issued in $1,000 minimums, with $5,000, $10,000, $50,000, $100,000, and $1 million denominations also available. They range in maturity from 10 to 30 years. A fixed rate of interest is paid semiannually. The interest earned is exempt from state and local taxes. Unlike T-notes, these bonds are sometimes subject to a special type of call. If a specific bond is callable, its maturity date and call date are both listed in hyphenated form in the newspaper. In the example described on page 124, the 12% bond due to mature in 2013 could be called in at any time starting in 2008.

§ HINT: Because government bonds come in so many maturities, stagger your portfolio to meet future needs and to take advantage of any rise in interest rates.

BUYING ON THE SECONDARY MARKET

After a Treasury issue is first sold, it then trades in the secondary or aftermarket—not on the major exchanges but over the counter. This type of trading is subject to the same market forces that affect corporate bonds (see Chapter 8) and stocks (see Chapter 13). And you will need a broker to handle your trades—all previously issued Treasuries must be purchased through securities dealers, commercial banks, or a stockbroker, not from the Federal Reserve Banks. Very often you will wind up buying directly from the broker's own portfolio of Treasuries and you may not have to pay a direct commission or transaction fee. Instead, the extra cost of the securities covers the brokers' costs and gives him a profit.

You may wish to buy in the secondary market if you want to have money come due on a certain date. In this case, check the Treasury listings in the newspaper to find a maturity date that meets your goals. You'll note that there's a "bid" and an "asked" figure. The bid price is what you're offered if you sell, while the asked is what it will cost you to buy. The figures in the paper, however, are for trades of $1 million. Since you'll most likely be buying less than a million, you'll wind up paying slightly more than the price listed in the newspaper and your yield will be slightly less. (See box)

Be certain you check with several brokers, including a discount broker. Charles Schwab, for example, charges $39 per transaction up to $150,000. That may or may not be a better deal than a full-priced broker.

HOW GOVERNMENT NOTES AND BONDS ARE QUOTED

ISSUE	BID	ASKED	CHANGE	YIELD
Feb. 95, 9	101–12	101–22	+04	8.46
Aug. 08–13, 12	127–22	127–28	−09	8.88
May 16, 7¼	84–27	84–31	−07	8.72
May 18, 9⅛	104–05	104–09	−06	8.71

SOURCE: Wall Street Journal.

HOW TO READ THE QUOTES

After a Treasury issue is first sold, it then trades in the secondary or aftermarket—not on the major exchanges but over the counter. The issues are quoted in dollars plus units of $1/32$ of a dollar (0.03125), with bid and asked prices daily. Newspapers list the bid, asked, change in price, volume, and yield.) The quotations are per $1,000 face value. The first line in the table above shows notes due in 1995 with a coupon of 9%, a bid price of 101–12 ($1,013.75), and an asked price of 101–22 ($1,016.88) with a yield of 8.46%. An investor who held these notes for four years until maturity will get $90 per year less the premium of $16.88, for a yield to maturity of 8.46% when redeemed in February of 1995.

The 12% bond due to mature in 2008–2013 has what is known as a double maturity, sometimes referred to as a call date. Its yield is calculated on the earlier maturity, 2008; however, at the Treasury's choice, the maturity may be extended to 2013. Notification appears in the newspaper, and in some cases by letter. All Treasury issues with this modified call feature can be identified in the paper by the hyphenated listing. A small "n" indicates that the issue is a note rather than a bond.

SELLING YOUR TREASURIES

If you hold Treasury issues in a Treasury Direct Account, you will have to transfer them out and into an account at a brokerage firm or bank. They then will sell the securities for a fee.

To transfer securities, fill out Form PD 5179, "Security Transfer Request," available from your Federal Reserve Bank or branch. You will need to include the routing number of the financial institution you will be using.

TAXES ON INCOME FROM SECURITIES

The income from securities is defined as: 1) the difference between the purchase price and either the face value of securities held to maturity or the market value of securities sold, given away, or otherwise disposed before maturity, and 2) the interest earned from the securities.

The income is subject to federal income tax but not state and local taxes. All income is reported to the IRS at the end of the year in which it is earned, with the exception of income earned on T-bills. This income is considered to be earned and reported to the IRS during the year the bills mature, are redeemed, sold, or given away.

SAVINGS BONDS

Savings bonds are an ultra safe and extremely easy way to put aside money. They are not just for timid investors or grandparents who are at a loss over what to give their grandchildren. Today these bonds offer several special tax breaks that make them ideal for those facing college tuition or retirement. And, they're inexpensive to purchase—the minimum is only $25.

From 1941 until 1979 the government issued Series E bonds. Starting in 1980, Series EE and Series HH bonds were issued.

➤ ADVANTAGES
- Easy to buy. You can buy EE savings bonds at your bank, through the Bureau of Public Debt, or through automatic payroll deduction plans, certainly a painless way to save. And, there are no fees or commissions involved, so all your money immediately goes to work for you.
- Low minimums. EE bonds have denominations ranging from $50 to $10,000, but you pay only half the face value. In other words, a bond with a $50 face value costs only $25; a $10,000 bond,

$5,000. The maximum annual investment in EE bonds is $30,000 face value per calendar year per person—that's $15,000 in cash.

- Safety. Savings bonds are backed by the full faith and credit of the U.S. government and are redeemed at full face value upon maturity. Even if you lose your bond, all is not really lost. You may get it replaced by writing to: Bureau of Public Debt, 200 Third St., Parkersburg, West Virginia, 26106-1328. Give as much information as you have: serial number; issuance date; name, address, and Social Security number of the original owner.
- Floating interest rates. EE bonds held 5 years or longer earn either a flat rate set by the government or 85% of the average yield on 5-year Treasury notes during the preceding six months, whichever is higher. The T-note based rate is adjusted every May and November to reflect current market rates. As of May 1, 1993, the rate for bonds held 5 years or more was 4%.

$ HINT: To get this current rate, call 1-800-US-BONDS.

The set rate you receive depends upon when the bonds were purchased. Those purchased after March 1, 1993 and held for 5 years have a rate of 4%. In other words, they will earn either 4% or 85% of the T-note rate, whichever is higher. However, EE bonds issued after November 1, 1986, and up until March 1, 1993, earn a minimum of 6% when held 5 years. Bonds issued on or after November 1, 1982, and before November 1, 1986, earn a minimum of 7.5% if held for at least 5 years.

$ HINT: The 4% floor, although 2% lower than it was, still makes EE bonds one of the better parking places for money you might want to tap during the next year or two. That's because the 4% rate is currently higher than rates being paid on money market funds and on 1-year CDs. Keep in mind, however, you must hold the bonds for 6 months. Then you can cash them in without penalty if rates go up and invest your money elsewhere.

- Easy to redeem. EE Bonds may be redeemed at any time after 6 months from issue date at most banks or other financial institutions. HH Bonds are redeemable at any Federal Reserve Bank or branch, or at the Bureau of the Public Debt in Parkersburg, West Virginia, any time after 6 months from issue.

- No probate. If, upon the death of an owner, there is a surviving co-owner or beneficiary named on the bonds, the bonds do not form a part of a decedent's estate for probate purposes. Subject to applicable estate or inheritance taxes, if any, they become the sole property of the survivor.

- Special tax breaks. The interest you earn on savings bonds is exempt from state and local taxes, and you have a choice when it comes to paying federal taxes. You can either pay the federal tax each year as the interest accrues, or wait and pay the tax when you cash in the bonds, give them to someone else, or when the bonds mature.

$ HINT: If you defer paying federal tax, that money, which would otherwise be going to the IRS, can be invested elsewhere.

There's yet another tax-related choice: you can exchange or roll over your EE bonds for HH bonds and continue delaying taxes on the amount you roll over until you cash in the HH bonds or they (the HH bonds) mature. However, the interest on HH bonds is paid out in semiannual installments and taxed in the year received. That rate since March 1, 1993, has been 4%.

HH bonds cannot be purchased. They are available only by exchanging at least $500 in Series E or EE bonds. Series HH bonds are issued in denominations from $500 to $10,000. Unlike EEs, they pay interest semiannually and are sold at full face value. You get your interest twice a year by Treasury check, and at redemption receive only your original purchase price.

- As a tax shelter. When you swap Es for EEs or HHs, the interest—unlike that from savings accounts, money market funds, and other bonds—does not have to be reported to the IRS annually until you cash them in. By swapping, you can postpone the tax on the accumulated interest for a number of years. When cashed in, the amount of the accrued income is stamped on the face of the HH

bonds, and from then on, you must pay taxes on the semiannual payments. To make the transfer, fill out form PD 3523.

▶ HOW INTEREST IS CALCULATED EE bonds do not pay out current interest to bondholders. Instead they sell for one-half their face value and are redeemed at full face value upon maturity. In other words, they are "accrual-type" bonds, which means that the interest is paid when the bond is cashed in—on or before maturity date, and not regularly over the life of the bond, as is the case with corporate bonds, Treasury notes, and bonds.

In March 1993, the Treasury changed the way interest is credited to new bonds. On bonds purchased prior to March 1993, the Treasury adds the interest earned to the bond's redemption value each month for the first 30 months. After that, it's added semiannually.

On EE bonds issued since March 1993, the interest is credited on the first of each month no matter how long you hold your bonds. That means timing the redemption of your bonds is less important than in the past, although you receive slightly more interest if you redeem them at the beginning of a month rather than at the end of a previous month.

In addition, the original maturity of newly issued EE bonds has been increased from 12 to 18 years—the longer maturity ensures that the bonds will double in value by maturity.

$ HINT: As long as short-term interest rates remain below 4%, hold onto your EE bonds.

Series HH bonds, which pay interest semiannually, also had their rates cut to 4%, which also applies to HH bonds issued after March 1, 1993. HH bonds issued from November 1986 until March 1992 earn a flat 6%. Older HH bonds continue to receive their previous guaranteed rates, either 8.5% or 7.5%, to the end of the maturity period.

$ HINT: If you have old EE bonds or if you converted EE bonds to HH bonds before the rate drop in 1993, KEEP THEM. The EE bonds you hold for 5 years or more will continue to earn their original minimum until their original maturity of 12 years from when you purchased them. And if you have old HH bonds paying 6%, they will continue to pay 6% for 10 years from when you purchased them. After that, these bonds will earn the current rate until final maturity.

➤ PAYING FOR COLLEGE. For generations Americans have used savings bonds as a way to pay for their children's college degrees. Before buying bonds for this purpose you should be aware of the tax rulings:

1   The first $600 of investment income a child receives is tax-free. This dollar amount is adjusted to reflect inflation, so it may change.

2   If the child is under age 14, the next $600 is taxed at the child's rate, which is probably 15%. And, investment income over $1,200 is taxed at the parent's rate, which is probably higher than the child's rate—most likely 28%, 31%, or 36%.

Because tax is deferred on EE bonds until they are redeemed, you can purchase them in a child's name and, assuming they are not cashed in before the child is 14, the interest will be taxed at the child's rate, which is presumably lower than the parent's.

☐CAUTION: If a parent is a co-owner of the bonds with the child, the parent is required to pay any tax due.

However, under certain circumstances it may make sense to report the interest income each year as it is earned; for instance, if the child has little or no other income, then, depending upon how many bonds the child owns and the amount of interest earned, there might be very little or no tax due at all.

Here's yet another tax consideration. Interest earned on EE bonds can be totally tax free, that is, free from state, local *and* federal income tax if the bonds are used to pay a child's college tuition. In order to qualify for this tax break, the bonds must be purchased in the parent's name, not the child's. And the parent must be at least 24 years old when the bonds are purchased. Bonds purchased before 1990 do not qualify.

$ HINT: Although grandparents cannot buy the bonds and meet the requirements for this tax break, they can, of course, give the money to the child's parents and let them buy the bonds.

When the parents redeem the bonds, the interest earned will be tax free if they are used to pay "qualifying educational expenses," which means

---

EE SAVINGS BONDS

PROS
↑ Safe; principal and interest guaranteed
↑ No fees or commissions
↑ If lost, replaced free of charge
↑ If held 5 years or more, get floating rate of interest with minimum of 4% guaranteed
↑ Federal taxes deferred
↑ No state or local taxes
↑ Market value does not drop when interest rates rise as with other bonds

CONS
↓ Floating rate minimum available only if bond held 5 years
↓ Cannot be used as collateral
↓ Limited purchase: $30,000 face value in 1 year per person
↓ Other vehicles may pay higher rates
↓ Cannot redeem during the first 6 months

---

tuition and fees (not room and board) at a college, university, technical institute, or vocational school.

For example, if parents redeem bonds worth $20,000 and pay $20,000 in tuition and fees, then all interest earned will be tax free; if only $10,000 is paid in education expenses, then just 50% of the interest will be tax exempt.

At the time, the child must be a dependent and the parent's income must fall within a certain dollar amount that is indexed to inflation. Currently the tax exemption begins to phase out above $66,200 of adjusted gross income on a joint return and disappears completely at about $96,200.

$ HINT: Keep "college" savings bonds separated from others you may own. Record the serial numbers, face amounts, and issue and redemption dates. When you redeem them, record the total dollar amount received (interest plus principal) and the name of the school to which you paid tuition.

THE YIELD CURVE

A yield curve is a diagram that illustrates the relation between bond yields and maturities on

YIELD CURVES OF TREASURY SECURITIES

This illustration shows the yield curve for Treasury securities of all maturities from 3 months to 30 years. Three yield curves, each for 3 different dates, are indicated by the different types of lines. Note that the yields for shorter term Treasuries have fallen considerably more than those with 10 to 30 year maturities. For example, the yield for 5 year notes fell from about 7.5% in April of 1991 to nearly 6% in April of 1992.

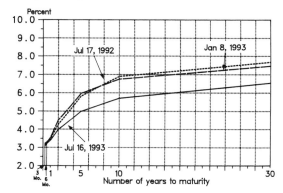

SOURCE: Market Reports Division (DFDATA).

a particular day. Use it to decide which type of bond to buy at a certain period. It is published daily in the *Wall Street Journal.*

To draw a yield curve, professionals set out the maturities of like bonds—all Treasuries or all AA rated corporates, on graph paper on a horizontal line, from left to right, starting with the shortest maturities (30 days) and continuing over days or years to the longest (30 years). Then they plot the yields on the vertical axis and connect the dots with a line that becomes the yield curve.

$ HINT: When short-term rates are more than a percentage point above long-term rates, the yield curve is inverted. A recession typically follows, usually within 6 months.

The curve is used to tell if short-term rates are higher or lower than long-term rates. When short-term rates are lower it is called a "positive yield curve." When short-term rates are higher,

it's a "negative" or "inverted yield curve." If there is only a modest difference between the two, it's known as a "flat yield curve."

Generally, when the yield curve is positive, investors who are willing to tie up their money long term are rewarded for their risk by getting a higher yield.

Although any fixed-income securities can be plotted on a yield curve, the most common one illustrates Treasuries, from a 3-month T-bill to a 30-year bond.

FOR FURTHER INFORMATION

Free pamphlets, "The Savings Bonds Question and Answer Book," "U.S. Savings Bonds Buyer's Guide," and "U.S. Savings Bonds: Now Tax-Free for Education," are available from:

Department of the Treasury
U.S. Savings Bond Division
Washington, DC 20226
1-202-377-7715

Basic information on Treasury bills is free from your nearest Federal Reserve Bank or:

Federal Reserve Bank of New York
Issues Division, 1st floor
33 Liberty Street
New York, NY 10045
1-212-720-6619

For material on the Treasury Direct program, call or write your area Federal Reserve Bank or write:

Bureau of Public Debt
Department A, Room 429
1300 C Street SW
Washington, DC 20239-1000
1-202-874-4000 (recorded message)

Buying Treasury Securities is available for $4.50 from:

Federal Reserve Bank of Richmond
Public Affairs Department
P.O. Box 27471
Richmond, VA 23261
1-804-697-8000

10 CONVERTIBLES: Income Plus Appreciation

These securities, which are part bond and part stock, are often a smart addition to one's portfolio—provided you are an experienced investor and willing to watch the market on a continuous basis.

A convertible is a bond that pays a fixed rate of interest with a unique feature—it can be exchanged for a specified number of the issuing company's common shares, if those shares move up to a certain price. In other words, you can have your cake and eat it too: you collect the high interest rate from the bond and, if the common shares rise sufficiently in price, make a profit by converting into the shares of the company's common. But if the common does not rise in price, you can simply keep collecting your bond's interest payments. (Unlike common stock dividends, which can be cut, postponed, or eliminated, a convertible's interest income is secure.)

Note: There are also some convertible preferred stocks, but they are not nearly as common as convertible bonds.

This conversion feature, however, does not come cheap. Convertibles cost more than the stock you can exchange it for. In fact they tend to trade at prices that are 5% to 20% or even 25% above that of the common stock into which they can be converted. The reason behind this premium over the conversion price is that convertibles tend to yield 3% to 5% more than common stock dividends, but less than what you would collect on the same company's "straight" bonds or preferred stock.

Before considering convertibles, you must know that:

1   If the issuing company's common stock goes up in price, the convertible reaches what is known as its "conversion price." At that point you can exchange your convertible for the common shares and pocket a profit.

2   If the issuing company's common stock goes down in price, your convertible will usually hold its value better than the common stock and you will still be collecting your regular income.

So this hybrid investment combines the security and fixed income of bonds (and preferred stocks) with the potential price appreciation of common stock. They pay higher income than common stocks and have greater price appreciation than regular bonds. Their convertibility factor links their price movement with that of the underlying stock, so even though a convertible bond has the low risk characteristics associated with "straight" bonds (safety of principal and regular interest payments), they usually fluctuate in price more than straight bonds. The bottom line: You give up some safety in exchange for potential capital gains.

Sometimes the issuing company calls the convertible bonds, forcing a conversion—but never below their conversion value. Bonds are generally called when interest rates fall so the corporation can save money by issuing new bonds at a lower rate.

$ HINT: If the CV is called when the market value of the stock is greater than the conversion value of the bond, you should opt to convert.

HOW CONVERTIBLES WORK

Company ABC needs to raise capital for expansion but does not want to dilute the value of its common stock by issuing new shares at this time. It also rejects selling a straight bond since it would be forced to pay the going interest rate, which for this example is 12%. Instead, management offers a bond that can be "converted" into its own common stock. Because of this desirable conversion feature, investors are willing to buy the CV bond at a lower rate of only

CONVERTIBLE BONDS

COMPANY/BOND	CV PRICE OF BOND*	PRICE OF COMMON	PRICE OF BOND	S&P RATING
Anadarko Petroleum 6¼, 2014	$34.20	$37	$111	BBB
Browning Ferris 6¼s, 2012	41.00	27	99	A
Hechinger 5½s, 2012	27.84	9	70	BBB−
Potomac Electric Power 7s, 2018	27.00	26	104	A+
Fifth Third Bancorp 4¼s, 1998	63.62	55	107	A+

* CV price of the bond is equal to the price at which you can convert the bond into stock.

SOURCE: Standard & Poor's *Bond Guide,* May 1993.

10%. Bonds are quoted as a percentage of par, or face value, which is $1,000, so this bond is listed as 100. This is the *market price,* the price at which the CV can be bought and sold to investors.

When Company ABC issues the CV bonds, its common stock is selling at $32 per share. Management decides its offering will be attractive to the public if each $1,000 bond can be converted into 25 shares of common. This is the *conversion ratio*—the number of shares of common stock you receive by converting one bond. The *conversion price* of the ABC bond is $40 (divide 25 into $1,000). The current value of

the total shares of ABC Corp. to which a bond can be converted is the *conversion value.* With ABC stock trading at $32 and a CV ratio of 25, the conversion value is $800.

On the day of issue, the difference between $40 (the conversion price) and $32 (the current market price) is $8. To determine the *conversion premium,* $8 is divided by $32 to yield 0.25, or a 25% CV premium. Another way to figure the conversion premium is to take the price of the bond ($1,000), subtract the CV value ($800), and divide the remainder ($200) by the CV value.

The *investment value* of ABC's CV is an estimated price, usually set by an investment advisory service, at which the bond would be selling if there were no conversion feature. For ABC it is 75.

The *premium-over-investment value* is the percentage difference between the estimated investment value and the market price of the bond. Here the investment value is 75 and the market price is 100, so the difference is 25, or 33% of 75. The premium-over-investment value is therefore 33.

HOW TO MAKE A PROFIT

IF THE STOCK GOES UP

In general, a CV's price will accompany the rise in price of the company's common stock, although it never rises as much. For example, let's say the

---

TIPS FOR INVESTING IN CVs

- Buy a CV only if you like the common stock.
- Avoid CVs of potential takeover companies; you may be forced to convert early.
- Buy only high-rated issues—BB or above as rated by Standard & Poor's or Ba by Moody's
- Know the call provisions; if a CV is called too early, you may not recover your premium.
- Select a CV whose common stock is expected to rise considerably in price.

underlying stock rises by 50%, from $32 to $48. To find the value of the CV bond, multiply the higher price by the conversion ratio: $48 × 25 = $1,200 (or 120, as bond prices are expressed). During the time in which this rise has taken place, the investor has received 10% interest on the bond and has participated in the appreciation of the common stock by seeing the value of the CV bond appreciate by 20%, from $100 to $120.

IF THE STOCK GOES DOWN

If the underlying stock falls in price, the CV may also fall in price, but less so. Let us assume that the price of ABC, instead of appreciating by 50% to $48, drops by 50% to $16 per share. Its conversion value is now only $400 ($16 × the CV ratio of 25). What happens to the price of the CV? The senior position of the bond as well as the 10% interest rate payable to bondholders serve as a brake on its decline in price. Somewhere between $100 and $40 the safety features inherent in a CV bond become operative, usually at the investment value, which in this case is 75. At 75 the bond's yield will rise to 13.33%.

$ HINT: When you want to make an investment but you fear that the company's common stock is too volatile and therefore risky, check to see if there are any convertible bonds or preferreds outstanding.

TO CONVERT OR NOT TO CONVERT

By and large, holders of CVs should stay with the security of the CV and not convert. Stock markets are uncertain, and prices of individual stocks have been known to fall 50% or even more. Therefore, the holder of a CV, which is senior to the common stock, should surrender or convert only under certain circumstances such as these:

- The company, in a restructuring, makes a tender offer for a large percentage of its outstanding common stock at a price well above the market price. The CV bondholder must convert to common stock in order to participate in this tender offer.
- In another type of restructuring, the company pays stockholders a special dividend equal to most of the price of the common stock. Here again, the CV

CONVERTIBLES

PROS
- ↑ When the stock market falls, CVs do not fall as much as the underlying stock.
- ↑ You can keep collecting regular income no matter what happens to the stock.

CONS
- ↓ You do not receive the full price gain when the stock goes up.
- ↓ You do not earn as much interest as you would had you bought the bond.
- ↓ When a takeover bid is made, the common stock usually soars in price.
- ↓ A proposed new takeover deal may eliminate CV holders' rights to exchange their bonds for stock.
- ↓ CVs are often issued by companies with poor ratings.

bondholder must convert in order to receive this special dividend. For example, in July 1988, USG Corp. paid for each common share outstanding $37 in cash, plus other securities, in a corporate restructuring.

- Corporations in cyclical businesses pay oversized year-end dividends. General Motors, for instance, did this for many years. To receive a special dividend, CV bondholders must convert prior to the ex-dividend date.

CV MUTUAL FUNDS

If you have limited capital or prefer to let someone else make the selections, there are mutual funds that use a substantial portion of their assets to buy CVs and, in some cases, to write options.

When considering CV mutual funds, keep these tips in mind:

- Usual minimum investment is $1,000.
- Shares can be purchased directly from the fund or from a stockbroker.
- Read the fund's prospectus before investing.
- Check the quality of the fund's underlying stocks.

- Convertibles offer a hedge against volatile changes in the stock market.
- Automatic reinvestment of distribution into additional fund shares is available.
- If you invest in a family of funds and your yield declines, you can switch to higher-yielding funds within the family.

HEDGING WITH CVs

For experienced investors, CVs offer excellent vehicles for hedging—buying one security and simultaneously selling short its related security. The hedge is set up so that if the market goes up, one can make more money on the purchase than one can lose on the sale, or vice versa if the market goes down. Such trading is best in volatile markets (of which there have been plenty in recent years).

Here's an example cited by expert Thomas C. Noddings: The CV debenture carries a 10% coupon and is convertible into 40 shares of common stock. The CV trades at 90; the common at 20. *Buy* 10 CVs at 90 at a cost of $9,000; sell short 150 common at 20—$3,000. Since the short sale requires no investment, the cost is $9,000 (not counting commissions).

- *If the price of the stock falls to 10,* the CV's estimated price will be 72, so there will be a loss of $1,800 ($9,000 − $7,200).

LEADING CONVERTIBLE BOND MUTUAL FUNDS

FUND	TOTAL RETURN, JANUARY 1 TO JUNE 30, 1993
American Capital Harbor Fund (1-800-421-5666)	7.99%
Putman Convertible Income Growth (1-800-354-4000)	9.32
AIM Convertible Securities (1-800-347-1919)	8.56
Calamos Convertible Income Fund (1-800-323-9943)	8.89
Value Line Convertible Fund (1-800-223-0818)	10.01
Phoenix Convertible Fund Series (1-800-243-1574)	5.04

But 150 shares of stock can be acquired for $1,500, for a profit of $1,500. Add $500 interest (10% for 6 months), and the net profit is $200.

- *If the price of the stock dips to 15,* the CV will sell at 80 for a $1,000 loss, but this will be offset by the $750 profit on the stock plus $500 interest, for a return of $250.
- *If the price of the stock holds at 20,* the CV will stay at 90. There will be no profit on either, but the $500 interest will represent an annualized rate of return of 11%.
- *If the stock rises to 25,* the CV will be worth 104, for a $1,400 profit, but there will be a $750 loss on the shorted stock. With the $500 interest, there'll still be a $1,150 profit.
- *And if the stock soars to 40,* the CV will trade at 160, for a whopping $7,000 gain, which will be offset by a $3,000 loss on the stock but enhanced by the $500 income, for a total of $4,500 on that $9,000 investment—all in 6 months!

Says Noddings: "Selling short stock against undervalued CVs can eliminate risk while offering unlimited gains if the stock advances."

Best bet with hedges of CVs: Try out the "if projections" on paper until you are sure that you understand what can happen. By and large, the actual transactions will follow these patterns. At worst, the losses will be small; at best, the profits will be welcome.

WRITING CALLS WITH CVs

Noddings also shows how to write calls with CVs. This is a conservative way to boost income and, when properly executed, involves minimal risks and fair-to-good gains. Since the CVs represent a call on the stock, they provide a viable base. Let's say that a $1,000 par value CV debenture can be swapped for 40 shares of common; the CV is at 90, the stock at 20; the calls, exercisable at 20, are due in 6 months and carry a premium of 2 ($200) each.

Buy 10 CVs for $9,000 and sell 3 calls. (Since the CVs represent 400 shares of stock, this is no problem.) The $600 premium will reduce the net investment to $8,400. *If the stock jumps to 40,* the CV will sell at 160, for a $7,000 gain. Add $500 interest to get $7,500 income. But there will be a $5,400 loss because the calls will have to be repurchased with a (tax-advantageous) deficit of $1,800 each. The net profit will thus be $2,100.

Warning: Writing calls on CVs is *not* for amateurs. To be worthwhile, this technique should (1) involve a substantial number of shares (at least 300), (2) be done with the aid of a knowledgeable broker who watches for sudden aberrations in price spreads, (3) be initiated with adequate cash or margin reserves that may be needed to buy back calls early, and (4) be undertaken only by individuals in a high enough tax bracket to benefit from the short-term losses.

FOR FURTHER INFORMATION

BOOKS

Thomas C. Noddings, *Superhedging* (Chicago: Probus Publishing Co., 1985).

NEWSLETTERS

Value Line Convertible Strategist
711 Third Avenue
New York, NY 10017
1-212-687-3965; 1-800-634-3583
48 times per year; $475

11

MUNICIPAL BONDS:
Last of the Tax Shelters

Municipals are tax-exempt debt obligations or IOUs issued by states, counties, cities, and other public agencies, such as school districts, sewer and water districts, airport, bridge and tunnel authorities, and highway authorities. Their great advantage is that the interest investors collect is exempt from federal income tax and, if the bonds are issued in the investor's state of residence, they are also exempt from state and local income taxes. For example, if you live in Minnesota, interest on "munis" (as they are called) issued by the state of Minnesota is exempt from federal and state income taxes. They are known as "double tax free" bonds. (Exceptions: Illinois, Iowa, Oklahoma, and Wisconsin impose some limitations on exemptions.) Munis issued by U.S. Territories—Puerto Rico, Guam, and the Virgin Islands—are tax-exempt in all states.

Because of their tax-exempt status, munis pay a lower interest rate than taxable corporate bonds. They are issued in units of $5,000 or, occasionally, $10,000. Most stockbrokers are reluctant to sell just one bond and many have $20,000+ minimums. Some discount brokers will accept small-sized orders. But to have an adequately diversified portfolio, you probably need $40,000 to $60,000. Certainly if you have only $20,000 you may want to invest through a mutual fund or unit investment trust, described at the end of this chapter.

The Clinton administration's pledge to boost tax rates on upper-income Americans is expected to give municipal bonds added appeal in 1994–1995. But before investing, you need to determine if these bonds make sense for your portfolio.

SHOULD YOU BUY MUNIS?

You don't have to be a millionaire to benefit from tax-exempt investments. On the other hand, municipal bonds make sense ONLY if the interest earned is more than the after-tax yield of a taxable investment. For most people, that means being in the 28% tax bracket or higher. Tax brackets are adjusted for inflation each year, but generally if your taxable income is about $25,000 for a single return or $40,000 for a joint return, you will be in the 28% bracket.

To really determine whether to buy a municipal or not, use this formula:

$$\text{taxable equivalent yield} = \frac{\text{yield from municipal}}{1 - \text{your federal tax bracket}}$$

For example, if a tax-exempt municipal bond has a 6% yield and you are in the 28% tax bracket, to match that yield you would need a taxable bond with a yield of at least 8.33%

$$1 - .28 = 0.72$$
$$6 - .72 = 8.33\%$$

As you can see, even though a taxable corporate bond might pay 7.5%, a muni paying only 6% is actually a better investment in this case. If you live in a high-tax state, such as New York, California, Minnesota, or Massachusetts, a municipal bond issued by your state would have even greater benefit.

Let's look at another example: If you're in the 31% tax bracket, a muni yielding 5.5% is the equivalent to a taxable bond yielding about 8%.

$$1 - .31 = .69$$
$$5.5\% - .69 = 7.97$$

Again, you would need a taxable bond yielding at least 8% to equal your tax-free muni with only a 5.5% yield.

☐CAUTION: There's no point, of course, in putting a tax-free municipal in an IRA or other tax-advantaged account.

Use this table for additional comparisons:

YOUR TAX BRACKET	28%	31%
Tax-exempt yield	Taxable equivalent yields	
4%	5.56%	5.80%
5	6.94	7.25
6	8.33	8.70
7	9.72	10.14

TYPES OF MUNICIPAL BONDS

If you decide to buy individual bonds, you'll find a number of choices:

➤ GENERAL OBLIGATION BONDS (GOS) Also known as public purpose bonds, these are sold to finance roads, schools, and government buildings. They are the most conservative of the municipals and are backed by the full taxing power of the issuer. The interest and principal are repaid to bondholders out of a government's "general" revenue, primarily its taxes. Therefore, they generally have the highest safety ratings but often the lowest yields.

➤ REVENUE BONDS These are issued to finance public works projects and their interest and principal are repaid ONLY from the revenues generated by the project that bonds were issued to build—an airport, highway, tunnel, toll bridge, or a sewage treatment plant, for example. Because of this limited source of income, they are generally regarded as less safe than GOs.

➤ TAXABLE MUNICIPALS For many years, all munis were tax-free, but that's no longer the case. Bonds issued to finance private business activities and ventures, such as shopping malls, sports stadiums, convention and trade shows, industrial parks and parking facilities, are exempt often from state and local taxes where issued, but subject to federal income taxes. Yet income from certain kinds of private activity bonds, such as those to build a hospital, is still fully exempt. These taxable municipals, or "private activity bonds" as they're also called, generally yield 2 to 3 percentage points more than fully tax-exempt municipals.

For investors in high tax brackets who have a sizeable amount of tax-sheltered income, interest from such bonds issued after August 7, 1986, may be subject to the alternative minimum tax (AMT). The AMT taxes so-called preference income above a certain level at a flat rate.

➤ ZERO COUPON MUNIS These bonds provide no interest income to the owner until they mature. Instead they are sold at a discount (below par) and you receive the full face value at maturity. Because they are sold far below face value, zero coupon munis are an inexpensive way for small investors to participate in the municipal bond market. "Stripped munis," as they are called, literally have their semiannual interest rate coupons stripped off. Both parts then are sold separately—the principal and the series of coupon interest payments. By dividing the bond into two pieces, maturities are created that otherwise would not exist. Prior to the existence of stripped munis, bondholders had to wait 20 to 40 years for a municipal bond to mature; zeros, on the other hand, mature in less than half that time. So when you buy a stripped muni, you are in essence buying a couponless bond with zero interest, hence the name "zero coupon."

These bonds have true tax advantages: If, for example, you buy a zero at $800, when it matures you'll receive the face value of $1,000, but there will be no federal income tax due on the $200 profit made during the holding period. Another advantage: bonds used for stripping are noncallable, so you know they can be held to maturity. (The call feature of bonds is explained beginning on page 116.)

Strips are sold by Salomon Brothers as M-Cats, by Goldman Sachs as Municipal Receipts, and by Morgan Stanley as M-Bears.

$HINT: Zero coupon bonds are an excellent way to pay for college or set money aside for retirement or other distant goals. Whoever owns the bonds does not have to pay federal income tax on them.

➤ ZERO COUPON CONVERTIBLE MUNIS Like other zeros, these sell at a deep discount to face value. They have a unique feature, however, and that is that at a certain time they convert into regular interest bonds.

For example, a 25-year zero coupon convertible muni bond pays out no interest during its first 10 years. Then in the tenth year, it converts into a regular municipal bond. At that point the investor starts to receive the stated interest rate in cash and continues to receive it for the remaining 15 years. At maturity, the bond returns its full face value of $1,000 to the investor. Both appreciation and interest income are free of federal income taxes.

◻ CAUTION: There are two major drawbacks: states may impose taxes on the imputed interest, and some zero coupon convertible munis can be called early.

➤ PREREFUNDED MUNIS Sometimes a bond issuer floats a second bond in order to pay off the first bond by the call date of the first bond. This is almost always done when interest rates have dropped and the issuer can now reduce its interest payments. The proceeds from the sale of the second bond are invested in Treasury securities that are selected to mature at the first call date of the first bond issued. These bonds are said to be pre-refunded. Because they are backed by Treasury securities, they are AAA-rated and regarded as very safe.

Example: New York State Urban Development 8⅞s, yield 7.3%, due to be called in 1996.

➤ INSURED MUNIS You can boost your safety by purchasing insured bonds. With these bonds, the insurance company agrees to pay the principal and interest to bondholders if the issuer defaults. The insurance policy lasts for the life of the bond.

STRIPPED MUNIS

PROS
↑ Can time your balloon payment
↑ No problem of where to reinvest income
↑ Noncallable
↑ Know exactly how much you will receive
↑ Shorter maturity dates than regular munis
CONS
↓ Interest is locked in; yields could rise
↓ Should be held to maturity
↓ Slim secondary market

Once a bond is insured, it is given an AAA rating by Standard & Poor's *even if the bond originally had a BBB rating.* So remember that if you are purchasing an AAA insured bond, it may really be a BBB bond with insurance.

Insured municipal bonds pay lower yields, usually 0.1 to 0.5 percentage points less than comparable uninsured bonds. If the insurer's rating drops, so do the ratings of all the issues that the company has insured.

$ HINT: Insurance does not protect you against market risks: If interest rates go up, the value of bonds still goes down.

To insure its bonds, the issuer pays an insurance premium ranging between 0.1% and 2% of total principal and interest. In return, the insurance company will pay the principal and interest to the bondholders should the issuer default. Generally, policies for new issues cannot be canceled, and the insurance remains active over the lifetime of the bond. With a bond fund or unit trust, the insurance is generally purchased for the entire portfolio. The oldest insurers are the American Municipal Bond Assurance Corp. (AMBAC) and the Municipal Bond Insurance Association (MBIA). Both are rated Aaa by Moody's and AAA by Standard & Poor's.

➤ VARIABLE-RATE OPTION MUNIS These are long-term municipals whose interest rates are adjusted, up or down, each year based on current market rates. You can usually cash in a variable-rate option muni on a daily, weekly, monthly, or yearly basis and get back what you paid for it. They are best if you know you might need your money within a year, or at least before the bond matures.

➤ SINGLE-STATE BONDS If you live in a high-tax state, look for munis issued by your own state and local governments. You can add as much as 1½ percentage points to your yield. Among the highest-taxed states are California, Connecticut, Massachusetts, Minnesota, and New York. Single-state municipal bond funds are listed in the table below.

Funds that specialize in single-state bonds must purchase bonds from a smaller pool than regular bond funds and consequently have less choice when it comes to bond grade, type, and maturity. This adds an element of risk to these bonds.

PICKING A MUNI BOND

These are the key points to keep in mind when building a portfolio of individual municipal bonds.

- Safety. Like corporate bonds, municipals are also rated for safety—or how likely they are to default—by Standard & Poor's and Moody's. The least risky are rated AAA or Aaa. And, of course, the higher the rating the less interest the bond issuer needs to pay to attract investors. The opposite is also true: the highest interest rates are paid on the riskiest bonds. (See page 112 for rating information.)

Before purchasing municipals, ask your stockbroker for a research report and bond ratings. Muni prices are rarely listed in the newspaper, so you must use an experienced, reliable broker. Stick with those rated BBB+ or above.

➤ MATURITY DATE   For bonds with the same rating, the shorter the maturity, the lower the yield and the greater the price stability. Unless you plan to buy municipals regularly, it is usually prudent to stick to those with maturities of less than 10 years. In many cases, these will be older bonds selling at a discount. Select maturities to match your financial goals.

- Type of bond. Start with general obligation bonds, which typically yield less than riskier municipals, or an insured bond.

Then consider revenue bonds backed by highly steady streams of income, such as utility bills. Suggested water revenue bonds and electric revenue bonds are given in the boxes on the following page. And keep in mind bonds of the Commonwealth of Puerto Rico. Their income is free from state, local, and federal taxes no matter where you live in the United States. To date, Puerto Rico has never defaulted on a bond issue.

- Unrated bonds. You may run across bonds that are not rated. An unrated bond is not necessarily high in risk. It is often unrated because the municipality is so small or has such modest debt its bonds have never been rated. If you personally know the community and if it is run well, you can add them to your portfolio. But plan to hold them to maturity as there probably is very little secondary market.
- Marketability. If you have to sell bonds before maturity, you want there to be an active secondary market. The most salable municipals are general obligation bonds of state governments and revenue bonds of large, well-known authorities. Smaller issues can be tough to sell.
- Call provision. Larger issues usually permit the bonds to be called, that is, redeemed before maturity. In fact, many municipals are issued with a 10-year call provision. If

LEADING SINGLE-STATE MUNICIPAL BOND FUNDS

STATE	MUTUAL FUND	YIELD (JULY 1993)	TOTAL RETURN (JAN–JUNE 1993)
Minnesota	Franklin Minnesota Insured (1-800-632-2180)	5.40%	6.54%
New York	Putnam New York (1-800-225-1581)	5.61	8.39
West Virginia	MFS Managed West Virginia (1-800-225-2606)	5.23	7.0
California	MFS Managed California (1-800-225-2606)	5.56	7.9
Oregon	Oregon Municipal Bond Fund (1-503-295-0919) (1-800-541-9732)	3.53	5.22

WATER REVENUE BONDS

ISSUER	S&P RATING	APPROXIMATE YIELDS
NY City Municipal Water	A−	5.75%
DuPage, IL Water Commission	A	5.25
Phoenix Water System	AA	4.60
Jackson, MS Water & Sewer	AAA*	5.15
Birmingham Water & Sewer (prerefunded)	AA	4.75

* MBIA insured.

your bond is called, you will have to reinvest that money, probably at lower rates. Try to buy bonds that cannot be called or have call protection. (See page 116.)

➤ SERIAL MATURITIES Unlike most corporate bonds, which usually have the same redemption date, municipals often mature serially: A portion of the debt comes due each year until the final redemption. Select maturities to fit future needs: college tuition, retirement, etc.

➤ BROKER'S REPUTATION If you get a hard sell on tax-exempts, especially by phone, be *very* cautious. Do business only with your regular broker, or one you trust.

You must shop around for the best price. In May 1992, the *Wall Street Journal* reported that an investor contacted eight securities firms regarding sale of a $10,000 face value Port Authority of New York and New Jersey bond. He was given prices ranging from $9,500 (Charles Schwab & Company) to $9,865 (Roose-velt & Cross). Several firms raised their bids when given competitive quotes. Moral: Don't take the first price offered. It's like selling jewelry or fine art—prices vary from dealer to dealer.

UNDERSTANDING THE RISKS INVOLVED

As with any bond, interest rate risk is a constant. If interest rates rise, the value of a municipal bond will fall. This presents a problem if you sell before the bond's maturity. It's not a problem, of course, if you hold until maturity because you will receive the bond's full face value.

In fact, interest rate risk is a greater problem than defaults for municipal bonds.

The second risk is that of default—if the issuer cannot make the interest and principal payments. To protect against default, purchase insured bonds.

ELECTRIC REVENUE BONDS

ISSUER	S&P RATING	APPROXIMATE YIELDS
South Carolina Public Service Authority	A+	5.80%
Intermountain Power Agency (UT)	AA−	5.85
Austin, TX, Combined Utility	A	5.00
New York State Power Authority	AA	4.75
Orlando Utilities Commission (FL)	AA	5.70
Muscaline Electric Revenue (IA)	AAA*	5.10

* Insured by AMBAC.

PUERTO RICO MUNICIPAL BONDS

ISSUER	S&P RATING	APPROXIMATE YIELDS
Puerto Rico Electric Power	A	5.40%
Puerto Rico Highway Authority	A	5.80
Puerto Rico Telephone Authority	A+	5.10
Commonwealth of Puerto Rico	A	5.00
Puerto Rico Public Building Authority	A	5.20

MUNICIPAL BOND MUTUAL FUNDS

For small investors, one of the best ways to buy municipals is through a mutual fund. Mutual funds provide diversification (by type, grade, coupon, and maturity), continuous professional management, the opportunity to add to your portfolio with relatively small dollar amounts, the ability to switch to other funds under the same sponsorship, and, most important, prompt reinvestment of interest to buy new shares and benefit from compounding.

Unless you have over $20,000 and can watch the market, a fund is the best way to invest in munis. The yields may be lower than you could obtain with individual bonds, but you won't be tempted to spend the income if you have the fund automatically reinvest it. Minimum investments are generally $1,000. (See Chapter 6 for details on selecting mutual funds.)

In a fund that is open-ended the portfolio contains bonds with varying maturities. The manager continually buys and sells bonds in order to improve returns, switching from short- to long-term maturities when yields are high and doing the opposite when yields decline. When interest rates shift quickly, some funds do extremely well; some do not. Keep in mind that your income from the fund will fluctuate, unlike that from an individual bond or a unit trust, where the yield is locked in.

▶ TYPES OF MUNICIPAL BOND MUTUAL FUNDS There are four types of mutual funds to consider:

- Nationally diversified tax-exempt funds. These hold bonds issued by states and municipalities through the country. Income is usually free from federal income taxes; some may be free from state and local taxes.

- Single state funds. These invest in bonds of a single state so investors who are residents of that state can have income that is free from federal and state taxes. Those that invest in municipal bonds are called "triple exempt" because income is free from local taxes.

With tax hikes very likely under the Clinton administration, residents of states with high taxes will find single state muni bonds and bond funds one way to cut the IRS bite. In Massachu-

INSURED MUNICIPAL BOND MUTUAL FUNDS

FUND	YIELD (JULY 1993)
Vanguard Muni Bond Insured Long Term (1-800-662-7447)	5.04%
Merrill Lynch Muni Insured Portfolio (1-609-282-2800)	5.42
American Capital Tax-exempt Insured (1-800-421-5666)	9.20
Dreyfus Insured Tax-exempt Bond Fund (1-800-645-6561)	5.81
Fidelity Insured Tax-free (1-800-544-8888)	4.95

10 TAX-EXEMPT BOND FUNDS	
FUND	YIELD (JULY 1993)
Calvert Tax-free Long Term (1-800-368-2748)	5.53%
Dreyfus Intermediate Tax-exempt (1-800-645-6561)	5.36
Fidelity Municipal Bond (1-800-544-8888)	4.80
Financial Tax-free Income (1-800-525-8085)	5.18
New York Muni Fund (1-800-225-6864)	4.85
T. Rowe Price Tax-free Intermediate (1-800-638-5660)	4.70
Scudder Managed Municipal (1-800-225-2470)	4.85
SteinRoe Intermediate Municipal (1-800-338-2550)	4.14
Value Line Tax-exempt Fund (1-800-223-0818)	5.13
Vanguard Long-Term Municipal (1-800-662-7447)	5.21

setts, for example, where the combined federal and state tax is almost 40%, it takes a taxable yield of 8.26% to equal a 5% tax-exempt yield from a state-issued municipal.

$ HINT: Before investing in a single state bond or bond mutual fund, check on the financial health of your particular state's economy. If you have any reservations, limit your holdings, perhaps to a 50-50 division between single state and multi-state funds.

■ Tax-free money market funds. These were discussed in Chapter 3. Income is free of federal taxes.

■ High yield funds. These invest in lower-rated tax-exempt bonds that are higher in risk and higher in yields. They are suitable only for investors who knowingly wish to assume a high risk for a high return.

MUNICIPAL BOND UNIT TRUSTS

These trusts have fixed portfolios of municipal bonds that remain in the trust until maturity, unless they are called. The trust aims to lock in the highest yield possible with good-quality issues at the time of the initial offering. Each trust has a limited number of shares for sale, but new trusts are continually being brought to the market. Sponsors also buy back existing units from investors who want to sell before the trust matures. The units are registered in the name

of the investor, and monthly, quarterly, or semiannual checks are mailed out to the holder. A handful of unit investment trusts have reinvestment privileges. Most provide income for a limited period—3, 5, 10, 20, or 30 years.

When the bonds mature, are sold (rarely), or are called, the principal is returned to the investor as a return of capital. If the sponsor feels a bond is endangering the trust's interest, it can be sold and proceeds paid out. Unit trusts, of course, are vulnerable to the risks of rising interest and early call on bonds in the portfolio.

Units can be sold in the secondary market, but doing so entails a commission. If interest rates have fallen, you could make a profit, but if they've gone up, you may not get back your original investment. Unit trust prices are based on the price of the securities in the portfolio and are determined either by the sponsor or by an independent evaluator. Nuveen, for instance, which has a number of trusts, sets the price on a daily basis. Although unit prices are not given in the newspaper, you can call the sponsor for up-to-date quotes.

There are two kinds of trusts: general and state. General trusts include bonds from various states and territories, while state trusts have bonds only from a single state, hence the name "single-state unit trusts." Income is generally free from state and local taxes in the issuing state as well as from federal taxes.

Unit trusts are usually sold in $1,000 units and have a one-time sales charge that typically ranges from 2% to 5% plus annual fees in the neighborhood of 0.15%. Both these costs are

---

MUTUAL FUND VS. UNIT TRUST

- A managed mutual fund is generally a better investment for people who expect to sell in less than 10 years. Check the 1-, 5-, and 10-year performance records of several before investing.
- Unit trusts are best for long-term holdings, especially when the initial yield is high enough that you want to lock it in.

A FREEBIE

The Franklin fund family has a free slide rule that lets you figure out your combined state and federal marginal income tax rate. The data are available for every state and for the 28%, 31% and 36% tax brackets. Call 1-800-342-5236.

---

factored into the yield. Mutual funds, by contrast, may be subject to a sales charge ("load") or not ("no load").

☐ CAUTION: Munis rated below A are regarded by many bond experts as risky. (The ratings are behind the true credit risk— they're a lagging indicator.) But because there is a shortage of municipals, many fund managers and others buy them anyway. Certain housing and health care bonds fall into this risk category. When buying a muni fund, trust, or individual bond, check the exact ratings.

YOUR TAXES AND MUNICIPALS

One of the unfortunate fallouts of the 1986 Tax Reform Act is that interest on some municipal bonds is now subject to taxation.

- Private activity bonds. Interest on these bonds, issued after August 7, 1986, to finance private business activities, such as shopping malls, is generally taxable at the federal level for individuals subject to the alternative minimum tax (AMT). The AMT affects investors in high tax brackets who also have a sizeable amount of tax-sheltered income. Interest on these private

activity bonds may be subject to the AMT. The AMT taxes so-called preference income above a certain level at a rate of 26% or 28%. Check with your accountant before investing in private activity bonds.

- An exception: bonds issued by private, nonprofit hospitals and universities, called 501(c) bonds, are not subject to taxation.
- Municipal bond income is indirectly taxable under certain circumstances for some retirees. Up to half of a retiree's Social Security benefits can be taxed if municipal bond interest income plus adjusted gross income plus half of Social Security payments is more than $32,000 for couples or $25,000 for singles. Again, check with your accountant.

FOR FURTHER INFORMATION

Muni Week
1 State Street Plaza
New York, NY 10004
1-212-943-8200
Weekly; $597 per year; $10 per copy

David L. Scott, *Municipal Bonds: The Basics and Beyond* (Chicago: Probus Publishing Co., 1992).

12

NONTRADITIONAL BONDS:
Maes, Junk, and Zeros

THE MAE FAMILY

High yields, safety, and convenience—that's what the various mortgage-backed securities in the Mae family offer. These securities, which are shares in pools of secured mortgages, are often called *pass-throughs* because the sponsor who packages the loans passes through the income (minus a modest fee) directly to investors. Payments are monthly, and yields tend to be 1.5+ points higher than those on comparable Treasury bonds, largely because the monthly payments include principal as well as interest. In this respect the Mae family does not behave like regular bonds, which provide a return of principal upon maturity. Instead you receive monthly checks that reflect both interest *and* principal. It is important to understand this distinction. Many investors mistakenly believe that these monthly checks are interest only. They are both interest *and* part payment of principal.

The pass-through technique allows individual investors to share the income derived from monthly mortgage payments and prepayments. They are similar to mutual funds in that investors do not own one particular mortgage but pieces of many mortgages.

Ginnie Maes are the only securities, other than U.S. Treasury issues, that carry the direct full faith and credit guarantee of the U.S. government. Others in the Mae group, described below, carry an indirect guarantee.

GINNIE MAEs

"Ginnie Mae" stands for the Government National Mortgage Association (GNMA), a wholly owned corporation of the U.S. government that functions as part of the Department of Housing and Urban Development. The objective of Ginnie Mae is to stimulate

housing by attracting capital and guaranteeing mortgages. A GNMA certificate represents a portion of a pool of 30-year FHA- or VA-insured mortgages. The GNMA provides payment of interest and principal on a monthly basis.

When a homebuyer takes out a mortgage, the house is pledged as collateral. The bank or savings and loan pools this loan with others of similar terms and rates, thus creating a package of mortgages worth $1 million or more. Ginnie Mae reviews the mortgages to make certain they meet certain standards and then assigns a pool number. Stockbrokers and others sell pieces of this pool, called certificates, to the public.

Homebuyers then make their payments (interest and principal) to the bank, which deducts a handling fee as well as a Ginnie Mae insurance fee. The rest of the money is "passed on" to the investors from the mortgage bankers.

Because GNMA certificates carry the guarantee of the U.S. government, they have made mortgage investments especially safe. And since certificates can be traded in the secondary market, they also offer liquidity.

The minimum investment for a GNMA is $25,000, with $5,000 increments thereafter. Monthly interest is considered ordinary income and is taxed, whereas monthly principal payments are considered a return of capital and are exempt from taxes. Monthly payments are *not* uniform—they are based on the remaining principal in the pool. As homeowners make their mortgage payments, the mortgage pool gets paid down, and although you receive the stated coupon interest, it is on a declining amount of debt. In other words, each month the proportion of interest received is slightly less and the proportion of principal slightly more. Over the long term, GNMAs are therefore self-liquidating. When the pool of mortgages is paid in full by homeowners, that's it. You don't receive a lump payment or a return of face value as you do with a zero or straight bond. *Note:* When interest rates fall, homeowners pay off their mortgages and refinance at lower rates. This means your Ginnie Mae is "called in" quickly.

You can purchase Ginnie Maes for less than $25,000 through mutual funds (discussion follows), or you can buy older Ginnie Maes in the secondary market. Older Ginnie Maes have been partially paid down and are usually bid down in value to compensate for the declining stream of income.

☐CAUTION: Ads for Ginnie Maes and their mutual funds often claim they are totally safe and 100% government guaranteed. This is not true. Ginnie Maes are *not* completely risk-free.

- The government does *not* guarantee the yield.
- The government does *not* protect investors against declines in either the value of the fund's shares or the yield.
- The government, however, *does* indeed protect investors against late mortgage payments as well as foreclosures. If homeowners default, you will still receive payments on time.

$HINT: If you're considering Ginnie Maes, bear in mind that the average 30-year Ginnie Mae is repaid in about 12 years.

GINNIE MAE MUTUAL FUNDS

For investors who don't want to invest $25,000, Ginnie Maes are available through unit investment trusts and mutual funds for as little as $1,000. In a unit trust, once the trust's portfolio is assembled, it's set. The portfolio manager cannot make adjustments, so if interest rates drop, you face exactly the same dilemma you do in owning a GNMA certificate. Unit investment trusts are explained in greater detail on page 141.

A Ginnie Mae mutual fund is not a pass-through security like the certificates. The fund itself receives interest and principal payments from the certificates in its portfolio. You then own shares in the fund, which in turn pays you dividends. The market value of your shares fluctuates daily, and the interest rate does, too.

☐CAUTION: The fund's yield is not fixed, nor is it guaranteed. If interest rates fall, as

GNMA ISSUES

RATE	BID	ASK	CHG.	YIELD
13.00				
13.50				
6.50	98-24	98-28	−22	6.70
7.00	101-10	101-12	−17	6.88
7.50	103-22	103-24	−13	7.07
8.00	105-27	105-29	−09	7.29
8.50	107-03	107-05	−05	7.62
9.00	108-03	108-05		7.98
9.50	109-10	109-12	+01	8.31
10.00	110-26	110-30	+01	8.59
10.50	112-10	112-14	+02	8.87
11.00	113-20	113-24	+02	9.18
11.50	115-00	115-04		9.47
12.00	116-00	116-04		9.80
12.50	117-00	117-08		10.12

SOURCE: Barron's, July 23, 1993.

mortgages are paid off, principal payments are received by the mutual fund. The manager then must reinvest this money, usually in lower yielding certificates. So, if interest rates are declining, your fund yield will fall also.

$HINT: Because of this volatility, John Rekenthaler, editor of *Morningstar Mutual Funds,* says investors should hold fund shares at least 3 to 5 years.

One advantage of a fund over a unit trust is that portfolio managers can shift the maturi-

---

HIDDEN RISKS IN GINNIE MAEs FOR RETIREES

- If you spend each monthly check, you are using up both interest and principal.
- You may want to reinvest your monthly payments. Finding a better rate with equal safety is often difficult.
- Monthly checks are not all the same, which is worrisome if you need a set dollar amount to live on.

ties of the certificates in the fund to reflect changing economic conditions. For example, if it appears that inflation is returning, they will move to shorter maturities to protect the return. And in certain types of funds, part of the portfolio can be shifted into other types of investments. The Kemper U.S. Government Securities Fund, for instance, also invests in intermediate Treasury bonds.

An advantage the funds have over straight Ginnie Mae certificates is that they will reinvest the principal payments received from homeowners in more fund shares if you so request.

Funds are best for investors who want high current income rather than capital appreciation. Plan on a long-term play, since these funds are volatile and subject to market risks.

☐CAUTION: In seeking high yields, many GNMA funds use almost speculative strategies, investing in put and call options, interest rate futures contracts, etc. Others invest in mortgage-related securities that do not carry the full government guarantee. Check the prospectus, and remember that a fund's shares may go down in value as well as its yield.

Ginnie Mae funds are offered by many of the large family funds, including Vanguard, Lexington, Franklin, Kemper, Fidelity, and T. Rowe Price. Their yields ranged from 5.6% to 7.5% as of 1993.

For every 1% change in interest rates, the value of the average Ginnie Mae fund will move in the opposite direction almost 6%. Therefore, Ginnie Maes are well suited to tax-deferred portfolios, where regular contributions over a period of time cushion the negative effect of price swings.

FREDDIE MACs

The Federal Home Loan Mortgage Corp., known as Freddie Mac, issues its own mortgage-backed securities, which are called participation certificates, or PCs. Freddie deals primarily in conventional single-family mortgages, which are backed by the Veterans Administration, but it also resells nongovernment-backed mortgages. If homeowners do not make their mortgage payments on time, you will receive your monthly payment on time, but you may have to wait several months to a year to receive your share

of the principal. A key difference between Freddie and Ginnie is that Ginnie Maes are backed by the U.S. government; Freddies are guaranteed by private mortgage insurance. Even though they're not quite as secure as GNMAs, they are considered very safe. Because of the discrepancy in safety, Freddie often pays slightly higher yields.

Freddie Mac PCs are sold for $25,000. Since the market is dominated by institutional investors, there are fewer mutual funds: Vanguard and Federated Investors are two. The U.S. AA Income Fund divides its assets between Ginnie and Freddie.

FANNIE MAEs

The Federal National Mortgage Association (FNMA, or "Fannie Mae") is a private shareholder-owned corporation that buys conventional mortgages, pools them in $1 million lots, and sells them in $25,000 units. Although not backed by the full faith and credit of the U.S. government, Fannies are AAA-rated by both

---

ESTIMATING A FANNIE MAE'S YIELD TO MATURITY

A Fannie Mae with: 10% coupon
price of 85 (85% of par)
11.76% current yield
25 years to maturity

1 Divide the amount of the discount by the number of years to maturity.

$$\frac{100 - 85 = 15}{25} = 0.60$$

2 Divide the result by 2 to factor in discounting.

$$0.60 \div 2 = 0.30$$

3 Add this number to the current yield.

$$0.30 + 11.76 = 12.06$$

4 This is your approximate current yield: 12.06%.

SOURCE: Fact magazine, February 1985.

Standard & Poor's and Moody's. Fannie Mae shares also trade on the NYSE.

Both Freddie Mac and Fannie Mae are corporations chartered by Congress and are *not* officially part of the federal government. Therefore, they do not carry the unconditional guarantee of Ginnie Mae. One advantage of this discrepancy in safety is a slightly higher yield. Another is that the mortgage pools are larger than the Ginnie Mae pools. The more mortgages, the more accurately you can predict how fast the principal will be returned.

After their initial offering, both Freddie and Fannie PCs trade in the secondary market.

CMOs

Collateralized mortgage obligations (CMOs) were introduced in 1983 by the Federal Home Loan Mortgage Corp. Their advantage is a more predictable payout of interest and principal than with Ginnie Maes. Instead of buying mortgage securities directly, you buy a AAA-rated bond. These bonds are sold against mortgage collateral comprised of GNMA- and FNMA-guaranteed mortgages. Each bond is divided into four classes, or tranches, having different dates of maturity ranging from 3 to 20 years. Each CMO has a fixed coupon and pays interest like a traditional bond—monthly or quarterly—*but,* and here's the difference, principal payments are initially passed through only to investors in the shortest maturity class, class A. Once that group has been paid in full, principal payments go to the next class. In the fourth and final class, investors get all interest and all principal in one lump sum.

These certificates generally have slightly lower yields than the regular pass-throughs, because the size and length of payments can be more accurately determined and you have some protection against prepayments. CMOs are available from larger brokerage firms in $5,000 units.

☐ CAUTION: Although CMOs improve on traditional mortgage securities by smoothing the rate of early principal payments, they are less liquid, more expensive to trade, and harder to track. They also entail record-keeping and reinvestment problems that most individuals want to avoid.

SALLIE MAEs

Created in Congress in 1972 to provide a nationwide secondary market for government guaranteed student loans, Sallie Mae (the Student Loan Marketing Association) is to students what Ginnie Mae is to homeowners. It issues bonds, rather than certificates, based on a pool of loans. Each bond is backed by Sallie Mae, and since its assets are made up of loans that have a government guarantee, these bonds are regarded as almost as safe as Treasuries. However, and this is key, this federal backing is only implied, not explicit. They yield about ¼% more than equivalent Treasury bonds.

Student Loan Marketing is a publicly owned company chartered by the government. Its stock trades on the New York Stock Exchange. Originally issued at $20 per share, it split a 2.5 for 1 in 1988; as of July 1993 it was selling at $44/share. It also issues floating-rate notes and convertible bonds. The need for student loans is expected to continue into the 1990s.

GOVERNMENT AGENCY BONDS

Despite lowered interest rates, there are still some bonds that are almost as safe as U.S. Treasuries and have respectable yields—government agency bonds. They are either affiliated with or owned by the government and so are mostly insured against default by some type of federal guarantee. No agency has defaulted on its debt. The distinguishing feature of government agency bonds is whether they are guaranteed by the government. Here's a guide to who's who in agency bonds:

■ *Fully guaranteed agencies.* Their bonds are guaranteed against default by the U.S. government:

1 Federal Housing Administration (FHA). Insures mortgages made by private lending firms to individual homebuyers, thus lowering the costs.

2 Government National Mortgage Association (GNMA). Ginnie Mae improves liquidity of the mortgage trading market by guaranteeing securities backed by pools of federally insured mortgages, for example, by the FHA.

3 Tennessee Valley Authority (TVA). U.S. government–owned utility providing electricity to the Tennessee River valley and area. Created in 1933 to promote regional growth.

- *Unguaranteed agencies.* These do not carry an unconditional guarantee. They are stockholder owned:

1 Federal Home Loan Mortgage Corporation (FHLMC or Freddie Mac). Increases liquidity of mortgage market by buying mortgages from lending institutions and selling them to individual investors.

2 Federal National Mortgage Association (FNMA or Fannie Mae). Performs same function as Freddie Mac.

3 Student Loan Marketing Association (SLMA or Sallie Mae). Improves liquidity of student loan market by providing financing to state student loan agencies and buying loans made by private sources.

- *Partially guaranteed agencies.* The United States and most other industrialized nations are obligated to contribute funds to these agencies:

1 Asian Development Bank. Makes loans to developing countries in Asia.

2 Inter-American Development Bank. Makes loans to developing nations in Latin America.

3 World Bank. Makes loans to developing countries throughout the world.

JUNK BONDS

If you're looking for very high yields, a solution is the so-called high-yield or junk bond, which yields substantially more than higher-quality, safer bonds.

Junk bonds are those rated BB or lower by Standard & Poor's and Ba or lower by Moody's. Some have no ratings at all. The world of junk bonds comprises new or old companies with uncertain earnings coverage of their fixed obligations (bond interest payments) along with blue chip companies that have been forced into heavy debt in order to fend off a takeover or to finance an acquisition or a buy-back of their own stock. For example, Kroger Co., in an effort to avoid a takeover attempt, paid its shareholders a special

---

A TWO-TIER SYSTEM

In 1993, the junk bond market shifted to a two-tier system and a recognition that not all junk is equal junk. This applies to mutual funds as well, as portfolio managers try to lure back investors by upgrading their holdings. Examples of junk bonds:

HIGH RISK

Loehmanns	12.45%
American Standard	10.12
Ornda Health	11.30
Stone Container	11.60

LOWER RISK

Kroger	9.12%
Embassy Suites*	8.56
Safeway Stores	8.90
Viacom Int'l.	7.94

* Guaranteed by Promus Corp.

---

distribution of $40 per share and financed it by raising its debt level to $4.6 billion.

When these situations occur in a blue chip company, a new set of circumstances comes into being:

- Low-earning or unprofitable assets are sold off.
- Costs are cut, reflecting corporate efforts to become "lean and mean."

The credit rating gradually improves as these changes are implemented. Thus a good junk bond is always one in which the coverage of fixed charges increases with time.

However, default is not out of the question, which is why, unless you have sufficient money with which to speculate, you should invest in junk bonds only through a mutual fund, where the element of risk is diversified.

JUNK BOND MUTUAL FUNDS

High-yield junk bond mutual funds offer professional management plus portfolio supervision. As with other mutual funds, track records vary, so care must be exercised. The publicity attached to the Ivan Boesky insider

JUNK BONDS TO CONSIDER IN 1994

COMPANY	S&P RATING	PRICE (SPRING 1993)
Coastal Corp. 11¾%; 2006	BB+	$116
Occidental Petrol. 11¾%; 2011	BBB	120
Safeway Stores 10%; 2001	B+	107
Orynx Energy 10⅜%; 2018	BBB−	110
MGM Grand Hotels 11¾; 1999	B+	110

trading scandals sent shock waves through the junk bond markets, but junk bonds have fared well despite the adverse publicity provoked by these and other notorious cases (see table above).

The sponsors of junk bond funds, of course, are quite apt to play up the diversification point and de-emphasize the risks involved. They make much of the fact that their portfolios are diversified and continually monitored so that issues in trouble can be jettisoned. This is, of course, absolutely true *if* the portfolio manager is astute. But there's another risk involved—the risk of changing interest rates. Like any fixed-income security, junk bond funds are vulnerable to

broad changes in interest rates, and as those rates rise, the value of the fund falls.

Some of the top-yielding junk bond funds are listed in the table. If one bond in a fund defaults, it means a decrease in the overall fund yield, certainly less of an impact than if you owned the bond directly. However, if several bonds default, the fund share price will suffer.

MUNICIPAL JUNK BONDS

High-yield municipal bond funds are another matter altogether, since tax revisions have made some municipals taxable. Check each fund's prospectus for its policy on taxable munis. Some of the best performers among the high-yield municipal funds are listed in the table below.

Junk bond munis are regarded as riskier than corporates. Corporates are frequently issued by new companies without a past history of earnings. Theoretically, these companies are on their way up. Munis that are low rated are more often than not the result of a fundamentally risky situation that is unlikely to improve.

Fund managers try to cut risks primarily by diversifying their portfolios according to both bond type and bond rating. A number of them limit their holdings of any one issue to 5% of the fund's total assets. Others offset risk by adding a mixture of investment-grade bonds. More frequent review of the portfolio—monthly or quarterly—is another risk-cutting technique. In selecting a junk bond fund, if you're concerned with risk, call the fund and inquire about the portfolio mix and management's position. Don't shy away solely because there are nonrated

HIGH-YIELDING JUNK BOND MUTUAL FUNDS

FUND	YIELD (JULY 1993)
Oppenheimer High Yield (1-800-525-7048)	10.46%
T. Rowe Price High Yield (1-800-638-5660)	8.82
American Capital High Yield (1-800-421-5666)	6.89
Prudential-Bache High Yield Corp. Fund (1-800-648-7637)	9.34
Fidelity Spartan High Income (1-800-544-8888)	7.29

HIGH-YIELDING MUNICIPAL BOND FUNDS

FUND	YIELD (JULY 1993)
Franklin High Yield Tax-free Income (1-800-342-5236)	6.75%
Fidelity Aggressive Tax-free Portfolio (1-800-544-8888)	5.84
SteinRoe High Yield Muni (1-800-338-2550)	5.35
T. Rowe Price Tax-free High Yield (1-800-638-5660)	6.07

issues: Some smaller municipalities have local appeal although they do not request a rating from Standard & Poor's or Moody's.

If you own shares in a high-yield bond fund, find out:

1   *Is the fund cutting its dividend?* This is not a bad sign, but instead indicates that the manager is raising cash and diversifying into higher-quality issues.
2   *What's the total return?* Don't gauge everything by yield. Get the fund's total return (income plus appreciation) and compare it to the group average.
3   *What's in the portfolio?* A fund that owns recession-resistant and noncyclical bonds is less at risk because these bonds are likely to meet their payments. (Noncyclical industries include health care, food, drug, and utilities.)

JUNK BOND UNIT INVESTMENT TRUSTS

Unit investment trusts are closed-end investment companies. Because they have fixed portfolios, their yields are more predictable than those of a mutual fund. However, they have far less flexibility in terms of adjusting the portfolio and getting rid of poor bonds. Since they are not actively managed, *investors are at risk* should there be a default. "The unit investment trust is fine for quality bonds but should be avoided for junk issues," warns Peter Hegel, bond expert at Van Kampen Merritt.

ADVICE FOR 1994

Junk bonds can be a mine field for the unsophisticated investor. Yet it's hard to say no to a 9% to 10% yield. Here are 9 ways to protect yourself if you decide to take the risk.

- Put no more than 10% of your portfolio in junk bonds.
- If you want to buy individual bonds, use a broker who knows the area well.
- Watch the market closely and be prepared to sell quickly and swallow losses.
- If you buy individual bonds, diversify among types: fallen angels (companies facing difficulties), emerging growth (companies that have yet to achieve quality ratings), and bonds of companies emerging from a leveraged buyout or takeover.
- Buy only publicly listed bonds—they are quoted daily and are much easier to buy and sell.
- Avoid bond issues under $75 million; they tend to be illiquid.
- Watch the price of the common stock that underlies your bonds. If it suddenly drops in price, it often forecasts trouble for the company's bond.
- Use a mutual fund for diversification unless you can afford to buy 10 to 15 bonds.
- If you buy a mutual fund, select it based upon total return, not just yield. A solid fund should generate capital gains along with income. Also, pick a well-diversified fund with no more than 2% to 3% of its assets in any one company's bonds. This broad base helps the fund to weather any adverse situations.

ZERO COUPON BONDS

Zero coupon bonds ("zeros") are an excellent choice if you know you will be needing a lump sum of money at a certain date in the future. These bonds, offered by corporations, municipalities and the U.S. government, are sold at a deep discount from face value ($1,000), and pay no interest. Worthwhile? Yes, as long as you understand the facts. These bonds are "stripped" of their interest coupons and, instead of being paid out, this interest is added to the principal every 6 months. So when zeros mature, you get this interest back in a balloon payment. In this respect they are much like EE savings bonds. In other words, they are fully redeemed at par or face value. The difference between the fractional price paid initially and the value at maturity is the return on your investment, that is, the yield to maturity. For example, a zero coupon Treasury selling for $121 will be worth $1,000 at maturity in 2004. That is a yield to maturity of 11.25%.

➤ TAXATION The annual appreciation (or undistributed interest) is subject to tax. *You must pay taxes* annually all along the way, just as if you had actually received the interest payments. Zeros tend to be volatile in price because of this compounding effect; in fact, since there are no interest payments to cushion market swings, zeros can fall dramatically in price when interest rates rise. Therefore, if you buy zeros, plan to hold them to maturity.

➤ WAYS TO USE ZEROS Zeros are tailor-made for retirement accounts, such as IRAs and Keoghs, so you can avoid paying taxes every year on interest you don't actually receive. For example, a Claremont Assoc. zero due 2000 sold at 52 ($520 per bond) with a yield of 8.9%. In December 2000, bondholders will receive $1,000 per bond.

Zeros are also ideal for saving for a specific goal, such as college tuition payments or a vacation home. If you use zeros to finance a child's college education, have your broker select ones that come due in the years your child will be in school. Better yet, put them in your child's name; when they mature, they'll be taxed at the child's lower rate after age 14.

➤ AVOIDING THE NEGATIVES Locking in your yield can turn out to be a disadvantage if interest rates rise over the life of your zero so that other investments are offering higher yields. To tackle the dual problem of rising interest rates and increasing inflation:

- Select zeros with medium-term maturities—3 to 7 years, possibly 10—and avoid being committed to an interest rate over the long term.
- Purchase zeros continually—say every year—as part of your IRA, to take advantage of changing rates.
- Purchase zeros with varying maturities to cover yourself in case interest rates decline.

$ HINT: Zero coupon Treasuries are backed by the full faith and credit of the U.S. government and are one of the safest and simplest ways to invest for your retirement. You lock in a fixed rate of return, thus eliminating unpredictability.

TYPES OF ZEROS

➤ GOVERNMENT ZEROS In 1982 Merrill Lynch devised the idea of Treasury zeros by purchasing long-term government bonds, placing them in an irrevocable trust, and issuing receipts against the coupon payments. This created a series of zero coupon Treasuries, one for every coupon date. In other words, Merrill "stripped" the interest coupons from the principal of the Treasury bond and sold each portion separately. Merrill called these TIGRs (Treasury Investment Growth Receipts). Then along came Salomon Brothers with their version—CATS (Certificates of Accrual on Treasury Securities). All are certificates held in irrevocable trust in a custodial bank.

➤ CORPORATE ZEROS These are not generally suggested for individual investors because of their potential credit risk: If the issuer defaults after you've owned the bond for some time, you've more to lose than with a straight bond since you've received no interest along the way.

➤ DINTS Deferred Interest Securities, also known as DINTS, are unique corporate zero coupon bonds that were issued by Exxon Shipping Company and General Motors Acceptance Corporation before the IRS ruled in 1983 that corporate zero interest was taxable. Their yields range between 8% and 9% with maturities in 2012 and 2015.

➤ TREASURY STRIPS In 1985 the government entered the act, introducing its own coupon-stripping program called STRIPS (Separate Trading of Registered Interest and Principal Securities). Because they are issued directly by the Treasury, they are safer than all other types of zeros. Yields are slightly less than those of TIGRs, LYONs, and CATS, because of the greater degree of safety. Treasury STRIPS must be purchased from a stockbroker.

Example: A 20-year bond with a face value of $20,000 and a 10% interest rate could be stripped into 41 zero coupon instruments: the 40 semiannual interest coupons plus the principal. The body upon maturity is worth the $20,000 face value. The other coupon zeros would be worth $1,000 each, or half the annual interest of $2,000 (10% of $20,000) on the payment date.

☐ CAUTION: Brokers and others may fail to emphasize that the price volatility of long-term Treasury zeros is above average. In fact, zero coupon Treasuries run a greater interest rate risk than straight Treasury coupon bonds of the same maturity.

➤ MUNICIPAL ZEROS Issued by state and local governments, these are exempt from federal taxes and also from state taxes in the state where issued. They are suggested for investors in high tax brackets. An A-rated muni zero

THE POWER OF COMPOUNDING:
How Much $1,000 in Zeros Will Grow, before Taxes, at Various Compounding Rates

MATURITY	SEMIANNUAL COMPOUNDING RATE				
	6%	7%	8%	9%	10%
5 Years	$1,343	$1,410	$1,480	$1,553	$1,629
10 Years	1,806	1,990	2,191	2,412	2,653
15 Years	2,427	2,807	3,243	3,745	4,322
20 Years	3,262	3,959	4,801	5,816	7,040
30 Years	5,892	7,878	10,520	14,027	18,679

SOURCE: Merrill Lynch.

issued by New York City, due 2008, with a yield of 6%, recently sold for $400.00. That means that in the year 2008 you would receive $1,000 for each $400 invested.

☐ CAUTION: Zeros issued with call features should be shunned.

➤ MORTGAGE-BACKED ZEROS These are backed by securities issued by Ginnie Mae, Fannie Mae, and Freddie Mac (see pages 144–146). The securities are secured by AAA-rated mortgages. You'll see some of them referred to as ABCs (agency-backed compounders).

☐ CAUTION: You may not get to hold your mortgage-backed security until maturity if mortgages are paid off early.

➤ ZERO COUPON CONVERTIBLES This hybrid vehicle allows you to convert the bond into stock of the issuing company. Merrill Lynch, the leading marketer of zero CVs, calls them LYONs (Liquid Yield Option Notes). Conversion premiums on LYONs are generally lower than on traditional coupon issues; therefore, they offer potential appreciation if the underlying stock moves up in price. LYONs are sold at a substantial discount from par. They give the holder the right, after a certain date, to sell the issue back to the issuer at the original issue price plus accrued interest. This so-called "put" feature can reduce some of the market risk that accompanies convertibles. (See Chapter 10 on convertibles.) For example, a Merrill Lynch LYON sold for $280 for a yield of 8.28%. It converts into 5.31 shares of common at $42.61.

➤ ZERO COUPON CERTIFICATES OF DEPOSIT These are really CDs but sell at discount and do not pay current interest. They are sold by banks and stockbrokers.

💲 HINT: Buy zeros that are the last callable issues in a particular series to partially protect yourself against call provisions.

➤ COLLEGE ZEROS A number of states issue tax-exempt zero coupon bonds as a way to help parents pay for their children's college education. They often have good yields and their interest is exempt from state taxes for the state's resi-

---

ZERO COUPON TREASURY BONDS

PROS
↑ Lock in fixed yield
↑ Maturity dates can be tailored to meet future needs
↑ Call protection available
↑ Predictable cash payment
↑ Guaranteed by U.S. government
↑ Tax-deferred in retirement accounts
↑ No reinvestment decisions
↑ Less expensive than most bonds

CONS
↓ If interest rates rise, you're locked in at a lower yield
↓ Inflation erodes purchasing power of the bond's face value
↓ Commissions and/or sales markups not always made clear
↓ Many zeros have call provisions permitting issuer to redeem them prior to maturity

dents. The first state to sell these bonds was Illinois—it sold a zero coupon general obligation bond. Some states sell these bonds on an annual or semiannual basis. Among those issuing bonds designed for college savings are: Arkansas, California, Connecticut, Delaware, Hawaii, Illinois, Indiana, Iowa, Kansas, Maryland, Missouri, New Hampshire, North Carolina, North Dakota, Tennessee, Texas, Vermont, Virginia, Washington, and Wisconsin. Other states expected to offer them soon (and may have by the time this book is published): Colorado, Louisiana, and Ohio.

The bonds vary in maturities and interest rates, but are united by the fact they are low in risk. Most are general obligation bonds, which are high in safety because they are backed by the taxing power of the state itself. Most are also noncallable, so if interest rates fall the state cannot call in your bond.

Although you can use the money you earn with these bonds for any purpose, the states often give added incentives if you use the proceeds to pay for college expenses at one of the state's own schools. Several states, for example, pay an added yield if you use the money to pay for an education in Illinois. Others do not count the income in their formulas for determining if you or your child is eligible for state financial aid.

These special education bonds, like other municipals, are sold through brokers, not by the states directly. Many states advertise its bonds when they are about to be issued. Some, such as Iowa, give announcements to public school students to take home to their parents. You must move quickly, however. These bonds tend to sell out quickly—often within a week or so.

These bonds are sometimes available in the secondary market. Tell your broker if you're interested; it may take him some time to locate the maturity you want.

ZERO COUPON FICO STRIPS

These zero coupon obligations derived from bonds issued by the federally sponsored agency FICO, the Financing Corp., first appeared on the scene in May 1988. They were the first zeros created from the bonds of a federally sponsored agency.

FICO was created by Congress to raise money for the ailing Federal Savings & Loan Insurance Corp. (FSLIC). FICO was authorized to raise about $11 billion over a 3-year period. The lead underwriter, Salomon Brothers, purchased $750 million of 10% bonds maturing in 30 years. It then stripped all 60 interest coupons from the bonds, creating 61 separate entities. Investors can purchase either the coupon strip or the principal strip.

The principal of these bonds is secured by U.S. Treasury securities that match the maturities on FICO bonds. Interest on the bonds is paid from assessments made on the Savings & Loan industry.

FICO zeros have higher yields than Treasury bonds. The longest-maturing FICOs pay the highest returns.

Although Standard & Poor does not assign credit ratings to FICOs, it has stated that it believes these bonds are "very high quality, the equivalent of AAA issues, based on a commitment of Congress to both FICO and FSLIC."

FICO strips trade over the counter and can be purchased from a stockbroker. Like other bonds, when interest rates rise, their value drops, and vice versa. The minimum face value of a FICO coupon strip is $1,000; of a principal strip, $20,000.

HOW TO BUY ZEROS AND MAES

A recent survey revealed the fact that brokers' fees for trading Ginnie Maes and zeros can vary by as much as 7%. And sometimes discount brokers are more expensive than full-service brokers, particularly for over-the-counter bonds, and less so for corporate and U.S. Treasury issues. (The vast majority of zero coupons trade over the counter.) Most brokers charge a commission ranging from $5 to $10 per bond. Stick to this range, which is fair, considering that even at $10 per bond the commission is only 1% of the bond's price.

☐ CAUTION: Ginnie Maes, zeros and other government agency bonds are often sold with unspecified commissions, so use a broker you trust and/or shop around. Ask them to spell out what your cash is—Get it in writing.

ZERO COUPON BOND MUTUAL FUNDS

Zeros, like straight bonds, rise in price when interest rates fall and fall when rates rise. And since they are even more sensitive to interest rates, they should be held until maturity. If this is not your plan, use a mutual fund. You'll avoid both being forced to sell early and paying a broker's commission.

Benham Target Maturities Trust (1-800-4 SAFETY)

Scudder U.S. Government Zero Coupon Target Portfolio (1-800-225-2470)

$HINT: To make certain you're getting a fair price when buying or selling bonds:
1 Find the price of the bond in the newspaper.
2 Call several brokers. Get the bid and asked price and what fees this includes. Find out if there are also commissions involved. If the bond is not listed in the paper, you'll have to call several more brokers to ascertain the true price range.
3 Try to negotiate with a full-service broker—if there's a discrepancy in the prices you're quoted.

FOR FURTHER INFORMATION

THE MAE FAMILY

Investor Relations Department
Federal Home Loan Mortgage Corp.
8200 Jones Branch Drive
McLean, VA 22102
1-800-424-5401

Investor Relations
Student Loan Marketing Association
1025 Thomas Jefferson Street NW
Washington, DC 20007
1-202-333-8000

CMOs

Pension Investment Memorandum: CMOs (free)
Research Division
Gabriele, Hueglin & Cashman
44 Wall Street
New York, NY 10005
1-212-607-4100; 1-800-422-7435

WHEN THE BULLS ARE RUNNING

At the heart of every portfolio are, of course, stocks. Whether you have only dreamed about owning a stock or whether you and your money manager are trading hundreds of shares every morning and afternoon, we suggest you read this entire section. The basic information is essential to the beginner and the lists of suggested stocks and the tips on trading options, getting in on new issues, and ways to make money with rights and warrants can help even the most wizened investor.

In Part Three you will learn about:
- Common and preferred stocks
- How to pick stocks that go up in price
- When to buy and when to sell
- Over-the-counter stocks
- Electric utilities and water company stocks
- High-dividend stocks
- Low-debt companies
- Options
- Stock rights and warrants
- New issues

13 | STOCKS: Common and Preferred

WHY OWN STOCKS?

The two basic tools of investing are stocks and bonds, or equity and debt, to use a little Wall Streetese. Bonds have been discussed in Part Two. The first part of this chapter is devoted to common stocks; then we describe preferred stocks. There are several truly compelling reasons for investing in stocks, and one or two reasons why you shouldn't—at least at certain times, in certain stocks. Sorting out the who, what, where, when, and how of making money in stocks hinges on two simple concepts that are frequently ignored in the excessively technical discussions of financial wizards and pundits.

- *Over the long run, stocks outperform bonds*—although sometimes it may indeed be a very long run. Both trade in the marketplace, which historically rewards risk rather than caution. There are, of course, periods when you're better off in T-bills or corporate bonds, but the fact that stocks are better profit-makers remains a truism of investing.
- *Stocks tend to keep pace with inflation.* With stocks, at least you have a fighting chance of staying even. Not so with bonds: Once you buy a bond, the interest rate is locked in. If, for example, oil prices go up, it doesn't matter—your bond will pay exactly the same whether crude is at $18 or $35 a barrel. (Bonds do compensate for this factor by moving up or down in price, however.) If you own shares in Exxon or Occidental Petroleum, however, you'll participate in the increase in oil prices through higher dividends *and* a rising price for your shares. Stocks, in fact, respond directly to inflation: If the buying power of your dollar is reduced to 50¢ by rampant inflation, you and everyone else

buying Exxon will have to pay more for the company's shares. At the same time, inflation will eat away at interest earned on fixed-income securities.

> ### SUCCESS WITH STOCKS
>
> Over the past 20 years, stocks, as measured by the S&P 500 Stock Index, provided an annualized return of 11.9% compared to 9% on 10-year Treasury bonds and 7.7% for 90-day Treasury bills. Inflation averaged 6.3% during this period.

TYPES OF STOCKS

There is no such thing as a stock that's always an excellent holding. It's a mistake to expect all things from any stock. A great number of investors are unaware of the fact that stocks are *not* all designed to do the same thing. In fact there are two distinct types of stocks: those that generate income and those that appreciate in price. Income-oriented stock, such as utility stocks, real estate investment trusts (REITs), and closed-end funds that trade on the exchanges, should be held primarily for income; you should not also expect appreciation from these issues, or at least not very much.

Stocks selected for appreciation are an entirely different matter. Within this growth category you must narrow your selection even further: to low-risk growth stocks or speculative stocks. Throughout this book you will find various lists of stocks suggested for growth, income, or total return.

SELECTED LOW-RISK STOCKS
These stocks were ranked #1 (highest) for safety by *Value Line* in the spring of 1993. Utility stocks are not included.

Abbott Labs	Lilly (Eli)
American Home	Long's Drug Stores
Products	McDonald's Corp.
AT&T	Minnesota Mining
Amoco Corp.	Mobil Corp.
Bristol-Myers Squibb	New Plan Realty Trust
CBS, Inc.	Pfizer Inc.
Chevron Corp.	Procter & Gamble
Clorox Co.	Royal Bank of Canada
Coca-Cola	Royal Dutch Petroleum
Deluxe Corp.	Sara Lee Corp.
1838 Bond-Debenture	Shell Canada
Emerson Electric	Tambrands, Inc.
Exxon Corp.	Texaco, Inc.
Foote, Cone & Belding	Toyota Motor (ADR)
Gannett Co.	Unilever
General Electric	Union Pacific
General Mills	Washington Post
Heinz (H.J.)	Washington REIT
Hershey Foods	Weiss Markets
Johnson & Johnson	Winn-Dixie Stores
Kellogg	

SOURCE: Standard & Poor's, May 1993.

- *Blue chip stocks* represent ownership in a major company that has a history of profitability and continual or increasing dividends with sufficient financial strength to withstand economic or industrial downturns. *Examples:* General Electric, Exxon, Du Pont, Procter & Gamble.
- *Growth stocks* represent ownership in a company that has had relatively rapid growth in the past (when compared with the economy as a whole) and is expected to continue in this vein. These companies tend to reinvest a large part of their earnings in order to finance their expansion and growth. Consequently, dividends are small in comparison with earnings. *Examples:* Cascade Corp., Tonka Corp., Brown & Co., Reader's Digest, and UST, Inc.
- *Cyclical stocks* are common stocks of companies whose earnings move with the economy or business cycles. They frequently have lower earnings when the country is in a slump and higher earnings when the economy is in a recovery phase. *Examples* of cyclical industries: aluminum, steel, automobiles, machinery, housing, paper, airlines, and travel and leisure.
- *Income stocks* have continually stable earnings and high dividend yields in comparison with other stocks. Income stocks generally retain only a small portion of earnings for expansion and growth, which they are able to do because there is a relatively stable market for their products. *Examples:* public utility companies, international oil companies, closed-end bond funds, and REITs.

Now you're ready to start selecting stocks for your own personal portfolio, keeping the following key consideration in mind: *Every investment involves some degree of risk.* Stocks vary in their degree of risk, depending on the stability of their earnings or dividends and the way they are perceived in the marketplace.

$ HINT: The general rule is that return is correlated to risk: The greater the risk, the greater the expected return.

HOW STOCKS WORK

When you buy shares in a company, you become part owner of that company, and you can make money in one of two ways: through dividends or through price appreciation when you sell your shares at a profit.

Dividends, a distribution of earnings, are generally declared when the company is comfortably profitable. The dollar amount is decided by the board of directors and is traditionally paid to shareholders quarterly.

A stock may appreciate for a variety of reasons, not all of which are completely rational:

- The company is profitable.
- It has an exciting new product.
- It is part of an industry that is performing well.
- It is the subject of takeover rumors or actual attempts.
- Wall Street likes it.

SIX CASH GENERATORS
(Stocks of companies that earned more cash than was needed to pay dividends and build plants)

STOCK	SYMBOL	PRICE	ACTIVITY
Forest Labs	FRX	$36	Drugs
Loews	LTR	101	Financial services
Primarica	PA	46	Financial
Reebok	RBK	35	Shoes
Tootsie Roll	TR	75	Candy
Wrigley (WM)	WWY	31	Gum

SOURCE: Value Line, May 1993.

If a corporation earns 15% on stockholders' equity (the money invested by shareholders), it ends the year with 15¢ per dollar more. After payment of a 5¢-per-share dividend, 10¢ is reinvested for future growth: research and development, new plants and equipment, new products and markets, etc. Thus the underlying value of the corporation doubles in about 7½ years. Eventually, these gains will be reflected in the price of the common stock. That's why the best investments are shares in companies that continue to make the most money!

As you might expect, it can fall in price for similar reasons and others: a poor earnings report, ineffective management, negative publicity, or even a mass dumping that feeds on itself, perhaps unrelated to the performance of the company.

Timing is an important factor in stock selection. In general there are times when you should move out of the market and times when you should be in high-yielding fixed-income securities. Just think about the world around you: Industries change with the times, and so do common stocks. Utilities face nuclear problems; the electronics and computer field has become overbuilt and competition is tough; the Koreans now make cheaper steel; the Japanese and Germans, better cars. Woe to the investor who psychologically locks into a stock as though it were a CD. To make a profit, always be prepared to sell your stock when the time is right.

$ HINT: The single most common mistake of investors is *inertia.* The market constantly changes, and no one stock (or any other investment) is right for all seasons. Do not buy a stock, even a solid blue chip, and then never look at it again. While your back is turned the company could be taken over, enter bankruptcy, or just have a bad year. In each case, you should be ready to take some form of action—buy more shares, sell all your shares, or sell some of your shares.

ADVANTAGES OF OWNING COMMON STOCKS

➤ GROWING VALUES Stocks are *live* investments. The market value of a common stock grows as the corporation prospers, whereas the face value of bonds remains the same, so that over the years, their real value, in terms of purchasing power, decreases.

The prices of bonds are almost completely controlled by interest rates and change almost immediately when rates do. When the cost of

FOUR STOCKS WITH LONGEST RECORD OF DIVIDENDS

Bank of Boston	1784
Fleet/Norstar Financial	1791
Midlantic	1805
First Maryland Bancorp	1806

SOURCE: Standard & Poor's Corp.

money rises, bond values drop to maintain competitive returns; when interest rates decline, bond prices rise. Bonds, therefore, are traded by yields; stocks, by what investors believe to be future corporate prospects.

➤ SAFETY Quality stocks are often almost as safe as corporate bonds. As long as the corporation meets quality standards—financial strength, growth, and profitability it will continue to pay dividends, usually with periodic increases; and with higher earnings, the value of its shares will increase. If a well-known corporation pays dividends for more than 20 years, its stock is certainly as durable as its bonds.

➤ GROWING DIVIDENDS This is important for investors who want ever-higher income. Almost all quality companies keep boosting their payouts because of higher earnings.

➤ LIQUIDITY Common stocks traded on major stock exchanges can be quickly bought or sold at clearly stated prices, the ranges of which are quoted in the financial press. You can instruct your broker to buy or sell at a specific price or at "market," which will be the best price attainable at that time. The complete transaction will take 5 working days, but immediately after the transaction, you can get exact data from your broker.

RISKS OF OWNING COMMON STOCK

There are, of course, risks associated with ownership of common stocks. The risks are far less with quality corporations and, to a large degree, can be controlled by setting strict rules for selling and by using common sense. As long as the company continues to make more money, its stock price is likely to rise, but this may take time, often longer than you are prepared to accept financially or mentally.

➤ PERMANENT LOSS OF CAPITAL You may lose all your profits and some of your capital. When you speculate in high-flying stocks that are temporarily popular, the odds are against success. Only a few strong-minded people have the courage to sell such stocks when they become overpriced. When such equities start down, many people hang on in hope of a comeback that seldom materializes.

$ HINT: *Speculation in stocks should be limited to half the money you can afford to lose.*

DIVIDENDS EVERY MONTH

You can receive a dividend check every month of the year by purchasing a group of stocks with different dividend-payment dates. The following is a list of issues broken down by payout dates. By purchasing stocks from each of the groups, you will have a portfolio of stocks producing dividend checks every month of the year.

January, April, July, October

Burlington Northern	Morgan (J.P.) & Co.
CIGNA	Northern States
Dexter	Power
Dow Chemical	Ogden
Eastman Kodak	Philip Morris
General Electric	Companies
Genuine Parts	SCEcorp
Heinz (H.J.)	Sears, Roebuck &
Kimberly-Clark	Co.
McKesson	Thomas & Betts

February, May, August, November

American Tel. &	Lincoln National
Tel.	Orange & Rockland
BellSouth	Utilities
Betz Laboratories	Penney (J.C.) Co.
Bristol-Myers	Procter & Gamble
Squibb	Rochester
Brooklyn Union Gas	Telephone
Clorox	Southwestern Bell
Colgate-Palmolive	TECO Energy
Consolidated	WPL Holdings
Natural Gas	

March, June, September, December

American Brands	K mart
American Home	Minnesota Mining
Products	& Mfg.
Amoco	Norfolk Southern
Atlantic Richfield	Potomac Electric
Deluxe	Power
Du Pont (E.I.)	South Jersey
Dun & Bradstreet	Industries
Exxon	Southern Indiana
General Motors	Gas & Electric
Indiana Energy	
International	
Business Machines	

SOURCE: Dow Theory Forecasts, 7412 Calumet Avenue, Hammond, IN 46324; 1-219-931-6480; 1993.

➤ STOCK MARKET RISK Regardless of whether you opt for income or appreciation, you certainly want all your stocks to be winners. This means avoiding ridiculous risks and instead incorporating *realistic risk* into your selections. A totally riskless portfolio is by its very nature doomed to mediocrity, since nothing exciting will happen to it. For risk-free investments, turn to EE savings bonds, bank CDs, or money market accounts.

You can, however, reduce your risk quotient and still make a profit with common stocks. Here are the best ways: (1) buy stocks with low betas (see page 161 for a full explanation of how beta works); (2) diversify by type of stock and industry; (3) spread out your risk over a number of stocks and industry groups; and (4) be defensive by moving in and out of the market when appropriate.

➤ INTEREST RATE RISK Certain stocks are "interest-sensitive," which means they are directly affected by changes in interest rates. These stocks include utilities, banks, financial and brokerage companies, housing and construction, REITs, and closed-end bond funds. You can cut your risk in these stocks by moving to other investments when interest rates are high or on the way up. The reason why these industries suffer during high-interest-rate seasons is because:

1 Utility companies have to pay more on monies borrowed for expansion or upgrading of facilities.
2 Banks and finance companies are forced to pay more on money deposited in their institutions as well as for money they borrow.
3 Building falls off because of higher interest rates.

8 WAYS TO ANALYZE STOCKS

These analytic tools are the most reliable for appraising a stock.

➤ EARNINGS PER SHARE For the average investor, this figure distills the company's financial picture into one simple number. Earnings per share is the company's net income (after taxes and preferred stock dividends) divided by the number of common shares outstanding. When a company is described as growing at a certain rate, the growth is then usually stated in terms of earnings per share.

Look for a company whose earnings per share have increased over the past 5 years; 1 down year is acceptable if the other 4 have been up. You will find earnings per share in *Moody's, Value Line, Standard & Poor's,* or the company's annual report.

➤ PRICE-EARNINGS RATIO (P/E) This is one of the most common analytic tools of the trade and reflects investor enthusiasm about a stock in comparison with the market as a whole. Divide the current price of a stock by its earnings per share for the last 12 months: that's the P/E ratio, also sometimes called the "multiple."

You will also find the P/E listed in the daily stock quotations of the newspaper. A P/E of 12, for example, means that the buying public is willing to pay 12 times earnings for the stock, whereas there is much less interest and confidence in a stock with a P/E of 4 or 5. A company's P/E is of course constantly changing and must be compared with its own previous P/Es and with the P/Es of others in its industry or category.

It is important to realize that the P/E listed in the paper is based on the last 12 months' earnings; however, Wall Street professionals refer to the earnings of the current year. So when considering a stock to buy or sell, remember to focus on its future, not its past.

Although brokers and analysts hold varying views on what constitutes the ideal P/E, a P/E under 10 is regarded as conservative. As the P/E moves above 10, you start to pay a premium. If the P/E moves below 5 or 6, it tends to signal uncertainty about the company's prospects and balance sheet.

Try to buy a strong company with favorable prospects and a conservative P/E *before* other investors become interested in it and run it up in price. Sometimes growth industries—for example, cellular telephones—fall into economic slumps and may provide this type of investment opportunity.

➤ BOOK VALUE This figure, also known as stockholders' equity, is the difference between a company's assets and its liabilities, in other words, what the stockholders own after all debts are paid. That number is then divided by the number of shares outstanding to arrive at book value per share. The book value becomes especially important in takeover situations. If book value is understated—that is, if the assets of the company are worth substantially more than the financial statements say they are—you may have found a real bargain that the marketplace has not yet recognized. (This is often true with in-the-ground assets such as oil, minerals, gas, and timber.)

➤ RETURN ON EQUITY (ROE) This number measures how much the company earns on the stockholders' equity. It is a company's total net income expressed as a percentage of total book value and is especially useful when comparing several companies within one industry or when studying a given company's profitability trends. To calculate a "simple" ROE, divide earnings per share by book value. A return under 10% is usually considered poor.

➤ DIVIDEND Check the current and projected dividend of a stock, especially if you are building an income portfolio. Study the payouts over the past 5 years as well as the current dividend. There are times when a corporation reinvests most of its earnings to ensure its future growth, in which case the dividend will be small. Typically, the greater the current yield, the less likelihood there is of stock price appreciation. However, it's best if a company earns $5 for every $4 it pays out.

➤ VOLATILITY Some stocks go up and down in price like a yo-yo, while others trade within a relatively narrow range. Those that dance about obviously carry a greater degree of risk than their more pedestrian cousins.

The measurement tool for price volatility, called *beta,* tells how much a stock tends to move in relation to changes in the Standard & Poor's 500 stock index. The index is fixed at 1.00, so a stock with a beta of 1.5 moves up and down $1\frac{1}{2}$ times as much as the Standard & Poor's index, whereas a stock with a beta of 0.5 is less volatile than the index. To put it another way, a stock with a 1.5 beta is expected to rise in price by 15% if the Standard & Poor's index rises 10% or fall by 15% if the index falls by 10%. You will find the beta for stocks given by the investment services as well as by good stockbrokers.

➤ TOTAL RETURN Most investors in stocks tend to think about their gains and losses in terms of price changes, not dividends, whereas those who own bonds pay attention to interest yields and seldom focus on price changes. *Both approaches are mistakes.* Although dividend yields are obviously more important if you are seeking income, and changes in price play a greater role in growth stocks, the total return on a stock is extremely important. It makes it possible for you to compare your investment in stocks with a similar investment in corporate bonds, municipals, Treasuries, mutual funds, and unit investment trusts.

12 STOCKS FOR LONG-TERM APPRECIATION

COMPANY	S&P RATING	PRICE (SPRING 1993)	P/E RATIO
Abbott Labs	A+	$25	14.7
Block (H&R)	A+	34	17.0
Bristol-Myers Squibb	A+	58	12.5
CSX Corp.	B	78	14.3
ConAgra	A+	24	14.5
Emerson Electric	A+	61	18.5
General Electric	A+	95	15.8
Merck & Co.	A+	34	14.5
Microsoft	B+	86	27.7
Procter & Gamble	A	48	18.0
Sara Lee	A+	25	18.5
Waste Management	A	33	17.4

To calculate the total return, add (or subtract) the stock's price change and dividends for 12 months and then divide by the price at the beginning of the 12-month period. For example, suppose you buy a stock at $42 a share and receive $2.50 in dividends for the next 12-month period. At the end of the period, you sell the stock at $45.00. The total return is 13%.

Dividend	$2.50
Price appreciation	+ 3.00
	$5.50 ÷ $42 = 13%

➤ NUMBER OF SHARES OUTSTANDING If you are a beginning investor or working with a small portfolio, look for companies with at least 5 million shares outstanding. You will then be ensured of both marketability and liquidity, because the major mutual funds, institutions, and the public will be trading in these stocks. You are unlikely to have trouble buying or selling when you want to. In a smaller company, your exposure to sharp price fluctuations is greater.

FINDING WINNERS

In addition to the eight analytical tools just described, you can boost your ability to build a winning portfolio by using these guidelines:

➤ CONTINUITY For investors who place safety first, the best common stocks are those of companies that have paid dividends for 20 years or more. Many have familiar names: Abbott Labs, Bristol-Myers, H. J. Heinz, Olin Corp., Philip Morris, Wells Fargo, and Woolworth.

Always check a company's annual report to see if (1) the dividends have increased fairly consistently as the result of higher earnings and (2) the company has been profitable in recent years and appears likely to remain so in the near future. It's great to do business with an old store, but only if the merchandise is up to date and priced fairly.

➤ INSTITUTIONAL OWNERSHIP Pick stocks chosen by the "experts"—managers of mutual funds, pension plans, insurance portfolios, endowments, etc. With few exceptions, these are shares of major corporations listed on the New York Stock Exchange.

Institutional ownership is no guarantee of quality, but it does indicate that some professionals have reviewed the financial prospects and for some reason (not always clear) have recommended purchase or retention. Without such interest, stocks are slow to move up in price.

In most cases, these companies must meet strict standards of financial strength, investment acceptance, profitability, growth, and, to some extent, income. But institutions still buy name and fame and either move in after the rush has started or hold on after the selling has started.

Institutions are not always smart money managers, but since they account for nearly three-fourths of all NYSE transactions (and a high percentage of those on the AMEX and OTC), it's wise to check their portfolios when you consider a new commitment.

$ HINT: Every investment portfolio should contain at least three stocks whose shares are owned by at least 250 institutions.

If you want to track portfolio changes, watch for reports on actions of investment companies in *Barron's.*

☐ CAUTION: Public information comes months after decisions have been made. By the time you get the word, prices may have risen so much that your benefits will be comparatively small. Or you may be buying just before the portfolio managers on Wall Street, realizing their mistake, start selling.

➤ MOST PROFITABLE COMPANIES An important standard of safety is high and consistent profitability. It can be determined by calculating the rate of return on shareholders' equity, a minimum annual average of 11%. By sticking to these real winners, you will always make a lot of money—in time.

A list of companies that are expected to achieve high total returns because of higher profits and current undervaluation appears on page 166.

➤ INDUSTRY LEADERS Companies that capture the business within their industry are creative, and well managed.

➤ STOCK SPLITS With many stocks at or near new highs, stock splits are on the rise. (The record was 225 in 1983.) In a purely technical way, a stock split provides no advantage to shareholders, but the history of the market shows that more often than not a stock will rise in price at about the time the directors vote a split. And, often an increase in the cash dividend accompanies a split. A stock split calls the public's attention to the company, to its earnings progress, and this often results in increased buying and eventually a higher price for the company's shares. And, with the new reduced price per share, small investors are attracted to the stock.

To find stock split candidates, look for a sharply higher market price, a history of stock splits or large stock dividends.

$ HINT: Standard & Poor's "The Outlook" generally publishes a list of stock split candidates once or twice a year.

GUIDELINES FOR SELECTING GROWTH STOCKS

- **Read the annual report backward.** Look at the footnotes to discover whether there are significant problems, unfavorable long-term commitments, lawsuits, etc.
- **Analyze the management's record** in terms of growth of revenue and earnings and, especially, return on stockholders' equity.
- **Find a current ratio of assets to liabilities of 2:1 or higher.** This indicates that the company can withstand difficulties and will probably be able to obtain money to expand.
- **Look for a low debt ratio with long-term debt no more than 35% of total capital.** This means that the company has staying power and the ability to resist cyclical downturns.
- **Compare a stock's price-earnings ratio** to those of other companies in the same industry. If their ratios are higher, this may be a sleeper. If the P/E multiple is above 20, be wary. Such stocks tend to be volatile.
- **Look for stocks with strong management,** little debt, and a return on investment high enough to generate internal growth.
- **Concentrate on companies whose earnings growth rate has been at least 15%** annually for the past 5 years and can be projected to be not much less for the next 2 years.

CALCULATING GROWTH RATES

ANNUAL RATE OF EARNINGS INCREASE PER SHARE	JUSTIFIED P/E RATIOS			
	5 YEARS	7 YEARS	10 YEARS	15 YEARS
2%	15	15	13	12
4	17	17	16	16
5	18	18	18	18
6	19	19	20	21
8	21	22	24	28
10	23	25	28	35
12	25	28	33	48

Note that there should be only a small premium when a low growth rate remains static over the years. A 5% annual gain in EPS justifies the same P/E no matter how many years it has been attained. But when a company can maintain a high rate of earnings growth, 10% or more, the value of the stock is enhanced substantially.

SOURCE: Graham and Dodd, *Security Analysis,* 4th ed. (New York: McGraw-Hill, 1962).

Keep in mind that (1) you are buying the future of the company, (2) increasing revenues are not enough (the real test is increasing profits), and (3) the stock market is built on hype, and that's easy with new companies that do not have a long, successful record.

ESTABLISHED COMPANIES

The corporation does not have to be young to have growth potential. There are opportunities with old companies where there's new management, a turnaround situation, or R&D-based developments. These developments are indicators of growth:

- **Strong position in an evolutionary market.** Find an industry or market that is bound to move ahead and check the top half dozen corporations. The leaders are probably the best bets, but do not overlook the secondary companies. They may provide a greater percentage gain on your investment.
- **Ability to set prices at profitable levels.** This is important in service industries where greater volume can bring

proportionately higher profits as overhead remains relatively stable. The same approach applies to companies making or distributing branded merchandise.

- **Adequate funds for R&D.** With few exceptions, future growth of any corporation is dependent on finding new and better products, more efficient methods of doing business, etc. Look for a company that is building for that sort of future.

- **Control of a market.** For example, General Electric is in a dominant position, not because of price but because of its ability to engineer new computers and office equipment and to provide good, continuing service at reasonable cost to the customer.

- **Strong technology base.** This is a valuable, but not essential, asset. Growth companies usually start with expertise in specific areas and then move out into other products and markets.

- **Growing customer demand.** This means a total market that is growing faster than the GNP. In the early years of new items, almost any company can prosper, because the demand is greater than the supply. Later, when production has caught up, the strong, better-managed firms will survive and expand their positions.

- **Safety is always important,** but with common stocks, the foremost consideration should be profitable growth: in assets, revenues, and earnings.

- **Improving profit margins.** This is an excellent test, because wider PMs almost always indicate increased earnings per share within a short period of time.

The gross profit margin (sometimes called the operating profit margin) shows a company's operating income, before taxes, as a percentage of revenues. It is listed in many annual reports and most statistical analyses. It can be calculated by dividing the operating income (total revenues less operating expenses) by the net sales. Generally, a gross PM of 12% indicates a company that deserves further study. Anything below that, especially when it is lower than the previous year, is a danger signal.

The gross profit margin is useful in comparing companies within a given industry. However, since it varies widely among industries, avoid interindustry comparisons. For example, supermarket stores have lower gross PMs than many others.

- **Plowed-back earnings.** The fastest-growing companies will almost always be the stingiest dividend payers. By reinvesting a substantial portion of its profits, preferably 70% or more, a company can speed expansion and improve productive efficiency. Any corporation that plows back 12% of its invested capital each year will double its real worth in 6 years.

- **Strong research and development.** The aim of research is knowledge; the aim of development is new or improved products and processes. A company that uses reinvested earnings largely for new plants and equipment will improve its efficiency and the quality of its products, but it may not grow as fast in the long run as a company that spends wisely to develop new and better products.

A prime test for aggressive growth management is whether the company is spending a higher than average percentage of its revenues for research and new process and product development. *With good management, dollars spent for R&D constitute the most creative, dynamic force for growth available for any corporation.* It is not unusual for the thousands of dollars used for research to make possible millions of dollars in additional sales and profits.

WHAT TO AVOID

To spot the nonachievers among companies in a growth industry, look for these danger signals:

- **Substantial stock dilution.** This means that a company repeatedly and exclusively raises funds through the sale of additional common stock, either directly or through convertibles. There's no harm in small dilution, especially when there are prospects that the growth of earnings will continue. But beware of any company with heavy future obligations. Too much dilution merely enlarges the size of the company for the benefit of management and leaves stockholders with diluted earnings.

- **Vast overvaluation as shown by price-earnings ratios of 30 or higher.** This is a steep price to pay for potential growth. Take your profits, or at least set stop-loss prices. When any stock sells at a multiple that is double that of the overall market (usually around 14.56), be cautious.

DISCOVERING BARGAINS

Benjamin Graham, in his book *Security Analysis*, looks for bargains in stocks, which he defines as the time when they trade at:

- A multiple of no more than twice that of the prevailing interest rate: that is, a P/E ratio of 16 vs. an interest rate of 8%
- A discount of 20% or more from book value
- A point where current assets exceed current liabilities and long-term debt combined
- A P/E ratio of 40% less than that of the S&P index P/E. Some examples of stocks with low P/Es as of early 1993 are listed below.

RISING EARNINGS AND DIVIDENDS

Despite some temporary setbacks, American business continues to make more money and to pay out higher dividends.

In selecting stocks, check the growth of earnings and dividends. Select companies that have posted rising earnings and dividends not for just a year or two but fairly consistently over a 5-year period.

- **Look for a high compound growth rate:** at least 15% to 20% annually. Compounding means that every year earnings are 20% higher than in the prior year. The table below shows a theoretical example of earnings growth of 20% compounded annually.

Example: To find earnings growth for any one year, subtract the earnings per share of the prior year from the earnings per share of the year in question. Then divide the difference by the base year (i.e., the prior year) earnings.

For example, a company earned $1.20 per share this year and, in the prior year, it earned $1.00 per share.

$$\begin{array}{r} \$1.20 \\ -\underline{1.00} \\ 0.20 \end{array} \div \$1.00 = 20\% \text{ growth rate}$$

In the next year, in order to maintain a 20% growth rate, it would have to report an increase

---

STOCKS SELLING AT MODEST P/E RATIOS

COMPANY	SYMBOL	PRICE	P/E
Avnet Inc.	AVT	$32	15.0
Bell Atlantic	BEL	55	16.5
Boeing Co.	BA	38	10.0
Chemical Banking	CHL	40	8.2
Chemical Waste Mgmt	CHW	13	19.0
Chrysler	C	40	10.5
Eastman Kodak	EK	55	16.0
Raymond James	RJF	24	7.6
Raytheon Co.	RTN	58	11.5
Reliance Group	REL	7	6.6

(As of May 1993.)

STOCKS WITH 25% EARNINGS GROWTH EXPECTED

COMPANY	SYMBOL	S&P RATING	PRICE
Adobe Systems	ADBE	B	$44
Air Express Int'l.	AEX	B	20
Atlantic Southeast Airlines	ASAI	B+	33
Beneficial Corp.	BNL	B+	70
Dreyer's Ice Cream	DRYR	B	21
Du Pont (EI)	DD	A−	52
Fleet Financial Group	FLT	B+	37
Harcourt General	H	A−	34
Limited Inc.	LTD	A+	23
Oracle Systems	ORCL	B	34
Reynolds & Reynolds	REY	B+	35
Rohm & Haas	ROH	B+	59
Shaw Industries	SHX	A−	36
Southwest Airlines	LUV	B	42
Spartan Motors	SPAR	B+	26
Thomas & Betts	TNB	B+	69
Witco Corp.	WIT	B+	53

(As of Spring 1993.)

of 20% of $1.20, or $1.20 × 0.20% = 24¢. Therefore, earnings expectations are $1.44 per share in the third year ($1.20 + 24¢ = $1.44).

HOW TO DETERMINE REAL GROWTH AND PROFITABILITY

Two fundamental measures of corporate growth and profitability are *earned growth rate* (EGR) and *profit rate* (PR). These reveal the ability of management to make the money entrusted to them by stockholders grow over the years. You can use the same technique.

➤ EARNED GROWTH RATE   The EGR is the annual rate at which the company's equity capital per

EARNINGS GROWTH RATE

Year 1	$1.00 × 20% = 0.20 = $1.20
Year 2	$1.20 × 20% = 0.24 = $1.44
Year 3	$1.44 × 20% = 0.29 = $1.73
Year 4	$1.73 × 20% = 0.35 = $2.08

WHAT ARE EARNINGS WORTH?

ANNUAL GROWTH RATE	WHAT $1.00 EARNINGS WILL BECOME IN 3 YEARS AT GIVEN GROWTH RATE	THE P/E RATIO YOU CAN PAY TODAY TO MAKE 10% ANNUAL CAPITAL GAIN AND EXPECT P/E RATIO IN 3 YEARS TO BE	
		15×	30×
4%	$1.12	12.6	25.3
5	1.16	13.1	26.2
6	1.19	13.4	26.8
7	1.23	13.9	27.7
8	1.26	14.2	28.4
9	1.30	14.7	29.3
10	1.33	15.0	30.0
12	1.40	15.8	31.6
15	1.52	17.1	34.3
20	1.73	19.5	39.0
25	1.95	22.0	44.0

SOURCE: Knowlton and Furth, *Shaking the Money Tree* (New York: Harper & Row, 1979).

common share is increased by net earnings after payment of the dividend—if any. *It is a reliable measure of investment growth because it shows the growth of the capital invested in the business.*

$$EGR = \frac{E - D}{BV}$$

E = earnings
D = dividend
BV = book value

The book value is the net value of total corporate assets, that is, what is left over when all liabilities, including bonds and preferred stock, are subtracted from the total assets (plant, equipment, cash, inventories, accounts receivable, etc.). It is sometimes called stockholders' equity and can be found in every annual report. Many corporations show the book value over a period of years in their summary tables. A good growth company will increase its equity capital at a rate of at least 6% per year.

To determine the EGR for a company, take the per-share earnings, say $5.73, and subtract the $3.34 dividend to get $2.39. Then divide this by the book value at the *beginning of the year.* Let's say it was $17.42. Thus, the EGR for that year was 13.7%:

$$EGR = \frac{5.73 - 3.34}{17.42} = \frac{2.39}{17.42} = 13.7\%$$

▶ PROFIT RATE The PR is equally important in assessing real growth, because it measures the ability of the corporate management to make money with your money; it shows the rate of return produced on shareholders' equity at corporate book value. It is calculated by dividing the earnings per common share by the per-share book value of the common stock, again at the *beginning of the year.*

Continuing the example above:

$$PR = \frac{5.73}{17.42} = 32.8\%$$

June 30: $\dfrac{11,100}{10,900} = 1.01$, or 1%

September 30: $\dfrac{13,500}{12,100} = 1.12$, or 12%

December 31: $\dfrac{15,000}{13,500} = 1.11$, or 11%

THE GROWTH STOCK PRICE EVALUATOR
How to Weigh Prices of Growth Stocks in Terms of Their Future Gains in Earnings or Cash Flow

IF— A STOCK NOW SELLS AT THIS MANY TIMES ITS CURRENT EARNINGS OR CASH FLOW:	—AND YOU BELIEVE ITS AVERAGE ANNUAL GROWTH IN EARNINGS OR CASH FLOW PER SHARE (COMPOUNDED) WILL BE: THEN—HERE IS HOW MANY TIMES ITS PROJECTED EARNINGS OR CASH FLOW PER SHARE 5 YEARS HENCE THE STOCK IS CURRENTLY SELLING AT:					
12	7.5	6.0	4.8	3.9	3.2	2.2	1.6
14	8.7	7.0	5.6	4.6	3.8	2.6	1.8
16	9.9	8.0	6.5	5.2	4.3	3.0	2.1
18	11.2	9.0	7.3	5.9	4.9	3.3	2.4
20	12.4	10.0	8.1	6.6	5.4	3.7	2.6
22	13.7	10.9	8.9	7.2	5.9	4.1	2.9
24	14.9	11.9	9.7	7.9	6.5	4.5	3.2
26	16.1	12.9	10.5	8.5	7.0	4.8	3.4
28	17.4	13.9	11.3	9.2	7.5	5.2	3.7
30	18.6	14.9	12.1	9.8	8.1	5.6	3.9
32	19.9	15.9	12.9	10.5	8.6	5.9	4.2
34	21.1	16.9	13.7	11.1	9.2	6.3	4.5
36	22.4	17.9	14.5	11.8	9.7	6.7	4.7
38	23.6	18.9	15.3	12.5	10.2	7.1	5.0
40	24.8	19.9	16.1	13.1	10.8	7.4	5.3
42	26.1	20.9	16.9	13.8	11.3	7.8	5.5
44	27.3	21.9	17.7	14.4	11.9	8.2	5.8
46	28.6	22.9	18.5	15.1	12.4	8.6	6.1
48	29.8	23.9	19.4	15.7	12.9	8.9	6.3
50	31.1	24.9	20.2	16.4	13.5	9.3	6.6

This evaluator can be used to make your own projections. It is most useful when studying fast-growing companies with above-average growth rates and cash flow, because it shows that if your growth assumptions are correct, the P/E ratio based on your cost today will be more modest.

Example: The stock of a small high-technology corporation is selling at 30 times current earnings. You estimate that over the next 5 years, earnings will grow at an average annual compound rate of 20%. The table shows that if this projection is correct, the stock will be selling at 12.1 times its anticipated 5-years-hence profits.

This evaluation technique can be reversed. Today the stock is selling at a multiple of 30, but you are not so sure about its future profits. From experience, you are willing to pay no more than 12 times future 5-year earnings for any growth stock. Checking the table, you find that the average annual growth rate must be 20% compounded annually to meet your investment standards. This stock just meets your criteria.

The Growth Stock Price Evaluator does *not* show the *future* price-to-earnings multiple or cash flow. They might be lower than, the same as, or greater than they are today.

Now use the quarterly figures according to the formula:

$$1.09 \times 1.01 \times 1.12 \times 1.11 = 1.37$$

The gain is $1.37 - 1 = 0.37 = 37\%$.

Thus 37% is the time-weighted rate of return, but the average rate of return is much lower.

GUIDELINES FOR SELECTING INCOME STOCKS

Dividend-paying stocks are not just for retirees and ultraconservative investors. They are important to everyone because they both boost the value of a stock and generally indicate that the company is a mature one, no longer in the throes of expensive expansion. A company that can afford to pay high dividends is no longer reinvesting all its profits in the company.

Another reason why high-dividend stocks are looked upon with such favor is that the dividend is likely to increase if the company's earnings grow—unlike a bond, whose coupon rate remains the same throughout its life.

$ HINT: Dividend-paying stocks fall less in price when the market falls. A study by Avner Arbel, professor of finance at Cornell University, shows that high-dividend stocks fell only 21% in the 1987 crash while nondividend payers dropped 32%.

To determine if a company is likely to continue making dividend payouts:

- Check the dividend-payout history for the past 10 years in *Standard & Poor's Stock Guide* or *Value Line Investment Survey.* Those with uninterrupted payouts are your best bet.

- Check the company's payout ratio: total dividends paid divided by net operating income. If the payout ratio is less than 50% the company will probably continue to pay dividends.

- Check the company's cash flow per share. If cash flow is three times the dividend payout, dividends will probably continue to be paid.

- Avoid or invest very carefully in stocks that have extraordinarily high yields for the industry group. Extremely high yields can signal trouble.

- Don't buy a high-yield stock near the ex-dividend date. That is the beginning of the time period during which purchasers of the stock cannot receive the next quarterly dividend, generally paid 3 to 4 weeks later. Usually stock prices are inflated just before the ex-dividend date, and on that date they tend to fall. If you buy the stock at an inflated price in order to receive the dividend, you may not break even since you'll be paying tax on the dividend income.

COMPANIES THAT HAVE PAID FIVE STRAIGHT YEARS OF HIGHER DIVIDENDS

	S&P RATING		S&P RATING
Beneficial Corp.	B+	General Electric	A+
Block (H&R)	A+	Heinz (H.J.)	A+
Coca-Cola Co.	A+	Kmart	A−
Crompton & Knowles	A+	Kimberly-Clark	A+
Deluxe Corp.	A+	May Dept Stores	A+
Du Pont	A−	NIKE, Inc.	B+
Federal National			
Mtge	A−	Pfizer, Inc.	A+
First of America Bank	A	Procter & Gamble	A
First Union Corp.	A	Wrigley (Wm), Jr.	A

(As of Spring 1993.)

SEVEN STOCKS WITH HIGH DIVIDENDS

Stocks with comparatively high dividends give income plus some protection against a falling stock market. Dow Chemical, for instance, has paid a dividend every year since 1911 and increased it over the past five years at a compound annual rate of 13.5%.

COMPANY	SYMBOL	BUSINESS	PRICE	YIELD
National City	NCC	banking	$50	4.2%
Bristol Myers Squibb	BMY	drugs	60	4.8
Dow Chemical	DOW	chemicals	55	4.8
American Brands	AMB	tobacco	31	6.3
Upjohn	UPJ	drugs	30	5.0
Hartford Steam Boiler	HSB	insurance	56	3.8
Royal Dutch	RD	petroleum	89	5.1

SOURCE: Quotron, May 1993.

$ HINT: Sign up for a company's dividend reinvestment plan so your dividends will automatically be reinvested in additional shares of stock. Most companies do not charge a brokerage fee for these purchases, and some companies offer a 5% discount off market price for shares purchased through dividend reinvestment. Approximately 1,000 companies have dividend reinvestment plans.

$ HINT: Call the investor relations division of any company you own shares in to see if it has a dividend reinvestment plan, or obtain the book *Directory of Dividend Reinvestment Plans* ($39.95) from:
Standard & Poor's Corp.
Direct Marketing
25 Broadway
New York, NY 10004
1-800-777-4858

This annually updated guide lists 700+ companies that offer such programs, telephone numbers, S&P rankings, and other details.

CYCLICAL STOCKS

The performance of so-called "cyclical" stocks is tied closely to the economic cycles. Those listed in the box above are expected to increase in price as the economy strengthens under the Clinton administration. However, industry groups such as building materials, diversified machinery, machine tools, and railroads are starting to see increased orders. The so called "smokestack" or basic industries, such as aluminum and chemicals, are slower to move. Nevertheless, a number of these companies have lowered their costs, reduced their debt, and trimmed interest expenses. Yet there's no guarantee that the cyclicals will perform as well as Wall Street says they will. And when they do make moves, they do it over a comparatively short time period. Before investing in any cyclical stock, check to see that the GNP is increasing, that unemployment has eased, that auto and retail sales are starting to rise.

- *Allied-Signal* (NYSE:ALD, $66). Diversified company in aerospace, automotive products, and engineered materials.
- *Arco Chemical* (NYSE:RCM, $45). Largest producer of propylene oxide needed in durable goods and construction.
- *Burlington Northern* (NYSE:BNI, $51). Coal and freight car hauling should increase with recovery.
- *Carpenter Technology* (NYSE:CRS, $48). Produces stainless steel used in construction and manufacturing.
- *Caterpillar Inc* (NYSE:CAT, $59). Premier manufacturer of construction equipment;

has modernized manufacturing facilities here and abroad; stock is poised for a turnaround.

- *Foster Wheeler* (NYSE:FWC, $30). Construction and engineering firm with sizeable overseas business.
- *Masco Corp* (NYSE:MAS, $34). Recovery in housing markets should boost its building products and home furnishings products.
- *Nalco Chemical* (NYSE:NLC, $33). Has a water treatment business that will benefit from new legislation and upsurge in business.
- *Temple-Inland* (NYSE:TIN, $46). A linerboard producer with strong balance sheet.
- *Worthington Industries* (OTC:WTHG, $27). Streamlined processor of steel products.

DOLLAR COST AVERAGING

One of the most difficult aspects of investing is timing—should you put money into stocks or mutual funds this week, next week, or months from now? There's a simple formula you can use to get around this age-old dilemma—dollar cost averaging. It involves investing the same amount of money in a stock or mutual fund at fixed intervals, monthly or quarterly, for instance. It may seem dull, but it requires some personal discipline in down markets when the temptation is not to invest.

Basically, what it does is force you to buy more of a stock or fund when its price is low and less when it is high. Over the long haul, your average cost will be lower than the average price of the security.

☐CAUTION: Although this is a fine technique, it will not turn a poor investment choice into a winner. If it keeps falling in price forever, you wind up buying more losses. To avoid this, select stocks and funds that have a record of long-term upward trends.

Most mutual funds require an initial investment of $1,000 or more, but subsequent investments may be as little as $100. You may be able to dollar cost average with a fund that automatically transfers a preset amount from your bank checking account into the fund's portfolio.

You can also dollar cost average with indi-

STOCK WITH DIVIDEND REINVESTMENT PLANS THAT PERMIT CASH INVESTMENTS	
STOCK	**MINIMUM DRP CASH PURCHASE**
Ameritech	$50
Atlanta Gas Light	25
Bristol-Myers Squibb	10
Brooklyn Union Gas	10
ConAgra	10
CPC International	10
Duke Power	25
General Electric	10
Merck & Co.	25
Mobil Corp.	10
Procter & Gamble	2
Southwestern Bell	50
Wisconsin Energy	25

vidual stocks. And if the shares are in your name (rather than held by your broker "in street name"), you may be able to participate in a dividend reinvestment plan. Over 750 companies have such plans in which your dividends are automatically reinvested in additional shares of stock rather than paying you the cash. Many of these companies also allow shareholders to make additional cash investments. This means you can dollar cost average without using a broker.

💲HINT: For a complete list of Dividend Reinvestment Plans, including addresses, phone numbers, details of the plan, and a 10-year total-return performance record, read the most recent edition of Standard & Poor's *Directory of Dividend Reinvestment Plans* at your library, or order from Standard & Poor's: 25 Broadway, New York, NY 10005; $39.95.

WHEN TO SELL A STOCK

Financial whiz kids and Wall Street gurus are always weaving complex theories about when to buy a stock. That's the easy part. They shy away from explaining when to sell, which is a much trickier business.

Although there's no foolproof system for making certain you always buy low and sell high, you can make an educated decision.

The first basic rule to follow in mastering the art of selling is to know precisely whether you bought the stock for growth or income.

1   *Growth.* If you purchased the stock for growth and price appreciation, hold it as long as the company's earnings keep rising at a steady pace. If profits slow down, find out why. Sell unless you discover a truly viable reason why profits will increase within the year.

2   *Income.* Keep the stock as long as the company is financially solid and its earnings per share exceed the dividend by at least 10% and they (i.e., earnings) are rising more than 5% a year. If earnings stagnate for several quarters, or if an independent rating agency (Standard & Poor's or Moody's), downgrade the firm's creditworthiness, seriously consider selling.

Other guidelines that work:

■   You should consider selling when you think the market is headed for a serious setback. But, of course, not all stocks react to a declining market to the same degree. So, to judge how much an individual stock fluctuates against broad market drops, check its beta in *Value Line Investment Survey.* The higher the beta, the more it moves and the faster you should sell (see list following).

■   You should also consider selling if you think the company is in serious trouble and its earnings prospects are poor and not likely to recover quickly.

■   If your stock suddenly drops in price by 20% or more within a short period—a month or less—you need to find out why and then consider selling.

■   If your stock has become overvalued—you can tell if its P/E suddenly moves up and is way above the average P/E of the S&P 500—find out if it's soared because of good news, in which case hold, or because it's out of line, in which case sell and take your profit.

These four indicators, all reported in the *Wall Street Journal* as well as most major newspapers, should be your signposts for selling.

■   *Stock prices are inflated.* This is indicated

CONSIDER INCREASING OR DECREASING YOUR POSITION IN AN INDIVIDUAL STOCK WHEN . . .

■ The price changes substantially.
■ New management takes over.
■ Earnings increases or decreases are announced.
■ A new product comes on line.
■ A merger or acquisition takes place.
■ The company is listed on or unlisted from one of the exchanges.
■ Substantial legal action is brought against the company.
■ Dividends are increased, cut, or canceled.
■ The P/E multiple changes dramatically.
■ The stock is purchased or sold by the institutions.
■ The company spins off unprofitable divisions or subsidiaries.

---

by a high P/E ratio for the S&P 500. In August 1987, just before the crash, it hit 23. Check the ratio regularly. In July 1993, it was 22.54.

■   *There's a rise in interest rates.* Escalating interest rates hurt stocks as money moves to CDs and bonds. Watch the 3-month T-bill rate and the Federal Reserve discount rate. The market tends to fall when the Fed has raised the discount rate three or four consecutive times. It also falls if the T-bill rate is double the S&P 500 dividend yield. In July 1993, the T-bill rate was 3.40% and the dividend yield on the S&P 500 was 2.82%.

■   *A recession is in the wings.* The market tends to decline 6 to 9 months before an economic slump. Watch the Department of Commerce's leading economic indicators, which are reported monthly. If they are down for 3 consecutive months, the market may soon follow.

■   *The market breadth is narrowing.* Often a group of stocks pushes the Dow Jones Industrial Average (or some other indicator) higher even though most other stocks are declining. This is called a narrowing of the market's breadth. You can spot this trend by following the advance/decline line that is reported in *Investor's Daily* and *Barron's*. It reflects the difference between the number of stocks that gain and lose each day. In August 1987 the market was moving up but the advance/decline line was moving down. In fact, the Dow reached a high of 2722 during that period.

CALCULATING YOUR RETURN

To know when to sell a stock, you should monitor your rate of return on each investment. To make this calculation, divide the total end value by the starting value, subtract 1, and multiply by 100:

$$R = \left(\frac{EV}{BV} - 1\right) \times 100$$

where R = rate of return
EV = value at end of period
BV = value at beginning of period

For example, in early January you bought 100 shares of OPH stock at a cost of $3,315 (price plus commissions and fees). During the year, OPH pays dividends of $3 per share. In December, the stock is at 45. For that year, the rate of return is 45%.

$$R = \frac{4,500 + 300}{3,315} = \frac{4,800}{3,315} = 1.45$$

The gain is 1.45 − 1 = 0.45 = 45%.

If you had held the stock for 2 years and the dividends rose in the second year to $3.50 per share but the stock price stayed at 45, the rate of return would be 55% over 2 years, or 27.5% per annum.

$$\frac{4,500 + 300 + 350}{3,315} = 1.55$$

The gain is 1.55 − 1 = 55% ÷ 2 = 27.5%.

To make similar calculations with a time-weighted rate of return (where the rates of return vary and there are additional investments over a period of time), use the same general formula but calculate each time frame separately.

For example, you started the year with a portfolio worth $10,000 and reinvested all income. At the end of March, your portfolio was worth $10,900; on June 30, it was up a bit to $11,100. On July 1, you added $1,000. At the end of the third quarter, the value was $13,500, and $15,000 at year-end. Here's how to determine the return.

March 30: $\dfrac{10,900}{10,000} = 1.09$, or 9%

KEEPING YOUR GAINS

Of course the most obvious way to keep your gains is simply to sell your investment when you've made a profit. This approach has several drawbacks—you have to pay taxes on the gain, and if the market goes up you won't benefit. Here are four ways to protect your position on the downside and profit on the upswings.

- *Enter stop orders.* Have your broker sell your stock if it drops to a particular price. This protects you against major declines.
- *Sell into strength.* Each time the market makes a major move on the up side, sell a portion of your holdings. For example, if you own 500 shares of Xerox and you have big gains, sell 100 shares each time it appreciates 10%. You reduce your risk, and at the same time you're selling your stock at higher prices.
- *Buy put options.* This gives you the right to sell 100 shares of a stock at a particular price within a certain time period, up to 9 months. These options set a selling floor. For example, if you own a $50 stock, you buy a put allowing you to sell 100 shares for $45 at any time within the next 6 months. The put costs about 75¢ per share and it limits your loss to $5 per share.
- *Switch to convertibles.* Move out of common stock into convertibles to lower your risk and still profit from a rise in the market.

Buy stocks for the long term.

PREFERRED STOCK

Individual investors usually gravitate toward preferred stocks because of their high, secure dividends. Many are issued by utilities.

LOW- OR NO-DEBT COMPANIES

SYMBOL	COMPANY	PRICE	YIELD	ACTIVITY
AGE	A. G. Edwards	$27	2.2%	Brokerage firm
IFF	Int'l. Flavors & Fragrances	113	2.7	Food flavoring
Ldg	Long's Drug Stores	34	3.3	Drugstore chain
LUB	Luby's Cafeterias	22	2.7	Restaurants
WMK	Weiss Markets	25	2.7	Supermarket
WWY	Wm. Wrigley Jr.	31	2.2	Chewing gum

SOURCE: Quotron, May 1993.

As their name implies, preferred stocks enjoy preferred status over common stocks. Preferred shareholders receive their dividend payments after all bondholders are paid and before dividends are paid on common shares. Like bonds, preferreds have a fixed annual payment, but it's called a dividend. It is set at a fixed dollar amount and is secure for the life of the stock. If a payment is skipped because of corporate losses, it will be paid later when earnings recover. That's why preferreds are sometimes called *cumulative,* because the dividends accumulate and must be paid out before common. Most preferreds are cumulative and are indicated by the initials "cm" in the stock guides.

There are also *noncumulative preferreds:* If a dividend is skipped, it is not recovered. It's best to avoid this type of preferred.

➤ PROS Although there have been a few incidents of corporations skipping preferred dividends, on the whole these securities have an excellent safety record. And if the yield is high, it remains permanently high.

➤ CONS Inflation and high interest rates can have a large negative impact on preferreds. That's because the dividend is fixed, and when rates rise, holders are locked in at the old lower rate. Not only are they shut out of rising interest rates, but the opportunity for substantial price appreciation of their shares is limited.

Although preferreds trade like bonds on the basis of their yields, unlike bonds they have no maturity date. With a bond you know that at a specified time you will get back your initial investment, the face value. There is no such assurance with a preferred. Market conditions are the sole determinant of the price you will receive when you sell.

SELECTING PREFERREDS

The basic criteria for selecting preferreds are *quality* of the issuing corporation, as shown by financial strength and profitability; *value,* as indicated by the yield; and *timing,* taking into account the probable trend of interest rates. Then:

- **Deal with a brokerage firm that has a research department that follows this group of securities.** Not every broker is familiar with preferreds, and many will not be able to provide enough pertinent information.

- **Recognize the inherent volatility because of limited marketability.** Preferreds listed on a major stock exchange may drop (when you want to sell) or rise (when you plan to buy) 2 or 3 points the day after the last quoted sale. If you have to sell in a hurry, this can be expensive. Preferreds sold over the counter (OTC) may fluctuate even more because of their thin markets. As a rule, place your orders at a set price or within narrow limits.

$ HINT: Ask your broker about *adjustable-rate preferreds.* The quarterly dividend fluctuates with interest rates and is tied to a formula based on Treasury bills or other money market rates.

$ HINT: *Participating preferreds* entitle shareholders to a portion of the company's profits. In *nonparticipating preferreds,* shareholders are limited to the stipulated dividend.

➤ QUALITY Choose preferred stocks rated BBB or higher by Standard & Poor's or Baa or higher by Moody's if you are conservative. But if you are willing to take greater risks, you can boost

SELECTED PREFERRED STOCKS

COMPANY	DIVIDEND	RECENT PRICE	RECENT YIELD
Alabama Power "C"	$8.16	$105	7.8%
Bank of Boston	2.15	26	8.1
Du Pont (E.I.) "A" "B"	4.50	74	6.1
Georgia Power "M"	2.50	28	8.8
Pennsylvania Power & Light "J"	8.00	103	7.8
Southern Calif. Edison "K"	7.58	100	7.6
Virginia Electric "H"	7.45	101	7.4

SOURCE: Quotron, prices, May 1993.

your income by buying BB-rated preferreds, such as Philadelphia Electric 7.80% cm pfd selling at 89 with a yield of 9.2%.

Usually, but not always, the higher rating will be given to companies with modest debt. Since bond interest must be paid before dividends, the lower the debt ratio, the safer the preferred stock. For example, look for utilities with balanced debt and then check the preferred stocks. Buy several different preferreds so you can benefit from diversification.

➤ CALL PROVISION This provision allows the company to redeem or call in the shares of a preferred, usually at a few points above par (face value). When the original issue carries a high yield, say over 10%, the company may find it worthwhile to retire some shares (1) when it can float new debt or issue preferred stock at a lower rate, say, 8% or (2) when corporate surplus becomes substantial. In both cases, such a prospect may boost the price of the preferred by a point or two.

☐CAUTION: Preferred stock, especially of small, struggling corporations, often has special call or conversion provisions. And utilities sometimes take advantage of obscure provisions in their charters to use other assets to call in their preferreds. You may end up with a modest profit, but if the redemption price is less than that at which the stock was selling earlier, you will lose money. Always check a preferred's call features.

➤ SINKING FUND Corporations use "sinking funds" to accumulate money on a regular basis in order to redeem the corporation's bonds or preferred stocks from time to time so that the entire issue is retired before the stated maturity date. For example, starting 5 years after the original sale, a company might buy back 5% of the stock annually for 20 years. The yields of such preferreds will usually be slightly less than those for which there is no such provision.

$ IF YOU DARE: Look for a company that has omitted dividend payouts for several years. It will probably be selling at a discount. Should earnings recover, it will pay off all

---

PREFERRED STOCK

PROS
↑ Generally pays higher dividends than common
↑ Receive your dividend before common stockholders
↑ Dividends generally cumulative; if dividend skipped, made up in future
↑ Know what your dividend income is
↑ Possibility of capital gain in price of stock
CONS
↓ If company's earnings rise, you don't share in increases unless it is a participating preferred
↓ Dividend fixed, with few exceptions
↓ Call provisions allow company to redeem your stock at stated price
↓ No protection against inflation

GETTING CURRENT INFO ON STOCKS

Call Standard & Poor's Research Reports ($10; 1-800-642-2858) or Schwab's Investment Reports Service ($5.50; 1-800-442-5111) to get five or more pages on each of about 4,000 publicly traded companies. Reports tell you how many analysts like the company and how many don't, plus earnings estimates, news about the company, future outlook the industry along with Standard & Poor's grade, ranging from one star (sell) to five stars (strong buy).

---

accumulated dividends, and the price of the stock is likely to rise.

$HINT: Buy participating preferreds to ensure receiving a percentage of any exceptional profit gain, as for example, if the corporation sells a subsidiary and has excess profits for the year.

CONTINUAL DIVIDENDS

Sharp investors may get as many as 12 dividends a year by rolling over preferred stocks. By buying shares just before the dividend date, they get the full payout. They sell the next day and buy another preferred with an upcoming dividend payment date. Because of the commission costs and need for constant checking, this technique is difficult for amateurs. Yet it can work well when it involves 500 shares or more and you work with a discount broker.

Timing is the key. After the payout date, the price of the preferred may drop almost as much as the value of the dividend. A 12% preferred thus might trade at 100 before the dividend date and drop back to just over 97 the next day. If you sell, you take a small loss. If you wait a week or so and are lucky in a strong market, you may be able to sell at 100. If you have the time, money, and a feel for this type of trading, you could make substantial profits.

$HINT: You can also purchase preferreds through the Lindner Dividend Fund, (1-314-727-5305), which is about 50% invested in preferreds. Its largest holdings are in utilities.

FOR FURTHER INFORMATION

Louis Engel & Brendon Boyd, *How to Buy Stocks* (Boston: Little, Brown & Co., 1982).

Lawrence J. Gitman and Michael D. Joehnk, *Fundamentals of Investing* (New York: HarperCollins, 1990).

Benjamin Graham & David L. Dodd, *Security Analysis*, 5th ed. (New York: McGraw-Hill, 1988) (updated by S. Cotile).

Richard J. Teweles and Edward S. Bradley, *The Stock Market* (New York: John Wiley & Sons, 1992).

Andrew Tobias, *The Only Investment Guide You'll Ever Need* (New York: Bantam, 1989).

Philip B. Capelle, *Investing in Growth* (Chicago: Probus Publishing Co., 1992).

Michael B. Lehman, *The Dow Jones–Irwin Guide to Using the Wall Street Journal* (Homewood, IL: Dow Jones–Irwin, 1990).

Charles D. Ellis, ed., *Classics: An Investor's Anthology* (Homewood, IL: Dow Jones–Irwin, 1989).

14 OVER-THE-COUNTER STOCKS

A good investment is not always an obvious one, dancing in the limelight of the New York Stock Exchange. Even the venerable Benjamin Graham, father of security analysis, subscribed to this theory. He advised investors to consider making one out of three securities in their portfolios an over-the-counter (OTC) stock. (The term *over the counter* stems from the days when securities were sold over the counter in banks and stores, right along with money orders and dry goods.)

This is an area of the market traditionally dominated by individual investors rather than the institutions, and over 11,000 securities trade OTC. Of these, approximately 4,700 are listed on NASDAQ (National Association of Securities Dealers Automated Quotation system), more than twice the number on the American and New York exchanges.

Since requirements for listing on NASDAQ are less stringent than for either the New York or American exchange (see box on page 177), the OTC companies tend to be smaller, newer, and less well known. This is reflected in their lower prices but higher risk level. And since fewer OTC stocks are owned by institutions or closely followed by analysts, research is not abundant on many of these issues, a fact that can work to your advantage, since it means neither Wall Street nor the public has run up the prices.

THE OTC MARKET

Unlike the New York and American stock exchanges, the OTC does not have a centralized trading floor. Instead, stocks are bought and sold through a centralized computer-telephone network linking dealers across the nation. There are two "divisions" of the OTC market: NASDAQ, a self-regulated trade group, which publishes daily quotes; and the National Quotation Bureau, a private company, which distributes daily data to brokers about small, thinly traded stocks, on what Wall Streeters call the "pink sheets" (because the data are printed on pink paper).

OTC trading is sometimes an expensive proposition. On the major and regional exchanges, specialists (who concentrate on particular stocks) match buy and sell orders received from brokerage firms. If no match is possible, the specialist usually fills the order from a personally held inventory. But when you trade OTC, your broker will fill your order from his or her inventory if there is one. Otherwise, your broker will buy the stock from another broker who makes a market in it and will then in turn sell it to you. The price is determined by a number of factors: the amount of stock the market maker has, the prices of recent trades, the markup, and the level of demand.

When you read the quotes in the paper, remember that the bid (or lower price) is what brokers or dealers are offering to pay for the stock. The higher (or asked figure) is what they will sell it for. The difference between these two numbers is the spread. On most exchanges, the spread is just a few pennies, but on the OTC the market makers actually negotiate the prices, and spreads are typically larger because of the greater risks involved.

$ HINT: The SEC requires all brokers who make a market in a stock to state their markup to clients. Be sure you ask.

GUIDELINES FOR SELECTING OTC STOCKS

- Start in your own backyard. Do research on companies in your region. Check with a local stockbroker for ideas. Read annual reports and visit the company personally.

- Buy only companies with established earnings growth and, if possible, low debt. Ideally, the assets–to–current liabilities ratio should be 2:1.
- Study wide economic and industrial trends and select companies that have a timely product or service.
- Find companies that have a market niche.
- Allow 2 to 10 months for price and/or earnings movement.
- Avoid penny stocks (stocks that sell for less than 50¢); the bid/asked price spread is often over 25%.

USING THE KEY INDICATORS

If and when you believe the big stocks are over-priced, it's time to move some of your portfolio into smaller issues. To help you time your move, watch these key indicators:

➤ NASDAQ COMPOSITE INDEX Listed in the major newspapers, its direction and progress can be compared with those of other major indexes. If its trend is up, the environment is favorable.

➤ OTC VOLUME Volume tends to verify the direction, up or down, of a market or individual issue. If the market rises on low volume, for example, generally the rise will be short.

➤ NEW HIGHS AND LOWS A number of new highs over new lows is a positive buy sign.

➤ BLOCK TRADING When trades of 10,000 shares or more take place, it probably signals institutional participation and future interest in the stock.

➤ S&P OTC 250 INDEX Like the NASDAQ index, Standard & Poor's indicates the overall direction of secondary issues. It is especially valuable to compare it to the S&P 500. Since the beginning of 1988, many OTC stocks have recovered from their lows of October–November 1987.

➤ SHADOW STOCK INDEX In January 1986 the American Association of Individual Investors, a nonprofit educational organization, introduced this index, which covers less well-known stocks. The market value of a company's outstanding stock must fall between $20 million and $100 million to qualify for inclusion. This means that all companies in the Shadow Stock Index have some sort of track record. Most trade OTC.

THE PINK SHEETS

This is also fertile territory for investors, but only for speculators, since these stocks are not listed on the NASDAQ electronic system, usually because of limited capitalization or the small number of shares outstanding. They are listed in *The Pink Sheets*, published daily by the National Daily Quotation Service. They give bid and asked prices for more than 11,000 OTC stocks. *The Pink Sheets* tells your broker who makes a market in the stock, although the prices are negotiable. These small and thinly traded companies offer high growth potential, which of course means high risk.

$ HINT: Look for local companies or firms that make products you like; chances are they will be trading over the counter.

☐ CAUTION: There are two key problems with pink sheet stocks: (1) The spreads between the bid and asked prices can be significant on thinly traded stocks, and (2) illiquidity is common.

REQUIREMENTS FOR LISTING OF STOCKS ON EXCHANGES

NEW YORK STOCK EXCHANGE
- Pretax income: $2.5 million for most recent year and $2.0 million for each of 2 preceding years
- Number of shareholders of 100 shares or more: 2,000
- Number of publicly held shares: 1.1 million
- Value of shares outstanding: $18 million

AMERICAN STOCK EXCHANGE
- Pretax income: $750,000 for previous year or 2 out of the last 3 years
- Number of shareholders: 800 (if 500,000 shares outstanding) or 400 (if 1 million shares outstanding)
- Value of shares outstanding: $3 million

NATIONAL ASSOCIATION OF SECURITIES DEALERS AUTOMATED QUOTATION SYSTEM (OVER THE COUNTER)
- Total assets: $4 million
- Number of shareholders: 300
- Number of publicly held shares: 100,000
- Stockholders' equity: $2 million

EIGHT OTC STOCKS FOR CONSIDERATION

- **Adobe Systems (ADBE)** Graphic software selling well
- **Amgen Inc. (AMGN)** Leading biotech products
- **Apple Computer (AAPL)** Strong demand for all its notebook computers
- **Comcast Corp. "A" (CMCSA)** Leading cable TV company
- **Microsoft (MSFT)** Windows fueling strong growth
- **Nordstrom Inc. (NOBE)** Specialty retailer popular with customers
- **QVC Network (QVCN)** TV shopping is explosive new field
- **Western Publishing (WPGI)** Publishes popular children's books

OVER-THE-COUNTER STOCKS

PROS
↑ In an OTC mutual fund, professional management, diversification, liquidity, possibility of switching into other funds within the same family
↑ Prices often low
↑ Potential capital appreciation
CONS
↓ May be thinly traded
↓ Can be difficult to sell when negative news appears
↓ Research difficult to find, sometimes nonexistent
↓ Losses can be large
↓ Value of fund shares can decline

$ HINT: Don't buy a pink sheet stock unless you can find adequate information on the company from reliable sources. Even then, stick to the well-researched OTC stocks that trade frequently.

SMALL CAP STOCKS

Another area that is often overlooked by investors is small cap stocks, those with a limited number of shares outstanding and small capitalization. (Capitalization is determined by multiplying the number of shares by the current market value of one share.) These are discussed in Chapter 23.

OTC MUTUAL FUNDS

FUND	TOTAL RETURN JANUARY 1 TO JUNE 30, 1993
Fidelity OTC Portfolio (1-800-544-8888)	−0.12%
T. Rowe Price OTC (1-800-638-5660)	6.05
American Capital Emerging Growth Fund (1-800-421-5666)	13.43

USING MUTUAL FUNDS

If you want a professional to make the buying and selling decisions in the OTC market, you can invest in one of several mutual funds. These funds invest in stocks of small companies. But remember, higher interest rates and inflation will hurt stocks.

Tips for selecting a fund:

- Invest only in a fund that has $100 million or less in assets. A larger fund may have to buy stocks of larger companies, or its portfolio may become too unwieldy to manage effectively.
- Portfolio turnover should be 30% per year or less.
- Check the prospectus and quarterly reports to make certain the fund is indeed investing in small companies with capitalization below $100 million.

FOR FURTHER INFORMATION

The 1993 NASDAQ Company Directory and Fact Book
NASD
Book Order Department
9513 Key West Avenue
Rockville, MD 20850
1-202-728-8000
$25

Lists all NASDAQ stocks with their symbols, their addresses, and telephone numbers.

> *Equities* (magazine)
> 145 E 49 Street, Suite 5B
> New York, NY 10017
> 1-212-832-7800
> Monthly; $36 per year

Contains studies of individual stocks.

> *Growth Stock Outlook* (newsletter)
> 4405 East-West Highway
> Bethesda, MD 20814
> 1-301-654-5205
> Twice monthly; $195 per year

Published by Charles Allmon; covers stocks with potential appreciation.

> *The OTC Profiles*
> Standard & Poor's
> 25 Broadway
> New York, NY 10004
> 1-212-208-8000; 1-800-221-5277
> $79 per year

Published quarterly; lists historical data and prices for the larger OTC companies. Check your library.

> *OTC Insight* (newsletter)
> 1600 School Street
> Moraga, CA 94556
> 1-510-376-1223
> Monthly; $295 per year

Scans data on 100 OTC stocks per month and provides sample portfolios.

> *Value Line OTC Special Situations*
> 711 Third Avenue
> New York, NY 10017
> 1-800-634-3583
> Bimonthly; $390 per year
> Trial: $39 (6 issues)

Reliable coverage of OTC and small cap stocks.

15 UTILITIES

Sometimes scorned as boring investments for widows and orphans, utility stocks deserve better press. A study by Standard & Poor's in 1992 revealed that over the last 20 years, shares of electric and gas utilities did better than the broader market. From 1982–1992, a period in which the stock market as a whole enjoyed a strong upturn, utilities again outperformed the market: the S&P Utilities returned 515% compared to 403% for the S&P 500.

Why did they do so well? During periods of high inflation, utilities passed along much of their increased operating costs to customers. And, during recessionary periods, industrial and commercial demand slowed, but not nearly as much as that for other industrial products.

The key point for you to keep in mind is that the group remains recession-resistant, since electricity, water, and gas are necessities.

However, utilities are no longer the staid, government-regulated monopolies they once were. They have been deregulated to some extent, and more deregulation is on the way. As this takes place, companies are both merging and expanding into other lines of business. This change creates the potential for greater profit and greater risk. Two electric utility companies, in fact, have gone bankrupt, and shareholders of several others have seen their stocks plummet. The Energy Policy Act that went into effect in October 1992 is expected to have some impact on utilities. The law requires power companies to give independent power producers access to their transmission lines. This means that industrial customers can shop around for the best price on electricity, and then have the local utility company deliver it to their factories and office buildings. This creates increased competition among utilities and increased risk for you as an investor.

Nevertheless, there are a number of well-managed, low-cost companies with long records of dividend growth. (See box, page 168.)

BRIGHT LIGHTS

There are a number of bright lights on the horizon.

- Construction programs have generally ended, which means stronger balance sheets.
- Many utilities are diversifying into nonutility areas, such as TECO Energy's move into shipping and transportation.
- Cash flows are up, thus enabling a number of companies to boost dividends, reduce high-cost debt, repurchase shares, or diversify.
- The group remains recession-resistant, since electricity, water, and gas are necessities. That means that in a recession, these stocks should suffer far less than most.

GUIDELINES FOR SELECTION

In the past, utility stocks moved pretty much as a group, but today the difference between the best and the poorest has widened and skepticism should be your guiding principle. When making a utility selection you should ask:

- How good is management?
- Is the dividend safe?
- What is the nuclear situation?
- What is the regulatory environment?
- What is the reserve margin? (Reserve margin is power capacity above peak-load usage; if it is especially high, the company may have unused plants and high costs. The industrywide average is around 25%.)

NINE UTILITIES WITH SECURE DIVIDENDS

COMPANY	SYMBOL	YIELD
Allegheny Power	AYP	6.2%
Brooklyn Union Gas	BU	5.3
Connecticut Natural Gas	CNG	4.8
Delmarva Power	DEW	6.7
FPL Group	FPL	6.5
Kansas City P&L	KLT	5.9
Orange & Rockland	ORU	5.4
Public Service Enterprises	PEG	6.3
Union Electric	UEP	5.9

SOURCE: Quotron, May 1993.

Moreover:

- Don't select a utility stock solely on the basis of its yield. (A high return often reflects Wall Street uncertainty about the safety of the dividend.)
- Do select stocks that have expectations for higher earnings and growth rates.
- If all other things are equal, select a utility that has a dividend reinvestment plan. You will save on commissions.
- Diversify. Buy utilities from several states, to avoid any one state's unfavorable regulatory policies.

You should also study:

- **Bond rating,** as determined by Standard & Poor's or Moody's. This is a measure of the company's financial strength.
- **Regulatory climate.** The attitude of state authorities toward permitting the utility to earn an adequate rate of return is an important factor.
- **Return on equity.** This is that basic standard of quality—the ability of management to make money with your money. It is often a reflection of the state authorities, who may or may not permit an adequate rate of return.
- **Main fuel.** This is a key criterion for many analysts. Utilities that use water (hydroelectric plants) have no cost worries.

Note: With utilities, state laws often prescribe actions that in other industries would be management's prerogative.

$ HINT: Look for utilities with strong internal cash flow that have completed construction programs.

NATURAL GAS STOCKS

Although these stocks have decent dividends, they are essentially a long-term growth investment. For many years, gas, a clean-burning fuel, has been thought to be the fuel of the future. Yet an oversupply and many warm winters have kept these stocks from rising much in price.

The Clinton administration is placing great emphasis on a clean environment, so the outlook for natural gas stocks is more positive than in the past. In fact, natural gas is becoming the politically correct fuel of choice, and the government is converting many of its vehicles to natural gas or other alternative fuels and many electric utilities view natural gas as a substitute for coal, especially for meeting the tighter emission standards. Some utilities are converting their out-of-date nuclear plants to use natural gas. The cogeneration market—where gas is used as an energy source for heating and electricity generation in commercial and industrial buildings—is seen as a positive trend for this industry.

Because many natural gas companies also own oil and gas exploration and production divisions, they have an added investment angle. Among the stocks to watch are:

- Apache
- Atlanta Gas Light
- Brooklyn Union Gas
- Coastal Corp.
- Enron
- Maxus Energy
- MCN Corp.
- Nicor Inc.
- Peoples Energy
- Washington Energy
- Williams Co.

TELEPHONE COMPANIES

This group is also suggested for long-term growth and appreciation, although some pay decent dividends. The Baby Bell holding companies, although still regulated, are also expanding into cellular, cable TV, and joint ventures in other countries. One of the strongest (at press time), US West, is doing extensive business in Great Britain and other countries.

THE BELL COMPANIES

As a result of the now historical AT&T breakup, there are eight different Bell companies. Shares of all are traded on the NYSE. Yields range from 6.2% to 3.6%.

Phone company stocks have changed little over the past year—some are slightly lower in price—yet they are much higher than after the 1987 crash.

SYMBOL	COMPANY	PRICE (MAY 1993)	P/E RATIO	YIELD
T	AT&T	$56	19	2.4%
AIT	Ameritech	76	16	4.8
BEL	Bell Atlantic	51	16	5.2
BLS	Bell South	53	16	5.2
NYN	NYNEX	84	13	5.6
PAC	Pacific Telesis	46	17	4.7
SBC	Southwest Bell	77	17	3.9
USW	U.S. West	42	15	5.1

SOURCE: Quotron, May 1993.

UTILITY MUTUAL FUNDS

If you don't want to select individual utilities, there are a number of mutual funds that invest in these stocks. As a group the funds have had negative returns only in 1987 and in 1990, both years when there were periods of rising long-term interest rates. They should continue to perform well, assuming inflation doesn't drive interest rates back up and through the roof. Historically, these funds perform best when long-term interest rates are declining, or at least stable.

The funds are not at all alike, so it is important that you read the prospectus before investing. For example, Putnam Utilities Growth & Income has 50% of its assets in utility bonds, while a more growth oriented fund owns natural gas and telephone issues whose growth potentially is generally greater than that of electric utilities. Some funds invest in foreign utilities and high yielding equities—IDS Utilities Income and Prudential Utility, for example. Frankling Utilities, the oldest utility fund, prefers electric utilities located in growth regions with favorable regulatory environments. Prudential Utility Fund, the largest fund in the group, invests in riskier special situation electrics.

$ HINT: The more diversified the fund's portfolio, the lower its interest rate sensitivity.

Some funds have two types of shares: Class A and Class B. Class A has a front-end load, while Class B usually has a 1% per annum 12b-1 fee to defray marketing expenses and levy a deferred sales charge if you redeem your shares within a certain number of years, often 5 or 6. If you know you're going to hold your shares 5 or 6 years, you're better off with the Class A shares so you can avoid the ongoing 12b-1 charges.

If you are retired you may want a fund that pays out dividends on a monthly basis.

SUGGESTED UTILITY FUNDS

FUND	YIELD (JULY 1993)	TELEPHONE
Colonial Utilities: A	4.57%	1-800-345-6611
Fidelity Utilities Income	3.88	1-800-544-8888
Franklin Utilities	5.02	1-800-342-5236
IDS Utilities Income	4.63	1-800-328-8300
Stratton Monthly Dividend	6.22	1-800-634-5726
Vanguard Utilities Income	4.91	1-800-662-7447

BUYING STOCK DIRECTLY

A number of utility companies allow customers to buy stock directly in the company, without a broker. Among those that do are:

- Centerior Energy
- Central Maine Power
- Dominion Resources
- Idaho Power
- Nevada Power
- San Diego Gas & Electric
- Central Hudson Gas & Electric
- Central Vermont Public Service
- Hawaiian Electric Industries
- Minnesota Power
- Philadelphia Electric
- Union Electric
- Wisconsin Energy

(*Note:* Call the investor relations department of your local utility company to see if you can purchase shares directly.)

WATER COMPANIES

Telephone and electric companies have always been in the spotlight, hogging center stage in the utility industry. Yet stocks of public water companies also deserve a place in the limelight. This group, which has low institutional ownership, over the years has turned in a solid performance.

- It provides a commodity everyone needs.
- It has no competition; there is no alternative to water.
- It has no nuclear exposure.
- Many water companies are profitably diversified.

Although there are an estimated 65,000 water companies in the United States, about 85% are municipally owned and regulated by city governments. That leaves about 350 investor-owned operations, and of these, only 17 have above $15 million in total capital. American Water Works is the largest. It serves over 1.4 million customers in 500 communities in 20 states. Its largest customer is Monsanto.

☐ CAUTION: If you decide to invest in a water company, keep in mind that rate increases are determined by area regulatory bodies and that various local situations, including the weather and the economy, have a major effect on earnings. Residential customers dominate the industry, and companies therefore tend to benefit from hot weather spells when Americans use more water. Companies must continually meet the water standards set by the Environmental Protection Agency.

The larger, better-known water firms are listed in the table below. You may also want to investigate your local water company—find out if it is publicly traded—but read the last two annual reports and the current quarterlies before purchasing shares.

UTILITY BONDS

When RJR Nabisco's CEO told the investment world that he planned to take his company private by floating new debt, the value of Nabisco's bonds immediately fell by nearly 20%. Suddenly investors in other high-grade corporate bonds were fearful, wondering if their bonds would do the same if a takeover or leveraged buyout came their way.

Certain bonds, however, are relatively free

WATER COMPANIES

COMPANY	EXCHANGE: SYMBOL	PRICE	YIELD
American Water Works	NYSE: AWK	$27	3.7%
Citizens Utilities	NYSE: CZU	24	0.8
Consumers Water	OTC: CONW	19	6.0
Philadelphia Suburban	NYSE: PSC	18	5.8
Southern California Water	OTC: SWTR	47	5.1
United Water Resources	NYSE: UWR	15	6.1

SOURCE: Quotron, May 1993.

SELECTED UTILITY BONDS

■ Michigan Bell Tel	7%	2012	102	AAA
■ NJ Bell Tel	7¼	2011	102	AAA
■ Georgia Power	7½	2002	103	BBB+
■ Bell South Telcom	7⅞	2032	105	AAA

(*Note:* the highest yield is offered by the bond with the longest maturity date.)

from takeover troubles: Treasury issues, for example, are not vulnerable to an LBO since it's unlikely anyone will try to take over the Treasury! Another fairly safe haven lies in high-rated utility bonds, whose yields tend to be slightly above those of Treasuries. Most utility bonds have high ratings because these corporations provide continually needed services and are recession-resistant. Bondholders receive interest semiannually, and as we go to press yields on new issues ranged from 6½% to 8%.

☐ CAUTION: Buy only bonds rated A or above and check the call feature. Most utilities have only 5-year call protection, whereas Treasuries are essentially noncallable. Avoid bonds of companies with nuclear or regulatory problems.

Many high-yielding utility bonds have special, early redemption clauses built into their issues. These call provisions permit a utility to buy back its bonds at face value or even a bit higher, but more often than not at prices below the current market. Utility companies are allowed to use these special "calls" to cut expenses by retiring high-yield or high-coupon bonds.

16 OPTIONS

A great many Americans have come to realize that stocks are a good way to achieve long-term total returns. Yet these same investors tend to avoid options because they feel they are too risky. Sometimes that's true. Options can be a fast-moving game, yet when used correctly, they can actually increase the profit on stocks you already own and/or reduce the potential for losses in a declining market. They also enable you to take advantage of the concept of leverage, for, with a small amount of money, you can control a large investment. However, you must be disciplined and adept to make options work.

$ HINT: Before actually allocating money to trading options, test several hypothetical examples on paper—follow them in the newspaper to see how options really work. Once you have done this learning exercise you are ready to take the plunge and spend real money.

Once you feel ready to trade, talk to your broker. Depending upon the brokerage firm, you may be asked for your net worth statement, or perhaps to open a margin account (see Chapter 25). And remember, to be successful with options you must be prepared to devote time watching the calendar.

WHAT ARE OPTIONS?

Options are the contractual right, but not the obligation, to buy or to sell something. A *put* is the right to sell, whereas a *call* is the right to buy. In a way options are a cross between trading in stocks and trading in commodities. They enable you to control a relatively large amount of stock with a relatively small amount of capital for a fixed period of time. To be more specific: An option represents the *right,* but not the obligation, to buy or sell a specific stock at a specific price, called the *strike* price for a

specified time. You do not need to own the stock to buy an option on it.

If, for example, you believe a stock will go up in price in the future, you can buy a call on it. This enables you to purchase 100 shares near its current price. On the other hand, if you have reason to believe the stock will fall in price, you can buy a put on that stock, which gives you the right to sell 100 shares near its current price. (You may also sell puts and calls.)

How long a time do options run? Most options are available for 3, 6, or 9 month periods, or remaining fractions thereof. (As their expiration date approaches, they may have as little as one or two weeks or days.)

However, in a small number of stocks there are options that last a year or two years. These long-term options are known as LEAPS, which stands for long-term equity appreciation security. All the same rules apply to LEAPS as to regular options, but the premiums you must pay for such extended times are higher. LEAPS are quoted in a separate section of the *Wall Street Journal* and financial press.

Example: AT&T LEAP expiring in January 1995, strike price $60, sold on the Chicago Board of Options, with the option at $3⅞ and the stock at $54 in the spring of 1993. (See page 187 for details on LEAPS.)

Now let's look at a very simple example of how options work. You bought a 3-month call on IBM at $100 when the stock was selling at $90. The option's selling price or premium was $300 (or $3 per share). One month later, IBM's shares move up to $110. You now have two choices (or options, hence the name of this vehicle): 1) you can exercise your option and buy the IBM shares at $100/share; or, 2) you can sell your call, which is now worth approximately $1,000, based on the price of IBM plus whatever the option is now worth—probably around $1,000. (When a stock rises in price, as in this example, the premium ($3) tends to diminish.)

You may wonder, Why not buy the 100 shares of IBM to begin with? It would have moved from $90 to $110 and you would have had a nice profit. First of all, you would have had to invest much more money—$9,000 rather than just $300. Had the stock dropped in price, you would have lost much more than you would with the option.

Options trade on the Chicago Board of Options Exchange, the American Stock Exchange, the Philadelphia Stock Exchange, the Pacific Stock Exchange, and the New York Stock Exchange. You may also buy and sell puts and calls on the major stock market indexes and on foreign currencies.

TERMS USED IN OPTION TRADING

Before moving on to some more sophisticated examples and techniques, let's review the terms involved.

- At the money: when a strike price is exactly the same as the price of the underlying stock
- Call: the right but not the obligation, to buy a stock at a specified price
- Closing transaction: buying or selling an option to close a previously held position
- Covered option: an option written against shares of a stock you already own. This is the most popular and a fairly conservative option strategy, letting you get a little more value out of your stock. It involves selling a call option on a stock that is already in your portfolio. The investor who buys the call then has the right to buy your shares (called the "underlying stock") at a predetermined strike price. In other words, the investor can "call" the stock away from you at a certain price. However, the investor will not exercise the call (that is, take possession of the shares) unless the stock rises above the option strike price.

When you sell a covered call option, you collect some income—the premium. If the price of the stock rises a lot, the investor will exercise the option and you then lose your stock and the ability to benefit from any further appreciation above the strike price.

☐CAUTION: This strategy works well if the stock price remains unchanged or stays under the strike price because then the option expires worthless and you've collected the premium plus any dividends.
- Diagonal spread: buying and selling options at the same time on the same stock, but with different expiration dates and difference strike prices
- Dividends and rights: As long as you own the stock, you continue to receive the dividends. That's why calls for stocks with high yields sell at lower premiums than those for companies with small payouts.

A stock dividend or stock split automatically increases the number of shares covered by the option in an exact proportion. If a right is involved (see Chapter 17), its value will be set by the first sale of rights on the day the stock sells ex-rights.
- Expiration date: options last 3, 6, or 9 months. Then they expire. The expiration date is the third Friday of the month in which it can be exercised.
- Horizontal spread: buying and selling options at the same time on a stock with the same strike price but with differing expiration dates
- In the money: an option that will make a profit if exercised
- Married put: a put on shares that you already own
- Naked option: opposite of a covered option; an option written (sold) against shares you do NOT already own
- Out of the money option: an option that will not be profitable to exercise
- Premium: an option's selling price. Premiums vary with the price of the underlying stock and its volatility.
- Put: the right to sell a stock at a specified price for a specified time
- Restricted option: This may occur when the previous day's price closed at less than 50¢ per option and the underlying stock price closed at more than 5 points *below* its strike price for calls or more than 5 points *above* its strike price for puts. Opening transactions (buying or writing calls) are prohibited unless they are covered. Closing transactions (liquidations)

are permitted. There are various exceptions, so check with your broker.

- Spread: buying and selling options on a stock at the same time in order to lock in a closing transaction and limit the risk involved
- Strike price: the price a stock must reach in order for the owner of the option to exercise the option
- alt: the price at which the option entitles its holder to buy (call) or sell (put) the underlying stock
- Vertical spread: buying and selling options on the same security with the same expiration dates but different strike prices

Note: Commissions: These vary with the number of contracts traded: For a single call, the maximum is often $25; for 10 calls, about $4 each. As a guideline, make your calculations, in multiple units, at $14 per contract, less if you use a discount broker. Ask your broker his rates *prior* to trading.

You may be able to save on commissions when you write calls for a premium of less than 1 ($100). A call traded at $15/16$ ($93.75) will cost $8.39 compared with $25 for one priced at 1 or higher.

LEAPS

Here's a leap you may not want to take. Long-Term Equity Anticipation Securities (LEAPS) are put and call options that expire in 2 or 3 years instead of the conventional 8 months for equity options. They are offered on about 100 large-cap stocks, on the S&P 500 and the S&P 100 indexes. About half of them trade on the CBOE, the rest on the Amex and Pacific stock exchanges. Each LEAPS has puts and calls on the underlying stock with at least three strike prices: in-the-money, at-the-money, and out-of-the money. At their start, the out-of-the-money strikes are approximately 20% to 25% away from the stock's market value. Initial prices tend to be under $10.

Let's look at how they work. This example is supplied by Standard & Poor's: You have a gain in Microsoft, selling at $84. You write a LEAPS call expiring in January 1995 with a strike price of $95. That means the option is 11 points "out of the money" or selling above the current market price. The call represents 100

shares, so you wind up with $1,300 for each. The buyer now can buy Microsoft shares from you at $95/share by January 1995.

Writing this call merely provides a cushion; it does not guarantee a profit. If the stock rises above $95 by the expiration date, the buyer will exercise the option and take your stock. At any price between $95 and $71, you will have a paper gain because of the $1,300 received for the call. If the stock falls, it can reach $71 before you have a paper loss.

Or you can buy a LEAPS put. Let's say you bought AT&T stock at $38¾. It's now March and the stock is at $58¾. You could buy a January put with a price strike of 60 for 5. Owning the put gives you the right to sell the stock at 60, which guarantees you an out price of at least $55. If AT&T goes to $61, the put goes to zero, but you can then sell your shares for a put price of $56. In any case, you will always get at least $55, which in this example would lock in 16¼ points or 81% of your $20 paper profit.

For more on the topic, read: *LEAPS: What They Are and How to Use Them* by Harrison Roth.

HOW PREMIUMS WORK

The cost of the option is quoted in multiples of $1/16$ for options priced below $3, ⅛ for those priced higher. To determine the percentage of

RELATIVE PREMIUMS
As Percent of Price of Underlying Common Stock When Common Is at Exercise Price

MONTHS TO EXPIRATION	LOW	AVERAGE	HIGH
1	1.8–2.6	3.5–4.4	5.2–6.1
2	2.6–3.9	5.2–6.6	7.8–9.2
3	3.3–5.0	6.7–8.3	10.0–11.7
4	3.9–5.9	7.9–9.8	11.8–13.8
5	4.5–6.8	9.0–11.2	13.5–15.8
6	5.0–7.5	10.0–12.5	15.0–17.5
7	5.5–8.2	10.9–13.7	16.4–19.2
8	5.9–8.9	11.8–14.8	17.7–20.6
9	6.4–9.5	12.7–15.9	19.0–22.2

HOW OPTIONS ARE QUOTED

NAME, EXPIRATION DATE, AND PRICE	SALES	HIGH	WEEK'S LOW	LAST	NET CHG.
EFG Apr30	1,317	$4^3/_4$	$2^3/_4$	$3^1/_8$	$-^1/_8$
EFG Apr30 p	996	$^9/_{16}$	$^1/_4$	$^3/_8$	$-^1/_{16}$
EFG Apr35	3,872	$1^1/_4$	$^3/_8$	$^1/_2$	$-^3/_{16}$
EFG Apr35 p	1,422	$3^1/_8$	$1^5/_8$	$2^{15}/_{16}$	$+^5/_{16}$
EFG Apr40	1,526	$^3/_{16}$	$^1/_{16}$	$^1/_8$	$-^1/_{16}$
EFG Apr40 p	2,219	$7^7/_8$	$5^7/_8$	$7^7/_8$	$+^3/_8$
EFG Jul30	426	6	$4^1/_2$	$4^1/_2$	$-^1/_2$
EFG Jul30 p	805	$1^3/_8$	$^7/_8$	$1^3/_8$	$+^1/_8$
EFG Jul35	1,084	3	2	$2^1/_{16}$	$-^3/_{16}$
EFG Jul35 p	870	$3^7/_8$	$2^3/_4$	$3^7/_8$	$+^1/_4$
EFG Jul40	1,145	$1^1/_8$	$^3/_4$	$^3/_4$	$-^1/_8$
EFG Jul40 p	523	$7^3/_4$	$6^1/_8$	$7^3/_4$	$+^3/_8$
EFG Oct35	346	$4^3/_8$	$3^1/_8$	$3^1/_4$	$-^1/_4$
EFG Oct35 p	261	$4^3/_8$	$3^1/_2$	$4^3/_8$	$+^3/_8$
EFG Oct40	137	$2^1/_4$	$1^5/_8$	$1^5/_8$	$-^1/_4$
EFG Oct40 p	326	$7^7/_8$	$6^1/_2$	$7^3/_4$	$+^1/_4$

Stock price: 32⅜. Table does not show open interest because of space limitations.

premium, divide the current value of the stock into the quoted price of the option. When there's a difference between the exercise price of the option and the quoted price of the stock, add or subtract the spread.

Here's how options were quoted in the financial pages when EFG stock was at 32⅜ (see the table above):

The April 30 call prices ranged from a high of $4^3/_4$ ($475) to a low of $2^3/_4$ ($275), and a closing price of $3^1/_8$ ($312.50) for a net change from the previous week of $-^1/_8$ ($12.50). There were 1,317 sales of contracts for 100 shares each.

The second line lists the action with April 30 puts: a high of $^9/_{16}$ ($56.25), a low of $^1/_4$ ($25), and a closing price of $^3/_8$ ($37.50). For the week, the net change was $-^1/_{16}$ ($6.25). There were 996 contracts traded.

Traders looking for quick profits were pessimistic, as shown by the heavy volume in puts: 1,422 contracts for the April 35s and 2,219 for the April 40s. But there were fairly sharp differences of opinion, as the April 35 puts were up $^5/_{16}$ and the April 40s up $^3/_8$.

Investors were more optimistic and appeared to believe that EFG stock was ready for an upswing: April 40 calls, due in a few weeks, were quoted at $^1/_8$, whereas the farther-out October 40s were quoted at $1^5/_8$. Much of the spread, of course, was due to the time factor.

The prices of the options reflect temporary hopes and fears, but over a month or two they will tend to move with the underlying stock. But do not rely solely on this type of projection: Near the expiration date, the prices of options move sharply.

One key factor to keep in mind is that the premium at the outset reflects the time factor. This will fall rapidly as the expiration date nears. In the last 3 months of a call, the premium can be cut in half because of the dwindling time.

WRITING CALLS

When you write or sell calls, you start off with an immediate, sure, limited profit rather than an uncertain, potentially greater gain, which is the case for puts. The *most* you can make is the premium you receive, even if the price of the stock soars. If you write calls on stock you own, any loss of the value of the stock will be reduced by the amount of the premium. Writing covered calls (on stock you own) is a conservative use of options. You have these choices.

➤ ON-THE-MONEY CALLS These are written at an exercise price that is at or close to the current price of the stock.

Example: In December, Investor One buys 100 shares of Company A at 40 and sells a July call, at the strike price of 40, for 3 ($300). He realizes that A's stock may move above 43 in the next 7 months but is willing to accept the $3 per share income.

Investor Two is the purchaser of the call. He acquires the right to buy the stock at 40 at any time before the expiration date at the end of July. He anticipates that A's stock will move up well above 43.

Investor One will not sustain a dollar loss until the price of A goes below 37. He will probably keep the stock until its price goes above 43. At this price, the profit meter starts ticking for Investor Two, so let's see what happens if company A's stock jumps to 50. At any time before late July, Investor Two can exercise his option and pay $4,000 for stock now worth $5,000. After deducting about $400 (the $300 premium plus commissions), he will have a net profit of about $600, thus doubling his risk capital.

Investor Two will sell the call at $2 and lose $1 per call. Investor One will end up with about $375: the $300 premium plus two dividends of $50 each minus the $25 commission for the sale of the call.

➤ IN-THE-MONEY CALLS In-the-money calls are those where the exercise price is below the price of the underlying stock. This is a more aggressive technique that requires close attention but can result in excellent profits.

Example: In January, Karen buys 300 shares of Glamor Electronics Co. (GEC) at 105 ($31,500) and sells three June 100 calls at 8 each ($2,400). If GEC stock drops below 100, she keeps the premiums and the stock. If it goes to 110, she can buy back the calls at, say, 11, $1,100 ($3,300 total), to set up a loss of $900.

➤ DEEP-IN-THE-MONEY CALLS These are calls that are sold at strike prices far *below* the current quotation of the stock—8 to 20 points below. Writing them is best when the investor is dealing in large blocks of stock because of the

almost certain commissions that have to be paid when the underlying stock is called. With this approach, the best selection is a stable, high-dividend stock. Your returns may be limited, but they are likely to be sure.

The technique used by professionals is called *using leverage:* When the exercise price of the call is below that of the current value of the stock, both securities tend to move in unison. Since the options involve a smaller investment, there's a higher percentage of return and, in a down market, more protection against loss.

Example: Pistol Whip, Inc. (PWI), is selling at 97⅞. The call price at 70 two months hence is 28, so the equivalent price is 98. If PWI goes to 105, the call will keep pace and be worth 35.

If you bought 100 shares of the stock, the total cost would be about $9,800. Your ultimate profit would be about $700, close to a 7.1% return. If you bought one option, your cost would be $2,800 and you would have the same $700 profit. Your return would be about 25%.

Note: All too often, this is more theory than practice. When an option is popular, it may trade on its own and not move up or down with the price of the stock. This separate value will shift only when the expiration date is near.

When one volatile stock was at 41 in March, the November 45 call was trading at $2\frac{1}{16}$. Three weeks later, when the stock fell to $35\frac{1}{2}$ (−16%), the call edged down to 2: a 3% decline. The professionals had moved in and set their own terms.

But remember that at times the price of the call may drop further percentagewise than that of the stock.

A variation of this use of deep-in-the-money calls is to create cost by basing the return on the total income received from premiums plus dividends.

Example: In January, one professional money manager seeking extra income for his fund bought 1,000 shares of Wellknown Chemical at 39½. He then sold April 35 options for 6⅞ each, thereby reducing the price per share to 32⅝. He could count on a 45¢-per-share dividend before the exercise date.

When the call is exercised at $35 per share, the profit on the $32.625 investment will be $2.375 plus the 45-cent dividend, or $1.825 for a return of 8.66% in a four month period.

➤ OUT-OF-THE-MONEY CALLS This is when the strike price is above the market price of the underlying stock for a call or the strike price is below the market price of the underlying stock of a put.

WRITING NAKED CALLS

Some calls are sold by speculators or investors who do not own the underlying stock. This is referred to as writing a naked call. The writer is betting that the stock will either remain at its current price or decline. He receives a premium, which he pockets if the stock does not rise above the call price. But if it does, he then *must* buy back his call at a loss.

$ HINT: Don't get involved unless you maintain a substantial margin account, have considerable experience, and feel confident that the price of a stock will stay flat or decline. It's risky, because if the stock hits the strike price before or at the exercise date, you are obligated to deliver the shares you do not own.

You can, of course, cover your position by buying calls, but if the stock price soars, the loss can be substantial. At best, your premium income will be reduced.

RULES FOR WRITING OPTIONS

- Define your goal.
- Work on a programmed basis.
- Concentrate on stocks that you would like to own.
- Set a target rate of return.
- Buy the stock first.
- Write long-term calls.
- Calculate your net return.
- Keep your capital fully employed.
- Be persistent.
- Watch the timing.
- Protect your capital.
- Use margin to boost profits.
- Watch the record date of high-dividend stocks.
- Keep a separate bookkeeping system.

One technique that works well is to write two out-of-the-money calls for every 100 shares you own. This gives you double premiums. Do not go too far out, because a lot can happen in a few months.

Example: You own 300 shares of Company XYZ at 32. The 35 call, due in 4 months, is 3, but you are not convinced that the market, or the stock, will rise soon. You sell six calls, pocket $1,800 (less commissions), and hope that the stock stays under 35. If it moves to 36, you can buy back three calls for, say, 1½ ($450) and let the stock go. But if the stock jumps to 40, you're in deep trouble.

BUYING CALLS

Investors buy calls in anticipation of an increase in the price of the underlying stock. If that happens, the call may also rise in price and you can sell at a profit. Buying calls means you can invest a fraction of the cost of the stock and obtain greater leverage. You also limit your risk since the most you can lose is the cost of the option.

$ HINT: The basic problem with buying options is that calls are wasting assets. At expiration date, their values can decline to zero if the stock price moves opposite to your expectations or stays fairly stable.

Example: On February 15, ABC's common is selling at $40 per share. An October 40 call can be purchased for $500 (100 shares at $5 per share). On April 15, ABC is selling at $46 per share and the October 40 call is trading at a value of $750. The investor, anticipating an increase in the value of ABC, had purchased the call for $500 and sold it for $750, realizing a $250 profit.

Here are the ways leverage works in this situation:

	STOCK	CALL
Bought—February 15	$4,000	$500
Sold—April 15	4,600	750
Profit	600	250
Return on investment	15%	50%

In this example, the call buyer can lose no more than the $500 he paid for the October 40 call, regardless of any decline in the stock, but he can lose the entire $500 if he is wrong. However, he may be able to resell his option in time to recover some of his cost. Keep in mind that if he had purchased the stock itself for $4,000 and it had gone down in price, he would have lost more than $500 if he had sold. If he decided to hold the stock and it appreciated, he would have another opportunity to make a profit.

A put buyer does not have to resell a profitable call but can instead exercise it and take delivery of the underlying stock. He can then sell the stock for a gain or hold it for long-term appreciation.

$ IF YOU DARE: In an up market, buy calls on up stocks on either of these terms:

- Long-term, out-of-the-money options at a low premium, typically 1 or less. By diversifying with four or five promising situations, you may be lucky enough to hit it big with one and make enough to offset the small losses on the others.

- Short- or intermediate-term in-the-money or close-to-the-money options of volatile stocks: 2 months to expiration date, a stock within 5% of the strike price, and a low time premium. If the price of the premium doubles, sell half your holdings. Advice from one expert: "Never pay a premium of more than 3 for a call on a stock selling under 50 or more than 5 for one trading over 60. Both prices should include commissions."

$ HINT: The strike price of the option and the market price of the stock should change by about half as many points as the change in the stock price: For example, if a 30 option is worth 5 when the stock is at 30, it should be worth 2½ when the stock falls to 25 and worth 8 when the stock moves up to 36.

PUTS FOR PROFIT AND PROTECTION

In a broad sense, a put is the opposite of a call: It is an option to *sell* a specified number of shares (usually 100) of a specified stock at a specified price before a specified date. Puts have the same expiration months and price intervals as listed calls. The put buyer profits when the price of the underlying stock declines significantly. Then he sells the put at a profit, with the holder buying the stock at the lower current market price and selling it at the higher exercise or striking price.

The value of a put moves counter to that of the related stock: *up* when the price of the stock falls, *down* when it rises. You buy a put when you are bearish and anticipate that the market or stock will decline. Vice versa with selling puts. As with all options, a put is a wasting asset, and its value will diminish with the approach of the expiration date.

Here again, the attraction of puts is *leverage*. A few hundred dollars can acquire temporary control of thousands of dollars' worth of stock. The premiums are generally smaller than those of calls on the same stock because of lower demand, reflecting the small number of people who are pessimistic. Sharp traders take advantage of this situation, because they realize that most people tend to be optimistic about the stock market.

➤ SELLING (WRITING) PUTS   This provides instant income but involves your responsibility to buy the stock if it sells, before the expiration date, at or below the exercise price.

Example: Ed owns Xanadu stock, now selling at 53, well above the purchase price. He's hopeful that the market will keep rising but decides to write a put at 50 for 2 ($200).

As long as the stock stays above 50, the put will not be exercised and Ed keeps the $200 per contract. But once the stock falls below 50, Ed must buy the shares or buy back the put, thus cutting or eliminating the opening profit.

➤ BUYING PUTS   These can be used to protect positions and, of course, to score a quick gain. The profits come when the price of the stock falls.

Example: In March, Ann becomes skittish about the stock now trading at 47. She buys a July put at the strike price of 50 for 4 ($400). This put has an intrinsic cash value of 3, because the stock is selling 3 points below the exercise price. In effect, she is paying 1 ($100) to protect her position against a sharp market or stock decline.

If Ann's prediction is right and the price of the stock drops, the value of the put will rise: to over 7 when the stock falls to 43.

In late July, the stock price is 45, so Ann sells the put for 5 for a $100 gross profit. If the price of the stock goes below 43, her profit will be greater.

As with calls, the important factor in profitable puts is the related stock. The best candidates for both writing and buying puts are stocks that:

- *Pay small or no dividends.* You are hoping that the value of the stock will decline. Dividends tend to set a floor because of their yields.

- *Sell at high price-earnings ratios.* These are more susceptible to sharp downswings than stocks with lower multiples. A stock with a P/E of 25 runs a greater risk of a quick decline than one with a P/E of 10.

- *Are historically volatile*—with patterns of sharp, wide swings in price. Stable stocks move slowly even in an active market.

- *Are unpopular with institutions.* At the outset, when selling starts, the price drops can be welcome. Later, however, when panic selling is over, there's likely to be minimal action, because there will be few buyers.

TECHNIQUES FOR HIGH ROLLERS

➤ SPREADS A spread is the dollar difference between the buy and sell premiums. Spreads involve buying one option and selling another short, both on the same stock. If the cost of the option is greater than the proceeds of the option sold, it is a "debit." If the reverse is true, it's called a "credit." If the costs and proceeds are the same, the spread is "even money." *Your goal:* to capture at least the difference in premiums—at least ½ point between the cost of options exercisable at different dates and/or at different prices. *Make your calculations on paper first,* and make no commitments until you are sure you understand the possibilities or probabilities.

Here's an example involving POP stock priced at 50 in April. The premiums for 50 calls are 3½ for July, 4 for October.

Sell July 50 for 3½	+$350
Buy October 50 for 4	− 400
Cash outlay	− 50
Commission	− 25
Total cost	−$ 75

If POP is below 50 in July, you keep $350 and still own an option worth $250 to $300.

If POP goes up by October, the option will be worth $500 or more, so you have a profit of $850.

If POP is at 60 at the end of July, that month's option will be worth 10, so you have to buy it back at a loss of about $650 plus in-and-out costs. But the October call might be at 14, so you could sell that for a gross profit of $1,000 to offset the July loss.

If the stock falls below 46½, you will lose money unless there's a recovery by October. But with such a stable stock in a rising market, this is not likely. The key factor is the small spread, which keeps the maximum loss low.

➤ PERPENDICULAR SPREAD Also called a price or vertical spread, it is based on buying and selling options with the same exercise date but different strike prices.

Example: Easy Rider (ER) is at 101¾. The market is moving up and you are bullish. Sell 10 ER October 100s at 12¼ and buy October 90s at 16⅞. This requires an outlay of $4,625. Your maximum loss will occur if ER plunges below 90.

If it goes to 95, you will still make $375. At 100 or higher, your profit will be a welcome $5,375, a 120% return on your investment.

If the market is declining, set up a bearish spread. Psychologically, the risk is greater, so it is best to deal with lower-priced stocks, selling at, say, 24⅝.

Buy 10 October 25s at 2⅛ and sell 10 October 20s at 5⅜. This brings in $3,250 cash. Since the October 20 calls are naked, you'll need $5,000 margin (but the premiums cut this to

MAKING YOUR OWN PUT

Options are flexible and can be combined so that the stock purchases, sales, or short sales protect positions and make profits. Here's an example, by Max Ansbacher, of how to create your own put.

Assume that in late summer, your stock is at 69⅞ and the January 65 call is 9¼. You sell short 100 shares of the stock and buy the call. Here are the possibilities:

- If the stock falls to 55 by the end of January, the call will be worthless, so you lose $925. But your profit from the short sale is $1,487.50 ($6,987.50 sale; $5,500 buy-back cost) for a net profit of $562.50 (not counting commissions and fees).

- The option limits your risk of loss on the short sale even if the stock price should rise. Thus if the stock jumps to 100, an unprotected short sale would mean a loss of $3,012.50 ($10,000 purchase price minus $6,987.50 received from the short sale).

- But with a short sale of the stock and a purchase of a call, the loss will be only $437: the purchase price of 9¼ ($925) minus $488 (the spread between the stock price of 69⅞ and the exercise price of 65)—again not counting costs.

$1,750) to control nearly $50,000 worth of stock.

If the stock goes to 22, you will make $1,250. At 20 or below, your profit is $3,250 for a 180% return. With perpendicular spreads, you know results at any one time. With horizontal spreads, there's the added risk of time.

➤ STRADDLE A straddle is a double option, combining a call and a put on the same stock, both at the same price and for the same length of time. Either or both sides of a straddle may be exercised at any time during the life of the option—for a high premium. Straddles are profitable when you are convinced that a stock will make a dramatic move but are uncertain whether the trend will be up or down.

Traditionally, most speculators use straddles in a bull market against a long position. If the stock moves up, the call side will be exercised and the put will expire unexercised. This is more profitable than writing calls, because the straddle premiums are substantially higher than those of straight calls.

But this can be costly in a down market. If the underlying stock goes down, there's a double loss: in the call and in the put. Therefore, when a straddle is sold against a long position, the straddle premium received must, in effect, protect 200 shares.

In a bear market, it is often wise to sell straddles against a short position. The odds are better.

Here's how one self-styled trader did it:

"In January, QRS stock was at 100. This was close to the last year's high, and since the stock had bounced as low as 65, I felt the best straddle was short term, so I picked a February expiration date. Simultaneously, I bought a call and a put, both at 100: 5 ($500) for the call and 4 ($400) for the put. With commissions (for buying and selling) of about $100, my exposure was $1,000.

"To make money, QRS had to rise above 110 or fall below 90. I guessed right. The stock's uptrend continued to 112. I sold the call for $1,300 and was lucky to get rid of the put at $50: profit—$350 in one month!

"I would do OK if the stock fell to 88. Then the call would be worth ½ but the put would bring at least $1,200, so I end up with about $250.

"The risk was that the stock's price would hold around 100. This would mean an almost total loss. But from experience I know that I'll lose on about 25% of my straddles, so I have to shoot for a high return on the other deals."

➤ STRIP A strip is a triple option: two puts and one call on the same stock with a single option period and striking price. A strip writer expects the stock to fall in the short term and rise over the long term. He offers to sell 100 shares that he owns above the market price or take 200 shares below the market. The premium is higher than for a straddle.

➤ STRAP This is also a triple option: two calls and one put on the same stock. The writer gets top premium—bullish over the long term but more negative than the strip seller on short-term prospects.

➤ INSURANCE To protect a profit, buy a put on stock you own. *Example:* Your stock has soared from 30 to 60, so you expect a setback. You buy a short-term put, at 60, for $400. If the stock dips to 50, the put will be worth 10 ($1,000), so you sell for a profit of $600 and still own the stock. If the stock keeps moving up to 70, the put expires worthless. You lose $400, but you have a paper profit of $1,000 on the stock, so you are $600 ahead.

➤ LOCK IN CAPITAL GAINS The same technique can be used to lock in a capital gain. By buying the put at 60 for $400, you reduce the stock value to 56. If it falls to 50, you sell the stock at the exercise price of 60 for $6,000. Deduct the $400 premium from the $3,000 profit (from cost of 30) and you still have $2,600. That's $600 more than if you had held the stock until its price fell to 50.

FOR FURTHER INFORMATION

Kenneth H. Shaleen, *Technical Analysis & Options Strategies* (Chicago: Probus Publishing Co., 1992).

Options Clearing Corporation
440 South LaSalle Street
Chicago, IL 60605
1-800-537-4258

Has a number of free brochures for the public. Call for a list.

American Stock Exchange
Derivative Securities Dept
86 Trinity Place
New York, NY 10006
1-800-THE-AMEX

Has general information brochures and "strategy sheets" describing in fairly easy, but detailed terms, how to make money with options.

17 STOCK RIGHTS AND WARRANTS

STOCK RIGHTS

Stock rights are a special type of option that permits current shareholders to buy more corporate securities, usually common stock, ahead of the public, without commissions or fees, and typically at a discount of 5% to 10%.

Most rights allow shareholders to buy new shares on the basis of the number of shares of common already held; therefore, two or more rights are often required to buy one new share. The price, given in the prospectus, is called the exercise or subscription price. It is always below the current market price.

Rights are a convenient way for corporations to raise additional capital at a modest cost. In a sense, they are a reward to shareholders. They are often used by utilities eager to issue more common stock to balance their heavy debt obligations. The discount makes it possible for investors (who obviously have confidence in the company) to acquire additional shares at a bargain price or to pick up a few extra dollars by selling the rights in the open market. But rights are worthwhile only when the additional money raised by the company can be expected to generate extra profits and eventually lead to higher dividends on the additional shares. This is an important aspect of judging rights, because essentially they represent a dilution of your ownership in the company.

To be eligible for rights, you must own the common stock on a stated date. Most offerings must be exercised within a short time, usually less than 30 days, so watch your mail, and if the shares are held by your broker, be doubly alert. Failure to take advantage of this opportunity is foolish and can be costly—causing loss of the actual value of the rights.

Rights have an intrinsic value, but they are also speculative because of the high leverage they offer: A 10% rise in the price of the stock can mean as much as a 30% jump in the value of the right. Or vice versa on the loss side.

Let's assume that the stock is trading at $28 per share, that shareholders get one right for every 5 shares, and that each right entitles the holder to buy 1 new share at $25 each.

$$VR = \frac{MP - EP}{NR + 1}$$

where   VR = value of right
MP = stock's market price
EP = exercise price
NR = number of rights needed to buy one share

To calculate the value of one right *before* the ex-date, add 1 to the number of rights:

$$VR = \frac{28 - 25}{5 + 1} = \frac{3}{6} = 0.50$$

Thus each right is worth 50¢, and the stock at this time is worth that much more to investors who exercise their rights.

After the stock has gone ex-right, there'll be no built-in bonus for the stock, and the right will sell at its own value, or possibly higher, if the price of the stock advances, lower if it declines.

ADVANTAGES TO SHARE-HOLDERS

- **Maintenance of ownership position.** If you like a company well enough to continue as a shareholder, pick up the rights. Historically, 80% of stocks bought with rights have outperformed the market in the year following the issue. That's logical; management was optimistic.

HOW RIGHTS ARE QUOTED

52 WEEKS					WEEK'S	
HIGH	LOW	STOCK	SALES 100s	YIELD	HIGH	LOW
68	42	XYZ Corp.	132	3.7	64	62¼
1	⅜	XYZ Corp. rts	27		⅞	½

- **Bargain price.** When Southwestern Public Service issued 29.2 million rights, the offer permitted shareholders to buy one additional common share at $10.95 for each 10 shares already held. At the time, the stock was trading at $11.50, so the new shares were available at a 4.8% discount. If you owned 1,000 shares, you could save about $55 on the deal, because there were no transaction costs.
- **Profits from rights themselves.** If you do not want to acquire more stock, you can sell the rights in the open market: through your broker or through a bank designated by the company. With Southwestern, each right was worth 4⅝¢ ($4.625 for each 100 rights).
- **Trading rights.** You can buy rights either to exercise or to speculate. Trading in rights starts as soon as the offer is announced. For a while, the prices of both the basic stock and the rights are quoted— the latter on a "when issued" (wi) basis, as shown with XYZ Corp. in the table. As a rule, it's best to buy rights soon after they are listed in the financial press; it's best to sell a day or two before the lapse date.

SPECIAL BENEFITS

There are two other investment advantages with rights. These give you the opportunity to purchase:

1 The stock with a very low margin in a special subscription account (SSA). This is a margin account set up to use the rights to buy extra stock within 90 days after the rights issue. To open an SSA, deposit rights—your own or purchased—with your broker.

In addition to no commission for exercising that purchase, the *advantages* are a 25% margin, compared with 50% for stocks, and a year to pay if you come up with 25% of the balance each quarter.

Example: You have rights to buy Kwick Kick common, selling at 63, for 56 on the basis of 1 new share for 10 old shares. You acquire 100 rights, so you need $5,600 to complete the purchase. You can borrow up to 75% ($4,200), so you can make the deal with only $1,400 in cash or collateral. Every 3 months you must reduce the outstanding balance by 25%.

The *disadvantages* of SSA are that the price of the stock may decline, so you will have to come up with more margin, and you cannot draw cash dividends or use the securities for collateral as long as they are in this special account.

Neither the receipt nor the exercise of the right results in taxable income to the stockholder. But you will have to pay taxes on ultimate profits when the stock is sold.

2 Oversubscription privileges. Some shareholders will not exercise their rights, so after the expiration date, you can buy these rights, usually on the basis of your original allotment. You must indicate your wish to participate in the oversubscription early, preferably when you send in your check for the new shares.

$ HINT: Rights offerings often put downward pressure on the price of the stock and therefore represent a good investment opportunity.

WARRANTS

Warrants, unlike options, are issued by the corporation typically with new issues, bonds, or preferred stock. They are traded on the exchanges.

A warrant is an option to buy a stated number of shares of a related security (usually common stock) at a stipulated price during a specified period (5, 10, 20 years, or, occasionally, perpetually). The price at which the warrant can be exercised is fixed above the current market price of the stock at the time the warrant is issued. Thus when the common stock is at 10, the warrant might entitle the holder to buy 1 share at 15. (This differs from a right, where the subscription price is usually lower than the current market value of the stock and the time period is typically several weeks.)

Since the two securities tend to move somewhat in parallel, an advance in the price creates a higher percentage gain for the warrant than for the stock.

Example: Let's say that the warrant to buy 1 share at 15 sells at 1 when the stock is at 10. If the stock soars to 20 (100% gain), the price of the warrant will go up to at least 5 (400% gain).

But the downside risk of the warrant can be greater than that of the stock. If the stock drops to 5, that's a 50% loss. The warrant, depending on its life span, might fall to ⅛, an 88% decline.

A warrant is basically a call on a stock. It has no voting rights, pays no dividends, and has no claim on the assets of the corporation. Warrants trade on the exchanges and are usually registered in the owner's name. Some warrants are issued in certificate form although most are not. On expiration date, a warrant loses all its trading value.

The value of a warrant reflects hope: that the price of the stock will rise above the exercise price. When the stock trades *below* that call price, the warrant has only speculative value: With the stock at 19 and the exercise price at 20, the warrant is theoretically worthless. But it will actually trade at a price that reflects the prospectus of the company and the life of the warrant. When the price of the stock rises above the specified exercise price, the warrant acquires a tangible value, which is usually inflated by speculation plus a premium, because it is a lower-priced way of playing the common stock. However, the closer a warrant gets to its expiration date, the smaller the premium it commands. Conversely, the longer the life of the warrant, the higher the premium if there is real

hope that the price of the stock will rise. After expiration, the warrant is worthless.

💲HINT: The main advantage warrants have over options is that they run for much longer. The longest an option lasts is 9 months. Warrants, however, run for years and some in perpetuity, which gives the investor a chance to speculate on a company over the long term at a relatively low cost. This time frame makes warrants less risky than options.

CALCULATING THE VALUE OF A WARRANT

The speculative value of a warrant is greatest when the warrant price is below the exercise price. If the stock moves up, the price of the warrant can jump fast. The table below shows guidelines set by warrant expert S. L. Pendergast for the maximum premium to pay. For example, when the stock price is at the exercise price (100%), pay at most 41% of the exercise price. Thus with a stock at the exercise price of 30, the maximum price to pay for a warrant (on a one-for-one basis) would be about 12. In most cases, better profits will come when the warrant is bought at a lower price.

An actual example is Atlas Corp. warrants that are perpetual; that is, they do not expire. They trade on the ASE at $3, with an exercise price of $15.625. The market price of the stock, as of July 1993, was $4½.

$$7 \div 15.625 = 46\%$$

$$3 \div 15.625 = 19\%$$

These percentages fall outside the acceptable buying range using the table below.

MAXIMUM PREMIUM TO PAY

STOCK PRICE AS PERCENT OF EXERCISE PRICE	WARRANT PRICE AS PERCENT OF EXERCISE PRICE
80	28
90	34
100	41
110	46

HOW TO SELECT PROFITABLE WARRANTS

Warrants are generally best in bull markets, especially during periods of great enthusiasm. Their low prices attract speculators who trade for quick gains. At all times, however, use these checkpoints:

➤ BUY ONLY WARRANTS OF A COMMON STOCK THAT YOU WOULD BUY ANYWAY If the common stock does not go up, there's little chance that the warrant's price will advance.

The best profits come from warrants associated with companies that have potential for strong upward swings due to sharp earnings improvement, a prospective takeover, newsmaking products or services, etc. It also helps if they are temporarily popular.

In most cases, the warrants for fast-rising stocks, even at a high premium, will outperform seemingly cheap warrants for issues that are falling.

At the outset, stick with warrants of fair-to-good corporations whose stocks are listed on major exchanges. They have broad markets.

When you feel more confident, seek out special situations, especially warrants of small, growing firms. Many of these "new" companies rely on warrants in their financing. Their actual or anticipated growth can boost the price of their warrants rapidly.

But be wary of warrants where the related stock is limited or closely controlled. If someone decides to dump a block of stock, the values can fall fast.

➤ BUY WARRANTS WHEN THEY ARE SELLING AT LOW PRICES The percentages are with you when there's an upward move, and with minimal costs the downside risks are small. But watch out for "superbargains," because commissions will eat up most of the gains.

Also watch their values and be cautious when their prices move to more than 20% of their exercise figure.

➤ WATCH THE EXPIRATION OR CHANGE DATE After expiration, the warrant has no value. If you're conservative, stay away from warrants with a life span of less than 4 years. When you know what you are doing, short-life warrants can bring quick profits if you are smart and lucky. But be careful. You could end up with worthless paper.

SOME POPULAR WARRANTS

COMPANY	EXERCISE PRICE TERMS	RECENT PRICE OF COMMON STOCK	RECENT PRICE OF WARRANT
ADT Ltd.	$10	$ 9	$1.50
Atlas Corp.	15.625	3.50	1.25
Beta Well	2.50	21	8.00*
Mercury Air	3.50	2.75	0.625

* For ½ share of common stock

SOURCE: Standard & Poor's *Stock Guide,* May 1993.

➤ AVOID DILUTION If there's a stock split or stock dividend, the market price of the stock will drop but the conversion price of the warrant may not change. The same caveat goes for warrants subject to call. Warrants of listed companies will generally be protected against such changes, but take nothing for granted.

Once in a while, warrants will be reorganized out of their option value. This occurs with troubled corporations taken over by tough-minded operators who are unwilling to pay for past excesses or to provide profits for speculators.

➤ SPREAD YOUR RISKS If you have sufficient capital, buy warrants in five different companies. The odds are that you may hit big on one, break even on two, and lose on the others. Your total gains may be less than if you had gambled on one warrant that proved a winner, but your losses will probably be less if you're wrong.

➤ LOOK FOR SPECIAL OPPORTUNITIES SUCH AS "USABLE" BONDS WITH WARRANTS ATTACHED Some bonds are sold along with detachable warrants. In many cases the bonds can be used at par ($1,000) in paying the exercise price. In other words, they can be used in lieu of cash to pay for the stock at the specified warrant price.

Should the bond trade at 90, a discount to par, the discounted price of the bond also discounts the exercise price of the warrant.

Except in unusual situations, all warrants should be bought to trade or sell and not to exercise. With no income, usually a long wait for appreciation, and rapid price changes, warrants almost always yield quick gains to speculators who have adequate capital and time to watch the market.

10 POINTS FOR EVALUATING WARRANTS

1 *Underlying stock price.* The higher the stock price, all other things being equal, the higher the value of the warrant.
2 *Stock volatility.* The higher the volatility of the underlying stock, the higher the value of the warrant. Volatile stocks are more likely to appreciate or depreciate substantially. A warrant, too, will benefit from appreciation.
3 *Dividend.* The higher the dividend on the underlying stock, the lower the value of the warrant. Warrant holders are not entitled to receive dividends paid to stockholders.
4 *Strike price.* The lower the exercise price, all other things being equal, the higher the value of the warrant.
5 *Time to expiration.* The longer the warrant's life, the higher the value of the warrant.
6 *Interest rates.* Higher rates tend to increase the value of warrants.
7 *Call features.* Call features shorten the life of the warrant and detract from its value.
8 *Usable bonds.* A usable bond can be used at par to pay the exercise price of a warrant. This gives a warrant added value.
9 *Ability to borrow the underlying stock.* This tends to depress the warrant's value.
10 *Takeovers.* If the company is taken over at a high price, warrants will appreciate.

NIKKEI WARRANTS

Warrants that allow investors to bet on the Japanese stock market were introduced at the start of 1990. These eight warrants, which trade on the American Stock Exchange, have at various times accounted for as much as 40% of the AMEX's daily volume.

WHERE TO FIND WARRANTS

WARRANTS ARE ISSUED:
- With bonds as a sweetener to buy them
- As part of initial public offering packages consisting of shares of common plus warrants
- In conjunction with mergers and acquisitions

WHERE TO FIND WARRANTS:
- Brokerage firm research lists
- Newspaper securities listings, where they are identified by the letters "wt"

Six of the eight are put warrants, which pay off in dollars if the Nikkei index of 225 Tokyo stocks falls below specified levels within a stated time period. The two call warrants came out in April 1990. (Put warrants represent a bet on the market dropping.) Since the eight were issued, new warrants have been brought to market by several brokerage firms. Prices of the put warrants rose 200% as the Nikkei declined 25%.

The popularity of the Nikkei warrants led Wall Street and investment bankers to issue warrant offerings tied to the London stock market, and others are expected to follow.

☐ CAUTION: Unless you have the time and expertise to follow foreign markets, this investment doesn't warrant your time and is best left to the Wall Street pros.

SELLING WARRANTS SHORT

Selling short means selling a security you do not own, borrowing it from your broker to make delivery. This is done in anticipation of a decline in price. Later you expect to buy it at a lower price and make the profit between that lower price and your original short sale.

But short selling is always tricky, and with warrants there can be other problems: (1) limited markets because of lack of speculator interest; (2) exchange regulations—e.g., the American Stock Exchange prohibits short selling of its listed warrants several months before expiration date; (3) the possibility of a "short squeeze"— the inability to buy warrants to cover your short sales as the expiration date approaches; (4) the possibility that the life of the warrants may be extended beyond the stated expiration date, advancing the date when the warrants become worthless, so a short seller may not be able to cover a position at as low a price as was anticipated.

FOR FURTHER INFORMATION

R.H.M. Survey of Warrants (newsletter)
R.H.M. Associates, Inc.
172 Forest Avenue
Glen Cove, NY 11542
1-516-759-2904
Weekly; $280 per year or $150 for 6 months

18 | NEW ISSUES

After the October 1987 crash, new issues, also known as initial public offerings (IPOs), plummeted and remained a small part of the market during the depths of the recession. As the economy began to recover in late 1992, so did the number of IPOs.

New issues continue to tempt many investors. If you're one of those, learn the facts and follow our guidelines for selecting fledgling companies to back. It is possible to make money in IPOs, but it requires far more research than most investments, as well as an understanding of the market. Norman G. Fosback, editor of *New Issues,* favors companies that have reported profits for at least 5 years and whose earnings are trending up.

If you don't buy an IPO when it's first issued, you can buy shares in the aftermarket when they trade OTC. If it's a weak market, chances are you won't pay much more, if anything; but in a hot market, expect a 20% to 25% increase in the aftermarket. If you are enamored of the issue but cannot buy at a reasonable price, follow the stock's progress carefully. Wait for the first blush to fade, and move in when it takes a tumble. Often a new company will lose its initial luster or report lower earnings, thus pushing the price down temporarily.

Learning about new issues is less difficult than you might think. A number of the larger brokerage firms publish a list of them on a regular basis, but unless you're a major client, you won't hear about them. Your broker or library may subscribe to the bible in the field, *Investment Dealer's Digest,* which lists all IPOs as they are registered with the SEC.

A good example of a successful IPO: Gaylord Entertainment Co., offered at $20.50 per share when it went public in October 1991. It was selling above $42 by July 1993. Gaylord owns

Nashville Network, an ad-supported cable TV service with country-western music, talk shows, etc. It's leading the "country craze."

THE UNDERWRITER

Your chances for success will be increased if you select IPOs from reputable investment bankers. First-class underwriters will not allow themselves to manage new issues that are of poor quality or highly speculative. Moreover, if a fledgling company runs into a need for additional financing, a first-rate banker will be ready to raise more capital. Thus the prime consideration is the reputation of the underwriters. However, this is not written in stone.

THE PROSPECTUS

Once you learn about a new issue, your first investigative step is to read a copy of the prospectus, generally available when an offering is registered with the SEC. (It's also called a "red herring" because of the red-inked warning that the contents of the report are not final.) Despite its many caveats, the prospectus will help you form a rough opinion about the company and what it may be worth. Look for:

➤ DETAILS ABOUT MANAGEMENT The success of a company is often determined by the quality of the management team. The officers and directors should have successful experience in the company and/or similar organizations; they should be fully involved in the firm and should not treat it as a part-time activity.

➤ TYPE OF BUSINESS New ventures have the best chance of success in growth areas, such as electronics, specialty retailing, and biotechnology. Software companies, environmental cleanup, waste disposal stocks, and health care are expected to do well. The risks are greatest with

201

companies in exciting but partially proven fields such as biotechnology, genetic engineering, and AIDS research. These companies are tempting but pay off only after heavy capital investments and successful R&D. Try to invest in an area you know something about or a business located near you. A good prospectus will also list some of the company's customers.

➤ FINANCIAL STRENGTH AND PROFITABILITY Apply the following criteria to the current balance sheet. Glance at the previous year's report to catch any major changes.

- Modest short-term debt and long-term obligations of less than 40% of total capital. With $40 million in assets, the debt should not be more than $16 million.
- Current ratio (of assets to liabilities) a minimum of 2:1 except under unusual, temporary conditions.
- Sales of at least $30 million to be sure that there's a market for products or services. Double-check if revenues exceed $50

million. That's the threshold for the big leagues, where competition is sure to heighten.

- High profitability: a return on equity of 20% annually for the past 3 years—with modest modifications if recent gains have been strong. This will assure similar progress in the future.

➤ EARNINGS The company should be able to service its debt. Look for the most recent P/E and compare it with P/Es of competitors, listed in the newspaper. If a P/E is significantly higher than the industry average of a similar-sized company, shares are overpriced. Robert S. Natale, editor of Standard & Poor's *Emerging & Special Situations* newsletter, states that a young company often hasn't had time to produce much in the way of earnings, so instead look for a ratio of total offering price to annual sales. On the whole, this market-capitalization-to-sales ratio should not be greater than 2:7.

➤ USE OF PROCEEDS Check out what the company plans to do with the newly raised capital. It should not be devoted to repaying the debt or bailing out the founders, management, or promoters. Most of it should be used to expand the business. If 25% or more is going toward nonproductive purposes, move on. Avoid firms whose management or a founding shareholder is selling a large percentage of the shares (30% or more).

$ HINT: Whenever the public is chasing after new issues beware of telephone solicitations from high-pressure salesmen who guarantee that you'll double your money once the company goes public. *Careful*: You're skating on thin ice.

MUTUAL FUNDS THAT INVEST IN SMALL, EMERGING COMPANIES

Alliance Quasar Fund
500 Plaza Drive (3rd floor)
Secaucus, NJ 07094
1-800-247-4154

American Capital
 Emerging Growth Fund
P.O. Box 418256
Kansas City, MO 64141
1-800-231-3638

Fidelity Growth Co.
 Fund
21 Congress Street
Boston, MA 02109
1-800-544-8888

Keystone S-4 Fund
Harkwell Emerging
 Growth
Box 2121
Boston, MA 02106
1-800-225-2618

New Horizon Fund
T. Rowe Price Associates
100 East Pratt Street
Baltimore, MD 21202
1-800-638-5660

Twentieth Century Ultra
 Investors OTC
P.O. Box 419200
Kansas City, MO 64141
1-800-345-2021

Vanguard Explorer Fund
P.O. Box 2600
Valley Forge, PA 19482
1-800-662-7447

FINDING OUT ABOUT IPOs

Many brokers will let their clients know about new issues that their firm either knows about or is underwriting. Make certain your broker knows of your interest. In addition, check the publications listed below. Several, such as *Barron's* and *Investment Dealer's Digest* cover IPOs along with all types of financial news. They will give you the following information:

- Name of stock and symbol
- Expected date
- Use of proceeds
- Name of underwriter
- Financial data and balance sheet

- Write-up of what the company has done and plans to do plus on evaluation of the IPO as an investment

FOR FURTHER INFORMATION

To help you spot the winners and avoid the losers when firms go public, you may want to read one of the following advisory newsletters for background data:

Emerging and Special Situations
Standard & Poor's Corp.
25 Broadway
New York, NY 10005
1-212-208-8000; 1-800-221-5277
Monthly; $228.50 per year
Three-month trial: $58

New Issues
Institute for Econometric Research
3471 North Federal Highway
Ft. Lauderdale, FL 33306

1-800-327-6720
Monthly; $95 per year

Barron's
200 Liberty Street
New York, NY 10281
1-800-628-9320
Weekly; $119 per year

Investment Dealers Digest
2 World Trade Center (18th floor)
New York, NY 10048
1-212-227-1200
Weekly; $375 per year

New Issues Performance Directory
50 Main Street
White Plains, NY 10606
1-800-477-3331
Every 10 days; $75 per year
Six-week trial: $39

Full page, advance reports on all IPOs plus follow-up in the after market for 9 months.

PART FOUR

HIGH RISK FOR HIGH RETURNS

There are occasions when a portion of your savings can be used for speculations. Recognize the hazards and limit your commitments to 15% of your capital. If you are smart—and lucky—enough to score, put half your winnings into a money market fund or certificate of deposit to build assets for future risks.

Speculations are not investments. This statement sounds simple-minded, but most people fail to make the distinction. Investments are designed to preserve capital and to provide income. The decisions are made on the basis of fundamentals: the quality and the value of the investment.

Speculations involve risks and are profitable primarily because of market fluctuations. They should *never* be included in retirement portfolios. They should be entered into only when you understand what you are doing *and with money that you can afford to lose.* Before getting into details about speculations:

- Recognize that there is usually a sound reason why a security is selling at a low price or paying a very low yield. Investors are not interested, so you must be certain that there are facts to justify higher future values.

- In making projections, cut in half the anticipated upward move and double the potential downswing.

- Speculate only in a rising market unless you are selling short. Worthwhile gains will come when more people buy more shares—not likely in a down market.

- Be willing to take quick, small losses, and never hold on in blind hope of a recovery.

- When you pick a winner, sell half your shares (or set a protective stop-loss order) when you have doubled your money.

  On the next few pages you will read about:

- Foreign stocks, bonds, currencies, and CDs

- Commodities

- Precious metals

- Financial futures and market indexes

- Splits, spin-offs, small caps, spiders, and stock buy-backs

FOREIGN STOCKS, BONDS, CDs, AND CURRENCIES

The electronic age makes the flow of money and information almost instantaneous, so whatever happens on the Hong Kong stock exchange or to the price of gold in London impacts directly on investors in Des Moines, Duluth, and Davenport. As we draw closer and closer to one global market, it is essential for investors to widen their horizons. If you're not convinced, just consider this fact: The U.S. stock exchanges now account for about 30% of the world's equity capitalization. Until 1986 that figure was always 50% or more.

At various times and in certain economic cycles, astute investors are able to make substantial profits by "going global" because of the international ripple effect: Each country's economic cycle is a separate one, so when one nation is in the midst of a poor stock market, others are inevitably thriving. Wise investors realize the advisability of not locking themselves into a narrow geographical investment sphere.

The European Economic Community of 1992, combined with the reunification of Germany into a single nation and the meetings among the leaders of the world, have focused all eyes on the emergence of a world increasingly based on free trade.

Timing overseas investments is tricky. A strong dollar makes foreign investments less profitable for Americans—but as the dollar levels off, it is a good point to enter the global arena.

☐ CAUTION: International investing is far more complicated than investing in the U.S. Stock markets in other countries have different listing requirements for stocks, often requesting fewer financial disclosures and having much looser accounting standards. More importantly, when you invest in a foreign stock, you invest also in foreign currency. Changes in the value of the dollar can reduce your profits or

reduce your losses. For example, if you buy a French stock for 42 French francs and the dollar is worth 4 francs, your cost is $10.50/share. If a year later the stock has risen to 50 francs, you may want to sell and take your profit. In the meantime, however, the dollar has also gotten stronger and is now worth 5 francs. If you sell you will actually get only $10/share and you will have a loss of 50 cents. The rule of thumb to bear in mind is:

- Foreign shares tend to do well if the dollar drops against the foreign currency. Even if the stock doesn't actually rise in price but the dollar declines against the currency of that country, you will make a profit when you sell. Why? Because the foreign currency you receive from the stock sale when converted into dollars, converts into more dollars than it cost you to buy the stock. If the stock should also independently rise in price, you will achieve even more profits.
- On the other hand, a decline in the foreign currency will eat into potential profits.

MAKING PROFITS

An investment in a foreign stock offers at least two ways to make a profit or loss:
- The price of the stock can go up (or down) in its local currency.
- The value of the foreign country's currency can rise (or drop) relative to the U.S. dollar, thereby increasing or decreasing the value of your stock.

The best situation obviously exists when the price of the stock rises *and* the value of the country's currency likewise rises against the dollar. An important fact to keep in mind is that a rising currency can sometimes save you from the pitfalls associated with a poor or only mediocre foreign stock.

Despite these compelling reasons for international investing, many otherwise clever investors still remain unschooled in the mechanics of successful investing in foreign stocks. The necessary guidelines, given here, can be mastered by anyone with the time and inclination to do so. But first let's examine the key pros and cons of international investing.

UNDERSTANDING CURRENCY RISKS

With all companies that have substantial foreign interests, there are extra risks resulting from gains or losses through foreign exchange. Since the company's earnings are in local currencies, they can lose a portion of their value when transferred back into dollars. The stronger the dollar, the lower the net earnings reported by the parent company. The impact can reduce profits by as much as 10%. Some international or foreign companies try to hedge against these currency swings by geographical or product diversification, but this can be expensive and is not always effective.

Currency fluctuations also affect the value of a company's nonmonetary assets (plant, equipment, inventories). When the dollar's value rises, that of the foreign currency declines. But the assets are shown at the exchange rates that were in effect when these items were purchased. That's why constant monitoring of the dollar's value is so important when going global. A good stockbroker or the international division of a large bank can keep you abreast of currency fluctuations and how they may affect your investments.

Although there are several methods for investing in foreign stocks, the three most popular are American Depository Receipts (ADRs), mutual funds, and multinational companies, which are discussed in the next chapter.

AMERICAN DEPOSITORY RECEIPTS (ADRs)

ADRs are negotiable receipts representing ownership of shares of a foreign corporation that is traded in an American securities market. They are issued by an American bank, but the actual shares are held by the American bank's foreign depository bank or agent. This custodian bank is usually but not always an office of the American bank (if there is one in the country involved). If not, the bank selected to be custodian is generally a foreign bank with a close relationship to the foreign company for which the ADRs are being issued.

ADRs allow you to buy, sell, or hold the foreign stocks without actually taking physical possession of them. They are registered by the SEC and are sold by stockbrokers. Each ADR is a contract between the holder and the bank, certifying that a stated number of shares of the overseas-based company have been deposited with the American bank's foreign office or custodian and will be kept there as long as the ADR remains outstanding. The U.S. purchaser

---

FOREIGN INVESTMENT

PROS
↑ Provides diversification
↑ Provides additional investment opportunities not available in U.S. markets
↑ Provides hedge against U.S. monetary or economic troubles such as inflation, dollar depreciation, slump in stock market
↑ As vitality shifts from one country to another, foreign firms may represent attractive alternatives

CONS
↓ Currency fluctuations
↓ Local political situations
↓ Less information available on foreign companies than on U.S. firms
↓ Foreign firms not required to provide the same detailed type of information as U.S. firms
↓ Different accounting procedures, which can make accurate evaluation complex
↓ Foreign brokers and foreign exchanges seldom bound by regulations as strict as those imposed by the SEC (every country has its own set of regulations)
↓ Quotes sometimes difficult to obtain

pays for the stock in dollars and receives dividends in dollars.

When the foreign corporation has a large capitalization, so that its shares sell for the equivalent of a few dollars, each ADR may represent more than 1 share: 10, 50, or even 100 shares in the case of some Japanese companies, where there are millions of shares of common stock.

ADRs are generally initiated when an American bank learns that there is a great deal of interest in the shares of a foreign firm. Or a foreign corporation may initiate action if it wants to enter the American market. In either case, the bank then purchases a large block of shares and issues the ADRs, leaving the stock certificates overseas in its custodian bank.

The most important test in a foreign company's selection of an ADR is whether a market exists in the United States for the shares. In other words, the ADR process is not designed to make a market for the shares of a foreign company so much as it is to make certain shares are available when there is sufficient demand from American investors.

If you decide to buy ADRs, select those actively traded in the United States—i.e., listed on one of the exchanges. Of the 800 ADRs available in May 1993, about one-fourth were listed, because not all foreign companies want to meet the disclosure requirements of or for listing. Those that are not listed trade over the counter. Their prices are not given in the newspaper, but are available from brokers.

IMPORTANCE OF DIVERSIFICATION

As with any investment, diversification greatly reduces the level of risk involved. With foreign stocks, it is especially important to avoid reliance on the performance of any one stock, one industry, or even one country. Risk reduction is best achieved by spreading your investment dollars in at least one of the following ways:

- *By country.* When some foreign stock markets fall, it is inevitable that others will rise. Diversification by country offers a hedge against a poor economic climate in any one area. Keep in mind that the U.S. market tends to be an anticipatory one,

LEADING ADRs

ADR	SYMBOL	PRICE SPRING 1993
Barclays plc	BCS	$27
British Airways	BAB	45
British Gas	BRG	48
British Petroleum	BP	55
Glaxo Holding plc	GLX	18
Honda Motor	HMC	25
Imperial Chemical Ind.	ICI	80
National Westminster	NW	44
News Corp., Ltd.	NWS	43
Novo-Nordisk	NVO	90
Shell Transport	SC	54
Smithkline Beecham plc	SBH	35
Unilever	UN	115

SOURCE: Quotron, May 1993.

reflecting what the American investor thinks will happen in the forthcoming months.

- *By type of industry.* Buying shares in more than one industry—high-tech, computers, oil, automobiles, etc.—likewise provides protection.
- *By company within the industry.* For example, an energy portfolio could include stocks from a number of companies located in the North Sea area, Southeast Asia, Canada, and the United States.
- *By region.* Diversify among the regions of the world. Never become too dependent on any one area.

Buy stocks with P/E ratios that are lower than those of comparable U.S. companies. There should always be a compelling reason to purchase a foreign security, such as a low P/E or a unique industry position.

1994 OPPORTUNITIES IN FOREIGN STOCKS

The collapse of the Berlin Wall in 1989 brought about a burst of enthusiasm for German and other European stocks. But since then there has

IN THE KNOW: 10 Terms to Impress
Your Broker

- **ADR** American Depository Receipt; document indicating you own shares in a foreign stock held by a U.S. bank. ADRs trade on the exchanges or over the counter.
- **Big Bang** October 27, 1986, when the London Stock Exchange ended fixed brokerage commissions.
- **Bourse** French word for stock exchange (from purse). Also used by exchanges in Switzerland and Belgium.
- **Denationalization** When a government-owned corporation is turned over to private ownership.
- **ECU** European currency unit; developed by nations of the European Common Market.
- **Eurobond** Bond issued in one European country's currency but sold outside that country.
- **Gilts** Government bonds and money market securities in Britain.
- **Out-sourcing** Shopping the world for the least expensive suppliers of parts or products and services.
- **SDRs** Special drawing rights; credits issued by the International Monetary Fund to its member countries; can be traded on the open market to stabilize the value of a currency in the foreign exchange market.
- **Supranationals** Agencies formed by groups of countries to help their economies: International Monetary Fund, World Bank.

been much investor gloominess about the troubles in Russia and the problems facing the rebuilding of Eastern Europe. Some say it could take 10 years to bring the economy of eastern Germany to western Germany's standards. And, of course, there's no guarantee that capitalism will improve the economies of the former East bloc countries.

However, European stock markets should be given serious investment consideration. There are rare buying opportunities here, especially for those who are willing to hold these securities long term.

In addition, Mexico and some other Latin American countries are making strong economic strides. Mexico, in particular, has returned to private ownerships and a more open trade policy. It will be a primary beneficiary of NAFTA. Suggested stocks are also listed in Chapter 1.

Below are some stocks to discuss with your broker. But remember, all are above average in risk.

- *Andina.* Santiago's Coca-Cola distributor.
- *Antofagasta Holdings.* A Chilean company with interests in railroads, water supply systems, banking and mining companies.
- *Attwoods plc.* Worldwide waste management company with thriving business in Germany.
- *Cemex.* A large Mexican producer and exporter of building materials.
- *CIFRA S.A. "B".* Mexico's largest retailer; also owns restaurants.
- *Copec.* Chile's major forest products company.
- *CCU.* Company has captured about 90% of Chile's beer market and over 25% of its soft drink business.
- *Enersis.* Provides electricity to both Santiago and Buenos Aires.
- *Telefonos de Chile.* Company has a booming business and may move into the cellular market outside Chile.

FOUR WAYS TO MAKE A PROFIT IN
OVERSEAS STOCKS

- When the price of a stock rises
- When a foreign currency rises against the U.S. dollar
- When you buy shares in a closed-end investment company at a discount to NAV and the discount narrows because of increased demand
- When both the stock and the foreign currency advance, creating a compounding effect

▶ INVESTING IN ISRAEL Because this country's fragile economy is being hurt by the large influx of Russian immigrants and its continuing domestic unrest, the best stocks to consider are those whose revenues are largely foreign derived. If you're in a position to assume some risk in your portfolio, here are three well-run companies.

- *Sciex Corp.* SCIX, $42. This nearly debt-free company makes imaging equipment for the publishing industry.
- *Lannet Data Communications* LANTF,

FOREIGN STOCK EXCHANGES

Amsterdam Stock Exchange
Bursplein 5
NL-1012 JW Amsterdam
Netherlands

Australia Stock Exchange
87-92 Pitt Street
Sydney, N.S.W. 2000
Australia

Frankfurt Stock Exchange
Frankfurter Wertpapierboerse
Boersenplatz 4
Postfach 100811
D-6000 Frankfurt ag Main 1
Germany

Hong Kong Stock Exchange
Exchange Square
GPO Box 8888
Hong Kong

Johannesburg Stock Exchange
17 Diagonal Street
Johannesburg 2001
South Africa

London Stock Exchange
Old Broad Street
London EC2N 1HP
England

Luxembourg Stock Exchange
11, Avenue de la Porte-Neuve
L-2227 Luxembourg

Madrid Stock Exchange
Plaza de la Lealtad, 2
Madrid, Spain

Milan Stock Exchange
Borsa Valori di Milano
Piazza degli Affari, 6
I-20123 Milan
Italy

Paris Stock Exchange
Bourse de Paris
4, place de la Bourse
F-75002 Paris Cedex 02
France

Singapore Stock Exchange
1 Raffles Place, 24-00
Singapore 0104

Tel Aviv Stock Exchange
54 Ahad Haam Street
Tel Aviv 65202
Israel

Tokyo Stock Exchange
Nihombashi-Kabuto-cho
2-1 Chuo-ku
Tokyo 103
Japan

Vienna Stock Exchange
Wiener Börsekammer
Wipplingerstrasse 34
A-1011 Wien 1
Austria

Zurich Stock Exchange
Bleicherweg 5
8021 Zurich
Switzerland

FOUR TOP INTERNATIONAL MUTUAL FUNDS		
FUND	TELEPHONE	TOTAL RETURN (1/1/93 TO 5/1/93)
Fidelity Overseas Fund	1-800-544-8888	+12.2%
G.T. Global Pacific Fund	1-800-824-1580	8.8
American Fund's New Perspective	1-800-421-0180	4.3
T. Rowe Price International Discovery Fund	1-800-638-5660	7.5

$19. Designs and manufactures computer networking systems; only 10% of revenues are Israeli-derived.

- *ECI Telecom Ltd.* ECLIF, $37. Producer of telephone circuit equipment for AT&T, British Telecom, MCI, etc. Well run company.

MUTUAL FUNDS

Perhaps the easiest way to go global, especially if you do not have the time or inclination to do your own research, is to purchase shares in one of the mutual funds specializing in foreign investments. In this way, you can participate in a diversified portfolio and, as with domestic mutual funds, you reap the advantages of professional management—in this case with foreign expertise. Although many of these funds are American owned and operated, they have foreign consultants providing up-to-date research on specific stocks as well as on the country's political situation and outlook.

Some funds consist entirely of foreign stocks; others mix foreign and American stocks. Most are members of a larger family of funds and thus offer the advantage of free switching from one fund to another (see boxes).

$ HINT: Before investing in any of these mutual funds, write or call for a copy of the prospectus. Investment philosophies of the funds vary widely from conservative to very aggressive.

EUROPEAN MUTUAL FUNDS

These open-minded mutual funds focus on blue chip stocks:

- *Financial Strategic European Portfolio.* 1-800-525-8085. A no-load fund that's ideal for small investors. It tends to favor British, German, and French stocks.
- *Vanguard International Equity Index Fund/European Portfolio.* 1-800-662-7447. Portfolio matches the weightings of the Morgan Stanley European Index. Large holdings in stocks traded on the largest European stock exchange, the London.
- *T. Rowe Price European Stock Fund.* 1-800-638-5660. A no-load fund whose managers have an outstanding record with other international funds.

CLOSED-END COUNTRY FUNDS

These funds are an excellent way for investors to participate in foreign bull markets without having to select individual stocks. However, they are not risk-free and should not be confused with international mutual funds.

These funds for the most part are *closed-end,* which is part of the reason why they remained in relative obscurity until recently. They are still less popular than their close cousin, open-end mutual funds, and there are fewer to select from: 120 closed-end foreign country sector funds versus nearly 2,000 open-end mutual funds.

Unlike open-end funds, which continually issue new shares to the public, closed-end funds sell their shares just once, when they begin operating. After that shares can be bought or sold only on stock exchanges or over the counter through a broker. Their prices then move up and down with investor demand just like any stock. Consequently, their price is often above or below net asset value (NAV), the value of the holdings in the portfolio divided by the number of shares. When the price of a fund is above NAV, it is being sold at a "premium"; when it falls below NAV, it's at a "discount" (see box on page 210).

BUYING AT A DISCOUNT

Closed-end funds provide investors with the possibility of buying a dollar's worth of common stock for less than $1. This occurs if you buy shares at a discount and thereafter the shares move up to or above NAV.

$ HINT: This can work negatively in reverse: If you're forced to sell your shares at the same or a larger discount, you'll lose money.

Most closed-end shares trade at a premium to NAV for a spell just after their initial public

CLOSED-END COUNTRY FUNDS

NAME	SYMBOL	PRICE/SPRING 1993
Asia Pacific	APB	$16
Austria	OST	8
Chile	CH	33
First Australia	IAF	10
First Iberian	IBF	7
First Philippine	FPF	12
Germany	GER	11
India Growth	IGF	13
Italy	ITA	10
Korea	KF	14
Malaysia	MF	17
Mexico	MXF	23
ROC Taiwan	ROC	8
Scudder New Asia	SAF	18
Singapore Fund	SGF	13
Spain	SNF	9
Swiss Helvetia	SWZ	15
Taiwan	TWN	21
Templeton Emerging Markets	EMF	18
Thai	TTF	20
Turkish Inv. Fund	TKF	7

SOURCE: Quotron, May 1993.

> ## FOREIGN COUNTRY SECTOR FUNDS
>
> **PROS**
> ↑ Professionally managed
> ↑ Offer diversification within a country, which reduces risk
> ↑ Provide a hedge against U.S. market
> ↑ Way to maintain position in overseas markets
> ↑ High liquidity
> ↑ May be able to buy shares at a discount
>
> **CONS**
> ↓ If foreign currency declines, value of your investment drops
> ↓ Value of stocks in fund can fall
> ↓ May be special taxes for Americans
> ↓ Political uncertainty
> ↓ Price of funds subject to fluctuations, like any stock
> ↓ Foreign markets less well regulated than U.S. market

offering. Then, if they continue to sell at premium, it's often because they've cornered the market. Generally, however, closed-end funds trade at a discount to NAV, partly because there are no salespeople keeping them in the public eye.

$ IF YOU DARE: Purchase closed-end shares at a discount and hold until they are selling at or above NAV. When funds reach NAV, they may become takeover targets or be converted into a regular mutual fund, at which point they are automatically repriced at 100¢ on the dollar.

FOREIGN BONDS

If you're income-oriented, you may want to own nondollar assets when the U.S. dollar is weak. Consider mutual funds that own foreign bonds. Your return is based on three factors: (1) the bond yields, (2) the price changes due to interest rate changes abroad, and (3) currency fluctuations. Since most individuals cannot monitor all three areas, mutual funds are the logical way to invest.

☐CAUTION: Although fund managers can move in and out of various countries, foreign bond funds are riskier than a U.S. one because of the myriad of economic and political variables. Therefore, put no more than 10% of your portfolio into one of these funds.

There are two kinds of funds: "international" bond funds with investments solely in foreign bonds; and "global" funds that hold positions in a variety of foreign and U.S. bonds. The ability to invest in U.S. as well as foreign bonds gives shareholders added protection because the fund manager can buy where yields and safety are highest.

☐CAUTION: A foreign bond is not an alternative to a U.S. government or corporate bond fund. It is riskier and subject to far greater price fluctuations. In a U.S. bond fund, an investor's total return (income plus price appreciation of the fund's shares) involves only two factors: (1) interest payments received by the fund on its bonds and (2) changes in the prices of the bonds themselves. The total return for foreign bonds is more complex: It involves the third crucial factor of currency risk, i.e., fluctuation. Some funds aim to keep this risk factor as low as possible by purchasing bonds of governments they believe to be politically and economically stable, even though

yields may be lower. Risk is further reduced when the average maturity of the bonds in the fund is relatively short. This gives the bonds less time in which to fluctuate in price. Short maturities—4 or fewer years—provide a quicker term payoff and the flexibility to buy or sell as interest rates or the economic situation in any one country changes.

HIGH YIELDS FROM GERMAN BONDS

As we go to press, German bonds are offering attractive yields; in fact, U.S. investors can lock in rates of around 6 to 7%. German time deposits, which are the equivalent of our bank CDs, offer another option. Their 6-month time deposits are yielding 8% versus about 4% on U.S. CDs.

You can contact German banks on your own, or use one of the large U.S. retail securities firms. Most brokerage houses have a $25,000 minimum on purchases of individual bonds. Merrill Lynch also has a unit investment trust composed of German fixed-income securities; the minimum is $5,000 with units available now on the secondary market.

Contact:
- Commerzbank
  Box 100505
  6000 Frankfurt am Main 1
  Germany
  telephone: 011-49-69-13620
- Merrill Lynch
- Dean Witter

GLOBAL INCOME FUNDS

High yields in short-term global income funds are enticing, but take care. This type of fund has risk and volatility. They invest primarily in high-grade foreign debt with maturities of 3 years or less and have some portion of their assets in dollar-denominated securities. They offer yields 2 to 4 percentage points above U.S. money market rates. But managers are constantly juggling three things: interest income, changes in the prices of the underlying securities, and currency changes.

☐CAUTION: These funds are best if you are able to accept modest price volatility. They are not a substitute for money market

MUTUAL FUNDS THAT INVEST IN FOREIGN BONDS

	YIELDS	
Fidelity Global Bond	7.79%	1-800-544-8888
GT Global Government Income	7.84	1-800-824-1580
PaineWebber Master Global	8.05	1-800-457-0849
Scudder International Bond	6.25	1-800-225-2470
T. Rowe Price International Bond	7.21	1-800-638-5660
Templeton Income	7.83	1-800-237-0738

NO-LOAD GLOBAL INCOME FUNDS

FUND	YIELD JULY 1993	TELEPHONE
Alliance Short-Term Multi Market	6.29%	1-800-227-4618
Blanchard Short-Term Global Income	6.90	1-800-922-7771
Fidelity Short-Term World Income	6.58	1-800-544-8888
Merrill Lynch Short-Term Global	6.03	1-800-637-3863
Prudential Short-Term Global	7.52	1-800-225-1852
Scudder Short-Term Global Income	6.68	1-800-225-2470

funds. Most also have high expense ratios, averaging about 1.5%, which is about three times that of domestic money funds.

WHY EXCHANGE RATES FLUCTUATE

Exchange rates among currencies fluctuate for a number of reasons. Here are the key factors to watch.

- *Inflation.* Rates move to reflect changes in the currencies' purchasing power.
- *Trade deficits.* Countries with large trade deficits usually have a depreciating currency. Inflation is often a cause of this deficit, making a country's goods more expensive and less competitive, which in turn reduces demand for its currency abroad.
- *Productivity.* If a country produces superior products, foreigners will pay more for them. Those products and the country's currency will tend to rise in value.
- *Interest rates.* High rates usually boost currency values in the short term by making these currencies appealing to investors. If high rates are the result of high inflation, in the long run the currency will fall in value.
- *Political instability.* Upheaval makes a country a hazardous place in which to invest.

INTERNATIONAL MONEY MARKET AND CURRENCY FUNDS

A more conservative way to invest overseas is through one of the handful of money market funds with portfolios denominated in foreign currencies. Like their domestic counterparts, these international money funds invest in short-term, top-quality money market instruments, such as foreign bank CDs, government issues, and high-quality corporate paper. They make money for investors by earning interest.

The best known among the international money funds is the Global Currency Portfolio, part of the International Currency Portfolio Group (ICP). This fund is able to profit from appreciation or depreciation of the dollar by moving its assets among CDs and other instruments in 16 different currencies, including that of the United States.

ICP runs two additional funds: the High Income Currency Portfolio, which invests in currencies of countries with the highest interest rates; and the Hard Currency Portfolio (1-800-354-4111).

Another foreign income fund that has posted impressive yields is Alliance Short-Term Multi-market Trust (1-800-221-5672).

FOREIGN CDs

One of the more conservative ways to bet on the falling dollar is to buy foreign currency

CDs; they're available at the large U.S. branches of overseas banks and the currency traders, such as Thomas Cook Foreign Exchange. Cook has a $50,000 minimum with 3- and 6-month maturities. Its product is called a "forward contract."

☐ CAUTION: Foreign CDs are a good investment *only* if the dollar is weak and/or the foreign interest rate is higher than you can get at home. If the dollar rises, you could suffer significant losses.

In some cases, interest rates are above those paid on U.S. bank CDs. If the dollar falls, your gain will be even greater. Details are available from any Thomas Cook office, or the Mark Twain Bank in St. Louis, MO (1-800-926-4922.)

A handful of banks now offer special accounts that allow depositors to easily invest in foreign CDs and foreign currency money market funds. Most banks offer these accounts primarily to business customers, with the exception of Citibank. Citibank offers two accounts: its Foreign Currency Money Market Deposit Account pays the overnight interest rate in each currency. Its Foreign Currency Time Deposit, like a CD, has maturities of 1 month to 1 year and pays a fixed rate. Both accounts are available in 7 currencies: British pounds, Japanese yen, Canadian dollars, Swiss francs, German marks, and New Zealand and Australian dollars. The minimum deposit is the equivalent of $25,000. These accounts are protected by federal deposit insurance—up to $100,000 each. Details: 1-800-321-CITI.

TRAVELER'S CHECKS

A low-cost way to play the game is to purchase traveler's checks in the currency you feel will rise against the dollar. Cash them in when that currency rises to pocket your gains.

The key disadvantage with traveler's checks is that you do not earn interest on your money.

CURRENCY OPTIONS

These operate like stock options (see Chapter 16). If you think a given currency will rise against the U.S. dollar, you buy a call. If you think it will fall, purchase a put.

Say you believe that the dollar will fall against the Japanese yen. By purchasing a call option on the yen, you gain the right to purchase a stated number of yen at a predetermined strike price in dollars. You have that right until the expiration date—usually at 3-month intervals.

☐ CAUTION: If the option exercise date comes up and the yen is below your strike price, your entire investment is lost.

The options, traded on the Philadelphia Exchange, are for 7 currencies: Deutsche mark (DM), pound sterling, Canadian dollar, Japanese yen, Australian dollar, French franc, and Swiss franc. The premiums run from $25 for a short-life out-of-the-money option to $2,000 for a long-term deep-in-the-money call or put.

The option represents the currency value against the dollar, so traders buy calls when they expect the foreign money to gain ground against the dollar and puts when they anticipate the reverse. The options expire at 3-month intervals.

The quotations are in U.S. cents per unit of the underlying currency (with the exception of the yen, where it's $1/100$¢): Thus, the quote 1.00 DM means 1¢ per mark, and since the contract covers 62,500 DM, the total premium would be $625.

➤ OPTIONS ON FUTURES These are now available on the Chicago Mercantile Exchange, where the currency futures are already traded. They are similar to regular options except that they give the holder the right to buy or sell the currencies themselves, *not the futures.*

The CME rules permit the speculator to do the following:

- Generate extra income by writing calls or selling puts (but this can be very expensive if you guess wrong and the option is exercised).
- Exercise the option at any time. But once you do so, you may not liquidate your option position with an offsetting option as you can do in futures trading. So you have to sell to, or buy from, the other party the required number of currency units at the option exercise price.

These options on futures sound risky—but only for the speculator. Business firms use them to hedge the prices of foreign goods at a future delivery date.

HOW TO SPECULATE IN FOREIGN CURRENCIES

Trading in foreign currencies can be exciting and profitable.

Futures contracts of foreign currency are traded on the International Monetary Market Division (IMM) of the Chicago Mercantile Exchange. Basically, positions are taken by importers and exporters who want to protect their profits from sudden swings in the relation between the dollar and a specific foreign currency. A profit on the futures contract will be offset by a loss in the cash market, or vice versa. Either way, the businessperson or banker guarantees a set cost.

The speculation performs an essential function by taking opposite sides of contracts, but unlike other types of commodities trading, currency futures reflect reactions to what has already happened more than anticipation of what's ahead.

For small margins of 1.5% to 4.2%, roughly $1,500 to $2,500, you can control large sums of money: 100,000 Canadian dollars, 125,000 German marks, 12.5 million Japanese yen, etc.

The attraction is leverage. You can speculate that at a fixed date in the future, the value of your contract will be greater (if you buy long) or less (if you sell short).

The daily fluctuations of each currency futures contract are limited by IMM rules. A rise of $750 per day provides a 37.5% profit on a $2,000 investment. That's a net gain of $705 ($750 less $45 in commissions). If the value declines, you are faced with a wipeout or, if you set a stop order, the loss of part of your security deposit. Vice versa when you sell short.

One of the favorite deals is playing crosses, taking advantage of the spread between different currencies: buying francs and selling liras short, etc. For example, when the German mark was falling faster than the Swiss franc relative to the U.S. dollar, an investor set up this spread:

April 15: He buys a June contract for 125,000 francs and sells short a June contract for 125,000 marks. The franc is valued at .6664¢, the mark at .5536¢. Cost, not including commissions, is the margin: $2,000.

May 27: The franc has fallen to .6461, the mark to .5120. He reverses his trades, selling the June contract for francs and buying the mark contract to cover his short position.

Result: The speculator loses 2.03¢ per franc, or $2,537.50, but he makes 4.16¢ per mark, or $5,200.00. The overall gain, before commissions, is $2,662.50, a return of 133% on the $2,000 investment—in about 6 weeks.

☐ CAUTION: Trading in foreign currencies can be exciting and profitable. It can also be hazardous to your financial health. Small margins tempt novices overlooking the fact that they are financially liable for the full extent of any losses. So:

- DON'T trade currencies or futures on currencies unless you know the full extent of your potential loss. Write it down.
- DON'T get involved at all unless you have a reliable and trustworthy stockbroker or adviser.

FOR FURTHER INFORMATION

FOREIGN STOCKS

➤ BOOKS You can add to your list of multinationals by studying one of the standard reference books such as Moody's *Handbook* and Standard & Poor's *Stock Market Guide* or *Value Line.* All three give the percentage of a company's earnings and sales derived from foreign operations. You should also read various company annual reports to learn what areas their sales come from. Earnings from Western Europe and Japan are currently more stable than those from Latin America.

The International Stock Exchange Official Yearbook, 1993–1994 edition; $395

Reed Business Publications
205 East 42nd Street, Suite 1705
New York, NY 10017
1-212-867-2080

Moody's International Manual & News Reports
Moody's Investors Service
99 Church Street
New York, NY 10007

1-212-553-0300; 1-800-342-5647
3-volume annual; $2,495

Contains financial information on over 5,000 companies and institutions in 100 countries.

> Thomas R. Keyes and David Miller, *The Global Investor: How to Buy Stocks Around the World* (Chicago: Dearborn Financial Publishing Co., 1990).

➤ PERIODICALS The following periodicals provide coverage of foreign markets as well as individual stocks:

- *Wall Street Journal*
- *Barron's National Business & Financial Weekly*
- *The Economist*
- *Investor's Chronicle and Financial World* (London)
- *Far Eastern Economic Review*
- *Japan Economic Review*
- *The Financial Times* (London)
  14 East 60th Street
  New York, NY 10022
  1-800-628-8088
  Daily; $420 per year
- *The Asian Wall Street Journal*
  Dow Jones & Company
  200 Liberty Street
  New York, NY 10281
  1-212-416-2000
  Weekly; $245 per year
- *Global Investor*
  Monthly; $325 per year
- *Euromoney* (London)
  Monthly; $350 per year

Both are available from:

Reed Business Publications
205 East 42nd Street, Suite 1705
New York, NY 10017
1-212-867-2080

➤ NEWSLETTERS The following newsletters regularly cover foreign stocks:

- *Capital International Perspective*
  Morgan Stanley
  1251 Avenue of the Americas
  New York, NY 10020
  1-212-703-2965
  16 times a year; $5,000 per year
- *Dessauer's Journal of Financial Markets*
  P.O. Box 1718
  Orleans, MA 02653
  1-508-255-1651
  Bimonthly; $195 per year; 1-year trial: $117
- *International Bank Credit Analyst*
  BCA Publications Ltd.
  3463 Peel Street
  Montreal, Quebec H3A 1W7
  1-514-398-0653
  Monthly; $695 per year

CLOSED-END FOREIGN FUNDS

The *Wall Street Journal's* Monday issue lists closed-end funds under its own category. You'll find the NAV, share price, and discount or premium as of the preceding Friday.

> *Investor's Guide to Closed-End Funds*
> Box 161465
> Miami, FL 33116
> 1-305-271-1900
> Monthly; $325 per year

> *Listing of Closed-End Funds*
> Investment Company Institute
> Publications Dept., Suite 600
> 1600 M Street NW, 6th floor
> Washington, DC 20036
> 1-202-955-3534
> Free; updated twice a year

20 COMMODITIES

The concept of buying and selling agricultural goods at a price agreed upon today, but with actual delivery of the goods sometime in the future, is a time-honored practice dating back to the early 19th century. But don't allow the long history of commodities trading lull you into thinking it's an easy way to make money. Trading commodities is one of the riskiest games on Wall Street—some studies indicate that well over half the people who invest in commodities lose their money. In fact, commodities futures are almost always 100% speculation because you must try to guess, months in advance, what will happen to the prices of good products, natural resources, metals, and foreign currencies.

The greatest appeal of trading commodities lies in the impressive amount of leverage they provide. Your broker will require you to meet certain net worth requirements and make a margin deposit. Nevertheless, there are low cash requirements: 5% to 10% of a contract's actual value, depending on the commodity and the broker's standards. That means $2,000 could actually buy, say, $29,000 worth of soybeans. So if you're good at it, you can make sizeable profits with very little money. However, don't get involved unless you have some money you can afford to lose, an ability to follow trends, and a lot of emotional stability and calmness. If prices move against you, your broker will require more money, and unless you have the cash readily available, he will sell out your position and you could suffer huge loses. To help reduce the risks involved, you can give your broker a stop-order loss on each futures contract, thus establishing a price at which you will automatically sell your position rather than suffer greater losses. (See Chapter 25 for details on stop-order sales.)

☐ CAUTION: Trading commodities is not an area for the novice, the conservative or the timid. Read the rest of this chapter with care and proceed with caution.

WHERE AND WHICH COMMODITIES ARE TRADED

- Chicago Board of Trade (CBOT)
  corn, Ginnie Mae mortgages, gold, oats, paper, plywood, silver, soybeans, soybean meal, soybean oil, Treasury bonds, wheat
- Chicago Mercantile Exchange (CME)
  broiler chickens, cattle, certificates of deposit, currencies, eggs, Eurodollars, gold, hogs, lumber, pork bellies, potatoes, silver coins, S&P 500 Index futures, Treasury bills
- Coffee, Sugar & Cocoa Exchange (New York City)
  aluminum, copper, gold, silver
- Kansas City Board of Trade
  wheat, Value Line Stock Index futures
- Mid America Commodity Exchange (Chicago)
  corn, gold, oats, soybeans, wheat
- Minneapolis Grain Exchange
  sunflower seeds, wheat
- New York Cotton Exchange
  cotton, orange juice, propane gas
- New York Futures Exchange (part of the NYSE)
  New York Stock Exchange Composite Index, options on futures
- New York Mercantile Exchange
  beef (imported), gasoline, gold, heating oil, palladium, platinum, potatoes, silver coins

WHAT ARE COMMODITIES FUTURES?

A futures contract is an agreement to buy or sell a certain amount of a commodity at a

AGRICULTURAL COMMODITIES CONTRACTS

COMMODITY	SYMBOL	ONE CONTRACT EQUALS
Soybeans	S	5,000 bushels
Soybean oil	BO	60,000 pounds
Soybean meal	SM	100 tons
Oats	O	5,000 bushels
Wheat	W	5,000 bushels
Corn	C	5,000 bushels
Silver	AG	1,000 troy ounces
Gold	K	1 kilogram

SOURCE: Chicago Board of Trade.

particular price within a given period of time. The price of the contract is established on the floor of a commodities exchange.

Futures are traded in many areas: grain, meat, poultry, lumber, meats, gold, foreign currencies, petroleum, Treasury bonds and notes, and even stock indexes.

You can make money in one of two ways: by "going long," which means buying a contract to take ownership of a product to be delivered on a certain date at a predetermined price; or by "going short," which means agreeing to hand over a product on a certain date at a predetermined price. To take your profits or to cut your losses, you cancel your contract by offsetting it with a contract for the opposite trade. In other words, a futures contract obligates the buyer to buy and the seller to sell *unless* the contract is closed out by an offsetting sale or purchase to another investor before the so-called settlement date. For example, if you had purchased a May 1994 wheat contract and you wanted to get out of the market, you would sell a May 1994 contract, thus closing out the position. The two positions cancel each other out. If you don't offset, you are obliged to take physical delivery. It would be cumbersome and costly to have wheat unloaded into your living room.

The theory or rationale behind futures trading is twofold: 1) futures are supposed to transfer risk from one party to another; and 2) they are designed to even out price fluctuations. Although this theory tends to be true in agricultural

markets, the proliferation of financial and stock index futures has led to increased volatility and speculation.

Farmers use futures are a hedge against changes in prices for agricultural prices; manufacturers use them to lock in the price of raw materials they need, such as orange juice, oil, rubber, corn, wheat, sugar. International traders lock in values for currencies. Others, especially institutional investors, use futures to protect against stock market drops using futures on indexes, such as S&P's 500 Stock Index.

HOW THE MARKET OPERATES

Commodity trading is different from investing in stocks. When you buy a common stock, you own a part of the corporation and share in its profits, if any. If you pick a profitable company, the price of your stock will eventually rise.

With commodities, there is no equity. You basically buy hope. Once the futures contract has expired, there's no tomorrow. If your trade turned out badly, you must take the full loss. And it's a zero sum game: For every $1 won, $1 is lost by someone else.

➤ HEDGING   Let's say a hog farmer has animals that will be ready for market in 6 months. He wants to assure himself of today's market price for these hogs, which he does by selling a contract for future delivery. When the hogs are ready for market, if the price has dropped, he will be forced to take a lower price on the actual hogs, but he will have an offsetting gain, because the contract he sold 6 months ago was at a higher price. In other words, he closes that contract with a profit.

- *The advantage to the sellers:* They have themselves locked in a price, thereby protecting themselves from any future fall in the price of hogs. In effect, they have transferred this price risk to the buyers.
- *The advantage to the buyers:* They also have locked in a price, thereby protecting themselves from any future rise in the price of hogs. The buyer in this hypothetical case might be a speculator, a meat packer, or a meat processor.

➤ MARGIN   Since payment is not received until the delivery date, a type of binder or good faith

---

SPECIAL TERMS IN COMMODITIES TRADING

- **Arbitrage**   Simultaneous purchase and sale of the same or an equivalent security in order to make a profit from the price discrepancy.
- **Basis**   The difference between the cash price of a hedged money market instrument and a futures contract.
- **Contract month**   Month in which a futures contract may be fulfilled by making or taking delivery.
- **Cross hedge**   Hedging a cash market risk in one financial instrument by taking a position in a futures contract for a different but similar instrument.
- **Forward contract**   An agreement to buy or sell goods at a set price and date, when those involved plan to take delivery of the instrument.
- **Hedge**   Strategy used to offset an investment risk that involves buying and selling simultaneously in the futures market.
- **Index**   Statistical composite that measures the ups and downs of stocks, bonds, and commodities; reflects market prices and the number of shares outstanding for the companies in the index.
- **Long position**   Futures contract purchased to protect the investor against a rise in cost of a future commitment or against a drop in interest rates.
- **Mark to the market**   Debits and credits in each account at the close of the trading day.
- **Open interest**   Contracts that have not been offset by opposite transactions or by delivery.
- **Physical**   The underlying physical commodity.
- **Selling short**   A popular hedging technique involving sale of a futures contract that the seller does not own. A commodity sold short equals a promise to deliver at a future date.
- **Spot market**   Also known as the actual or physical market in which commodities are sold for immediate delivery.
- **Spread**   Holding opposite positions in two futures contracts with the intent of profit through changes in prices.

---

deposit is required. It is called "margin." The margin in the world of commodities is only a small percentage of the total amount due, but it serves as a guarantee for both buyer and seller. Unlike margin for stocks, which is an interest-bearing cost, margin for commodities is a security balance. You are not charged interest, but if the price of your futures drops by a certain percentage, more money must be deposited in the margin account or your position will be closed out by your broker.

In reality, most futures trading is not this simple. More often than not, the opposite side of each transaction is picked up by speculators who believe they can make money through favorable price changes during the months prior to delivery.

➤ TRADING LIMITATIONS The commodity exchanges set "day limits," based on the previous day's closing prices, specifying how widely a contract's trading price can move. The purpose of these limits is to prevent excessive short-term volatility and therefore also to keep margin requirements low. But trading limits can also lock traders into positions they cannot trade out of because the contract held is either up or down to the daily limit.

For example, an investor buys one gold contract (100 ounces) at $500 per ounce on June 30. On July 1 gold falls to $470 an ounce. The trading limit on gold is $20 per day, which means that on that day gold can be traded anywhere from $480 to $520 per ounce. Since the price has dropped below $480, trading is halted and the investor is locked into his position, unable to sell on that day. On the next day, July 2, the trading limits change to $460 to $500.

> PRICE QUOTATIONS Commodity prices are printed in the papers in various ways. In general you'll find the "high" (highest price of the day), the "low," and the "close." "Net change" refers to the change from the prior day's settlement price. The final column gives the high-low range for the year. Grain prices are given in cents per bushel; for example, wheat for December may be listed at a closing price of 3.71 per bushel.

STEPS TO TAKE

> GET CURRENT INFORMATION There is no inside information about commodities. All statistics are available in government reports, business and agricultural publications, newsletters, and special services. Always check two or three for confirmation and then review your conclusions with your broker. It will help to become something of an expert in both the fundamental and technical aspects of a few major commodities. When you become experienced, you can move into other areas where information is not so widely available.

> CHOOSE AN EXPERIENCED BROKER Deal only with a reputable firm that (1) has extensive commodities trading services and (2) includes a broker who knows speculations and can guide you. Never buy or sell as the result of a phone recommendation until it has been confirmed in written or printed form.

> ZERO IN ON A FEW COMMODITIES Preferably those in the news. For instance, during the drought in the Midwest in spring 1988, soybeans and grains experienced wild price gyrations.

COMMODITIES

PROS
↑ Large potential capital gains
↑ High amount of leverage available
↑ Small initial investment
↑ High liquidity

CONS
↓ Extremely risky
↓ Requires expertise
↓ Highly volatile
↓ Must continually monitor position
↓ Could lose total investment

Watch for such movements and remember that in commodities "the trend is your friend."

> AVOID THIN MARKETS You can score when such a commodity takes off, but the swings can be too fast and may send prices soaring or plummeting, and the amateur can get caught with no chance of closing a position.

> LOOK FOR A RATIO OF NET PROFIT TO NET LOSS OF 2:1 Since the percentage of losses will always be greater than that of profits, choose commodities where the potential gains (based on confirmed trends) can be more than double the possible losses.

> PREPARE AN OPERATIONAL PLAN Before you risk any money, test your hypothesis on paper until you feel confident that you understand what can happen. Do this for several weeks to get the feel of different types of contracts in different types of markets.

With an active commodity, "buy" contracts at several delivery dates and calculate the potential profits if the price rises moderately.

> NEVER MEET A MARGIN CALL When your original margin is impaired, your broker will call for more money. Except in most unusual circumstances, do not put in more money. Liquidate your position and accept your loss. This is a form of stop-loss safeguard. When a declining trend has been established, further losses can be expected.

> BE ALERT TO SPECIAL SITUATIONS Information is the key to profitable speculation. As you become more knowledgeable, you will pick up many points, such as these:

- If there's heavy spring and summer rain in Maine, buy long on potatoes. They need ideal weather.
- If there's a bad tornado over large portions of the Great Plains, buy wheat contracts. Chances are the wheat crop will be damaged, thus changing the supply and demand.

> TRADE WITH THE MAJOR TREND, AGAINST THE MINOR TREND With copper, for example, if you project a worldwide shortage of the metal and the market is in an uptrend, buy futures when the market suffers temporary weak spells. As long as prices keep moving up, you want to accumulate a meaningful position.

The corollary to this is never to average down. Adding to your loss position increases the number of contracts that are returning a loss.

By buying more, you put yourself in a stance where you can lose on more contracts if the price continues to drop.

Generally, if the trend is down, either sell short or stay out of the market.

➤ WATCH THE SPREADS BETWEEN DIFFERENT DELIVERY DATES In the strong summer market, the premium for January soybeans is 8¢ per bushel above the November contract. Buy November and sell January.

If the bull market persists, the premium should disappear and you will have a pleasant limited profit. Carrying charges on soybeans run about 6½¢ per month, so it is not likely that the spread will widen to more than 13¢ per bushel. Thus with that 8¢ spread, the real risk is not more than 5¢ per bushel.

➤ NEVER SPREAD A LOSS Turning a long or short position into a spread by buying or selling another contract month will seldom help you and in most cases will guarantee a locked-in loss. When you make a mistake, get out.

$ HINT: If you don't dare play the commodities game yourself, invest in one of the publicly traded commodity funds. They're diversified and professionally managed. You could, of course, lose money if the fund performs poorly, but you'll never be subject to margin calls.

➤ WATCH THE PRICE PEAKS AND LOWS Never sell at a price that is near the natural or government-imposed floor, and never buy at a price that is near its high.

Similarly, do not buy after the price of any commodity has passed its seasonal high or sell after it has dropped under its seasonal low.

➤ RISK NO MORE THAN 10% OF YOUR TRADING CAPITAL IN ANY ONE POSITION And risk no more than 30% of all capital in all positions at any one time—except when you have caught a strong upswing and can move with the trend. These limits will ease the effect of a bad decision. Few professionals count on being right more than half the time.

➤ BE SLOW TO LISTEN TO YOUR BROKER Unless the recommendations are backed by absolutely clear analyses. In most cases, by the time you get the word, smart traders have made their moves. To be successful, you must anticipate, not follow. The same caveat applies to professional newsletters.

COMMODITY FUTURES OPTIONS

COMMODITY	SYMBOLS	ONE CONTRACT EQUALS
Options on T-bond futures	CG, PG	One T-bond futures contract
Options on soybean futures	CZ, PZ	One soybean futures contract
Options on corn futures	CY, PY	One corn futures contract
Options on silver futures	AC, AP	One 1,000-ounce silver futures contract
Options on 10-year Treasury futures	TC, TP	One 10-year Treasury futures contract

SOURCE: Chicago Board of Trade.

➤ USE TECHNICAL ANALYSIS Especially charts, because timing is the key to speculative success, and with commodities, what has happened before is likely to be repeated.

COMMODITY FUNDS

There are a number of commodity futures funds open to individual investors. In addition to the fact that professionals make the buy and sell decisions, these funds diversify your investment dollars among many types of commodities, and your losses are limited to the amount you invest. Minimums range widely: the Cornerstone Fund (1-212-392-8837) requires $6,300, while the Trout Trading Fund (1-312-372-9262) requires $1 million.

Professional management, however, does not guarantee success and does not come cheap: funds have hefty sales fees plus annual management fees that can take anywhere from 10% to 20% of the fund's equity. Before investing in a fund, check its performance record in one of the publications listed in "For Further Information." And read the fund's prospectus, paying particular attention to its performance figures.

$ HINT: Although most commodity funds permit investors to get out, either monthly or quarterly, do not invest unless you plan

---

TIPS ON INVESTING IN COMMODITY FUNDS

Read the prospectus to determine:
- The average annual performance
- Rules regarding redeeming shares
- Net worth and income requirements for investing
- Fees
- If the adviser is registered with the Commodities Futures Trading Commission; if not, do business elsewhere

---

to stay in for at least a year. On a short-term basis, commodities are more volatile than stocks, fluctuating as much as 5% to 10% per month. Funds also have hefty fees: Sales charges range from 5% to 8% of your initial investment plus an annual management fee.

COMMODITY ADVISERS

One avenue for help is the trading adviser. These professionals must be registered with the Commodity Futures Trading Commission. They charge in one of two ways: a percentage, usually 6%, of the funds turned over to them, or an incentive fee, typically 15% of any profits generated by the adviser.

$ HINT: Select an adviser who has an annual rate of return of at least 25% for a minimum of 3 years.

Burlington Hall Asset Management, in Hackettstown, NJ, offers a software program, called "La Porte Asset Allocation System," that evaluates trading advisers. For details, call: 1-908-852-1694.

Performance records of major advisers are also tracked by several of the publications listed below.

FOR FURTHER INFORMATION

Commodity Traders Consumer Report
1831 Howe Avenue
Sacramento, CA 95825
1-800-999-CTCR
Bimonthly; $198 per year; one trial issue: $35

Tracks commodities advisers and provides useful information on how to trade.

Managed Account Reports
220 Fifth Avenue
New York, NY 10001
1-212-213-6202
Monthly; $299 per year; one free sample copy

Tracks commodity funds.

Dwight A. Jackson, *The Individual Investor's Guide to Commodities* (Chicago: Probus, 1991).

21 PRECIOUS METALS

Some say it's a hedge against inflation; doomsayers sweat it's our only protection against the inevitable downfall of our entire economic system. And in between are those who believe in diversification. Precious metals have a place, albeit it a small place, in every portfolio *as long as one realizes they are volatile—you have to know when to sell or else be willing to hold long term.*

If you decide to invest, here are your choices:

- BULLION You can buy actual bars of the metal itself, called ingots, through larger banks, brokerage firms, and major dealers. It must be assayed (certified for weight and purity) before reselling. Bullion requires storage and does not pay dividends or benefit from compounding
- BULLION CERTIFICATES Unless you want to fill up your living room with bars or coins, buy certificates. The minimum is typically $1,000, and they are sold at roughly 3% over the price of the metal.
- BULLION COINS Not to be confused with rare coins, these have very little or no value as a collectible. Bullion coins, issued by the United States and a handful of other countries (see box on page 225), also must be stored. Their price is based on their gold content, whereas rare coins purchased at auctions or from dealers have a numismatic value, which is based upon their age, rarity, and popularity.
- MINING STOCKS Another route is to purchase the individual stocks of mining companies. Stocks offer potential price appreciation and dividend income, yet leave you subject to political upheavals, mining strikes, and the overall trend of the stock market.

Mining stocks tend to rise faster in price than the gold itself when the market is up and they usually drop faster than the metal when its price drops.

- MUTUAL FUNDS Funds specializing in precious metals are one of the easier ways to invest. However, this is not a "pure" play because you are buying partial shares of stocks of companies that mine metals. Your profit will depend on how well the fund is managed.
- OPTIONS Options on metals and mining stocks are listed in the newspaper. (See Chapter 16 for more on options.)
- FUTURES CONTRACTS These are available on precious and industrial metals and are the riskiest choice because they involve betting on the future direction of prices. With a gold, silver, or platinum futures contract, you agree to buy or sell a certain quantity at a specified price. You are required to put up 5% to 10% of the value of the contract as "margin." Although you control a large amount of metal for a relatively small amount of money, you can lose your entire investment if your bet is wrong. (See Chapter 22 for more on Futures.)

The true gold buffs shun mutual funds, stocks, and certificates, maintaining that if the world caves in, only the real tangible metals will be valuable. If you're less of a purist, then you may be content with a certificate or shares of a stock or a fund. After all, gold, silver, and platinum do not pay dividends and can never benefit from compounding.

☐ CAUTION: Put no more than 5% to 8% of your portfolio in precious metals.

GUIDELINES FOR BUYING

Here are the key facts to keep in mind:

GOLD
To enhance your potential profits in gold, watch for changes in these leading indicators:

- Political situation in South Africa
- The trend of inflation and the Consumer Price Index
- Movement of interest rates
- Direction of the dollar
- Third-world debt and related banking problems
- Changes in gold production

Remember, gold vies with the dollar as the world's safest currency. When the dollar is strong, gold tends to be low in price and vice versa.

In 1960, gold was $35 per ounce; in 1970, also $35 per ounce; in 1980, $612 per ounce; in 1990, $383; and as we go to press, $391.

BEFORE BUYING A PRECIOUS METAL

Follow these guidelines and heed these warnings:

- Paper trade for at least 1 month. Make decisions, calculate margins, set stop-loss prices, and monitor how well you are doing in theory.
- Never commit more than 5% of your risk capital to metals. If you are trading contracts, keep the balance in a money market account to meet any margin calls.
- Read the commodity columns in the *Wall Street Journal* and *Barron's*. Ask several dealers to send you their research reports.
- Track the direction of interest rates, inflation, and the spot prices of the metals. (Spot price is the cash price for metals that are delivered at once.)
- Never give discretionary powers to anyone in the business.
- Never place an order over the phone with someone who has called you cold.

SILVER
Silver is primarily an industrial metal; its price is directly related to supply and demand and less (as is the case with gold) to inflation, interest rates, and politics. Silver is used in coins, jewelry, and silverware, but its greatest demand is in the photographic, elec-

NO LOAD GOLD FUNDS		
FUND	TOTAL RETURN Jan-June 1993	TELEPHONE
US Gold Shares	104.00%	1-800-873-8637
Bull & Bear Gold Investors	73.72	1-800-847-4200
US World Gold	70.00	1-800-873-8637
Lexington Gold Fund	69.19	1-800-526-0056
Vanguard Spec Portfolio-Gold	65.19	1-800-662-7447

tronic, dental, and medical fields. Its industrial uses are so great, in fact, that the world consumes as much silver as is mined.

In 1980 the Hunt brothers tried to corner the market in silver, and at that time the price soared to $48 an ounce only to fall rapidly. As we go to press it's around $5.03 an ounce. The American silver bullion coin is called the Silver Eagle.

PLATINUM

Although platinum has generally been considered more valuable than gold or silver because of its limited availability, it has never been as popular with investors. Its primary uses are in the electronics, chemical, and automobile industries. It is an essential ingredient in the production of catalytic converters for pollution control in cars.

Its use as an antipollutant is expected to create more demand as emission control regulations become increasingly strict in both the United States and Europe. Platinum coins include the Noble, Canadian Maple Leaf, and Australian Koala.

BUYING METALS BY PHONE

Although you should never succumb to a high-pressure salesman, you can buy bullion bars and coins by phone from reliable dealers; however, check prices and fees first.

- *Wilmington Trust Refined Investments* allows clients to use their VISA or MasterCard to buy precious metals, provided you store the metals with them. Call: 1-800-223-1080. (Their 24-hour Quoteline gives the latest spot prices: 1-302-427-4700.)
- *Merrill Lynch's "Blueprint"* program has a minimum purchase of only $100 with $50 thereafter. Call: 1-800-637-3766.
- *Benham Certified Metals* has a discount brokerage division. The minimum for silver is $1,000 and $2,000 for gold and platinum. Call: 1-800-447-4653.
- *Rhode Island Hospital Trust National Bank* of Providence sells coins, bars, and certificates. Call: 1-800-343-8419.

FOR FURTHER INFORMATION

Dow Theory Letters
P.O. Box 1759
La Jolla, CA 92037
1-619-454-0481
$250 per year

Your Introduction to Investing in Gold and *Your Introduction to Investing in Silver*
The Gold and Silver Institute
1112 16th Street NW
Washington, DC 20036
1-202-835-0185
$5 each

FINANCIAL FUTURES AND MARKET INDEXES

FINANCIAL FUTURES

If trading corn and pork bellies is too tame, you can move along to another type of commodity: interest-bearing securities, such as Treasury bonds and notes, CDs, and Ginnie Maes. For amateurs, financial futures and stock indexes are just about the riskiest areas of Wall Street. Yet professional money managers use them as investment tools, as a way to hedge their portfolios. Just as agribusinesses rely on commodities futures, so money managers and others use financial futures to protect their profits.

Financial futures trading requires an ability to predict correctly the short-term or intermediate movements of interest rates, because futures involve debt issues whose values move with the cost of money; that is, with interest rates. With tiny margins (as small as $800 to control $1 million), a shift of ½% in the interest rate can double your money—or lose most of your capital.

The swings of financial futures are often dramatic, but the forecast of higher interest rates by only one financial guru can send these contracts down as fast as a punctured balloon.

If you are a modest investor, skip this chapter. If you have over $100,000 in a portfolio, read it rapidly. If you are a speculator who can afford to lose half your stake, study the explanations and then deal with an experienced broker.

HOW FINANCIAL FUTURES WORK

Basically, these are contracts that involve money. They are used by major investors, such as banks, insurance companies, and pension fund managers, to protect positions by hedging: What they gain (lose) in the cash market will be offset by the loss (profit) in the futures market.

The terms and rules of trading are set by the exchanges.

A financial futures contract is in essence a contract on an interest rate. The most popular are Treasury bills, bonds, and notes; Ginnie Maes; and CDs. They are sold through brokers or firms specializing in commodities. Contract sizes vary with the underlying security and the exchange, but they range from approximately $20,000 to $1 million. However, since margin requirements are low, sometimes only 5% to 10% of total value, your actual outlay is surprisingly little, relatively speaking.

The value of a financial futures contract is determined by interest rates:

- When rates rise, the price of fixed-income securities and the futures based on them *fall*.
- When rates decline, these investments *rise* in value.

$ HINT: Place stop orders with your broker. These provide instructions to close out your position when the price falls to a certain level, which will help limit any potential losses.

U.S. TREASURY BOND FUTURES

Since their introduction in 1977, U.S. T-bond futures have become the most actively traded futures contract worldwide. Although there are various other financial futures traded, we will illustrate the principle with T-bonds and T-notes. ("For Further Information" at the end of this chapter lists more in-depth studies of trading financial futures.)

Like all futures contracts, T-bond futures contracts are standardized (see box on page 228). Their only variable is the price, which is established on the floor of the Chicago Board of

Trade. Bond prices, of course, move in inverse relationship to interest rates: When rates rise, bond prices fall. Speculators and others use T-bonds to take advantage of anticipated interest rate changes; hedgers focus more on reducing and managing risk for their portfolios.

▶ IF YOU EXPECT INTEREST RATES TO FALL Such an expectation implies that bond futures will rise. This means you'll want to take a long position in order to take advantage of the potentially rising bond market (to be long on a contract is to buy it; to short a contract is to sell). For example, if bond futures are now trading at 72% of par, you go long one $100,000-face-value bond contract. If bond prices then rise to 74% of par, you offset your original long position by going short for a profit of 2 points, or $2,000.

Long one contract @ 72 or $72,000
Short one contract @ 74 or $74,000
Profit: $2,000

▶ IF YOU EXPECT INTEREST RATES TO RISE You then take a short position. Then when bond prices fall to 69, you can offset your original position by going long for a $3,000 profit.

Short one contract @ 72 or $72,000
Long one contract @ 69 or $69,000
Profit: $3,000

▶ SPREADS Speculators usually trade financial futures by going long on one position and short on another with both contracts due in the same month. But you can also use spreads: buying one contract month and selling another. This technique is used when there's an abnormal relation between the yields and thus the prices of two contracts with different maturities. These situations don't come often, but when they do, they can be mighty rewarding, because the gains will come from a restoration of the normal spread.

Example: An investor notes that June T-bonds are selling at 80-11 (each $1/32$% equals $3.125 of a standard $100,000 contract) and that September's are at 81-05. The basis for quotations is an 8% coupon and 15-year maturity.

Based on experience, he decides that this $26/32$ difference ($81^5/_{32} - 80^{11}/_{32} = {}^{26}/_{32}$) is out

of line with normal pricing. He *sells* the September contract and *buys* the June one. In a couple of weeks, prices begin to normalize: The September contract edges up to 81-08 and the June one surges to 80-24. Now he starts to cash in: He loses $3/32$ ($93.75) on the September contract but gains $13/32$ ($406.25) on the June one: $312.50 profit minus commission.

RULES TO FOLLOW

If you have money you can afford to lose, time enough to keep abreast of developments in the financial world, strong nerves, and a trustworthy, knowledgeable broker, trading in financial futures may be rewarding and surely will be exciting. Of course, if you're involved with substantial holdings, you probably are already familiar with hedging, so you can stick to protective contracts. Otherwise, follow these rules:

- *Make dry runs on paper for several months.* Interest rates change slowly. Pick different types of financial futures each

---

U.S. TREASURY BOND FUTURES

Trading unit: $100,000 face value of U.S. T-bonds

Deliverable: U.S. Treasury bonds with a nominal 8% coupon maturing at least 15 years from delivery date if not callable; if callable, not for at least 15 years from delivery date

Delivery method: Federal Reserve book entry wire transfer system

Par: $1,000

Price quote: Percentage of par in minimum increments of $1/32$ point, or $3.125 per "tick," e.g., 74-01 means $74^1/_{32}$% of par

Daily price limit: $^{64}/_{32}$ or $2,000 per contract above or below the previous day's settlement price

Delivery months: March, June, September, or December

Ticker symbol: US—traded on Chicago Board of Trade

week and keep practicing until you get a feel for the market and risks and, over at least a week, chalk up more winners than losers.

- *Buy long when you look for a drop in interest rates.* With lower yields, the prices of all contracts will rise.
- *Sell short when you expect a higher cost of money.* This will force down the value of the contracts, and you can cover your position at a profit.
- *Set a strategy and stick to it.* Don't try to mix contracts until you are comfortable and making money.

§ HINT: Set stop and limit orders, not market orders. A market order is executed immediately at the best possible price. A stop order, to buy or to sell at a given price, becomes a market order when that price is touched. A limit order is the maximum price at which to buy and the minimum at which to sell.

OPTIONS ON FUTURES

Another way to participate in the futures market is through options (see Chapter 16). A futures option is a contract that gives you the right to buy (call) or sell (put) a certain futures contract within a specified period of time for a specified price (called the premium).

▶ OPTIONS ON COMMODITIES FUTURES Options are traded on futures for agricultural commod-ities, oil, livestock, metals, etc. Quotes are listed in the newspaper under "Futures Options." These involve far less money than contracts do: roughly, $100 for an option compared to $1,800 for a futures contract. There are no margin calls, and the risk is limited to the premium. But these are for professionals and gamblers. If you ride a strong market trend, you can make a lot of money with a small outlay and rapid fluctuations, or you can make a modest profit by successful hedging. *Be cautious and limit your commitment.* It's easy to con yourself into thinking you're a genius when you hit a couple of big winners fast, but unless you bank half of those profits, you will lose money over a period of time if only because of the commissions.

▶ OPTIONS ON FINANCIAL FUTURES Options are also traded on some interest-bearing securities, such as Treasury bills and notes. T-bond options, for example, are traded on the Chicago Board of Trade. The T-bond futures contract underlying the option is for $100,000 of Treasury bonds, bearing an 8% or equivalent coupon, which do not mature and are noncallable for at least 15 years. When long-term interest rates fall, the value of the futures contract and the call option increases while the value of a put option de-creases. The opposite is true when long-term rates rise.

Premiums for T-bond futures options are quoted in $\frac{1}{64}$ths of 1% (1 point). Thus $\frac{1}{64}$ point equals $15.63 ($100,000 $\times$ 0.01 $\times$ $\frac{1}{64}$). A premium quote of 2–16 means $2^{16}/_{64}$, or [(2 $\times$ 64) + 16] $\times$ $15.63, or $2,250.72 per option.

CONTRACT SPECIFICATIONS OF FUTURES				
	U.S. TREASURY BONDS	10-YEAR U.S. TREASURY NOTES	GNMA-CDR	GNMA II
Basic trading unit	$100,000 face value	$100,000 face value	$100,000 principal balance	$100,000 principal balance
Price quotation	Full points (one point equals $1,000) and 32nds of a full point			
Minimum price fluctuation	$\frac{1}{32}$ of a full point ($3.125 per contract)			
Daily price limit	$^{64}/_{32}$ (2 points or $2,000) above or below the previous day's settlement price			
Date introduced	Aug. 22, 1977	May 3, 1982	Oct. 20, 1975	1984
Ticker symbol	US	TY	M	GT

SOURCE: Chicago Board of Trade.

The profit is the premium you receive when the option is sold minus the premium paid when you purchased the option.

➤ SETTING UP HEDGES Options provide excellent opportunities to set up hedges if you plan your strategy and understand the risks and rewards. Here's an example cited by Stanley Angrist in *Forbes.*

In March, the June T-bond contract is selling at 72–05 (72⅝). Calls at 72, 74, and 76 are quoted at premiums of 2–06, 1–20, and 0–46, respectively; puts at 68, 70, and 72 are available at 0–30, 0–61, and 1–54. You think that the market will remain stable, so you make these paper projections of hedges with a margin of $3,000:

Sell June 72 call	$2,093.75
Sell June 72 put	1,843.75
Total income	$3,937.50

If the T-bond is still worth 72 on the June strike date, both options will expire worthless, so you have an extra $3,937.50 minus commissions.

Sell June 74 call	$1,312.50
Sell June 70 put	953.13
Total income	$2,265.63

GOVERNMENT INSTRUMENT FUTURES CONTRACTS

COMMODITY	SYMBOL	ONE CONTRACT EQUALS
U.S. Treasury bonds	US	Face value at maturity: $100,000
10-year T-notes	TY	Face value at maturity: $100,000
GNMA	M	$100,000 principal balance
30-day Treasury repo	—	$2.5 million face value
90-day Treasury repo	—	$1 million face value
Zero coupon T-bonds	—	Discounted
Zero coupon T-notes	—	Discounted

SOURCE: Chicago Board of Trade.

This is less risky, and less profitable, because both options will expire worthless if the last-day price is between 70 and 74.

Sell June 76 call	$ 718.75
Sell June 68 call	468.75
Total income	$1,187.50

If the final price is between 68 and 76, you will do OK. You swap a lower income for a broader price range.

STOCK INDEXES

You can also trade stock index options and stock index futures options.

These are the fastest-growing area of speculations and make it possible to play the market without owning a single share of stock. They combine the growth potential of equities with the speculative hopes of commodities.

With a stock index, you are betting on the future price of the composite of a group of stocks: *buying* if you anticipate a rise soon, *selling* if you look for a decline. You put up cash or collateral equal to about 7% of the contract value versus 50% for stocks. All you need is a little capital and a lot of nerve. A minor jiggle can produce sizable losses or gains. And there are also options that require even less money.

To emphasize the speculative nature of indexes, some brokerage firms advise their brokers to limit trading to individuals with a net worth of $100,000 (exclusive of home and life insurance).

These stock indexes currently have futures contracts and/or options on futures available:

- **Standard & Poor's 500 (SPX):** stocks of 500 industrials, financial companies, utilities, and transportation issues, all listed on the NYSE. They are weighted by market value. This means each stock is weighted so that changes in the stock's price influence the index in proportion to the stock's representative market value. Contracts are valued at 500 times the index. They are traded on the Chicago Mercantile Exchange. Generally, this is the index favored by big hitters, as contracts are extremely liquid and it's widely used to measure institutional performance. *Options* on the SPX trade only on the Chicago Board of Options Exchange (CBOE).

- **Standard & Poor's 100:** a condensed version of the S&P 500 index (known as OEX). It is weighted by capitalization of the component corporations, all of which have options traded on the CBOE. The value is 100 times the worth of the stocks.
- **Value Line Composite (XVL):** an equally weighted geometric index of about 1,700 stocks actively traded on the NYSE, AMEX, and OTC. Contracts are quoted at 500 times the index. This tends to be difficult to trade because of a thin market on the small Kansas City Board of Trade. Options trade on the Philadelphia exchange.
- **AMEX Market Value Index (XAM):** measures the changes in the aggregate market of over 800 AMEX issues. The weighting is by industry groups: 32% natural resources, 19% high technology, 13% service, 11% consumer goods. No one company accounts for more than 7% of the total.
- **Major Market Index (XMI):** based on 20 blue chip NYSE stocks and price-weighted so that higher-priced shares have a greater effect on the average than lower-priced ones. Options trade on the American exchange.
- **AMEX Oil & Gas Index (XOI):** made up of the stocks of 30 oil and gas companies, with Exxon representing about 17%. Options trade on the AMEX.
- **Computer Technology Index (XCI):** stocks of 30 major computer companies, with IBM accounting for about half and Hewlett-Packard, Digital Equipment, and Motorola another 16%. Options trade on the American.
- **NYSE Composite Index (NYA):** a capitalization-weighted average of about 1,500 Big Board stocks. Options trade on the New York Stock Exchange.
- **Standard & Poor's Computer & Business Equipment Index (OBR):** a capitalization-weighted average of a dozen major office and business equipment companies, with IBM about 75%, Digital Equipment, Wang, and NCR about 18%.
- **Technology Index (PTI):** a price-weighted index of 100 stocks of which 45 are traded OTC. Very volatile. Options trade on the Philadelphia Stock Exchange.
- **Gold & Silver Index (XAU):** options trade on the Philadelphia Stock Exchange.
- **National OTC Index (NCMP):** options trade on the Philadelphia Stock Exchange.
- **NYSE Beta Index (NHB):** options trade on the New York Stock Exchange.

GUIDELINES FOR SUCCESS

- *Follow the trend.* If the price of the index is higher than it was the day before, which in turn is higher than it was the previous day, go long. If the reverse, sell short.
- *Set stop-loss prices at 3 points below cost.* If they are too close, one erratic move can stop you out at a loss even though the market may resume its uptrend soon.
- *Recognize the role of the professionals.* To date, most contracts have been traded by brokerage houses active in arbitrage and spreads and in hedging large block positions. Only a handful of institutional managers have done more than experiment. So the amateur is competing with top professionals who have plenty of capital and no commissions to pay and who are in positions to get the latest information and make quick decisions.
- *Study the price spreads.* Contracts for distant months are more volatile. In a strong market, buy far-out contracts and short nearby months; in a weak market, buy the closer months and short the distant ones.
- *Be mindful that dividends can distort prices.* In heavy payout months, these discrepancies can be significant.
- *Use a hedge only when your portfolio approximates that of the index:* roughly a minimum of $250,000 (very rarely does a major investor buy only 100 shares of a stock). In most cases, any single portfolio has little resemblance to that of the index.

HOW OPTIONS ON STOCK INDEXES WORK

These are the ultimate in speculations. For a few hundred dollars, you can control a cross section of stocks worth $75,000 or so. The action is fast and exciting. The options, both calls and puts, have expiration dates every 3 months, they are quoted at intervals of 5 points, and their premiums reflect hopes and fears, the time premiums declining with the approach of the strike date. There are no margin calls, and the risks are limited.

Example: An investor has $60,000 worth of quality stocks and anticipates a drop in the overall stock market. The Standard & Poor's 500 index is at 151.50. She sells short one September contract. By mid-September the index is up to 153, so she didn't need the protection. She paid $150 for insurance, but the value of her holdings was up about $600.

With volatile stocks, options on the special indexes can be useful. You're bullish (but hesitant) on high-tech stocks. Here's what to do, according to *Indicator Digest:*

- In January the XCO options index is at 100.79. You buy a March 100 call at 4⅜ and sell a March 105 call at $1^{13}/_{16}$: a net cost of $2^{9}/_{16}$ points, or $256.25 (not counting commissions).
- If the XCO trades at 105 or above at expiration (about +4%), you make 2¼ points ($225)—more than an 80% gain. The maximum loss will be the cost of the spread if the index trades at 100 or less at expiration.

With all options on indexes, settlements are made in cash. When the option is exercised, the holder receives the difference between the exercise price and the closing index price on the date the option is exercised.

▢CAUTION: This can be far from the price the day the assignment notice is received. A hedge can lose on both the long and short side!

FOR FURTHER INFORMATION

Al Gietzen, *Real-Time Futures Trading* (Chicago: Probus, 1992).

Mark J. Powers, *Inside the Financial Futures Markets* (New York: John Wiley & Sons, 1991).

Edward W. Schwartz, *Financial Futures* (Homewood, IL: Dow Jones–Irwin, 1986).

William and Susan Nix, *The Dow Jones–Irwin Guide to Stock Index Futures and Options* (Homewood, IL: Dow Jones–Irwin, 1984).

Contact the following exchanges for pamphlets on futures trading:

The Options Exchange
400 South La Salle
Chicago, IL 60605
1-312-786-5600

Chicago Board of Trade
Literature Services Department
141 West Jackson Blvd.
Chicago, IL 60604
1-312-435-3500

Chicago Mercantile Exchange
30 South Wacker Drive
Chicago, IL 60606
1-312-930-1000

Chicago Mercantile Exchange
67 Wall Street
New York, NY 10005
1-212-363-7000

23 SPLITS, SPIN-OFFS, SMALL-CAPS, SPIDERS, AND STOCK BUY-BACKS

This catchall chapter is simultaneously geared to experienced investors and those with money set aside for speculation. Opportunities are investments and speculations. The definition depends on the type of security, the quality of the corporation, and the trading techniques used.

- **Splits.** Companies that split their stocks can be excellent investments when these splits are justified by profitable growth. The techniques used in buying and selling, however, can be speculative: That is, when it appears that a company may split its stock, the price of its shares will usually rise rapidly and, after the split, fall sharply. The long-term investor who bought the shares when undervalued will probably benefit automatically. The speculative investor, however, buys as the prospects of a split catch Wall Street's fancy and sells at a quick profit right after the announcement.

- **Spin-offs.** When a company divests itself of a subsidiary, the investor in the parent company automatically owns stock in the new company as well. This provides possible price appreciation.

- **Small-caps.** Companies with a small number of shares can be investments when you know, and have confidence in, the owners, but they are speculations when there are problems because of limited capital, poor management, or threats of acquisition.

- **Spiders.** A unit investment trust that tracks the performance of the Standard & Poor's 500 Stock Index. It trades on the American Stock Exchange.

- **Bankrupt companies.** Bankrupt stocks offer speculative investors an opportunity to make money if the company pulls itself together or restructures successfully.

- **Stock buy-backs.** Companies often buy back their own shares to maintain control. This procedure often boosts the stock's price.

COMPANIES THAT SPLIT THEIR STOCKS FREQUENTLY

One of the most rewarding and exciting investments can be a corporation that increases the number of its shares of common stock: issuing 1 or more shares for each outstanding share. Such splits usually occur when:

- The price of such a stock moves to a historic high so that individual investors are unwilling or unable to buy shares. Psychologically, a stock trading at 50 will attract far more than double the number of investors who are willing to pay 100.

- A small, growing company, whose shares are traded OTC, wants to list its stock on an exchange where the rules for listing are far tougher. The NYSE, for example, requires a minimum of 1.1 million common shares and at least 2,000 shareholders with 100 shares or more. Such a listing broadens investment acceptance as many institutions prefer the liquidity of an established market, and more individuals can use the shares as collateral for margin loans.

- A corporation seeks to make an acquisition with minimal cash or debt.

- The price of the stock reaches $75 per share. The most attractive range for most investors is $20 to $45 a share, so few splits are declared when the stock price is that low.

- Management becomes fearful of an unfriendly takeover. When the top officials hold only a small percentage of the outstanding shares, a stock split will make more shares available at a lower price and thus, it is hoped, lessen the likelihood of a raid.

■ Earnings are likely to continue to grow, which means that the price of the shares will keep rising. With more stock, the per-share profits will appear smaller—for a while.

■ The company has a record of stock splits. This indicates that the directors recognize, and are familiar with, the advantages of adding shares to keep old stockholders and attract new ones.

SPIN-OFFS

These take place when the parent company divests itself of a division, which may be unrelated to the rest of the business or may not fit into the parent company's future plans. The new division becomes an independent company. The parent company then issues shares in this new corporation to shareholders of the parent company in proportion to their original investment. Now they hold shares in two companies instead of one.

The theory behind a spin-off is that the division will be better off operating independently and that the parent company will be better off without this particular division. A prime example: General Mills' spin-off of its fashion and toy divisions. Similarly, after Allied Corp. and Signal Corp. merged, the parent company selected a number of businesses in which it was less interested and spun these off as an entity called Henley Group. Thus shareholder value was maintained and the parent company's objectives were met.

If you have a good sense of timing, you may be able to cash in on spin-offs. Most follow a fairly similar pattern:

■ When a new stock is spun off, it tends to be sold by the shareholder recipients.

■ Afterwards, the spun-off stock tends to rise in price as its true value is realized.

That corporate spin-offs create shareholder wealth has been verified by several studies. The Pennsylvania State University's Department of Finance found that performance of parent companies' shares outpaced the benchmark indexes, and in one out of seven cases, the spin-offs eventually attracted premium-priced takeover bids. A University of Texas Graduate School of Business study found that shares of spin-offs fell 4% to 10% during the first days of trading and then moved up. That time period is obviously optimum buying time.

§ IF YOU DARE: Buy spin-off shares after they decline, if you have faith in the company, and hold for the long term or until they have rebounded close to their initial price.

SMALL-CAP STOCKS

Small-cap companies typically have a capitalization of $150 million or less. With blue chips up in price, small-caps, like OTC issues, offer a defensive position against a market correction, as well as an alternative to paying high premiums for quality stocks. They have outperformed larger stocks in the early stages of the last eight bull markets.

Second-tier stocks have been pushed to the foreground because of the diminishing supply of moderately priced blue chips due to the large number of takeovers and leveraged buyouts that took place in the late 1980s. This trend removed common shares from the trading arena.

Small-caps are not without their problems, however. They are not heavily followed by Wall Street pros, which means little readily available research, but that also means they're often undiscovered and still low in price.

When corporations have a limited number of shares, their stock prices can move sharply: up when there's heavy buying, down when there's concerted selling. Theoretically, when a company has fewer than 500,000 shares, it should be an excellent speculation. Typically, the price-earnings ratios are low and the dividends sometimes relatively high. These firms are often targets for merger or acquisition and thus profitable long-term speculations.

If you prefer to have a professional select small-cap stocks, then investigate one of the mutual funds that specialize in these companies (see box page 235).

➤ TEN OVERLOOKED SMALL-CAP STOCKS FOR 1994 Small-cap stocks typically have faster earnings growth rates than large-cap companies. Their capitalizations range from several million dollars to $600 million versus the median capitalization of $2.6 billion for the S&P 500 and $766 million for the S&P MidCap 400 Index. Statistics compiled by Ibbotson Associates show that since 1954, in every 12-month period following a recession, small-company stocks have outperformed large-company stocks. Although these issues could benefit from the expected improvement in the economy, they are indeed speculative and should be considered as a way to diversify your portfolio and not as your only holdings.

- *Amtel Corp.* (OTC: ATML; $26) A producer of logic and memory semiconductors; serves rapidly growing markets such as cellular telephones and portable computers. Company has an aggressive new products program.
- *Analytical Surveys* (OTC: ANLT; $4) A leader in the digital mapping business; could benefit from increased spending on our infrastructure.
- *Banyan Systems* (OTC: BNYN; $19) Specializes in systemwide networking software products that allow PC users to access other networks. Revenues are growing rapidly, but stock is fairly risky.
- *Blair Corp.* (AMEX: BL $48) Mail-order retailer of reasonably priced clothes; annual revenues of $500 million, with net profit margins of 7%, double the industry standard. Expanding market: senior citizens and recession-conscious consumers.
- *BPI Environmental* (OTC: BPIE; $6) Company makes thin plastic sheeting for bags that take up far less of the landfill space of regular bags. Should benefit from new environmental protection laws.
- *Clarcor* (NYSE: CLC $19) Some 35% of

sales derived from making custom containers for consumer goods, such as metal Band-Aid boxes. Almost has a monopoly on this business.

- *Giddings & Lewis* (OTC: GIDL; $21) Machine tool maker; acquired Cross & Trecker in 1991, making it the largest North American producer of automated machine tools and assembly equipment. Expanding business in Europe.
- *Gaylord Container* (AMEX: GCR; $2½) Makes corrugated packaging products and is just coming out of Chapter 11 bankruptcy.
- *Lamson & Sessions* (NYSE: LMS; $5) This manufacturer of industrial equipment is likely to see increased earnings as the United States spends more on repairing its infrastructure.
- *Noise Cancellation Technologies* (OTC: NCTI; $4) Has its own unique way of reducing noise pollution in industry; a very speculative but interesting stock.

➤ SMALL-CAP MUTUAL FUNDS The average small-cap fund posted solid gains in 1992 and into the early months of 1993 and then plunged on fears that President Clinton's economic proposals would dampen the recovery. Although their returns continue to gyrate, they should not be ignored by investors willing to take some risks in their portfolios.

$ HINT: To cushion the uncertainty related to small-cap companies: 1) Only put up to 25% of your equity money in these funds; 2) plan to stay invested a minimum of three years; 3) select small-cap funds that aim to preserve capital, such as those listed in the box below.

SMALL-CAP STOCK FUNDS THAT TAKE LOW RISKS

These funds purchase less volatile, low P/E stocks and hold on average 35 to 40 stocks from a wide number of different industries.

FUND	TOTAL RETURN JAN-JUNE 1993	TELEPHONE
Fasciano	2.06%	1-800-848-6050
Fidelity OTC	−0.12	1-800-544-8888
Nicholas II	−0.08	1-414-272-6133
Pennsylvania Mutual	+4.00	1-800-221-4268
Winthrop-Focus Aggressive Growth	+2.90	1-800-225-8011

SPIDERS

Leave it to Wall Street to come up with another animal product (see LYONS in Chapter 12). The Spiders crawled out of the financial web on January 29, 1993, when they became available on the American Stock Exchange.

SPDRs (Standard & Poor's Depository Receipts) are shares in a unit investment trust that tracks the performance of the Standard & Poor's 500 Index. Their key advantage is that they enable you to buy the Standard and Poor's 500 just as if it were a single share of stock. They actually provide all the diversity and market-tracking ability of an index fund, and they have the plus of being liquid since they are a widely held and actively traded stock. (Index funds are designed to give you an opportunity to earn market returns by buying all or a portion of the securities in a market index. See page 87 for a discussion of index funds, including those that mimic the Standard & Poor's 500.)

Since Spiders trade like stocks, they are subject to price fluctuations. The Standard & Poor's 500 as of spring 1993 was around 450; Spiders at the same time were priced at approximately one-tenth of the index valuation, at 45. The symbol for Spiders that trade only on the American is SPY.

How do you decide whether to buy a Standard & Poor's index fund or this Spider? It depends upon the amount of your investment and how long you plan to hold it. Keep these factors in mind:

- You buy shares in an index fund directly from the sponsor at the net asset value (the total of the fund's holdings divided by the number of shares outstanding).
- Spiders must be bought through stockbrokers, which entails a commission. They are also sold with a bid/asked spread.
- Index funds may have a load or sales fee or may be of the no-load variety.
- Spider management expenses are deducted from the quarterly cash distribution and are capped at $1/20$th of 1%.
- Index funds often have an annual account maintenance fee—Vanguard's, for example, is $10.
- Most people who invest in funds have their dividends reinvested.

- Spiders distribute all dividends on a quarterly basis so you do not have the benefit of increasing your holdings through accrual.
- The Spider dividend rate as of spring 1993, was only about 2.5%—about the same as bank savings rates.
- With an index fund, you pay taxes on capital gains distributions once a year.
- With Spiders, you pay tax on any capital gains only when you sell your position.

$ HINT: *If you are a frequent trader:* Spiders seem to be a better bet, even taking brokerage commissions into consideration. You can trade them all day long, while with index funds (or any funds, for that matter) purchases and redemptions are based only on end-of-the-day prices.

Stephen Bloom, vice president for new market development at the American Stock Exchange, gives this example:

If you wanted to sell when the market opened on Monday, October 19, 1987, you could have sold Spiders (had they existed then) early in the morning when the Standard & Poor's 500 was at 270, down from the opening of 283, for only a 5% loss on the day. On the other hand, if you wanted to get out of a Standard & Poor's 500 index fund, you wouldn't have been able to do so until the end of the day at the closing price, which was 225. With a fund you would have had a 20% loss.

Index funds, however, are more cost-efficient over time. Of the nearly 30 funds that track the Standard & Poor's 500, the largest in which individuals can invest is the Vanguard Index Trust 500. Although it has no load, it takes 19 basis points off dividends for operating expenses and you must pay a $10 annual maintenance fee. With a Spider, you pay a brokerage commission, and a management fee of 20 basis points is taken out of dividends.

However, Vanguard limits its investors' trades to two purchases and sales a year. Buy and sell requests are mailed only, not relayed by telephone or fax. This creates a time lag between when transactions are ordered and executed. Most other index funds allow more frequent trades, but they have made these transactions very expensive in order to discourage them. This does not make them an appropriate choice for those who like to trade on a daily or even weekly basis.

By way of contrast, Spiders trade continually, so if you're the type who carefully tracks market movements, you can make profits during the day in a Spider.

STOCKS SELLING BELOW BOOK VALUE

As explained on page 160, book value is the net worth per share of common stock: all assets minus all liabilities. When the stock price is below book value, it is at a bargain level in that: (1) the corporation may be worth more dead than alive: if it were liquidated, shareholders would get more from the sale of assets than the current value of the stock; and (2) the company may be a candidate for a takeover.

The usefulness of book value as a criterion depends on the type of corporation. Steel firms and manufacturers of heavy machinery have huge investments in plants and equipment, so they usually have a high book value. But they rarely make much money.

By contrast, a drug manufacturer or retailer will have a low book value but will often have excellent earnings. The trick in using book value effectively is to find a company whose stock is trading below that figure and is making a comeback that has not yet been recognized in the marketplace.

In such a situation, you will get a double plus: buying assets at a discount, and a higher stock price due to better profits. Just make sure that the assets are real and that the earnings are the result of management's skill, not accounting legerdemain.

BANKRUPT COMPANIES

When corporations fall upon hard times, their misfortunes can signal investment opportunities for the strong willed. Before these companies revive, their stocks and bonds are often available at bargain prices. What are your chances for success? Edward Altman, professor of finance at New York University's business school, released a report in early 1990 showing that investors who bought bonds of companies that declared bankruptcy or defaulted on meeting their payments averaged nearly 30% in compounded annual returns over the past 4 years.

$ HINT: You can invest in bankrupt companies through Fidelity Special Situations (1-800-544-8888), a mutual fund that puts about 10% of its assets in distressed companies.

If you'd like to select your own stocks, begin by looking at management. If a company has gone through restructuring and the new team is competent, the value of the stock will rise. It takes time for the improved performance to be recognized.

- *Look for corporations that have resources and a strong position in their field.* The broader the customer base, the greater the chance of success.

- *Diversify with at least three holdings.* If you're lucky, one will prove to be a winner, the second will stay about even, and the loss on the third will be small. Hopefully, that right choice will pay off well enough to make all the risks worthwhile.

EIGHT SELECTED STOCKS SELLING WELL BELOW BOOK VALUE

COMPANY	SYMBOL	PRICE	% PRICE TO BOOK VALUE
British Steel (ADR)	BST	$14	44%
Brown & Sharpe	BNS	8	53
Conner Peripherals	CNR	13	76
Dime Savings Bank	DME	7	50
Glenfed	GLN	3	17
Penn Central	PC	26	74
Prowler International	PS	8	65
Rohr Inc.	RHR	9	34

SOURCE: Value Line, May 1993.

STOCK DIVIDENDS

Stock dividends are extra shares issued to current shareholders, usually on a percentage basis: That is, a 5% stock dividend means that 5 new shares are issued for every 100 old shares. Such a policy can be habit-forming, and most companies continue the extra distributions year after year because it conserves cash, keeps shareholders happy, and provides an easy, inexpensive way to expand the number of publicly owned shares and, usually, stockholders.

It's pleasant to receive such a bonus, but be sure that the payout is justified. The actual dollar profits of the corporation should keep rising. If they stay about the same or decline, stock dividends may be more for show than growth. To evaluate a stock dividend in terms of a company's earning power and the stock's current price:

1   Find the future earnings yield on the current stock price. Use anticipated earnings per share for the current year. If the projected profits are $3 per share and the current price of the stock is 50, the earnings yield is 6%: $3 ÷ 50 = 0.06.

2   Add the stock dividend percentage declared for the current year to the annual cash dividend yield. If the stock dividend is 5% and the cash dividend is 2%, the figure is 7%—the total dividend yield.

If the second figure (7%) exceeds the first (6%), a shareholder faces earnings dilution and probable price weakness *unless* the corporate prospects are strong.

But if the profits are $5 per share, the earnings yield is 10%. Since this is more than the total dividend yield (7%), the stock dividend is not excessive.

■   *Buy soon after emergence from Chapter 11.* At that point, there's the greatest uncertainty and maximum risk, but also a low base for future gains.

According to the National Institute of Business Management, investors can identify a com-

pany preparing for a strong comeback by looking for these traits:

■   A large tax loss carryforward that can be written off against future earnings, thus sharply boosting after-tax profits
■   Substantial salable assets relative to debt, indicating that the securities will appreciate even if the company is partially or completely liquidated
■   A new management team, especially one with turnaround experience
■   Selling off of unprofitable divisions or buying of profitable new ones
■   Restructuring of debt to improve cash flow
■   Reduced leverage
$ IF YOU DARE: Since many institutions shy away from stocks of troubled companies, individual investors willing to assume the high degree of risk involved can sometimes make large profits in turnaround situations. To be on the safe side of an unsafe situation, wait until the company has announced a reorganization plan, or buy secured debt of the company.

STOCK BUY-BACKS

A corporate action that has become fairly popular is the stock buy-back. And as a shareholder you generally benefit when a company repurchases some of its shares. That's because buy-backs are very often a sign that the company's cash flow is improving and that management views its company's stock as undervalued by the overall market.

If the shares of repurchased stock are returned to the status of Treasury shares, then the number of the company's outstanding shares is reduced. This should eventually raise per share profits and boost the price of the remaining outstanding shares.

Companies buy back their shares primarily for one of three reasons: to have stock available for employee stock-ownership programs, for executive stock options, or for making acquisitions.

By purchasing its shares in the open market, the company avoids diluting shareholder equity, which would be the case if it issued new stock.

Various studies show that the best price impact comes from what is called a "Dutch auction." This is a type of self-tender in which the shareholder is asked to specify the lowest per-share price he will accept within a range set by the seller. A study at the University of Rochester's Graduate School of Business found that Dutch auctions generally provide returns of about 8% versus the Standard & Poor's 500, while open-market repurchases, which can take many months to complete, give excess returns of about 2%.

☐CAUTION: Not all corporate buy-backs are a positive sign. If the company borrows money to reacquire its shares, it is taking on additional interest expenses, which may offset the benefit of increased per-share earnings.

⑤HINT: Standard & Poor's weekly publication, *The Outlook* occasionally runs a list of stock repurchase programs, indicating which stocks they favor for investor's portfolios.

FOR FURTHER INFORMATION

David Alger, *The Raging Bull: How to Invest in the Growth Stocks of the 90s* (Homewood, IL: Business One Irwin, 1992).

PART FIVE

YOU AND YOUR ACCOUNT

You might think you've done enough once you've learned which investments are best and when to buy and sell them. Yet surprisingly, your education will not be complete then. After you've set your financial goals, selected various securities, and worked out a balanced portfolio, you need to correctly implement your plan, to put it into action in the most effective way possible.

The financial planner or broker you select, the firm you use, and the type of account you have make the difference between success and failure, between being in charge of your money or merely letting someone else, often a stranger, pull the strings. So, before you start trading securities, read this section carefully, or if, unfortunately, you are in the midst of a situation you're displeased with, study the suggestions for changing brokers and arbitrating disputes.

In this section you will learn:

- How to find, interview, and select the best professionals
- How to settle discord with your broker
- Whether to use a full-service broker or a discount broker
- The advantages of regional stockbrokers
- How to change brokers
- The type of brokerage account that's best for you
- What types of orders to use and when
- Easy ways to build a profitable portfolio
- Whether or not to have a margin account
- How to do your own research
- Dividend reinvestment plans
- Dollar cost averaging

24 FINDING THE BEST PROFESSIONAL HELP

If you are willing to spend time in research and analysis, to adhere to the sound investment principles outlined in this book, and to use good old common sense, you can be a successful investor. Yet there are certain times when professional help is useful, even essential: for *direction* when you are starting out; for *confirmation* when you become more experienced; and for *management* when you have sizeable assets and no time to oversee them.

Nevertheless, you should be cautious about letting anyone else manage your money without first understanding your goals. It's your money, you worked hard to earn it, and in most cases, you know your risk tolerance and future needs better than anyone else. So, before turning your money over to someone else to manage, review Chapter 2 and make certain you have clarified your financial goals in your own mind.

There are three general categories of people whose job it is to help you with your investments: financial planners, stockbrokers, and investment advisers. Below are guidelines for selecting the best in each category, but a word of general advice first:

Don't use a financial planner, broker, or investment adviser who:

- Has a criminal record or a history of securities-related complaints. Check with your state Securities Agency, or contact The National Association of Securities Dealers, P.O. Box 9401, Gaithersburg, MD 20898 (1-202-728-8000), and ask for an information request form.
- Has no staff or operates from a post office box or telephone answering service. Insist on visiting the office, and then check out the person's ties with other professionals. No one planner can master the U.S. Tax Code, pension laws, stocks, bonds, real estate, and insurance.

FINANCIAL PLANNERS— GETTING THE RIGHT ONE

If you feel you need help with your overall financial decision-making, you may want to turn to a generalist, known as a financial planner. Planners, unlike stockbrokers, become involved with your entire estate—stocks, bonds, mutual funds, real estate, insurance, trusts, tax plans, even collectibles. Most planners work independently or in a group practice, although many are on the staffs of accounting firms, brokerage houses, banks, insurance companies, or mutual funds.

A good financial planner will begin by looking at your net worth, reviewing key documents relating to your assets and debts. He should have a checklist to be certain everything is covered: bank and brokerage firm statements, insurance records, mortgage papers, titles and deeds, tax returns, pension plans, a list of valuable objects, estimates of monthly living expenses, and so forth.

He next should review your goals. You need to be forthcoming about your investments, your job and possible promotions, what you might inherit, your retirement plans, as well as any major expenses you will be incurring. He should draw up, along with your help, a workable budget to help you meet your goals.

By putting all of this together, the planner can then advise you on appropriate investments, what insurance you do or do not need (health, disability, property, and damage), if you need to rewrite your will, set up trusts, or make other plans for passing your wealth to others. He should also discuss whether or not you should invest in real estate, and if you are saving enough toward retirement. He should spot errors in how you've been handling your finances, if you have: the wrong kinds of insurance, too risky a portfolio, a poorly executed will or estate plan, or sloppy tax returns.

This analysis is generally presented in writing, with suggestions on ways to improve your financial picture. Some planners then put into motion all aspects of the plan; others turn to professionals, such as an accountant for tax purposes, an attorney for trust plans, stockbrokers, insurance experts, and others.

These generalists, who help you develop an overall financial plan and then implement it with you, are not licensed or regulated by the government. Most work independently or in a small practice. Unless a planner is a stockbroker, he or she does not advise on stocks and bonds. Instead, the planner favors mutual funds or refers you to a broker.

At least 200,000 people call themselves financial planners according to the Consumer Federation of America, but only 15% to 20% have ever completed a course in the field. With no federal regulations and no nationwide accreditation requirements, it's not easy to weed through the crop. Before you turn your money over to a planner, read this section carefully. There are three basic categories of financial planners—determined by what they charge clients.

➤ FEE-ONLY These planners charge either an annual fee, based on your assets and investment activity, or an hourly fee, ranging from $75 to $250+. Annual reviews may be another 25% to 50% of the initial fee. Fee-only planners give advice but may or may not sell products; therefore they are not burdened by potential conflict of interest in promoting a particular investment, such as stocks, insurance, or limited partnerships. However, you still have to pay for any securities you eventually purchase, and of course you are charged for the plan, whether you follow it or not.

➤ COMMISSION ONLY Some planners do not charge a fee but receive a commission on the investments they sell—for example, on a mutual fund or insurance product. With a commision-only planner, you benefit from one-stop shopping. Since any financial plan entails investments with a commission, you can do it all with the same person. However, the commission-only planner may have a vested interest in selling particular commission products. If you have a

good relationship with your planner, this need not be a problem.

➤ FEE PLUS COMMISSION Many planners charge a fee for their overall plan and a commission on investments you purchase. In many cases the commission is lower than with a commission-only planner, simply because under this arrangement the adviser also receives a fee. In addition, the fee is almost always lower than with a fee-only planner.

$ HINT: Always get a written estimate of what services you can expect for what price before making a commitment to a planner.

Unless you have a complicated situation, don't pay more than 1% of the assets involved for a financial plan.

FINDING THE BEST PLANNER

Unless you know an exceptional financial planner personally, confine your search to those who have demonstrated their seriousness by obtaining one of the several designations offered in the field. For example, those who have the designation CFP after their names have studied and been awarded this certification by the International Board of Standards & Practices for Certified Financial Planners. Other degree programs and designations are listed below. Although meeting the requirements is not a guarantee of brilliance, it does represent dedication to the field.

Most of these associations will provide a list of members in your area.

- APFS (Accredited Personal Financial Specialists) for CPAs who concentrate on financial planning:

  American Institute of CPAs
  Personal Financial Planning Division
  1211 Avenue of Americas
  New York, NY 10036

- CFP (Certified Financial Planners) More than 22,000 planners are listed with the Board of Standards and Practices for Certified Financial Planners of the College for Financial Planning (in Denver). To qualify, members pass six, three-hour exams based on a year or two of home study; to stay listed, CFPs must be full-time planners and participate in continuing education. About 30 colleges offer courses to prepare students for the CFP exam.

- International Board of Standards & Practices for Certified Financial Planners. Contact:

  1660 Lincoln Street
  Denver, CO 80264
  1-303-830-7543

  About 7,000 CFPs make up membership in the Institute of Certified Financial Planners, also in Denver. Contact: 1-800-282-PLAN.

- IAFP (The International Association for Financial Planning) in Atlanta has some 15,000 members, about 1,000 of whom are in the Registry of Financial Planning Practitioners. IAFP members must have at least 3 years of experience and meet other qualifications.

  International Association for Financial Planning
  2 Concourse Parkway
  Atlanta, GA 30328
  1-404-395-1605

  If you call 1-800-945-IAFP, you can get the name of five planners in your area.

  $ HINT: If you have any reservations about a planner, contact the North American Securities Administrators Association at 1-202-737-0900, your state attorney general's office, or your local Better Business Bureau to see if complaints or lawsuits have been filed against him.

- NAPFA (National Association of Personal Financial Advisors) An organization for fee-only planners. For a list of planners in your area, call or write the association:

  1130 Lake Cook Road
  Buffalo Grove, IL 60089
  1-800-366-2732

STOCKBROKERS

These are representatives or agents who act as an intermediary between a buyer and a seller of securities. Brokers, who receive commissions for their services, are sometimes partners in a brokerage firm, but if not, they are called registered representatives (reps) and are regular employees. Brokers and registered reps must first be employed by a member firm of the National Association of Security Dealers (NASD) and then pass a comprehensive exam. Only upon successful completion of the exam is the broker registered and allowed to buy and sell securities for customers.

INVESTMENT ADVISERS

This professional may be a financial planner but not all financial planners are investment advisers. An investment adviser recommends stocks, bonds, or mutual funds that are appropriate to your goals and risk level. If you give the adviser a discretionary account, he or she will buy and sell securities without first consulting you. Or you may require that he consult with you regarding trades. Many investment advisers require high minimums—at least $100,000. Annual fees start at 1½% to 2% of the assets up to $500,000, with a sliding scale of lower fees on heftier accounts. You also pay brokerage costs. Investment advisers do not become involved in other aspects of your financial life, although you want to match your tolerance for risk and financial goals with those of the adviser. Some advisers are conservative, others extremely aggressive.

Ask your lawyer, accountant, or stockbroker for names of reliable investment advisers. You can also get a list by writing to:

Investment Counsel Association of America
20 Exchange Place
New York, NY 10005
1-212-344-0999

FINDING THE BEST STOCKBROKER OR ADVISER

Select a financial adviser the same way you do your doctor: with great care and caution. Your financial well-being is second only to your physical health. Don't be tempted by tips you hear at cocktail parties or Little League baseball games. By following these steps, you will find the person best suited to guide your financial future.

Step 1 Ask for names from friends and colleagues whose business judgment you respect.

Step 2 Ask your lawyer and accountant for referrals.

Step 3 If you have a contact at a particular firm, ask the manager or president for the names of two or three brokers.

The number one consideration in choosing any type of investment adviser is comfort: Select someone you respect, whose advice you are willing to follow, who operates in a professional manner (with integrity, intelligence, and information), who answers your questions and eases your doubts and fears.

These criteria eliminate brokers hustling for commissions; salespeople who make quick recommendations without considering your assets, income obligations, and goals; and everyone who promises large, fast returns.

Look for the following:

➤ PERFORMANCE OVER THE LONG TERM Select someone with at least 5 years' experience in order to cover both bull and bear markets. Anyone can be lucky with a few stocks for a few years, but concentrate on an individual or firm whose recommendations have outpaced market averages by at least 2 percentage points: higher in *up* markets, lower in *down* periods. This applies to total returns—income plus appreciation or minus depreciation—and refers primarily to stocks but is a sound guideline for debt securities. A minimum expectation of return on investment from an investment adviser should range between 15% and 20%, including income and appreciation.

Superior performance should be a continuing criterion. Every 6 months, compare the returns on your investments with those of a standard indicator: for *bonds,* the Dow Jones Bond Average or, for tax-frees, the Dow Municipal Bond Average; for *stocks,* Standard & Poor's 500 (which is broader and more representative than the Dow Jones Industrial Average). Then subtract the commissions you paid to see whether you're getting your money's worth.

➤ REPUTATION Comments from old customers are most valuable for helping you learn how you are likely to be treated, including promptness and efficiency of service and reports. Is extra cash moved quickly into a money market fund? Are orders executed promptly and correctly? Are dividends posted immediately? Are monthly reports issued on time?

➤ COMPATIBILITY Choose advisers whose overall investment philosophy matches your objectives of income or growth. If you're conservative,

stay away from a swinger who constantly comes up with new issues, wants you to trade frequently, suggests speculative situations, and scoffs at interest and dividends.

If you're aggressive, look for someone who keeps up on growth opportunities and is smart enough to recognize that no one should always be fully invested in equities and not to recommend bonds or liquid assets under unfavorable stock market conditions.

➤ STRATEGIES AND TECHNIQUES Find out by asking questions such as these:

- **Where do you get investment ideas?** From in-house research or from brokerage firms?
- **What are your favorite stock-picking strategies?** Out-of-favor stocks with low price-earnings ratios? Small company growth stocks? Larger corporations whose shares are now undervalued according to predictable earnings expectations?
- **How diversified are the portfolios?** Do you shoot for big gains from a few stocks or seek modest profits from a broader list?

➤ WILLINGNESS TO SELL Successful investing relies on two factors: how much you make and how little you lose. Check the composition of several portfolios for the past 5 years. If they are still holding glamor stocks bought at peaks and now near lows, move on! Don't stick with professionals who ignore their losses.

➤ SAY NO After you've made a choice, **don't be afraid to say no** if you don't understand or if you lack confidence in the recommendations. Nothing is more important than trust when you are dealing with money. You can forgive a few mistakes, but if they mount up, cancel the agreement. Remember, it is your money and you have every right to call the shots.

INTERVIEWING POTENTIAL PLANNERS, ADVISERS, AND BROKERS

Whatever you do, don't select someone to help you with your investments by walking into a firm cold off the street. And never sign on with the first person you talk with. Set up interviews with several candidates. Go to the interview prepared with a series of questions and compare how each of your potential advisers answers them.

Jay J. Pack, a broker and author of *How to Talk to a Broker,* suggests the following six basic questions:

- What do you suggest that I do with my $25,000 (or whatever amount you have)? Beware of the person who suggests you put it all in one product.
- How long have you been in business? With this firm?
- Will you give me several references so that I may check on your record?
- What will it cost me to use your help? Get specifics about fees and commissions, in writing.
- What sort of return can I expect from my investment?
- What research materials do you rely on?

Any good planner, adviser, or broker should:

- Be willing to meet with you in person for a free consultation
- Provide you with references or sample portfolios
- Ask you about your net worth, financial goals, and tolerance for risk
- Offer you several alternatives and explain them
- Be able to refer you to other professionals for specific help
- Set up a schedule for reviewing your securities, assets, and overall financial picture
- Answer your phone calls promptly

$ HINT: The NASD will tell you if a broker or his or her firm has been slapped with a disciplinary action or convicted of a crime. Unresolved complaints are not provided. Call: 1-800-289-9999.

DISCOUNT STOCKBROKERS

If you like to make your own buy-and-sell decisions, do your own research, and can operate independently of a full-service brokerage firm, it is possible to save between 30% and 80% on your commissions by using a discount broker.

These no-frills operations are able to offer lower rates because they do not provide research, they hire salaried order clerks and not commissioned brokers, and they maintain low overheads. Yet many have a surprisingly complete line of investment choices available: In addition to stocks and bonds, many handle Treasury issues, municipals, options, and mortgage-backed securities and will set up self-directed IRAs or Keoghs. The country's largest discounter, Charles Schwab & Co., also offers to trade mutual fund shares. Shearman Ralston and Securities Research have distinguished themselves in the field by publishing a monthly market report newsletter and offering modest amounts of research free to customers.

Several discounters have also moved into the computer field: Quick & Reilly, Charles Schwab, and Fidelity Brokerage Services market software programs enabling customers to place trades from their home computers, to receive stock quotes, and even to evaluate their portfolios.

As a general rule, you will be able to save $25 to $75 when doing a 300-share trade. But discounters set up varying schedules, so it definitely pays to shop around when selecting a firm. With some—called value brokers—the rates escalate with both the number of shares and their price. With others—called share brokers—rates are tied solely to the number of shares traded. You will save more with lower-priced shares if you use a value broker and with higher-priced stocks if you use a share broker.

As guidelines, use a discount broker if you:

- Have a portfolio of $100,000
- Trade at least twice a month in units of 300 shares or more
- Feel so confident of your stock market skill that you do not want someone else to monitor or question your decisions
- Are sure that the savings in commissions are worthwhile: at least 20% below rates negotiated with regular stock brokerage firms
- Are not involved with special securities such as convertibles, options, or warrants, where accurate information is difficult to obtain

If you are a heavy trader, play it both ways: Get information from your regular broker, and handle large deals through the discount house.

Don't assume that all discount firms are alike. Always ask what services are offered in addition to buying and selling stocks at a dis-

DISCOUNTERS

Baker & Co., Cleveland, OH
(1-800-321-1640; 1-800-362-2008 in
Ohio); $40 minimum

Fidelity, Boston, MA (1-800-544-3939; 1-
800-544-6767 in Massachusetts); $38
minimum

Pacific Brokerage Services, Los Angeles,
CA (1-800-421-8395);
$25 + $4 service fee minimum

Quick & Reilly, New York, NY
(1-800-221-5220; 1-800-522-8712 in
New York); $37.50 minimum

Charles Schwab & Co., San Francisco, CA
(1-800-435-4000); $39 minimum

Shearman Ralston, Inc., New York, NY (1-
800-221-4242; 1-212-248-1160 in New
York); $40 minimum

Securities Research, Inc., Vero Beach, FL
(1-800-327-3156); $35 minimum

Muriel Siebert & Co., New York, NY
(1-800-872-0711); $37.50 minimum

StockCross, Inc., Boston, MA
(1-800-225-6196; 1-800-392-6104 in
Massachusetts); $25 plus 8.5¢ minimum

Jack White & Co., San Diego, CA
(1-800-233-3411; 1-619-587-2000); 833
+ 3¢ minimum

Wilmington Brokerage Services, Wilmington, DE (1-800-345-7550;
1-302-651-1011); $39 minimum

SHOULD YOU USE A DISCOUNT BROKER?

YES, IF:
- You have investment savvy.
- You enjoy following the stock market and have time to do so.
- You have clear ideas about what to buy and sell, and when.
- You subscribe to an investment service or to serious professional periodicals.
- You follow technical indicators.
- You read market news on a regular basis.
- You trade often.
- You are not afraid to make mistakes.

NO, IF:
- You cannot decide what to buy and sell.
- You require investment advice.
- You are too busy to follow the market.
- You are nervous about things financial.
- You are inexperienced.

SOURCE: Jay J. Pack, *How to Talk to a Broker* (New York: Harper & Row, 1985).

- Receive independent research reports by fax, phone, and mail
- Trade your account by modem and access stock market research through its software

COMMISSIONS: FULL-RATE FIRMS VS. DISCOUNT BROKERS

	200 SHARES @ 25	300 SHARES @ 20	500 SHARES @ 18	1,000 SHARES @ 14
Merrill Lynch	129.50	157.00	214.50	293.60
Shearson	128.00	154.25	222.25	347.75
Prudential	140.92	167.08	232.60	348.95
Dean Witter	122.13	145.52	205.86	322.82
Charles Schwab	81.00	87.00	96.00	111.00
Fidelity Brokerage	80.75	86.75	95.75	110.75
Quick & Reilly	60.50	65.00	81.50	94.00

count. For example, Charles Schwab & Co., headquartered in San Francisco, makes it possible for clients to:
- Purchase any of 600 no-load and low-load mutual funds through any of its 175 branch offices
- Place buy and sell orders 24 hours a day
- Purchase fixed-income securities, including Treasuries, municipals, and corporate bonds

package, available to those with an IBM-compatible computer
- Get a no-fee CMA-type account, called the Schwab One Account, free checking, and a VISA debit card
- Trade stocks, get price quotes, and check on your account through TeleBroker, an automated service available to customers with touch-tone phones

REGIONAL STOCKBROKERS

Regional brokerage firms, those with home bases outside New York, are recognized for their personal touch, local knowledge, and independent nature. Many are excellent in picking stocks. That's because regional brokers are in positions to spot promising unnoticed stocks and bonds of local companies, ones Wall Street firms either ignore or do not follow closely. For investors, this means a chance to buy a stock before the rest of the investment world becomes bullish.

The regionals also pride themselves on better service. Brokers tend to stay longer at these firms, which lessens the chances of a rookie or broker-of-the-day handling your account. They also have the freedom to sell products of other firms—mutual funds, unit investment trusts, limited partnerships, and so forth.

$ HINT: To check out a regional firm, read the annual report to see if it's been profitable during bull and bear cycles (see list on page 249).

GETTING YOUR BROKER'S RESEARCH

The advantage of a full-service broker is access to investment research that separates companies on the rise from those that are heading down. Reports on individual companies as well as industry groups are prepared by analysts. Assigned to follow a particular industry, analysts interview corporate executives, study financial reports, and identify trends, potential problems, and new developments. Their reports are the basis of investment decisions made by your broker.

Reports produced by analysts are a mixed bag—some are financial tables of little use to individuals, while others contain useful comments on a company's stock. Some are brilliant; most are ordinary. Many analysts tend to run with the pack. To overcome this tendency, take the advice to "hold" a stock and interpret it as "OK to sell."

If your broker recommends a stock, always ask for the most recent report on the company. Or, if you hear about a potentially interesting buy, find out if the firm has taken a position on it. If you are a regular customer, your broker should send you the firm's weekly or monthly roundup reports, which cover a number of stocks. If your broker resists sending these to you, maybe you should look for another broker. (However, don't expect the firm's best reports if you make only a handful of trades a year.)

A publication that merits reading by serious investors is *Wall Street Transcript*, which taps into the research departments of nearly every brokerage firm and investment house. It often reprints in full their major reports and summarizes many others each week. Brokers regularly read the "roundtable" feature, which covers discussions among three or four analysts who follow a single industry. There is one roundtable per issue. Since a one-year subscription now costs $1,890, you may want to read the copy at your library or broker's office.

BEWARE OF THE PONZI SCHEME

Every year, intelligent people are taken in by seemingly attractive, smart embezzlers through the Ponzi scheme—a swindle in which the first few investors are paid interest out of the proceeds of later investors. The latter end up with zero when the balloon breaks and the swindler pockets the remaining money. Ponzi schemes masquerade as tax shelters, deals in precious metals, gold and diamonds, real estate, and collectibles.

A sure sign: a guarantee of far higher interest rates or returns than the prevailing market is paying.

REGIONAL BROKERAGE FIRMS

FIRM	TELEPHONE	FIRM	TELEPHONE
Advest Inc. 280 Trumbull Street Hartford, CT 06103	1-203-525-1421 1-800-243-8115	Janney Montgomery Scott Inc. 1801 Market St. Philadelphia, PA 19103	1-215-665-6000 1-800-526-6397
J. C. Bradford & Co. 330 Commerce Street Nashville, TN 37201	1-615-748-9000 1-800-251-1060	Legg Mason Wood Walker 111 South Calvert Street Baltimore, MD 21202	1-410-539-0000 1-800-368-2558
Alex Brown & Sons Co. 135 East Baltimore Street Baltimore, MD 21202	1-410-727-1700 1-800-638-2596	McDonald & Co. 800 Superior Avenue Cleveland, OH 44114	1-216-443-2300 1-800-553-2240
Crowell, Weedon & Co. 624 South Grand Avenue Suite 2600 Los Angeles, CA 90017	1-213-620-1850	Piper, Jaffray & Hopwood 222 South 9th Street Minneapolis, MN 55402	1-612-342-6000 1-800-333-6000
Dain Bosworth Inc. Dain Bosworth Plaza 60 South 6th Street Minneapolis, MN 55402	1-612-371-2711	Raymond James & Associates 880 Carillon Parkway St. Petersburg, FL 33716	1-813-573-3800 1-800-248-8863
D. A. Davidson & Co. P.O. Box 5015 Great Falls, MT 59403	1-406-727-4200 1-800-332-5915	Rauscher Pierce Refsnes, Inc. Plaza of the Americas 2500 RPR Tower Dallas, TX 75201	1-214-978-0111
Edward D. Jones & Co. 201 Progress Parkway Maryland Heights, MO 63043	1-314-851-2000	Sutro & Co. 201 California Street San Francisco, CA 94111	1-415-445-8500 1-800-652-1030
A. G. Edwards & Sons, Inc. One North Jefferson Avenue St. Louis, MO 63103	1-314-289-3000	Van Kasper & Co. 50 California Street San Francisco, CA 94111	1-415-391-5600 1-800-652-1747
Interstate/Johnson Lane 121 West Trade Street Charlotte, NC 28202	1-704-379-9000	Wheat First Securities Box 1357 Richmond, VA 23211	1-804-649-2311 1-800-627-8625

TOP RESEARCH

If you decide to do your own research or supplement that offered by your stockbroker or adviser, three publication services will be enormously helpful. They are expensive, so you may want to use them at your library or broker's office before buying your own copies.

MOODY'S

Moody's Investors Service
99 Church Street
New York, NY 10007
1-212-553-0300
1-800-342-5647

A leading research and information service aimed primarily at the business community, Moody's (a Dun & Bradstreet Corporation company) is known throughout the world for its bond ratings and factual publications. It is not an investment advisory service.

➤ MOODY'S MANUALS The company publishes 8 manuals on an annual basis. Each is continually updated, some as often as twice a week. The manuals cover 20,000 U.S. and foreign corporations and 15,000 municipal and government entities. Each one gives financial and operating data, company histories, product descriptions, plant and property locations, and lists of officers. The 8 are:

- *Bank and Finance.* Covers 14,000 financial institutions, including insurance companies, mutual funds, banks, and real estate trusts.
- *Industrial.* Covers every industrial corporation on the NYSE and AMEX plus 500+ on regional exchanges.
- *OTC Industrial.* Covers 3,200 industrial companies traded on NASDAQ or OTC.
- *OTC Unlisted.* Covers 2,000 hard-to-find companies not listed on NASDAQ's National Market System.
- *Public Utility.* Covers every publicly held U.S. gas and electric utility, gas transmission, telephone, and water company.
- *Transportation.* Covers airlines, railroads, oil pipelines, bridge and tunnel operators, bus and truck companies, and auto and truck rental and leasing firms.
- *International.* Covers 5,000+ international corporations in 100 countries.
- *Municipal and Government.* Covers 15,000 bond-issuing municipalities and government agencies; includes bond ratings.

➤ MOODY'S HANDBOOKS These soft-cover books, published quarterly, give concise overviews of 2,200 corporations. Useful for instant facts and financial summaries. They are called *Handbook of Common Stocks* and *Handbook of OTC Stocks.*

➤ OTHER PUBLICATIONS *Moody's Dividend Record.* Detailed reports on current dividend data of 18,300 stocks; updated twice weekly.

Moody's Industry Review. Ranks 4,000 leading companies in 145 industry groups.

Moody's Bond Record. Monthly guide to 56,000 fixed-income issues including ratings, yield to maturity, and prices.

Moody's Bond Survey. Weekly publication on new issues.

➤ A WORD ABOUT MOODY'S BOND RATINGS Their purpose is to grade the relative quality of investments by using 9 symbols ranging from

Aaa (the highest) to C (the lowest). In addition, each classification from Aa to B (for corporate bonds) sometimes has a numerical modifier: The number 1 indicates that the security ranks at the highest end of the category; the number 2, in the middle; and the number 3, at the lower end.

STANDARD & POOR'S

Standard & Poor's Corp.
25 Broadway
New York, NY 10004
1-212-208-8000
1-800-221-5277

For over 120 years Standard & Poor's has been providing financial information, stock and bond analysis, and bond rating and investment guidance. Its materials are used by investors as well as the professional and business community.

➤ MAJOR PUBLICATIONS
- *Corporation Records.* Seven volumes covering financial details, history, and products of 12,000 corporations. One volume, *Daily News*, provides continually updated information 5 days a week about these publicly held corporations.
- *Stock Reports.* Analytical data on 4,000 corporations. Includes every company traded on the NYSE and AMEX plus 1,500 over-the-counters. There are 2-page reports on each company.
- *Industry Surveys.* This 2-volume looseleaf is continually updated and covers 20 leading U.S. industries. Surveys cover all aspects of an industry including market trends, earnings, and government regulations.
- *Stock Guide.* A small paperback containing 48 columns of statistical material on 5,100 stocks. A broker's bible.
- *The Outlook.* A weekly advisory newsletter covering the economic climate, stock forecasts, industry predictions, buy-and-sell recommendations, etc. Presents a "master list of supervised stocks" with 4 separate portfolios: long-term growth, promising growth, cyclical and speculative stocks, and income stocks.

- *Trendline Publications.* Publishes marketing behavior charts providing investors with a visual look at a company's performance. Includes charts of indexes and indicators.

▶ OTHER PUBLICATIONS *CreditWeek, Bond Guide, Commercial Paper Ratings Guide, Standard & Poor's Register of Corporations, Directors and Executives and Security Dealers of North America.*

▶ A WORD ABOUT STANDARD & POOR'S RATINGS Standard & Poor's rates bonds from AAA (the highest) to D (bonds in default). Those with ratings between AAA and BBB are considered of investment quality. Those below BBB fall into the speculative category. Ratings between AA and CCC often have a + or − to indicate relative strength within the larger categories.

Standard & Poor's rates stocks from A+ (highest) to A (high), A− (above average), B+ (averge), B (below average), B− (lower), to C (lowest). With the exception of banks and financial institutions, which are rated NR (no ranking), most publicly owned corporations are listed. *Never invest in any company rated below B+.*

VALUE LINE

Value Line, Inc.
711 Third Avenue
New York, NY 10017
1-212-687-3965
1-800-634-3583

An independent investment advisory, Value Line, Inc., publishes one of the country's leading investment advisory services, the *Value Line Investment Survey,* as well as several other publications and the Value Line index.

▶ MAJOR PUBLICATION *The Value Line Investment Survey,* begun in 1935, is a weekly advisory service published in a 2-volume looseleaf binder. It covers reports on each of 1,700 common stocks divided into 94 industry groups.

A report on each industry precedes the individual stock reports. Each stock is given two rankings: one for "timeliness" (the probable relative price performance of the stock within the next 12 months) and one for "safety" (the stock's future price stability and its company's current financial strength). Within these two categories each stock is assigned a rank from 1 (the highest) to 5 (the lowest). Here's what the rankings mean:

▶ VALUE LINE TIMELINESS

RANK 1 (highest) Expect the stock to be one of the best price performers relative to the 1,700 other stocks during the next 12 months.

RANK 2 (above average) Expect better than average price performance.

RANK 3 (average) Expect price performance in line with the market.

RANK 4 (below average) Expect less than average price performance.

RANK 5 (lowest) Expect the poorest price performance relative to other stocks.

▶ VALUE LINE SAFETY

RANK 1 (highest) This stock is probably one of the safest, most stable, and least risky relative to the 1,700 other stocks.

RANK 2 (above average) This stock is probably safer and less risky than most.

RANK 3 (average) This stock is probably of average safety and risk.

RANK 4 (below average) This stock is probably riskier and less safe than most.

RANK 5 (lowest) This stock is probably one of the riskiest and least safe.

▶ OTHER PUBLICATIONS *The Value Line OTC Special Situations Service.* Covers fast-growing smaller companies. Published 24 times a year.

Value Line Options. Evaluates and ranks nearly all options listed on the U.S. exchanges. Published 48 times a year.

Value Line Convertibles. Evaluates and ranks for future market performance 580 companies and 75 warrants. Published 48 times a year.

SETTLING DISPUTES: ARBITRATION

As with all businesses, there are individuals who either deliberately or carelessly give poor advice. In the brokerage business, integrity is paramount—all the exchanges have strict rules, and most firms have compliance officers whose responsibility it is to monitor trading, make sure that full information is provided to all clients, and act promptly when there are deviations.

The trouble comes when the customer does

not understand an investment or when the broker is not clear about all the facts or has not made them clear to the client. When the price of the securities goes down, recriminations start. If you take a flier, you can't blame the broker for your mistake. But brokers may be at fault if they cross the line between optimism and misrepresentation.

The areas in which problems most often arise are options, commodities, and margin accounts, or what are called "other, esoteric" investments. Every broker is required to know each customer and not put any customer in an inappropriate, high-risk investment. A client's net worth, income, investment objectives, and experience help determine what is suitable.

If you have a problem with your broker, begin by trying to settle it informally with your broker. If the problem remains unresolved, take the following action:

Step 1: Talk to the broker's supervisor or

HOW TO PROTECT YOURSELF

- Keep track of all your trades, including monthly statements.
- Note all important conversations with your broker in a diary.
- Contact your firm's manager if there's a problem—the company wants to keep, not lose customers.
- If you're not satisfied, contact an experienced lawyer; ask about fee structure.
- Figure out your brokerage losses plus the lawyer's fee. Is it worth taking the next step?

BEFORE YOU UNDERTAKE ARBITRATION . . .

Arbitration is a long and often unpleasant procedure and should never be entered into casually.

According to Jay J. Pack, author of *How to Talk to a Broker:*

- The odds for an arbitration settlement in your favor are typically 50-50.
- You will improve your chances if you are prepared ahead of time. Gather proper documentation and other evidence to support your case.
- In 1987 the SEC ruled that arbitration results are binding. Therefore, if you decide to go to arbitration and the case is not decided in your favor, you cannot turn around and sue your broker.
- Act immediately if you are planning to go to arbitration. Arbitrators won't look favorably upon your complaint if you wait to see whether the investment in question goes up in price.

For further information, see sources listed at the end of this chapter.

---

branch manager. Brokerage firms do not want to earn bad reputations with the public or have a number of vociferous, complaining clients.

Step 2: Write a letter of complaint to the broker and the firm's compliance officer, with a copy to the branch manager. Request a written response from the compliance officer.

Step 3: Send a copy of the letter to the state securities administrator. The North American Securities Administrators Association is the national organization for all 50 state securities officials. Call NASAA for the person in your state: 1-202-737-0900.

Step 4: Contact the SEC, Office of Consumer Affairs, 450 5th Street NW, Washington, DC 20549. If your problem involves a commodities or futures contract, a copy of the complaint letter should go to the Commodity Futures Trading Commission, Office of Public Information, 2033 K Street NW, Washington, DC 20581.

Step 5: Finally, send a copy to the exchange involved (see Appendix E for addresses).

Step 6: If you cannot resolve your complaint through phone calls and letters—and if it involves a great deal of money, you probably can't—the next step is arbitration.

When you opened your brokerage account, you signed a customer's agreement form of some sort. Many forms specify which arbitration body will hear a case if there is a dispute. Contact that body.

Arbitration panels sponsored by the industry's self-regulatory bodies consist of three people, and only one can be affiliated with the securities industry. Arbitrators have awarded punitive damages of as much as $1 million. They often also award attorneys' fees.

By contrast, the American Arbitration Association has absolutely no connection to the brokerage industry. Check your brokerage agreement. Although it may be more impartial, filing with the AAA is also more costly—from $300 for a dispute involving $20,000 or less to $3,750 for disputes of $500,000 or more. At the National Association of Security Dealers, it is $30 for $1,000 or less and $1,250 for amounts over $500,000.

$ HINT: In May 1990, the U.S. Supreme Court upheld a ruling that allows securities dealers to refuse to open accounts for clients who do not agree in advance to settle disputes through arbitration rather than by suing. Arbitration is generally quicker and less costly than a long court battle. See "For Further Information" at the end of this chapter.

FOR FURTHER INFORMATION

ARBITRATION

Director of Arbitration
New York Stock Exchange
20 Broad Street
New York, NY 10005
1-212-656-3000

Director of Arbitration
National Association of Security Dealers
33 Whitehall Street
New York, NY 10004
1-212-480-4881

Office of Consumer Affairs
Securities & Exchange Commission
450 Fifth Street NW
Washington, DC 20549
1-202-272-7440

American Arbitration Association
140 West 51st Street
New York, NY 10020
1-212-484-4000

Coping with the Crash: A Step-by-Step Guide to Investor Rights
North American Securities Administrators Association
Massachusetts Avenue NW
Washington, DC 20001
1-202-737-0900

Lists telephone numbers and addresses of state administrators and federal agencies. Free.

BROKERS

Jay J. Pack, *How to Talk to a Broker* (New York: Harper & Row, 1985).

The 1993 Discount Brokerage Surveys (rates 100+ brokers)

Mercer, Inc.
379 West Broadway
New York, NY 10012
1-212-334-6212
$34.95 + $2.50 shipping

Tips on Selecting a Stockbroker
Council of Better Business Bureaus, Inc.
Publications Dept.
4200 Wilson Boulevard, 8th floor
Arlington, VA 22203
1-703-276-0100
$1 plus SASE business-sized with 87¢ postage

FINANCIAL PLANNERS

Consumer's Guide to Financial Independence
International Association for Financial Planning
2 Concourse Parkway
Atlanta, GA 30328
$1.00

Selecting a Qualified Financial Planning Professional
Institute of Certified Financial Planners
7600 East Eastman Avenue
Denver, CO 80231
Free

Tips on Financial Planners
Council of Better Business Bureaus, Inc.
Publications Dept.
4200 Wilson Boulevard, 8th floor
Arlington, VA 22203
$1 plus SASE with 87¢ postage

Fee-only Planners
National Association of Personal Financial
  Advisors
1130 Lake Cook Road
Buffalo Grove, IL 60089
1-800-366-2732
Free

*Investment Swindles: How They Work and
  How to Avoid Them*
National Futures Association
Public Affairs Dept.
200 West Madison Street
Chicago, IL 60606
1-312-781-1300
Free

25 MANAGING YOUR BROKERAGE ACCOUNT

In the previous chapter you learned how to select a top-notch pro to help you buy and sell securities and manage your overall portfolio. Once you've lined up this adviser, you're not off the hook. You still have some decisions to make— such as what type of account to use, what types of orders to place, and the degree to which you want to be involved in running your account, all topics covered in this chapter.

YOUR ACCOUNT

First you must decide between a *margin account* and a *cash account*. Most investors should and do use a cash account. In a cash account you pay for your securities within 5 business days after the transaction.

A margin account is not only more risky, since it involves borrowing, but it can lead to actual dollar losses if you do not monitor your position on a regular basis. Margin accounts are discussed in detail later in this chapter.

➤ DISCRETIONARY OR NONDISCRETIONARY ACCOUNTS If you are just beginning to work with your broker, do not, repeat, *not* sign a discretionary account agreement. This type of account gives the broker the power to buy and sell securities without consulting you first. Discretionary accounts should be used only with brokers you have worked with for a number of years and you trust more than your own mother. Not surprisingly, discretionary accounts often cause problems—customers think the broker is churning their accounts (executing too many trades merely to rack up commissions) or not buying the right types of securities. The customer may or may not be right. Mismanagement of an account is hard to pinpoint, but it does happen. So don't let it become a possibility— stick with a cash account instead.

➤ IN STREET NAME Your broker will also ask you if you want your securities held in "street name"—that is, held with the firm—or if you want them registered in your own name with the certificates sent directly to you. If you decide to take physical possession of your securities, you will have to wait several weeks for them to arrive. If they are in street name, they become simply a computerized book entry at your firm, and your dividends and any stock splits are automatically collected and recorded for you.

$ HINT: If securities are in the broker's custody, transfer of shares when you sell them is easier than if the stock is registered in your name. Then you have to deliver the actual certificates to the broker's office.

➤ JOINT ACCOUNTS Before you open your account, check with your lawyer, especially if you are involved in estate planning. You may want to establish a joint account.

In a *joint tenancy with the rights of survivorship*, if one person dies, the other receives all the securities and cash in the account. The assets bypass probate and go directly to the survivor, although estate taxes may have to be paid.

In a *tenancy-in-common account*, the deceased's share of the account goes to the deceased's heirs, not to the joint account holder. The survivor must then open a new account.

If you have children, you may want to open a *Uniform Gifts to Minors account*. Whoever establishes the account names a "custodian" for the minor—very often they name themselves. All trading activity is then done by the custodian for the child's benefit. When the child reaches majority (age 18 or 21) he or she can legally take control of the account.

HOW TO SWITCH BROKERS

One of the most time-consuming and sometimes awkward tasks investors face is switching brokers. Transferring assets from one firm to another ought to be easy, but it often occurs at a tortoise-like pace. Delays sometimes last weeks or months, and occasionally investors lose money because securities dropped in value during the transit process.

Here's how to head off delays and trouble.

- Your new broker will ask for a list of what's held in your old account. Have that ready. Give him a copy of your last monthly statement, or fax it to him to accelerate the process. Under the rules of the National Association of Securities Dealers and the New York Stock Exchange, the old broker must deliver the holdings in 5 to 10 days.

- If that deadline cannot be met, the old brokerage firm must send the new one cash equaling the market value of the securities under what is called a "fail-to-deliver contract." This money enables the customer to trade. When the securities arrive, the money is returned. (Fail-to-deliver contracts are required by the NASD under a 1986 ruling adopted because of the number of customer complaints about transfers.)

➤ HANDLING SNAGS Problems, of course, do arise. The key reasons are that (1) assets cannot be moved quickly, such as an IRA that requires a change of custodians or proprietary investments, such as a mutual fund run by the transferring brokerage firm; (2) the account has assets with virtually no value—bankrupt companies or companies with other technical problems; or (3) the old broker stalls—he or she may be annoyed that you're leaving, on vacation, or no longer with the firm. Talk first with the old broker, then with the supervisor. Ask why there is a hang-up. Prod gently, then firmly. You'll find most firms are accustomed to making this type of transaction within two weeks.

➤ SOLUTIONS If a serious delay occurs, you can complain to your old broker's supervisor, the NASD, and the SEC. Complaints to the NASD should be filed with the district office nearest the receiving broker. Contact the NASD in Gaith-ersburg, MD (1-301-590-6500) for the address of its nearest office. The SEC will contact the brokers and ask for an update. To complain, contact the Office of Consumer Affairs, SEC, 450 Fifth Street NW, Washington, DC 20549 (1-202-272-7440).

If you lose money because of a delay and your former broker won't help out, your only recourse is to use the NASD's arbitration service. For the proper forms, write to the NASD's Arbitration Office, 33 Whitehall Street, New York, NY 10004 (1-212-858-4488). Expect to spend between $30 and $1,250, depending on the amount involved. Cases take about 6 to 10 months to complete, and the decision is binding.

TYPES OF STOCK MARKET ORDERS

Once you have opened your account you're ready to trade. Although both dividend reinvestment plans and dollar cost averaging, discussed later on, are sensible ways to buy shares of stocks or mutual funds, they only work for securities you already own. When adding to your holdings or selling stocks, you need to know what type of order to place.

Most investors simply call their broker and place an order, called a market order. However, there are several other ways to go about it. Armed with a little more information, you can place a specific type of order and thereby protect your portfolio.

➤ MARKET ORDER This is the most common type of order. It tells your broker to buy or sell at the best price obtainable at the moment, or at the market. If the order is to buy, the broker must keep bidding at advancing prices until a willing seller is found. If the order is to sell, the broker offers it at increasingly lower prices. With a market order, you can be certain that your order will be executed.

➤ LIMIT ORDER Usually a market order is sufficient, but when prices are fluctuating, it is wise to enter a limit order, which tells the broker the maximum price you're willing to pay, or if you're selling, the minimum you'll accept. For example, if you put in a limit order to buy a stock at 20 when the stock is trading at 22, your order will not be filled unless the stock falls to 20 or lower.

➤ DAY ORDER This is an order to buy or sell that expires unless executed or canceled the same day it is placed. All orders are day orders unless you indicate otherwise. The key exception is a "good until canceled order."

➤ GOOD UNTIL CANCELED ORDER Also known as an open order, this is an order that remains in effect until executed or canceled. If it remains unfilled for long, the broker generally checks to see if the customer is still interested in the stock should it reach the designated or target price.

➤ SCALE ORDER An order to buy or sell specified amounts of a security at specified price increments. For example, you might want to buy 5,000 shares but in lots of 500 each in stages of ¼ points as the market falls. Not all brokers will accept scale orders since they involve so much work.

➤ STOP ORDER An order to buy (or sell) if the stock trades at a certain price. If the stock reaches this price your order is automatically triggered and becomes an order to buy (or sell) "at the market." A stop order may also be placed with a price limit to avoid its being executed at a substantially different price than the price of the stop.

➤ STOP-LOSS ORDERS An order that sets the sell price below the current market price. Stop-loss orders protect profits already made or prevent further losses if the stock falls in price.

☐CAUTION: Both the New York and American stock exchanges have the power to halt stop orders in individual stocks to prohibit further sell-off in a declining stock. However, they very rarely use this power and in fact did not do so during the 1987 market crash.

HOW TO USE STOP ORDERS

Stop orders basically provide protection against the unexpected by forcing you to admit your mistakes and thus cut your losses. In effect, they say that you will not participate above or below a certain price. For example, if you bought a stock 6 months ago at $50 per share and it's now at $75, you can set a stop-loss order to sell at $60. Then, should it fall in price, you know that your broker will sell you out at $60. Stop orders are useful for the following purposes.

➤ TO LIMIT LOSSES ON STOCKS YOU OWN You buy 100 shares of Allied Wingding at 50 in hopes of a quick gain. You are a bit queasy about the market, so at the same time you enter an order to sell the stock at 47⅜ stop. If AW drops to 47⅜, your stop order becomes a market order and you've limited your loss to 2⅝ points per share.

Traders generally set their loss targets at 10% below cost or recent high. Those who are concerned with long-term investments are more cautious and prefer a loss figure of about 15%: say, 42⅜ for a stock bought at 50.

§HINT: For best results, set stop prices on the down side and have courage enough to back up your decisions. Once any stock starts to fall, there's no telling how far down it will go. Cut losses short and let your profits run.

➤ TO ENSURE A PROFIT A year ago you bought 100 shares of a stock at 42 and it is now at 55. You are planning a vacation trip and do not want to lose too much of your paper profit, so you give your broker an order to sell at 51 stop, good until canceled. If the market declines and the sale is made, you will protect most of your 9-point-per-share gain.

Similarly, the stop order can protect a profit on a short sale. This time, you sell short at 55. The price falls to 40, so you have a $15-per-share profit. You look for a further price decline but want protection while you're away. You enter a buy order at 45 stop. If the stock price does jump to 45, you will buy 100 shares, cover your short position, and have a $1,000 profit (assuming that the specialist is able to make the purchase on the nose).

➤ TO TOUCH OFF PREDETERMINED BUY, SELL, AND SELL-SHORT ORDERS If you rely on technical analysis and buy only when a stock breaks through a trend line on the up side and sell or sell short when it breaks out on the down side, you can place advance orders to "buy stop," "sell stop," or "sell short stop." These become market orders when the price of the securities hits the designated figure.

Example: Your stock is at 48¾ and appears likely to shoot up. But you want to be sure that the rise is genuine, because over the years there's been resistance at just about 50. You set a *buy stop order* at 51⅜. This becomes a *market order* if the stock hits the price 51⅜.

HOW TO SET STOP PRICES

Broadly speaking, there are two techniques to use:

➤ SET THE ORDER AT A PRICE THAT IS A FRACTION OF A POINT ABOVE THE ROUND FIGURE At 50⅛, for example. Your order will be executed before the stock drops to the round figure (50), which most investors will designate.

☐ CAUTION: There is no guarantee that your stock will be sold at the exact stop price. In a fast-moving market, the stock may drop rapidly and skip the stop price, and thus the sale will be at a lower figure than anticipated.

➤ RELATE THE STOP PRICE TO THE VOLATILITY OF THE STOCK This is the *beta*. In making calculations, the trader uses a base of 1, indicating that the stock has historically moved with the market. A stock with a beta of 1.1 would be 10% more volatile than the overall market; one with a beta of 0.8 would be 20% less volatile than the market. If your stop price is too close to the current price of a very volatile stock, your order may be executed prematurely.

Use these guidelines for relating your stop order to the volatility or beta of your stock:

- Under 0.8, the sell price is 8% below the purchase price.
- Between 0.8 and 1, the stop loss is set at 10% below the cost or recent high.
- 1.1 to 1.3: 12% below
- 1.4 to 1.6: 14% below
- Over 1.6: 16% below

Example: XYZ stock is acquired at 50. Its beta is 1.2, so the stop loss is set at 44: 12% below 50. If the market goes up, the stop is raised for every 20% gain in the stock price. At 60, the sell order would be 53: 12% below 60.

The lower the price of the stock, the greater the probable fluctuations; the higher the price of the stock, the smaller the swings are likely to be.

Thus Teledyne, at 150 with a 1.1 beta, would normally have a stop-loss price of 132, but because of its high price, it would probably be about 139.

SELLING SHORT

Selling short is a technique that seeks to sell high and buy low—or reverse the order of what most investors seek to do. It's speculative but can be used as a protective device. You sell stock you do not own at the market price in anticipation of a drop in price. You borrow the stock from your broker, who either has it in inventory, has shares in the margin account of another client, or borrows the shares from another broker. If the stock drops to a lower price than the price at which you sold it short, you buy it, pocket the profit, and return the stock you borrowed to your broker.

Example: The stock of Nifty-Fifty, a high-technology company, has soared from 20 to 48 in a few months. A report from your broker questions whether NF can continue its ever-higher earnings. From your own research—of the company and the industry—you agree and decide that after the next quarter's report, the price of the stock will probably fall sharply. You arrange with your broker to borrow 500 shares and sell these shares at 48.

Two months later, the company announces lower profits, and the stock falls to 40. Now you buy 500 shares and pocket a $4,000 profit (less commissions). Or if you're convinced that the price will continue to go down, you hold out for a lower purchase price.

This technique seems easy, but short selling is one of the most misunderstood of all types of securities transactions and is often considered un-American and dangerous, as indicated by the Wall Street aphorism "He who sells what isn't his'n buys it back or goes to pris'n." Yet when properly executed, selling short can preserve capital, turn losses into gains, defer or minimize taxes, and be profitable.

§ HINT: With few exceptions, the only people who make money with stocks in a bear market are those who sell short.

Here's another example. Say that in anticipation of a bear market, you sell short 100 shares of AW at 50. To reduce your risk if you are wrong and the market rises, you enter an order to buy 100 shares of AW at 52⅞ stop. If the stock price advances that high, you'll limit your loss to $287.50 (plus commissions).

With a stop-limit price, you specify a price below which the order must *not* be executed. This is useful with a volatile stock in an erratic market. Then if the price of the stock slips past the stop price, you won't be sold out.

Say you enter an order to sell 100 AW at

50 stop, 50 limit. The price declines from 50½ to 50. At that point, your order becomes a *limit* order at 50, *not a market order.* Your stock will *not* be sold at 49⅞, as can happen with a stop order at 50.

Short selling is not for the faint of heart or for those who rely on tips instead of research. You may have some nervous moments if your timing is poor and the price of the stock jumps right after you sell short. But if your projections are correct, the price of that stock will fall— eventually. You must have the courage of your convictions and be willing to hang on.

RULES AND CONDITIONS FOR SELLING SHORT

Because it's a special technique, short selling of all securities is subject to strict operational rules:

➤ MARGIN   All short sales must be made in a margin account, usually with stock borrowed from another customer of the brokerage firm under an agreement signed when the margin account was established. If you own stock, you can sell "against the box," as will be explained. The minimum collateral must be the greater of $2,000 or 50% of the market value of the shorted stock.

§ HINT: For those who want to feel more comfortable with a short sale, it's best to maintain a margin balance equal to 90% of the short sale commitment. This will eliminate the necessity for coming up with more cash.

➤ INTEREST   There are no interest charges on margin accounts.

➤ PREMIUMS   Once in a while, if the shorted stock is in great demand, your broker may have to pay a premium for borrowing, usually $1 per 100 shares per business day.

➤ DIVIDENDS   All dividends on shorted stock must be paid to the owner. That's why it's best to concentrate on warrants and stocks that pay low or no dividends.

➤ RIGHTS AND STOCK DIVIDENDS   Because you are borrowing stock, you are not entitled to rights or stock dividends. You must return all stock rights and dividends to the owner.

If you know or suspect that a company is going to pass or decrease its payout, you can get an extra bonus by selling short. The price of the stock is almost sure to drop. *But be careful:*

The decline may be too small to offset the commissions.

➤ SALES PRICE   Short sales must be made on the uptick or zero tick: that is, the last price of the stock must be higher than that of the previous sale. If the stock is at 70, you cannot sell short when it drops to 69⅞ but must wait for a higher price: 70⅛ or more.

Exception: The broker may sell at the same price, 70, provided that the previous change in the price was upward. There might have been three or four transactions at 70. A short sale can be made when the last different price was 69⅞ or lower. This is called selling on an even tick.

CANDIDATES FOR SHORT SALES

In choosing stocks for short sales, professionals use computers to analyze economic, industry, and corporate factors—plus guesswork based on experience. Amateurs must rely on simpler indicators such as these:

- **Insider transactions.** That is, if officers and directors of the corporation have sold stock in the previous few months. The assumption is that when the number of insiders selling exceeds the number buying, the stock is at a high level and these knowledgeable people believe a decline is ahead.

- **Volatility,** as measured by the beta of the stock. This is the historical relation between the price movement of the stock and the overall market. A stock that moves with the market has a beta of 1.0; a more volatile issue is rated 1.5 because it swings 50% more than the market.

  The more volatile the stock, the better it may be for short selling. You can hope to make your profit more quickly.

- **Relative strength,** or how the stock stacks up with other companies in the same or similar industries. This calculation takes into account the consistency and growth of earnings and whether the last quarter's profits were lower or higher than anticipated by Wall Street. These data are available from statistical services such as Value Line and Standard & Poor's Earnings Forecast.

When corporate earnings are lower than the professional forecasts, the stock will almost always fall sharply. Helene Curtis Industries stock dropped over 11 points, even though its annual earnings rose to $1.96 from $1.40, simply because this was below expectations. Catching such a situation so that you can sell short early will depend on your own projections, which can be based on news stories or information that you have gleaned from your personal contacts.

WHAT TO SELL

As a rule of thumb, the best candidates for short selling are (1) stocks that have zoomed up in a relatively short period; (2) one-time glamour stocks that are losing popularity; after reaching a peak, these stocks will be sold rapidly by the institutions, and since these "professionals" follow the leader, the prices can drop far and fast; (3) stocks that have begun to decline more than the market averages; this may be an indication of fundamental weakness; (4) warrants of volatile stocks, which are selling at high prices.

WHAT NOT TO SELL

The least attractive stocks for short selling are (1) thin issues of only a few hundred thousand outstanding shares; a little buying can boost their prices, and you can get caught in a squeeze and have to pay to borrow, or buy back, shares; (2) stocks with a large short interest: more than the volume of 3 days' normal trading; they have already been pressured downward, and when the shorts are covered, this extra demand will force prices up.

SELLING AGAINST THE BOX

This is a favorite year-end tactic that can freeze your paper profits and postpone taxes. You sell short against shares you own. The short sale brings in immediate cash and the profit (loss) is deferred until the short position is covered—next year. Here's how it works:

On March 1, Mary buys 100 shares of XYZ Corp. at 40. By July the stock is at 60, but the market is weakening and Mary gets nervous. She sells short 100 shares of XYZ with her own shares as collateral.

Her long position (the 100 shares bought at 40) remains in a margin account, where it represents collateral.

Her short position is made in a different "short account."

What are Mary's choices?

1   If the stock stays around 60, she may elect to deliver her stock against her short sale, which was made at 60, after January 1. This will postpone taxes until the new year and will also give her a 20-point profit (60 − 40 = 20).

2   If the stock drops from 60 to 50, she can deliver her stock and take a 20-point profit (60 − 40 = 20) as in choice 1, or she can take a 10-point profit by buying back her short sale. In this case she remains an investor in the company with the original stock at a cost of 40.

Commissions should be considered in selling against the box; they become a factor.

Under the wash sale rule (see Chapter 32), there will be no tax loss if the short sale is covered by buying the same or identical securities within 30 days before or after the date of the original short sale. In other words, if Mary sells short at 60 and then her stock moves up in price within a short period of time and she covers the short sale by purchase within 30 days, the loss is *not* a tax loss; it is simply added to her original cost (40 per share). If she covers the short sale by purchase after 31 days, the loss is valid for tax purposes.

SOURCE: Joel Fein, ISI Group, Inc.

GUIDELINES FOR SUCCESSFUL SHORT SELLING

DON'T buck the trend. Do not sell short unless both the major and intermediate trends of the market—or, on occasion, those of an industry—are down. Make the market work for you. You may be convinced that an individual stock is overpriced, but do not take risks until there is clear, confirmed evidence of a fall in the market and in your target stock.

DON'T sell short at the market when the stock price is heading down. Place a limit order at the lowest price at which you are willing to sell short.

DO set protective prices. *On the up side,* 10% to 15% above the sale price, depending on the volatility of the stock. In most cases, a quick small loss will be wise.

Be careful with stop orders. You may be picked off if the stock price rises to the precise point of the stop order and then declines.

DON'T short several stocks at once until you are experienced and have ample funds and time enough to check daily. Start with one failing stock; if you make money, you will be ready for further speculations.

DO rely on the odd-lot selling indicator. This is available from several technical advisory services or can be set up on your own. It is calculated by dividing the total odd-lot sales into the odd-lot short sales and charting a 10-day moving average. When the indicator stays below 1.0 for several months, it's time to consider selling short. When it's down to 0.5, start selling.

Conversely, when the indicator rises above 1.0, do not sell short and cover your positions. And if you hesitate, cover all shorts when a 1-day reading bounces above 3.0.

DO set target prices but be ready to cover when there's a probability of an upswing. There will usually be a resistance level. If this is maintained with stronger volume, take your profit. You can't afford to try to outguess the professionals.

BREAKING EVEN

Before you hang on to a stock in hopes that its price will rise so that you can break even, check the following table. A stock must rise 100% to

IF A STOCK DROPS THE FOLLOWING PERCENTAGE	IT NEEDS TO RISE THIS PERCENTAGE FOR YOU TO BREAK EVEN
5% (100 to 95)	5% (95 to 100)
10% (100 to 90)	11% (90 to 100)
15% (100 to 85)	17% (85 to 100)
20% (100 to 80)	25% (80 to 100)
25% (100 to 75)	33% (75 to 100)
30% (100 to 70)	42% (70 to 100)
40% (100 to 60)	66% (60 to 100)
50% (100 to 50)	100% (50 to 100)
60% (100 to 40)	150% (40 to 100)
75% (100 to 25)	300% (25 to 100)

correct a 50% decline! If your stock declines from 100 to 50, it has dropped 50%. But it will take a doubling in price (a 100% increase) to rise from 50 back to 100. *Moral:* Take losses early; set stop orders to protect profits; stop dreaming.

PROGRAM TRADING

An ongoing situation individual stock investors should be aware of is "program trading," a complicated strategy used by institutions whereby computers trigger buy and sell orders. During the past 5 years it has added to market volatility and was blamed for much of the market's drop in October 1987.

THE TRIPLE WITCHING HOUR

Four times a year, three "items" expire on the same day: stock index futures, index options, and stock options. Program traders take offsetting positions, and a huge burst of buying and selling takes place, sometimes just before the market closes. There's no way to determine if the result will push the market up or down. This occurs on the third Friday of March, June, September, and December.

Program trading is the result of the introduction of index options, index futures, and computers to Wall Street. It takes advantage of the price gap between index futures and option prices and the market value of the stocks making up the indexes.

The trader uses computers to follow the price differentials and then to sell automatically at a specified point. When a number of big institutions follow the same strategy, the market swings can be large. Here are two typical trading situations:

- If the value of the S&P 500 futures contract drops below the market price of the stocks that make up the index and the spread (or price gap) becomes wide enough, computers send out automatic signals to sell stocks. This huge sell order can lead to a drop in the price of the stocks.
- If the prices of the S&P 500 stocks fall behind the futures on the index, the computers will signal to buy these stocks and sell the futures when the spread reaches a certain amount. This can lead to a rise in stock prices.

SPACE YOUR TRADES

If you are making a large investment (500 shares or more) in any one stock, consider spacing out your purchases over a period of several days or even weeks. The commissions will be higher, but you'll gain a time span in which to review your investment decisions without committing all your funds. And if you decide that your choice was wrong, you can cancel the rest of the order.

EX-DIVIDEND DATE

Always check the ex-dividend dates before you sell. This will ensure extra income benefits.

Ex-dividend means without dividend. On the stock tables, this is shown by the symbol

"x" after the name of the company in the "sales" column.

The buyer of a stock selling ex-dividend does not receive the most recently declared dividend. That dividend goes to the seller. With Consolidated Edison, the date is shown in Standard & Poor's *Stock Guide* as below.

Once a dividend is ex-dividend, shareholders then look to the next dividend to be declared.

Going ex-dividend is actually a two-step process. The new dividend is payable to those who are "holders of record" as of a certain date. To be a holder of record, one must buy the stock at least 5 business days before the record date. On the fourth business day prior to the record date, the stock trades ex-dividend; that is, without dividend. Step two involves payment of the dividend by the corporation to the holders of record. This payment occurs 2 or 3 weeks after the official record date.

Once you have decided to sell a stable stock, you may want to delay the sale until a few days after the ex-dividend date, so you can earn the dividend. On the ex-dividend date, the stock will usually drop by the amount of the dividend but will tend to make it up in the following few days.

Ex-rights means without rights. As outlined in Chapter 17, rights offer stockholders the opportunity to buy new or additional stock at a discount. The buyer of a stock selling ex-rights is not entitled to this right after the ex-right date.

BUILDING YOUR PORTFOLIO

The simplest, easiest way to buy shares of a stock—once you own it, that is—is through a *dividend reinvestment plan*, so we'll discuss that approach first. *Dollar cost averaging* is another automatic way to add to your portfolio holdings. Neither dividend reinvestment nor dollar cost averaging requires a great deal of

NAME OF ISSUE	DECLARED	EX-DIV.	RECORD	PAYMENT
Consolidated Edison	4/28	5/13	5/19	6/15/1993

AVOID ODD-LOT TRANSACTIONS

When you deal with odd lots of stocks— fewer than 100 shares—you may have to pay a premium, typically ⅛ point. This goes to the specialist handling the transaction. However, you may not be penalized if the issue is handled directly by the broker and it involves shares of a company for which the firm makes a market.

work or thought on your part once you've actually purchased the stock or mutual fund for your portfolio.

DIVIDEND RE-INVESTMENT

In this plan, offered by most blue chip companies, dividends are automatically reinvested in shares of a company's stock without a brokerage fee. A number also offer a 5% price discount on new stock purchases. This service is offered by corporations to strengthen stockholder relations

SOME CORPORATIONS WITH DIVIDEND REINVESTMENT PLANS: 1994

AT&T	Indiana Energy
Bell South	Kellogg
Bristol-Myers Squibb	Kroger Co.
Citicorp	McDonald's
Clorox	MMM
Commonwealth	Morgan (J.P.)
Edison	NYNEX
Duke Power	PepsiCo
DuPont	Piedmont Nat. Gas
Exxon	Raytheon
General Electric	Sears, Roebuck
Green Mountain	Southwestern Bell
Power	Texas Utilities
Hawaiian Electric	United Water Resources
Ind.	Universal Foods
Heinz	Wells Fargo
IBM	WPL Holdings
Illinois Power	Xerox Corp.

and raise additional capital at low cost; for investors, it is a handy, inexpensive means for regular saving. It avoids the nuisance of small dividend checks and forces regular investments. It's good for growth but not for current income, because you never see the dividend check. Many corporations permit extra cash deposits, ranging from $10 to $3,000 each dividend reinvestment time. There is usually an annual cap ranging anywhere from $10,000 to $100,000 per year.

Under such a plan, all dividends are automatically reinvested in the company's stock. The company then credits the full or fractional shares and pays dividends on the new total holdings.

Because these cash dividends are reinvested automatically at regular quarterly intervals, they resemble dollar cost averaging and turn out to be a way to buy more shares of a stock when its price is low. Full as well as fractional shares are credited to your account.

☐CAUTION: You must pay income taxes on the dividends reinvested just as though you had received cash. If you buy the stock at a discount from its current market price, the difference is regarded as taxable income.

💲HINT: For more information, read *Buying Stocks Without a Broker*, Charles B. Carlson (New York: McGraw-Hill); $16.95 + $3 shipping from: Dow Theory Forecasts, Inc. 7412 Calumet Avenue, Hammond, IN 46324.

DOLLAR COST AVERAGING (DCA)

This, the most widely used direct-investment formula plan, eliminates the difficult problem of timing when to buy and sell. You purchase a fixed dollar amount of stocks at specific time intervals: 1 month, 3 months, or whatever time span meets your savings schedule. Consequently, your average cost will always be lower than the average market price. This is because lower prices always result in the purchase of more shares.

For example, if you invest $100 per month regardless of the price of the shares, the lower the market value, the more shares you buy. The stocks you buy fluctuate in price between 10 and 5 over 4 months. The first month you buy 10 shares at $10 each for a total of $100. The

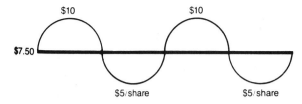

Total invested: $400
40 shares @ $5 = $200
20 shares @ $10 = 200
$400

STOCKS FOR DOLLAR COST AVERAGING:
1994

American Home Products	Long's Drug Stores
Archer-Daniels-Midland	Merck & Co.
Becton Dickinson	PepsiCo, Inc.
Caterpillar	Pfizer, Inc.
Clorox Co.	Pitney-Bowes
Coca-Cola	Procter & Gamble
Disney (Walt)	Reader's Digest
Dow Jones	Reebok
Eastman Kodak	Rockwell Int'l.
Exxon	Rollins, Inc.
General Electric	Rubbermaid, Inc.
Goodyear Tire	Scott Paper
Heinz	Smucker
IBM	Upjohn Co.
Iowa Gas & Electric	Winn Dixie Stores
Lilly (Eli)	Wrigley (Wm.)
Long Island Lighting	Xerox Corp.

second month you buy 20 shares at $5 each, and so on. At the end of 4 months you have acquired 60 shares for your $400 at an average cost of $6.67 per share (400 ÷ 60). *Note:* During this same period, the average price was $7.50.

With DCA, the type of stock acquired is important. You want quality stocks that have these general characteristics:

- **Volatility** . . . but not too much. Preferably, the 10-year-high price should be 2½ times the low. These swings are more common with cyclical stocks such as motors, machinery, and natural resources, but they can also be found with industries whose popularity shifts: drugs, electronics, and food processors.

  In bear markets, your dollars buy more shares, but your paper losses on stock already held will be high, so you will have to have a stout heart and confidence enough to maintain your commitment. That's where quality counts.

- **Long-term growth.** These are stocks of companies that can be expected to continue to boost revenues and earnings and outperform the overall stock market. If your stock fails to keep pace with the market comeback, you will lose the main advantage of DCA. Look for stocks that are more volatile on the up side than on the down side.

- **Steady, ample dividends.** It is true that dividends, as such, have little to do with formula plans, but they can help to provide regular sums needed for periodic investments, especially when you find it difficult to scrape up spare cash.

  With the right stocks and modest commitments, you may find that in a few

years, the dividends will be enough to meet those periodic payments.

When you use margin, you can buy more shares with the same savings, but you will have to pay interest on your margin account. However, the interest charged will be partially offset by the dividends you receive.

$ HINT: Start your program a week or two before the date you expect to receive a dividend check from the company whose stock you plan to buy.

- **Better than average profitability.** The average profit rate of the company over a decade should be at least 10%. It's fine to be able to buy more stock when the price is low, but there's little benefit if its value does not move up steadily over the years. Corporations able to show consistent profitable growth will always be worth more in the future. With DCA, you are striving to accumulate greater wealth. This can always be done best by buying stocks of companies that make better than average profits.

- **Good quality.** This means stocks of companies rated A− or higher by Standard & Poor's. With such criteria, you will avoid companies with high debt ratios

REVERSE DOLLAR COST AVERAGING

SHARE PRICE	$100 PER MONTH: NO. SHARES SOLD	10 SHARES PER MONTH: INCOME
10	10	$100
5	20	50
10	10	100
20	5	200
10	10	100
5	20	50
	75	$600
Average redemption price per share	$8	$10

and, usually, those whose prices swing sharply.

$ HINT: Shares of mutual funds are excellent vehicles for DCA. They provide diversification, generally stay in step with the stock market as a whole, and usually continue to pay dividends.

REVERSE DCA

This is a technique that is best used after retirement when you begin to liquidate shares of a mutual fund. Instead of drawing a fixed dollar amount (as most retirees do), you sell a fixed number of shares. The average selling price will come out higher that way.

For illustration only, the table above shows the values of fund shares that fluctuate widely over a 6-month period. To get $100 income, you must sell 10 shares in the first month, 20 in the second, etc. Over the half-year, you liquidate 75 shares at an average price of $8.

But if you sell a fixed number (10) of shares each month, your income will vary: $100 in month 1, $50 in month 2, $200 in month 4. Overall, you will cash in only 60 shares at an average redemption price of $10.

This can be dangerous for two reasons: (1) You won't get the same dollars every month, but over the same period of time you will receive as much and have more shares still invested. Yet when the price of the shares drops,

you will have to unload more shares and will have fewer assets invested in the fund. (2) You cannot know in advance the correct number of shares to sell; if you have to change the formula, you may be in trouble.

$ HINT: This system is arithmetically correct but may be difficult for people who do not have additional income to live on in months when fund per-share price is low.

➤ ADVANTAGES Over the years, the average cost of all shares will be less than the average price at which you bought them. But you lose the fun and pride of judgment-based investing.

☐ CAUTION: When stock prices are falling, consistent purchases are a form of averaging down—generally a poor policy unless you are convinced that there will be a turnaround soon.

➤ DISADVANTAGES Formula plans sound simple, but they can be difficult to maintain. Most investors cannot convince themselves to sell when things are going well and to buy when the market action is unfavorable. These plans will seldom let you achieve a big killing, but they can stop you from being killed.

ONE-STOP INVESTING

If you have a brokerage account, a money market fund, and a major credit card, as well as some type of checking account, you may find it useful and economical to wrap it all together and put it into a combo, or central assets, account. In this way, all your financial transactions will be handled under one roof—at a bank or brokerage firm—which saves you time, red tape, and sometimes money, too.

A typical central assets account consists of one versatile package that can include stocks, bonds, your IRA, a money market fund, and credit or debit card transactions. But you must be able to meet the minimum amount set by the brokerage firm or bank, which ranges from $5,000 to $20,000.

For a yearly fee (zero to $200) the sponsoring bank or brokerage firm will provide unlimited checkwriting privileges on a money market account; an American Express, VISA, or MasterCard account; a line of credit; a securities brokerage account; and an all-inclusive monthly statement. An important additional benefit,

DIRECTORY OF CENTRAL ASSETS ACCOUNTS

Citibank: Citigold Account
(1-800-285-1701)
Dean Witter: Active Assets Account
(local office)
A. G. Edwards: Total Asset Account
(1-800-677-8380)
Fidelity: Ultra Service Account
(1-800-343-8721)
Kidder Peabody: Premium Account
(1-800-543-3377)
Merrill Lynch: Cash Management Account
(1-800-262-4636)
Paine Webber: Resource Management Account (1-800-762-1000)
Prudential-Bache: Prudential Command
Account (1-800-222-4321)
Charles Schwab: One Account
(1-800-421-4488)
Shearson Lehman Hutton: Financial
Management Account (local office)
Smith Barney: Vantage Charter Account
(1-800-221-3434)

known as the "sweep" feature, automatically transfers or sweeps any idle cash (from the sale of a security, from a CD that matured, or from dividends) into a high-paying money market fund. This system not only relieves you of keeping track of the money but, more important, prevents any loss of interest between transactions.

A central asset account comprises seven basic ingredients:

- A brokerage account in which securities can be bought and sold at regular commissions
- Automatic investment of idle cash into money market funds
- A checking account, usually with free checks; minimum amounts vary
- A debit or credit card that can be used for purchases, loans, or cash
- A line of credit, that is, the privilege of borrowing against your credit or debit card

- Quick loans secured by the margin value of the securities held in the account, with interest charged at slightly above the broker call rate
- Composite monthly statements showing all transactions and balances

Here's how a central assets account works. Let's say you have 300 shares of Eastman Kodak that you want to sell. You call your broker with directions to make the transaction. Money from the sale is immediately invested in a money market fund, where it earns around 4%. The transfer of money from your securities account to the money market fund is done automatically by computer.

Then a few weeks later you write a check for $800. You do so against your money market fund, leaving a balance of several thousand dollars. You felt this was an adequate balance— and it was, until you had a sudden emergency and needed to use that amount plus $1,500. So your broker arranged for a loan using your remaining securities as collateral. This was done in your margin account. By having an umbrella account, you avoided hours of time and miles of red tape that are customarily involved in obtaining a bank loan.

Many of the larger brokerage firms offer customers one of several funds in which to park their idle cash: a regular money market fund; a U.S. government fund, which is slightly safer but also has lower yields; and a tax-free money fund for those in high-tax brackets.

The traditional monthly statement includes:

- A list of securities held in the account
- Securities bought or sold with an indication of profit or loss
- Amount of commission paid to the broker
- Dividends received
- Interest received from the money market fund
- Number of money market fund shares
- Amount of margin loans either advanced or paid off
- Credit and debit card transactions
- Data required in preparing your income tax returns

Before you leap into a central assets account, check out the following:

- Minimum required to open the account
- Annual fee
- Commission charged

- Margin loan rate (explained below)
- Method for handling debit and credit card transactions
- Frequency of sweeps into money market funds
- Number of money market funds to choose from
- Minimum amount for writing checks
- Clarity of monthly statements
- Any extras offered

You should also keep in mind some of the disadvantages of this type of account. First of all, most components of a combo account are available elsewhere. Credit card holders already have credit lines and cash advances. Debit cards can be a disadvantage, because they provide a shorter "float period"—that is, less free credit time than for a standard credit card. With the latter, you can stretch your credit or payment time up to at least 30 days, sometimes 60 or 90.

Some investors find that such easy access to money and loans makes it possible for them to spend more than they should. If you fall into this category, steer clear of the central assets account.

The Better Business Bureau in many areas has free material on central asset accounts, banks, and brokerage services. Contact your local office.

MARGIN ACCOUNTS

Leverage—using borrowed funds to supplement your own commitments—is a key factor in making money make money. With *real estate*, it's making a small down payment and having a large mortgage; with *securities*, it's buying on margin: using cash, stocks, convertibles, bonds, etc. as collateral for a loan from your broker. When the borrowing is kept at a reasonable level and the interest costs are modest, buying on margin can enhance profits, because your money is working twice as hard since you put up only part of the cost. Margin, then, is trading on credit and a way of using borrowing power to take a larger position in the stock market.

Leverage in the stock market is not as simple as it sounds. Successful use of margin requires sophistication, sufficient resources to absorb substantial losses when the prices of the

securities decline, and the temperament to handle debt.

THE RULES

When you open a margin account and sign a margin agreement and loan consent, you are giving your broker permission to lend the securities in your account.

Your stocks in a margin account are held "in street name," which means in the broker's firm. Therefore, you cannot put your stock certificates in your vault. You may also be subject to "margin call" if you use the assets in your account to the point where you have no more credit, or if the value of your portfolio falls below a minimum amount. Then your broker will ask you to reduce some of the loan. If you cannot come up with the cash or additional securities, your broker may have to sell some of your remaining stock.

Margin accounts are governed by the Federal Reserve Board's Regulation T, the New York Stock Exchange, the National Association of Securities Dealers, and individual brokerage house rules.

EXCHANGE AND FEDERAL MARGIN REQUIREMENTS

Assuming you put up cash in the amount of $10,000 in each case, you could buy on margin:
- $20,000 worth of *marginable stocks*
- $20,000 worth of *listed corporate convertible bonds*

You can invest on margin in nearly every issue on the New York and American stock exchanges and in nearly 2,000 over-the-counter securities. To open an account, you must sign a margin agreement that includes a consent to loan securities. The margin account agreement states that all securities will be held "in street name"; that is, by the broker. The consent to loan means that the broker can lend your securities to others who may want them for the purpose of selling short.

1   Under the rules set forth by the Federal Reserve Board, the initial requirement for margin on stocks is 50%. So to buy $10,000 worth of securities you must put up at least $5,000. Greater leverage is allowed on government bonds, where you can borrow up to 95%.

2   The New York Stock Exchange, however, has stricter requirements. It asks members to demand that investors deposit a minimum of $2,000 in cash or its equivalent in securities in order to open a margin account. That means that if you want to buy $3,000 in stock, your initial margin requirement is actually 66⅔%, or $2,000, rather than the $1,500, or 50%, that the Federal Reserve Board requires.

3   Some brokers set even higher requirements.

All brokers hold securities purchased on margin in "street name."

The New York Stock Exchange also requires that the equity in the account be maintained at 25% to 30% at all times. This is called a "minimum maintenance margin." When the value of your portfolio drops below this level, your broker will issue a margin call, and you will have to come up with more cash or the

---

DO NOT HAVE A MARGIN ACCOUNT IF:

- You lack the temperament.
- You are dealing in small amounts of money.
- You cannot absorb a loss.
- Your portfolio consists primarily of income equities.
- You tend to buy and hold stocks.

TO MINIMIZE RISKS:

- Set stop orders above the 30% loss point.
- Borrow less than the maximum.
- Buy on margin only in a bull market.
- Watch for increases in the broker loan rate.
- Check the prices of your margined stock at least once a week to avoid a surprise margin call.

CALCULATING YOUR YIELD WHEN BUYING ON MARGIN

To determine exactly what yield you get by buying on margin, you must ascertain the return on your actual investment: the *margin equivalent yield.* You can calculate this from the accompanying formula.

The *cash yield percent* (CY%) is the return on securities bought outright. The same formulas can be used for both pre-tax and after-tax yields.

$$MEY = \left(\frac{100}{\%M} \times CY\%\right) - \left[\left(\frac{100}{\%M} - 1\right) \times DI\%\right]$$

where MEY = margin equivalent yield
       %M = % margin
       CY% = cash yield %
       DI% = debit interest %

Example: You are on a 50% margin base, receive 12% cash yield from dividends, and pay 20% in your debit balance.

$$MEY = \left(\frac{100}{50} \times 12\right) - \left[\left(\frac{100}{50} - 1\right) \times 20\right]$$

$$MEY = (2 \times 12 = 24)$$

$$- [(2 - 1 = 1) \times 20 = 20]$$

$$MEY = 24 - 20 = 4\%$$

Thus the 12% return, with margin, dwindles to 4%.

---

broker will sell enough securities in your account to bring it up to the required level.

Example: Let's say you want to buy 200 shares of a $50 stock. In a regular cash account, you would put up $10,000 ($50 × 200 = $10,000). But in a margin account, you only have to put up 50% of the purchase price, or $5,000 plus commission. Your broker lends you the other $5,000 and charges you interest on it.

➤ LOAN RATE Mounting interest charges can take a big chunk out of profits in a margin account, especially if you hold your stocks a long time. You are charged interest daily based on the *broker call rate,* the rate the banks

MARGIN CALL

If your firm requires a 30% minimum maintenance rather than 25%, to find out if you're approaching a call, multiply the price of the stock at the time you purchased it by 0.71. If it's reached that price, your phone will ring.

charge brokers for money. The interest the broker then charges you may run from 0.5% to 2.5% above the broker loan rate, which is currently ranges from 6¼ to 7¼%. The more active and the larger your account, the lower the rate is likely to be. Dividends, of course, can help offset some of the interest.

$ HINT: The interest you pay on your margin account is tax-deductible to the extent that it is offset by investment income— dividends and capital gains. So to deduct $2,000 in interest, you must report at least $2,000 in investment income.

☐ CAUTION: The New York Stock Exchange may set special margin requirements calling for more cash or securities or require full cash payments in very volatile stocks.

➤ SPECIAL MISCELLANEOUS ACCOUNT If you have excess cash or equity in your margin account, this is known as a special miscellaneous account (SMA). It is created by the deposit of more than 50% of the purchase price of stocks or securities bought on margin, by the accumulation of dividends, or by a rise in the value of the margined portfolio. As long as the value of your margined portfolio is at or above the minimum maintenance margin, you may use your SMA to buy additional securities, but if your account is below the minimum margin maintenance requirement your broker will use your SMA to meet the margin call.

$ HINT: If you use margin, don't let your equity fall below 50%. In a volatile market, you can get in trouble very fast.

ADDITIONAL REGULATIONS

- Margin rules have been extended to some mutual funds.
- Individuals are allowed to have more than one margin account at the same brokerage house under certain circumstances, which vary from firm to firm. Check with your broker.
- Not all securities traded over the counter are marginable. Stocks under $5 usually cannot be margined.
- The NYSE sets special loan limits for individual issues that show unusual volume, price fluctuations, or rapid turnover, to discourage undue speculation.
- Customers whose accounts show a pattern of "day trading" (purchasing and selling the same marginable issues on the same day) are required to maintain appropriate margin before the transactions are made.
- Each brokerage firm sets its own margin requirements for nonconvertible bonds, municipal bonds, and U.S. government bonds.

$ HINT: You may use your margin account to borrow from your broker for purposes other than to buy stocks and bonds. The rates are almost always lower than a consumer bank loan, and there is no monthly repayment of the loan payments.

PART SIX

FINANCING YOUR LIFE-STYLE

Whether you're a baby boomer, an empty nester, single, a new parent, or in the senior citizen category, you need to arrange your finances to suit your life-style. In this section we look at the most important areas of financial planning as they relate to your particular needs:

- Housing: residential, rental, second homes
- Mortgages: how to get the best rate
- Paying for college: for your kids and yourself
- Adjusting to adult children returning home
- Helping aging parents
- Retirement plans, IRAs, Keoghs, 401(k)s
- Getting the most out of Social Security
- Understanding GICs
- Insurance and annuities
- Retirement living: adult communities, nursing homes, reverse mortgages
- Investment gifts

The recession brought about a sharp decline in real estate values in many parts of the country. At the same time, mortgage interest rates are favorable. And, until prices approach their highs of the 1980s, there are still excellent opportunities, both in property itself and in real estate stocks.

WHAT TO DO IN THIS REAL ESTATE MARKET

1 *If you want to buy, start looking.* The slump in residential and commercial property has led to a large number of distress sales. The real estate auction continues to have a big inventory of foreclosure properties. Public notices of default sales are posted at some city halls and frequently announced in local newspapers. And due to the savings and loan debacle, the federal government is now one of the country's biggest real estate brokers and is auctioning thousands of homes through the Resolution Trust Corporation (RTC).

$ HINT: For a free list of repossessed properties in your area, call 1-800-782-3006. For other RTC publications, call 1-800-431-0600.

Government agencies and mortgage lenders also often list with local brokers; many accept smaller than usual down payments.

$ HINT: For a list of foreclosed properties offered by Fannie Mae (Federal National Mortgage Association), write to: Foreclosures, Box 13165, Baltimore, MD 21203

■ If you're investing to rent, pick a location within a day's drive; it's easiest to be a landlord if your property is nearby.

2 *What about refinancing?* With lower interest rates, the question of refinancing your mortgage pops up. The rule of thumb is do not refinance unless the new rate is at least 2 percentage points lower than the old one. This guideline, however, overlooks a critical factor: how long you plan to stay in your home. The sooner you intend to move, the greater the rate differential between the two loans must be for refinancing to pay off. Why? You will probably pay 3% to 4% of the total loan in points and closing fees on a new loan, and it will take 2 to 4 years to recoup the up-front charges.

3 *Try a lease option.* If you own a house you would like to sell but haven't been able to, or if you want to buy but can't quite afford the down payment, a "lease-option" plan may solve the problem. Under this arrangement, the potential buyer moves into the house as a tenant, paying monthly rent. The rent, however, is considerably higher than normal, sometimes even double. The extra is credited toward the down payment. Some landlords also require an up-front cash payment. At the end of a specified time, typically 1 to 4 years, the tenant finds a mortgage and buys the house. If he cannot, the owner keeps the extra payments. Most of these arrangements are made through ads in local newspapers.

☐ CAUTION: Make certain the lease includes an exclusive contract that the property will be sold to the tenant for a set price when the lease expires and states whether or not the deposit is refundable. An option to buy could prove worthless unless a sales contract is attached to the lease and the

CALCULATING BENEFITS OF REFINANCING

If you have a $150,000 mortgage payable over 30 years at 10.5%, your monthly payments are $1,372. If after 3 years you refinance the mortgage balance, about $147,400, at 8.5% payable over 27 years, your monthly payments will be reduced by $210, to $1,162. However, you also must account for administrative fees and other costs: refinancing $147,400 will probably cost $2,710 ($500 in fees plus $2,210 for 1.5 points, a percentage of the loan amount).

Balance that against what you save in monthly payments: those refinancing costs will be recovered in about a year ($2,710 divided by $210 = 12.9 months). After that, your gross monthly cash flow is improved by $210 and your total interest paid over the life of the mortgage is reduced significantly.

Example courtesy of Thomas Hakala, partner of KPMG Peat Marwick in New York City.

contract has been signed in advance by the seller.

4 *Buying in an unknown area.* Whether it's rental property or a home for yourself, get a "destination appraisal" before buying in unfamiliar territory. Otherwise you might move in and find out six months later that an office building is going to be built nearby. Prepurchase appraisals range in price from $200 to $400. They let buyers know about hidden problems as well as give them an idea of the going prices.

$ HINT: To find a qualified appraiser, call the Society of Real Estate Appraisers at 1-312-335-4100 and request *Directory of Designated Members.*

YOUR HOME AS A TAX SHELTER

Once you own a home, you can use it to shelter taxes.

First, you can postpone gains made on the sale of your principal residence as long as you buy another that costs at least as much as the one you sold within 2 years of the sale date. If your new home costs less, you must pay taxes on the lesser of either the house sale profits or the difference between the prices of the old and new homes.

Second, you can continue to defer these taxes, provided you do not move more frequently than once every 2 years, unless the move is job related.

Third, when you reach age 55, you can take advantage of a special one-time tax break: a $125,000 capital gains exemption from your taxes. You must have lived in the home for 3 out of the past 5 years, unless you've been living in a nursing home. In that case, you must have lived at home for just one of the previous 5 years to escape tax on a sale. You can claim the $125,000 exclusion only once, and a married couple cannot claim the break when one spouse has already used his or her exclusion before the marriage. However, only one spouse must be over 55 to claim the exclusion on a jointly held home. When the home is not jointly owned, the spouse whose name is on the deed must be over 55 at the time of sale.

To make certain you whittle down the size of any eventual tax bill, keep good records. When your home is sold at a profit, the difference between the net sale price and the seller's "basis" in the property is the amount that is subject to tax. The basis is calculated as the price paid for the property plus closing costs, such as title insurance, incurred in making the purchase. Add to this expenses for capital improvements made over the years, but subtract any depreciation or casualty losses claimed. A capital improvement is anything that adds to the value of the property, for example, replacing a roof, fences, gates, central air conditioning, or a burglar alarm. Painting and repairs are maintenance expenses, however, and do not increase the owner's basis in the property. So keep canceled checks, copies of invoices relating to capital improvements, and notices of co-op apartment assessments.

$ HINT: Call the IRS at 1-800-TAX-FORM to get a copy of Publication 523, *Tax Information On Selling Your Home.*

HOME EQUITY LOANS

Interest on up to $100,000 of a home equity loan or a home equity line of credit is fully deductible as long as the loan is secured by your principal home or a second home that you own.

The elimination of deductibility of personal interest (on credit card loans, for example) has added to the appeal of home equity loans. And because this type of loan is secured by your home, interest rates are often lower than those charged on other borrowing.

$ HINT: Call the IRS at 1-800-TAX-FORM to get a copy of Publication 963, *Home Mortgage Interest Deduction.*

Home equity lines of credit—basically a repackaging of a second mortgage loan—have grown in popularity since the 1986 Tax Reform Act was passed. Because the deductibility of interest on most consumer loans has been eliminated and because interest paid on debt secured by your personal residence is deductible, banks are promoting these "credit line" types of loans to pay for big-ticket items such as cars, college education, and vacations.

☐ CAUTION: Use a home equity line of credit only if necessary. Your home could be repossessed if you fail to make payments.

With a home equity line of credit, the bank allows borrowers to apply for a loan, pay closing costs just once, and then borrow money as needed. You can usually borrow up to 80% of the home's appraised value minus any existing mortgages. Interest is higher than on first loans, but it is assessed only on money you actually draw. Fees and closing costs tend to be low because of lender competition.

$ HINT: Interest rates are usually tied to prime, so look for a loan with an interest rate cap.

GETTING RENTAL INCOME

Rental property, whether it's a condo in Florida, a ski house in Montana, or a center-hall colonial in the suburbs, if purchased after January 1, 1987, does not fare as well as before. It must be depreciated over a much longer period of time. The write-off period, formerly 19 years on residential property, has been stretched out to 27½ years (31½ years for commercial property). In the past, as a landlord, you could

***

DEDUCTIONS YOU MAY TAKE ON RENTAL PROPERTY

- Maintenance
- Depreciation
- Repairs
- Utility bills
- Insurance

***

deduct the total value of your investment over 19 years, writing off greater amounts in the first years, but now you must take deductions in equal amounts each year over 27½ years. *Note:* Depreciation can only be taken on the cost of the buildings, not on the underlying land.

If property produces rent, the income or losses generated are considered "passive," which means you cannot offset salary or investment income with these rental losses, with one exception: If your adjusted gross income is under $100,000 ($50,000 for married couples filing separately), the tax law allows you to write off up to $25,000 a year in rental property tax losses against other income, including your salary—*provided you actively manage the property.* This special $25,000 allowance is phased out as you become wealthier; if your adjusted gross income exceeds $150,000 ($75,000 for married couples filing separately), there is no such break.

$ HINT: Recalculate the return you receive on any property. If your property generates a loss *and* your income is less than $150,000, make certain you satisfy the IRS requirement of being an "active" participant in order to get the loss allowance.

To be considered an active manager, you must own 10% of the property involved as well as make decisions on repairs, rents, and tenants. If you hire a manager but provide guidance, you will still be considered active provided you can document your involvement to the IRS.

In considering rental property, keep in mind that the restrictions for deducting losses mean you must invest in property that produces a positive cash flow; that is, rents must be greater than costs.

If you make more than $150,000 annually, you can still reap some benefits, because the changes pertain to tax reporting, not to your cash flow. This means that if your rental income covers mortgage payments, the only plus you've lost is the tax shelter aspect. In the meantime, keep a running account of your losses and apply them when you eventually sell the property or to offset passive income from limited partnerships or other rental income.

VACATION HOMES FOR PROFIT

If you do not rent out your vacation home, you can deduct interest on your mortgage up to the original purchase price plus the cost of improvements.

Your vacation home is considered a "residence" *if you use it personally for more than 14 days a year or more than 10% of the time you rent it out* (at a fair market rate), whichever is greater. Time that you spend on repairs and upkeep does not count toward personal or rental use. Deductions for rental expenses on a "residence" are for the most part limited to the income received. The IRS formula is precise; check with your accountant.

$HINT: If you rent out for no more than 14 days a year, the income is tax-free and you are not even required to report it, but the expenses, other than property taxes and interest, are not deductible.

SEAFARING LOOPHOLE

Although tax reform eliminated interest deductions on most consumer credit loans, yacht owners and houseboat dwellers got a break. If your boat qualifies as a personal residence by having a head, galley, and sleeping facilities, you can probably deduct interest on any loan you take out to buy the floating home. Have your accountant check Code section 163(h) 5(A) (i) II, which governs interest deductions for qualified residences.

If you rent out more than 14 days or 10% of the time, the house is classified as rental (not residential) property. If the property was placed in service prior to January 1, 1987, you can still use the 19-year accelerated depreciation schedule, which allows larger deductions in early years. Otherwise, you must use the 27½-year depreciation schedule. Rental expenses cannot be used to offset regular income since they are considered passive losses. Under the 1986 law, these expenses can be deducted only from passive income from other rental properties or from limited partnerships and *not* from your wages, salary, or portfolio income. *Note:* There is an exception for those whose adjusted gross income is $150,000 or less, as explained earlier.

$HINT: If your income is too high to benefit from the $25,000 active rental allowance, you may be better off converting a "rental" vacation home into a "residential" property and writing off the full amount of the mortgage interest.

TIME-SHARES

Time-sharing, which combines vacationing with a very small degree of investing, should be viewed cautiously if not with complete skepti-

WHERE TO FIND BARGAINS IN RENTAL REAL ESTATE

- Someone desperate to sell—who has already moved, is being transferred, or has purchased another piece of property.
- An REO (real estate owned), also known as a foreclosure. Local bankers maintain listings. Prices are often well below market.
- Estate liquidations and family breakups.
- Distressed properties sold through sheriff's sales, IRS seizures for back taxes, and other forced sales.
- Discounted mortgages. These are existing loans sold by the lender for less than the balance owed. Check with real estate brokers, or place an ad in the newspaper. Review state foreclosure laws carefully.

cism. When you buy a time-share, you purchase the right to use a studio, apartment, or house in a vacation complex year after year. Time-shares are usually 1- to 4-week periods. For example, you may purchase a 2-week time slot in Aspen for a fixed period, say the first 2 weeks in January, or for a floating period that changes from year to year.

The primary advantage is cost. It's an affordable way to vacation—1 week can range from $2,000 to $25,000+ depending on the location, season, and facilities. There is often an annual maintenance fee as well. You pay only for the days you use your space, and in most situations you can sublet if you are unable to occupy your time-share. The interest on your mortgage is tax-deductible.

Many time-share investors have been disappointed that their property did not escalate in value as much as traditional real estate. The resale potential of time-shares depends on their location, how well they're managed, and the market.

The concept of time-sharing is less popular today than when it first came to the public's attention more than 20 years ago. Since then it has suffered as a result of industry mismanagement and a period when dishonest operators were more common than they are now. Federal and state regulations now protect the investor, so it is possible that time-sharing will regain some popularity. However, with the widespread trend toward co-ops and condos, this remains a less than timely investment.

☐CAUTION: Buy a time-share for vacationing, not primarily as an investment.

$ HINT: Call or write:
National Timeshare Council
1220 L Street NW, 5th floor
Washington, DC 20005
1-202-371-6700

They have a number of consumer publications.

THE MORTGAGE MAZE

One thing that has not changed over the years is the fact that getting a mortgage is one of the largest financial commitments most people make. To help get through the mortgage maze, review these most popular types.

HOW TO AVOID DROWNING IN A MORTGAGE

1 *Shop around.* Call several banks and mortgage companies and find out what they are offering. Compare details carefully. Don't rely only on your real estate broker's recommendation.

2 *Do your math.* You must figure out the exact amount you will pay each month for each type of mortgage. When doing the numbers for ARMs, assume interest rates will rise the maximum.

3 *Look for hidden traps.* Read the mortgage document before signing on. Among the traps to look for in the fine print: a bank that requires permission for borrowers to obtain a second mortgage or a home equity line of credit; a clause requiring you to sell your old house before the bank will let you close on a new one; any add-on charges and fees.

4 *Make extra payments.* Assume a mortgage only if it lets you make payments above the stated required amount. This reduces the length of your mortgage and will save you thousands of dollars in interest, since the prepaid amount is applied to the principal.

➤ FIXED-RATE MORTGAGE The old standby, the 30-year fixed-rate mortgage, remains the most popular type of real estate loan. Interest rate and monthly payments are fixed for the life of the loan, which protects buyers from increased monthly payments when interest rates rise. On the other hand, when rates drop, it often pays to refinance this type of mortgage in order to get lower monthly payments.

$ HINT: Shop carefully for a fixed-rate mortgage, because even a small rate difference affects your monthly payments.

This mortgage is generally considered a good choice for those planning to remain in their houses a number of years. The borrower knows what the payments will be, and equity builds up steadily over time.

A variation on this theme is the *15-year fixed-rate mortgage.* The good news here is that the debt is paid off in half the time it would be with a 30-year mortgage, and the total interest cost of the loan is lower. The bad news: Monthly payments are higher. On a $100,000 loan, for instance, the monthly payment would be $1,106 on a 15-year mortgage at 10.5% versus $953 on an 11%, 30-year loan. The major advantage of a 15-year mortgage is that you build equity faster and save on interest costs. This makes it a logical choice for those near retirement who want to be free of mortgage payments and/or those with sufficient disposable income to handle higher monthly payments.

➤ BIWEEKLY MORTGAGE This is another way to build equity more quickly and reduce interest costs. Instead of paying down your mortgage on a monthly basis, you do so every 2 weeks. The biweekly payments are half of what a monthly payment would be, but there's the equivalent of one more monthly payment per year. In other words, 26 biweekly payments equal 13 monthly payments. Most lenders require that biweekly payments be automatically deducted from your bank account.

➤ ADJUSTABLE-RATE MORTGAGES Called ARMs for short, this mortgage generally offers lower initial rates than fixed-rate home loans, but the interest rate and the monthly payment are adjusted periodically according to terms specified by the lender. Most peg the rate to an index based on short-term Treasury bill rates. Many ARMs are adjusted annually, semiannually, or once every 3 years over a 5-year period, and thereafter remain fixed. With others, the rate remains fixed for one or more years and then is adjusted annually. In most cases, the increase in interest is capped and cannot be adjusted by more than 2 points over the life of the loan. Some ARMs have a conversion feature allowing borrowers to convert (for a fee) to a fixed-rate mortgage, usually between the second and fifth year.

$ HINT: ARMs are particularly well suited to young people who anticipate growth in income and those who do not plan to stay in the same home for more than a few years.

➤ SEVEN-YEAR TWO-STEP It may sound like a dance, but it's a mortgage with fixed monthly payments for the first 7 years at a rate ¼ to ½ a percentage point less than those on a 30-year fixed. After 7 years, the rate is adjusted to market level.

$ HINT: This mortgage is suggested for buyers who are fairly confident they will be moving.

TIPS ON MORTGAGES

While the purpose of this chapter is to discuss real estate as an investment, a key part of successful investing is leverage—that is, your mortgage. For current rates and information, keep up to date by reading the popular press and talking to bank loan officers. To help you make informed decisions, consult these sources.

➤ FINDING A MORTGAGE
HSH Associates
1200 Route 23
Butler, NJ 07405
1-800-UPDATES

This group operates a mortgage hotline (1-201-838-8197), which lists the national average rates on a variety of mortgages. For $20 HSH will send you a listing of mortgage rates in your area plus a 44-page planning kit. HSH covers 50 metropolitan areas.

➤ REFINANCING Tables to determine if you should refinance or pay off your mortgage early appear in *Consumer's Guide to Refinancing Your Mortgage.*

Mortgage Bankers Association of America
1125 15th Street NW, 5th Fl.
Washington, DC 20005
1-202-861-6500

➤ PREPAYMENT Design your own mortgage prepayment plan with *The Banker's Secret.* The book ($14.95 plus $3 handling) or book and software package ($42.95) is available from:

Good Advice Press
Post Office Box 78
Elizaville, NY 12523
1-914-758-1400; 1-800-255-0899

➤ ADJUSTABLE-RATE MORTGAGES For a copy of *Introducing a New ARM for Today's Home-owner,* contact:

Public Information
Federal Home Loan Bank Board
3900 Wisconsin Avenue NW
Washington, DC 20016
1-202-752-7124

➤ VACANT LOTS Know your legal rights and avoid problems by reading the Department of Housing and Urban Development's brochure *Buying Lots from Developers.*

> HUD
> Program Information
> 451 7th Street SW, 8th floor
> Washington, DC 20410
> 1-202-708-1420
> Free

☐CAUTION: Make certain that any "points" you pay in connection with your mortgage are for interest (1 point equals 1% of the loan amount). As long as you pay points up front, with a separate check, they are tax-deductible in the year you buy the property. Points that are really origination fees are not deductible until you sell your property for a profit. Points paid for refinancing a mortgage are not deductible in full in the year they were paid. They must be deducted over the term of the mortgage. This is particularly important now, because lenders are sending reports to the IRS.

SWAPPING PROPERTY

The 1986 tax law gave a boost to a rather obscure yet legal technique that allows real estate investors (in theory) to sell one piece of investment property and buy another while deferring capital gains taxes. In fact, you can swap any number of times and not pay taxes until you actually sell for cash. The exchange must be completed within 180 days.

§HINT: Discipline yourself to invest the money that would have gone to pay the capital gains tax.

To qualify for this tax deferral you must:

- Exchange like pieces of property.
- Use the property for business or hold it as an investment; your home does not qualify, nor does an interest in a real estate limited partnership.

If the two pieces of property involved in a swap are not of equal monetary value, cash or an additional piece of property is used to make up the difference. *Note:* The cash or extra property is a taxable transaction.

HOW TO REDUCE YOUR PROPERTY TAXES

Experts estimate that 60% of all homeowners pay too much property tax. Take time to study your taxes and if you suspect you're being overcharged, file a challenge.

➤ THE MOST COMMON MISTAKES Errors in paperwork and/or math are widespread. So go in person to the tax assessor's office and ask to see the worksheet used when your property was evaluated. You have a legal right to examine this document. Check for:

1 *Typographical errors.* The assessment amount on the worksheet should match the assessment on the tax bill.
2 *Measurements.* Dimensions and square footage should be accurate.

After checking out the figures, look at how your property was evaluated. The assessed value of property, adjusted by the local tax assessment

---

SELECTED REITs

STOCK	SYMBOL	PRICE	YIELD	DIV AS % OF CASH FLOW
American Health Prop.	AHE	$26	8.5%	86%
Meditrust	MT	33	7.6	97
MGI Properties	MGI	14	5.7	60
New Plan Realty	NPR	23	5.6	na
Property Capital Trust	PCT	4	7.0	47
Weingarten Realty Invst	WRI	41	5.0	92

(As of spring 1993.)

office, is almost always lower than the market value. To find out if you are being overassessed, ask what the *adjusted* assessment value is plus what *multiplier* was used to make the adjustment. For instance, if your tax bill shows an assessed value of $100,000 and the multiplier is 2, then your home is really assessed at $200,000. If you believe your home is worth less than $200,000, challenge the assessment by following these steps:

1 Find out the assessed values of comparable property in your neighborhood. This is public information.

2 Get the actual selling prices of similar homes in the "Recorder of Public Deeds" office at your town hall.

3 Find copies of any existing professional appraisals of your property. (Your bank is likely to have this document.)

4 Get a new appraisal to document the fact that the value of your home is lower than its appraised value.

Present these facts to the assessor. If your appeal is denied, you can present your case to a board of review for an impartial opinion. Ask the assessor for an appeal form and the filing deadline.

FOR FURTHER INFORMATION

Julian Block, *The Homeowner's Tax Guide* (Runzheimer International, 1992).

INVESTING IN REAL ESTATE STOCKS

Although the real estate market across the country has been battered, in some areas it's beginning to make a slow comeback. That means it's the right time for investors willing to invest long-term and assume above average risk to add real estate stocks to their portfolios. Let's begin by taking a look at Real Estate Investment Trusts (REITs).

REITs are like mutual funds—they own a variety of properties or mortgages on properties. Their shares trade on the stock exchanges. Some are high in risk, but others are considered relatively sound investments and they offer an easier way to participate in commercial real estate than direct ownership, say of an office building.

REITs frequently focus on specific geographical areas and on particular property types. As we go to press, health care REITs are among the best investments. Three of the top performers with impressive dividend yields are:

- Nationwide Health Properties (NHP); $38/share; 6.2% yield
- Meditrust (MT); 33; 7.5
- Health & Rehabilitation Properties (HRP); 13½; 9.4
- Another consideration: American Strategic Income Portfolio (NYSE: ASP), which has a yield of 8.1%, and is selling at $16½ per share. This closed-end fund invests 70% to 75% of its portfolio in discount mortgages, such as those of the Resolution Trust Corp., and the rest in government-backed mortgages such as those issued by Ginnie Mae and other government agencies.
- *ARMS.* Adjustable rate mortgage mutual funds are a relatively new and fast-growing type of investment vehicle that invests primarily in adjustable rate mortgage securities issued by Ginnie Mae, Fannie Mae, and Freddie Mac (see Chapter 12). Because the rates on ARM securities are adjusted periodically, prices are less volatile than fixed-income securities. However, some investment uncertainty is created by the varying patterns of mortgage prepayment by property owners.

The yield on ARM securities generally tracks the ebb and flow of short-term interest rates, but is typically 1.5% to 2% higher.

Two ARM mutual funds that impose no sales charges are Benham's Adjustable Rate Government Securities (1-800-472-3389) with a 6.62% yield, and T. Rowe Price's Adjustable Rate U.S. Government (1-800-541-8832) with a 7.02% yield.

27 FAMILY FINANCES

THE HIGH COST OF CHILDREN

For many people, nothing is ever as exciting as having a baby—or as expensive. It's certainly one of life's most costly endeavors. Depending on where you live and how extravagant you want to be, raising a child from birth to age 18 can set you back anywhere from $47,000 to $120,000. And that's before college bills. So there's no question that having a baby will drastically change your financial life.

The best way to enjoy parenthood is to have enough money to care for your child, to maintain the life-style you and your spouse had before baby made three, and to minimize as many financial sacrifices as possible. The biggest sacrifice for most couples is the loss of the mother's income, since the majority of women take 3 to 6 months off for the first child. Yet, armed with a sensible financial plan, you can minimize the dollar drain and fully enjoy the newest member of your family.

➤ PRENATAL TO AGE 2 As soon as you know you'll be having a baby, both you and your spouse should find out what your respective firms offer in terms of maternity leave, including possible benefits for the father. Then check your health coverage. Whether you have a private policy or one sponsored by your firm, determine precisely what medical costs for the first 2 years are covered.

$HINT: Borrow maternity and baby clothes as well as equipment from friends, or buy from second-hand shops, discount stores, and outlets. And don't be shy: Encourage baby showers. Your family and friends may pitch in and purchase some of the big-ticket items for you. Use family members to baby-sit or join a baby-sitting

cooperative and share the task with other parents.

Build up your savings as soon as you know you'll be having a baby. Stash all or part of one salary in a money market fund and practice living on one salary, which will be the case when the baby arrives.

If you already have a nest egg, divide it into two categories: Put half into a money market fund so you can draw on it to pay immediate bills when the baby is born, and put the remainder into a revolving certificate of deposit program, purchasing CDs with staggered maturity dates. Save all cash gifts the baby receives. You'll need to get the baby a Social Security number to put them in his or her name.

➤ AGES 2 TO 5 Now that the start-up costs of having a baby have been absorbed, use these years to replace or add to your savings, especially

SAVINGS BONDS PAY FOR COLLEGE

The earlier you start saving, the more you will have when your child is ready for college.

CHILD'S AGE	VALUE AT AGE 18, BASED ON MONTHLY ALLOTMENTS OF:	
	$50	$100
1	$14,579.32	$29,158.64
6	9,233.20	18,466.40
10	5,656.16	11,312.32
12	4,069.28	8,138.56

The values in this table are based on the guaranteed interest rate of 4% per annum, compounded semiannually.

SOURCE: The Treasury, U.S. Savings Bond Division.

if you plan to move to a larger home. If you have not done so, you and your spouse should try to put at least 3% to 5% of your take-home pay in safe investments, such as Treasuries. You'll also need this money if you have a second child. Make certain you have adequate life and disability insurance to provide for your child, up to and through college. Finally, make out your wills and name guardians for the baby.

➤ ELEMENTARY SCHOOL YEARS When your child reaches age 6, you have approximately 12 years left in which to save money for college. Begin immediately adding to the college fund established when he or she was born. An early start will pay off. For example, a zero coupon Treasury that matures in 18 years can be purchased for approximately $150. When it comes due you will receive $1,000.

➤ JUNIOR AND SENIOR HIGH SCHOOL Encourage your child to earn his or her own money. Do not pay for everything. Instead, teach your child how to save and pay for certain items. And remember, children learn by what they see regularly—make sure you are not living off credit and neglecting to save while encouraging your child to do so.

$ HINT: Start to investigate financial aid for college by ordering a free copy of "Planning for College" from the Investment Company Institute, 1600 M Street NW, Washington, DC 20036.

PAYING FOR COLLEGE

Most children have plenty of toys, clothes, bikes, and even cars, but very few have a nest egg to pay for one of life's biggest expenses: a college degree. It takes more than good grades to get through school: During the 1980s, the average cost of attending college doubled, with tuition, room and board, and books increasing almost 10% a year. And there's no sign that it will slow down.

Early planning certainly eases the pain, as the time value of money works to everyone's advantage. For instance, if parents want to accumulate $35,000 by the time their child reaches age 18, based on a fixed interest rate of 9%, compounded monthly, they must save $73.08 per month, if the child is now 1 year old. If they wait until the child is 14, that figure jumps to $608.48 a month.

Yet the picture's not all that hopeless. There are a number of ways to stockpile money and find financial aid. Here's what parents and grandparents can do to meet college costs.

➤ STEP ONE Know who should own the nest egg. Money earmarked for college can be held in an adult's name, in the child's name, or in trust with the child named as beneficiary. Putting the money in the adult's name is, of course, the easiest, and it gives the adult complete control over the money and how it is used. It's also advantageous when it comes to seeking financial help: Most financial aid formulas require the student to contribute 35% of his or her assets to college costs annually, while parents are expected to contribute far less, usually only 5%.

☐ CAUTION: All the income and capital gains in the account are taxed at the parent's rate, which is almost always higher than the child's rate.

Money can also be transferred to the child through the Uniform Gifts to Minors Act (UGMA), adopted in almost all states, and the Uniform Transfers to Minors Act (UTMA), available in over 30 states. The key difference between them is the type of property an adult can transfer to a child. UTMA allows any kind of property—real estate, personal property, securities, cash—to be given as a custodial gift, whereas UGMA restricts custodial gifts to bank deposits, securities (including mutual funds), and insurance policies.

Both are simple to set up and administer. Almost any bank, mutual fund company, stockbroker, or attorney can do so. The custodian, who can be a parent or someone else named by the person funding the trust, controls the money until the child becomes of legal age (18 or 21, depending on the state). The custodian can invest, manage, or even dispose of the gifted property on the minor's behalf.

☐ CAUTION: At age 18 or 21, the money must be turned over to the child, who can then use it any way at all—to buy a car, join the circus, or, ideally, pay for college.

There are other types of tax-advantaged trusts for sizable amounts of money that an accountant or attorney can explain.

➤ STEP TWO Understand the tax law. The so-called kiddie tax seriously affects college nest eggs. Study the box below and talk to an accountant or tax lawyer before deciding who should hold the assets for college. For example, if the child is under age 14, it's advantageous to put the money in the child's name only as long as the income it earns does *not* exceed the annual $1,000 income cap.

➤ STEP THREE Consider gifts. A parent, grandparent, or anyone else can give a child up to $10,000 a year without paying gift taxes. If parents or grandparents have sizable estates that they plan to leave to the family, such a gift reduces future estate taxes. Grandparents can also make cash gifts in any amount and pay no gift tax *as long as* the gift goes for tuition and is paid directly to the college. And a grandparent can give an additional $10,000 free of gift tax to pay for room and board.

➤ STEP FOUR Set up a savings plan. Save a certain amount every month. Parents who find this difficult or who lack the discipline to do so on their own can establish an automatic payroll-deduction plan at work so that a set amount is taken out of paychecks on a regular basis and is used to purchase EE savings bonds or is transferred to a high-yielding money market fund. Both are low in risk. The current yield on money market funds is around 5.58% and is effective through October 31, 1992. EE bonds pay a guaranteed minimum rate of 6% if held at least 5 years. After that the rate is adjusted every 6 months. Although the interest on these bonds has always been exempt from state and local taxes, it's now exempt from federal taxes if the bonds are purchased after January 1, 1990, and are used to pay college tuition. However, the parents' total income must fall below a certain dollar amount when the bonds are cashed in. This income cap is adjusted annually for inflation. Bonds purchased in this tax-free education plan cannot be held in the child's name.

$HINT: For details, send 50¢ for *U.S. Savings Bonds: Now Tax-Free for Education,* #449Y, to: Consumer Information Center, Pueblo, CO 81002.

➤ STEP FIVE Consider other investments. Certain investments are particularly suited for a college nest egg because they grow in value over time. One of the most popular is zero coupon bonds, described on page 149. Growth stocks and mutual funds are suitable for long-term investments. Conservative choices include certificates of deposit and Treasury bonds and notes. Deferred

annuities can be purchased so that they start paying out income when tuition bills come due. An added advantage: Earnings inside an annuity grow tax-deferred until the money is paid out.

➤ STEP SIX Look into baccalaureate bonds. A growing number of states offer special municipal zero coupon bonds to help parents. They are sold at a discount from face value and do not pay interest until they mature. At that time, the bondholders receive the principal plus earned interest in one lump sum. Their great advantage: Parents know exactly how much money is coming due on a certain date. Some states even pay a cash bonus when the bonds mature if the child attends a state college. These bonds are exempt from federal taxes and, for state residents, from state and local taxes. Call your stockbroker or your state's treasury department for current details.

➤ STEP SEVEN Investigate special college deals. Tuition prepayment plans allow parents to pay a flat one-time dollar amount that is guaranteed to cover the cost of schooling later on. These plans eliminate the risk that inflation will boost tuition bills out of sight.

$HINT: Before signing up, ask the following questions: Can the money be transferred to another member of the family? What does the plan cover—tuition only, or other costs? Is the plan insured or guaranteed? Is there an on-campus residency requirement? Is the money available in an emergency? What if the child elects to go to another school?

Many schools will also arrange for bills to be paid on an installment basis, typically with monthly payments over a 10-month period, for a nominal fee.

➤ STEP EIGHT Apply for financial aid. Although it's tough to get, some financial aid is available, even to middle-income families. When visiting college campuses or writing for catalogs, ask each school about its financial aid packages. A statement of the family's financial resources must be submitted along with the application.

☐CAUTION: Keep in mind that shifting money into a child's name may jeopardize aid.

Many people assume incorrectly that they won't qualify for financial aid. The three most common misconceptions are: (1) The money I've saved in my retirement account will count against my child's chances of getting aid. *Wrong:*

Money from 401(k)s, IRAs, and Keoghs is *not* counted in the formula for determining aid. (2) If one child was rejected, the other will be too. *Wrong:* Families with more than one child in school often have a better chance than those with just one in college. (3) Older people returning to college or those who are going for the first time aren't financial aid candidates. *Wrong:* Older students are just as eligible as traditionally aged students.

➤ STEP NINE Borrow if you have to. Meeting the staggering costs may mean borrowing. Check these three relatively low-cost sources first: (1) Many companies allow employees to borrow from their 401(k) retirement plans to pay college bills. The major advantage: Interest payments are made into the account, not to a bank. (2) Borrow against a universal life insurance policy. Policyholders pay premiums to the company, which are then invested in an account where they grow tax-deferred. When it's time to pay tuition, policyholders can withdraw the cash balance or borrow against it. Loan rates are almost always lower than bank rates. (3) Home equity loans offer a tax break in that the interest is tax deductible.

$HINT: For a free brochure on using home equity loans, send a stamped, self-addressed envelope to: Public Relations Dept., Credit Union National Association, Inc., Box 431, Madison, WI 53701.

PLUS (Parent Loan for Undergraduate Students) loans do not require parents to show financial need, although they must have a good credit history. These loans are made by private financial institutions, not the government. Other similar loans are available. The college financial aid office will give you information on them.

➤ STEP TEN Have the student help out. Encourage children to shoulder some of the expenses by saving money from jobs or working part time. Another cost-cutting choice: Attend a school that offers a work-study program in which students alternate working and attending classes, so they earn money as they go along. Among the leading such schools are Drexel in Philadelphia, the University of Detroit, and Northeastern University in Boston. Students can also commute and eliminate the cost of room and board, or attend a community college for the first two years, where the tuition is much lower than at a four-year school. Military schools supported

---

HOW A CHILD'S MONEY IS TAXED	
IF THE CHILD IS:	THEN
Under age 14	The first $500 of income is tax-free; $501 to $1,000 of income is taxed at the child's tax rate, usually 15%
Age 14 or older	All income is taxed at the child's rate

---

by the government, such as West Point, Annapolis, or the Air Force Academy, provide free education if, in return, the student pledges a certain number of years of military service. These schools are difficult to get into, but most other colleges and universities offer ROTC, which is open to all and covers most school expenses.

FOR FURTHER INFORMATION

- *Paying for Your Children's College* and *The College Guide for Parents*, both $12.95, are available, along with other publications on financial planning, from: The College Board, 1-212-713-8150.
- *Don't Miss Out; The Ambitious Student's Guide to Financial Aid*, from: (Alexandria, VA: Octameron Press); 1-703-836-5480; $6 + $1.75 shipping.
- *Paying for College: A Step by Step College Planning Guide,* is free from T. Rowe Price, 1-800-638-5660.

BOOMERANG KIDS, OR ADULT CHILDREN WHO COME HOME

Your child may wend his or her way back home after college, bringing the stereo, posters, and a pile of dirty clothes. He or she may plan to stay just for the summer or longer—until landing an apartment, a job, a spouse, or all three. Or your child may have no plan at all. You face a philosophical decision about money at this point: Should you be an indulgent parent and provide free housing, a car, spending money, a lavish wardrobe? Even though you say it's because you're a loving parent, such moves actually encourage dependence and continue to keep your son or daughter in the role of child. Alternatively, you can treat the stay as you would that of any other adult boarder: charging room and board, drawing up a simple contract, and encouraging adult behavior and self-reliance.

Check insurance coverage for adult children living at home:

- *Medical.* If the plan where you work does not include grown dependents, then your child will need individual coverage, unless he or she is working and is covered there.
- *Automobile.* Drivers under age 25 typically add to the premium costs of family vehicles.
- *Personal liability.* You may want to take out an umbrella policy that will supplement your coverage for accidents around the house as well as in the family car.

From time to time, even when the nest is empty, you may receive requests for additional financial help—for graduate school, a downpayment on a car or house, or a wedding. If your child has a trust fund or a secure job, encourage the child to use his or her own money, perhaps with some help from you. If you're in a quandary about how much to help, set dollar and time limits and divide the responsibility. You may want to make a no- or low-interest loan. At this point, you must also think about your own financial needs, about saving for retirement or to help your elderly parents if they need it. Although you want to be supportive, emotionally and financially, you also want to encourage self-reliance—what you set out to do when you taught your toddler how to cross the street and tie shoelaces.

These judgment calls are not easy to make; they are filled with emotion. It's particularly hard to say no to your own children. But keep in mind that setting limits is sensible and reasonable, for both of you. Regardless of the choice you make, when you make a loan you should get a written IOU spelling out the amount of the loan, interest, and terms of repayment.

$ HINT: If you need additional advice, read *Boomerang Kids: How to Live with Children Who Return Home*, by Jean Okimoto and Phyllis Steggal (Boston: Little, Brown and Co., 1987).

TRADING PLACES: HELPING YOUR PARENTS

When age or a serious illness hits one's parents, children must often step in and help out. But as in anything financial, the results will be far superior if some planning takes place before a crisis hits. Your parents have three sources of support: their own assets, help from their children or other relatives, and the government. Here's what you can do to make certain all three are fully used.

First, talk. While your parents are still fit, discuss their plans for the future. If you need help breaking the ice, refer to the pamphlet *Tomorrow's Choices: Preparing Now for Legal, Financial and Health Care Decisions* available free from the American Association of Retired Persons, AARP Fulfillment, 601 E Street NW, Washington, DC 20049. Hold any discussions on parent's turf or a neutral place, such as a lawyer's office. Among the topics to cover:

- *Assets and liabilities* Ask parents to make a complete list of bank accounts, stocks, bonds, mutual funds, CDs, life insurance policies, safe deposit boxes, real estate, and other holdings. Debts should be listed as well.
- *Income* Review sources of income: Social Security, investments, pensions. Is it enough?
- *Wills* Each parent should have a separate will and all wills should have been updated since the 1986 Tax Reform Act, following relocation to a new state, a death, divorce, or birth in the family.
- *Important papers* Where are documents stored? Who has the key to the safe deposit box? Get names and telephone numbers of attorney, accountant, stockbroker, insurance agent, financial planner, and clergy. Is there a burial plot? Where is the deed?
- *Insurance* Determine whether parents are adequately insured or overinsured. Parents 65 or older are eligible to enroll in Medicare, a federal health insurance program. Still, supplemental insurance may be required to fill in the gaps. For an explanation of benefits and exclusions under the Medicare program, ask your

doctor for a copy of *Medicare: What It Will and Will Not Pay For,* published by the American Society of Internal Medicine; or call the association at 1-202-289-1700.

- *Housing* Be prepared to help your parents move to a new, smaller home, a retirement community, or perhaps even a nursing home. Read *Choosing a Nursing Home: A Guide to Quality Care,* free with a self-addressed, stamped envelope from the American Association of Homes for the Aging, 901 E Street NW, Washington, DC 20004; (see also Chapter 28).

- *Incapacity* If no provisions are made for physical or mental incapacity, the court can declare parents incompetent and appoint a guardian or conservator. So get a lawyer to draw up one or more durable powers of attorney to ensure that a person the parents trust will manage their financial and medical welfare if they cannot. Parents can confer the power on each other and also name, as successor, one of their children. The powers can be broad or narrow: The appointed individual can manage all finances, for instance, or merely have checkwriting privileges. A medical durable power of attorney enables an appointed trustee to make health care decisions on the parents' behalf.

Short of getting power of attorney, a joint checking account, usually with a spouse or child, can provide funds for an incapacitated individual.

Discuss drawing up a living will that specifies medical measures to be taken or not taken in case of terminal illness.

Consult a knowledgeable attorney regarding joint ownership of property and various types of trusts. A revocable living trust, for example, in which a parent is the trustee but makes provisions for a successor trustee, provides money management in case the parent becomes mentally or physically disabled.

PROVIDING FINANCIAL HELP

Review these suggestions with a lawyer familiar with estate planning.

- *Hire parents* Children who own a business can hire parents to work on a part- or full-time basis. This is a good way to provide fit parents with income while receiving tax benefits.

- *Make tax-free gifts* Anyone can give as much as $10,000 ($20,000 if given jointly with a spouse) without incurring a gift tax. If parents don't want to accept a gift, try making a loan instead. The money can eventually be repaid from the estate or sale of their home.

- *Increase investment income* Money in low-yielding bank accounts or CDs should be transferred to higher yielding money market funds.

- *Tap equity in their home* (see Chapter 28) One final note—you are not alone. Thousands of children face similar situations. Children of Aging Parents, Woodbourne Office Campus, 1609 Woodbourne Rd., Suite 302A, Levittown, PA 19057 will put you in touch with a support group in your area. Membership is $15 a year, or send $2 and a SASE. Call: 1-215-945-6900.

GOING BACK TO SCHOOL

Some say that youth is wasted on the young. The same might be said about a college education, which is one reason why so many adults return to school with enthusiasm, absorbing new information and skills. If you're planning to return to college or professional school, be prepared for the fact that tuition is probably higher than when you last sat in a classroom. And, keep in mind that raising money takes time; start as early as possible. Here are some tips for funding your schooling:

- Ask the school you're applying to about special tuition deals. Many state institutions reduce tuition for nontraditional and/or adult students.

- As soon as you're accepted into a program, contact the school's financial aid officer. This person typically knows the most about sources of money.

- Many states have loan programs for students pursuing careers as teachers, with "forgiveness" features for those who wind up in the classroom, as well as incentives for professionals the state needs—usually medicine, nursing, and special and bilingual education. Write to the appropriate state department of higher education. For addresses see: *Need a Lift? Educational Opportunities, Careers, Loans, Scholarships, Employment,* $2 from the American Legion, Box 1050, Indianapolis, IN 46206.

- *Perkins Loans* are available for both undergraduates and graduate students. They are distributed by the school's financial aid office.
- *Stafford Student Loans* are federally guaranteed student loans made by banks, S&Ls, and credit unions. Interest rates are 8% for the first four years, 10% thereafter. Get a loan application from a lender and send it to the college.
- *Supplemental loans.* Banks provide federally guaranteed loans of up to $4,000 per academic year to students who are not dependents. Obtain application from banks.

§ HINT: For quick information about loans and procedures, call 1-800-4-FEDAID; for information about other public student loans, call the Student Loan Marketing Association at 1-800-831-5626.

- *Private loans,* unlike public funds, do not carry income limits or have needs tests provisions. Approval is based on the creditworthiness of the applicant or, if necessary, on the participation of a reliable cosigner. The three leading sources are:
- *Nellie Mae loans.* New England Education Loan Marketing Corp.; 1-800-634-9308.
- *PLATO.* Personal Loans for Accredited Teaching Organizations; 1-800-767-5626.
- *TERI.* The Education Resource Institute; 1-800-255-8374.

Also consult: *Directory of Financial Aids for Women* by Gail Schlachter, Reference Service Press, San Carlos, CA; 1-415-594-0743; and *Don't Miss Out: The Ambitious Student's Guide to Financial Aid,* $45 + $4 shipping.

Those who are working or home with children will find "Weekend Colleges" designed to meet their needs. Classes are held on Friday evenings, Saturdays, and Sundays, depending upon the school. Some, like Trinity College in Washington, DC, provide on-campus babysitting and rent dorm rooms for only $15/night. Others,

like The College of St. Catherine in St. Paul, MN, allow adult students to pay tuition using their Visa or MasterCard and spread out the bills over three payment periods—for which there is a small interest charge.

§ HINT: Read IRS Publication #508, *Educational Expenses* to learn what expenses qualify as income tax deductions.

INVESTMENT GIFTS

Financial gifts are a wonderful, easy way to defray the cost of raising a family, buying a house, paying for college, even funding retirement. The next time you're asked, "What do you want for your birthday?," or when you're wondering what to give a recent graduate, a newlywed couple or a retiree, the answer may be a financial gift. Throughout this book we have suggested specific stocks, bonds, and mutual funds—any that fall within the conservative category make sound presents. To simplify matters, here are 9 suggestions.

- Stock in a company the recipient knows. *Suggestions:* the publisher, Reader's Digest; the gum maker, William Wrigley & Co.; the cereal giant, Kellogg Co.; and the shoemaker, Reebok. Check with several discount brokers to compare the commissions for buying a small number of shares (see list on page 247) or use A.G. Edwards (1-314-289-3000) where one-share commission on trades of $100 or less is only 16% of the stock's price.
- EE Savings Bonds. Available at your local bank with no commission or fee. These ultra-safe bonds, when held 5 years, are guaranteed a 4% rate, or 85% of the T-note rate, whichever is higher. Bonds are available for as little as $25. (See Chapter 9 for more on using savings bonds as a tax deferred investment.)
- Shares in a mutual fund. Pick a no-load fund with a good track record. The MIM Funds (1-800-233-1240) and the Berger Funds (1-800-333-1001) both have minimums of $250. (See Chapter 6 for more fund suggestions.)
- Stock or bond in a local utility company. They are a known entity, are generally recession-proof, and have above average yields. Some utilities sell shares of stock

(but not bonds) directly to investors, so you avoid a brokerage commission. (See Chapter 15.)

- Zero coupon bond. These sell at a substantial discount from the $1,000 face value, yet the owner will receive the full $1,000 when the bond matures. Treasury zeros are especially safe. (See Chapter 12 for details.)

- Tuition for a course in investing or financial planning. Check local colleges, YMCAs, and other schools in your area. Beware of courses taught by financial products salespeople; some may be prospecting for customers.

- A session with a financial planner. Call the International Association of Personal Financial Advisors (1-800-366-2732) or the Institute of Certified Financial Planners (1-800-282-7526) for referrals to planners in your area.

- Subscription to a financial publication. (See page 2 for suggestions.)

- Financial software programs. *Quicken* will balance a checkbook, prepare budgets, and track investments. *For the Record* stores your personal history, financial and estate plans, and lists where to find key documents and possessions. (See Appendix A for additional software information.)

28 RETIREMENT LIVING

As retirement draws near, most people begin to reevaluate their housing needs. So should you, if you haven't already done so. The house you bought 20, 30, or 40 years ago may indeed be your most valuable asset, one that you can put to active use to provide income and security as well as shelter.

TO MOVE OR NOT TO MOVE

Your rambling three-story Victorian was probably perfect for raising a family, but now it may be empty most of the time. Perhaps you'd like to sell and move to smaller quarters, all on one floor, maybe in a warmer climate. Or you may be so attached that you don't want to move but would like to make better use of the space. Either way, you can profit from the fact that you own a valuable piece of property.

Among the investment-related alternatives to consider are:

- Selling and moving to a less expensive, smaller house or apartment
- Renting out part of your house
- Sharing your house with a friend or relative, especially if you live alone
- Remodeling to create a separate, self-contained apartment, either to live in or to rent
- Selling and moving to a retirement or planned community

If you're thinking of this last possibility, be certain that you want to live with people all the same age. If so, select a place where you have friends or can easily make new ones, where you are near work if you would like to work part-time or as a consultant, and where you have the kinds of activities you enjoy close at hand—golf, swimming, schools, etc. Adequate transportation and health facilities are also important when relocating.

If you buy into a community, select one that is accredited by the American Association of Homes for the Aging, preferably one that has a waiting list. Both are indications of a well-run establishment. Among the other points to check out before making a financial commitment are:

- Management's experience and reputation
- The corporation's balance sheet
- Potential price increases
- Restrictions on use of the property (pets, children, car space, visitors)
- Any deed restrictions

$ HINT: If you are age 55 or older, $125,000 of the proceeds of the sale of a house that is your primary residence is tax-free. This is a once-in-a-lifetime tax break.

FREEING UP THE ASSETS IN YOUR HOUSE

Here is a thumbnail sketch of techniques that can turn your house into a source of income. For more on each one, check the source list at the end of this chapter. And regardless of which path you take, consult your accountant or tax lawyer well in advance. Laws change, and state regulations vary widely.

➤ SELLING TO THE CHILDREN You can sell your house to your children and then lease it back, paying them a fair market value. This gives them the tax advantages associated with real estate as well as your rental money with which to meet their costs. You can invest the money from the sale, perhaps in an annuity or other vehicle that provides you with a steady stream of income.

➤ MOVE TO A RENTAL THAT MAY GO CO-OP OR CONDO Check the local and state laws first. In many areas, when a rental building converts to co-op or condo, tenants over a certain age can stay on forever as renters. This is known as a noneviction plan. If the rent is modest, this could be to your financial advantage.

➤ TAKE OUT A MORTGAGE ON YOUR HOME Then invest the proceeds. You can deduct the interest portion of your mortgage payments.

$HINT: Be cautious about selling your home, especially to someone outside your family, and certainly if it is your only residence. Your house is immune from claims by the government, even if you or your spouse apply for Medicaid, particularly if one of you lives in it. Cash is not.

➤ GET A REVERSE MORTGAGE This is a home loan in reverse that allows you to take the equity in your home and turn it into regular monthly income without giving up your property. A reverse mortgage is designed to help elderly homeowners who are house rich but cash poor. The monthly amount is deducted with interest from the accumulated equity in the home. Each month the equity declines. The loan is paid off when the house is sold or the owner dies.

Nationally, about 150,000 home equity conversion loans have been made since they began in the early 1980s. Of these, about 10,000 have been made through private banks. Federally insured reverse mortgages are available in 41 states.

"Short-term" reverse mortgages tend to run 3 to 10 years, which can be a problem if you outlive the loan—you must repay the loan in full, refinance, or sell.

"Long-term" reverse mortgages establish payments until the owner dies or sells the house. The amount received monthly is based on the value of your home, your age, prevailing interest rates, and the percentage of future increases in the value of the house that you agree to share with the lender or bank. If, for example, you own a $100,000 house and are 65 years of age, depending upon the type of reverse mortgage you take out, your monthly check could range from $207 to $496.

☐CAUTION: Keep in mind that a reverse mortgage means leaving less for heirs.

Before signing any papers, have a lawyer and an accountant review all terms.

➤ CONTINUING CARE RETIREMENT COMMUNITIES If you are concerned that your parents, or you, may need nursing services but not a nursing home, consider CCRCs, a flexible, although fairly expensive, form of long-term care insurance. As of early 1993, about 275,000 people with an average age of 82 live in these communities. CCRCs offer a range of leisure activities as well as residential and nursing services.

In a typical CCRC, you do not purchase your home, but you pay a hefty entry charge plus a monthly fee. The fee covers nursing care for residents who need it. If you don't need the care, or if you move out, it is very unlikely that you will get your money back because you are *not* buying real estate as much as you are buying a service.

Examples: (call for up-to-date figures)

- *Type A facility* provides unlimited nursing care. Median entry charge for a one-bedroom apartment is $71,000 with a monthly fee of $1,150. At the high end of the range: $195,000 to $250,000 for two bedrooms with a monthly fee of $4,200.

- *Type B facility* provides specified level of long-term care, often 60 days a year; after that you pay $50 to $150 per day for care. Median entry charge is $51,000; monthly fee is $1,000.

- *Type C facility* provides a "fee-for-service" plan with access to nursing facilities—but you pay full rate. Medicare will cover short-term care only. In some facilities, residents pay for meals. Median entry price: $42,000 plus a $800 monthly fee.

Predicting your illness or that of your parents is not easy to do. But your decision can be guided by other more "known" factors. For instance: Can you or your parents afford to pay the monthly fees for as long as the CCRC resident lives? Select a CCRC that's in sound financial shape; ask to see its audited financial statement and review it with a knowledgeable accountant. Know under what circumstances the monthly fees can rise, or if there are any refunds in the event you or your parents move or do not need long-term care. Determine what happens to the fee and the unit if one parent moves to the health center.

$ HINT: Choose a CCRC that has a seal of approval from the American Association of Homes for the Aging (AAHA). Of the 700 CCRCs in the United States, about 110 have been so accredited. For a list, send a SASE to: CCRC, 901 E Street NW, Washington, DC 20004.

IF YOU RETIRE EARLY, ARE FIRED, OR LAID OFF

In recent years a great many American corporations have eliminated thousands of blue- and white-collar jobs. No one, not even top executives, are immune to cutbacks. Those who planned to glide into retirement are cast adrift. Those on the fast track are suddenly being derailed. If you're one of the many Americans who has been "let go," you face a number of important financial decisions. Although it is beyond the scope of this book to guide you through this period in your life, the following financial tips may help make life a bit easier.

1 Make a realistic budget and stick to it. Prepare for leaner times. Cut back on luxury items, eating out, taxis, and the like.

2 Keep any severance pay in a liquid account, such as a money market fund. If you received a sizable amount, put half in a fund and half in a high yielding closed-end bond fund (see page 98 for a list).

3 If you are given the choice of taking severance in a lump sum or payments, it's generally best to opt for the lump sum and invest it so it starts earning interest. This way you won't need to worry about your ex-employer's financial condition. If it's near year-end, it may be better to schedule payments so you can defer income into the next year.

4 Do not make the common mistake of using the severance check to pay off the mortgage. You may need this money, and a mortgage is usually one of the lowest-rate loans around with interest tax deductible.

5 If you receive a large sum from your 401(k) or other retirement plan, try not to touch it. That money has never been taxed. If you take it out now, you will pay income tax on it plus a 10% penalty if you're under age 59½. In many cases, profit sharing and stock option plans can be left with the company. However, if you suspect that your pension might be underfunded, provide for a direct transfer to your IRA to avoid the 20% withholding. It will continue to grow on a tax-deferred basis with no penalty. Keep this IRA money separate from any other IRAs; if you take a new job, you can roll it over into the new employer's plan.

6 Don't be too proud to take unemployment insurance if you were fired. (You cannot collect if you leave voluntarily.) You and your employer have helped fund this benefit over years; now you're certainly entitled to use it.

7 In a true emergency you may have to use some of your retirement savings.

8 Keep track of job hunting expenses; some of these may be deducted from your taxable income as "miscellaneous itemized deductions." Check with your accountant for details. Among the expenses to track are recruitment and agency fees, transportation, telephone calls, and resumé preparation.

9 Keep your health insurance. In 1986 a federal law was enacted requiring employers sponsoring group health plans to offer employees and their dependents the opportunity to extend their health coverage at group rates. This is called "continuation coverage" and it lasts for 18 months, longer if you are disabled. You will have to pay the costs, but they will be far less than taking out your own policy. If you are forced to take out your own policy, look into group rates offered by professional associations, unions, or an alumni association. If you are self-employed, look into membership in the National Association for the Self-Employed; call 1-817-589-2475 or 1-800-232-NASE.

10 Don't panic. Most problems have solutions and people willing to help you find them. Join a local group comprised of others who are out of work. There's much to be gained by sharing your situation with others. The worst thing you can do is to bury your head in the sand and hide from the reality of what has happened.

FOR FURTHER INFORMATION

For a list of reverse mortgage programs and a fact sheet, send a self-addressed, stamped envelope to the National Center for Home Equity Conversion. It also has a useful book, *Retirement Income on the House,* available at libraries or for $29.45 from the Center.

National Center for Home Equity Conversion
7373 147 M Street
Apple Valley, MN 55124
1-612-953-4474

HomeMade Money: Consumers' Guide to Home Equity Conversion
AARP Home Equity Information Center
601 E Street NW
Washington, DC 20049

American Association of Homes for the Aging
901 E Street NW
Washington, DC 20004
1-202-783-2242

Free literature plus a directory of member homes.

Continuing Care Retirement Communities
American Association of Retired Persons
601 E Street NW
Washington, DC 20049
1-202-434-2277
Free

Discusses contacts, payment plans, and financial matters, plus how to evaluate communities

Tax Information for Older Americans
IRS Publication #554
1-800-TAX-FORM
Free

29 SOCIAL SECURITY, RETIREMENT, AND PENSION PLANS

The time to start planning for a financially secure retirement is the day you receive your first paycheck, although few of us ever do. But don't agonize over the fact; just avoid further delays and start now. This chapter is not intended to be a complete retirement guide, but the information here will help you lay the financial groundwork that makes the difference between merely getting along and continuing life at full tilt.

HOW MUCH WILL YOU NEED?

Retirees are living much longer now—a person retiring in 1994 at age 60, is expected to live about another 25 years or more. This means that accumulating enough money to carry you through those years is critical. The combination of a pension and Social Security may equal only 40% to 60% of preretirement income, so the balance must come from personal savings and/ or part-time work. In addition, the higher your annual earnings, the less percentage-wise may be replaced by Social Security. Inflation, too, will erode retirement funds: At 4% a year, $1,000 will be worth only $380 in 25 years.

To maintain your current standard of living, your pension, investment income, and Social Security must add up to 70% to 80% of your last year's salary.

§ HINT: To retire at your current standard of living, begin saving 10% of your income while you're in your twenties and thirties. As soon as possible—and certainly by age 40—begin increasing that by at least 1% each year. When your children are out of college, boost savings to 15% per year until retirement.

WHAT DIFFERENCE DOES $1,000 MAKE?

You might not think that just $1,000 a year could make a difference in your retirement nest egg—it's a little less than $20 a week. Yet if starting on your 45th birthday you save $1,000 each year and earn 6% annually, by the time you're 65 you'll have almost $39,000, not taking into consideration income taxes. Obviously your best bet is to save the money in a tax-exempt investment or tax-deferred account such as an IRA, SEP, or Keogh.

Annual Interest Rate	20 years	10 years	5 years
5%	$33,775	$13,124	$5,794
6%	38,993	13,972	5,975
7%	44,211	14,810	6,156
8%	49,423	15,645	6,335

SOURCE: Case Western Reserve University

SOCIAL SECURITY

HOW SOCIAL SECURITY WORKS

Although we all spend a lot of time talking and thinking about Social Security, few of us know how the system works. It is a social insurance program that provides old-age benefits for retirees and their survivors, disability insurance for workers, and survivor benefits for dependents. It is called an "entitlement" because

Congress has set eligibility requirements—age and years worked.

The system is financed by matching contributions from employers and employees. Employees currently pay 6.2% of their earnings, up to a maximum of $57,600, into two separate trust funds: 5.6% into the Old Age and Survivors Insurance (OASI) fund and 0.6% into the Disability Insurance fund (DI). Employers match this amount. (Together the funds are known as the OASDI program.)

Every day, dedicated payroll tax revenues are deposited in the OASDI fund. Social Security benefits are paid from these funds and any money not needed is invested daily in U.S. government bonds and earns interest.

For many years, Social Security was financed on a current-cost basis or a "pay as you go" plan. Since 1983, however, it has been operating under a "partial reserve" type of funding that aims to take in more money than is paid out in order to build up the necessary reserves to pay the benefits of the large number of retired baby boomers who will begin collecting benefits in 2012.

In order to plan your retirement investments intelligently, start by taking a close look at your Social Security situation. Then build around this basic data. It may seem like a nuisance, but

ignoring Social Security records could lead to lower benefits than you're legitimately entitled to, since benefits are based on the Social Security Administration's records of what you have earned. It's up to you, and not the Social Security Administration, to find out if your records are accurate. Serious errors could cost you thousands of dollars in benefits.

STEPS YOU MUST TAKE

➤ STEP 1   Request a written statement of earnings. Call the Social Security Administration, 1-800-772-1213, or visit your local office to get a copy of Form SSA-7004, "Request for Social Security Earnings and Benefit Estimate Statement." Fill it out, sign it, and mail it back. In a few weeks, you will receive a computerized statement showing all earnings credited to your account. It will give a year-by-year listing of earnings from 1983 on, with a lump-sum total for your working years.

Check the information for errors. If you suspect an error, contact your Social Security office. Provide them with copies of as much data as possible, including dates of employment, wages received, employer's name and address, copies of W-2 forms, and paycheck stubs. The most common error results from incorrect reporting by your employer, unreported name changes because of marriage, or clerical errors at the Social Security Administration.

$ HINT: If for some reason you cannot find your old W-2 forms, try to get copies from the employer you had at the time of the error. If you fail, you can get a certified copy of any tax return from the last six years for $4.25 by sending Form 4506 to the Internal Revenue Service Center where you filed your return.

In 1989, Congress virtually eliminated the three-year statute of limitations on errors, so you can now correct mistakes, even those the Administration previously refused to address.

➤ STEP 2   Request this statement periodically, especially if you have changed employers, or if you have more than one employer.

➤ STEP 3   File an application three months before you want retirement benefits to begin. You

---

FOR ADDITIONAL HELP

- To reach one of the 4,200 Social Security representatives who help the public, call 1-800-772-1213. The lines are least busy between 7 A.M. and 9 A.M. and 3 P.M. and 7 P.M. Social Security representatives can answer most questions and will also send you helpful publications.
- Several hundred lawyers specialize in resolving Social Security problems related to disability benefits. They are members of the National Organization of Social Security Claimants' Representatives, which operates a nationwide referral service. For a member in your area, call 1-800-431-2804.

should file for disability or survivor benefits as soon as possible after disability or death occurs. Start any application by calling 1-800-772-1213. Social Security will not start sending your benefits until you file an application. Most applications can be taken by telephone. If you are late in filing an application, it's possible you may be paid only some of your benefits. Social Security seldom goes back more than 12 months, no matter how long ago you could have started receiving benefits had you filed on time.

Keep in mind these points about Social Security:

- Working spouses who pay Social Security taxes earn their own benefits.
- Nonworking spouses qualify for a retirement benefit that is equal to half what their retired spouses receive.
- You can supplement your retirement income by working, but any amount earned over $10,200 will reduce benefits for retirees aged 65 to 69; earnings above $7,440 reduce benefits for those under age 65. If you are 70, there is no limit. If your earnings go over these limits, Social Security withholds $1 in benefits for every $2 of earnings above the limits when you are under age 65. Between ages 65 to 69, $1 in benefits is withheld for every $3 of earnings.
- Investment income is not taxed for Social Security purposes.
- Social Security payments rise 3% for each year you delay collecting them. This credit escalates until it reaches 8% in 2008.
- No matter how old you are, benefits may be taxed if your modified adjusted gross income exceeds the base amount: $32,000 for filers of joint returns, $0 for marrieds filing separately who lived with their spouse at any time during the year, and $25,000 for all other filers. The formula for determining how much is taxed is: the lesser of (1) one-half the net Social Security benefits or (2) one-half the amount by which modified adjusted gross income plus half the Social Security benefits exceeds the base amount.

Now that you know what you're likely to receive from Social Security, you're undoubtedly impressed with the fact that you will need a great deal more to continue a comfortable lifestyle after age 65! Other ways to build a retirement nest egg are covered later in this chapter.

WHEN TO BEGIN TAKING SOCIAL SECURITY

Are you wondering whether to start collecting Social Security benefits at age 62 or waiting until you're 65? If you begin taking checks as early as possible, your benefits will be reduced by 20% for life. Yet in some cases it pays to begin early. It takes about 12 years of bigger checks to catch up with the total payments made to the early retiree. And if you invest the early payments, the break-even point is still further away. According to a study done at Widener University in Chester, Pennsylvania, by Paul Marshall and Robert Myers:

- If you plan to work after age 62 and you expect to make more than the earnings limit for Social Security recipients, you are better off delaying benefits.
- The current tax law is in favor of waiting for full benefits if your income, including half of your Social Security benefits, is high enough to trigger a tax on your benefits. If your income is over $32,000 on a joint return or $25,000 on a single

HOW AN IRA CAN PAY OFF

If you invest $2,000 a year and you are in the 28% tax bracket, here's what you'll earn in an IRA versus in a taxable investment. The figures assume that you'll earn 7% annually on the money invested.

	IN AN IRA	IN A TAXABLE INVESTMENT
5 years	$12,306	$11,617
10 years	29,567	26,473
15 years	53,776	45,469
20 years	87,730	69,759
30 years	202,146	140,537

SOURCE: Chase Manhattan Bank.

return, as much as half of your benefits will be taxed.

- Chances are you will live long enough to reap the money you passed up by not collecting benefits at age 62. You break even after 12 years of higher benefits, or at age 77. According to the National Center for Health Statistics, the life expectancies for 62-year-olds are as follows:
  White females: 83.1 years
  Black females: 81 years
  White males: 78.9 years
  Black males: 77.1 years

Obviously, as life expectancies for Americans increase, the advantage of taking lower benefits at age 62 diminishes.

INDIVIDUAL RETIREMENT ACCOUNTS (IRAs)

Whenever you work for yourself or a company, you can build a retirement nest egg with an IRA. In fact, if you've been stashing away $2,000 a year since 1981, when IRAs were made available to all workers even if they had a pension plan, you have a sizable amount of money on hand. Your philosophy should be shifting too—away from thinking of your IRA as savings to be ignored or placed in a CD toward realizing that it's an investment requiring diversification and thoughtful management.

Where you should invest it depends on several factors: the current economic environment, your age, other sources of income, and your appetite for risk. The closer you are to retirement, of course, the less risk you should take. You must also decide if you are temperamentally suited to manage your account or if you need a professional. In general, high-yield conservative investments should form the basic core of most IRAs, but there are exceptions and variations. A part of your IRA should go into other vehicles such as growth stocks, which protect your nest egg from reduced returns when interest rates are low and yet take advantage of a rising stock market.

Only a few investments are excluded by law from IRAs: collectibles (such as gems, stamps, art, antiques, and Oriental rugs), commodities, and leveraged investments (those made

with borrowed cash). The 1986 Tax Reform Act permits inclusion of U.S. legal tender gold and silver coins acquired after December 31, 1986, but they must be held by a custodian, not the IRA owner. You may borrow money to put in your IRA, but margined stocks, commodity futures, and mortgaged real estate are out. Among the tax-advantaged investments that make no sense in an IRA are municipal bonds, tax shelters, and deferred annuities.

Originally, the $2,000 annual deduction was available to all who earned at least that much in salary form. That's no longer true:

- If your adjusted gross income (before IRA contribution) is over $50,000 ($35,000 for singles) *and* you or your spouse is an active participant in an employer's pension plan, you are no longer entitled to any IRA tax deduction, but you can make nondeductible contributions.
- If your gross adjusted income (before IRA contribution) is between $40,000 and $50,000 ($25,000 to $35,000 for singles) *and* you or your spouse is an active participant in an employer's pension plan, your IRA deduction is reduced.
- If you or your spouse is not an active participant in such a plan, you can still deduct the full $2,000 IRA contribution.
- Full $2,000 deduction is available to workers who are active participants in employer-maintained retirement plans only if their adjusted gross income is below $25,000 for singles and $40,000 for those filing jointly.

The following retirement programs disqualify you from making a fully deductible IRA contribution: Keogh, SEP, money-purchase pension plan, profit-sharing plan, defined-benefit plan, 401(k), employee stock option plan, government employee retirement plan, 403(b) (teachers' annuity), 457s (municipal employee retirement plan), and Taft-Hartley plan (union employee retirement plan).

$ HINT: Oppenheimer Fund Management has a free calculator that lets you determine the growth of an IRA depending on the size of annual contributions, the number of years contributions are made, and various assumed rates of return. Call: 1-800-525-7048.

SHOULD YOU HAVE AN IRA?

If you no longer qualify for the $2,000 tax deduction, you may decide it's not worth contributing to your IRA anymore. This is a mistake for most investors. Over the long run, your money will accumulate on a tax-deferred basis, more than offsetting the fact that it's not an immediate tax deduction. And, of course, it is a forced way of saving. In general, the higher the rate you earn on your IRA and the higher your tax bracket, the more valuable this shelter is. And there's no guarantee that Congress won't raise the tax brackets before you retire.

$ HINT: Contributions that do not qualify as a tax deduction should be paid into a separate IRA to avoid confusion.

Make your IRA contribution as early as possible in the new year—this will boost the value of your account in the long run. Most people delay until April 14 to fund their IRA because they either feel that they can't spare the $2,000 or they can't decide where to invest the money.

$ HINT: Use an automatic plan with a mutual fund or your stockbroker. Plan to deposit $167 each month, even if it's into a money market fund. You will have accumulated $2,000 within a year, painlessly.

$ HINT: If you can only make nondeductible IRA contributions, you may want to consider a deferred annuity contract. These, too, allow you to accumulate interest and dividend earnings tax-free. Two added pluses: There is no limitation on the amount you can invest.

Note: The 10% early withdrawal penalty applies to annuities—but only to the amount includable in income, which is less than the total amount of withdrawal.

SELF-DIRECTED IRAs

When your IRA contains $5,000 to $10,000, you're ready to benefit from diversification. Consider doing so through a self-directed account, which can be set up at a brokerage firm for $25 to $35 plus a yearly fee. Designed for those who want to guide their own accounts, it allows you to invest in stocks, bonds, limited partnerships, options, Treasuries, zeros, or mortgage-backed securities. If you want advice on managing the portfolio, use a full-service broker; otherwise, save on commissions with a discount broker. A self-directed account takes time and vigilance on your part, yet it offers the greatest degree of flexibility along with the greatest potential for appreciation. It also involves the most risk.

☐ CAUTION: Avoid investments that are attractive largely for tax advantages, such as tax-exempt municipal bonds. Since IRAs are already sheltered from taxes, the exemption is wasted. In addition, all income, including tax-free yields, will be taxed when withdrawn.

$ HINT: The Cleveland Electric Illuminating Co. was the first company to establish an IRA for those who buy the stock through its

---

FOUR STOCK MUTUAL FUNDS FOR YOUR IRA

Unless you're very close to retirement, you can afford to devote 20% to 40% of the total amount of your IRA to low to moderate risk stock or balanced funds; the latter hold both stocks and bonds. The following four funds charge low IRA custodial fees and have had 10-year annual returns above the average for equity funds, which was 13%. None have initial sales charges.

FUND	10 YR ANNUAL RETURN TO 1/1/93	TELEPHONE
IAI Regional	19.9	1-800-945-3863
CGM Mutual	15.6	1-800-345-4048
Wellington	14.6	1-800-662-7447

FOUR INCOME FUNDS FOR YOUR IRA

FUND	YIELD SPRING 1993	AVERAGE 1-YEAR	ANNUAL RETURN 3-YEAR
T. Rowe Price Growth & Income	3.69%	15.6%	13.7%
USAA Mutual Income	7.08	14.7%	13.7%
Vanguard Preferred Stock	7.80	12.1	14.1
Wellesley Income (Vanguard)	6.26	17.9	13.9

dividend reinvestment plan. There are no brokerage commissions, and dividends can be automatically reinvested. Check with the electric utility company in your area.

YOUR IRA AND YOUR HEIRS

If you're blessed with sufficient income from other sources, you may want to leave IRA funds to your heirs. Although the IRS views IRAs primarily as a retirement benefit, not a death benefit, the new mortality tables help those who want to leave money behind by making it possible for them to withdraw less money from their IRAs. You must start withdrawing money by April 1 of the year after you turn 70½; otherwise, you face a stiff 50% excise tax on excess accumulations. Study the table on page 294 and check with your accountant or financial planner to determine your withdrawals.

☐CAUTION: An IRA left to a beneficiary is fully taxable to the heir. If it is left to an heir under age 14, it is taxed at the parents' rate. These funds cannot be rolled over, and thus another tax benefit is eliminated.

STOCKS FOR YOUR IRA: 1994

An IRA holds plenty of appeal for building retirement funds. These stocks combine good capital gains potential with attractive yields, dividend growth prospects, and above-average safety.

STOCK	REASON
American Home Products	Top dividend record
AT&T	Long-term growth
Bell South	Growing service region
Bristol-Myers Squibb	Attractive drug issue
Citizens Utilities B	Provides utility growth
Coca Cola	Solid overseas sales
Consolidated Natural Gas	Energy play
Kellogg	Recession-resistant company
Morgan (J.P.) & Co.	Leader in banking field
Royal Dutch Petroleum	Energy play; high yield
Southwestern Bell	Appeal of cellular business
WPL Holdings	Expanding via acquisition

IRA ROLLOVER

If you receive a partial or lump-sum distribution from a qualified retirement plan or tax-sheltered annuity, you may roll it over into an IRA. The amount you roll over may not include your after-tax contributions to the plan. But you may roll over all or only part of the distribution that would otherwise be taxable. Once in the IRA rollover, the savings continue to accumulate tax-free until payouts start—permissible after age 59½, mandatory at 70½. The transfers must be made within 60 days after the distribution. Be extremely careful when rolling over or transferring these funds, especially if the transfer is to yourself. The safest method is from trustee to trustee.

Note: Rollover from a single IRA can be made only once in a one-year period (one-year waiting period between distributions applies separately to each IRA) but for direct trustee-to-trustee transfers, the one-year waiting period does not apply.

AVOID PENALTIES

If for any reason you have inadvertently put too much money into your IRA, take it out immediately. For each year the excess remains in the account, a 6% excise tax is levied on both it and earnings. Earnings on the excess must be reported as income in the year earned. The excess and earnings on the excess may also be subject to a 10% penalty when withdrawn.

YOUR COMPANY PENSION PLAN

The next scheduled stop on your road map for an enjoyable retirement should be your company pension plan. The crash of 1987 proved to all of us that the value of even the best-run pension plan can decrease, just as a personal portfolio can. So even if you have little or no control over where your plan is invested, you need the facts. Ask. Find out what you can expect to receive. The answer will help you determine what additional savings you will need to live comfortably in your later years.

Here are 12 questions you should gather the answers to during the course of 1993:

- Am I eligible to receive retirement benefits? If not now, when will I be?

IRA BASICS

- Annual contribution: $2,000 of earned income if under age 70½.
- You can wait until April 15 to make your contribution for the previous year.
- If you and your spouse both work, you may each have an IRA.
- You can contribute a total of $2,250 to a spousal account; this amount can be split between accounts as long as neither gets over $2,000.
- IRA money must be invested with an IRS-approved custodian, such as a bank, savings and loan, stockbroker, mutual fund, or insurance company.
- You can open as many IRA accounts as you like using a different custodian or investment each year and thus spreading out your risk.
- There is a 10% penalty for withdrawing money before you are 59½. There is an exception to penalty for withdrawals in the form of equal periodic payments over its expectancy.
- Money withdrawn from IRAs funded by deductible contributions is taxed as ordinary income. (Only the earnings from IRAs funded by nondeductible contributions are taxed as ordinary income upon withdrawal.) If you withdraw before age 59½, you pay both the tax *and* the 10% penalty.
- You must withdraw money starting at age 70½ or be penalized.

- What type of retirement plan do I have, defined benefit or defined contribution? (A defined-contribution plan gives you some flexibility regarding where the money is invested, but it doesn't guarantee you any set amount when you retire. A defined-benefit plan is less flexible, but it guarantees you a certain amount when you retire.)
- What choices do I have about where my pension is invested? How many times a year can I move my money from one place (usually a mutual fund) to another?

- What are the penalties for early withdrawal?
- Can I borrow money from my plan? How much? At what rate?
- Can I make contributions to my plan to build up the dollar amount? How much? How often?
- How much is my plan worth today?
- How much do you estimate it will be worth when I retire?
- How will the benefits be paid out? What are the advantages and disadvantages of taking it in a lump sum?
- What happens if I become disabled? If I die?
- What happens to my pension if the firm is bought by another company or if the firm closes down?
- What is the estimated amount I will receive on a monthly basis when I retire?

$ HINT: If you have no pension plan, you're not alone. According to AARP, thousands of Americans are in this situation. The organization has two booklets that will help you: *Working Options* and *Planning Your Retirement.* Order from: AARP Fulfillment Office, 601 E Street NW, Washington, DC 20049.

There are several fundamental types of retirement programs available to employees. Programs for the self-employed—Keoghs and SEPs—are discussed later on in this chapter.

- *Defined-benefit plans.* These are the traditional type of pension plans that pay a fixed retirement benefit, such as 50% of your final salary, determined by a formula. The advantage here is that you know what your final pension will be.
- *Defined-contribution plans.* Popularly called profit-sharing plans. The company decides how much it wants to contribute each year. Amounts are contributed to individual employee accounts. The employee's final benefit is not determined in advance, but depends upon the amount of money accumulated in his or her account prior to leaving the company. In a self-directed plan, you, the employee, assume responsibility for whether the money is invested in stocks, bonds, or money market accounts.
- *Money-purchase plans.* The company contributes a fixed percentage of your salary into an individual benefit account. You decide how it should be invested.
- *401(k) plans.* You voluntarily contribute part of your own salary into individual accounts. The tax advantages are explained below. The company often supplements your contribution by matching a percentage of employee contributions.
- *Combination plans.* Your company may set up more than one plan, say, for example, a pension plan and a profit-sharing plan. The most common combination is a money-purchase plan to which the company makes an annual contribution equal to, say, 10% of salary, combined with a profit-sharing plan to which the company has the option of contributing up to another 15%.
- *Medical benefit plans.* Many companies pay medical benefits to retirees.
- *Employee stock ownership plans (ESOPs).* An ESOP is a retirement program that invests contributions in the company's own stock. The ESOP buys company stock with money obtained from a third-party lender, thus giving the company in effect the proceeds of a bank loan. The bank loan is repaid through annual contributions to the ESOP.

401(k) PLANS

This plan, also known as a "salary-reduction" plan, is offered by nearly four out of five major firms. Employers like it because it reduces the firm's pension costs by encouraging employees to save more themselves. Employees like it because they can set aside untaxed dollars in a special account and their employer will add to their contribution.

HOW THEY WORK

1 Your employer sets up the plan with a regulated investment company, a bank trust department, or an insurance company.
2 You set aside part of your salary into a special savings and investment account.

ALCOA—A LEADING 401(k) PLAN

Compare your company's plan with Alcoa's, one of the best in the nation.

- *Matching.* Each division determines how much it will match; it ranges from 50% to 100% of up to 6% of the employee's salary.
- *Investments choices.* Guaranteed investment contracts (GICs)
  American Balanced (a growth and income fund)
  Investment Company of America (a growth and income fund)
  Amcap (a growth fund)
  New Perspective (a global fund)
  Alcoa stock
- *Features.* Automated phone system for account balance and for executing transactions. Sales fees on all mutual funds are waived.

You have several options, typically a guaranteed fixed-rate income fund, a stock fund, a bond fund, or short-term money market securities. The amount set aside is *not* counted as income when figuring your federal income tax. For example, if you earn $50,000 and put $5,000 into a 401(k), you report only $45,000 compensation. In addition, earnings that accumulate in the 401(k) plan do so free of tax until withdrawn.

3 Many companies match employee savings, up to 5% or 6%. Most often a firm chips in 25¢ to 50¢ for each $1 the employee saves. Employer contributions can be up to 25% or $30,000, whichever is less.

4 The maximum you could contribute in 1993 was $8,994. There is a 10% penalty for withdrawing funds before age 59½. The maximum contribution is adjusted annually for inflation.

5 If you change jobs or take out the balance in a lump sum after age 59½, you can take advantage of 5-year averaging, another tax break. (You treat the total payout as though you received it in 5 annual installments.) Entire tax calculated under 5-year averaging is payable in one year.

6 You can withdraw money without paying a penalty:
- When you reach 59½
- If you separate from service and you are age 55 when the distribution occurs
- If you are disabled
- If you need money for medical expenses that are greater than 7.5% of your adjusted gross income

WHAT TO INVEST IN

As with any investment portfolio, make it a point to diversify. If your plan does not offer many choices, you can diversify in your IRA or regular brokerage account.

If you are 10 years or more from retirement, a large portion of your 401(k) should be in stocks or stock mutual funds. Over almost any 15-year period, they have outperformed interest-paying investments. So, don't shy away from stocks because of the risk involved. (See box of suggested stock funds on page 296.)

As retirement approaches, gradually swing more toward conservative investments, but do not completely abandon stocks. Stocks continue to protect you from inflation. The percentage of your stock portfolio should equal 100 minus your age. (See box of suggested income funds on page 297.)

Don't over invest in your company's stock. You've seen what has happened to even the bluest of the blue chips: stocks of IBM, General Motors, and other major companies have taken a nosedive. It is a serious mistake to have more than 40% of your assets in your company's stock, since your job is also dependent upon the company.

Many 401(k) plans offer the same mutual funds that are sold to the public, in which case getting information on their performance is not difficult. But some plans put money into funds run by banks, insurers or private money managers. In this case you must turn to your benefits director for information. Ask for each vehicle's investment objective, largest holdings, fund manager's name and long-term and year-to-year performance records. If you can't get adequate answers, don't invest in that particular fund.

$ HINT: There are about 600 private-label mutual funds sold only through insurance companies and pension plans. Some of them have names that sound like those of banks or other funds. Yet you will not find their performance figures listed in most financial publications. To track their performance records, read: "Morningstar's Variable Annuity/Life Performance Report," $55/year; 1-800-876-5005, or: "Annuity & Life Insurance Shopper," $45/ four issues; 1-800-521-5110; or pick up a copy of *Barron's* on the newsstand.

TAKING MONEY OUT OF YOUR 401(k)

Regulations that went into effect January 1, 1989, make it tougher to take money out of your 401(k). Even if you meet the so-called hardship qualifications, you must have no other sources of income reasonably available, and you will still have to pay the 10% early withdrawal penalty unless the money is going for medical expenses that exceed 7.5% of your adjusted gross income. *Hardship reasons that will satisfy the IRS are:*

- Medical expenses for you, your spouse, or dependents
- Down payment on your principal home
- Post-secondary tuition for you, your spouse, or dependents
- Prevention of foreclosure on or eviction from principal residence
- Funeral costs for a member of the family

BORROWING FROM YOUR 401(k)

Balances up to half the funding but not more than $50,000 can be borrowed under many plans. You pay interest on the loan to your own account, typically a percentage point less than what banks charge on secured personal loans, which, as we go to press, averages just below 11.90% nationally. By law, 50% of your balance must stay in the account as security against the loan. The loan must be repaid at least quarterly and fully within 5 years, unless the money goes for buying a principal residence.

◻CAUTION: You lose tax-deferred compounding until you repay the loan, so if you own a home, get up to $100,000 from a tax-deductible home equity loan instead.

Whatever amount you borrow usually must be paid back within 5 years, although extensions are usually granted if the loan is helping you purchase your principal residence.

LEAVING YOUR 401(k)

Before you leave your company, find out the exit rules. 1) If you take the money from your 401(k), you'll owe taxes on everything except any after-tax contributions made. 2) If you are under age 55, there is also a 10% penalty on the taxable amount. 3) You may be able to leave your money in the company's plan. 4) You may be able to have it transferred to the 401(k) of your new employer. 5) You can also shift the money into an IRA. If you decide to do this, make certain the money transferred directly from the 401(k) to the IRA and NOT TO YOU. If you personally take the payout and roll it over into an IRA, 20% of your money will be withheld for taxes by the IRS. And, don't put any other money into the IRA created for your 401(k) funds. If you do, you lose the right to transfer the funds into a new employer's 401(k) later on.

YOUR 403(b) AND 457 PLAN

Some 17 million Americans are eligible for these two plans that differ slightly from 401(k)s.

- *403(b) Plans.* These are for employees of colleges, universities, hospitals, research institutes, schools, and other nonprofit organizations. In fact, the country's largest retirement plan—the $114-billion Teachers Insurance and Annuity Association and College Retirement Equities Fund (TIAA-CREF) is a 403(b). Rules for contributions, rollovers, taking money out before age 59½, and hardship withdrawals are almost identical to those for a 401(k).
- *457 Plans.* These are sponsored by state and local governments and nonprofit organizations. They are considerably different from 401(k)s in that matching contributions from the employer are rare and the maximum you can contribute annually is $7,500, not $8,994. The money you contribute remains the property of the employer until you leave

your job and thus is subject to the claims of the employer's creditors. Rules for taking money out under hardship conditions are tougher than with a 401(k)—buying a house or paying for college do not qualify. Nor can you borrow from a 457. When you leave your job, you cannot make a tax-free rollover of your funds to an IRA. The one advantage: there's no penalty for withdrawing funds if you leave your job before you turn 59½.

GUARANTEED INVESTMENT CONTRACTS (GICs)

Few people realize that the most popular investment in most 401(k) and company pension funds is a *guaranteed investment contract,* or GIC. GICs are fixed-rate, fixed-term debt instruments sold only by insurance companies to corporate pension plans. They offer a stated, fixed rate of return for a specific period typically one to five years. They are the life insurance industry's equivalent of bank CDs, although they are not federally insured. They tend to yield ⅔ of a percentage point more than Treasuries.

HOW THEY WORK

GICs run as long as the retirement manager likes, generally 1 to 10 years. The insurance company invests the cash it raises in a number of conservative investments, such as long-term bonds, public utility bonds, real estate and mortgages, and, to some extent, stocks. The rate of return is guaranteed by the issuer, but no specific pool of funds backs a GIC and most are not backed by federal insurance or government guarantees. Instead, the assets of the insurance carrier back the principal contract, so any default of an underlying issue or drop in interest rates is absorbed by the insurance company.

Most employees who select where to invest their retirement funds select GICs but know little about them, since the contracts are sold to institutions, not individuals. Make sure you learn about them. (They may also go by other names, such as "guaranteed fund," "stable return fund" or "benefit accumulation contract.")

If rates rise, as with any fixed-income ve-

hicle, you are locked into a lower yield. If rates fall, you benefit.

CHECK THE QUALITY

As a member of a 401(k) plan you are legally entitled to at least annual reports from your plan manager on how your plan is performing. Check for the names of the insurance companies that sold the GICs. Then turn to A. M. Best Co., which publishes ratings of insurance companies, including those that sell GICs. In addition, Standard & Poor's and Moody's rank the insurance companies. Find out if the parent life insurance company or a pension subsidiary issues your GIC. If the subsidiary has any financial problems, will the parent company bail it out? Some states, including New York, have regulations requiring bailout of failed insurers. Call the state insurance commissioner in the state where the insurer is domiciled.

$ HINT: For information on the financial health of an insurance company, call: A.M. Best, 1-908-439-2200; Weiss Research, 1-800-289-9222; Moody's, 1-212-553-0377; or Standard & Poor's, 1-212-208-1527.

☐ **CAUTION:** GICs guarantee only the interest rate; the ability to pay is not guaranteed and depends upon the creditworthiness of the insurance company.

During 1990, several insurers, most notably First Executive Corp. of California, ran into financial trouble because they had more than 5% of their assets in junk bonds. If you're concerned about your 401(k) plan in a GIC, find out exactly where that money is invested. Begin your inquiry with your plan administrator, usually your company's employee benefits department. Ask which insurance companies and banks are represented in the plan's GIC portfolio and what portion of the portfolio each insurer accounts for. Some plans place all fixed-income money with one insurer, but of course it's safer if it's spread among several insurers, which is more often the case with large companies than smaller ones.

The most important question to ask is how much of the money is in a portfolio of troubled junk bonds. The quality of an issuer's portfolio is reflected in its credit rating—the higher the rating the less likely the company and its GICs will run into trouble. Your plan administrator should be able to give you the credit rating of *each* issuer. Top-rated insurance companies will have an AAA rating. Beware of issuers with ratings below single A.

§ HINT: If you don't like what you learn, ask about making a change. Most plans allow investment choices to be changed several times a year. Although you probably cannot select among GICs, you can move money into stocks, bonds, and cash.

PLANS FOR THE SELF-EMPLOYED: KEOGHS AND SEPs

If you run an unincorporated business, either full time or as a moonlighter, you can reduce your income tax by saving for retirement. This is accomplished by putting some of these earnings each year into a Keogh plan or a simplified employee pension (SEP). In both you can defer federal income tax on your contributions and all the money accumulated from investment returns. The money is taxed when you withdraw it.

To qualify for a Keogh plan or a SEP, your earnings must come from your business or from fees for services you provided. The IRS will recognize you as self-employed if the companies that paid you send you Form 1099-MISC, which is used to report nonemployee compensation, instead of the Form W-2.

KEOGH PLANS

Keoghs work much like IRAs but have several added advantages. You can put away as much as $30,000 a year and, as with an IRA, your Keogh contribution is deductible from income when calculating your taxes. Earnings are not taxed until withdrawn. If you have a Keogh, you may also have an IRA.

To get your annual deduction, however, you must have the Keogh in place by the end of that year, although dollar contributions don't have to be completed until you file your income tax return.

One disadvantage to keep in mind: If you, as a self-employed person, establish a Keogh for yourself, you must extend its benefits to your employees. In fact, employees must get comparable benefits on a percentage basis: For example, if you put in 15% of earned income for yourself, you must match that 15% for each employee.

There are several types of Keoghs:

- *Defined-contribution plan.* In this type, you decide how much to put in. In other words, the annual contribution is predetermined and what you receive upon retirement is variable, depending on how well you've invested the deposits. You can contribute up to a maximum of 25% of compensation, not to exceed $30,000 a year. This plan may be either a *profit sharing plan* or a

- *Money-purchase plan.* The amount you can contribute is sometimes given as 20% of earned income or as 25% of compensation minus your Keogh contribution, which works out to 20% of net earnings. Limit is lesser of $30,000 or 20% self-employed individuals net earnings. For example, if you make $100,000, you can contribute $20,000 ($100,000 minus $20,000 contribution = $80,000 compensation; 25% of $80,000 = $20,000). In a money-purchase plan you must hew to this percentage no matter how hard-pressed you may be. In other words, the percentage contribution initially established must continue in the future. Although this plan gives you the most mileage by letting you determine the annual contribution at a fixed rate that is as high as 20% (25% of "net" income), you must stick to this percentage in lean years as well as prosperous ones.

- *Profit-sharing plan.* The most you can contribute and deduct here amounts to the lesser of $30,000 or 13.043% of your net self-employed earnings. This plan gives you the flexibility to contribute less than the maximum or even nothing at all, from year to year.

- *Combination plan.* To keep your right to make maximum contributions without committing yourself to them every year, you can open two accounts: a profit-sharing and a money-purchase plan. Set your obligatory money-purchase plan at

7% of income. Then, in good years, you can put up to 13% in the profit-sharing plan.

- *Defined-benefit plan.* If you've only recently started to make a high income, you can shelter much of it. The limit is the lesser of $112,221 or 100% of the average compensation for the highest 3 consecutive years of self-employment income, in a defined-benefit plan. This plan is best for those with surplus income. For example, if you're earning $55,000 from a sideline business, you may be able to shelter it all from taxes. A defined-benefit plan is designed to pay a predetermined benefit each year after you retire. A pension actuary determines how much you need to deposit each year to provide for your benefits. This amount is adjusted for inflation. This type of Keogh is smart for those over 50, since there are fewer years left in which to put aside retirement funds.

➤ FEES AND FILINGS Starting and maintaining a defined-benefit Keogh plan is expensive. Pension specialists may charge several thousand dollars to set one up and then $750 or so a year to administer the plan. Profit-sharing and money-purchase plans, on the other hand, may cost nothing or only a few dollars to set up and run.

If you have a Keogh plan with more than $100,000 in the plan or more than one participant, you must file a special tax form with the IRS on or before July 31 each year. If you work alone, this is not complicated—fill out the appropriate lines on Form 550EZ—but if your plan covers several employees, consult a tax pro.

- *Investment choices.* With a profit-sharing or money-purchase Keogh you have a number of investment choices available to you, just as you do with an IRA. Banks, mutual funds, stockbrokers, and life insurance companies all sponsor Keoghs. Use one that has a prototype plan on file so your paperwork will be limited.

Defined-benefit Keoghs must be invested to meet the rules of the Employee Retirement Income Security Act (ERISA). You can still use a wide variety of investments, but they will be subject to scrutiny by federal regulations.

HOW MUCH INCOME YOU CAN PUT AWAY

KEOGH DEFINED-CONTRIBUTION PLANS:
Money-purchase: The lesser of 20% or $30,000
Profit-sharing: The lesser of 13.0435% or $30,000

KEOGH DEFINED-BENEFIT PLAN: as much as 100%; maximum of $112,221.

SEP
Regular plan: The lesser of 13.0435% or $30,000
Salary-reduction plan: The lesser of 15% or about $8,000

➤ WITHDRAWALS You must start taking money out of your Keogh or SEP by April 1 of the year after you turn 70½. (You can keep contributing after that date, however.) Lump-sum withdrawals from Keoghs after age 59½ (but NOT from SEPs) are eligible for 5-year forward averaging, which can reduce your tax bite. If you were born before 1936, you can use the even more advantageous 10-year averaging.

SIMPLIFIED EMPLOYEE PENSION PLANS (SEPs)

There is another type of tax-saving retirement plan for the self-employed that has received far less publicity than either the IRA or Keogh, yet it permits employer contributions greater than $2,000 a year. Called a *simplified employee pension plan* (SEP), it is suitable for small businesses and sole proprietors. Designed to cut red tape, it's considerably easier to set up and administer than a Keogh. Although its initial purpose was to encourage small and new firms to establish retirement programs, self-employeds without Keoghs can use it too. The deadline for setting up a SEP is April 15, just as it is with a regular IRA or the extension date if you file for one. (With a Keogh, the date is December 31.)

When an employer—which can be you as

MOVING YOUR IRA, SEP, OR KEOGH

As your account grows or as market conditions change, you may want to invest your dollars elsewhere. The IRS has strict rules to follow.

A TRANSFER

- If you arrange for a direct transfer of funds from one custodian to another, there is no limit on the number of switches you can make.
- Plan on transfers taking at least a month. Banks, brokerage firms, and even some mutual funds are often backlogged with paperwork.
- Get instructions early on, ideally in writing, from both the resigning and accepting sponsor. Pay fees and notarize necessary papers immediately. Keep track of details as well as deadlines; don't depend on the institution to do this for you.

A ROLLOVER

- You may take personal possession of your money once a year for 60 days.
- If you hold the money longer than 60 days, you'll be subject to the 10% penalty.

a sole proprietor—establishes a SEP, the employee then opens an IRA at a bank, mutual fund, or other approved institution. The employer can put up to 15% of an employee's annual earnings in the SEP, to a maximum of $30,000. The contributions made on your behalf are not included in total wages on your W-2, and no deduction for the amount contributed in your behalf is allowed.

Note: Contributions for an owner-employee are limited to 13.0435% of contribution to a maximum of $30,000.

ANNUITIES AND YOUR PENSION

If you're close to retirement or changing jobs, you're faced with the issue of how to handle the balance in your pension account. There are three basic choices: (1) cashing it in for a lump-sum distribution, (2) taking it in monthly payments, and (3) rolling it over into an IRA. Your accountant should be consulted prior to making a final decision.

- With a *lump-sum payment,* you will have control over your investment choices and you may also be able to take advantage of the 5- or 10-year averaging tax formula.
- If you decide on *monthly payments,* your employer uses your pension dollars to buy an annuity. As discussed on pages 314–317, annuity returns vary widely. Find out. Of course, you can also buy your own individual annuity.
- With an *IRA rollover,* your money will grow tax-free until withdrawn, starting no later than age 70½.

If you elect an annuity, you can specify how your pension savings will be invested: for *fixed income,* where the holdings will be bonds and mortgages to provide a set sum each month, or *variable income,* where the investments are split between bonds and stocks and the returns will vary, depending on how well the portfolio performs.

If you have a defined-benefit plan (see page 299), in which the amount of distribution is guaranteed, you will probably have these four choices:

1 *Straight-life (single-life) annuity.* This is the classic annuity in which you get a fixed monthly payment for the rest of your life, whether you live 5 days, 50 years, or more. *Best for:* singles with no dependents and people with dependents who are unlikely to outlive them. It offers the highest monthly payment. Some plans also offer a guaranteed minimum of 5 years of payment, which are made to your beneficiary if you die within 5 years of retiring.

2 *Joint and survivor annuity.* You get a fixed monthly payment during your lifetime, and if you predecease your spouse, he or she receives a set percentage of that monthly amount for the rest of his or her life. However, the younger your spouse and the higher his or her percentage, the smaller the current payment you'll receive. Since 1984, this plan is required by law to make a minimum 50% payment to the surviving spouse of married retirees. A married

person can select a different option only if the spouse provides written consent within 90 days of the person's retirement date.

3 *Period-certain annuity.* This annuity makes payments for your entire life, but if you die within a certain number of years, your surviving dependent receives your full monthly pension for the remaining years. *Best for:* those who need to provide for a current dependent who will eventually become independent. Also ideal for people with spouses who are expected to live only a few years.

4 *Lump-sum certain.* Although this is not usually offered in defined-benefit plans, you should know its ramifications. Here you relieve your company of its legal obligation to pay you a lifetime monthly retirement benefit. In exchange, it gives you one large lump sum. This single payment is based on the average life expectancy for someone your age and a given interest rate. Of course, the older you are and the higher the rate, the lower the lump sum. *Best for:* retirees with other resources who are not terribly dependent on their pension, and for those in poor health who will not be receiving annuity payments for very long.

FINDING WORK

According to a study by the Commonwealth Fund, a New York philanthropic group, about 2 million retired Americans over age 50 want to work, but they're not looking for jobs—they think employers will say they're too old. Wrong! The study points out that certain employers are clamoring for mature workers. The best jobs are found by word of mouth—so talk to everyone about your interest in working.

- *Banks.* Older workers are excellent as tellers and customer service representatives. The Bank of America, Citibank, and others actively seek older workers.
- *Hotels.* Over one-third of Days Inn's employees are 55 and older. Their absentee rate is only 3%. Other chains, including Marriott, are following Days Inn's example.
- *Home health care.* Demand for home

health aids is soaring—physical therapists, companions, preparation and delivery of meals.

- *Travel agencies.* Since one in four pleasure trips is taken by someone age 55 or older, the gray-haired employee is a plus in this industry. Take a six- to eight-week course at a travel agent school. And you get extra perks: reduced hotel rates and airfares.
- *Hardware stores.* Builders Emporium, Hechinger, and Home Depot all rely heavily on older employees who have fix-up experience.
- *Tax return preparers.* The IRS hires people during tax time; so do accounting firms.
- *Temp agencies.* Kelly, Adia, and Volt actively recruit employees over 55. Demand for accountants is strong during the first quarter of the year; engineers can land short-term projects; office assignments are unending.

$ HINT: If you work as a temp you can get around the fact that Social Security benefits are cut when annual wages are over $7,080 for someone under age 65 or $9,720 for someone age 65 to 69—when your income reaches that amount, you simply delay going to work until next year.

You should know that it is unlawful to be turned down for a job because of age—if you're 40 and older. If you feel you've been discriminated against because of age, write:

Equal Employment Opportunity Commission (EEOC)
1801 L Street, NW
Washington, DC 20507

FOR FURTHER INFORMATION

Retirement Income Guide
A. M. Best Company
A. M. Best Road
Oldwick, NJ 08858
1-908-439-2200
Twice a year; $55 per year

Lauraine Snelling, *Start Your Own Business After 50—or 60—or 70!* (Bristol Publishing Enterprises, 1991), $8.95.

"A Step By Step Guide to Planning Your
  Retirement"
(IRA Fact Kit)
Fidelity Investments
1-800-544-8888
Free

"Retirement Planning Kit"
T. Rowe Price
100 East Pratt Street
Baltimore, MD 21202
1-800-638-5660
Free

*Deciding What to Do With Your Company
  Retirement Money*
T. Rowe Price
1-800-IRA-5000
Free

Walter W. David, *The 50 Plus Guide to
  Retirement Investing*
(Homewood, IL: Business One Irwin, 1992).

Retirement Plans for the Self-Employed
IRS Publication #560
1-800-TAX-FORM
Free

"Working Options—How to Plan Your Job
  Search, Your Work Life" and "How to
  Stay Employable: A Guide for the Mid-
  life and Older Worker"

American Association of Retired Persons
AARP Fulfillment Center
P.O. Box 22796
Long Beach, CA 90801-5796

INSURANCE AND ANNUITIES

It may never have occurred to you, but you can turn your life into a tax shelter. Certain types of life insurance double as an investment, a tax-deferred way to save, and as coverage on your life. That's because Congress preserved the tax-free buildup of savings (called "cash value") inside both insurance policies and annuities, making them one of the few ways left to defer taxes since the 1986 Tax Reform Act was passed.

There are other advantages to this type of tax shelter: In a crisis you can cash in your policy and get most of your money back. With some policies, you can withdraw part of your cash value or borrow against the policy at below market rates, save for future expenses, and, of course, provide for your beneficiaries.

In this chapter we concentrate on *insurance as an investment.* However, do not overlook health and disability coverage, both of which should be part of your overall financial planning. Both annuities and life insurance are long-term investments, and many impose heavy sales charges and early surrender fees. If you decide to purchase either life insurance or an annuity, deal only with a financially stable company, one rated A or A+ by A. M. Best Co., the nationwide rating service. Most libraries and all insurance salespeople have the A. M. Best rating service.

☐ CAUTION: *This is not idle advice:* In 1991, First Executive Corp., a Los Angeles-based holding company that owns four life insurers with $18 billion in assets, failed and was taken over by the state of California.

TERM INSURANCE

There are two basic types of life insurance plans—*term* and *cash.* Term, which is not an investment, provides pure life insurance protection for a specified time, usually 1, 5, 10, or 20 years or up to age 65. It has absolutely no savings feature. When the policyowner dies, the beneficiary of a term policy receives the full face value of the policy.

Term insurance must be renewed every term, generally once a year. If you stop paying premiums, then the insurance coverage also stops. Premiums are relatively low when you are young but move up significantly with your age. Although there is no cash buildup inside a term policy, a "convertible" term policy can be converted, for a higher premium, into a cash value policy without requiring you to meet new medical standards. Term is initially cheaper than other types of policies for the same protection. It is best for those who need coverage for a certain time period—parents of young children, home buyers, etc.

$ HINT: Make certain any term policy you buy has a "renewable" provision. Then you do not have to prove you are insurable each time.

CASH VALUE OR WHOLE LIFE INSURANCE

Cash value policies, also called straight or permanent life, are part insurance and part investment since they have a savings feature. You pay a premium based on your age when you purchase the policy, and this amount remains fixed as long as the policy is in effect. Premiums are paid monthly, annually, or quarterly. During the early years, the premium exceeds the insurance company's estimated cost of insuring your life. Then after several years the surplus and interest are channeled into a cash or surplus fund. You do not select where your cash value is invested—the insurance company does—usu-

GETTING THE BEST RATES

Insurance Information, Inc., will do a search of term rates for a $50 fee. It guarantees it will save you at least $50 over your current policy or the $50 will be refunded. Call: 1-800-472-5800.

ally in conservative, fixed-rate, long-term bonds and mortgages and blue chip stocks. The insurance company uses part of this cash fund to pay administrative costs and any agent's commission. If you cancel your policy, you receive the cash value (or most of it) in a lump sum.

Because of the cash reserve feature, premiums for whole life insurance are generally higher than those for term.

TYPES OF WHOLE LIFE INSURANCE

- *Modified life:* Premium is relatively low in the first several years but escalates in later years. Designed for those who want whole life but need to pay lower premiums when they are young.
- *Limited-payment whole life:* Provides protection for the life of the insured, but the premiums are payable over a shorter period of time. This makes the premiums higher than for traditional whole life.
- *Single-premium whole life:* Provides protection for the insured's life, but the premium is paid in one lump sum when you take out the policy.
- *Combination plans:* Policies are available that combine term and whole life within one contract. Generally premiums for combination plans do not increase as you get older.
- *Universal life:* Can pay premiums at any time in virtually any amount subject to certain minimums.
- *Variable life:* The cash value fluctuates according to the yields earned by the fund in which the premiums are invested.

☐CAUTION: Keep in mind that sales charges are high, consuming 50% or more of the first year's premium.

When the policyowner dies, the beneficiary receives *only* the face value of the policy and not the cash reserve. This face value is a predetermined amount, selected when you buy the policy. The latter is used to pay off the claim. For example, if the face value of your policy is $200,000, but the cash value has built up to $175,000, the insurance company needs to put up only $25,000 to pay off the claim.

You can borrow from your cash reserve, typically at low rates, currently in the neighborhood of 5% to 8%, and still be insured. The loan is repaid either prior to death or is deducted from the death benefit.

Taxes on your cash reserve are deferred until it is withdrawn or surrendered, and then you pay only on the amount of cash that exceeds the total amount of premiums you paid in.

TERM VS. CASH

When purchasing life insurance, keep in mind that commissions are highest for whole life. Agents, aware of this fact, may try to steer you away from term, saying it is really only a temporary solution. However, term almost always provides the most insurance coverage for the price and is initially cheaper.

Yet term premiums become extremely expensive as you get older. If your family is adequately covered by your pension and other sources of income, you could conceivably drop term in your later years.

Term tends to be best for those who need large amounts of coverage for a given time span: parents of young children, for example, or homeowners.

$ HINT: Purchase a term policy that is convertible *and* renewable. Then switch to whole life as your age and family circumstances change.

UNIVERSAL LIFE

Universal life, a fairly new form of whole life, has grown in popularity because of its unique and flexible features:
1 The death benefit, i.e., the face value, can be increased or decreased.

2 The premium payments can vary, subject to a basic minimum. You can elect to pay annually, quarterly, or monthly.

3 You can use money from your cash buildup value to meet premium payments.

4 You can borrow against the cash value at low interest rates.

5 You can cash in the policy at any time and receive most of your savings.

With universal life, part of each premium is used to cover sales commission and administrative fees; this is called a load charge. The rest of your premium is invested in various low-risk vehicles. With some universal life policies you can designate how much you want to go for insurance and how much into savings. The company, however, determines the rate of return, which is often tied to an index, such as the Treasury bill rate. Rates generally are guaranteed for 1 year but when changed will not fall below the minimum stated in the policy—about 4% to 5%.

Some companies now offer a variable universal life plan that lets you switch your investments among several mutual funds sponsored by the insurance company.

At the present time, standard universal life policies are paying between 7½% and 9%, although the yield is actually less after fees and commissions are deducted.

☐CAUTION: Sales fees and other costs can eat up as much as 50% of your first year's premium and between 2% and 5% annually thereafter. So plan to hold your policy at least 10 years.

No-load universal life is now being offered by some companies. The premiums are less because, of course, there are no commissions. However, you must buy your policy through a salesperson, such as a financial planner, who receives a fee. No load, however, does not mean no cost. There are still administrative costs and other fees.

VARIABLE LIFE

Another relatively recent type of cash value insurance is variable life. Its premiums are fixed; however, the death benefits and the cash value vary based on how successfully your cash reserve is invested. Most companies offer a number of choices, including stocks, bonds, and

money market funds, as well as the opportunity to switch from one to another.

With this type of insurance, you have the potential of a far greater return than with other types of cash value policies, but there is also substantially more risk.

☐CAUTION: If your investment choices turn out to be poor, you could conceivably wind up with less cash value in a variable policy than with other types of insurance.

There are two types of variable: scheduled premium and flexible premium. Premiums in the scheduled premium plans are fixed, both in timing and dollar amount. With a flexible premium plan, you can change both the timing and the amount.

TIPS FOR INVESTING IN LIFE INSURANCE

A recent study by the Federal Trade Commission concluded that (1) life insurance is so complicated that the public is practically unable to evaluate the true costs of various policies; (2) the savings portions of cash value policies that do not pay dividends offer an extremely low rate of return; (3) prices for similar policies vary widely; and (4) the public loses large amounts of money when they surrender cash value policies within the first 10 years.

As a result of these FTC conclusions, the National Insurance Consumer Organization (NICO), an independent consumer advocacy group, devised these guidelines for selecting an insurance policy.

- *Don't buy if you don't need it.* If you are without dependents you probably don't need life insurance, and don't buy a policy to cover your children's lives.
- *Buy only annual renewable term insurance.* If you buy term, purchase only this type.
- *Don't buy credit life insurance.* This pays off your loan when you die and is way overpriced in most states, although New York is an exception.
- *Don't buy mail-order life insurance* unless you compare its price to annual renewable term and find it less expensive.
- *Don't let an agent talk you into dropping an old policy.* If it still pays dividends you may be better off borrowing out any cash

RATING THE INSURANCE COMPANIES

The insolvencies of several companies have highlighted the importance of dealing with an A-rated company. Check these sources:
- Best's Insurance Reports
  A.M. Best Co.
  Oldwick, NJ 08858
  1-900-420-0400 ($2.50/min)
- Standard & Poor's Insurance Rating Service
  25 Broadway
  New York, NY 10004
  1-212-208-8000
- Weiss Research, Inc.
  2200 North Florida Mango Rd
  West Palm Beach, FL 33409
  1-800-289-9222

value and reinvesting it elsewhere at higher rates.

Weiss Research, based in West Palm Beach, Florida, was the first rating agency to give Executive Life, a subsidiary of the failed First Executive Corp, a negative rating. In August 1989, while A. M. Best and Standard & Poor's were still giving Executive Life top ratings, Weiss gave the company a C−. In early 1990, Weiss downgraded Executive Life to a D. In April 1991, Weiss gave the following three insurers a D+ rating because of their substantial junk bond holdings and excessive interest rate guarantees:

Equitable Life Assurance Society of the U.S.
Kemper Investors Life
First Capital Life Insurance Company

$ HINT: Consumers can obtain a rating over the phone for $15 per company, a 1-page *Personal Safety Brief* for $25, or an 18-page *Personal Safety Report* for $45 from: Weiss Research, Inc.; 1-800-289-9222.

HOW MUCH INSURANCE DO YOU NEED?

When you decide to buy any kind of insurance, don't automatically rely on an agent's advice. They have an inherent desire to sell you as much coverage as possible. Instead, begin with these general guidelines and then adapt them to your particular situation. Keep in mind that the amount of life insurance you should have is related to other coverage.

➤ LIFE Depends upon how many people need your financial help. If you have several small children, you want enough coverage to support them until they are 18 or through college, but if you are single, put your money elsewhere. The rule of thumb is 65% to 75% of the breadwinner's income—but this does not all have to come from life insurance. Because insurance needs are so individual, even the old formula—which said your coverage should equal 5 times your total annual take-home pay—no longer holds. Instead, assess your assets, liabilities, and income requirements using the worksheet in *A Consumer's Guide to Life Insurance*, available free from American Council of Life Insurance, 1-202-624-2000.

➤ HEALTH You need a major medical policy that covers at least 80% of doctor and hospital bills above your deductible. Avoid a policy that has exclusions for expensive diseases such as cancer.

➤ DISABILITY Get a policy that replaces 60% to 80% of your net income. Select one that will pay out when you cannot work at your *own*

INSURANCE TIPS

DO:
- Take the maximum deductible you can afford.
- Ask if you qualify for a discount.
- Get coverage through a group when possible; it's cheaper.

DON'T:
- Buy narrow policies; they frequently duplicate coverage you may have in other policies.
- Switch from one policy to another without studying the costs; fees and commissions are high.
- Use life insurance only for an investment; your first goal is coverage, then investment.

occupation, not when you cannot do any type of work.

➤ AUTO Meet these minimums: $100,000 for one injury; $300,000 total per accident, and $50,000 for property damage. If your car has lost at least one-third of its initial value, consider canceling collision. Your state may require you to be covered against uninsured motorists. Ask if discounts are available for safe drivers, non-smokers, honor-roll students, graduates of driver education courses, and owners of cars with airbags.

➤ HOMEOWNERS Be covered for at least 80% of the replacement cost of your home, not including land value, plus a minimum of $100,000 for liability. Ask if discounts are available for those with smoke alarms, deadbolt locks, and fire extinguishers.

➤ UMBRELLA POLICY If your assets are above $100,000, you have a swimming pool, throw lots of parties, race cars, or are vulnerable to lawsuits, take out an umbrella policy for $1 million.

BORROWING AGAINST LIFE INSURANCE

Although your agent may say you can borrow up to 95% of the cash value of your policy at below market rates, the true cost of the loan is not always clear. (The cash value is the sum by which the premiums and the dividends earn money above the insurer's estimated cost of coverage.) Read the fine print first, and watch in particular for dividend cuts. Some policies continue paying the same dividends on the entire cash value, but many cut earnings on that portion of cash equal to the loan amount. This is known as a "two-tier" dividend treatment.

☐CAUTION: You do not have to pay back a policy loan, but generally all outstanding loans plus interest are deducted from the amount paid to the beneficiary.

Loans taken out against single-premium life policies are called "zero percent loans." Because you pay a large single premium up front ($5,000 to $100,000+), you begin earning large dividends immediately; consequently, the policy has a high cash value sooner than other types of life insurance. These loans are "wash loans," because the insurer charges the same rate for the loan

---

as it pays on the policy—if you borrow against the earnings.

☐CAUTION: This money of course is not earning interest while being borrowed. Single-premium policies have many twists, so check the prospectus carefully for penalties and other restrictions.

To determine the actual cost of borrowing from your life insurance policy, subtract the after-loan rate from the rate you earned before the loan. Add to that figure the stated policy loan rate. This is the true cost of borrowing.

Preloan rate − Postloan rate

   12%   −   6.5%

              + Policy loan rate = Loan cost
           +   8%   =   13.5%

SWITCHING YOUR LIFE INSURANCE POLICY

Before changing your policy, take time to compare the death benefit, annual premium, initial rate of cash buildup, and, most importantly, the net yield—what your money earns after all charges and fees.

For help analyzing the rate of return, write:

National Insurance Consumer Organization
121 North Payne Street
Alexandria, VA 22314
1-703-549-8050

For $35 for the first proposal and $25 for each additional one, NICO will analyze the rate of return on your current cash value policy.

MEDIGAP INSURANCE

This supplemental policy is designed to fill the gaps between your medical bills and what Medicare covers. Before you buy such a policy, be clear about what Medicare now covers:

- Hospital stays after a deductible and copayments; check for limitations
- Up to 100 days in a skilled nursing facility; with some copayments
- Hospice-care benefits for the terminally ill; check for certain limitations
- Home health care
- 80% of approved doctor's charges after a $100 deductible

(*Note*: The rulings are continually being revised.)

$ HINT: "The Medicare Handbook" has complete explanation of coverage. Call: 1-800-772-1213 for a free copy.

Whether or not you need a Medigap policy depends on what other coverage you already have. Review your existing policies carefully, and take full advantage of the "free look" provision recommended by the National Association of Insurance Commissioners (NAIC), which gives you 30 days to change your mind after purchasing a policy. Most states have adopted this provision. Follow these guidelines:

- Buy one comprehensive policy, not several with possible overlapping coverage.
- Buy a policy that is renewable for life.
- Find out about exclusions for preexisting conditions and waiting periods.
- Turn down any policy that says it is government sponsored or guaranteed; it's not.
- Write a check only to the insurance company, not the agent. If your policy does not arrive in 30 days, call your state insurance office.

A Medigap policy is not worth the premiums to anyone who uses doctors who accept "Assignment"—that is, doctors who agree to take whatever Medicare approves as their full payment. Ask your doctor.

WHO NEEDS COVERAGE:If you have assets between $100,000 and $1 million, excluding your home *and* you want to pass it on to heirs. If you have more than $1 million you can pay for care yourself; under $100,000; Medicaid will pay after your money runs out.

Heed the words of Robert Hunter, president of the National Insurance Consumer Organization in Alexandria, VA, "I wouldn't pay more than $700 a year for a Medigap policy."

NURSING HOME INSURANCE

As you (or members of your family) approach your late 60s or 70s, part of retirement planning should deal with long-term care. Depending on your financial situation, you may want to consider this new type of insurance. According to the American Health Care Association, the national average for nursing home costs are $80 a day, or about $31,000 a year. Many senior citizens incorrectly believe that Medicare will pick up the total bill. It does not.

Although an insurance policy may initially seem the logical solution, this particular field is complex and riddled with problems. Read the brochures listed at the end of this chapter before purchasing a policy.

More than 100 companies now sell long-term care coverage, according to the Health Insurance Association of America. And although

---

INSURANCE QUOTE FIRMS

Insurance quote firms provide four or five of the lowest-cost policies in their computer files. Most deal only with highly rated companies. Some operate in all states; others are licensed only in certain areas.

Insurance Information
Cobblestone Court #2, Rte. 134
South Dennis, MA 02660
1-800-472-5800

Insurance Quote
3200 North Dobson Road, Building C
Chandler, AZ 85224
1-800-972-1104

SelectQuote
140 Second Street, 5th floor
San Francisco, CA 94105
1-800-343-1985

NURSING HOME INSURANCE PROVIDERS

COMPANY	TELEPHONE
CNA Box 593925 Orlando, FL 32859	1-800-327-2430
AMEX Life Assurance Co. Box 2060 San Rafael, CA 94912	1-800-456-7766

the National Association of Insurance Commissioners has issued guidelines for policies, insurers are not legally forced to abide by them. This means you must do some serious research before purchasing a long-term care policy. The companies listed in the box above may be a good place to begin gathering information, as are the sources listed at the end of this chapter. Before taking out a policy, discuss the matter with your insurance agent or financial planner and study at least two, preferably three, different plans before making a final decision.

The downside of long-term health care policies is that if you never need this care, the premiums paid are not recoverable. However, a new type of policy, which uses the structure and guarantees of whole life insurance, recently came onto the market. With a single premium of $10,000 or more, you can purchase a death benefit that also doubles as an account for paying for the cost of long-term care. It is available on a single life or joint basis, and if an insured needs nursing home care, the policy will pay up to 2% (4% for both insureds) of the death benefit for these costs. It is available from the Golden Rule Insurance Company in Lawrenceville, IL (1-800-950-4474).

TIPS FOR EVALUATING INSURANCE POLICIES

Select a policy that:
- Covers these three areas: skilled, intermediate, and custodial care.
- Does not require being hospitalized before receiving long-term care. Those with Alzheimer's, for instance, are not usually hospitalized before entering a home.
- Covers long-term care in the home.
- Guarantees renewability for life.
- Covers "organically based mental conditions" (e.g., Alzheimer's).
- Has an inflation clause—you want to have your benefits ride up with the cost of living.
- Covers any type of health-care facility, not just a Medicare-certified nursing home.

NEW NURSING HOME INSURANCE RULINGS

Many long-term insurance care policies have flaws. To address them, the National Association of Insurance Commissioners adopted new guidelines in 1993 and over the next year or so, states are expected to adopt the voluntary rules. Meanwhile, you should look for policies that already meet the NAIC standards.

One rule requires insurers to let buyers designate up to three people to be notified if a policy is about to lapse because of nonpayment. (The designees would not be liable for payment.) The new rules also require an insurer to reinstate a policy for a period of at least 5 months after termination, if the lapse was due to mental or physical impairment of the insured. *Note:* AMEX Life Assurance, for example, offers a 9-month reinstatement period, but not all insurers do.

Another new rule would bar insurers from describing premiums as "level" unless they are set for life. Many insurers use the term even though they have the right to raise rates.

$ HINT: For more information, get of copy of the free booklet, "A Shopper's Guide to Long-Term Care Insurance," by writing to: NAIC, 120 West 12th Street, Suite 1100, Kansas City, MO 64105.

ANNUITIES: A SAVINGS ALTERNATIVE

If you'd like to stockpile tax-deferred savings for your retirement years, then take a close look at an annuity—it's one of the few investment vehicles that survived the 1986 Tax Reform Act relatively unscathed. Annuities have all the benefits of an IRA, but no $2,000 cap on annual contributions, and with most you can continue to invest on an after-tax basis beyond age 70. The minimums are low, often only $1,000, and with most you can invest as much as you like. However, annuities are complicated, riddled with fees, charges, rules, and restrictions, so do your homework first.

THE BASICS

An annuity is simply a contract between you and an insurance company in which you pay a sum of money and in return receive regular payments, for life or for a stated period of time. The money grows on a tax-deferred basis until you begin receiving it, typically after age 59½. At that point you can postpone the tax bite by annuitizing; that is, converting your assets into a monthly stream of income. Then, only that portion of the payout representing growth or interest income is taxed.

Annuities are often confused with life insurance. They are not the same. An annuity provides a steady stream of income while you are alive, while a life insurance policy pays off upon your death and benefits your heirs.

There are two basic types of annuities: fixed and variable.

➤ FIXED ANNUITIES With a fixed annuity the premiums are invested in fixed-rate instruments, usually bonds or mortgages. Your money earns a fixed rate of return that is guaranteed for a certain time period, anywhere from 1 to 5 years, occasionally longer. After the guarantee period is over, your assets are automatically rolled over for a new time period at a new rate. The new rate will have moved up or down, depending upon the general direction of interest rates. Fixed annuities are best in times of high interest rates, when you can lock in good yields.

Most fixed annuities have a "floor" or guaranteed rate below which your return will not drop. This floor, often tied to the T-bill rate or other index, lasts the life of the annuity.

☐ CAUTION: Watch out for any plan that entices investors with an initially high teaser rate and then reduces it drastically when the guarantee period is up. And make certain when you roll over that the new rate is equal to that being paid to new customers.

➤ VARIABLE ANNUITIES A variable annuity, which works rather like a tax-deferred mutual fund, has more pizzazz as well as more risk. Your premiums are invested in stocks, bonds, real estate, money market instruments, and managed portfolios, thus offering the potential of a higher return than with a fixed annuity. You can direct your assets among portfolios (or have the insurance company do so for you). Your return varies, depending upon the portfolio's performance, hence the name variable annuity.

PAYING FOR AN ANNUITY

You can select either a single-premium annuity, in which case you make a one-time payment, or an installment or flexible premium, which you pay for in stages over time. You can also purchase an annuity long before you retire, which is known as a deferred annuity, or close to retirement, known as an immediate annuity. An immediate annuity, in which payments begin almost at once, is often used by those who receive a lump-sum payment from a company pension plan. In a deferred payment annuity, no payments are made until at least a year or more after you've paid your premium.

VARIABLE ANNUITIES WITH A RATINGS	
COMPANY/INSURER (CONTRACT NAME) TELEPHONE	*S&P RATING
MFS/Sun Life (N.Y.) (Compass 2-NY-VA) 1-800-343-2829	AAA
American Skandia Life (LifeVest-VA) 1-800-752-6342	AA
Hartford Life Ins. (The Director-VA) 1-800-862-6668	AAA
Guardian Ins. & Annuity (Guardian Investor-VA) 1-800-221-3253	AAA
Keyport Life Ins. (KEYFLEX 4-VA) 1-800-437-4466	A+
Putnam/Hartford Life Ins. (Putnam Capital Mgr-VA) 1-800-862-6668	AAA
Union Central Life (Carillon Account-VA) 1-513-595-2600	A−
Nationwide Life Ins. (Best of Amer 2, 3 & 4-VA) 1-800-321-6064	AAA

All annuities have two phases: accumulation and payment.

GETTING YOUR MONEY BACK

When you reach 59½ your money is returned to you in one of several ways: in a lump sum, in regular monthly payments, or as lifetime income for you and your spouse. Payments vary depending on the amount you have contributed, your age, the length of time your money has been compounding, and the rate of return on the portfolios. Taxes must be paid on all payouts.

☐CAUTION: If you withdraw money before age 59½ there is a 10% IRS tax penalty.

SURRENDER CHARGES

Cashing in your annuity early is expensive. As mentioned above, there's a 10% IRS penalty for

money taken out before you reach 59½. In addition, most insurance companies let you take out only up to 10% of your assets before they impose a surrender charge. Go beyond that 10% and you'll be slapped with a fee, typically 6% of the withdrawal during the 1st year, going down to 0% by the 7th year. (One plan, The Specialty Manager from Western Capital Financial in Los Angeles, lets you cash out up to 15% with no fee. Call: 1-800-423-4891.)

The combination of surrender charges and a 10% penalty means an annuity *must* be viewed as a long-term investment.

☐CAUTION: Look for a plan that has a "bailout" clause so you can cash out with no surrender charge *if* the insurer lowers the renewal rate by more than 1% below the initial rate.

SELECTING AN ANNUITY

Annuities are not federally protected or guaranteed. If you need that type of security, you should purchase a bank CD, which is covered by FDIC insurance, or Treasury securities, which are backed by the full faith and credit of the U.S. government. With an annuity, you must depend on the financial strength of the insurance company. It should have an A or A+ A. M. Best rating. (Most large libraries carry this rating book, or you can ask the insurance company what its rating is.)

It's a good idea to check the ratings periodically, since insurance companies can be downgraded. Remember, Baldwin United, which filed for bankruptcy just over 6 years ago, once had an A+ rating! (The company had approximately $3.4 billion in annuities. The investors did not lose their principal, but a great many did not have access to it for several years.)

$HINT: If your company's rating drops, you can make a tax-free exchange into another annuity. Called a 1035 exchange, it is similar to a tax-free IRA rollover.

Additional protection is provided in all 50 states—but not in Washington, DC. If one insurer goes bankrupt, the state fund assesses charges against other insurance companies in the state to cover investor losses. Call your state insurance commission to determine if you live in one of these states. Coverage is generally limited to

$300,000 per life insurance policy or $100,000 per annuity—*Find out!*

CHECKING AN ANNUITY'S PER-FORMANCE

Before selecting an annuity, gather information on the insurer by consulting one of the sources in the box on page 311 and then find out its performance figures.

- The current rates for over 180 fixed annuities are tracked by Comparative Annuity Reports (P.O. Box 1268, Fair Oaks, CA 95628.) A copy of the monthly newsletter, which provides an overview of the top ten programs is $10; a full report, $50.
- Returns on variable annuities are tracked by Lipper Analytical Services (Summit, NJ; 1-908-273-2772) and then reported weekly in *Barron's.*
- Since Lipper does not take into account sales charges, you may want to consult the latest monthly survey by Variable Annuity Research & Data Services (VARDS) of Miami. VARDS, which tracks the total returns of 700 annuity funds, subtracts management fees in calculating performance figures. Call: 1-305-252-4600.
- "Morningstar's Variable Annuity/Life Performance Report," $55 per year; available at libraries or call: 1-800-876-5005.
- "Annuity & Life Insurance Shopper," $45 for four issues; call: 1-800-521-5110.
- ☐ CAUTION: The tax-deferred advantages of an annuity do not come cheap. Sales charges, surrender fees, management costs, and other expenses can eat away at your return. You can reduce some of these costs by purchasing a no- or low-load annuity.

FOR FURTHER INFORMATION

INSURANCE

Glenn Daily, *The Individual Investor's Guide to Low-Load Insurance Products.* (International Publishing Corp., 1991), $19.95.

For a copy of *A Consumer's Guide to Life Insurance*, contact:

> The American Council of Life Insurance Company Services
> 1001 Pennsylvania Avenue NW
> Washington, DC 20004
> 1-202-624-2000
> Free

For the organization's list of publications, as well as "Rate of Return" data, contact:

> NICO
> 121 North Payne Street
> Alexandria, VA 22314
> 1-703-549-8050

For details and an evaluation of rates, bailout provisions, and suitability of over 30 insurance companies offering single-premium whole life, single-premium annuities, term, and universal life insurance, contact:

> Tax Planning Seminars
> Frank Miller
> 2 Echelon Plaza, Suite 220
> Voorhees, NJ 08043
> 1-800-445-6914

LONG-TERM CARE INSURANCE

> *Long Term Care: A Dollars and Sense Guide*
> United Seniors Health Cooperative
> 1331 H Street NW
> Washington, DC 20005
> 1-202-393-6222
> $10

> *How Do I Pay for My Long-Term Care?*
> Berkeley Planning Associates
> 440 Grand Avenue, Suite 500
> Oakland, CA 94610
> 1-510-465-7884
> $7.77

> *Consumer's Guide to Long Term Care Insurance*
> Health Insurance Association of America
> 1025 Connecticut Avenue NW
> Washington, DC 20036

1-202-223-7780
Free

The Association will also send you a list of private insurers offering long-term health care policies in your state.

MEDIGAP
INSURANCE

Guide to Medigap Policies
The Health Insurance Association of America
1025 Connecticut Avenue NW
Washington, DC 20036
1-202-223-7780

Medigap (#D13696)
AARP Fulfillment
601 E Street NW
Washington, DC 20049

Guide to Health Insurance for People with Medicare
Consumer Information Center
Box 100
Pueblo, CO 81002
$1

PART SEVEN

TAXES AND YOUR INVESTMENTS

The U.S. Congress is continually overhauling the tax code. Unless you know the basic changes in the 1993 act, you could unwittingly lose hundreds of dollars to the IRS. It is particularly crucial that every financial decision you make be made only after reading the following two chapters *and* consulting with your tax adviser.

These chapters explain the pertinent parts of the law and how it relates to investments and also shows you how to take advantage of the 1993 changes. Among the topics covered are:

- New tax rates
- Margin loans
- AMT
- Taxes on investments
- Sources of tax-free income
- Last-minute tax savers

31 DEALING WITH YOUR TAXES

By a slim margin—two votes in the House and the Vice President's tie-breaking vote in the Senate—the Omnibus Budget Reconciliation Act of 1993 was passed. Here's a summary of those new provisions that relate to your investments.

INDIVIDUAL TAX RATES

Retroactive to January 1, 1993, the new tax law adds a fourth individual income-tax rate of 36%. It applies to taxable income over $140,000 for married couples filing jointly, $115,000 for single taxpayers, $127,500 for heads of household, and $70,000 for married individuals filing separate returns.

In addition, a 10% surtax is imposed on taxable income over $250,000 ($125,000 for married individuals filing separate returns). The surtax effectively raises the top individual tax rate to 39.6%.

To ease the pain, you can pay your additional 1993 taxes, attributable to the rate increases, in three annual installments beginning on or before the due date, but without extensions. No interest or penalties will be imposed if your installments are paid in full before April 15, 1994, 1995, and 1996, respectively.

ALTERNATIVE MINIMUM TAX

This tax was designed to make certain that Americans with high incomes and high deductions would still have to pay an appropriate amount of income tax. That means no matter how rich you are, no matter how many loopholes or tax shelters you participate in, if you have a high income, you still must pay a minimum amount of federal income tax. The AMT is actually a separate, parallel tax system under which many of the deductions and credits allowed under the regular tax are modified or eliminated. The AMT calculation begins with your regular taxable income as reported on Form 1040, to which certain AMT "adjustments" and "tax preference items" are added. You pay the AMT only if it exceeds your regular income tax. The 1993 Act increased the ATM. A two-tier structure now exists: a 26% rate applies to the first $175,000 of AMT income above an exemption amount; on amounts above $175,000, the rate is 28%. The level of income exempt from ATM was increased to $45,000 for married filing a joint return, $33,750 for unmarried individuals, and $22,500 for married individuals filing separate returns.

The most common way to incur the AMT is to make investments that take advantage of or even exploit tax shelter provisions of the tax code, such as accelerated depreciation methods for real estate, passive losses from passive activities. However, other more common investments also provide AMT adjustments and tax preference items, such as private activity municipal bonds (either direct ownership or through a mutual fund), charitable gifts of appreciated property (such as real estate or securities), incentive stock options and real estate investment trusts that use accelerated depreciation on their holdings.

CAPITAL GAINS

You can take some comfort in the fact that the maximum tax rate on net capital gain (i.e., net long-term capital gain less net short-term capital loss) remains at 28%. This widens the spread between the tax on ordinary income and capital gains to as much as 11.6% for individuals subject to the 39.6% income-tax rate. This means that investments with the potential to yield capital gains are now much more attractive. In

1993 TAX RATES AND BRACKETS

	SINGLE TAXPAYERS	MARRIED TAXPAYERS FILING JOINTLY
15%	$0–22,100	$0–36,900
28%	$22,101–53,500	$36,901–89,150
31%	$53,501–115,000	$89,151–140,000
36%	$115,001–250,000	$140,001–250,000
39.6%	over $250,000	over $250,000
	HEADS OF HOUSEHOLD	MARRIED FILING SEPARATELY
15%	$0–29,600	$0–18,450
28%	$29,601–76,400	$18,451–44,575
31%	$76,401–127,500	$44,576–70,000
36%	$127,501–250,000	$70,001–125,000
39.6%	over $250,000	over $125,000

other words, consider making investments that will generate income from capital gains, such as individual growth stocks, mutual funds that invest in growth stocks, real estate and other assets that are likely to appreciate in price. You won't owe tax on the appreciation of these assets until they are sold, so in effect your taxes are being deferred while your personal wealth is growing. And, as a special break, the new tax law grants a maximum capital gains tax rate of just 14% on profits earned by individual investors in certain small businesses, when stocks in these companies are held for five years or longer. Your stockbroker can provide a list of small business stocks. To qualify, the stock must have been issued after the date of the enactment of the new tax law. The gain eligible for this break is limited to the greater of ten times the stock's basis or $10 million of gain. The issuing corporation must meet a $50 million or less "aggregate gross assets" test to qualify.

☐ CAUTION: Don't let the appeal of this low, 14% capital gains rate, sometimes expressed as a 50% capital gains exclusion (28% ÷ 2 = 14%), make you oblivious to the high risks involved in investing in start-up businesses. Experts estimate that nearly half of the nation's new businesses fail within the first few years of operation.

SMALL BUSINESS INVESTMENTS

The new law gives two incentives for investment in small businesses. The first is a 50% capital gains exclusion on sales or exchange of qualified small business stock held more than five years, effective for stock issued after August 10, 1993. Gain eligible for exclusion is limited to the greater of ten times the stock's basis, or $10 million of gain from stock in that corporation.

The second incentive is a new rule allowing for deferral of gain from the sale of publicly traded stock that is rolled over into a specialized small business investment company. Check with your accountant for specific details.

SOCIAL SECURITY BENEFITS

The new law includes a tax hike for many Social Security recipients. Beginning in 1994, up to 85% of benefits will be subject to tax when income exceeds $34,000 for unmarried persons; $44,000 for married persons filing jointly; $0 for married persons filing separately. The existing 50% inclusion rule will continue to apply when income is between $25,000 and $34,000 for singles and $32,000 and $44,000 for married couples filing jointly. The income includes not only adjusted gross income but also tax-exempt interest income and one-half of Social Security or Railroad Retirement Tier 1 benefits.

TIMELY MOVES: WISE YEAR-END INVESTMENT STRATEGIES

TAX STRATEGIES

- If you have been buying or selling commodities, a different set of tax rules applies. Check with your accountant, as this ruling is extremely complicated.
- If you own stock in a corporation whose long-term outlook is favorable but whose stock has dropped in price, you may want to take a loss for tax purposes but not give up your position entirely. You can buy more stock now at the lower price and sell your original holdings 31 days later. (You must wait the 31 days in order to avoid the "wash sale rule," which prevents loss deductions on sale and repurchase transactions made within 31 days. You can buy it back after 31 days.) The risk involved is of course that the stock could continue to fall in price.
- If you own stock that has gone way up in price since you purchased it and you feel it is near its peak and you want to lock in your profit but not pay taxes this year, you can "sell short against the box" (see page 258). In other words, you can keep your stock until the covering date next year, when you will be taxed. This is known as "closing the transaction." The gain is always taxed in the year the transaction is closed.

BOND SWAPS

Another year-end strategy that can help save on taxes is a bond swap. You'll find that under certain circumstances it pays to sell bonds worth less than their initial cost in order to set up a tax loss and then reinvest that same money in a similar bond. By converting a paper loss to an actual loss, you can offset any taxable gains earned in more profitable investments. In the process of swap-

DEDUCTIONS FOR THE INVESTOR

You can deduct the amount over 2% of adjusted gross income for certain expenses incurred to produce and collect income and to manage or maintain property held to make income. Among these deductible-as-itemized deductions are:
- Subscriptions to investment publications
- Cost of books on investing and taxes
- Clerical expenses
- Insurance on investment property
- Safe deposit box rent or home safe if used to hold securities
- Fees for accounting or investment advice and for legal advice if related to tax or investment matters
- Expenses directly related to tax (but not investment) seminars, including transportation
- Travel expenses to visit your broker, your safe deposit box, and your tax accountant or lawyer for investment or income-tax purposes
- Computers: The cost of a computer used in managing your investments is sometimes deductible. (If you use your computer for business over 50% of the time, you can depreciate it over 5 years.)
- IRA or Keogh account custodial fees

ping, you may also be able to increase your yield.

If you're thinking of a bond swap, don't wait until the last days of the year. It may take your broker several weeks to locate an appropriate bond.

Bond swaps involve two steps:
1 Selling bonds that have declined in price
2 Replacing these assets with similar (but not substantially identical) bonds

By immediately purchasing similar bonds for approximately the same price as the ones you sold, you restore your market position and your income.

➤ TAX BREAKS Even if you didn't make a killing in the market this year, if you took some investment profits, a bond swap can help reduce your tax bite. Here's how it works:

If you own bonds purchased when interest rates were lower, they are probably worth less in the secondary market today. If you sell them, you can take a loss that can be used, dollar for dollar, to offset any capital gains. If you have no long- or short-term capital gains, the loss can be used to offset up to $3,000 of taxable income, on a dollar-for-dollar basis. If your loss is greater than that, it can be carried over into the next year.

A bond swap enables you to keep your position by buying comparable bonds selling for approximately the same price.

In order for the IRS to recognize a loss for tax purposes, you must buy bonds of a different issuer or with a substantially different maturity date or coupon.

➤ STATE INCOME TAX A bond swap is also useful if you move from a state with no income tax to one that has an income tax. Buy municipal bonds issued by the new state that are not subject to state taxes.

➤ SWAPPING COSTS Unlike stocks and most other securities, where commissions are noted separately from the purchase or sale price, municipal bonds have their commission included in the price of the bond. Commissions range from $5 to $20 per $1,000-face-value bond, which means that a swap involving $50,000 worth of bonds could entail a commission somewhere between $500 and $2,000.

SHIFTING INCOME TO CHILDREN

According to the new tax law, unearned income of a child aged 14 or less, regardless of the source, is taxed at the parent's rate when this income exceeds $1,200 per year. But the first $600 is not taxed, and the next $600 is taxed at the child's rate. If the child is over 14, all income is taxed at the child's rate, presumably lower than the parent's.

The new law has in effect put an end to the value of the Clifford trust, which was one of the most popular ways to reduce taxes by transferring assets to children.

If you wish to give money to your children but you don't want it to be taxed at your rate, you are limited to a handful of choices. One, of course, is tax-free municipal bonds. Another is U.S. EE savings bonds. In the latter case, interest is not taxed until the bonds are cashed in. Then, when your child turns 14, you can change the portfolio mix and periodically cash in the bonds, since the income will then be taxed at the child's rate.

$ HINT: Earnings in Clifford trusts set up after March 1, 1986, will be taxed to the donor regardless of the beneficiary's age.

If you have already transferred investments to a child under age 14, you may want to put these investments into municipals or zero coupon bonds.

$ HINT: You can still make a tax-free loan up to $10,000 ($20,000 for a couple) to each member of your family per year. It is also possible to loan up to $100,000 if tax avoidance is not one of the principal purposes. Imputed interest is then limited to the borrower's investment income. This is a popular way for parents to help children buy property.

If you are involved in income shifting, keep careful records indicating that you have separate accounts for your children.

LAST-MINUTE TAX MANEUVERS

Despite New Year's resolutions and other good intentions, most people put off organizing their tax return materials until the first week in April. If you're serious about reducing your tax bite, you should start at the end of the year. Here are 10 last-minute moves that will pay off:

■ *Shift income.* You have until December 31 to shift money to reduce your taxable income for the following year and at the same time avoid the gift tax. The law allows you to give anyone up to $10,000 a year ($20,000 for a married couple) tax free. Although there is no gift tax on the transfer, there will be income tax on any earnings the gift generates. (Gifts are not a deduction from income.) Note: The recipient of the income must have immediate access to the funds transferred. Check with your accountant for exceptions.

■ *Set aside retirement money.* If you have income from your own business or from free-lance work, set up a Keogh retirement account at a bank or brokerage firm. The dollar amount you contribute is tax deductible directly from your taxable income and the principal grows on a tax-deferred basis. You must open your Keogh before the end of the year but you do not need to make a dollar contribution until you actually file your tax return.

■ *Contribute early to your IRA.* Put aside money now to fund your IRA or Keogh plan. Tax is deferred on the income earned from the day you contribute until withdrawal. If you delay making your 1993 contribution until the last minute, you are giving up months of compounded tax-deferred income.

■ *Add up your deductions.* Take time to determine if you have spent enough on tax-deductible items to qualify for write-offs. Miscellaneous deductible expenses must be greater than 2% of your adjusted gross income in order to be itemized. Unreimbursed medical expenses must add up to more than 7.5% of your AGI to be deductible. If you are still far away from these minimums (known as "floors"), try to postpone these expenses until next year when you may have enough to deduct then. On the other hand, if you are near these thresholds, consider making additional expenditures that will lift you above the floor. *Note:* Some municipal bonds are subject to the AMT; check with your accountant.

■ *Establish a charitable remainder trust.* The philanthropic should consider a remainder trust in which you give appreciated securities, such as stocks, bonds, or property, to a charity in exchange for a qualified annuity. As the donor, you receive an immediate charitable deduction. The amount is determined by IRS tables. This type of annuity is not subject to premature withdrawal penalties or new pension excise tax. Since rulings are complex, work out this particular tax move with a knowledgeable accountant.

■ *Defer capital gains tax on property.* Until Congress decides otherwise, you can still swap one piece of investment property for another, deferring capital gains tax until the property is sold for cash. The pieces exchanged must be comparable and used for business or investment purposes. (Your home does not qualify.) If the two properties are not of equal value, and cash or an additional piece of property has been included in the swap to make up the difference, both are taxable.

■ *File correct estimates.* If you underestimate this particular tax, you face a penalty, but if you overestimate you lose the earning power of that money. To be safe, estimate 100% of last year's tax liability—the actual amount reported on your return or, if required, 90% of current liability. Check with your accountant. Then, even if your income goes up, you will not be penalized.

■ *Pre-pay property and state and local income taxes by December 31.* If you pay 100% of your state tax liability by December 31 you can deduct it on this year's federal income tax return.

■ *Make charitable contributions with appreciated investments.* If you are considering making a charitable contribution, do so by December 31, and use appreciated investments, such as stocks or bonds. Your capital gains tax will be forgiven and you can get a deduction.

■ *Defer income.* Delay receipt of self-employment income or year-end bonuses; or delay billing customers so payments are made to you after December 31.

☐ CAUTION: If you are subject to the alternative minimum tax, check with your accountant first before using this option.

OTHER RULES TO KEEP IN MIND

➤ STATE AND LOCAL TAXES Except for sales tax, these taxes continue to be fully deductible.

➤ INVESTMENT EXPENSES These, including tax planning, the cost of this book, tax-return preparation, investment publications, and other miscellaneous items are deductible only for amounts in excess of 2% of your adjusted gross income.

> CHARITABLE DEDUCTIONS Unless you itemize, you cannot deduct your charitable contributions.
> MEDICAL EXPENSES You can deduct unreimbursed medical expenses only to the extent that they exceed 7.5% of your adjusted gross income.

SOURCES OF TAX-FREE INCOME

By carefully planning your investment strategies, you can easily increase the amount of tax-free or tax-deferred money you receive every year. Here are 10 ways to do just that:

- *IRAs.* You don't pay any tax on the earnings in an individual retirement account until you withdraw the funds. Interest earned is reinvested and thus continues to compound on a tax-deferred basis.
- *Life insurance.* As with an IRA, the interest income earned inside a life insurance investment is tax-deferred until you cash in the policy.
- *Disability insurance.* If you paid your own disability insurance premium, the benefits from accident or health insurance policies are tax-free. However, if your employer paid the premiums, any income you receive from the policy is taxable.
- *Municipal bonds.* Interest earned on muni bonds is free from federal income tax. You may have to pay a state tax if you purchase bonds issued by a state other than your state of residence—for example, if you live in Minnesota and purchase a bond for New York State, you may have to pay Minnesota tax on the income.
- *Real estate.* Some real estate investments yield depreciation deductions over the life of the property.
- *Savings plans, annuities, and pension plans.* Any investment made with after-tax income is tax-free when you withdraw it or when you receive a payment that represents the return of your investment. Or, to state it another way, the principal is tax-free, although the income earned on the principal is generally taxed.

- *Social Security.* Disability, retirement, or surviving spouse income may be tax-free, depending on your other income. Taxpayers with income greater than $32,000 ($25,000 for singles) have to pay tax on up to half of their Social Security income. A maximum of half of this income is tax-free. (Note: Under the 1993 law, up to 85% is taxable if couples have income over $44,000; for individuals, over $34,000.)
- *Tax-deferred annuities.* Sometimes called single-premium deferred annuities. The money invested with an insurance company in this type of annuity and the interest earned is deferred until you cash in and receive that income.
- *Tax-free money market funds.* Mutual funds whose portfolios consist of very short-term municipal notes offer tax-free income.
- *U.S. Treasury issues.* Treasury bonds, notes, bills, and savings bonds are exempt from tax at the state level no matter what state you live in. However, there is a federal tax due on these investments.

FOR FURTHER INFORMATION

These publications are available free of charge at your local IRS office or by calling 1-800-TAX-FORM (3676). For a complete list of all IRS brochures, ask for publication 910, *Guide to Free Tax Services.*

523 Tax Information on Selling Your Home
527 Residential Rental Property
530 Tax Information for Home Owners including Condominiums and Cooperative Apartments
550 Investment Income and Expenses
554 Tax Information for Older Americans
560 Retirement Plans for the Self-employed
564 Mutual Fund Distributions
575 Pension and Annuity Income
590 Individual Retirement Arrangements (IRAs)
915 Social Security Benefits

ALPHABETICAL DIRECTORY OF YOUR INVESTMENTS AND THEIR TAX STATUS

The information that follows is general in scope and intended as an introductory explanation of how taxes affect your investments. Remember, the IRS recognizes three types of income:

- *PORTFOLIO or INVESTMENT: dividends and interest*
- *ACTIVE INCOME: salaries, wages, fees, commissions, and personal services*
- *PASSIVE INCOME: From businesses you don't actively manage and from rental property. Note: Passive losses cannot offset active or portfolio income; they can offset only passive income.*

You should always consult your accountant about specific problems.

ANNUITIES

- Interest earned can accumulate tax-free until withdrawn. When it is withdrawn, only the interest earned is taxed, not your initial investment.
- If you withdraw money prior to age 59½, there is a 10% tax penalty. With qualified employer-sponsored annuities, there is no 10% penalty if you immediately transfer the money to a qualified annuity with another company.
- For other rulings, check your policy.

ANTIQUES, ART, COINS, GEMS, STAMPS, AND OTHER COLLECTIBLES

- Profits made upon sale are subject to federal income tax at the regular rate of 15%, 28%, or 31%. If the asset is held long term, the maximum tax is 28%. The purchase price is subject to state and local sales tax.

BONDS (AGENCY ISSUES)

- Interest income is subject to federal tax.
- Interest income on some agency issues is exempt from state and local taxes. Ask your broker or accountant.

BONDS (CORPORATE)

- Interest income is subject to federal, state, and local taxes.
- Gains made when bonds are sold are taxed at regular rates with a maximum of 28% if held long-term.
- Losses can be used to offset other net gains you may have, plus up to $3,000 of wages, salary, and other "ordinary" income.

BONDS (MUNICIPAL)

- Interest earned on most munis is exempt from federal income tax and from state and local taxes for residents of the state where the bonds are issued.
- Most states tax out-of-state bonds.
- Bonds issued by the Commonwealth of Puerto Rico and the District of Columbia are exempt from taxes in all states.
- Interest earned on certain "private-activity" bonds that were issued after August 7, 1986, is a tax preference item to be included in the calculation of the alternative minimum tax (see page 316). If you are not subject to the AMT, you will not pay taxes on these particular bonds.
- Some bonds are now subject to federal tax but remain exempt at the state and local levels—these include bonds to help finance convention centers.
- Illinois, Iowa, Kansas, Oklahoma, and

Wisconsin tax any municipal bonds issued in their state.

- Interest earned on fully tax-exempt bonds can have a tax cost when held by retired people receiving Social Security. If you are retired and if your adjusted gross income plus half your Social Security plus tax-exempt interest income is over $25,000 for a single return or $32,000 for a joint return, interest earned on the tax-exempt bonds *is* effectively taxable.

BONDS (PREMIUM)

- If you purchase a bond at a premium, you can only use any amortizable premium to offset your interest income. In other words, you can no longer use the premium as a deduction against other types of income. The amortized premium is subtracted directly from the interest you earn on the bond, rather than deducted as a separate expense subject to the investment interest expense limitations.

BONDS (ZERO)

- Taxes must be paid on the so-called imputed interest that accrues annually, even though, of course, no interest is actually paid to the bondholder.
- Because you must pay tax as though you had received interest, zeros are well suited for IRAs and Keoghs where interest income is deferred from taxes until withdrawn and for children over 14 not subject to the kiddie tax.
- Zero coupon municipals are usually exempt from federal taxes and from state and local taxes when bonds are issued in the investor's state.
- Zero coupon Treasuries are exempt from state and local taxes.

CERTIFICATES OF DEPOSIT (CDs)

- Any interest earned is subject to federal, state, and local taxes.
- Interest is taxed in the year it is available for withdrawal without substantial penalty. Interest can be deferred on a CD with a term of 1 year or less. If you invest in a 6-month CD before July 1, the entire amount of interest is paid 6 months later and taxable in the year of payment. However, if you invest in a 6-month CD after June 30, only the interest actually paid or made available for withdrawal without penalty is taxable in the year issued. The balance is taxable in the year of maturity. The interest, however, must specifically be deferred to the year of maturity by the terms of the CD.

CHILDREN'S INVESTMENTS

- This tax applies only to children under age 14 with investment income over $1,200. Such children must compute their tax on Form 8615 at their parent's top rate unless the parent elects to report the income directly on his or her own return. In other words, the kiddie tax is based on the parent's taxable income. Income in custodial accounts is treated as the child's income and is subject to the kiddie tax, but income the child earns from wages or self-employment is not subject to the kiddie tax.

COMMERCIAL PAPER

- Any interest earned is subject to federal, state, and local taxes.
- *Exception:* Commercial paper issued by state and local governments is usually, but not always, exempt from federal as well as state and local taxes.

COMMODITIES AND FUTURES CONTRACTS

- Profits and losses are taxed at 60/40 rates: 60% long-term and 40% short-term and reported at the end of the year. Losses may be carried back to the 3 prior years to offset any futures contract gains (but not other income) from those years.
- Profits become taxable at the end of the year, even if you have not closed out your position. The IRS, in effect, will tax you on your paper profits.
- In some cases, you can deduct paper

losses, even of positions still open. These rules may apply to contracts subject to the mark-to-the-market rule. Check with your accountant.

CONVERTIBLE STOCKS AND BONDS

- There is no gain or loss when you convert a bond into a stock or preferred stock into common stock of the same corporation, IF the conversion privilege was granted by the bond or preferred stock certificate.

CREDIT UNION ACCOUNTS

- Even though depositors are actually shareholders of the credit union and the money earned is known as a dividend, your earnings are regarded as interest and subject to federal, state, and local taxes.

DIVIDEND INCOME

Dividends and interest you receive are reported to the IRS by the company on various versions of form 1099: dividends on Form 1099-DIV, interest on Form 1099-INT, and original issue discount on Form 1099-OID. You also will receive copies from the company and must report the amounts shown on your tax return. The IRS will use its forms to check the income you report.

- *Cash dividends.* If you receive dividends from IBM, GE, Pepsi, or any other corporation, the amount is reported by the company directly to the IRS. You, in turn, receive Form 1099-DIV from each corporation telling precisely how much you received for the year.
- *Stock dividends.* If you own common stock in a company and receive additional shares as a dividend, it is usually not taxable. Exceptions: if you can take either stock or cash or if it is a taxable class of stock. Your company will notify you if it is taxable.
- *Dividend reinvestment plans.* If you sign up to have your dividends automatically reinvested in the company's stock and if you pay fair market value for these shares, the full cash dividend is taxable.

The IRS maintains that since you could have had cash but elected not to, you will be taxed the same year you receive the dividend.

- *Return of capital.* Corporations sometimes give a return of capital distribution. If this is the case it will be so designated on your 1099 slip. Most return of capital is not taxed; however, your basis of stock must be reduced by whatever the amount is. If a return of capital exceeds basis, the excess is taxable and the basis is reduced to zero.
- *Insurance dividends.* Any dividends you may receive on veterans' insurance are *not* taxed, and dividends received from regular life insurance are generally not taxed. However, if you are in doubt, check with your accountant or insurance company.
- *Other types of dividends.* Money market mutual funds pay what is called a dividend, and you should list it as such on your tax return.

If you have an interest-bearing checking account with a savings and loan or a credit union, you may collect interest, although it is sometimes referred to as dividend income. Be aware: If this interest is reported on the 1099 slip as dividends, you too should report it as dividend income.

EQUIPMENT-LEASING PARTNERSHIPS

- Income is subject to federal, state, and local taxes.
- Since it is a partnership, items of income and deductions are passed through, and are thus subject to the at-risk rules. Interest expense may be used to the extent of interest, dividend and other net investment income.
- Deductions generated by the partnership will help shelter some of the income derived from lease payments. The key deduction is depreciation for the cost of the equipment. If the partnership borrows to pay for the equipment, interest may also be deductible.
- When deductions are greater than income, resulting losses cannot be used to shelter your salary, wages, interest, and dividend

income or profits made in the stock market. The partnership losses can only be used to shelter income from other passive activities.

- If you do not have passive income (i.e., interest in a partnership or S corporation where you do not actively participate in the business), you can carry these losses forward and use them when the equipment-leasing deal has excess income or when the investment is disposed of.
- If the partnership is publicly traded, income and loss require special treatment; check with your accountant.

FOREIGN CURRENCY

- If you have a foreign bank account or a foreign securities account, you must indicate this on Form TDF 90-22.1 if the value of the accounts at any time during the year was over $10,000.

GINNIE MAE, FREDDIE MAC, AND FANNIE MAE CERTIFICATES

- The interest portion of the monthly payments you receive is subject to federal, state, and local taxes.
- Profits from the sale of any mortgage-backed security are taxed as well.

GOLD AND SILVER

- If you buy gold or silver coins or bullion, most states impose state and local sales tax. In many cases you can sidestep this tax if you do not take delivery but leave the metal with the dealer and buy certificates instead.
- Profits from the sale of gold and silver are taxed at regular rates, generally as capital gains, but this is under review.
- Dividends from precious metals stocks and mutual funds are taxed at regular rates, in the same manner as other dividends.
- Profits from futures and options: see "Commodities."
- An exchange of gold for gold coins or silver for silver coins usually qualifies as a tax-free exchange of like-kind investment

property—for example, if you exchange Mexican pesos for Austrian coronas. However, exchanging silver for gold is not tax-free nor is exchanging collectible coins for bullion coins (i.e., exchanging coins whose value is based on rarity, etc. for coins whose value is based on weight of metal).

HISTORIC REHABILITATION

- The credit is 20% or 10% of qualified rehabilitation expenditures, depending on the building (10% for nonresidential buildings put into service prior to 1936 and 20% for all certified historic structures).
- The tax credit is not a deduction: It provides a dollar-for-dollar reduction in the actual amount of income tax you owe.
- The tax credit is applicable only to depreciable buildings—those used in a trade or business or held for the production of income, such as a commercial or residential rental property. A nondepreciable building may qualify as a certified historic structure *if* it is the subject of charitable contributions for conservation purposes.
- A *certified historic structure* is any structure that is listed individually in the National Register of Historic Places, maintained by the Department of the Interior, *or* located in a registered historic district and certified by the Secretary of the Interior.
- A *registered historic district* is any district that is listed in the National Register of Historic Places *or* designated under a state or local statute that has been certified by the Secretary of the Interior as "containing criteria which will substantially achieve the purpose of preserving and rehabilitating buildings of significance to the district."

INVESTMENT CLUBS

- If the club is considered a corporation, it reports and pays a tax on the club's earnings. As an individual, you report dividend distributions made by the club to you. If the club is a partnership, the club files a partnership return that includes the tax consequences of its transactions and the shares of each member. The club does not pay a tax. You and the other members pay tax on your shares of dividends, interest, capital gains, and any other income earned by the club. You report your share as if you earned it personally. *Note*: You may deduct as itemized deductions your share of the club's investment expenses, subject, of course, to the 2% AGI floor.

IRAS AND KEOGHS

- See Chapter 29.

LAND

- Any profits made when land is sold are taxable.
- Rental income is subject to regular income tax, although it may be partially offset by deductible expenses, property costs, and mortgage interest payments.
- Land does not qualify for depreciation deductions.
- Check with your accountant regarding the status of income-producing land vis-à-vis the current passive loss rules, as these rulings are complex.

LIFE INSURANCE

- When you purchase whole life insurance, part of your premium goes toward the purchase of insurance; the rest is an investment. The earned income on the investment portion builds up tax-deferred until you cash in the policy. If you die before you cash in, and the benefits are paid to your children or spouse, this buildup becomes completely income tax-free, not just tax-deferred.

☐CAUTION: Single-premium annuities or life insurance policies, where you pay only one premium, no longer qualify for this tax-deferred treatment.

- If you purchase a single-premium contract after June 30, 1988, and you borrow from

the contract, the loan is treated as a distribution of income on which you must pay regular income tax and, in most cases, a 10% penalty on the taxable portion. (There's no 10% penalty if distributions are made after you reach 59½ or if you are disabled or if the distribution is part of a life annuity.) The same rules apply to a partial surrender of the contract, a cash withdrawal, or the distribution of dividends that are not retained by the insurance company as a premium if received on or after the annuity starting date. If received before the annuity starting date, special rules apply. Check with your accountant.

- These rules generally apply also to any life insurance plans ("modified endowment contract") that you fund with fewer than seven annual payments of equal size.
- You must also pay income tax on distributions from single-premium contracts purchased on or after June 21, 1988, to the extent that the distributions exceed your contract investment. Distributions of less than $25,000 made after your death to cover your burial are not taxed.

LOW-INCOME HOUSING

- Tax credits are available to those who buy, build, or rehabilitate low-income housing.
- The credits can offset regular income tax, subject to certain limits, but are phased out if your adjusted gross income is over $200,000. If your income exceeds $250,000, there are no credits. This income limitation does not apply to property placed in service after 1989.
- For newly constructed properties not federally subsidized, the annual credit is adjusted monthly for projects placed in service after 1987. For acquisition of existing buildings and/or where federal subsidies are used, it is 4%.

☐CAUTION: This can be a high-risk investment and should be examined carefully by a knowledgeable professional. Avoid projects of inexperienced developers.

MARGIN LOANS

- Interest you pay on money borrowed from your broker for investment purposes is deductible only to the extent that it is offset by investment income (from dividends, interest income, and royalties). For example, if you want to deduct $1,500 worth of interest on your margin loan, you must report at least $1,500 of investment income to the IRS.
- You must use the money borrowed to make an investment in order to deduct the interest. Keep careful records to document the fact that you used the money for an investment.
- ☐CAUTION: If you borrow to hold municipal bonds or any other tax-exempt investment, interest (or margin) expense is *not* deductible.

MONEY MARKET DEPOSIT ACCOUNTS

- Interest earned is subject to federal, state, and local income taxes.

MONEY MARKET MUTUAL FUNDS

- Interest is subject to federal, state, and local taxes.
- With tax-exempt money market funds, interest is exempt from federal tax and possibly from state and local tax if the fund buys securities in the investor's state.

MUTUAL FUNDS

- Dividend income and capital gains distributions are usually taxed at federal, state, and local levels, except for tax-free or municipal bond funds.
- Income from municipal bond funds is exempt from federal tax and is also exempt from state and local taxes if the securities in the portfolio are issued in the taxpayer's state.
- Mutual fund companies must send investors a year-end statement documenting all distributions and their tax status (Form 1099 and/or Form 1099-B).
- A dividend declared in December by a mutual fund is taxable in the year declared IF it is paid before February 1 of the following year.
- All fund capital gains distributions are considered long-term.

Income received from a tax-exempt municipal bond fund is usually tax-free, but capital gains distributions are taxable. Tax-free dividends are not shown on Form 1099-DIV, but capital gains are shown on Form 1099-DIV and must be reported. When selling shares in a tax-exempt bond fund, you make a taxable sale on which you realize a capital gain or loss.

- When you sell your fund shares at a profit, this gain is taxed at the applicable income rate of either 15%, 28%, or 31%, with a maximum rate of 28% for long-term holdings.
- Losses can be used to offset gains and up to $3,000 in salary, wages, and ordinary income.
- Most funds make their largest distributions at the end of the year; call the 800 number to verify. Avoid buying fund shares just before major distributions. The fund's NAV or share price immediately drops by the amount of the distribution. By waiting for a fund to go ex-dividend, you can buy in at a lower share price and avoid paying tax. Consult IRS Publication 564, "Mutual Fund Distributions."

OIL AND GAS PARTNER-SHIPS

- In year 1 of a drilling program, investors may receive a write-off for 60% to 90% of their investment. This deduction is derived from "intangible drilling costs"—labor, fuel, chemicals, nonsalvageable items.
- If oil is found, deductions are also derived from capital expenditures for materials and equipment (pumps, tanks, etc.). These deductions must be written off over the lifetime of the assets.
- When oil is found, income earned from the partnership is subject to regular tax rates. However "depletion" deductions may

shelter 15% of the gross income of the property, subject to certain limitations.

- In an oil and gas limited partnership, you cannot use losses or write-offs in excess of income to shelter your salary or portfolio income. You can, however, use write-offs against income from this or another tax-sheltered partnership. You can also carry the write-offs forward to a year when the partnership has excess income.
- However, when the partnership interest is ended or when you dispose of your investment, any tax losses can be used to offset other income.
- *Exception:* Investors with "working interests" in oil and gas partnerships (as opposed to a limited partnership investment) can use tax losses to shelter wages, salary, and ordinary income. The risk, of course, is that your entire net worth is exposed. In a limited partnership, your risk is limited to the amount you invest.
- Deductions for intangible drilling costs and depletion are preference items and used in calculating the AMT. Check with your accountant.

OPTIONS

- Rulings are extremely complicated—consult an accountant.

POINTS

- See "Real Estate."

PREFERRED STOCKS

- See "Stocks."

PUBLIC LIMITED PARTNER-SHIPS

- If a limited partnership trades publicly, income earned is not passive but is considered portfolio income, and current losses cannot be used to offset income from other public partnerships.

- Because a partnership is a pass-through entity, reportable income may be greater than actual cash distributions.

REAL ESTATE

- Until tax reform, the absolute deductibility of mortgage interest was viewed as an inalienable benefit of home ownership. But the 1986 Act and rules passed since then have changed all that. There are now two kinds of mortgage debt: acquisition indebtedness and home equity indebtedness.
- *Acquisition debt.* This is money used to purchase or substantially improve a residence. You may deduct all mortgage interest costs on up to a total of $1 million in acquisition debt for primary and secondary residences purchased or refinanced after October 13, 1987.
- *Home equity debt.* This is money you borrow using your home as collateral. You may deduct interest on home equity loans up to $100,000. The proceeds of this loan can be used for any purpose.
- *Points.* Lenders charge "points" above the regular interest rate to increase their fees and get around state limits. Whether points are deductible as interest depends on what the charge covers. You may deduct points if the payment is solely for your use of the money and not for services performed by the lender, which are separately charged. Points do *not* include fees for services such as appraisal fees, notary fees, and recording fees. Points should be paid separately by check. Points associated with refinancing a loan are not fully deductible in the year paid but must be deducted ratably over the life of the loan.
- Gain on the sale of your principal residence may be deferred if the proceeds are invested in another principal residence that you buy or build within a time period beginning 2 years before the date of the sale and ending 2 years after the sale date. To defer the full amount of the gain, the cost of the new residence must be at least equal to the adjusted sales price of the old residence.

- *The $125,000 capital gains exclusion.* This has been expanded, so that if you are age 55 or older and you sold your home after September 30, 1988, you may be able to exclude up to $125,000 of the capital gain from your income even if you did not use the house as a principal residence for 3 of the 5 previous years. New rules offer an exception for a homeowner who, because of physical or mental handicaps, lived in residential care facilities, provided he or she lived in the principal residence for 1 of the 5 years before it was sold.

REAL ESTATE INVESTMENT TRUSTS (REITs)

- Although REITs generally do not pay taxes themselves, you as an investor do. Most dividends are taxable, even those that represent capital gains distributions from the sale of property.
- There is an exception: Dividends paid out of the shareholders' equity and treated as a return of your original investment are not taxed.
- When you sell your REIT stock, any gains realized are taxed at regular rates.
- Losses from a REIT stock can be used to offset gains, plus up to $3,000 of salary, wages, and ordinary income.

REAL ESTATE LIMITED PARTNERSHIPS (RELPs)

- Partnerships generate deductions based on depreciation, operating expenses, and interest, but they can be used by investors to shelter only income from this partnership or from another passive activity, not ordinary income.
- Excess deductions cannot be used to offset taxes you owe on your salary, wages, interest and dividend income, or stock market profits.
- Income from a partnership that is greater than the deductions allowed is taxed at regular rates.
- Profits made from the sale of property are taxed at regular rates, subject to the 28% maximum on long-term gains.

RENTAL REAL ESTATE

- Rental income and profits when property is sold are taxed at regular rates.
- Much rental income can be sheltered by deductions and expenses, such as mortgage interest, property taxes, depreciation, maintenance, repairs, and travel to and from the property. You can write off the cost of residential properties over a period of 27½ years, or 39 years for commercial property placed in service after May 13, 1993.
- Up to $25,000 per year in tax losses can be used to offset your wages, salary, and other income, provided that your adjusted gross income is under $100,000. This $25,000 cap is reduced 50¢ for each dollar by which your adjusted gross income exceeds $100,000. By the time your income hits $150,000, the cap is at zero. You must, however, pass the active participation test to receive this benefit.
- If your adjusted gross income is over $150,000, you can use tax deductions only up to the amount of rental income received that year. If there are any excess losses, they can be carried over until such time as you have excess income. These losses, however, can be used to offset income from other passive activities.
- To claim losses, you cannot have less than a 10% ownership in rental property.

SAVINGS ACCOUNTS

- Interest earned is taxable even though you do not present your passbook to have the interest entered. *Note*: Dividends on deposits or accounts in some institutions are reported as interest income: mutual savings banks, cooperative banks, domestic building and loan associations, and savings and loan associations.

SAVINGS BONDS

- Interest is exempt from state and local taxes.
- Federal income tax can be deferred on Series EE bonds until the bond is redeemed or matures.
- If you roll over your Series EEs into Series

HHs, federal tax on the accrued interest can again be deferred until the HH bonds either mature or are redeemed.

- Interest earned on Series HH bonds is taxed each year.
- If you elect to pay the federal tax due each year on Series EE bonds, you pay on the annual increase in redemption value of the bond. However, once you begin paying, you must continue doing so for the bonds you presently own plus any new ones you buy.
- *Children's accounts.* If a child is under age 14 the first $600 of investment income is not taxed. The next $600 is taxed at the child's rate. Any investment income over $1,200 per year is taxed at the parent's tax rate, which is presumably higher. Starting at age 14, the income is taxed at the child's lower rate. By timing bonds to come due after the child turns 14, you can save on taxes.
- EE savings bonds purchased after January 1, 1990, by a bondholder at least 24 years old, and used to pay college tuition for yourself, your spouse, or dependent children, are free from federal income tax provided you fall within recently established income guidelines. Since the guidelines are inflation-indexed, check with your tax adviser to see if you can take advantage of this tax break.

STOCK INDEX OPTIONS AND FUTURES

- Profits are generally taxed the same as commodities—60/40 rule for gains and losses and a 3-year carryback for losses.
- Profits on futures and options become taxable at the end of the year, even if you have not closed out your position. In effect, the IRS will tax you on paper profits.
- In some cases you can deduct paper losses, even of positions still open. Check with your accountant.

STOCK RIGHTS

- If you sell your rights, the profit is taxed.
- If you exercise the rights, you will

eventually pay tax, but not until you sell the new stock.

- If you receive stock rights (as opposed to purchasing them in the market) and then let them expire, you cannot claim a deduction for the loss.
- If you purchase rights in the market and let them expire as worthless, you can deduct the loss.

STOCK SPLITS

- Stock splits are not dividends; they do not represent a distribution of surplus funds as do stock dividends. Therefore, stock splits are not taxable.

STOCKS

- Profits from the sale of stocks and dividends earned are taxed at regular rates.
- Losses from sales may be used to offset any gains you have plus up to $3,000 of salary, wages, and other ordinary income.
- Interest on margin loans may be claimed as an itemized deduction. Check with your accountant.
- Gain on the exchange of common stock for other common stock (or preferred for other preferred) of the same company is not taxable. An exchange of preferred stock for common, or common for preferred, in the same company, is generally not tax-free, unless the exchange is part of a tax-free recapitalization.
- You may deduct as a capital loss the cost basis of securities that became worthless during the year. *Note*: It is deductible *only* in the year it became completely worthless. To support this deduction, you must show that it had some value the previous year and that it became worthless in the current year—showing that the company went bankrupt, stopped doing business, or is insolvent. Check with your stockbroker.

STOCKS (FOREIGN)

- If you have foreign tax withheld from dividends of a foreign stock, you are entitled to a credit. To determine how much, divide your taxable foreign income by your total income, then multiply by the amount of U.S. tax. *Example:* You receive taxable foreign income of $5,000 and your total taxable income is $100,000. Divide $5,000 by $100,000 and multiply that by $28,000 (the estimated U.S. tax on $100,000). The maximum tax credit you could claim would be $1,400. Your credit would be the lesser of the amount withheld and the maximum credit calculated. Any amount disallowed in the current year may be carried forward.

- You can also list foreign taxes as an itemized deduction on line 7 of Schedule A. But you must choose one method or the other.

TREASURY BILLS

- Interest income is subject to federal tax but not state and local taxes.
- The income earned is subject to taxation the year in which it matures or in which you sell it.
- With T-bills, the dollar difference between the original price and the amount you receive when you redeem the bill is regarded as the interest income.
- You can defer income from one year to the next by purchasing a T-bill that matures in the new calendar year.

TREASURY BONDS

- Interest is subject to federal tax but free from state and local tax.
- Losses from sales can be used to offset any capital gains you have plus up to $3,000 of salary, wages, and other ordinary income.

TREASURY NOTES

- Interest income is subject to federal income tax but exempt from state and local tax.
- Any profit made when T-notes are sold is taxed.
- Any losses from sales can be used to offset any gains you have plus up to $3,000 of salary, wages, and ordinary income.

VACATION HOMES

- *If a home is solely for personal use,* you can deduct mortgage interest and real estate taxes, as you can with your principal residence. Mortgage interest is not deductible on third or fourth homes unless they are rental properties.
- You can deduct mortgage interest on loans up to the amount of your original purchase price plus improvements. Special rules apply to refinancing.
- *If a home is used for pleasure and rental,* your tax liability varies, depending on how long you rent it out and how long you use it. If you rent it out for no more than 14 days per year, there is no tax on the rental income. You do not even have to report it.
- If you use your home more than 14 days a year or 10% of the number of days rented, whichever is greater, your property qualifies as a second home. Mortgage interest and property taxes become deductible. Rental expenses can be deducted, but only up to the amount of rental income. If you have excess expenses, they can be carried forward.
- If your personal use of your house is 14 days or less a year or 10% of the number of days the house is rented out, whichever is greater, the house is a rental property (see "Rental Real Estate"). Remember, you cannot deduct more than the rental income received, nor can you deduct mortgage interest in excess of rental income, because that is allowed only if the home falls under the second home category. (This is a simplification of a fairly complicated rule. Consult an accountant.)
- When you sell a vacation home, profits are taxed at regular rates. But they do not qualify for the preferential treatment that your primary residence does. With a primary residence, taxes on the profits of a sale can be deferred as long as the profits are reinvested in a principal residence that costs at least as much as the sale price of the previous home. The special one-time $125,000 exemption of gains from the sale of a primary residence

available to those age 55 or older is not extended to the sale of vacation homes. Losses from sales of vacation homes are not deductible.

WARRANTS

- Profits made when warrants are sold are taxed at regular rates.

- If your warrant expires worthless, the cost of the warrant can be used to offset capital gains plus up to $3,000 of salary, wages, and other ordinary income.

- If the warrant is converted to stock shares, no taxes are due on the transaction. Cost of warrant, if any, is added to cost of stock purchased.

PART EIGHT

YOUR CUSTOMIZED PORTFOLIO

You've now read over 300 pages about investing, provided you started at the beginning and plowed straight through to this point. Yet all reading and no action won't make you rich. It's now time to actually pick specific investments that will work for you. In this special section you will find suggestions for what to buy—and why. Although we've divided the sample portfolios by lifestyle, you should read all of them and mix and match investments that seem right to you. If you're worried or nervous about making a move, resist sitting on the sidelines. It may seem safe, but earning 2 to 3% in a savings account is not safe since it barely equals the current rate of inflation. Calm your investment jitters by heeding the advice of the great Cowboy-Humorist Will Rogers: "Even if you're on the right track, you'll get run over if you just sit there."

Sample portfolios follow for those who are:

- Just out of school
- Newly married, or living with a significant other
- Raising a family
- Empty nesters
- Retired, or just about to be
- Have, or are starting, a small business

Plus, how to protect your portfolio during tough economic times.

Sometimes we spend more time thinking about what car or dishwasher to purchase than we do about our own portfolios. We pore through consumer magazines, talk to friends, test-drive endless models, read the ads. We need to spend the same research and enthusiasm on buying the right stocks, bonds and mutual funds. The investments you should own, like a car, depend upon certain personal factors—your age, your income, your family status, your feeling about risk and what other cars or equities you already own.

Bear in mind that as you grow older, your investment needs will change along with your income and your responsibility to others. That means you must review your portfolio on a regular basis. Your financial goals, too, will change. So stocks, bonds or mutual funds that do not meet your changing goals should be sold and replaced with ones that do.

The following sample portfolios contain ideas that are geared toward the various stages of your life. Many of them, particularly the stocks, should be held at least a year or more; the bonds, until maturity or their call date. The portfolios are divided into five lifestyle categories:
- those who are just out of school
- those who are newly married or coupled
- those having a family
- those who are empty nesters
- those approaching or in retirement
- those who have their own business

Even though all the suggestions are above average in quality and risk level, major world events, market conditions and interest rates shift rapidly, so actively monitor your portfolio year-round and discuss your stock and bond selections with a reliable pro.

$ HINT: Read all the portfolios even though you may fall into only one category; the

investment recommendations are transferable.

IF YOU'RE JUST OUT OF SCHOOL

This is a time for new beginnings—you're on your own, perhaps for the first time in your life, and although your income is probably modest, it's likely to increase quite quickly. Your responsibilities are limited—perhaps only to you and your cat—so you can focus your financial attention on building up a solid cash base. Follow these 10 steps to achieve financial independence:

Step 1. Set financial goals (see suggestions in the box on pages 16–17).

Step 2. Open a bank account. If you're new in the area, try the same institution your company uses.

Step 3. Get a credit card and pay all bills on time to establish a good credit rating.

Step 4. Open a money market mutual fund. A list of high-yielding funds appears on page 31.

Step 5. Sign up for the automatic payroll savings plan where you work and have 3% to 5% of your paycheck transferred into your money market fund.

Step 6. After you've accumulated cash to cover three months' worth of living expenses you're ready to invest. (Aim to keep housing costs to 30% or less of take-home pay.) Begin by purchasing several short-term CDs with different maturities, either at a local bank for convenience or with an out-of-the-area bank that has higher rates. Check *Barron's* (a weekly) or Friday's *Wall Street Journal* for a list of the nation's top-yielding CDs.

Step 7. Purchase 100 shares of stock in the

PORTFOLIO FOR THE RECENT GRAD

INVESTMENT	AMOUNT	DETAILS
Money market account	3-months' living expenses	Add cash gifts, bonuses, freelance income
Certificates of deposit	Due in 3 and 6 months	Roll over only if rates go up
Company you work for *or*	100 shares	Use employee stock purchase plan
Snapple Beverage, Advanced Micro Devices, Nike, PepsiCo, Club Med, J.P. Morgan, Kellogg	100 shares	Monitor carefully and reinvest dividends
Electric utility	100 shares	Reinvest dividends
IRA	$2,000	Stock, CD, Treasuries

company you work for, if you have faith in its future, using the company's stock purchase plan, if one exists. You'll avoid a broker's commission and you may be able to buy shares at a discount.

Alternative: Buy 100 shares of a company whose product you use or like, or one that is within the industry where you work. *Suggestions:* Snapple Beverage, Nike, PepsiCo, Club Med, J.P. Morgan, and Kellogg. Use this as a learning experience, as your introduction to the stock market.

Step 8. Study the financial condition of your local electric or gas utility company. Read the annual report and check the rating in *Value Line.* If the utility is rated #1 or #2 in safety, add 100 shares to your portfolio. If your particular utility is not a smart investment, select one of those listed in Chapter 15 on utilities.

Step 9. After a year or two you can afford to take greater risks with your money. Consider the sample portfolios that follow and incorporate those choices that you find appealing, keeping in mind that it is essential to diversify—between types of investments as well as types of industries.

Step 10. Open an IRA so fifty years from now you'll have a sizeable retirement fund. Put in $2,000 all at once or in smaller monthly or quarterly payments.

$ HINT: Look into a "Smart Loan" Account which enables college grads to consolidate their student loans into a single loan. Payments in the first four years (when interest is typically higher) are cut by nearly 40%. Students can stretch repayment term from 10 to 15 years. INFO: Sallie Mae (Student Loan Marketing Association) 1-800-524-9100.

IF YOU'RE NEWLY MARRIED OR LIVING WITH A SIGNIFICANT OTHER

Now that you've added someone else to your life, review and revise your financial goals. Draw up a new set of your own as well as some joint goals. Just because you are part of a team doesn't mean that all your goals must match. Some can be his or hers, and some should be united. Decide whether to invest jointly or separately or do a little of both, keeping in mind

---

GOALS FOR THE RECENT GRAD

- Pay off college loans
- Build up a cash nest egg
- Buy a car
- Save for a vacation
- Save for graduate school or an advanced degree

PORTFOLIO FOR THE NEWLY COUPLED

INVESTMENT	AMOUNT	DETAILS
Company you work for	100 shares	Use employee purchase plan, when available
Electric utility company	100 shares	Reinvest dividends
U.S. Treasury notes or zeros	$5,000 minimum	Hold until maturity
Municipal bonds or UIT	$1,000 minimum	Hold until maturity
Neuberger & Berman Partners Fund	$1,000 minimum	Call 1-800-367-0770
IRA	$2,000	Stock, CDs, Treasuries
PepsiCo	100 shares	Price: $38 Yield: 1.7%
Sysco Corp.	100 shares	Price: $26 Yield: 1.0%
Montgomery Street Income Securities, Inc.	200 shares	Price: $21 Yield: 7.9%
Intel	100 shares	Price: $52 Yield: 0.4%
Marvel Entertainment	100 shares	Price: $35 Yield: none

Prices are as of July 23, 1993.

that your dual incomes give you doubled investing and saving power.

Step 1. Review the portfolio for the recent grad. All suggestions there should be part of your financial life, too.

Step 2. Focus on the housing issue. You've probably been renting, but now together, by putting aside 3% to 5% of both your salaries, you can save a sizable amount for a down payment on a house or co-op. Begin by purchasing Treasury notes with two- to four-year maturities. Put the semiannual monthly interest payments in your money fund. This cash plus your CDs can be combined with your Treasuries when the latter come due.

Alternative: Treasury zeros require less cash to purchase. For example, those with a 8.2% coupon due February 1997 are priced at just 73. You'll receive $1,000 per note in 1997 (but no interim interest payments). However, you must pay federal taxes each year as if you received the income.

Step 3. Because you have a lot of time to build assets, securities should be primarily for growth, not income, at this point in your life. Check the list of suggested stocks in the box. Regard them as long-term holdings, yet monitor

earnings trends regularly and be prepared to sell.

Step 4. If you are in the 28% tax bracket, put 10% to 15% of your investments in municipal bonds or a tax-free unit investment trust.

Step 5. If you and your spouse spend weekends going to flea markets, auctions, or garage sales, consider becoming a knowledgeable collector. Every year the "Investor's Almanac" section of this book contains ideas for building a savvy collection. Check your library for previous editions.

➤ PEPSICO. (PEP) This leading soft drink company continues to report increased earnings. It is well positioned overseas to reap benefits of the growing international market for its products and in Mexico, where it is the largest food company. It has a solid balance sheet and strong management.

➤ SYSCO CORP. (SYY) This company distributes food to restaurants, hospitals, hotel/motel chains, and educational institutions. The largest company of its type in the U.S., Sysco is virtually recession-proof.

➤ MONTGOMERY STREET INCOME SECURITIES, INC. (MTS) A closed-end diversified investment company with 75% of assets in high-quality debt instruments. These shares, with their impressive 7.9% yield, are suitable for the most conservative investors, regardless of age.

➤ INTEL CORP. (INTC) A leading manufacturer of integrated circuits; also sells computer systems. Sales are surging; costs are kept relatively low.

➤ MARVEL ENTERTAINMENT (MRV) Derives earnings from sale of comic books and baseball and other trading cards. Recent purchase of Fleer Corp., a producer of baseball cards and gum, makes Marvel a leader in the field.

IF YOU HAVE A FAMILY

Nothing is ever quite as exciting or expensive as raising a family. Depending upon where you live and how extravagant you are, raising a child from birth to 18 can set you back between $50,000 and $100,000+. Then add college expenses, currently running $6,000 to $30,000 per year, and the total bill for four years is more than the cost of many houses.

Step 1. As soon as you know you're going to have a family, check your firm's maternity leave and possible benefits for the father as well as your health coverage.

Step 2. Put all or part of the mother-to-be's salary in a money market fund or other liquid investment and practice living on one salary, which may be the case when the baby arrives, at least at the beginning.

Step 3. Then put half of your money market fund into a series of CDs, staggered to come due at various dates, for example, one every two months after the baby is born. This will provide an influx of much-needed cash.

Step 4. Start a college education fund before the baby leaves the hospital's nursery. Begin by putting all gifts of cash or securities the baby receives in a custodial account under the Uniform Gifts to Minor Act in the baby's name. You'll need to get your child a Social Security number. When he or she reaches adulthood (18 or 21, depending upon the state), this money must be turned over to the child. (See Chapter 31 for tax implications.)

Step 5. At this stage your portfolio should be both income- and growth-oriented—income, to cover extra costs of the family, and growth, to make it possible to move into a larger home, add on to your present one, save for college tuition, and finance any expansion of your

PORTFOLIO FOR THOSE WITH A FAMILY

INVESTMENT	AMOUNT	DETAILS
Company you work for	100 shares	Use employee purchase plan
Electric utility company	100 shares	Reinvest dividends
Municipal bonds or UIT	$1,000 minimum	Hold until maturity
Neuberger & Berman Partners Fund	$1,000 minimum	Sell when you've reached your profit point
U.S. Treasury notes	$5,000 minimum	Use if needed to purchase house or pay child expenses
IRA	$2,000	Stocks, CDs, Treasuries
American Capital Bond Fund	200 shares	Price: $21 Yield: 8%
*WMX Technology	100 shares	Price: $33 Yield: 1.9%
Abbott Labs	100 shares	Price: $25 Yield: 2.7%
Pacific Telesis	150 shares	Price: $49 Yield: 4.5%
Wrigley (Wm)	100 shares	Price: $33 Yield: 1.2%

* Formerly, Waste Management
Prices are as of August 7, 1993.

family. See the suggested stocks and bonds in the table.

$ HINT: If you have a teenager who is working summers or part-time, consider putting up to $2,000 of his earnings into an IRA and reimburse him with spending money. This provides a small tax deduction on your child's tax return and you will have started him on a smart savings program. But explain that he cannot use the IRA money for college education or a downpayment on a future house since withdrawing money before age 59½ incurs a penalty.

➤ AMERICAN CAPITAL BOND FUND (ABC) This diversified closed-end management fund states its investment objective to be income and conservation of capital. ABC invests solely in nonconvertible debt securities. Approximately 82% of its assets are in high-quality instruments. These shares, with their 8.2% yield, should be held for income.

➤ WMX TECHNOLOGY (WMX) A leader in garbage collection and waste disposal, earnings should increase as smaller companies leave the field.

➤ ABBOTT LABS (ABT) Leading maker of health-care products, drugs and diagnostic tests, including Similac, Sucaryl, Murine. Domestic and foreign business is thriving while a cost-conscious management is devoting funds to research. A long-term holding.

➤ PACIFIC TELESIS (PAC) This company has strong telephone operations in California, as well as a foothold in the cellular business that is growing at a rate of over 50% annually. Any dividend increases can easily be covered by strong cash flow. Its yield of 4.5% is high for a common stock.

➤ WRIGLEY (WM) The world's largest manufacturer of chewing gum. The company has no debt, no pension liability, and a steady growth rate. William Wrigley and family own about 27% of the stock. Conservatively managed with a continually popular, cheap product.

IF YOU'RE AN EMPTY NESTER

These are the peak payout years of your life, whether you are married or single, with or without adult children. You can now afford to focus on maintaining a comfortable life-style, caring for your own aging parents, fueling an expanding business or career. During this period your income is probably the highest it will ever be, which enables you to make more aggressive investments than when you were footing the bill for college education or just getting started. Look at a second home or rental property, additional growth-oriented stocks, precious metals, and even some junk bonds. Fund your 401(k) or Keogh plan to the fullest and set up a tax-deferred annuity, keeping in mind that tax-free issues are all-important at this stage.

➤ SMUCKER (J.M.) CO. (SJM) Holds dominant market share in fruit spreads (about 40%) and is benefiting from growing shift in eating habits toward lower-calorie and fat-free foods. Conservatively managed.

PORTFOLIO FOR AN EMPTY NESTER

INVESTMENT	AMOUNT	DETAILS
Smucker (J.M.) Co.	100 shares	Price: $27 Yield: 1.8%
Hong Kong Telecom	100 shares	Price: $41 Yield: 4.4%
Meditrust	200 shares	Price: $34 Yield: 7.4%
AT&T 8.125s 2022, 105	5 to 10 bonds	Reinvest income for retirement or to buy real estate
Con Edison 6.625s 2002, 100	5 to 10 bonds	Reinvest income
Government zeros	5 to 10 bonds	Pick maturity dates to match your retirement

Prices are as of July 23, 1993.

ALTERNATIVE PORTFOLIO SUGGESTIONS FOR ALL AGES

- *Buy Embassy Suites bonds*, 10⅞s, due 2002, selling at 113. Five bonds at 113 each will cost $5,650. Annual income from these junk bonds will be approximately $543.
- *Buy Puerto Rico aqua and sewer municipal bonds*, 7.00s, due 2019, priced at $100. Total cost for ten bonds is $10,000. Annual income will be approximately $700. Puerto Rican municipals are exempt from local, state, and federal taxes in all 50 states.
- *Buy government zeros*, due August 2003, with a yield of 6.2%. Cost per bond is $540. Total cost for $10,000 worth of bonds is $5,400. In the year 2003 you will receive the full $10,000.
- *Dreyfus Strategic Gov't Fund (DSI)*. This closed-end bond fund trades on the NYSE and invests in U.S. and foreign government debt. Its shares in August 1993 were $11½ for an 8.3% yield.

➤ HONG KONG TELECOMMUNICATIONS ADRs (HKT) Most communications between China and the rest of the world are through this company's transmission facilities. Demand for its services are growing rapidly and company has exclusive rights in many areas.

➤ MEDITRUST (MT) One of the nation's largest health care REITs (real estate investment trust), it owns 116 properties, including nursing homes. Well managed, it has steady cash flow from its holdings and investments. The dividend has been raised for the last 24 quarters. Note the solid yet high yield.

IF YOU'RE RETIRED OR ABOUT TO BE

Now the emphasis should be on income plus some growth. Safety should be paramount unless you have sufficient money from an inheritance or sale of your home. Top-rated bonds, blue chip stocks, and high-yielding securities are most appropriate during these years. In addition to the specific suggestions that appear in the table, take a look at these investments:

➤ TREASURY BONDS. As we go to press, U.S. Treasury bonds with the longer maturities, i.e.,

PORTFOLIO FOR THOSE RETIRED OR ABOUT TO BE

INVESTMENT	AMOUNT	DETAILS
American Electric Power	200 shares	Price: $38
		Yield: 6.3%
AT&T 7⅛s, 2002 at 102	5 to 10 bonds	Use interest income or reinvest
Mutual of Omaha Interest Shares	200 shares	Price: $15
		Yield: 7.5%
1838 Bond Deb. Fund	150 shares	Price: $24½
		Yield: 7.0%
Shering-Plough	100 shares	Price: $67
		Yield: 2.0%
Oryx Corp. 10⅜s 2018, 108	5 to 10 bonds	Monitor these junk bonds
Long Island Lighting pfd c	100 shares	Price: $102
		Yield: 7.5%
Royal Dutch Petroleum	50 shares	Price: $93
		Yield: 5.3%

Prices are as of July 23, 1993.

FOR ANY PORTFOLIO
The Top Yielding Stocks in the Dow

At any time when you have accumulated enough cash, use this simple strategy that almost always beats the market: On a given day, say January 2nd, buy equal amounts of the 10 highest-yielding stocks in the Dow Jones industrial average. Then, on that same date each year, replace any that have fallen out of the top ten.

STOCK	PRICE	YIELD
Westinghouse	$17	4.2%
General Motors	39	4.1
IBM	92	5.3
Union Carbide	14	5.3
Texaco	63	5.1
Sears	40	5.0
Chevron	71	4.6
Eastman Kodak	44	4.5
Exxon	64	4.5
American Express	22	4.4

Prices as of August 7, 1992.

---

those due in 30 years, are yielding a little under 7.5%.

➤ HIGH-YIELD BONDS If you are willing to assume some risk, put a small portion (up to 5%) in a high-yield or junk bond mutual fund or select your own.

➤ ZERO COUPON BONDS to mature at or soon after your retirement date. Put these in your tax-sheltered pension plan, where taxes are deferred. Remember, zeros do not pay annual interest, but you must pay annual taxes on the imputed income.

➤ GINNIE MAES OR FANNIE MAES that pay high yields (7 to 8½%) through monthly checks. Most pass-throughs are fully paid out in less than 15 years, so time your certificate purchase to coincide with your retirement. If you are younger, look into CMOs, a similar investment with more predictable payout dates, described in Chapter 12.

➤ SCHERING-PLOUGH (SGP) Worldwide manufacturer of prescription and over-the-counter

drugs, animal health care and biotechnology products. Operating margin has been expanding unrelentingly since 1981 and even in difficult market, earnings were up to 18%.

➤ ORYX ENERGY. These bonds are issued by a large producer of gas and oil. It also explores for oil in the U.S. and Europe. These bonds, rated BBB–, fall into the high junk bond category.

➤ ROYAL DUTCH PETROLEUM (RD) Company is in a turnaround situation as costs have been greatly reduced and earnings are increasing. The 5.3% yield, high for a common stock, compensates for temporarily slow capital gains.

IF YOU HAVE OR ARE STARTING A SMALL BUSINESS

It may not seem logical but an economic slump can be a good time to start a business. Lowered interest rates and a plentiful labor pool with people willing to work for reasonable salaries can be viewed in a positive light. If you already own a business and your credit is good, it's also an advantageous time to borrow and expand, with interest rates lower than they have been in some time. Despite what you may hear, banks are willing to grant loans to solid businesses. Before doing either, take these steps.

Step 1. Address personal financial needs. No one should be in business for themselves if there's any question about where money for the kids' education or the next mortgage payment is coming from. We increase our nest egg suggestion for business owners: you should have enough money set aside in a money market fund or CDs to cover at least one year's worth of personal living expenses. (Ordinarily that time frame is six or nine months, depending upon the economy and one's age.)

Step 2. Take care of personal medical and disability insurance. Under federal law, you have the right to continue medical coverage for eighteen months after leaving a job, at your expense. Since premiums for a group policy are lower than for individual coverage it is wise to arrange to continue coverage by paying the premiums yourself. Then you're on your own. Bear in mind that various benefits—health, life and disability insurance plus paid vacations,

---

PORTFOLIO FOR BUSINESS OWNERS

INVESTMENT	DETAILS
Money market account	9-months' living expenses
and/or	
Certificates of deposit	9-months' living expenses
IRA ($2,000/annually)	Stocks, CDs, Treasuries

Discuss these high yield choices with your investment advisor. Be certain to diversify, ideally with stocks and bonds both represented.

American Capital Bond Fund (NYSE: ACB)	Price: $21
	Yield: 8%
American Electric Power (NYSE: AEP)	Price: $38
	Yield: 6.3%
AT&T 7⅛s due 2002 selling at 104	Solid utility bond
Long Island Lighting pfd C	Price: $102
	Yield: 7.5%
1838 Bond Deb. Fund (NYSE: BDF)	Price: $24½
	Yield: 7.0%
Webb (Del) 9¾s 2003, selling at 106	Hold for income
Safeway Stores 10s 2001, selling at 110	Hold for income
Meditrust (NYSE: MT)	Price: $29
	Yield: 8.7%
Montgomery Street Income Securities (NYSE: MTS)	Price: $21
	Yield: 7.9%
Mutual of Omaha Interest Shares (NYSE: MUO)	Price: $15
	Yield: 7.5%
Putnam Premier Income Trust (NYSE: PPT)	Price: $8
	Yield: 8.5%*

* Some of this yield is actually a return of capital. Portfolio has some high risk holdings. Prices as of July 23, 1993.

---

make up almost one-third of most employees' annual salaries. So for you to stay even, your business must generate more than just your salary.

Your portfolio should be geared to provide income to weather any downturns in your business and to provide collateral should you wish to use part of it to obtain a loan. (There are two ways to finance a business: debt financing consists of loans that the business must repay; equity financing consists of money given to a business in exchange for an ownership share in the business. In most cases, a balance between the two is ideal. Too much debt necessitates a huge cash flow to pay the interest on the loans and too much equity means you've

given away control and perhaps too much ownership.)

The suggestions in the box above are aimed primarily at providing income as well as securities that can be used as collateral for a loan or sold if you should need an infusion of capital. Please note that the first 3 securities suggestions should be taken care of before attempting the rest.

HINT: Order IRS publication #334, Tax Guide for Small Businesses, free, by calling 1-800-829-3676
#583, Taxpayers Starting a Business
Free
#917, Business Use of a Car
Free

PROTECTING YOUR PORTFOLIO DURING HARD TIMES

The recession has affected virtually every American: some have lost jobs, others have failed to see wages materialize or have had their hours or salaries frozen, even cut back. Just about everyone is worried about finances. Whether or not you've been hit by the recession, it's prudent to know what steps to take to protect your family's money during tough times, now or later.

BUILD UP YOUR NEST EGG

If you're worried about your job security, start now to build up a sufficient nest egg to see you through hard times. Set aside a monthly sum immediately after paying the rent or mortgage. Don't wait to save until later. Useful steps:

1   Use automatic savings plans. Sign up for payroll deduction programs. Arrange for automatic transfers from checking to savings or to money market funds. Purchase EE Savings Bonds this way as well.
2   Pay cash for purchases. Avoid using credit cards, which often leads to overspending, debt buildup, and high interest rate charges.
3   Use retirement plans for forced savings. Voluntary contributions to 401(k) plans, IRAs, Keoghs and others not only defer taxes but they are tax-advantaged ways to save, since contributions may be funded with pre-tax dollars.
4   Increase tax withholding. Get a bigger tax refund by boosting salary withholding. Then use the refund for savings.
☐CAUTION: Overwithholding operates like an interest-free loan to the government, since no interest is paid on the refund check.

OTHER STRATEGIES

If you are already experiencing financial difficulties:

1   Go on a crash budget.
2   Review avenues of income and fixed and variable expenses.

3   Trim variables, such as entertaining, travel, eating out, dry cleaning.
4   Stop outrageous spending.
5   Talk to the children. If you or your spouse has lost a job or has a sudden cutback in income, it's important to let children know the truth, but without frightening them. After all, they will be affected too. Reassure them that recessions are cyclical and hard times won't last forever.
6   Claim benefits. If you are laid off and entitled to unemployment compensation, do not be embarrassed to collect. After all, you've been paying to fund the system for many years.
7   Trim debt. Paying off high-rate loans, such as credit card debt, is critical. Be certain to pay all credit card balances within 30 days to avoid interest charges. And, consolidate high-rate debt to obtain a more favorable interest rate.
8   Ease up on savings. Delay contributions to 401(k) and other voluntary savings plans if cash is tight.
9   Pinch pennies. Conspicuous consumption, so in vogue during the 1980s, is out and sensible spending for the 1990s is in.
10   Eat home more. Or, if dining out, have drinks and dessert at home.

FINDING EXTRA CASH

You may discover that you need extra cash to tide yourself over. Here are some suggestions:

1   Review your portfolio and first sell securities that are not performing well. If need be, slowly sell other securities, holding until last the best performers.
2   Consider a home equity line of credit.
☐CAUTION: It is virtually impossible to get this type of loan when you are out of work. If you fear losing your job, process the loan now. There's no obligation to use it, although you will incur some expense in setting it up.
3   Borrow against the cash value in any life insurance policies.
4   As a last resort, borrow from 401(k) plans. Hold off tapping this source as long as possible because it's hard to replace these funds, which you will need upon

retirement. Most companies let employees borrow up to 50% of the amount vested, or $50,000, whichever is less. Typically you repay the money in installments through payroll deductions. Finance charges are based on current market rates—expect to pay prime plus one or two percentage points. Terms vary, so check with your benefits officer.

☐CAUTION: Don't withdraw money from your IRA or Keogh plan if you are under age 59½. Not only is there regular income tax on such withdrawals, but there's a 10% penalty on top of that.

INVESTMENT ANALYSIS AND INFORMATION SOURCES

Now that you are well acquainted with the various types of investments available, the next step, of course, is deciding which ones to select for your personal portfolio. Do you want common stocks? If so, which ones? Perhaps you would benefit from bonds or convertibles. Yet selecting the best and avoiding the worst require skill and knowledge. That's where investment analysis enters the picture.

In this section you will learn the various techniques used by the experts in selecting all types of securities. You will come to know how to recognize the potential profit in stocks, bonds, and mutual funds and how to spot the winners and avoid the losers. Among the topics covered are:

- Reading a company's balance sheet and annual report
- Getting the most out of statistics
- Following technical analysis
- Studying the charts
- Using software programs

In Parts Three and Four we explained the various types of stocks and the analytical tools for evaluating securities. You may want to review these points as you now learn precisely how to select top-quality securities on your own, including:

- Knowing the stock exchanges, indexes, and averages

A

MANAGING AND INVESTING YOUR MONEY WITH A COMPUTER

A personal computer can be a helpful tool for financial planning, investing, and even preparing tax returns. It not only does the obvious—make number crunching faster and easier—but with the right software you can gain access to a large amount of research ordinarily reserved for the professionals.

There's all sorts of help available—programs for check writing, tax filing, getting current stock and mutual fund data, doing a budget, even talking to other investors and experts. No one program, however, does it all and no combination of programs can replace intelligent, sensible decision-making. So look upon your computer as an additional way to improve your financial bottom line, and not as a substitute for thinking. Use it in conjunction with the basic investment guidelines you've learned by reading this book and other resources.

Following is an overview of some of the best software and on-line programs, starting with the simplest programs first—those that do check writing. Read what we have to say, talk with knowledgeable friends who use financial software programs, check your public library (many have programs you can practice with) and then call the sources for the promotional literature. (*Note:* we have not given prices for software since they range widely depending upon where you purchase the program.)

Before purchasing any software you need to consider two things: 1) how complex are your financial affairs; and 2) what format does your computer accept—DOS, Windows, or Macintosh?

CHECKBOOK MANAGEMENT

- *Microsoft Money.* Has a great deal of built-in assistance for keeping track of your checkbook and budget. Its on-screen

graphic resembles a checkbook. You fill in the necessary information and the calculations are done automatically.

- *Quicken.* This best seller is just about the easiest to learn and use. It sorts financial information into budgeting and tax categories for record-keeping purposes. The data can then be transferred to most major tax-preparation software packages. Small businesses can add on a payroll program, "QuickPay," for an extra $60.
- *Quicken for Windows.* This version has an extra feature for the same price called "IntelliCharge." Users can apply for a Visa Gold Card; all charges placed on the card are then electronically sent via modem to your computer and automatically sorted into the two categories.
- *QuickBooks.* Similar to Quicken, but with a simple accounting program useful if you have a home office or small business. It uses the same checkbook entry plan as Quicken, but adds on business features such as invoicing, accounts payable, accounts receivable.

FINANCIAL PLANNING

- *Andrew Tobias's Managing Your Money.* One of the most comprehensive and popular financial planning packages available. In addition to doing checkbook, budget, and portfolio management, it tracks stocks, has an address keeper, a calendar, a to-do list, a simple word processor and a tax planner. The program also calculates mortgage payments and can help you determine whether it's better to buy or lease a car or home. A well-written and enjoyable-to-read manual.

TAXES

You'll have to spend about two hours learning a tax program, but it does make filling out returns easier. None of the programs answers every question—you may still have to consult IRS publications or even a professional.

- *Andrew Tobias's TaxCut.* A question and answer format that gets you to the right IRS forms and then leads you through the forms with help screens. Keeps track of important receipts and tax information throughout the year. Prints out IRS-approved forms on any printer.

- *Kiplinger Taxcut.* This takes the "Andrew Tobias' TaxCut" program and adds material from the tax editor of *Kiplinger's Personal Finance* magazine. This extra help, written in easy-to-follow language, makes calculations much easier. The package also includes the "Kiplinger TaxEstimator" program for tax planning and a copy of Kiplinger's 476-page tax guide, *Sure Ways to Cut Your Taxes.*

- *MacInTax.* Has a question-and-answer format and a useful, easy-to-follow help program. For another $19.95, you can file tax returns electronically for faster refunds.

ON-LINE SERVICES

With a home computer and a modem, you can tap into the telephone lines and into an amazing amount of up-to-the-minute financial information—stock prices, mutual fund values, earnings estimates, analysts' opinions, historical information, research reports. You can even place stock orders through on-line discount brokerage firms. Or you can join a discussion group and ask your financial questions of on-line experts.

Once you have the necessary hardware, you pay an initial setup fee and an as-you-go fee or a flat monthly fee. Here's data on several of the leading on-line services for investors.

- *CompuServe.* No start-up cost; $25 to $50 for software, which is offset by a usage credit. Monthly flat fee is $8.95. Extended services: $8/hour or $16/hour. Additional surcharges for other features.

  This service is vast, with current and historical market quotes, fundamental and technical data on U.S. and foreign stocks, mutual funds, as well as material from newsletters and journal articles.

  A flat monthly fee covers basic quotes and company earnings data, mutual funds, news, sports and weather.

  For other information and browsing, including research on stocks, there's an hourly connect-time fee. The "Company Analyzer," which searches all the financial data bases for data on a single company, is also additional.

☐CAUTION: Costs can quickly mount up.

On-line stock trading, mutual fund purchases and other brokerage services through Quick & Reilly, Spear Rees & Co., and E Trade.

- *Dow Jones News/Retrieval.* No start-up cost. $25 monthly fee for unlimited nonprime-time access to quotes and news or to selected stock and mutual fund info. For both, $45. Access to other data bases during nonprime time is 15¢/minute.

  Although designed for professionals and serious investors, a flat fee, after-hours arrangement enables you to access what otherwise is an expensive, top-notch service, getting Dow Jones news as well as current and historical stock quotes. For an additional $20, you can access Standard & Poor's reports, mutual fund performance data, and financial analysts' reports. For a per/minute charge, there is additional Dow Jones' data, including its vast library of news articles.

  On-line trading with Fidelity for $12/month fee per account.

- *Prodigy.* Start-up kit $30 to $50 plus

YOUR BEST BUY

If all you want are the day's closing stock and mutual fund quotes, GEnie, from General Electric, is the cheapest on-line service with a $4.95/month flat fee. If you sign up for a Charles Schwab account, you get 100 free real-time quotes, more if you make trades.

$14.95/month for basic service; it's another $14.95/month for "Strategic Investor." First month's fee included with start-up kit.

A general on-line, graphic-intensive service, with numerous charts. The monthly fee gives you most of the service, news, weather, shopping, current stock market news, quotes, libraries of investing articles, discussion forums with experts providing answers to financial questions. For an extra monthly fee you get access to "Strategic Investor" for in-depth research on stocks and funds.

B

BEHIND THE SCENES:
How to Read Annual Reports

All annual reports are the single most important tool in analyzing corporations to decide whether to buy, hold, sell, or pass by their securities. In a few minutes, you can check the corporation's quality and profitability and, with closer study, learn a great deal about the character and ability of management, its methods of operation, its products and services, and, most important, its future prospects. If you own securities of the corporation, you will receive a copy of the annual report about 4 months after the close of its operating year. If you are considering becoming a shareholder, get a copy from your broker or by writing the company (get the address from Standard & Poor's, Value Line, Moody's, or other reference books at your library).

First, skim the text, check the statement of income and earnings to see how much money was made and whether this was more than that of previous years, and review the list of officers and directors for familiar names. Later, if you're still interested, you can follow up the points of interest.

The statements will always be factually correct, but the interpretations, especially those in the president's message, will naturally be the most favorable within legal and accounting limits.

If you are considering a stock to buy, look at 3 years' annual reports. Here's what to be aware of:

➤ TRENDS In sales, earnings, dividends, accounts receivable. If they continue to rise, chances are that you've found a winner. *Buy* when they are moving up; *review* when they plateau; *consider selling* when they are down.

➤ INFORMATION *From the tables:* corporate financial strength and operating success or failure. *From the text:* explanations of what happened during the year and what management projects for the future. If you don't believe management, do not hold the stock.

➤ POSITIVES New plants, products, personnel, and programs. Are the total assets greater and liabilities lower than in previous years? If so, why—tighter controls or decreases in allocations for R&D, marketing, etc.?

If the profits were up, was the gain due to fewer outstanding shares (because of repurchase of stock), to nonrecurring income from the sale of property, or to higher sales and lower costs?

➤ NEGATIVES Plant closings, sales of subsidiaries, discontinuance of products, and future needs for financing. Not all of these will always be adverse, but they can make a significant difference with respect to what happens in the next few years.

If the profits were down, was this because of the elimination of some products or services? Price wars? Poor managerial decisions?

➤ FOOTNOTES Read these carefully because they can point up problems. Be cautious if there were heavy markdowns of inventory, adverse governmental regulations, rollovers of debt, and other unusual events.

➤ BALANCE SHEET To see whether cash or liquid assets are diminishing and whether accounts receivable, inventories, or total debts are rising. Any such trend can serve as a yellow flag, if not a red one.

➤ FINANCIAL SUMMARY Not only for the past year but for the previous 5 years. This will provide an overall view of corporate performance and set the stage for an analysis of the most recent data.

In the stock market, *past is prologue.* Few companies achieve dramatic progress or fall on hard times suddenly. In most cases, the changes have been forecast. The corporation with a long, fairly consistent record of profitable growth can be expected to do as well, or better, in the years ahead and thus prove to be a worthwhile holding. The erratic performer is likely to move from high to low profits (or losses). And the faltering company will have signs of deterioration over a 2- or 3-year period.

READING THE REPORT

When you review the text, you will get an idea of the kind of people who are managing your money, learn what they did or did not do and why, and be able to draw some conclusions about future prospects.

➤ BEGIN WITH THE SHAREHOLDERS' LETTER This message from the chairman outlines the company's past performance and its prospects. Compare last year's letter with this year's facts. Did the company meet its previously stated goals? Beware of the chairman who never mentions any problems or areas of concern. If there were failures, there should be logical explanations. Management is not always right in its decisions, but in financial matters, frankness is the base for confidence. If previous promises were unfulfilled (and that's why you should keep a file of past annual reports), find out why. If the tone is overly optimistic, be wary. If you are skeptical, do not hold the stock or buy.

➤ WATCH FOR DOUBLE-TALK Clichés are an integral part of business writing, but they should not be substitutes for proper explanations. If you find such meaningless phrases as "a year of transition" or some of the locutions listed in the box on page 355, start getting ready to unload. There are better opportunities elsewhere.

➤ STUDY THE BALANCE SHEET This presents an instant picture of the company's assets and liabilities on the very last day of the fiscal year. Divide the current assets by the current liabilities to get the current ratio. A ratio of 2:1 or better signals that there are enough assets on hand to cover immediate debts. (We return to balance sheets in Appendix C.)

➤ LOOK AT LONG-TERM DEBT Divide long-term debt by long-term capital (i.e., long-term debt plus shareholders' equity). If it is below 50%, the company is probably solid, but, of course, the more debt, the less cash to help weather rough times.

➤ REVIEW ACCOUNTS RECEIVABLE Listed under current assets, this figure reflects the payments for products or services that the company expects to receive in the near future. If receivables are growing at a faster pace than sales, it may indicate that the company is not collecting its bills fast enough.

➤ LOOK AT CURRENT INVENTORIES If inventories are rising faster than sales, the company is creating or producing more than it can sell.

➤ LOOK AT NET INCOME PER SHARE Note if this figure, which reflects earnings, is trending up or down.

➤ COMPARE REVENUES AND EXPENSES If expenses are greater than revenues over time, management may be having trouble holding down overhead. Discount earnings increases that are due to a nonrecurring event, such as sale of a property or division. Nonrecurring items should be explained in the footnotes. The footnotes also reveal changes in accounting methods, lawsuits, and liabilities.

➤ STUDY THE QUALITY AND SOURCE OF EARNINGS When profits are entirely from operations, they indicate management's skill; when they are partially from bookkeeping, look again. But do not be hasty in drawing conclusions. Even the best of corporations may use "special" accounting.

Examples: In valuing inventories, LIFO (last in, first out) current sales are matched against the latest costs so that earnings can rise sharply when inventories are reduced and those latest costs get older and thus lower. When oil prices were at a peak, Texaco cut inventories by 16%. The LIFO cushion, built up over several years, was a whopping $454 million and transformed what would have been a drop in net income into a modest gain.

Such "tricks" are one reason why stocks fall or stay flat after annual profits are reported. Analysts are smart enough to discover that earnings are more paper than real.

➤ READ THE AUDITOR'S REPORT If there are hedging phrases such as "except for" or "subject to," be wary. These phrases can signal the inability to get accurate information and may forecast future write-offs.

➤ LOOK AT FOREIGN CURRENCY TRANSACTIONS These can be tricky and often difficult to understand. Under recent revisions of accounting rules, it's possible to recast them retroactively when, of course, they can be favorable. One major firm whose domestic profits had been

HOW TO TRANSLATE THE PRESIDENT'S MESSAGE

Here are some of the techniques used in writing annual reports to phrase comments in terms that tend to divert the reader's attention away from problems.

WHAT THE PRESIDENT SAYS	WHAT THE PRESIDENT MEANS
"The year was difficult and challenging."	"Sales and profits were off, but expenses (including executive salaries) were up."
"Management has taken steps to strengthen market share."	"We're underselling our competitors to drive them out of the market."
"Integrating the year's highs and lows proved challenging."	"Sales were up; profits went nowhere."
"Management worked diligently to preserve a strong financial position."	"We barely broke even but were able to avoid new debts."
"Your company is indebted to the dedicated service of its employees."	"We don't pay 'em much, but there's not much else to cheer about."

CONSOLIDATED STATEMENT: FRED MEYER, INC.

FISCAL YEAR ENDED ($ IN THOUSANDS EXCEPT PER-SHARE AMOUNTS)

	JANUARY 31, 1991	FEBRUARY 1, 1991	FEBRUARY 2, 1991 (53 WEEKS)
Net sales	$1,688,208	$1,583,796	$1,449,108
Cost of merchandise sold	1,200,379	1,135,836	1,053,689
Gross margin	487,829	447,960	395,419
Operating and administrative expenses	430,469	397,841	354,914
Income from operations	57,360	50,119	40,505
Interest expense, net of interest income of $1,679, $2,983, and $3,090	11,945	17,652	19,565
Income before income taxes and extraordinary items	45,415	32,467	20,940
Provision for income taxes	21,350	13,000	8,000
Income before extraordinary items	24,065	19,467	12,940
Extraordinary items	(1,530)		2,649
Net income	$ 22,535	$ 19,467	$ 15,589
Earnings per Common Share			
Income before extraordinary items	$ 1.15	$ 1.06	$ .73
Extraordinary items	(.07)		.15
Net income	$ 1.08	$ 1.06	$ .88
Weighted average number of common shares outstanding	20,870	18,355	17,790

lagging went back 4 years with its overseas reports and boosted its per-share profits to $7.08 from the previously reported $6.67 per share.

Most international corporations have elaborate systems for hedging against fluctuations in foreign currencies. These are relatively expensive, but they tend to even out sharp swings in the value of the dollar.

➤ CHECK FOR FUTURE OBLIGATIONS You may have to burrow in the footnotes, but with major companies, find out about the pension obligations: the money that the firm must pay to its retirees. One way to boost profits (because this means lower annual contributions) is to raise the assumed rate of return on pension fund investments.

➤ CALCULATE THE CASH FLOW Add after-tax earnings and annual depreciation on fixed assets and subtract preferred dividends, if any. Then compare the result with previous years. Cash flow is indicative of corporate earning power because it shows the dollars available for profits, new investments, etc.

➤ BEWARE OF OVERENTHUSIASM ABOUT NEW PRODUCTS, PROCESSES, OR SERVICES Usually, it takes 3 years to translate new operations into sizable sales and profits. And the majority of new projects are losers.

➤ PAY SPECIAL ATTENTION TO THE RETURN ON EQUITY (PROFIT RATE) This is the best measure of management's ability to make money with your money. Any ROE above 15% is good; when below, compare the figure with that of previous years and other firms in the same industry. Some industries seldom show a high rate of return: for example, heavy machinery because of the huge investment in plants and equipment, and utilities because of the ceiling set by public commissions.

➤ WATCH OUT FOR EQUITY ACCOUNTING Where earnings from other companies, which are more than 20% owned, are included in total profits. There are no cash dividends, so the money cannot be used for expansion or payouts to shareholders. This maneuver can massage the reported earnings, but that's about all. Teledyne, a major conglomerate, reported $19.96 per share profits, but a close examination revealed that $3.49 of this was from equity accounting— phantom, not real, earnings.

FOR FURTHER INFORMATION

How to Read a Financial Report, 1990 (pamphlet), free from any Merrill Lynch office.

George T. Friedlob and Ralph E. Welton, *Keys to Reading an Annual Report* (Hauppauge, NY: Barron's Educational Series, 1989).

DETERMINING VALUE

The idea is to buy low and sell high. This sounds easy, but it isn't. You must determine what is *low* and, to a lesser degree, what is *high.* That's where value comes in. The surest way to make money in the stock market is to buy securities when they are undervalued and sell them when they become fully priced. *Value shows the range in which a stock should be bought or sold and thus provides the base for investment profits.*

Value itself is based on financial "facts," as stated in the corporate reports. Projections, by contrast, are based on analyses of past performance, present strength, and future progress. When you select quality stocks on the basis of value (or undervaluation), you will almost always make money—perhaps quickly with speculative situations, more slowly with major corporations. You can identify value *if* you understand the basics of financial analysis, our next step.

HOW TO ANALYZE FINANCIAL REPORTS

Financial analysis is not as difficult as you may think, and once you get into the swing of things, you can pick the few quality stocks from the thousands of publicly owned securities. If you are speculation-minded, you can find bargains in securities of mediocre or even poor corporations.

Several basic figures and ratios show the company's current and prospective financial condition, its past and prospective earning power and growth, and therefore its investment desirability or lack of desirability.

Publicly owned corporations issue their financial reports on an annual, semiannual, or quarterly basis. Most of the information impor-

tant to the investor can be found in (1) the balance sheet; (2) the profit and loss, or income, statement; and (3) the change in financial position or "flow of funds" data. In each of these three sections you should look for:

- *The key quantities:* net tangible assets, changes in working capital, sales costs, profits, taxes, dividends, etc.
- *The significant rates and ratios:* price-earnings multiples, profit rates, growth in net worth, earnings, dividends, etc.
- *The comparison of a corporation with a standard:* that of its industry, the stock market, the economy, or some other broader base.

The following data and explanations are digested from *Understanding Financial Statements,* prepared by the New York Stock Exchange. They do not cover every detail but will get you started. For a copy, write to the address given on page 68, or ask your broker for one.

INCOME AND RETAINED EARNINGS

Here's where you find out *how the corporation fared for the past year* in comparison with the two previous annual reporting periods: in other words, how much money the company took in, how much was spent for expenses and taxes, and the size of the resulting profits (if any), which were available either for distribution to shareholders or for reinvestment in the business. Income and retained earnings are the basis for comparisons, both between years for this company and between firms in the same or similar business.

SALES

How much business does the company do in a year? With public utilities, insurance firms, and service organizations, the term "revenues" is often used instead of sales.

In the past year, corporate sales in the sample corporation shown were up $5.8 million, a gain of 5.3%, not quite as good as the 5.5% rise the year before. Net income per share (middle) was also just slightly better: $0.4 million (to $9.9 from $9.5), +4.2%. Check these figures against those of the industry and major competitors. They may be better than they appear.

COSTS AND EXPENSES

➤ COST OF GOODS SOLD The dollars spent to keep the business operating. The $3.2 million more was less than the $5.8 million increase in sales.

➤ SELLING, GENERAL, AND ADMINISTRATIVE EXPENSES The costs of getting products or services to customers and getting paid. These will vary with the kind of business: high for consumer goods manufacturers and distributors because of advertising; lower for companies selling primarily to industry or government.

➤ DEPRECIATION A bookkeeping item to provide for wear and tear and obsolescence of machinery and equipment, presumably to set aside reserves for replacement. The maximum calculations are set by tax laws. Typically, a straight-line accounting method might charge the same amount each year for a specified number of years.

With companies in the natural resource business, the reduction in value is called depletion, and it too is calculated over a period of years.

By changing the type of depreciation, a

STATEMENT OF INCOME AND RETAINED EARNINGS ($ millions)
"Your Company"

	DECEMBER 31 YEAR-END		
	CURRENT YEAR	**PREVIOUS YEAR**	**2 YEARS AGO**
SALES	$115.8	$110.0	$104.5
Less:			
COSTS AND EXPENSES			
Cost of goods sold	$ 76.4	$ 73.2	$ 70.2
Selling, general, and administrative expenses	14.2	13.0	12.1
Depreciation	2.6	3.5	2.3
	$ 93.2	$ 89.7	$ 84.6
OPERATING PROFIT	$ 22.6	$ 20.3	$ 19.9
Interest charges	1.3	1.0	1.3
Earnings before income taxes	$ 21.3	$ 19.3	$ 18.6
Provision for taxes on income	11.4	9.8	9.5
Net income (per common share for year: current, $5.24; last, $5.03; 2 years ago, $4.97)*	$ 9.9	$ 9.5	$ 9.1
RETAINED EARNINGS, BEGINNING OF YEAR	42.2	37.6	33.1
Less dividends paid on:	$ 52.1	$ 47.1	$ 42.2
Preferred stock ($5 per share)	(.3)	(.3)	—
Common stock (per share: this year, $3.00; last year, $2.50; 2 years ago, $2.50)	(5.4)	(4.6)	(4.6)
RETAINED EARNINGS, END OF YEAR	$ 46.4	$ 42.2	$ 37.6

  * After preferred share dividend requirements.

company can increase or decrease earnings, so always be wary when this happens.

OPERATING PROFIT

Operating profit consists of the dollars generated from the company's usual operations without regard to income from other sources or financing. As a percentage of sales, it tells the profit margin: a rising 19.5% in the last year compared with 18.5% the year before.

➤ INTEREST CHARGES The interest paid to bondholders. It is deductible before taxes. The available earnings should be many times the mandated interest charges: in this case, a welcome 17 times before provision for income taxes (i.e., $22.6 \div \$1.3 = 17$).

➤ EARNINGS BEFORE INCOME TAXES The operating profit minus interest charges. When companies have complicated reports, this can be a confusing area.

➤ PROVISION FOR TAXES ON INCOME The allocation of money for Uncle Sam—a widely variable figure because of exemptions, special credits, etc., from about 5% for some companies to 34% for industrial corporations.

➤ NET INCOME FOR THE YEAR *The bottom line.* This was 4.2% better than the year before—about the same as recorded in the previous period. This was no record breaker and works out better on a per-share basis: $5.24 vs. $5.03.

One year's change is interesting, but the true test of management's ability comes over 5 years.

Use this figure to make other comparisons (against sales: 8.5% vs. 8.6% the year before) and then relate this to returns of other companies in the same industry. The average manufacturing corporation earns about 5¢ per dollar of sales, but supermarkets are lucky to end up with 1¢ against shareowners' equity: the profit rate (PR). Here, the PR was a modest 13%.

To find the earnings per share, divide the net income (less preferred dividend requirements) by the average number of shares outstanding during the year. This is the key figure for most analysts. It is also used to determine the price-earnings (P/E) ratio: divide the market price of the stock by the per-share profits. If the stock was selling at 30, the P/E would be 10—slightly above the average of most publicly owned shares.

➤ RETAINED EARNINGS The dollars reinvested for future growth, always an important indica-

tion of future prospects. If the company continues to boost this figure, its basic value will increase. At the same PR, earnings will increase, and eventually so will the value of the common stock.

Here the company keeps plowing back more: $4.6 million in the current year versus $4.5 million the year before. (Subtract the retained earnings at the beginning of the year from retained earnings of the previous year: $37.6 − $33.1 = $4.5.)

➤ DIVIDENDS The amount paid out to shareholders for the use of their money. The $5 per share paid on the preferred stock is fixed. The payments for the common move with profits: last year up 50¢ per share to $3.00 from the flat $2.50 of the 2 prior years.

Note that this statement shows earnings retained as of the beginning and end of each year. Thus the company reinvested $46.4 million for the future.

BALANCE SHEET ITEMS

Now that you know what happened in the last year, it's time to take a look at the financial strength (or weakness) of the corporation. On page 360 is a typical balance sheet. Use it as the basis for reviewing annual reports of the companies in which you own, or plan to own, securities. The headings may vary according to the type of industry, but the basic data will be similar—and just as important.

CURRENT ASSETS

Items that can be converted into cash within 1 year. The total is $48.4 million this year, $4.2 million more than last year.

➤ CASH Mostly bank deposits, including compensating balances held under terms of a loan—like keeping a savings account to get free checking.

➤ MARKETABLE SECURITIES Corporate and government securities that can be sold quickly. In the current year, these were eliminated.

➤ RECEIVABLES Amounts due from customers for goods and services. This is a net amount after a set-aside for items that may not be collected.

➤ INVENTORIES Cost of raw materials, work in process, and finished goods. Statements and foot-

BALANCE SHEET ($ millions)
"Your Company"

ASSETS	DEC. 31 CURRENT YEAR	DEC. 31 PRIOR YEAR	LIABILITIES AND STOCKHOLDERS' EQUITY	DEC. 31 CURRENT YEAR	DEC. 31 PRIOR YEAR
Current Assets			**Current Liabilities**		
Cash	$ 9.0	$ 6.2	Accounts payable	$ 6.1	$ 5.0
Marketable securities	—	2.0	Accrued liabilities	3.6	3.3
Accounts and notes receivable	12.4	11.4	Current maturity of long-term debt	1.0	.8
Inventories	27.0	24.6	Federal income and other taxes	9.6	8.4
Total current assets	$ 48.4	$ 44.2	Dividends payable	1.3	1.1
			Total current liabilities	$ 21.6	$ 18.6
Property, Plant, and Equipment					
Buildings, machinery, and equipment, at cost	104.3	92.7	**Other Liabilities**		
Less accumulated depreciation	27.6	25.0	Long-term debt	3.6	2.5
	$ 76.7	$ 67.7	5% sinking-fund debentures, due July 31, 1990	26.0	20.0
Land, at cost	.9	.7			
Total property, plant, and equipment	$ 77.6	$ 68.4	**Stockholders' Equity**		
			5% cumulative preferred stock ($100 par: authorized and outstanding, 60,000)	6.0	6.0
Other Assets			Common stock ($10 par: authorized, 2,000,000; outstanding, 1,830,000)	18.3	18.3
Receivables due after 1 year	4.7	3.9	Capital surplus	9.6	9.6
Surrender value of insurance	.2	.2	Retained earnings	46.4	42.2
Other	.6	.5	Total stockholders' equity	$ 80.3	$ 76.1
Total other assets	$ 5.5	$ 4.6			
Total Assets	$131.5	$117.2	**Total Liabilities and Stockholders' Equity**	$131.5	$117.2

notes describe the basis, generally cost or current market price, whichever is lower. To handle the additional business, these were up over those of the previous year.

PROPERTY, PLANT, AND EQUIPMENT

The land, structures, machinery and equipment, tools, motor vehicles, etc. Except for land, these assets have a limited useful life, and a deduction is taken from cost as depreciation. With a new plant, the total outlays were $11.6 million more, with depreciation up $2.6 million.

OTHER ASSETS

Identifiable property is valued at cost. Intangibles such as patents, copyrights, franchises, trademarks, or goodwill cannot be assessed accurately, so they are omitted from the computation of tangible net worth or book value.

If an increase in sales does not follow an increased investment, management may have

STATEMENT OF CHANGES IN FINANCIAL POSITION ($ millions)
"Your Company"

	DEC. 31 CURRENT YEAR	DEC. 31 LAST YEAR	DEC. 31 2 YEARS AGO
FUNDS PROVIDED			
Net income	$ 9.9	$ 9.5	$ 9.1
Changes not requiring working capital:			
Depreciation	2.6	3.5	2.3
Increase in other liabilities	1.1	2.0	1.4
Funds provided by operations	$13.6	$15.0	$12.8
Proceeds from long-term debt	7.0	—	—
Proceeds from sale of 5% cumulative preferred stock	—	6.0	—
Total funds provided	$20.6	$21.0	$12.8
FUNDS USED			
Additions to fixed assets	$11.8	$ .5	$ 6.2
Dividends paid on preferred stock	.3	.3	—
Dividends paid on common stock	5.4	4.6	4.6
Payments on long-term debt	1.0	15.0	—
Increase in noncurrent receivables	.8	.1	.3
Increase in other assets	.1	—	.2
Total funds used	$19.4	$20.5	$11.3
Increase in working capital	$ 1.2	$ .5	$ 1.5
CHANGES IN COMPONENTS OF WORKING CAPITAL			
Increase (decrease) in current assets:			
Cash	$ 2.8	$ 1.0	$ 1.1
Marketable securities	(2.0)	.5	.4
Accounts receivable	1.0	.5	.8
Inventories	2.4	1.0	1.3
Increase in current assets	$ 4.2	$ 3.0	$ 3.6
Increase in current liabilities:			
Accounts payable	$ 1.1	$ .9	$ .6
Accrued liabilities	.3	.5	.2
Current maturity of long-term debt	.2	.1	.5
Federal income and other taxes	1.2	1.0	.8
Dividends payable	.2	—	—
Increase in current liabilities	$ 3.0	$ 2.5	$ 2.1
Increase in working capital	$ 1.2	$ .5	$ 1.5

misjudged the ability to produce and/or sell more goods, or the industry may have reached overcapacity. If a company's plant and equipment show little change for several years during a period of expanding business, the shareholder should be cautious about the company's progressiveness. In this example, both fixed and total assets grew steadily.

LIABILITIES

Divided into two classes: current (payable within a year) and long-term (debt or other obligations that come due after 1 year from the balance sheet date).

➤ ACCOUNTS PAYABLE Money owed for raw materials, other supplies, and services.

➤ ACCRUED LIABILITIES Unpaid wages, salaries and commissions, interest, etc.

➤ CURRENT LONG-TERM DEBT Amount due in the next year. This usually requires annual repayments over a period of years.

➤ INCOME TAXES Accrued federal, state, and local taxes.

➤ DIVIDENDS PAYABLE Preferred or common dividends (or both) declared but not yet paid. Once declared, dividends become a corporate obligation.

➤ TOTAL CURRENT LIABILITIES An increase of $3 million needed to finance expansion of business.

➤ LONG-TERM DEBT What's due for payment in the future less the amount due in the next year. Although the total was reduced to $20 million, an additional $6 million of debentures was issued.

STOCKHOLD-ERS' EQUITY (or CAPITAL)

All money invested in the business by stockholders as well as reinvested earnings.

➤ PREFERRED STOCK Holders are usually entitled to dividends before common stockholders and to priority in the event of dissolution or liquidation. Dividends are fixed. If cumulative, no dividends can be paid on common stock until the preferred dividends are up to date.

Here each share of preferred was issued at $100, but its market value will move with the cost of money: up when interest rates decline, down when they rise.

➤ COMMON STOCK Shown on the books at par value, an arbitrary amount having no relation to the market value or to what would be received in liquidation.

➤ CAPITAL SURPLUS The amount of money received from the sale of stock in excess of the par value.

➤ RETAINED EARNINGS Money reinvested in the business.

➤ TOTAL STOCKHOLDERS' EQUITY The sum of the common par value, additional paid-in capital, and retained earnings less any premium attributable to the preferred stock: what the stockholders own. The increase of $4.2 million is a rise of about 5%—not bad, but not as much as should be the mark of a true growth company.

CHANGES IN FINANCIAL POSITION

This presents a different view of the financing and investing activities of the company and clarifies the disposition of the funds produced by operations. It includes both cash and other elements of working capital—the excess of current assets over current liabilities.

The balance sheet shows that the working capital has increased by $1.2 million (current assets of $48.4 million exceeded current liabilities of $21.6 million by $26.8 million at the end of the year versus $25.6 million the year before).

Sales and net income were up; the contribution to working capital from operations decreased to $13.6 million vs. $15 million the year before. This was narrowed to $.4 million by the proceeds of the $7 million in long-term debt, $1 million more than the proceeds from the sale of preferred stock the year before.

The difference between the funds used last year and the year before was $1.1 million, reflecting a heavier investment in productive capacity against a larger repayment of long-term debt the year before.

With increased capacity, the company should be able to handle higher sales. The additional cash may be a good sign, but when too much cash accumulates, it may indicate that management is not making the best use of its assets. In financially tense times, cash is still always welcome.

SEVEN KEYS TO VALUE

1 **Operating profit margin (PM)** The ratio of profit (before interest and taxes) to

KEYS TO VALUE

	CURRENT YEAR	PRIOR YEAR
1 Operating profit margin	19.5%	18.5%
2 Current ratio	2.24	2.38
3 Liquidity ratio	41.7%	44.1%
4 Capitalization ratios:		
Long-term debt	19.7%	20.8%
Preferred stock	6.0	6.3
Common stock and surplus	80.3	72.9
5 Sales to fixed assets	1.1	1.2
6 Sales to inventories	4.3	4.5
7 Net income to net worth	12.3%	12.5%

sales. As shown on the statement of income and retained earnings, the operating profit ($22.6) divided by sales ($115.8) equals 19.5%. This compares with 18.5% for the previous year. (Some analysts prefer to compute this margin without including depreciation and depletion as part of the cost, because these have nothing to do with the efficiency of the operation.)

When a company increases sales substantially, the PM should widen, because certain costs (rent, interest, property taxes, etc.) are pretty much fixed and do not rise in proportion to volume.

2   Current ratio   The ratio of current assets to current liabilities is calculated from the balance sheet: $48.4 ÷ $21.6 = 2.24:1. For most industrial corporations, this ratio should be about 2:1. It varies with the type of business. Utilities and retail stores have rapid cash inflows and high turnovers of dollars, so they can operate effectively with low ratios.

When the ratio is high, say 5:1, it may mean that the company has too much cash and is not making the best use of these funds. They should be used to expand the business. Such corporations are often targets for takeovers.

3   Liquidity ratio   Again referring to the balance sheet, the ratio of cash and equivalents to total current liabilities

($9 ÷ $21.6 = 41.7%). It should be used to supplement the current ratio, because the immediate ability of a company to meet current obligations or pay larger dividends may be impaired despite a high current ratio. This 41.7% liquidity ratio (down from 44.1% the year before) probably indicates a period of expansion, rising prices, heavier capital expenditures, and larger accounts payable. *If the decline persists, the company might have to raise additional capital.*

4   Capitalization ratios   The percentage of each type of investment as part of the total investment in the corporation. Though often used to describe only the outstanding securities, capitalization is the sum of the face value of bonds ($26.0) and other debts *plus* the par value of all preferred and common stock issues ($18.3 + 6.0 = $24.3) *plus* the balance sheet totals for capital surplus ($9.6) and retained earnings ($46.4).

Bond, preferred stock, and common stock ratios are useful indicators of the relative risk and leverage involved for the owners of the three types of securities. For most industrial corporations, the debt ratio should be no more than 66⅔% of equity, or 40% of total capital. Higher ratios are appropriate for utilities and transportation corporations.

In this instance, looking at the balance sheet, the long-term debt plus preferred stock ($26.0 + $6.0 = $32.0) is 87.2% of the $27.9 equity represented by the common stock ($18.3) and surplus ($9.6), and 30.1% of total capital.

5   Sales-to-fixed-assets ratio   Using both the statement of income and retained earnings and the balance sheet, this ratio is computed by dividing the annual sales ($115.8) by the year-end value of plant, equipment, and land before depreciation and amortization ($104.3 + $0.9 = $105.2). The ratio is therefore 1.1:1. This is down from 1.2:1 the year before.

This ratio helps to show whether funds used to enlarge productive facilities are being spent wisely. A sizable expansion in facilities should lead to larger sales volume. If it does not, there's something wrong. In this case, there were delays in getting production on stream at the new plant.

6   **Sales-to-inventories ratio** Again referring to both statements, you can compute this ratio by dividing the annual sales by year-end inventories: $115.8 ÷ $27 = 4.3:1. The year before, the ratio was 4.5:1.

This shows inventory turnover: the number of times the equivalent of the year-end inventory has been bought and sold during the year.

It is more important in analyzing retail corporations than in analyzing manufacturers. A high ratio denotes a good quality of merchandise and correct pricing policies. A declining ratio may be a warning signal.

7   **Net-income-to-net-worth (return on equity) ratio** One of the most significant of all financial ratios. Derived by dividing the net income from the statement of income and retained earnings ($9.9) by the total stockholders' equity from the balance sheet ($80.3). The result is 12.3%: the percentage of return that corporate management earned on the dollars entrusted by shareholders at the beginning of each year. Basically, it's that all-important PR (profit rate).

This 12.3% is a slight decrease from the 12.5% of the prior year. It's a fair return: not as good as that achieved by a top-quality corporation but better than that of the average publicly held company. *The higher the ratio, the more profitable the operation.* Any company that can consistently improve such a ratio is a true growth company. *But be sure that this gain is a result of operating skill, not of accounting legerdemain or extraordinary items.*

RATIOS AND TRENDS

Detailed financial analysis involves careful evaluation of income, costs, and earnings. But it is also important to study various ratios and trends, both those within the specific corporation and those of other companies in the same industry. Analysts usually prefer to use 5- or 10-year averages. These can reveal significant changes

and, on occasion, point out special values in either concealed or inconspicuous assets.

➤ OPERATING RATIO The ratio of operating costs to sales. It is the complement of *profit margin* (100% minus the PM percentage). Thus if a company's PM is 10%, its operating ratio is 90%. It's handy for comparing similar companies but not significant otherwise.

PMs vary with the type of business. They are low for companies with heavy plant investments (Ingersoll-Rand) and for retailers with fast turnovers (The Limited) and high for marketing firms (Gillette).

➤ INTEREST COVERAGE The number of times interest charges or requirements have been earned. Divide the operating profit (or balance available for such payments before income taxes and interest charges) by the annual interest charges.

According to the statement of income and retained earnings, the interest (fixed charges) was covered 17.4 times in the past year and 20.3 times in the previous year. This is a high, safe coverage. If earnings declined to only 6% of the past year's results, interest would still be covered. As a rule, a manufacturing company should cover interest 5 times; utilities, 3 times.

Keep in mind that when a company (except utilities or transportation firms) has a high debt, it means that investors shy away from buying its common stock. To provide the plants, equipment, etc., that the company needs, management must issue bonds or preferred shares (straight or convertible to attract investors). There are some tax advantages in following such a course, but when the debt becomes too high, there can be trouble during times of recession. All or most of the gross profits will have to be used to pay interest, and there will be nothing or little left over for the common stockholders.

By contrast, speculators like high-debt situations when business is good. With hefty profits, interest can be paid easily, and the balance comes down to the common stock. Typically, airlines with heavy debt obligations for new planes do well in boom times. An extra 10% gain in traffic can boost profits by as much as 30%.

➤ PAYOUT RATIO The ratio of the cash dividends to per-share profits after taxes. Fast-growing corporations pay no or small dividends because they need money for expansion. Profit-

COMPANIES WITH STRONG CASH FLOWS	
COMPANY NAME	LINE OF BUSINESS
Abbott Laboratories	Health care products
Bristol-Myers Squibb	Drugs
Calgon Carbon Corp.	Activated carbons
A.G. Edwards & Sons	Securities broker
Federal Signal Corp.	Signal manufacturer
Gibson Greetings Inc.	Greeting cards
J.M. Smucker Co.	Jams, jellies
Tootsie Roll Industries	Candy

able companies pay out from about 25% to 50% of their profits. Utilities, which have almost assured earnings, pay out more. But be wary when those dividends represent much more than 70% of income.

It's pleasant to receive an ample dividend check, but for growth, look for companies that pay small dividends. The retained earnings will be used to improve financial strength and the operating future of the company. *And they are tax-free.*

➤ PRICE-TO-BOOK-VALUE RATIO The market price of the stock divided by its book value per share. Since book value trends are usually more stable than earnings trends, conservative analysts use this ratio as a price comparison. They check the historical over- or undervaluation of the stock, which in turn depends primarily on the company's profitable growth (or lack of it).

Because of inflation, understatement of assets on balance sheets—and, in boom times, the enthusiasm of investors—often pushes this ratio rather high. On the average, only stocks of the most profitable companies sell at much more than twice book value. Investors believe that these corporations will continue to achieve ever-higher earnings. But if the stock prices rise too high, their decline, in a bear market, can be fast and far.

➤ PRICE-EARNINGS (P/E) RATIO Calculated by dividing the price of the stock by the reported earnings per share for the past 12 months. Such projections can be made *only* for stocks of quality corporations with long, fairly consistent records of profitable growth. They will not work for shares of companies that are cyclical, erratic, or untested. There can be no guarantee that these goals will be attained as soon as anticipated. Wall Street is often slow to recognize value and always takes time to come to intelligent decisions.

➤ CASH FLOW A yardstick that is increasingly popular in investment analysis. Reported net earnings after taxes do not reflect the actual cash income available to the company. Cash flow shows the earnings after taxes *plus* charges against income that do not directly involve cash outlays (sums allocated to depreciation, depletion, amortization, and other special items).

A company might show a net profit of $250,000 plus depreciation of $1 million, so cash flow is $1,250,000. Deduct provisions for preferred dividends (if any), and then divide the balance by the number of shares of common stock to get the cash flow per share.

Two types of cash flow are important:

- *Distributable cash flow:* the amount of money that the company has on hand to pay dividends and/or invest in real growth. If this is negative, there are problems. If it's positive, fine, *unless* the company pays out more than this figure in dividends and is thus liquidating the firm.
- *Discretionary cash flow:* distributable cash flow minus dividends, that is, how much money is left to grow with, after allocations for maintenance and dividends. Companies do not actually set aside such funds, but they must ultimately have the money in some form—cash savings or borrowing.

HOW TO DETERMINE A PRUDENT P/E RATIO

Analysts usually justify their recommendations by adjusting the multiple of the price of the stock by estimated rate of future growth or by cash flow per share rather than by reported earnings. In both cases, these are attempts to justify a predetermined decision to buy. The projections appear plausible, especially when accompanied by tables and charts and computer printouts. But in most cases, they are useful only as background and not for the purpose of making decisions on the proper level to buy or later to sell. The calculations depend a good deal on market conditions and your own style, but here's one approach for those "supergrowth" stocks that will be suggested by your friends or broker.

Example: According to your financial adviser, the stock of a "future" company now selling at 40 times its recent earnings will be trading at "only 16 times its projected earnings 5 years hence *if* the company's average earnings growth is 20% a year." (See price evaluator, page 367.)

If you are speculating with this type of "hot" stock, you should compare it with other opportunities and on some basis decide how reasonable this projection really is.

A handy formula is

Prudent P/E ratio = GRTQM

G = growth
R = reliability and risk
T = time
Q = quality
M = multiple of price to earnings

➤ GROWTH The company's projected growth in earnings per share over the next 5 years. The basic compound interest formula is $(1 + G)^5$, where G is the projected growth rate, as shown in the price evaluator and prudent P/E multiples table. This omits dividend yields because they are usually small in relation to the potential capital appreciation.

➤ RELIABILITY AND RISK Not all projected growth rates are equally reliable or probable. A lower projected growth rate is likely to be more reliable than a very high projected one (30% to 50% a year).

Logically, you can assign a higher reliability rating to a noncyclical company (utility, food processor, retailer) than to a corporation in a cyclical industry (aluminum, machinery, tools).

➤ TIME Another factor is the assumed length of the projected growth period. If you can realistically anticipate that the company will continue its rate of growth for the next 10 years, a 10% rate for its stock is more reliable than a 15% rate for a company whose growth visibility is only 3 to 5 years.

If you are uncertain about the corporation's consistency, you should assign it the greater risk.

➤ QUALITY As you know, this is the single most important investment consideration.

➤ MULTIPLE OF PRICE TO EARNINGS This is a comparative measurement. The first step is to determine the P/E for an average quality nongrowth stock. This is done by relating the current yield on guaranteed, fixed-income investments (savings accounts, corporate bonds) to the P/E multiple that will produce the same yield on the nongrowth stock.

$$P/E = \frac{D}{IR}$$

P/E = price/earnings ratio
D = dividend as percentage payout of earnings
IR = interest rate

Thus a stock yielding 8% on a 70% payout of profits must, over a 5-year period, be bought and sold at 7 times earnings to break even on capital and to make as much income as could be obtained over the same period via the ownership of a fixed-income investment continually yielding 10%:

$$P/E = \frac{7}{10} = .7$$

Note: This is *not* a valid comparison in terms of investment alone. Since the nongrowth stock carries a certain amount of risk in comparison to the certainty of a bond or money market fund, the stock should sell at a lower multiple, probably 5 to 6 times earnings.

Other key items used in analysis are:

➤ EARNINGS GROWTH RATE A formula that gives the rate at which a company's profits have increased over the past several years. You can find the earnings growth rate in annual reports or from your broker. Then divide it by the P/E and compare this number with the Standard & Poor's 500 to decide whether to buy or sell. Keep in mind that in good years the average growth rate for the Standard & Poor's 500 stock index has been 16% and the average P/E 8, so the index for the purposes of this formula should be divided by 2.

For example, let us assume that Company XYZ has an earnings growth rate of 40% per year. Its P/E is 20; its index is therefore 2, only equal to the Standard & Poor's average—nothing to get excited about.

PRUDENT PRICE-EARNINGS MULTIPLES FOR GROWTH STOCKS

IF YOU PROJECT EARNINGS PER SHARE (AFTER TAXES) TO GROW IN NEXT 5 YEARS AT AN AVERAGE COMPOUNDED RATE OF:	WITH THESE QUALITY RATINGS* THESE ARE APPROXIMATE PRUDENT MULTIPLES THAT REPRESENT THE MAXIMUM CURRENT PRICE TO PAY:				
	B	B+	A−	A	A+
5%	12.0	12.9	13.7	15.0	16.7
6%	12.5	13.4	14.3	15.8	17.4
7%	13.0	14.0	14.9	16.5	18.2
8%	13.6	14.5	15.6	17.1	18.9
9%	14.1	15.1	16.2	17.8	19.7
10%	14.6	15.7	16.8	18.5	20.4
15%	17.4	18.7	20.1	22.0	24.5
20%	20.2	21.8	23.4	25.7	28.6
25%	23.0	24.7	26.6	29.3	32.7
30%	25.2	27.3	29.4	32.5	36.2
35%	28.5	31.0	33.5	37.1	41.5
40%	31.9	34.8	37.7	41.7	46.7

*Standard & Poor's designations. If not rated, use B; if a new, untested firm, use a conservative rating based on comparison with similar companies, preferably in the same industry.

Another company, the LMN Corporation, has an earnings growth rate of 40% also; however, its P/E is 15, so its index comes out to be 2.6. Because this ratio is above the Standard & Poor's index of 2, it is an apparent bargain.

➤ PERCENTAGE BUYING VALUE This is a variation of the formula developed by John B. Neff of the Windsor Fund. It uses the current yield plus the rate of earnings growth divided by the current P/E ratio. If the result is 2 or more, the stock is worth buying:

$$CY = \text{current yield}$$
$$EG = \text{earnings growth}$$
$$P/E = \text{price-earnings ratio}$$
$$PBV = \text{percentage buying value}$$

$$\frac{CY + EG}{P/E} = PBV$$

$$\frac{1.4 + 20}{22} = 9.7\% = \text{buy}$$

$$\frac{8.6 + 2}{7.7} = 1.32\% = \text{sell or do not buy}$$

➤ RETURN ON EQUITY AND P/E: TOTAL RETURN Most investors tend to think about their gains and losses in terms of price changes and not dividends, whereas those who own bonds pay attention to interest yields and seldom focus on price changes. Both approaches are mistakes. Although dividend yields are obviously more important if you are seeking income, and changes in price play a greater role in growth stocks, knowing the *total return* on a stock makes it possible for you to compare your investment in a stock with a similar investment in a corporate bond, municipal, Treasury, mutual fund, etc.

To calculate the total return, add (or subtract) the stock's price change and the dividends received for 12 months and then divide that number by the price at the beginning of the 12-month period.

Example: An investor bought a stock at $42 per share and received dividends for the 12-month period of $2.50. At the end of 12 months, the stock was sold at $45. The total return was 13%.

Dividend	$2.50
Stock price change	$3.00
	$5.50 ÷ $42 = 13%

➤ CORPORATE CASH POSITION Developed by Benjamin Graham, granddaddy of fundamentalists.

- Subtract current liabilities, long-term debt, and preferred stock (at market value) from current assets of the corporation.
- Divide the result by the number of shares of common stock outstanding to get the current asset value per share.
- If it is higher than the price per share, Graham would place the stock on his review list.

CHECKPOINTS FOR FINDING UNDERVALUED STOCKS

- A price that is well below book value, asset value, and working capital per share
- Ample cash or liquid assets for both normal business and expansion
- A current dividend of 4.5% or more
- Cash dividends paid for at least 5, and preferably 10, years without decrease in dollar payout
- Total debt less than 30% of total capitalization

STOCKS SELLING AT MODEST P/E RATIOS

COMPANY	SYMBOL	PRICE	P/E
Avnet Inc.	AVT	$32	15.0
Bell Atlantic	BEL	55	16.5
Boeing Co.	BA	38	10.0
Chemical Banking	CHL	40	8.2
Chemical Waste Mgmt	CHW	13	19.0
Chrysler	C	40	10.5
Eastman Kodak	EK	55	16.0
Raymond James	RJF	24	7.6
Raytheon Co.	RTN	58	11.5
Reliance Group	REL	7	6.6

(As of May 1993.)

- Minimum current dividend protection ratio of at least 1:4 ($1.40 earnings for each $1.00 in dividends), preferably higher
- A P/E ratio lower than that of prior years and preferably below 10 times projected 12-month earnings
- A company that sells at 4 or 5 times cash flow and that generates excess cash, which can be used to expand or repurchase its stock
- Inventories that are valued lower than their initial cost or their immediate market value (check Value Line or S&P for figures)

LOW P/Es PAY OFF

Investors often get excited about stocks with high P/Es. They figure the stocks are so popular that their prices will keep on rising. But the facts prove otherwise: Stocks with low P/Es (seemingly those with the worst prospects) outperform those with high multiples.

Low P/Es are often found in mature industries, in low-growth and blue chip companies. In general, low-P/E companies pay higher dividends, although there are many exceptions.

High P/Es, by contrast, tend to be found in newer, aggressive growth companies, which are far riskier than those with lower P/Es.

$ HINT: Look for companies with high sales per share in cyclical industries (auto, aluminum, rubber) that are temporarily depressed. When industry conditions change and profit margins increase, the turnaround in earnings can be dramatic.

COMPANIES REPURCHASING THEIR STOCK

When corporations set up a program to buy back their shares, it's a bullish sign. Over a 12-month period, one survey showed, 64% of such stock outpaced the market.

Repurchase of a substantial number of shares automatically benefits all shareholders: Profits are spread over a smaller total, there's more money for dividends and reinvestments, and there's a temporary price increase for the stock in many cases.

FOR FURTHER INFORMATION

Charles H. Brandes, *Value Investing Today* (Homewood, IL: Dow Jones–Irwin, 1989).

Rose Marie Bukics, *Financial Statement Analysis* (Chicago: Probus Publishing Co., 1992).

Technical analysis (TA) is a way of doing securities research using indicators, charts, and computer programs to track price trends of stocks, bonds, commodities, and the market in general. Technical analysts use these indicators to predict price movements.

If you understand the basics of both technical and fundamental analysis, you'll have a great advantage as an investor.

TA is neither as complex nor as esoteric as many people think. It's a tell-it-as-it-is interpretation of stock market activity. The technician glances at the fundamental values of securities but basically concentrates on the behavior of the market, industry groups, and stocks themselves—their price movements, volume, trends, patterns; in sum, their supply and demand.

Basically, TA is concerned with what *is* and not with what *should be.* Dyed-in-the-wool technicians pay minimal attention to what the *company* does and concentrate on what its *stock* does. They recognize that over the short term, the values of stocks reflect what people *think* they are worth, not what they are really worth.

Technical analysts operate on the assumption that (1) the past action of the stock market is the best indicator of its future course, (2) 80% of a stock's price movement is due to factors outside the company's control and 20% to factors unique to that stock, and (3) the stock market over a few weeks or months is rooted 85% in psychology and only 15% in economics.

THE DOW THEORY

There are a number of technical theories, but the granddaddy is the Dow theory. It is the oldest and most widely used. As with all technical approaches, it is based on the belief that stock prices cannot be forecast accurately by fundamental analysis but that trends, indicated by price movements and volume, can be used successfully. These can be recorded, tracked, and interpreted because the market itself prolongs movements: Investors buy more when the market is rising and sell more when it's dropping.

This follow-the-crowd approach enables the pros to buy when the market is going up and to sell or sell short when the market turns down. For amateurs, such quick trading is costly because of the commissions involved and the need for accurate information. But when properly used, TA can be valuable in correctly timing your buy and sell positions.

The Dow theory is named after Charles H. Dow, one of the founders of Dow Jones & Company, Inc., the financial reporting and publishing organization. The original hypotheses have been changed somewhat by his followers, but broadly interpreted, the Dow theory signals both the beginning and end of bull and bear markets.

Dow believed the stock market to be a barometer of business. The purpose of his theory was not to predict movements of security prices but rather to call the turns of the market and to forecast the business cycle or longer movements of depression or prosperity. It was not concerned with ripples or day-to-day fluctuations.

The Dow theory basically states that once a trend of the Dow Jones Industrial Average (DJIA) has been established, it tends to follow the same direction until definitely canceled by *both* the Industrial and Railroad (now Transportation) Averages. The market cannot be expected to produce new indications of the trend every day, and unless there is positive evidence to the contrary, the existing trend will continue.

Dow and his disciples saw the stock market as made up of two types of "waves": the *primary*

TECHNICAL VS. FUNDAMENTAL ANALYSIS

Technical analysis focuses on the changes of a company's stock as illustrated on daily, weekly, or periodic charts. Volume or number of shares traded is included, and from this "technical" information future price movements are forecast.

Fundamental analysis of industries and companies, by contrast, centers on the outlook for earnings and growth. Analysts study such factors as sales, assets, earnings, products, services, potential markets, and management.

wave, which is a bull or bear market cycle of several years' duration, and the *secondary* (or *intermediary*) *wave,* which lasts from a few weeks to a few months. Any single primary wave may contain within it 20 or more secondary waves, both up and down.

The theory relies on similar action by the two averages (Industry and Transportation), which may vary in strength but not in direction. Robert Rhea, who expanded the original concept, explained it this way: "Successive rallies, penetrating preceding high points with ensuing declines terminating above preceding low points, offer a bullish indication . . . (and vice versa for bearish indication). . . . A rally or decline is defined as one or more daily movements resulting in a net reversal of direction exceeding 3% of either average. Such movements have little authority unless confirmed by both Industrial and Transportation Averages . . . but confirmation need not occur in the same day."

Dow did not consider that his theory applied to individual stock selections or analysis. He expected that specific issues would rise or fall with the averages most of the time, but he also recognized that any particular security would be affected by special conditions or situations.

These are the key indicators of the Dow theory:

- **A bull market is signaled as a possibility** when an intermediate decline in the DJIA stops above the bottom of the previous

intermediate decline. This action *must be confirmed* by the action of the Transportation Average (DJTA). A bull market is confirmed after this has happened and when on the next intermediate rise *both* averages rise above the peaks of the last previous intermediate rise.

- **A bull market is in progress** as long as each new intermediate rise goes *higher* than the peak of the previous intermediate advance and each new intermediate decline stops *above* the bottom of the previous one.

- **A bear market is signaled as a possibility** when an intermediate rally in the DJIA fails to break through the top of the previous intermediate rise. A bear market is *confirmed* (1) after this has happened, (2) when the next intermediate decline breaks through the low of the previous one, and (3) when it is confirmed by the DJTA.

- **A bear market is in progress** as long as each new intermediate decline goes *lower* than the bottom of the previous decline and each new intermediate rally fails to rise as high as the previous rally.

A pure Dow theorist considers the averages to be quite sufficient to use in forecasting and sees no need to supplement them with statistics of commodity prices, volume of production, car loadings, bank debts, exports, imports, etc.

➤ INTERPRETING THE DOW THEORY The Dow theory leaves no room for sentiment.

A primary bear market does not terminate until stock prices have thoroughly discounted the worst that is apt to occur. This decline requires three steps: (1) "the abandonment of hopes upon which stocks were purchased at inflated prices," (2) selling due to decreases in business and earnings, and (3) distress selling of sound securities despite value.

Primary bull markets follow the opposite pattern: (1) a broad movement, interrupted by secondary reactions averaging longer than 2 years, where successive rallies penetrate high points with ensuing declines terminating above preceding low points; (2) stock prices advancing because of demand created by both investors and speculators who start buying when business conditions improve; and (3) rampant speculation as stocks advance on hopes, expectations, and dreams.

$HINT: A new primary trend is not actually confirmed by the Dow theory until *both* the DJTA and the DJIA penetrate their previous positions.

➤ CRITICISM There are analysts who scoff at the Dow theory. They point out that the stock market today is vastly different from that in the early 1900s when Dow formulated his theory. The number and value of shares of publicly owned corporations have increased enormously: In 1900, the average number of shares traded *annually* on the NYSE was 59.5 million. Now that's the volume on a very slow *day.*

The sharpest criticism is leveled against the breadth, scope, and significance of the averages. The original Industrial index had only 12 stocks, and today's 30 large companies do not provide a true picture of the broad, technologically oriented economy. Critics point out that the Transportation Average is also unrepresentative, because some of the railroads derive a major share of their revenues from natural resources, and the airlines and trucking companies are limited in their impact. Add the geographic dispersal of industry, and Transportation is no longer a reliable guide to the economy.

Finally, the purists argue that government regulations and institutional dominance of trading have so altered the original concept of individual investors that the Dow theory can no longer be considered all-powerful and always correct.

To most investors, the value of the Dow theory is that it represents a sort of think-for-yourself method that will pay worthwhile dividends for those who devote time and effort to gaining a sound understanding of the principles involved.

➤ WHAT'S AHEAD In July 1993, Richard Russell, publisher of the newsletter *Dow Theory Letters,* and the leading authority on the Dow theory, told his readers, "Two new stock groups (have) turned up from below zero, *money center banks* and *electric utilities.* Note that both these groups are interest-rate sensitive. In order of strength, the leaders in banks are: Citicorp, Bank of New York, Bankers Trust, Chemical Bank, Republic of New York. As for the electrics, they are, in order of strength: General Public Utilities,

Consolidated Edison, Niagara Mohawk, American Electric Power, Philadelphia Electric, Duke Power, and Central and Southwest. All yield over 5%."

Russell also noted a small "yet quiet and persistent move *out* of financial assets and into tangible (real) assets, (such as) diamonds and gold." He lists the gold stocks in order of strength as: American Barrick, Placer Dome, Pegasus Gold, Echo Bay Mines and Homestake. (*Source: Dow Theory Letters.*, P.O. Box 1759, La Jolla, CA 92038; $250 per year.)

PSYCHOLOGICAL INDICATORS

Keeping in mind that the stock market is rooted 15% in economics and 85% in psychology, some analysts predict the future by using such technical indicators as these:

➤ BARRON'S CONFIDENCE INDEX (BCI) This is published weekly in the financial news magazine *Barron's.* It shows the ratio of the yield on 10 highest-grade bonds to the yield on the broader-based Dow Jones 40-bond average. The ratio varies from the middle 80s (bearish) to the middle 90s (bullish).

The theory is that the trend of "smart money" is usually revealed in the bond market before it shows up in the stock market. Thus, *Barron's Confidence Index* will be *high* when shrewd investors are confident and buy more lower-grade bonds, thus reducing low-grade bond yields, and *low* when they are worried and stick to high-grade bonds, thus cutting high-grade yields.

If you see that the BCI simply keeps going back and forth aimlessly for many weeks, you can probably expect the same type of action from the overall stock market.

➤ OVERBOUGHT-OVERSOLD INDEX (OOI) This is a handy measure, designed by *Indicator Digest,* of a short-term trend and its anticipated duration. Minor upswings or downturns have limited lives. As they peter out, experienced traders say that the market is "overbought" or "over-sold" and is presumably ready for a near-term reversal.

➤ GLAMOUR AVERAGE Another *Indicator Digest* special, this shows what is happening with the institutional favorites, usually trading at high multiples because of their presumed growth potential and current popularity (in a bull market). By and large, this is a better indicator for speculators than investors.

➤ SPECULATION INDEX This is the ratio of AMEX-to-NYSE volume. When trading in AMEX stocks (generally more speculative) moves up faster than that in NYSE (quality) issues, speculation is growing. It's time for traders to move in and for investors to be cautious.

BROAD-BASED INDICATORS

➤ ODD-LOT INDEX This shows how small investors view the market, because it concentrates on trades of fewer than 100 shares. The small investor is presumably "uninformed" (a somewhat debatable assumption) and so tends to follow established patterns: selling as the market rises; jumping in to pick up bargains when it declines. The signal comes when the odd lotter deviates from this "normal" behavior.

When the small investor distrusts a rally after a long bear market, that investor gives a bullish signal: Initial selling is normal, but when this continues, it's abnormal and a signal to the pros to start buying.

➤ MOVING AVERAGE LINES You can also watch the direction of a stock by comparing its price to a *moving average* (MA). A moving average is an average that's periodically updated by dropping the first number and adding in the last one. A 30-week moving average, for example, is determined by adding the stock's closing price for the current week to the closing prices of the previous 29 weeks and then dividing by 30. Over time, this moving average indicates the trend of prices.

A long-term moving average tends to smooth out short-term fluctuations and provides a basis against which short-term price movement can be measured.

Moving averages can be calculated for both individual stocks and all stocks in a group— say, all those listed on the NYSE or all in a particular industry. Technical analysts use a variety of time frames: 10 days, 200 days, 30 weeks, etc. In most cases they compare the moving average with a regular market average, usually the Dow Jones Industrial Average. For example:

■ As long as the DJIA is *above* the MA, the outlook is bullish.

■ As long as the DJIA is *below* the MA, the outlook is bearish.

■ A confirmed downward penetration of the MA by the base index is a *sell* signal.

■ A confirmed penetration of the MA is a *buy* signal.

Beware of false penetrations, and delay action until there is a substantial penetration (2% to 3%), upward or downward, within a few weeks. In other words, don't be in a hurry to interpret the chart action.

MAs are vulnerable to swift market declines, especially from market tops. By the time you get the signal, you may have lost a bundle, because prices tend to fall twice as fast as they rise.

If you enjoy charting, develop a ratio of the stocks selling above their 30-week MA. When the ratio is over 50% and trending upward, the outlook is bullish. When it drops below 50% and/or is trending down, there's trouble ahead.

$ HINT: The longer the time span of the MA, the greater the significance of a crossover

BY DOLLAR VOLUME

NAME	$VOL(THS)	CLOSE	CHANGE
IBM	698573	42¼	− 3⅜
TelefMex	601612	49⅜	+ 1⅜
Motorola	523507	88¼	+ 1¾
Sears	520517	50⅜	+ 4⅝
PhilipMor	495038	47⅜	− ⅜
GenElec	488125	97¾	− 2⅛
Merck	466867	32⅝	− ½
AmT&T	457922	63½	+ ⅜
Chrysler	450354	45	− ⅜
RoylDutchP	413020	92⅝	+ 2¼
Compaq	412845	50¼	+ 6½
GenMotor	405680	46¾	− 1
ColgatePalm	401782	X49½	− 4⅞
JohnsJohns	379272	38⅜	− ⅞
Citicorp	378872	31¾	
BrisMyrsSqb	350522	57	
Disney	343809	39¼	+ 1½
PepsiCo	321569	37¾	+ 2⅛
FordMotor	300019	52⅛	+ ¾
Exxon	299259	65⅛	+ 1⅝

SOURCE: Barron's, July 23, 1993.

signal. An 18-month chart is more reliable than a 30-day one.

➤ BUYING POWER   Buying power basically refers to the amount of money available to buy securities. It is determined by the cash in brokerage accounts plus the dollar amount that would be available if securities were fully margined. The bottom line: The market cannot rise above the available buying power.

The principle here is that at any point investors have only so much money available for investments. If it's in money market funds and cash, their buying power is stored up and readily available, not only to move into stocks but to push up prices. By contrast, if most investor buying power is already in stocks, there's little left for purchasing more stocks. In fact, in this situation investors could actually push the price of stocks down should they begin to sell.

Buying power is shown by these indicators:
- Rising volume in rallies. Investors are eager to buy, so the demand is greater than the supply, and prices go up.
- Shrinking volume on market declines. Investors are reluctant to sell.

With this technical approach, volume is the key indicator: It rises on rallies when the trend is up and rises on reactions when the trend is down.

§ HINT: Volume trends are apt to reverse before price trends. Shrinking volume almost always shows up before the top of a bull market and before the bottom of a bear market.

One other measure of buying power is the percentage of cash held in mutual funds. The Investment Company Institute in Washington, D.C., publishes this figure every month. In general, the ratio of cash to total assets in mutual funds tends to be low during market peaks, because this is the time when everyone is eager to buy stocks. The ratio is high during bull markets.

§ HINT: When cash holdings, as compiled by the Investment Company Institute, are above 7%, it's considered favorable; 9% to 10% is out-and-out bullish.

➤ MOST ACTIVE STOCKS   This list is published at the top of daily or weekly reports of the NYSE, AMEX, and NASDAQ, and it gives the high, low, and last prices and change of 10 to 15 volume leaders. Here's where you can spot popular and unpopular industry groups and stocks.

Forget about the big-name companies such as Exxon, GE, and IBM. They have so many shares outstanding that trading is always heavy. Watch for repetition: of one industry or of one company. When the same names appear several times in a week or two, something is happening. Major investors are involved: buying if the price continues to rise, selling if it falls.

Watch most-actives for:
- *Newcomers,* especially small- or medium-sized corporations. When the same company pops up again and again, major shareholders are worried (price drop) or optimistic (price rise). Since volume requires substantial resources, the buyers must be big-money organizations. Once they have bought, you can move in, *if* the other fundamentals are sound.
- *Companies in the same industry.* Stocks tend to move as a group. Activity in computer retailers such as IBM and Apple *could* signal interest in this field.

➤ PERCENTAGE LEADERS   This list is published weekly in several financial journals. It's primarily for those seeking to catch a few points on a continuing trend.

Although the value of the percentage leaders list has diminished recently because of the high gains scored by takeover or buyout candidates, it is still a way to spot some potential winners and to avoid losers. If you're thinking about making a move, check this list first. You may find several yet undiscovered stocks moving up in price.

➤ ADVANCES VERSUS DECLINES (A/D)   This is a measure of the number of stocks that have advanced in price and the number that have declined within a given time span. Expressed as a ratio, the A/D illustrates the general direction of the market: When more stocks advance than decline on a single trading day, the market is thought to be bullish. The A/D can be an excellent guide to the trend of the overall market and, occasionally, of specific industry or stock groups. The best way to utilize A/D data is with a chart where the lines are plotted to show the cumulative difference between the advances and the declines on the NYSE or, for speculative holdings, on the AMEX. The total can cover 1

NYSE BIGGEST % MOVERS

WINNERS

NAME	SALES	CLOSE	CHANGE	% CHG.
Valhi	95,300	$5\frac{3}{8}$	$+\ 1\frac{1}{8}$	$+\ 26.5$
DiagnstPdt	154,500	$21\frac{1}{2}$	$+\ 4\frac{1}{8}$	$+\ 23.7$
BoltBerNew	1,884,900	$9\frac{3}{4}$	$+\ 1\frac{3}{4}$	$+\ 21.9$
BrookeGp	226,200	$3\frac{3}{4}$	$+\ \frac{5}{8}$	$+\ 20.0$
DowneySL	308,400	$21\frac{5}{8}$	$+\ 3\frac{3}{8}$	$+\ 18.5$
FrptMcRes	1,798,900	$20\frac{1}{8}$	$+\ 3\frac{1}{8}$	$+\ 18.4$
McDonDoug	2,692,100	$84\frac{1}{2}$	$+\ 12\frac{1}{2}$	$+\ 17.4$
CrysBrnds	595,900	$2\frac{5}{8}$	$+\ \frac{3}{8}$	$+\ 16.7$
USAirGp	5,020,700	$17\frac{1}{4}$	$+\ 2\frac{3}{8}$	$+\ 16.0$
BaroidCp	1,420,800	$7\frac{1}{4}$	$+\ 1$	$+\ 16.0$
BannerAero	42,400	$5\frac{1}{2}$	$+\ \frac{3}{4}$	$+\ 15.8$
Compaq	8,631,800	$50\frac{1}{4}$	$+\ 6\frac{1}{2}$	$+\ 14.9$
OutbrdMar	627,800	$19\frac{3}{8}$	$+\ 2\frac{1}{2}$	$+\ 14.8$
UniCareFnl	419,000	22	$+\ 2\frac{3}{4}$	$+\ 14.3$
FairchldCp	104,700	4	$+\ \frac{1}{2}$	$+\ 14.3$
Datapoint	1,216,600	$7\frac{1}{8}$	$+\ \frac{7}{8}$	$+\ 14.0$
FisherPrice	923,400	$23\frac{1}{4}$	$+\ 2\frac{3}{4}$	$+\ 13.4$
CarterWal	760,000	$30\frac{1}{2}$	$+\ 3\frac{3}{8}$	$+\ 12.4$
TerraInd	1,192,500	$4\frac{5}{8}$	$+\ \frac{1}{2}$	$+\ 12.1$
SizzlerInt	370,400	$9\frac{3}{8}$	$+\ 1$	$+\ 11.9$

LOSERS

NAME	SALES	CLOSE	CHANGE	% CHG.
Portec	364,700	10	$-\ 3\frac{5}{8}$	$-\ 26.6$
ChinaTire	2,709,300	$13\frac{1}{4}$	$-\ 3\frac{3}{4}$	$-\ 22.1$
Unifi	4,369,200	$25\frac{1}{8}$	$-\ 6\frac{7}{8}$	$-\ 21.5$
Indresco	2,075,800	11	$-\ 3$	$-\ 21.4$
Amdura	46,100	$2\frac{1}{8}$	$-\ \frac{1}{2}$	$-\ 19.0$
DelValFnl	16,600	$1\frac{5}{8}$	$-\ \frac{3}{8}$	$-\ 18.8$
YorkInt	2,524,900	$32\frac{5}{8}$	$-\ 7\frac{3}{8}$	$-\ 18.4$
PHPHlthcare	109,600	7	$-\ 1\frac{1}{2}$	$-\ 17.6$
IntertanInc	1,483,600	$5\frac{1}{2}$	$-\ 1\frac{1}{8}$	$-\ 17.0$
AmShipBldg	13,600	$1\frac{7}{8}$	$-\ \frac{3}{8}$	$-\ 16.7$
Handleman	872,500	$10\frac{3}{4}$	$-\ 2\frac{1}{8}$	$-\ 16.5$
PaxarCp	587,700	16	$-\ 3$	$-\ 15.8$
HotelInvTr	58,500	2	$-\ \frac{3}{8}$	$-\ 15.8$
RalstonPur	1,848,100	39	$-\ 7$	$-\ 15.2$
Toastmstr	82,000	$5\frac{5}{8}$	$-\ 1$	$-\ 15.1$
NetwkEqpt	417,200	$7\frac{1}{8}$	$-\ 1\frac{1}{4}$	$-\ 14.9$
WMSInd	2,610,600	$23\frac{3}{8}$	$-\ 3\frac{7}{8}$	$-\ 14.2$
NoTelecm	3,467,100	$21\frac{3}{4}$	$-\ 3\frac{1}{2}$	$-\ 13.9$
PopeTalbot	710,600	$20\frac{7}{8}$	$-\ 3\frac{3}{8}$	$-\ 13.9$
Vencor	401,500	$26\frac{1}{4}$	$-\ 4\frac{1}{4}$	$-\ 13.9$

AMEX BIGGEST % MOVERS

WINNERS

NAME	SALES	CLOSE	CHANGE	% CHG.
IntrmagGen	2,179,900	$14\frac{1}{4}$	$+\ 5\frac{1}{4}$	$+\ 58.3$
PresRltyA	7,600	$6\frac{1}{2}$	$+\ 1\frac{3}{4}$	$+\ 36.8$
HlthProf	1,034,800	$3\frac{11}{16}$	$+\ \frac{15}{16}$	$+\ 34.1$
ECIEnvr	245,100	$3\frac{15}{16}$	$+\ 1$	$+\ 34.0$
PresRltyB	47,900	$6\frac{1}{4}$	$+\ 1\frac{9}{16}$	$+\ 33.3$
RxMed	319,900	4	$+\ \frac{7}{8}$	$+\ 28.0$
IntPwrMach	47,200	$2\frac{7}{8}$	$+\ \frac{9}{16}$	$+\ 24.3$
TuckerFA	82,800	$5\frac{7}{8}$	$+\ 1\frac{1}{8}$	$+\ 23.7$
LittlefldAd	331,800	14	$+\ 2\frac{1}{4}$	$+\ 19.1$
AngelesPtMtg	44,100	13	$+\ 2$	$+\ 18.2$
CIIFnl	75,200	$5\frac{7}{8}$	$+\ \frac{7}{8}$	$+\ 17.5$
DaxorCp	44,300	$6\frac{7}{8}$	$+\ 1$	$+\ 17.0$
GamaBio	21,200	$3\frac{5}{8}$	$+\ \frac{1}{2}$	$+\ 16.0$
UtdGuardn	16,700	$5\frac{5}{8}$	$+\ \frac{3}{4}$	$+\ 15.4$
Merimac	73,200	$9\frac{1}{8}$	$+\ 1\frac{1}{8}$	$+\ 14.1$
CoastDistr	88,200	$7\frac{5}{8}$	$+\ \frac{7}{8}$	$+\ 13.0$
JupiterNtl	62,200	35	$+\ 3\frac{7}{8}$	$+\ 12.4$
CSTEntmt	445,500	$2\frac{7}{8}$	$+\ \frac{5}{16}$	$+\ 12.2$
Middleby	4,500	$2\frac{3}{8}$	$+\ \frac{1}{4}$	$+\ 11.8$
BushInd	188,100	$15\frac{3}{4}$	$+\ 1\frac{5}{8}$	$+\ 11.5$

LOSERS

NAME	SALES	CLOSE	CHANGE	% CHG.
Medeva	2,582,400	$6\frac{3}{4}$	$-\ 6\frac{1}{4}$	$-\ 48.1$
AmRestrtPtrs	42,700	$10\frac{1}{2}$	$-\ 3\frac{1}{2}$	$-\ 25.0$
BakerMichael	98,500	$8\frac{7}{8}$	$-\ 2\frac{7}{8}$	$-\ 24.5$
Cognitron	121,400	$4\frac{1}{2}$	$-\ 1\frac{1}{4}$	$-\ 21.7$
ViralTest	355,800	$1\frac{11}{16}$	$-\ \frac{7}{16}$	$-\ 20.6$
BarrLabs	132,900	$15\frac{3}{4}$	$-\ 3\frac{5}{8}$	$-\ 18.7$
Tipperary	204,800	$4\frac{3}{16}$	$-\ \frac{15}{16}$	$-\ 18.3$
JanBellMkt	1,132,400	$9\frac{3}{4}$	$-\ 2\frac{1}{8}$	$-\ 17.9$
HondoO&G	252,200	$8\frac{1}{8}$	$-\ 1\frac{3}{4}$	$-\ 17.7$
RymacMtg	51,600	$1\frac{13}{16}$	$-\ \frac{3}{8}$	$-\ 17.1$
StlyesVideo	263,800	$17\frac{1}{4}$	$-\ 3\frac{3}{8}$	$-\ 16.4$
Xytronyx	179,100	$9\frac{7}{8}$	$-\ 1\frac{7}{8}$	$-\ 16.0$
PLCSys	112,800	$4\frac{1}{8}$	$-\ \frac{3}{4}$	$-\ 15.4$
CrossATA	245,600	$14\frac{3}{4}$	$-\ 2\frac{5}{8}$	$-\ 15.1$
BensonEyecr	114,400	$6\frac{3}{8}$	$-\ 1\frac{1}{8}$	$-\ 15.0$
TritonGpwi	5,000	$2\frac{1}{8}$	$-\ \frac{3}{8}$	$-\ 15.0$
Lumex	57,400	$12\frac{1}{8}$	$-\ 2\frac{1}{8}$	$-\ 14.9$
HalseyDrug	125,200	$4\frac{3}{8}$	$-\ \frac{3}{4}$	$-\ 14.6$
ColumbLabs	352,400	$3\frac{3}{4}$	$-\ \frac{5}{8}$	$-\ 14.3$
EdistoRes	143,500	9	$-\ 1\frac{1}{2}$	$-\ 14.3$

NASDAQ BIGGEST % MOVERS

WINNERS

NAME	SALES	CLOSE	CHANGE	% CHG.
GtSoBcp	61,400	43	+ 14	+ 48.3
VentCtyBcp	76,900	$3^1/_4$	+ $^3/_4$	+ 30.0
BachmnInfo	236,800	4	+ $^7/_8$	+ 28.0
WestportBcp	2,600	$3^1/_2$	+ $^3/_4$	+ 27.3
MedQuist	109,300	$5^7/_8$	+ $1^3/_4$	+ 27.0
MartinColor	527,200	$13^3/_4$	+ $2^3/_4$	+ 25.0
RotoRtr	91,300	$28^3/_4$	+ $5^3/_4$	+ 25.0
SportHero	57,300	$2^1/_2$	+ $^1/_2$	+ 25.0
BTRRlty	41,700	$3^3/_4$	+ $^3/_4$	+ 25.0
BTShip	99,300	$2^7/_8$	+ $^9/_{16}$	+ 24.3
Gencor	21,480	$8^3/_4$	+ $1^1/_2$	+ 24.0
Intrgroup	2,000	13	+ $2^1/_8$	+ 23.8
PacRimHldg	221,400	4	+ $^3/_4$	+ 23.1
CasinoData	965,600	$12^1/_4$	+ $2^1/_4$	+ 22.5
JGInd	2,000	$2^3/_4$	+ $^1/_2$	+ 22.2

LOSERS

NAME	SALES	CLOSE	CHANGE	% CHG.
Ezcorp	5,641,700	$10^1/_2$	− $10^1/_2$	− 50.0
AllstFnl	2,186,000	$7^1/_8$	− $6^3/_8$	− 47.2
ComrcBcpCA	41,800	2	− 1	− 33.3
CincMicrw	305,200	3	− $1^3/_8$	− 31.4
UnivSeism	96,300	$3^1/_{16}$	− $1^3/_{16}$	− 27.9
PanAtlRe	2,200	$6^1/_2$	− $2^1/_2$	− 27.8
WetSealA	234,200	$4^1/_4$	− $1^1/_2$	− 26.1
TapistronInt	476,200	6	− 2	− 25.0
RamapoFnl	9,000	$2^5/_8$	− $^7/_8$	− 25.0
Chemtrak	330,100	$6^1/_2$	− 2	− 23.5
CorpSftwr	316,400	$8^3/_4$	− $2^1/_2$	− 22.2
Intersolv	278,300	$5^1/_4$	− $1^1/_2$	− 22.2
FstAlbny	56,500	7	− 2	− 22.2
SaltonMaxim	44,000	$1^3/_4$	− $^1/_2$	− 22.2
SymTekSys	9,700	$2^3/_4$	− $^3/_4$	− 21.4

SOURCE: *Barron's*, July 23, 1993.

week, 21 days, or whatever period you choose, but because you're looking for developing trends, it should not be too long.

The table on page 376 shows a week when the advance/decline ratio was approximately 10 to 7, generally a positive trading day. On Wednesday, declines outnumbered advances by a small percentage, but new highs outnumbered new lows by a greater amount than on the prior day.

Many analysts prefer a moving average (MA) based on the net change for the week: 3,484 advances and 4,403 declines, for a net difference of 919. To make plotting easier, you can start with an arbitrary base, say 10,000, so the week's figure would be 9,081 (10,000 − 919).

The following week there's a net advance of 1,003, so the new total would be 10,084, etc. When you chart a 20-week MA, divide the cumulative figure by 20. When you add week 21, drop week 1. *Result:* a quick view of market optimism or pessimism.

To spot trouble ahead, compare the A/D chart with that of the DJIA. If the Dow is moving up for a month or so but the A/D line is flat or dropping, that's a negative signal. Watch out for new highs and lows on the A/D

chart. Near market peaks, the A/D line will almost invariably top out and start declining before the overall market. At market lows, the A/D line seldom gives a far-in-advance warning.

Be cautious about using the A/D line alone. Make sure that it is confirmed by other indicators or, better yet, confirms other signals.

▶ VOLUME Trading volume, or the number of

LONDON'S *FINANCIAL TIMES* INDEX

The *Financial Times* Index is a British version of the Dow Jones Industrial Average. It records data on the London Stock Exchange: prices, volume, etc. Because it reflects worldwide business attitudes, it's a fairly reliable indicator of what's ahead, in 2 weeks to 2 months, for the NYSE.

There are, of course, temporary aberrations due to local situations, but over many years it has been a valuable technical tool. Since London is 5 hours ahead of New York, early risers benefit the most.

shares traded, is an important indicator in interpreting market direction and stock price changes. Changes in stock prices are the result of supply and demand, that is, the number of people who want to buy a stock and the number who want to sell. The key point here is that a rise or fall in price on a small volume of shares traded is far less important than a move supported by heavy volume. When there's heavy trading on the up side, buyers control the market, and their enthusiasm for the stock often pushes its price even higher.

⑤ HINT: Volume always precedes the direction of a stock's price.

➤ MOMENTUM This indicator measures the speed with which an index (or stock) is moving rather than its direction. Index changes are seldom if ever abrupt, so when an already rising index starts to rise even faster, it is thought likely to have a longer continuing upward run.

To measure momentum effectively you need to compare current figures to an index or previous average such as a 30-week moving average or the S&P 500.

➤ NEW HIGHS OR LOWS Every day the newspaper prints a list of stocks that hit a new price high or low for the year during the previous day's trading activity. Technical analysts use the ratio between the new highs and the new lows as an indication of the market's direction. They believe that when more stocks are making new highs than new lows, it's a bullish indication. If there are more lows than highs, pessimism abounds.

⑤ HINT: You should not use these figures as an absolute prediction of the future course of the market, because for a while a number of the same stocks will appear again and again. Also, the further into the year it is, the more difficult it is for a stock to continually post new highs.

These figures are most effective when converted to a chart and compared with a standard average. As long as the high and low indicators stay more or less in step with the Dow Jones Industrial Average or the S&P 500, they are simply a handy confirmation. But when the high-low line starts to dip while the average moves up, *watch out:* Internal market conditions are deteriorating.

This index of highs and lows exposes the underlying strength or weakness of the stock

NYSE ADVANCES AND DECLINES: HIGHS AND LOWS

NYSE	WED	TUE	WK AGO
Issues traded	2,267	2,282	2,268
Advances	821	1,010	883
Declines	881	698	829
Unchanged	565	574	556
New highs	72	62	91
New lows	13	19	10

SOURCE: Wall Street Journal

market, which is too often masked by the action of the DJIA. In an aging bull market, the DJIA may continue to rise, deceptively showing strength by the upward moves of a handful of major stocks; but closer examination will usually reveal that most stocks are too far below their yearly highs to make new peaks. At such periods, the small number of new highs is one of the most significant manifestations of internal market deterioration. The reverse is the telltale manner in which the total number of new lows appears in bear markets.

USING THE INDICATORS

Never rely on just one technical indicator. Only rarely can a single chart, ratio, average, MA, or index be 100% accurate. When an indicator breaks its pattern, look for confirmation from at least two other guidelines. Then wait a bit: at least 2 days in an ebullient market, a week or more in a normal one. This won't be easy, but what you are seeking is confirmation. These days a false move can be costly.

This emphasis on consensus applies also to newsletters, advisory services, and recommendations. If you select only one, look for a publication that uses—and explains—several indicators. Better yet, study two or three.

CHARTS: A VALUABLE TOOL FOR EVERYONE

Charts are a graphic ticker tape. They measure the flow of money into and out of the stock market, industry, or specific stock. They spotlight the highs and lows and point up how volume rises and falls on an advance or decline, illustrating the long-term patterns of the market and individual stocks.

Charting is simple, but interpretation can be complex. Even the strongest advocates of technical analysis (TA) disagree about the meaning of various formations, but they all start with three premises: (1) what happened before will be repeated, (2) a trend should be assumed to continue until a reversal is definite, and (3) a chart pattern that varies from a norm indicates that something unusual is happening. More than almost any other area of TA, chart reading is an art and a skill rather than a solid body of objective scientific information. It is an aid to stock analysis but not an end.

Charts are not surefire systems for beating the market, but they are one of the quickest and clearest ways to determine and follow trends. But all charts provide after-the-fact information.

The best combination for maximum profits and minimum losses is fundamental analysis supplemented by graphic technical analysis. Charts report that volume and price changes occur. Proper interpretation can predict the direction and intensity of change, because every purchase of every listed stock shows up on the chart.

Watch the bottom of the chart as well as the progress lines. This shows volume, and *volume precedes price.* A strong inflow of capital eventually pushes up the price of the stock; an outflow of dollars must result in a decline. To the charted results, it makes no difference who is doing the buying or selling.

Keeping in mind that charts are not infallible. Use them to:

- **Help determine when to buy and when to sell** by indicating probable levels of support and supply and by signaling trend reversals
- **Call attention, by unusual volume or price behavior,** to something happening in an individual company that can be profitable to investors
- **Help determine the current trend:** up, down, or sideways, and whether the trend is accelerating or slowing
- **Provide a quick history of a stock** and

show whether buying should be considered on a rally or a decline
- **Offer a sound means for confirming or rejecting** a buy or sell decision that is based on other information

$ HINT: Charts are history. By studying past action, it is often possible to make a reasonably valid prediction of the immediate future.

WIDELY USED CHARTS

The most commonly used types of charts are point-and-figure (P&F) and bar charts. For best results, they should be constructed on a daily or weekly basis.

If you have time, charting can be fun and highly educational. All you need is a pad of graph paper: plain squares for P&F charts, logarithmic or standard paper for bar charts.

P&F CHARTS
P&F charts are one-dimensional graphics. They show only price changes in relation to previous price changes. There are no indications of time or volume. The key factor is the change in price direction.

Some professionals think that P&F charts are oversimplified and consider them useful only as short-term guides and as a quick way to choose between two or three selections.

In making a P&F chart, the stock price is posted in a square: one above or below another, depending on the upward or downward movement of the price. As long as the price continues in the same direction, the same column is used. When the price shifts direction, the chartist moves to the next column.

In the chart shown on page 378, the stock first fell in a downward sequence from 68 to 67 to 66. Then it rose to 67, so the chartist moved to column 2. The next moves were down to 62, up to 63 (new column), and so on. Most chartists start the new column only when there is a distinct change, typically 1 point, but for longer projections, 2 or 3 points.

Note how a pattern is formed with various resistance levels where the price of the stock stayed within a narrow range (57–56 and later 48–47). The chart signals each shift from such a base: down from 56 to 51; up from 47 to 52.

The best way for an amateur to learn about

POINT AND FIGURE CHART

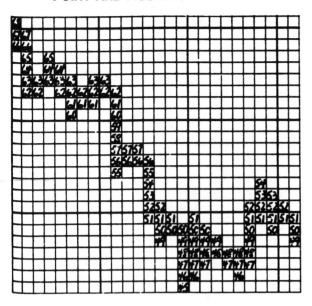

BAR CHART

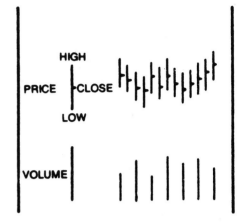

P&F charts is to copy them. Take a stock that has been plotted for many years and slowly recopy its action on a piece of graph paper. Then draw in the trend lines: the uptrend line on the high points, the downtrend line along the low points. Then draw your channels, which are broad paths created by the highs and lows of a definite trend. (Without a trend your channel will be horizontal.)

P&F charts have disadvantages: They do not portray intraday action or consider volume. The financial pages report only the high (62), low (59¼), and close (61½). This does not show that the stock might have moved up and down from 60 to 62 several times during the day.

Despite the omission of volume on P&F charts, many technical analysts feel that volume should always be checked once there is a confirmed trend on the chart. Rising volume on upward movements and dwindling sales on the downside usually indicate that the stock has ample investor support. It's always wise to be on the same side as volume.

BAR CHARTS
These graphics record changes in relation to time. The horizontal axis represents time—a day, week, or month; the vertical coordinates refer to price. To follow volume on the same chart, add a series of

vertical lines along the bottom. The higher the line, the greater the volume. On printed charts, adjustments are made so that everything fits into a convenient space.

In plotting a bar chart, enter a dot to mark the highest price at which the stock was traded that day; add another dot to record the low. Draw the vertical line between the dots to depict the price range, and draw a short horizontal nub to mark the closing price. After a few entries, a pattern will begin to emerge.

HEAD-AND-SHOULDER CHARTS
Almost every chartist has favorite configurations. They include such descriptive titles as the rounding bottom, the flag, the pennant, the tombstone top, the Prussian helmet formation, the megaphone top, and the lattice formation. One of the most popular formations is *head and shoulders* (H&S).

Oversimplified, the head-and-shoulders chart portrays three successive rallies and reactions, with the second reaching a higher point than either of the others. The failure of the third rally to equal the second peak is a warning that a major uptrend may have come to an end. Conversely, a bottom H&S, formed upside down after a declining trend, suggests that an upturn lies ahead.

➤ LEFT SHOULDER This forms when an upturn of some duration, after hitting a climax, starts to fall. The volume of trading should increase with the rally and contract with the reaction. *Reason:* People who bought the stock on the up-

HEAD-AND-SHOULDERS CHART

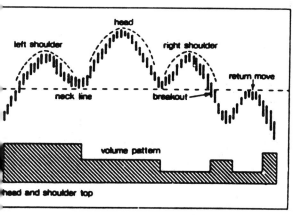

trend start to take profits. When the technical reaction takes place, people who were slow to buy on the first rally start buying on the technical reaction.

➤ HEAD This is a second rally that carries the stock to new highs and is followed by a reaction that erases just about all the gain. Volume is high on the rally, yet lower than when forming the left shoulder. *Reason:* Investors who missed both the earlier actions start buying and force new highs.

This is followed by another drop as those who hesitated earlier see the second reaction and start acquiring the stock as it is sold by early buyers.

➤ RIGHT SHOULDER The third rally fails to reach the height of the head before the reaction. This is a sign of weakness. Watch the volume. If it contracts on a rally, it's likely that the price structure has weakened. If it increases, beware of a false signal.

➤ BREAKOUT This occurs when the stock price falls below the previous lows. At this point, most of the recent buyers have sold out—many of them at a loss.

No H&S should be regarded as complete until the price breaks out below a line drawn tangent with the lows on the left and right shoulders. This is called the neckline.

INTERPRETING CHARTS

The charts from Securities Research Company (SRC) shown at right and on page 380 are typical of those available from technical services. They can be valuable tools to improve the selection of securities and especially the timing of purchases and sales. Similar graphics are available for industry groups and stock market averages.

Do *not* buy any stock when the chart shows a confirmed downtrend. Buy *up* stocks in *up* groups in an *up* market. And unless you are holding for the long term, consider selling when there's a downtrend in the stock, the industry, and the market.

SRC offers two books of charts on stocks: blue for long-term trends over 12 years, red for short-term trends over 21 months. By using both, you get a better idea of the character, history, and probable performance of the stock.

LONG-TERM CHARTS

Ⓐ CAPITALIZATION Information on the corporation: dollars of bonds and preferred stocks (in millions); number of common shares outstanding (in thousands); and book value per common share.

Ⓑ EARNINGS AND DIVIDENDS Per-share data scaled from $1.40 to $5.50.

Ⓒ DIVIDENDS The annual rate of interim divi-

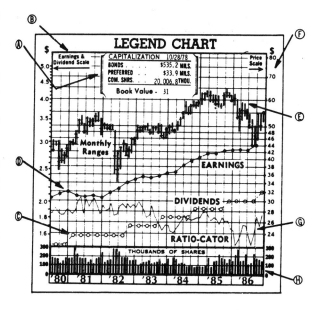

SOURCE: Securities Research Company, A Division of United Business Service Company, 208 Newbury Street, Boston, MA 02116.

dend payments. The circles mark the month in which the payments were made. Extra or irregular payouts (not shown) are typed in.

Ⓓ EARNINGS On a per-share 12-month-ended basis as shown by the solid black line. Dots indicate whether the company issues quarterly, semiannual, or annual earnings reports.

Ⓒ MONTHLY RANGES Shows the highest and lowest prices for the stock each month. Crossbars indicate the closing price.

Ⓕ PRICE SCALE This shows the dollar price of the stock, against which the monthly ranges are plotted.

Ⓖ RATIO-CATOR A guideline used by SRC. The plottings are obtained by dividing the closing price of the stock by the closing value of the DJIA on the same day. The resulting percentage is multiplied by a factor of 4.5 to bring the line close to the price bars and is read from the right-hand scale. The plotting indicates whether the stock has kept pace, outperformed, or lagged behind the general market.

Ⓗ VOLUME The number of shares traded, in thousands, each month on an arithmetic scale. Volume comes before price.

SHORT-TERM CHARTS

Here the data are similar to those of the longer-term charts but cover the action for only 21 months.

➤ EARNINGS For the last 12 months. Read from the left border to find the changes in dollar-per-share profits.

➤ DIVIDENDS On an annual basis; ✕ indicates the ex-dividend date, ◯, the dividend payment date.

➤ MOVING AVERAGE FOR 39 WEEKS Each dot represents the average of the closing prices of the 39 most recent weeks. When used with the price bars, it helps you determine trends as well as buying and selling points.

➤ RATIO-CATOR Shows the relative performance of the stock. It is calculated by dividing the closing price of the stock by the closing value of the DJIA on the same day and then multiplying by 7.0.

Note: In plotting the short-term chart, the price range, earnings, and dividends are shown on a uniform ratio scale: that is, the vertical linear distance for a 100% move is the same any place on the chart regardless of whether

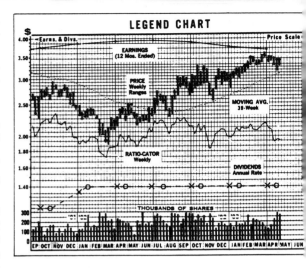

SOURCE: Securities Research Company, A Division of United Business Service Company, 208 Newbury Street, Boston, MA 02116.

the rise was from $5 to $10 or from $20 to $40. Thus all charts of all stocks are comparable.

USING TREND LINE CHARTS

The key to the successful use of charts, and most technical analysis, is the premise that *a trend in force will persist until a significant change in investor expectations causes it to reverse itself*—or as Martin Pring puts it, "on the assumption that people will continue to make the same mistakes they have made in the past." To discern that trend, the chartist draws lines connecting the lowest points of an upward-moving stock and the highest points of a downward-moving stock. This trend line is a reliable indicator about 80% of the time, because it predicts the immediate action of the stock or market.

The shrewd investor rises with the trend: buying when there's a confirmed upward move, considering selling when there's a definite downswing. Generally, the stock will move along that line—regardless of the direction. There will be interim bounces or dips, but most stocks hold to that pattern until there is a clear change.

Trend lines establish bases. The uptrend line becomes a support level below which an upward-moving stock is not likely to fall. The downtrend line marks a resistance level above which the stock is not likely to rise.

$ HINT: Before you invest—or speculate—in any stocks, check the chart and draw trend lines. Buy when the trend is up; hold or do not buy when it is moving down. The best profits always come when you buy an up stock in an up industry in an up market—clearly evident from trend lines on charts. And, of course, when you sell short, it's the opposite.

Technical analysis, especially charts, can be a valuable aid to timing if you remember these three points:

- Unless you are extremely optimistic and can afford to tie up your money for a while, *never* buy any stock until its chart is pointing up.
- *Always* check the chart action before you sell. You may think that the high has been reached, but the chart may disagree and make possible greater gains.
- If the chart shows a downtrend, consider selling. If it's a good investment, you can buy the stock back later at a lower price. If it's not, you'll save a lot of money.

Properly employed, technical analysis can be an important adjunct to fundamental investing and, more often than not, it will keep you humble!

FOR FURTHER INFORMATION

Robert D. Edwards and John Magee, *Technical Analysis of Stock Trends* (Boston: John Magee, Inc., 1992).

Martin Pring, *Technical Analysis Explained,* 3rd ed. (New York: McGraw-Hill, 1991).

T.H. Stewart, *How Charts Can Make You Money: Technical Analysis for Investors,* 2nd ed. (Chicago: Probus Publishing, 1990).

Robert W. Colby and Thomas A. Meyers, The Encyclopedia of Technical Indicators (Homewood, IL: Business One Irwin, 1992).

E

WHERE, WHAT, WHEN:
Exchanges, Indexes, and Indicators

In keeping with Wall Street jargon and financial reporting, initials are used frequently. Here are some of the most widely used:

EXCHANGES

➤ NYSE: NEW YORK STOCK EXCHANGE 11 Wall Street, New York, NY 10005; 1-212-656-3000. This is the oldest and largest exchange in the United States. To be listed, a corporation must:
- Demonstrate earning power of $2.5 million before federal income taxes for the most recent year and $2 million pre-tax for each of the preceding 2 years
- Have net tangible assets of $18 million
- Have market value of publicly held shares of $18 million
- Report a total of 1.1 million common shares publicly held
- Have 2,000 holders of 100 shares or more

➤ AMEX: AMERICAN STOCK EXCHANGE 86 Trinity Place, New York, NY 10006; 1-212-306-1000. These corporations are generally smaller and less financially strong than those on the NYSE. The firm must have:
- Pre-tax income of at least $750,000 in its last fiscal year or in two of the last three
- Stockholders' equity of $4 million
- 500,000 shares of common, exclusive of holdings of officers or directors
- 800 public stockholders or a minimum public distribution of 1 million shares together with a minimum of 400 holders of 100 or more shares
- Market price of $3 minimum with $3 million market value

➤ OTC: OVER THE COUNTER This is the market for securities that are not listed on major exchanges. The trading is conducted by dealers who are members of NASD (National Association of Securities Dealers, 1735 K Street NW, Wash-

ington, DC 20006; 1-202-728-8000) and who may or may not be members of other exchanges. Trading is by bid and asked prices. The primary market is NASDAQ (National Association of Securities Dealers Automated Quotations), which consists of about 4,700 of the most actively traded issues. Some 11,000 other stocks are quoted in daily financial summaries.

➤ CBOE: CHICAGO BOARD OPTIONS EXCHANGE La Salle at Van Buren, Chicago, IL 60005; 1-312-786-5600. The major auction market for calls and puts, primarily on NYSE stocks, and recently for special types of options such as those on Treasury bonds and on the S&P 100 and 500.

➤ ACC: AMEX OPTIONS EXCHANGE 86 Trinity Place, New York, NY 10006; 1-212-306-1000. The division of AMEX that trades puts and calls, almost entirely on NYSE-listed and OTC stocks.

➤ CBT: CHICAGO BOARD OF TRADE   141 West Jackson Boulevard, Chicago, IL 60604; 1-312-435-3500. A major market for futures contracts: commodities, interest rate securities, commercial paper, etc.

➤ CME: CHICAGO MERCANTILE EXCHANGE 30 South Wacker Drive, Chicago, IL 60606; 1-312-930-1000. Futures contracts for commodities.

➤ COMEX: COMMODITY EXCHANGE (FORMERLY NEW YORK COMMODITY EXCHANGE) 4 World Trade Center, New York, NY 10048; 1-212-938-2900. Futures and options of a limited number of commodities and metals (gold, silver, and copper).

➤ NYCE: NEW YORK COTTON EXCHANGE 4 World Trade Center, New York, NY 10048; 1-212-938-2650. Trading in futures in cotton and orange juice.

➤ IMM: INTERNATIONAL MONETARY MARKET; 1-312-930-1000. A part of the Chicago Mercantile Exchange. Trades in futures of foreign currency and U.S. Treasury bills.

OTHER STOCK EXCHANGES

U.S.

Boston Stock Exchange   1-617-723-9500
1 Boston Place, 38th floor
Boston, MA 02108

Cincinnati Stock Exchange   1-513-621-1410
36 E. 4th Street, Suite 906
Cincinnati, OH 45202

Midwest Stock Exchange   1-312-663-2222
440 S. LaSalle Street
Chicago, IL 60605

Pacific Stock Exchange   1-415-393-4000
301 Pine Street
San Francisco, CA 94104
           or
233 South Beaudry Avenue   1-213-977-4500
Los Angeles, CA 90012

Philadelphia Stock Exchange   1-215-496-5000
1900 Market Street
Philadelphia, PA 19103

CANADIAN

Alberta Stock Exchange   1-403-262-7791
300 Fifth Avenue SW
Calgary, Alberta T2P 3C4

Montreal Stock Exchange   1-514-871-2424
800 Victoria Square
Montreal, Quebec H4Z 1A9

Toronto Stock Exchange   1-416-947-4700
Exchange Tower
2 First Canadian Place
Toronto, Ontario M5X 1J2

Vancouver Stock Exchange   1-604-643-6590
609 Granville Street
Vancouver, British Columbia
   V7Y 1HY

Winnipeg Stock Exchange   1-204-942-8431
2901 One Lombard Place
Winnipeg, Manitoba R3B
   0Y2

➤ KCBT: KANSAS CITY BOARD OF TRADE 4800 Main Street, Suite 303, Kansas City, MO 64112; 1-816-753-7500. Trades in futures of commodities and Value Line futures index.

➤ NYFE: NEW YORK FUTURES EXCHANGE 20 Broad Street, New York, NY 10005; 1-212-656-4949.

A wholly owned subsidiary of the NYSE that trades in the NYSE Composite Index futures contract.

➤ NYME: NEW YORK MERCANTILE EXCHANGE 4 World Trade Center, New York, NY 10048; 1-212-938-2222. Trading in futures of petroleum, platinum, and palladium.

FEDERAL AGENCIES

➤ SEC: SECURITIES AND EXCHANGE COMMISSION 450 Fifth Street NW, Washington, DC 20549; 1-202-272-7440. A federal agency established to help protect investors. It is responsible for administering congressional acts regarding securities, stock exchanges, corporate reporting, investment companies, investment advisers, and public utility holding companies.

➤ FRB: FEDERAL RESERVE BOARD 20th and C Streets NW, Washington, DC 20551; 1-202-452-3000. The federal agency responsible for control of such important investment items as the discount rate, money supply, and margin requirements.

➤ FDIC: FEDERAL DEPOSIT INSURANCE CORPORATION 550 17th Street NW, Washington, DC 20429; 1-800-424-5488. An agency that insures bank deposits.

➤ SAVINGS ASSOCIATION INSURANCE FUND 550 17th Street NW, Washington, DC 20429; 1-800-424-5488. An agency that insures deposits with savings and loan associations.

➤ CFTC: COMMODITY FUTURES TRADING COMMISSION 2033 K Street NW, Washington, DC 20581; 1-202-254-6387. This is a watchdog for the commodities futures trading industry.

STOCK MARKET AVERAGES

AVERAGES VS. INDEXES

➤ DOW JONES AVERAGES The most popular indicators of the direction of the stock market, these were devised in 1884 by Charles H. Dow, a founder and first editor of the *Wall Street Journal*. The makeup of the Dow Jones averages appears in the box on page 377. Each is simply an average price of the stocks in the group, derived by adding up the prices and dividing by the number of stocks represented. Initially

STOCKS IN DOW JONES AVERAGES AS OF MAY 1993

Industrials (DJIA)

Alcoa	International Business
Allied Signal	Machines
American Express	International Paper
AT&T	McDonald's Corp.
Bethlehem Steel	Merck & Co.
Boeing	Minnesota Mining &
Caterpillar	Mfg.
Chevron	J.P. Morgan
Coca-Cola	Philip Morris Co.
Disney	Procter & Gamble
Du Pont, E.I.	Sears, Roebuck
Eastman Kodak	Texaco, Inc.
Exxon Corporation	Union Carbide
General Electric	United Technologies
General Motors	Westinghouse Electric
Goodyear Tire	Woolworth (F.W.)

Transportation (DJTA)

Airborne Freight	Federal Express
Alaska Air Group	Norfolk & Southern
American President	Roadway Service
Lines	Ryder Systems
AMR Corp.	Santa Fe Southern
Burlington Northern	Pacific
Carolina Freight	Southwest Air
Consolidated Freightways	UAL Corp.
Consolidated Rail	Union Pacific Corp.
CSX Corp.	U.S. Air Group
Delta Airlines	XTRA Corp.

Utility (DJUA)

American Electric Power	Niagara Mohawk Power
Arkla, Inc.	Pacific Gas & Electric
Centerior Energy	Panhandle Eastern Corp.
Commonwealth Edison	Peoples Energy
Consolidated Edison	Philadelphia Electric
Consolidated Natural Gas	Public Service
Detroit Edison	Enterprises
Houston Industries	SCE Corp.

the divisor was 11; then in the 1920s it became 30 when the number of stocks was increased from 11 to 30; today it's .559. Each average measures the stocks' performance during one day. When one of the companies in the average

declares a stock split or dividend, the divisor is reduced in size to accommodate the change.

For many years the Dow Jones Industrial Average hovered around 100, peaking at 386 in 1929 just prior to the crash. After the crash it climbed back up slowly, never moving much past 200 until World War II, when it hit 700. In 1966 it reached 1000. It fell again to 570 in 1974 only to return to 1000 two years later. In August 1987 the Dow posted an all-time high of 2722.42, but 2 months later, on October 19, it plunged a record 508 points to 1738.74. Since then there have been numerous ups and downs. In early July 1988 it reached 2158.61, the highest point since the October crash. A year later, in July 1989, it was 2456.56. As we go to press, it is 3525.22.

The Dow is often criticized for the fact that a high-priced stock, such as IBM, has a greater impact on the index than lower-priced issues. In other words, the stocks are *not* equally weighted, so on any given day, a fluctuation of significance in one or two high-priced stocks can distort the average. As a result, the Dow is useful for tracking the direction of the market over the long term but is often less reliable on a daily or even weekly basis. With only 30 stocks, it is also thought to be too small.

➤ STANDARD & POOR'S 500 INDEX This index addresses some of the criticism of the Dow and has challenged its premier position. The S&P 500, devised in 1957, is weighted according to the market value of each stock in the index. Covering 500 stocks, it is computed by multiplying the price of each stock by the number of shares outstanding. This gives larger and more influential corporations more weight.

Despite their different approaches, the averages and the index move together most of the time, especially on major swings.

S HINT: Keep in mind that the Dow figure is about 10 times larger than the S&P 500. That's because S&P tried to devise an index that was more nearly comparable to the average dollar price of all stocks traded on the NYSE.

➤ DOW JONES INDUSTRIAL AVERAGE (DJIA) The oldest and most widely used stock market average. It shows the action of 30 actively traded blue chip stocks, representing about 15% of NYSE values, on a weighted basis: for example,

IBM at 110 carries more than 3 times the weight of Woolworth at 35.

The DJIA is determined by dividing the closing prices by a divisor that compensates for past stock splits and stock dividends. The average is quoted in points, not dollars.

➤ DOW JONES TRANSPORTATION AVERAGE (DJTA) This is made up of the stocks of 20 major transportation companies.

➤ DOW JONES UTILITY AVERAGE (DJUA) This consists of 15 major utilities to provide geographic representation. With more firms forming holding companies to engage in oil and gas exploration and distribution, its value is greater as a point of reference than as a guide to the market's evaluation of producers of electricity and distributors of gas.

➤ DOW JONES COMPOSITE INDEX Also called the 65 Stock Average, this combines the other three indexes and consists of 30 industrials, 20 transportation, and 15 utility stocks. It is not widely followed.

➤ STANDARD & POOR'S COMPOSITE INDEX OF 500 STOCKS A market-value-weighted index showing the change in the aggregate value of 500 stocks, it consists mainly of NYSE-listed companies with some AMEX and OTC stocks. There are 400 industrials, 60 transportation and utility companies, and 40 financial issues. It represents about 80% of the market value of all issues traded on the NYSE but actually reflects the action of a comparatively few large firms. Options on this index trade on the Chicago Board Options Exchange and futures on the Chicago Mercantile Exchange.

➤ STANDARD & POOR'S 400 MIDCAP INDEX Introduced in June 1991, this index is comprised of 400 domestic companies. The median market capitalization of stocks in the index is $610 million vs. about $2.2 billion for stocks in the S&P 500. It is a market-weighted index (stock price times shares outstanding).

➤ STANDARD & POOR'S 100 STOCK INDEX This consists of stocks for which options are listed on the Chicago Board Options Exchange. Options on the 100 Index are listed on the Chicago Board Options Exchange and futures on the Chicago Mercantile Exchange.

➤ WILSHIRE 5000 EQUITY INDEX This is a value-weighted index derived from the dollar value of 5,000 common stocks, including all those listed on the NYSE and AMEX and the most active OTC issues. It is the broadest index and thus is more representative of the overall market. Unfortunately, it has not received adequate publicity. The Wilshire is prepared by Wilshire Associates in Santa Monica, Calif. No futures or options are traded on the Wilshire.

➤ NYSE COMPOSITE INDEX A market-value-weighted index covering the price movements of all common stocks listed on the Big Board. It is based on the prices at the close of trading on December 31, 1965, and is weighted according to the number of shares listed for each issue. The base value is $50. Point changes are converted to dollars and cents to provide a meaningful measure of price action. Futures are traded on the NYFE and options on the NYSE itself.

➤ NASDAQ-COMPOSITE INDEX This represents all domestic OTC stocks except those having only one market maker. It covers a total of 3,500 stocks and is market-value weighted. No futures or options are traded.

➤ VALUE LINE COMPOSITE INDEX This is an equally weighted index of 1,700 NYSE, AMEX, and OTC stocks tracked by the *Value Line Investment Survey*. Designed to reflect price changes of typical industrial stocks, it is neither price- nor market-value weighted. Options trade on the Philadelphia Exchange and futures on the Kansas City Board of Trade.

➤ AMEX MAJOR MARKET INDEX Price-weighted, which means that high-priced stocks have a greater influence than low-priced ones, this is an average of 20 blue chip industrials. It was designed to mirror the Dow Jones Industrial Average and measure representative performance of these kinds of issues. Although produced by the AMEX, it includes stocks listed on the NYSE. Futures are traded on the Chicago Board of Trade.

➤ AMEX MARKET VALUE INDEX This is a capitalization-weighted index that measures the collective performance of more than 90% of AMEX-listed companies, including ADRs, warrants, and common stocks. Cash dividends are assumed to be reinvested. Options are traded on the AMEX.

➤ DOW JONES BOND AVERAGE This consists of bonds of 10 public utilities and 10 industrial corporations.

MARKET INDICATORS, INDEXES, AND AVERAGES

Whether you're bullish, bearish, or uncertain, you can get a reading on the direction of the market, interest rates, and the overall economy by following some of the key statistics (or indicators) regularly churned out by Wall Street and Washington. These should be regarded not as gospel but rather as tools to help you make informed and intelligent decisions about your investments and for timing moves between stocks, bonds, and cash equivalents. Make a point of jotting down these numbers on your own chart and track the trends. You will see definite patterns between the market, interest rates, and the money supply. (The indicators are presented in alphabetical order.)

ECONOMIC INDICATOR	COMPOSITION	WHAT IT PREDICTS
Consumer price index (CPI)	The average price of consumer goods and services	The direction of inflation and changes in the purchasing power of money
Dollar index	The value of the dollar as measured against major foreign currencies	Domestic corporate profits and multinational earning power
Dow Jones Industrial Average (DJIA)	30 major companies whose stock is held by many institutions and individuals; index is price-weighted so that moves in high-priced stocks exert more influence than those of lower-priced stock	Action of the stock market, which in turn anticipates future business activity
Employment figures and payroll employment	Number of people working or on company payrolls	Potential consumer spending, which in turn affects corporate profits
Gross domestic product (GDP)	Total goods and services produced in United States on an annual basis; inflation can distort the accuracy of this figure, so subtract inflation from GDP to get "real" GDP	General business trends and economic activity
Index of industrial production (IIP)	Shown as a percentage of the average, which has been tracked since 1967; base is 100	Amount of business volume
Money supply:		
M1	Currency held by the public plus balances in checking accounts, NOW accounts, traveler's checks, and money market funds	Extent of consumer purchasing power and liquidity of public's assets, used by Federal Reserve as a gauge for predicting as well
M2	M1 plus time deposits over $100,000 and repurchase agreements	as controlling the pace of the economy; when M1 shows a big increase, the Fed usually reduces
M3	M2 plus T-bills, U.S. savings bonds, bankers' acceptances, term Eurodollars, commercial paper	the money supply, which sends interest rates up; Fed reduces M1 by selling Treasuries; tightening of M1 serves to curb inflation; an increase in M1 fuels inflation

ECONOMIC INDICATOR	COMPOSITION	WHAT IT PREDICTS
Standard & Poor's 500 stock index	Indexed value of 500 stocks from NYSE, AMEX, and OTC; more useful than the Dow Jones Industrial Average because it's broader; includes 400 industrials, 40 public utilities, 20 transportations, and 40 financials; stocks are market-value weighted; that is, price of each stock is multiplied by the number of shares outstanding	Direction of the economy and the market; good leading indicator because the market tends to anticipate future economic conditions
Three-month Treasury bill rate	Interest rate paid to purchasers of T-bills	General direction of interest rates; gives indication of the Federal Reserve system's fiscal policy; for example, during a recession, the Fed increases the amount of currency in circulation, which serves to lower the T-bill rate; during inflation, currency is reduced and the T-bill rate rises; rising interest rates tend to reduce corporate profits because of the increased costs of borrowing; therefore, a continual rise in T-bill rates presages a decline in the stock market; falling rates help stock and bond prices
Wage settlements	Percentage changes in wages that come about because of new labor contracts	Price changes for goods and services; sharply higher wage settlements result in higher inflation rates

➤ BARRON'S CONFIDENCE INDEX Weekly index of corporate bond yields published by *Barron's,* the financial newspaper owned by Dow Jones. It shows the ratio of the average yield of 10 high-grade bonds to the Dow Jones average yield on 40 bonds. The premise is that when investors feel confident about the economy they buy lower-rated bonds.

➤ BOND BUYER'S INDEX Published daily, it measures municipal bonds.

GLOSSARY: WALL STREET JARGON MADE SIMPLE

adjustable rate mortgage (ARM): A mortgage whose interest rate shifts, typically twice a year, to reflect general changes in interest rates.

after-tax contributions: Money that you've paid income tax on that is contributed to your savings plan; also called voluntary contributions. Because you have paid taxes on this money when you earned it, it cannot be mingled with the pretax money you or your employer contributed to your savings plan.

alternative minimum tax: A special income tax for high earners with certain tax-exempt investments.

American Depository Receipts (ADRs): Certificates of ownership of foreign stocks that are held by American banks.

amortization: Gradual reduction of a debt by a series of periodic payments. Each payment includes interest on the outstanding debt and part of the principal.

annuity: A contract, usually sold by an insurance company, that makes periodic payments to the person who holds it (the annuitant) at a future date, usually beginning at retirement. A fixed annuity pays a guaranteed rate; a variable annuity produces investment returns that are tied to the performance of the market. An immediate income annuity begins income payments right away. A deferred annuity can be fixed or variable and keeps your investment growing, shielded from taxes until you begin withdrawals.

arbitrage: Profiting from price differences when a security, currency or commodity is traded on different markets. Also, to buy shares in a company that is about to be taken over and sell short the shares of the acquiring company.

asked price: The lowest price at which a security is offered for sale.

asset: A possession that has present and future financial value to its owner.

ATMs: Automated teller machines, located primarily at banks. Upon insertion of a magnetically coded bank identification card, the computer-controlled machine dispenses cash that you request or deposits money to your account and indicates the status of your account on a viewing screen. No teller is necessary. The majority of ATMs are open 24 hours.

back-end load: A commission paid when you sell mutual fund shares; also known as redemption fees. They may be eliminated after you've owned your shares a certain number of years.

basis point: One hundredth of 1%; used in discussing bond yields.

bearer bond: A bond certificate held by the owner with coupons that are detached and presented in order to collect the interest due. It is not registered to an owner on the books of the issuer; it is owned by the person holding or bearing the certificate.

beneficiary: The person(s) named to receive your benefits in the event of your death.

beta: A number that compares the volatility of a stock with that of the overall market.

bid price: The highest price which a buyer is willing to pay for a security.

blue chip: The common stock of a well-known national company with a history of earnings growth and dividend increases, such as Exxon or General Electric.

bond: A security that represents debt of the issuing corporation. Usually the issuer is required to pay the bondholder a specified rate of interest for a specified time and then repay the entire debt (also known as face value) upon maturity.

book value: The current net worth of a company—i.e., its assets minus its liabilities divided by the number of shares on the market. If a stock's price is lower than its book value and the company is financially solid, it is considered a bargain.

bull and bear cycles: The up-and-down movements of the stock market. A bull believes that prices will rise and buys on that assumption. A bull market is a period when stock prices are advancing. A bear believes that security or commodity prices will decline. A bear market is marked by declining prices.

bullion: Gold or silver sold in bars called ingots.

bullion coins: A coin whose value resides only in the precious metal it contains. See also *numismatic coins.*

call: An option for the right to buy a stock.

call date: A feature of many bonds giving the issuer the right to call in or redeem the bonds before their maturity date.

capital: Also called capital assets; property or money from which a person or business receives some monetary gain.

capital gains: Profits from the rising price of an investment.

cash equivalents: The generic term for assorted short-term instruments such as U.S. Treasury securities, CDs and money market fund shares, which can be readily converted into cash.

central asset or combo account: Brokerage, money market fund and checking account combined with a credit card. Offered by both banks and brokerage houses, some central asset accounts include forms of life insurance, mortgages, traveler's checks and other special features.

certificates of deposit: Also called CDs or "time certificates"; official receipts issued by a bank stating that a given amount of money has been deposited for a certain length of time at a specified rate of interest. CDs are insured by the U.S. government for up to $100,000.

charts: Records of price and volume trends as well as the general movement of stock and bond markets, economic cycles, industries and individual companies, updated continually. Chartists believe that past history as expressed on a chart gives a strong clue to the next price movement. They "read" the lines to determine what a stock has done and may do.

closed-end fund: Mutual funds that issue lim-

ited numbers of shares and then are traded on stock exchanges as common stocks.

commodities: Anything in which contracts for future delivery may be traded, such as precious metals, food, grain, oil, U.S. Treasury securities, foreign currencies and stock indexes.

common stock: See *stock, common*

compound interest: The amount earned on the original principal plus the accumulated interest. With interest on interest plus interest on principal, an investment grows more rapidly.

convertibles: Bonds, debentures or preferred stock that may be exchanged or converted into common stock.

correction: A reverse downward in the prices of stocks, bonds or commodities.

cost of living adjustment: A boost in wages, Social Security or a pension designed to offset the impact of inflation.

credit card: A plastic card issued by a bank or financial institution that gives the holder access to a line of credit to purchase goods or receive cash. Repayment may be required in full in 30 days or in installments. Compare with *debit card.*

custodian: The financial institution responsible for the safekeeping of your investment assets.

debit card: A deposit access card that debits the holder's bank account or money market account immediately upon use in purchasing. There is no grace period in which to pay; payment is transferred immediately and electronically at the moment of purchase.

defined-benefit plan: A pension that promises to pay a specified amount to all employees who complete a set number of years of work. In many plans, employers make all the contributions and invest them.

defined-contribution plan: Usually called a 401(k) or salary-reduction plan. It allows employees to contribute up to 10% of their pretax salaries to various investment funds. The account grows tax-free, but employees who select funds that perform poorly have no recourse.

discount rate: The interest rate the Federal Reserve charges member banks; it provides a floor for interest rates that banks then charge their customers.

disinflation: A reduction in the rate of ongoing inflation.

dividends: A portion of the company's net profits distributed to its shareholders; usually a fixed amount for each share of stock held and paid quarterly in cash; dividends also may be in the form of property, script or stock. Dividends must be voted on by the company's directors before each payment.

DJIA (Dow Jones Industrial Average): Price-weighted average of 30 blue chip stocks, representing overall price movements of all stocks on the New York Stock Exchange.

effective annual yield: Rate of return earned on your savings if you do not incur service charges or penalties.

employee stock ownership: Called an ESOP plan, it encourages workers to buy their employer's stock, usually at a reduced price.

equity: Stocks or ownership interest held by shareholders in a corporation as opposed to bonds. In a brokerage account, the market value of securities minus the amount borrowed.

face value: Value of a bond or note when issued. Corporate bonds are usually issued with $1,000 face value; municipals with $5,000; T-bills with $10,000. Also called par value.

FDIC (Federal Deposit Insurance Corporation): An independent agency of the U.S. government whose basic purpose is to insure bank deposits.

financial futures: Contracts to deliver a specified number of financial instruments at a given price by a certain date, such as U.S. Treasury bonds and bills, GNMA certificates, CDs and foreign currency.

401(k) plan: One that allows an employee to contribute pretax dollars to a company pool, which is invested in stocks, bonds or money market instruments; also known as a salary reduction plan.

front running: A trader knowing in advance of a block trade that will affect the price of a security and buying to profit from the trade.

futures: See *commodities.*

going public: When a private company first offers shares to the public.

guaranteed investment contract: Known as a GIC, it is a contract between an insurance company and a corporate savings or pension plan that offers a fixed rate of return on the capital invested over the life of the contract. It is not federally insured.

index: A statistical yardstick that measures a whole market by using a representative selection of stocks or bonds. Changes are compared to a base year. Futures are sold on stock indexes, such as the S&P 500.

index arbitrage: Profiting from the difference in prices of the same security. In program trading, traders buy and sell to profit from small price discrepancies, using computers that monitor both the S&P 500 stock index and futures contracts on the index. When there is a larger than normal gap, the computers notify the traders to sell.

index future: A contract to buy or sell an index (S&P 500, for example) at a future date. An index is not an average. See also *index.*

individual retirement account: Called an IRA, this personal fund defers taxes on the money put in and any income it generates until the owners begin withdrawing their money, which they cannot do without penalty before the age of 59-1/2.

inflation: An increase in the average price level of goods and services over time.

institutions: Organizations that trade huge blocks of securities, such as banks, pension funds, mutual funds and insurance companies.

interest: Money paid for the use of money. See also *discount rate; prime rate.*

IRA rollover: A technique allowing employees to avoid taxes by transferring lump-sum payments from a 401(k) or a profit-sharing plan into an IRA within 60 days.

junk bonds: High-risk, high-yielding bonds, rated BB or lower.

LBO (leveraged buyout): The purchase of a corporation by using a large amount of debt, much of it short-term bank loans secured by the assets of the company being acquired. After the buying is completed, the acquired company issues bonds to pay off a portion of the debt taken on in the takeover.

liability: A debt; something owed by one person or business to another.

limited partnership: Investment organization in which your liability is limited to the dollar amount you invest; a general partner manages the project, which may be in real estate, farming, oil and gas, etc.

liquid: Cash or investments easily convertible into cash, such as money market funds or bank deposits.

lump-sum distribution: Payment of a retirement account's complete holdings at once, usually when one leaves a job.

"Mae" family: Various mortgage-backed securities either sponsored or partially guaranteed by a handful of government agencies or private corporations, such as the Government National Mortgage Association (GNMA, or "Ginnie Mae") and the Federal Home Loan Mortgage Corporation ("Freddie Mac").

margin: The amount a client deposits with a broker in order to borrow from the broker to buy stocks.

mark to the market: The value of any portfolio based on the most recent closing price of the securities held.

mature: To come due; to reach the time when the face value of a bond or note must be paid.

money market fund: A mutual fund that invests only in high-yielding, short-term money market instruments such as U.S. Treasury bills, bank CDs and commercial paper. Shareholders receive higher interest on their shares than in a bank money market deposit account.

Moody's: A trademark for issuance of ratings on the relative investment quality of corporate and municipal bonds and for the company's financial publications.

municipal bonds: Debt obligations of state and local entities. For the most part, the interest earned is free from federal income tax and often from state and local taxes for residents.

mutual fund: An investment company in which investors' dollars are pooled with those of thousands of others. The combined total is invested by a professional manager in a variety of securities; shares are sold to the public.

net asset value (NAV): The price at which you buy or sell shares of a mutual fund. To determine NAV, mutual funds compute their assets daily by adding up the market value of all securities owned by the fund, deducting all liabilities, and dividing the balance by the number of shares outstanding. The NAV per share is the figure quoted in the newspaper.

net worth: Total value (of cash, property, investments) after deducting outstanding expenses and amounts owed.

no-load fund: An open-end investment company that sells shares directly to customers without applying a sales charge.

option: The right to buy (call) or sell (put) a certain amount of stock at a given price (strike price) for a specified length of time.

over-the-counter (OTC) stock: A security not listed or traded on a major exchange. Transactions take place by telephone and computer network rather than on the floor of an exchange.

point: A measure of a price change. With a stock, a point change means a change of $1; with a bond that has a $1,000 face value, it refers to a $10 change.

points: Upfront fee charge by the lender in a real estate deal; separate from interest but designed to increase the overall yield to the lender. A point is 1% of the total principal amount of the loan; on a $100,000 mortgage, 2 points would equal $2,000.

preferred stock: See *stock, preferred.*

premium: Amount by which a bond sells above its par or face value.

price/earnings (P/E) ratio: Price of a stock divided by its earnings per share. Also known as the multiple, it gives investors an idea of how much they are paying for a company's earnings power.

prime rate: Interest rate banks charge their largest and most financially solid business clients; lower than rate charged to consumers.

principal: Face amount of a debt or mortgage on which interest is either owed or earned; balance due on an obligation as separate from interest.

profit-sharing plan: An agreement by which a company makes annual contributions out of its profits to an account for each employee. This money is invested in stocks, bonds or money-market securities. The funds are tax-deferred until the employee leaves the company.

prospectus: A summary of data on an issue of securities, including mutual funds, that will be sold to the public, enabling investors to evaluate the security and decide whether or not to buy. The SEC regulations determine what information must be set forth in every prospectus.

put: An options contract giving the investor the right to sell a specified number of shares by a certain date at a certain price.

real return: The inflation-adjusted rate of return on an investment. If an investor earns a 12% return during a year when inflation is 3%, the real return is 9%.

SEC (Securities and Exchange Commission): A federal agency with power to enforce federal laws pertaining to the sale of securities and mutual fund shares and the governing of the exchanges, stockbrokers and financial advisers.

sharedraft: Interest-bearing checking account at a credit union.

secondary: The market in which existing securities are traded after their initial public offering. Also called the aftermarket.

selling short: Sale of a security that must be borrowed to make delivery. Usually involves the sale of securities that are not owned by the seller in anticipation of making a profit from a decline in the price of the security.

SIPC (Securities Investor Protection Corporation): An independent agency established by Congress to provide customers of most brokerage firms with protection similar to that provided by the FDIC for bank depositors, in the event that a firm is unable to meet its financial obligations.

spread: The difference between the bid and asked prices of a security; the difference in yields between two fixed-income securities.

stock, common: A security that represents ownership in a corporation.

stock, preferred: A stock that pays a fixed dividend and has first claim on profits over common stocks for payment of that dividend. The dividend does not rise or fall with profits.

stock right: A short-term privilege issued by a corporation to its existing stockholders granting them the right to buy new stock at a stated price.

stockbroker: An agent who handles the public's orders to buy and sell stocks, bonds, commodities and mutual funds. A broker may be a partner of a brokerage firm or a registered representative, who is an employee of a brokerage firm. Brokers charge a commission for their services.

strike price: The dollar amount per share at which an option buyer can purchase the underlying stock or a put option buyer can sell the stock. Also called the exercise price.

takeover: When the controlling interest of a corporation is taken over by a new company. Takeovers can be friendly or hostile.

tax bracket: The point on the income tax rate schedules where one's taxable income (income subject to tax after exemptions and deductions) falls. It is expressed as a percentage to be applied to each additional dollar earned over the base amount for that bracket. The current tax brackets for individuals are 15%, 28% and 31%.

tax-deferred: Taxes postponed until a later date. Pretax money invested in retirement plans is tax-deferred but *not* tax-exempt or tax-free, which means that no taxes will ever have to be paid.

tax shelter: An investment that allows one to realize tax benefits by reducing or deferring taxable income.

total return: Dividend or interest income plus any capital gain; a better measure of an investment's return that just dividends or interest.

Treasuries: Bills, notes and bonds backed by the U.S. government and sold through the Department of the Treasury. The interest they pay investors is exempt from state and local taxes.

triple tax-exempt bonds: Municipal bonds exempt from federal, state and local taxes for residents of the states and localities that issue the bonds.

vested benefits: The nonforfeitable dollar amount in a pension plan that belongs to the employee even if he/she leaves the job. An employee typically becomes vested after five years with the same firm.

warrant: A security, usually issued with a bond or preferred stock, giving the owner the privilege of buying a specified number of shares of a stock at a fixed price, usually for a period of years.

yield: The income paid or earned by a security divided by its current price. For example, a $20 stock with an annual dividend of $1.50 has a 7.5% yield.

zero coupon bond: A bond that pays no current interest but is sold at a deep discount from face value. At maturity, all compounded interest is paid and the bondholder collects the full face value of the bond (usually $1,000). EE savings bonds are zeros.

INDEX

AARP (American Association of Retired Persons), 284
ACC (AMEX Options Exchange), 382
Accounting, equity, 356
Accounts
  brokerage. *See* Brokerage accounts
  central asset, 266–267
  checking. *See* Checking accounts
  discretionary, 255
  joint, 255
  margin, 267–269
  money market deposit, 26, 52
  nondiscretionary, 255
  NOW, 25–26
  retirement. *See* Individual retirement accounts (IRAs)
  savings. *See* Savings, savings accounts
  tenancy-in-common, 255
  Treasury direct, 121–122
  for Uniform Gifts to Minors, 255
Accounts payable, 362
Accounts receivable, 354, 359
Accredited Personal Financial Specialists (APFS), 243
Acronyms, for exchanges and agencies, 382–383
Advances versus Declines (A/D), 373–374
Agricultural commodities contracts, 219
Alt, 187
American Association of Retired Persons (AARP), 284
American depository receipts (ADRs), 207–208
American Institute of CPAs, 243
American Stock Exchange. *See* AMEX (American Stock Exchange)
AMEX (American Stock Exchange), 382
  Major Market Index, 385
  Market Value Index (XAM), 231, 385
  Oil & Gas Index (XOI), 231
  Options Exchange (ACC), 382
Annual reports, 353–356

Annuities, 314–318, 326
  joint and survivor, 305–306
  lump-sum certain, 306
  period-certain, 306
  single-life (straight-life), 305
Antiques. *See* Collectibles
Appraisals, 101–102
Arbitrage, 220
ARMs (adjustable-rate mortgages), 277
Assets, 15–16, 359–362
  fixed, 363–364
Auctions, 100–107
Auditor's reports, 354

Balance sheets, 353, 354, 357–368
Banks, 23–33
  certificates of deposit (CDs) in, 26–33
  checking accounts in. *See* Checking accounts
  failure of, 41–44
  investments in, protecting, 39–44
  money market deposit accounts in, 26, 52
  relationship banking, 23–24
  services of, 23–24
Bar charts, 378
Barron's Confidence Index (BCI), 371, 387
Basis, 220
BCI (Barron's Confidence Index), 371, 387
Bear markets, 109, 370. *See also* Bond(s)
Beneficiaries, mutual funds and, 71
Beta. *See* Volatility
Bills
  short-term, 64
  Treasury securities, 123–124
    CDs versus, 27–28
Blue chip stocks, 64, 157
Bond(s), 326–327
  baccalaureate, 282
  Bond Buyer's Index, 387
  call protection, 116–117
  closed-end funds. *See* Closed-end funds
  convertible. *See* Convertible

    bonds (CVs)
  corporate, 12–13, 110–120, 326
  deferred call, 117
  described, 110
  discounts on, 110, 115
  Dow Jones Bond Average, 385
  electric revenue, 139
  Eurobonds, 209
  flower, 115
  foreign. *See* Foreign investments
  freely callable, 117
  general obligation (GOS), 136
  government agency, 146–147
  individual, mutual funds versus, 51–53
  junk, 147–149
  long-term, 64
  marketability of, 116
  maturities of, 64, 110, 114–115
  municipal. *See* Municipal bonds
  and mutual funds. *See under* Mutual fund(s)
  noncallable, 117
  nontraditional, 143–153
  optional maturity, 115, 137
  prospectus for, 112
  purchasing considerations, 111, 112–114
  ratings of, 112–113, 114, 137
  record-keeping for, 65–66
  refunding provisions, 117–118
  revenue, 139
  risks with, 116
  savings. *See* Savings bonds
  secured, 113
  series. *See* Savings bonds
  single-state municipal, 137
  sinking fund provisions, 118
  special types, 115–116
  stocks versus, 156
  swaps of, 118–119, 322–323
  Treasury. *See under* Treasury securities
  utility company, 183–184
  water revenue, 139
  Yankee, 116
  yields, 111–112, 114
  zero coupon. *See* Zero coupon securities, bonds

Book value, of stocks, 160–161, 237
Brokerage accounts, 221
  discount brokerage firms, 63
  managing, 255–269
    dollar cost averaging, 263–265
    ex-dividend dates, 262
    margin accounts, 267–269
    one-stop investing, 265–267
    program trading, 261–262
    selling short, 258–261
    stock market orders, 256–258
    stop prices, setting, 258
    switching brokers, 256
  safety of, 46–47
  types of, 255
Brokered CDs, 30–31, 52
Budgeting, 15–17
Bullion, 224
Bull markets, 155, 370. See also
  Stock(s)
"Bump-up" CDs, 28–29
Buying power, 373

Calls, 185, 188–191. See also Warrants
  buying, 190–191
  of convertible bonds (CVs), 130,
    133–134
  deep-in-the-money, 189
  margin, 269
  naked, 190
  protection of, 116–117
  writing, 188–190
  yield and, 113
Capital gains
  mutual funds and, 70–71, 96–97
  $125,000 exclusion, 333
  and options, 194
  taxes on, 7, 320–321
Capitalization ratios, 363
Capital surplus, 362
Cash flows, 18, 356, 365, 367
CD. See Certificates of deposit (CDs)
Central asset accounts, 266–267
Certificates of deposit (CDs), 52, 64,
  327
  alternatives to, 10–13
  in banks, 26–33
  brokered, 30–31, 52
  bump-up provisions, 28–29
  foreign, 214–215
  junk, 29
  low interest rates and, 10–11
  money market funds versus, 35
  out-of-state, 31–33
  step-up provisions, 29
  Treasury bills versus, 27–28
  true rate of interest on, 29–30
  unique, 27–29
  zero coupon, 29
Certified Financial Planners (CFP),

243–244
Certified historic structures, 329
CFP (Certified Financial Planners),
  243–244
Charitable contributions, 324, 325
Charitable remainder trusts, 324
Charts, 376–381. See also Technical
  Analysis (TA)
  bar, 378
  head-and-shoulder, 378–379
  long-term, 379–380
  P&F (point-and-figure), 377–378
  short-term, 379–380
  trend line, 380–381
Checking accounts, 24–25
  money market funds versus, 35
  NOW accounts, 25–26
  personal computers and, 350
Chicago Board of Trade (CBT), 218,
  382
Chicago Board Options Exchange
  (CBOE), 382
Chicago Mercantile Exchange
  (CME), 215, 218, 382
Children. See also Family finances
  cost of, 280–284
  gifts to, 282
  income taxes for, 281–283, 323,
    327, 334
  selling home to, 288
Closed-end funds, 73, 78, 94–99
  bond funds, 13, 95, 119–120
  country funds, 211–212
  purchasing, 96
  returns on, 96–97
  selling, 98–99
  types of, 95–96
Closing transaction, 186
CMOs (Collateralized mortgage
  obligations), 146
Coffee, Sugar & Cocoa Exchange,
  218
Collateral, 113
Collateralized mortgage obligations
  (CMOs), 146
Collectibles, 100–107, 326
College, paying for, 281–283
  savings bonds and, 128, 280
College zeros, 151–152
COMEX (Commodity Exchange),
  382
Commercial paper, 327
Commissions
  for professional advisors, 243,
    246–248
  sales, 61–63, 246–247
Commodities, 218–223
  COMEX (Commodity Exchange),
    382
  and futures contracts, 218–219,
    222–223, 327–328

Commodity Futures Trading
  Commission (CFTC), 383
  options on, 229–230
  market operation of, 219–221
  pros and cons of, 221
Commodity Exchange (COMEX),
  382
Commodity Futures Trading Commission (CFTC), 383
Common stock. See Stock(s), common
Companies
  bankrupt, 233, 237–238
  corporate bonds, 12–13, 150,
    326
  financial reports for, 357–368
  and pension plans, 298–300
Compounding. See Interest, compound
Computers, personal, 350–352
Computer Technology Index (XCI),
  231
Contract month, 220
Conversion. See Convertible bonds
  (CVs)
Convertible bonds (CVs), 53, 328
  calls with, 133–134
  CV mutual funds, 132–133
  described, 130–131
  hedging with, 133
  investment value of, 131
  municipal bonds, 136–137
  premium-over-investment value,
    131
  profiting from, 131–132
  pros and cons of, 132
  zero coupon, 136–137, 151
Cost of goods sold, 358
Costs, of investing, 61–63
Costs and expenses, corporate,
  358–359
Coupon rates, 110, 113. See also
  Interest rates
Covered option, 186
CPAs (Certified Public Accoun-
  tants), 243, 244
Credit card securities, 116
Credit guarantees. See GNMA (Gov-
  ernment National Mortgage
  Association)
Credit unions, 37–38
  depositor earnings, tax status of,
    328
  failure of, 39–44
Cross hedge, 220
Cumulative preferred stock. See
  Stock(s), preferred
Currencies, foreign. See Foreign cur-
  rencies
Currency funds, 214
Currency options, 215

Current assets, 359
Current ratio, 163, 363

Day order, 257
Debt. *See also* Bond(s)
  acquisition, 332
  home equity, 332
  long-term, 173, 354, 362
  low, stocks with, 173
Deferred Interest Securities (DINTS),
  150
Delivery dates, 222
Denationalization, 209
Depreciation, 358–359
Diagonal spread, 186
DINTS (Deferred Interest Securities),
  150
Disability insurance, 311
Discounts, on bonds, 110, 115
Diversification, 21, 53, 55, 58
  foreign investments and, 206, 208
  mutual funds and, 69
Dividend(s), 158–161, 186, 192, 264,
  328, 359
  continual, 175
  ex-dividend dates, 262
  high, stocks with, 169
  mutual funds and, 70–71, 96
  reinvestment of, 66, 262–263, 328
  secure, utilities with, 181
  on shorted stock, 259
  and warrants, 199
Dollar cost averaging (DCA), 21, 54,
  72, 170, 263–265
  mutual funds and, 70
  reverse, 71–72
Dow Jones Averages, 383–385
Dow Jones Composite Index, 385
Dow Jones Industrial Average
  (DJIA), 384–385
Dow theory of technical analysis,
  369–371
Dow Jones Transportation Average
  (DJTA), 385
Dow Jones Utility Average (DJUA),
  385

Earned growth rate (EGR), 166–167
Earnings, 354, 366–367
  per share, 160
Economic indicators. *See* Indicators
Economic trends, 55–56. *See also*
  Indicators
The Educational Resource Institute
  (TERI), 286
EGR (earned growth rate), 166–167
Elderly investors, protection from
  fraud, 49–50
Electric revenue bonds, 139
Employment, lay-offs/terminations,
  290

Equipment certificates, 115
Equipment leasing partnerships, tax
  status of, 328–329
Equity, return on, 356
Equity accounting, 356
Equity funds, 80
Eurobonds, 209
Europe, investments in. *See* Foreign
  investments
European currency unit (ECU),
  209
Exchange rates, 214. *See also* For-
  eign currencies
Exchanges, 210, 382–383. *See also*
  individual exchanges
Ex-dividend dates, 262
Expenses, 76, 354, 358–359
Expiration date, of options, 186

Face value, 110
Family finances, 280–287. *See also*
  Children
  boomerang kids, 283–284
  children, cost of, 280–284
  college, 281–283
  investment gifts, 286–287
  parents, assisting, 284–285
  portfolios for, 341–342
  school, going back, 285–286
Fannie Maes (Federal National
  Mortgage Association),
  145–146, 147, 329
FDIC (Federal Deposit Insurance
  Corporation), 23, 26, 39–44,
  383
Federal Agencies, 383
Federal Deposit Insurance Corporation (FDIC), 23, 26, 39–44,
  383
Federal Home Loan Mortgage Corporation (FHLMC) participation
  certificates, 145, 147, 329
Federal Housing Administration
  (FHA), 146
Federal National Mortgage Association (Fannie Maes), 145–146,
  147, 329
Federal Reserve Board (FRB), 43,
  383
Federal Savings and Loan Insurance
  Corporation (FSLIC), 26,
  39–44, 383
Fees. *See also* Commissions
  for mutual funds, 74–75
FHA (Federal Housing Administration), 146
FHLMC (Federal Home Loan Mortgage Corporation) participation certificates, 145, 147, 329
FICO (Financing Corp.), stripped
  bonds, 152

FIFO (first in, first out), asset costing
  method, 66
Financial advisors. *See* Professional
  help
Financial futures. *See* Futures,
  financial
Financial planners, 242–244. *See*
  also Professional help
Financial position, changes in, 361,
  362
Financial reports, analyzing,
  357–359
First in, first out (FIFO), asset costing method, 66
Foreign currencies, 206–207, 329
  mutual funds and, 214
  options and, 215
  speculation in, 216
  transactions involving, 354–356
Foreign investments, 206–217
  American depository receipts
    (ADRs), 207–208
  bonds, 212–213
  certificates of deposit (CDs),
    214–215
  closed-end country funds,
    211–212
  currencies and. *See* Foreign cur-
    rencies
  European stock market and, 8
  income funds, 213–214
  money market funds, 214
  mutual funds for, 211, 213–214
  1994 opportunities, 208–211
  pros and cons of, 207
  stocks, 208–211, 334–335
  traveler's checks, 215
Forward contract, 220
457 plans, 301–302
401(k) retirement plans, 299–301,
  302–303
403(b) retirement plans, 301–302
Freddie Mac PCs (Federal Home
  Loan Mortgage Corp. participation certificates), 145, 147,
  329
FSLIC (Federal Savings and Loan
  Insurance Corporation), 26,
  39–44, 383
Futures
  commodities, 218–219, 222–223,
    327–328
  financial, 227–230
  New York Futures Exchange
    (NYFE), 383
  options on, 215
  and precious metals, 224

General expenses, 358
GICs (Guaranteed investment contracts), 302–303

Gifts
  to children, 282
  financial, 282, 286–287
Gilts, 209
Glamour average, 371–372
GNMA (Government National Mortgage Association), 143–145, 329
  mutual funds, 144–145, 146
Goals, investment, 3, 14–17, 20
Gold, 225, 329
  Gold & Silver Index (XAU), 231
  mutual funds for, 80
Good until canceled order, 257
Government agency bonds, 146–147
Government closed-end bond funds, 95, 97
Government National Mortgage Association (GNMA), 143–145, 329
  mutual funds, 144–145, 146
Government Zeros, 150–151
Growth stocks, 7, 64, 157, 171
  guidelines for selecting, 163, 165–168
  mutual funds for, 80
Guaranteed investment contracts (GICs), 302–303

Head-and-shoulder charts, 378–379
Health care industry, investments in, 9–10
Health insurance, 311
  boomerang kids and, 284
  medigap insurance, 313
  nursing home, 313–314
  for parents, 284
Hedging, 219, 220, 230
  with convertible bonds (CVs), 133
"High rollers", options and, 192–194
Historic rehabilitation, tax status of, 329
Horizontal spread, 186
Housing, 272–274. See also Real estate
  home equity loans, 274, 332
  homeowners insurance, 312
  low income, tax status of, 330
  mortgages, 276–278
  for older parents, 285
  rental income from, 274–275, 333, 335
  retirement. See Retirement
  as tax shelters, 273
  time-shares, 275–276
  vacation homes for profit, 275, 335–336

Identifiable-cost, asset costing method, 66–67

IMF (International Monetary Fund), 209
Income, 357–359
  active, 326
  capital gains, mutual funds and, 70–71, 96–97
  deductions for tax purposes, 322, 324, 325
  deferred, 124, 324
  distribution, mutual funds and, 70–71
  dividends, mutual funds and, 70–71, 96
  net, 364
  passive, 326
  regularity of, mutual funds and, 71
  reinvestment, mutual funds and, 70–71
  rental, from housing, 274–275
  taxable, reducing, 6–7
Income funds, 80
  global, 213–214
Income stocks, 157, 168–169, 171
Income taxes. See Taxes
Index(es), 220. See also specific indexes
  advances versus declines, 373–374
  buying power, 373
  funds, 12, 80, 87–88
  glamour average, 371–372
  of leading economic indicators, 56, 386
  momentum, 376
  most active stocks, 373
  percentage leaders, 373
  stock, 230–232, 334
  trading volume, 375–376
Indicators, 55–56
  broad-based, 372–376
  economic, 386–387
  key, 177
  psychological, 371–372
Individual retirement accounts (IRAs), 295–298, 325
  and heirs, 297
  moving accounts, 305
  mutual funds and, 70
  need for, 296
  operation of, 295
  and rollovers, 7, 297
  rules regarding, 295
  self-directed, 296–297
  taxable investments compared, 294
  year-end tax planning and, 324
Inflation, 116
  effects of, 3
  stock performance and, 156
Initial public offerings (IPOs), 201–203

Initials, for exchanges and agencies, 382–383
Insider transactions, 259
Insurance
  deposit, rules for, 40–42
  life. See Life insurance
  medigap, 313
  nursing home, 313–314
  Old Age and Survivors (OASI), 293
  social. See Retirement, and Social Security
  term, 308, 309
Insurance companies, investments with, protecting, 48–49
Interest, 259
  accrued, 66
  compound, 4, 16, 25
    CD's and, 27
  investments providing, 67
  true rate of, on CDs, 29–30
Interest expense, 359, 364
Interest rate risk, 160
Interest rates, 199
  changing, appropriate actions for, 36–37
  coupon rates, 110, 113
  financial futures and, 227–228
  low, avoiding, 10–11
  savings bond calculations, 127–128
  yields versus, 23
International Association for Financial Planning (IAFP), 244
International Monetary Fund (IMF), 209
International Monetary Market (IMM), 382
In the money, 186, 189
Inventories, 354, 359–360, 364
Investment advisors. See Professional help
Investment clubs, 63–65, 329–330
Investment gifts, 286–287
Investment pyramid, 14–22, 82
Investment(s). See also Portfolio(s)
  antique fishing lures, 102–103
  Bonds. See Bond(s)
  collectibles, 100–107
  costs of, 61–63
  dos and don'ts for successful, 57–61
  expense deductibility, 324
  foreign. See Foreign investments
  fund sources for, 55
  goals for, 3, 14–17, 20
  in health care industry, 9–10
  information availability on, mutual funds and, 71
  insurance as. See Life insurance
  mistakes with, 21–22

mutual funds. *See* Mutual funds
oriental rugs, 105–107
protecting, 39–50
providing interest payments,
    ranked by risk level, 67
for retirement. *See* Retirement
safety of, 23–38
Stickley furniture, 103–105
Stock(s). *See* Stock(s)
strategies for, 6–13
tax status of, directory, 326–336
Investors, types of, 54–55. *See also*
    Pyramid investment
IPOs (initial public offerings),
    201–203
IRAs. *See* Individual retirement
    accounts (IRAs)

Joint accounts, 255
Junk bonds, 147–149
Junk CDs, 29

Kansas City Board of Trade (KCBT),
    218, 383
KEOGH retirement plans, 303–304,
    305
Kiddie tax, 281–282, 283

Land, sales of, 330
Leaps (long-term equity apprecia-
    tion securities), 185, 187
Leases, 272
Liabilities, 15–16, 362
Library, financial, 2
Life insurance, 308–314, 325, 330
borrowing against the policy,
    312
cash value (whole life) insurance,
    308–310
switching policies, 312
term insurance, 308
universal, 309–310
variable, 310
Limited partnerships, 332
Limit order, 256
Liquidity, 159
Liquidity ratio, 363
Load fund(s), 62, 74–75
back-end, 75, 78
deferred, 75
front-end, 78
reinvestment, 75
Loans
for college costs, 283
home equity, 274
from insurance policies, 312
Perkins, 286
London Stock Exchange, 209
Long position, 219, 220
Long-term equity appreciation secu-
    rities (leaps), 185, 187

Major Market Index (XMI), 231
Management. *See* Portfolios
Margin, 219–220, 259
margin accounts, 267–269
margin calls, 221
margin loans, 331
purchasing on, 54, 81
Marketable securities, 359
Market indexes. *See* Index(es), stock
Market order, 256
Mark to the market, 220
Married put, 186
Maturities, 110, 113
of bonds, 114–115
long, when to purchase, 56–57
money market funds and, 36
optional maturity bonds, 115,
    137
risk and, 46
serial, 139
yields and, 111–112
zero coupon CDs and, 29
Medical expenses, 325
Medicare, 284
Medigap insurance, 313
Mid America Commodity Exchange,
    218
Minneapolis Grain Exchange, 218
Momentum, 376
Money market deposit accounts, 26,
    52, 331
Money market mutual fund(s),
    31–36, 52, 64, 80, 331
as CD alternative, 10–11
foreign, 214
general, 35
government-only, 35
investments in, protecting, 45–46
management expenses for, 62
picking, 35–36
socially responsible, 87
tax-free, 35–36
Moody's Investor Service, 249–250
Mortgages, 276–278
adjustable-rate (ARMs), 277
fixed-rate, 276–277
and retirement planning, 289
reverse, 289
securities backed by, 143–146
zero coupon, 150
Moving average lines, 372–373
Municipal bonds, 135–142, 326–327
buying decision, 135–136
fees for, 63
insured, 137
junk, 148–149
mutual funds for, 11–12, 80,
    140–141
risks of, 139
selecting, 138–139
serial maturities and, 139

single-state, 137
stripped, pros and cons of, 137
taxes and, 6–7, 135–136, 142
types of, 136–138
unit trusts for, 141–142
variable-rate option, 137
zero coupon, 136–137, 150–151
Munis. *See* Municipal bonds
Mutual fund(s), 69–93, 224, 331
advantages of, 69–71
beta of, 76–77
bond funds, 11–12, 80, 119–120,
    132–133, 140–141
capital gains on, 96–97
closed-end. *See* Closed-end funds
of convertible bonds (CVs),
    132–133
European, 211
fees for, 61–62
for foreign investments, 211,
    213–214
front-end load, 78
of GNMA mortgages, 144–145
index funds, 87–88
versus individual securities,
    51–53
initial public offerings (IPOs) and,
    202
investments in, protecting, 44–46
junk bond, 147–148
managers of, leaving, 90
mixed, 80
money market. *See* Money market
    mutual fund(s)
of municipal bonds. *See* Munici-
    pal bonds, mutual funds for
no-load, 74, 77
number to be owned, 81–82
open-end, 73
operating methods, 72–73
for over-the-counter stocks (OTC),
    178
portfolio construction, 82–85
purchasing, 77–79
record-keeping for, 66–67
sector funds, 85
selecting, 73–77
selling, 90
small-cap, 236
systematic withdrawal plans
    (SWPs) and, 71–72
taxes and, 6–7, 88–90
total returns on, 10
types of, 79–81
for utility stocks, 182
volatility of, 76–77

NAFTA (North American Free Trade
    Accord), investments benefit-
    ing from, 8–9
Naked option, 186

NASDAQ (National Association of Securities Dealers Automated Quotation System), 176
Composite Index, 385
National Association of Investors Corporation (NAIC), 64–65
National Association of Personal Financial Advisors (NAPFA), 244
National Credit Union Administration (NCUA), 37, 39–44
National OTC Index (NCMP), 231
National Quotation Bureau, 176
Natural gas company stocks, 181
NAV (net asset value), 10, 72–73, 78, 94
Negotiable order of withdrawal (NOW) accounts, 25–26
Nellie Mae loans (New England Education Loan Marketing Corp.), 286
Net asset value (NAV), 10, 72–73, 78, 94
Net income, 359, 364
Net-income-to-net-worth ratio. See Returns, on equity (ROE)
Net worth, 15–16, 364
New England Education Loan Marketing Corp. (Nellie Mae loans), 286
New York Cotton Exchange (NYCE), 218, 382
New York Futures Exchange (NYFE), 218, 383
New York Mercantile Exchange (NYME), 218, 383
New York Stock Exchange (NYSE), 218, 231, 382
Composite Index, 218
Nikkei index, 199
1994, special advice for, 6–13
1993 Tax Act, 6–7
North American Free Trade Accord (NAFTA), investments benefiting from, 8–9
Notes
floating-rate, 115
short-term, 64
Treasury securities, 124
NOW (Negotiable order of withdrawal) accounts, 25–26
Nursing homes, 285, 313–314
NYA (NYSE Composite Index), 231, 385
NYSE Beta Index (NHB), 231
NYSE Composite Index (NYA), 231, 385
NYSE (New York Stock Exchange). See New York Stock Exchange (NYSE)

Odd-lot index, 372
Oil and gas partnerships, tax status of, 331–332
Old Age and Survivors Insurance (OASI), 293
On-line services, 351–352
On-the-money calls, 189
Open interest, 220
Operating profit margin (PM), 362–363
Operating ratio, 364
Option funds, 80
Options, 185–194, 224
and calls
buying, 190–191
writing, 188–190
Chicago Board Options Exchange (CBOE), 382
defined, 185–187
on financial futures, 215, 229–230
"high rollers" and, 192–194
premiums and, 187–188
and profit protection for, 194
and puts, 191–192
restricted, 186–187
on stock indexes, 231–232
stock rights, 195–196
straps (triple options), 193–194
strips (triple options), 193
triple, 193–194
warrants. See Warrants
Oriental rugs, 105–107
OTC. See Over-the-counter stocks (OTC)
Out of the money, 186, 190
Out-sourcing, 209
Overbought-Oversold Index (OOI), 371
Over-the-counter stocks (OTC), 176–179, 382, 385
key indicators and, 177
mutual funds for, 178
The Pink Sheets, 177–178
selection guidelines, 176–177
small cap stocks, 178

Parent Loan for Undergraduate Students (PLUS), 283
Participation certificates (PCs), 145
Par value, 110
Passive income, 326
Pass-through securities, 143–147, 329
Payout ratio, 364–365
Pension Benefit Guaranty Corporation (PBGC), 48
Pension plans, 7, 47–48, 298–300. See also Retirement
Percentage buying value, 367
Percentage leaders, 373

Perkins loans, 286
Perpendicular spreads, 192–193
Personal computers, 350–352
Personal Loans For Accredited Teaching Organizations (PLATO), 286
P&F (point-and-figure) charts, 377–378
Physical, 220
The Pink Sheets, 177–178
Platinum, 226
PLUS (Parent Loan for Undergraduate Students), 283
Point-and-figure (P&F) charts, 377–378
Points, 332. See also Real estate
Poison puts, 113
Portfolios. See also Investments
building, 262–263
for couples, new, 339–341
customized, 338–347
for empty nesters, 342–343
for families, 341–342
management fees, 75
management of, 69, 73–74
protecting, 346–347
quality of, 36
for recent graduates, 338–339
for retirees, 343–344
setting up, 53–55
for small business owners, 344–345
upgrading, 59–60
Precious metals, 80, 224–226, 329
Preferred stock, 172–175, 362
Premiums, 110, 186, 259
options and, 187–188
for warrants, 197
Prepayments, on mortgages, 277. See also Pass-through securities
Prerefunded municipal bonds, 137
Price-earnings ratio (P/E), 160, 163, 165, 192, 365–368
Price quotes, 78, 125
Price-to-book-value ratio, 365
Professional help, 242–254
arbitration, 251–253
financial planners, 242–244
finding, 244–246
research, 248–251
stockbrokers, 244–249
Profit, operating, 359, 362–363
Profit margin (PM), 164, 362–363
Profit rate (PR), 167–168, 356
Profit-sharing KEOGH plans, 303
Program trading, 261–262
Property, plant and equipment, 360
property taxes, 278–279
swapping, 278

Prospectus, 77
for bonds, 112
for stocks, 201–202
Psychological indicators, 371–372
PTI (Technology Index), 231
Public limited partnerships, 332
Puts, 185, 191–192
Pyramid investment, 14–22. *See also*
Investors, types of

Quality
of bonds, 112–114, 137
of investments, risk reduction
and, 53
of portfolios, 10, 36

Ratios, 362–365
Real estate, 7, 332–333. *See also*
Housing
markets, 272–273
points, 332
real estate investment trusts
(REITs), 278–279, 333
rental income from, 333, 335
stocks in, 279
Real estate investment trusts
(REITs), 278–279, 333
Real estate limited partnerships
(RELPs), tax status of, 333
Receivables, 354, 359
Record-keeping, 65–67
Refinancing, of mortgages, 272, 277
Refunding provisions, 117–118
Registered historic district, 329
REITs (Real estate investment
trusts), 278–279, 333
"Relationship banking", 23–24
Rental income, 274–275, 333, 335
Repurchase of stock. *See* Stock buy-
backs
Research and development, 164
Retained earnings, 357–359, 362
Retirement, 288–318
annuities for, 305–306
and company pension plans,
298–300
early, 290
financial needs during, 292
457 plans, 301–302
401(k) plans, 299–301, 302–303
403(b) plans, 301–302
guaranteed investment contracts
(GICs), 302–303
housing options, 288–290
continuing care communities,
289–290
individual funding of, 7
IRAs. *See* Individual retirement
accounts (IRAs)
KEOGH plans, 303–304, 305
pensions, 7, 304–306

portfolios for, 343–344
for the self-employed, 303–305
simplified employee pension
plans (SEPs), 304–305
and Social Security, 7, 292–295
checking personal status,
293–294
described, 292–293
receiving, when to start,
294–295
Social Security, taxes on, 321–322
working during, 306
year-end tax planning and, 324
Returns
calculating, 172
on equity (ROE), 161, 181, 356,
364, 367
yields versus, 10, 76
Revenue bonds, 136, 139
Revenues. *See* Sales
Reverse dollar cost averaging, 265
Rights, on stock, 195–196, 259
Risk, 159, 160. *See also* Investors,
types of
high, for high returns, 205–239
maturities and, 46
reduction of, in portfolios, 53–54
risk-return relationship, 10
"Rule of 72", 4

"Salary reduction" plan. *See* 401(k)
retirement plans
Sales, 354, 357–358, 363–364
Sales-to-fixed-assets ratio, 363–364
Sales-to-inventories ratio, 364
Sallie Maes (Student Loan Marketing Association), 146, 147
Savings
annuities for. *See* Annuities
for college costs, 282
mutual funds and, 70
savings accounts, 24, 52, 333
money market funds versus,
35
savings bonds, 11
Savings Association Insurance
Fund, 383
Savings bonds, 11, 52, 286, 333–334
advantages of, 126–127
for college, 128, 280
interest calculations for, 127–128
Savings & Loan (S&L) associations,
26, 39–44
Scale order, 257
SDRs (Special drawing rights), 209
Secondary market, 110, 125
SEC (Securities and Exchange Commission), 383
Sector funds, 81, 85, 212
Securities, 51–53. *See also* Investments; Portfolios

Securities and Exchange Commis-
sion (SEC), 383
Securities Investor Protection Cor-
poration (SIPC), 32, 46–47
Self-employed persons, 303–305
Selling against the box, 260
Selling expenses, 358
Selling short, 133, 219–220,
258–261
warrants and, 199–200
Senior citizens, 7. *See also* Retire-
ment
SEPs (simplified employee pension
plans), 304–305
Serial maturities, 139
Series bonds. *See* Savings bonds
72, "Rule of", 4
Seven-year two step mortgages,
277
Short position. *See* Selling short
Silver, 225, 329
Gold & Silver Index (XAU), 231
Simplified employee pension plans
(SEPs), 304–305
Sinking funds, 118, 174
Small business investment, and
taxes, 321
Socially conscious funds, 81, 85–87
Social Security. *See* Retirement,
Social Security
SPDRs (Standard & Poor's Deposi-
tory Receipts), 233, 236
Special drawing rights (SDRs), 209
Speculation, 205–239
Speculation Index, 372
Spiders, 233, 236
Spin-offs, 233, 234
Splits, 233–234, 334
Spot market, 220
Spreads, 61–63, 187, 192–193, 220,
222
Stafford student loans, 286
Standard & Poor's Corp., 250–251
Composite Index of 500 Stocks,
385
Computer & Business Equipment
Index (OBR), 231
Depository Receipts (SPDRs), 233,
236
500 Index (SPX), 230, 384
400 Midcap Index, 385
100 Index (OEX), 231, 385
Standard & Poor's Stock Guide,
168
"Step-up" CDs, 29
Stockbrokers, 30–31, 244–249. *See
also* Brokerage accounts
Stock buy-backs, 233, 238–239, 368
Stock exchanges, 210, 382–383. *See
also* individual exchanges
Stockholder's equity, 362

Stock indexes. *See* Index(es), stock
Stock market
   European. *See* Foreign investments
   valuation of, 7–8
Stock Market Averages, 383–387
Stock market risk, 160
Stock options. *See* Options
Stock(s), 156–203, 286, 334. *See also*
   Convertible bonds (CVs);
   Stockbrokers
   active, 373
   analysis methods, 160–170
   beta of, 7–8, 161
   blue chip, 64, 157
   book value of, 160–161, 237
   bought directly from companies,
     63, 64
   buy-backs of, 233, 238–239, 368
   for capital appreciation, 161
   cash generating, 158
   common, 156–172, 362
     advantages of, 158–159
     risks of, 159–160
     and stock rights, 195–196
   cyclical, 157, 169–170
   described, 157–158
   dividends. *See* under Dividend(s)
   dollar cost averaging. *See* Dollar
     cost averaging (DCA)
   fees for, 62–63
   foreign. *See* Foreign investments
   growth. *See* Growth stocks
   high dividend, 169
   income, 168–169
   individual, mutual funds versus,
     51–53
   initial public offerings (IPOs),
     201–203
   of low/no debt companies, 173
   low risk, 157
   mining company, 224
   most active, 373
   natural gas company, 181
   new issues of, 201–203
   options to buy or sell. *See* Options
   over-the-counter. *See* Over-the-
     counter-stocks
   percentage buying value and, 367
   preferred, 172–175, 362
   price-earnings ratio (P/E). *See*
     Price-earnings ratio (P/E)
   price-to-book-value ratio, 365
   real estate, 279
   reasons for owning, 156
   record-keeping for, 65
   repurchase of, 233, 238–239, 368
   rights to, 195–196, 259, 334
   selling, timing of, 170–172
   small-cap, 178, 233, 234–235
   splits, 233–234, 334

   technical analysis of. *See* Techni-
     cal analysis (TA)
   telephone company, 181–182
   types of, 156–157
   undervalued, 367–368
   of utilities. *See* Utility companies,
     stocks in
   value of, 357, 362–364, 367–368
   volatility of. *See* Volatility, of
     stocks
   water company, 183
   winners, finding, 162–166
Stock splits, 162, 334
Stop-loss orders, 257–258
Straddles, 193
Straps (triple options), 193–194
Street name, securities held in, 255
Strike price, 186, 187, 199. *See also*
   Options
Stripped bonds
   FICO (Financing Corp.), 152
   municipal, pros and cons of, 137
   Treasury, 150
STRIPS, Treasury, 150
Strips (triple options), 193
Student Loan Marketing Association
   (Sallie Maes), 146, 147
Student loans, 146, 147, 286
Supranationals, 209
Swaps
   of bonds, 118–119, 322–323
   of property, 278
Switching privileges, mutual funds
   and, 69
Systematic withdrawal plans
   (SWPs), mutual funds and,
   71–72

Taxable municipal bonds, 136
Tax Act of 1993, 6–7
Taxes, 320–336, 362
   alternative minimum, 320
   capital gains, 7, 320–321
   and children, income shifted to,
     281–282, 283, 323
   computers for preparing returns,
     351
   deductions from income, 322,
     324, 325
   gifts to children, 282
   individual tax rates, 320
   and investments, directory of,
     326–336
   mutual funds and, 88–90
   property, 278–279
   provisions for, 359
   rate changes for 1994, 6–7
   returns using computers, 351
   shelters from, housing as, 273
   and small business investment,
     321

   on Social Security, 321–322
   state and local, 324
   tax-free income. *See* Tax-free
     income
   Treasury securities and, 125, 126
   year-end strategies for, 321–324
Tax-free income, 6–7, 11–12, 35–36.
     See also Municipal bonds
   mutual funds and, 89–90
   sources of, 325
   Treasury securities, 125, 126
Technical analysis (TA), 369–381
   broad-based indicators, 372–376
   Dow theory, 369–371
   psychological indicators, 371–372
Technology Index (PTI), 231
Telephone company stocks,
   181–182
Tennes*see* Valley Authority (TVA),
   147
TERI (The Educational Resource
   Institute), 286
Thin markets, 221
Time-shares, 275–276
Total return, 76, 161–162, 367
Trading limitations, 220
Trading volume, 375–376
Traveler's checks, foreign, 215
Treasury direct accounts, 121–122
Treasury securities, 12, 52, 121–129,
   335
   bills, 123–124
     CDs versus, 27–28
   bonds, 124–125, 326
     financial futures and, 227–228,
      230
     zero coupon, 150, 151
   Federal Reserve Banks (FRB),
     123
   financial futures and, 227–228,
     230
   mutual funds for, 81
   notes, 124
   purchasing, 121–123, 125
   sales commissions on, 62
   savings bonds, 126–128
   selling, 125–126
   STRIPS, 150
   taxes on income from, 126
   Treasury direct accounts, 121–122
   yield curve, 128–129
   zero coupon bonds, 150, 151
Trends
   charts and, 380
   corporate, 221, 353, 364–365
   economic, 55–56
Triple witching hour, 261
Turnover, 75
TVA (Tennes*see* Valley Authority),
   147
12b-1 fees, 75, 79

Umbrella policy insurance, 312
Underwriters, 201
Uniform Gifts to Minors accounts, 255
Unit trusts
  junk bond, 149
  municipal bond, 141–142
Universal life insurance, 309–310
U.S. Treasuries. *See* Treasury securities
Utility companies
  bonds from, 183–184
  Dow Jones Utility Average (DJUA), 385
  mutual funds for, 182
  with secure dividends, 181
  stocks in, 64, 180–183

Vacation homes, 275, 335–336
Value, of stocks, 357

Value Line, Inc., 251
  Value Line Composite Index (XVL), 231, 385
  Value Line Investment Survey, 97, 168
Vertical spread, 187
Volatility
  of mutual funds, 76–77
  of stocks, 7–8, 161, 199, 259, 264
Volume, trading, 375–376

Warrants, 196–200, 336
  Nikkei, 199
  selecting, 198–199
  value of, 197
Water company stocks, 183
Water revenue bonds, 139
Whole life (cash value) insurance, 308–310
Wills, 284

Wilshire 5000 Equity Index, 385
World Bank, 209

Year-end, tax strategies for, 321–324
Yields, 23, 76
  on bonds, 111–112, 114
  chasing, 21
  margin buys and, 268
  and risk, 10
  on Treasury securities, 124, 128–129

Zero coupon securities
  bonds, 63, 136–137, 149–153, 287, 327
  CDs, 29
  municipal bonds, 136–137, 150–151

INDEX OF SECURITIES

(Note: Closed-end funds are listed here as they trade as stocks.)

Abbott Laboratories, 9, 157, 161, 341, 342, 365
ACM Govt Income Fund, 97, 119
Adams Express, 98
Adobe Systems, 166, 178
Advanced Micro Devices, 339
A.G. Edwards, 173, 365
Airborne Freight, 384
Air Express International, 166
Alabama Power "C", 174
Alaska Air Group, 384
Alcoa, 384
Alexander & Baldwin, 8
Allegheny Power, 181
Allied-Signal, 169, 384
AMBAC Inc., 7
American Brands, 159, 169
American Capital Bond Fund, 341, 342, 345
American Capital Convertible Fund, 98
American Electric Power, 343, 345, 384
American Express, 344, 384
American Home Products, 157, 159, 264, 297
American President Lines, 384
American Strategic Income Portfolio, 279
American Telephone & Telegraph, 157, 159, 182, 263, 297, 384
American Water Works, 183
Ameritech, 170, 182
Amgen Inc., 178
Amoco Corp., 157, 159
AMR Corp., 384
Amtel Corp., 235
Analytical Surveys, 235
Andina, 209
Antofagasta Holdings, 209
Apache, 181
Apple Computer, 178
Arco Chemical, 169
Archer-Daniels-Midland, 264
Arkla, Inc., 384
Asia Pacific Fund, 212
Atlanta Gas Light, 170, 181
Atlantic Richfield, 159
Atlantic Southeast Airlines, 166
Attwoods plc, 209

Austria Fund, 98, 212
Avnet Inc., 165, 368

Bank of Boston, 158, 174
Banyan Systems, 235
Barclays plc (ADR), 208
Becton, Dickinson, 13, 264
Bell Atlantic, 165, 182, 368
BellSouth, 159, 182, 263, 297
Beneficial Corp., 166, 168
Bethlehem Steel, 384
Betz Laboratories, 159
Beverly Enterprises, 9
Biomagnetic Technologies, 9
Biomet Inc., 9
Blair Corp., 235
Block (H&R), 8, 161, 168
Blue Chip Value Fund, 98
Boeing Co., 165, 368, 384
BPI Environmental, 235
Bristol-Myers Squibb, 9, 13, 157, 159, 161, 169, 170, 263, 297, 365
British Airways (ADR), 208
British Gas (ADR), 208
British Petroleum (ADR), 208
British Steel (ADR), 237
Brooklyn Union Gas, 159, 170, 181
Brown & Sharpe, 237
Bruno's, Inc., 8
Burlington Northern, 9, 159, 169, 384

Calgon Carbon Corp., 365
Carolina Freight, 384
Carolina Power & Light, 63
Carpenter Technology, 169
Caterpillar Inc., 169, 264, 384
CBS, Inc., 157
CCU, 209
Cemex, 209
Centerior Energy, 183, 384
Central Hudson Gas & Electric, 183
Central Maine Power, 183
Central Power & Light, 13
Central Vermont Public Service, 63, 183
Chemical Banking, 165, 368
Chemical Waste Management, 165, 368

Chevron Corp., 157, 344, 384
Chile Fund, 212
Chrysler, 165, 368
CIFRA S.A., 209
CIGNA, 159
Citicorp, 263
Citizens First Bancorp, 63
Citizens Utilities, 183, 297
Clarcor, 235
Cleveland Electric Illuminating Co., 63
Clorox Co., 157, 159, 263, 264
Club Med, 339
Coastal Corp., 181
Coca-Cola Co., 157, 168, 264, 297, 384
Colgate-Palmolive, 159
Comcast Corp., 178
Commonwealth Edison, 263, 384
ConAgra, 161, 170
Connecticut Natural Gas, 181
Conner Peripherals, 237
Consolidated Edison, 384
Consolidated Freightways, 384
Consolidated Natural Gas, 159, 297, 384
Consolidated Rail, 384
Consumers Water, 183
Copec, 209
CPC International, 170
Crompton & Knowles, 168
CSX Corp., 161, 384

Delmarva Power, 181
Delta Airlines, 384
Deluxe Corp., 157, 159, 168
Detroit Edison, 384
Dexter, 159
Dime Savings Bank, 237
Disney (Walt), 64, 264, 384
Dominion Resources, 183
Donnelley (RR) & Sons, 9
Dow Chemical, 159, 169
Dow Jones, 264
Dreyer's Ice Cream, 166
Dreyfus Closed-end Strategic Municipal Bond Fund, 13
Dreyfus NY Muni Income Fund, 98
Dreyfus Strategic Govt Income Fund, 13, 343

Duff & Phelps Utility Fund, 98
Duke Power, 63, 170, 263
Dun & Bradstreet, 159
Du Pont (E.I.), 159, 166, 168, 174, 263, 384

Eastman Kodak, 159, 165, 264, 344, 368, 384
Eaton Vance, 8
ECI Telecom Ltd., 211
1838 Bond Debenture, 13, 98, 157, 343, 345
Eli Lilly, 13
Emerson Electric, 157, 161
Enersis, 209
Enron, 181
Exxon Corp., 63, 157, 159, 263, 264, 344, 384

Federal Express, 384
Federal National Mortgage, 168
Federal Signal Corp., 365
First Australia, 212
First Boston Income, 119
First Iberian, 212
First Maryland Bancorp, 158
First of America Bank, 168
First Philippine Fund, 212
First Union Corp., 168
Fleet Financial Group, 166
Fleet/Norstar Financial, 158
Florida Progress Corp., 10
Flowers Industries, 8
Foote, Cone & Belding, 157
Forest Labs, 158
Fort Dearborn Income, 119
Foster Wheeler, 170
Foundation Health Corp., 9
FPL Group, 181
France Growth Fund, 8

Gannett Co., 157
Gaylord Container, 235
General Electric, 13, 157, 159, 161, 168, 170, 263, 264, 384
General Mills, 157
General Motors, 159, 344, 384
Genuine Parts, 159
Georgia Power "M", 174
Gerber Products, 9
Germany Fund, 212
Gibson Greetings, 365
Giddings & Lewis, 235
Glaxo Holding plc (ADR), 208
Glenfed, 237
Global Income Plus, 98
Goodyear Tire, 264, 384
Green Mountain Power, 263
Growth Fund of Spain, 8

Harcourt General, 166

Hartford Steam Boiler, 169
Hawaiian Electric Industries, 63, 183, 263
Health & Rehabilitation Properties, 279
Heinz (H.J.), 157, 159, 168, 263, 264
Hershey Foods, 157
High Yield Income, 119
Honda Motor (ADR), 208
Hong Kong Telecommunications (ADR), 342, 343
Houston Industries, 384

Idaho Power, 183
Illinois Power, 263
Imperial Chemical Industries (ADR), 208
India Growth Fund, 212
Indiana Bell Telephone, 13
Indiana Energy, 159, 263
Intel, 340, 341
International Business Machines, 159, 263, 264, 344, 384
International Flavors & Fragrances, 173
International Paper, 384
Iowa Gas & Electric, 264
Italy Fund, 212

John Hancock Income Securities, 119
John Nuveen Co., 6
Johnson & Johnson, 157

Kansas City Power & Light, 181
Kellogg, 64, 157, 263, 286, 297, 339
Keystone International, 9
Kimberly-Clark, 9, 159, 168
Kmart, 159, 168
Korea Fund, 212
Kroger Co., 263

Lamson & Sessions, 235
Lannet Data Communications, 210
Lilly (Eli), 157, 264
Limited Inc., 166
Lincoln National, 159
Loews, 158
Long Island Lighting, 264, 343, 345
Long's Drug Stores, 157, 173, 264
Luby's Cafeterias, 8, 173

McDonald's Corp., 64, 157, 263, 384
McKesson, 159
Malaysia Fund, 212
Manor Care, 10
Marvel Entertainment, 340, 341
Masco Corp., 170
Maxus Energy, 181
May Department Stores, 168
MBIA Inc., 7

MCN Corp., 181
Meditrust, 279, 342, 343, 345
Merck & Co., 161, 170, 264, 384
Mexico Fund, 212
MFS Govt Markets, 119
MFS Special Value Fund, 98
Microsoft, 161, 178
Midlantic, 158
Minnesota Mining & Manufacturing, 157, 159, 263, 384
Minnesota Power & Light, 63, 183
Mobil Corp., 64, 157, 170
Montgomery Street Income Securities, Inc. 340, 345
Morgan (J.P.) & Co., 159, 263, 297, 339, 384
Mutual of Omaha Interest Shares, 343, 345

Nalco Chemical, 170
National City, 169
National Westminster (ADR), 208
Nationwide Health Properties, 279
Nevada Power, 183
New Plan Realty Trust, 13, 157
News Corp., Ltd. (ADR), 208
Niagara Mohawk Power, 384
Nicor Inc., 181
NIKE, Inc., 168, 339
Noise Concellation Technologies, 235
Nordstrom Inc., 178
Norfolk & Southern, 159, 384
Northern States Power, 159
Novo-Nordisk (ADR), 208
Nuveen California Muni Value Fund, 98
NYNEX, 182, 263

Ogden, 159
Old Kent Financial, 8
Oracle Systems, 166
Orange & Rockland Utilities, 159, 181

Pacific Gas & Electric, 384
Pacific Telesis, 182, 341, 342
Panhandle Eastern Corp., 384
Penn Central, 237
Penney (J.C.) Co., 159
Pennsylvania Power & Light "J", 174
Peoples Energy, 181, 384
PepsiCo, Inc., 263, 264, 339, 340
Petrol & Resources Fund, 98
Pfizer Inc., 157, 168, 264
Philadelphia Electric, 183, 384
Philadelphia Suburban, 63, 183
Philip Morris Companies, 159, 384
Piedmont Natural Gas, 263
Pitney-Bowes, 264
Potomac Electric Power, 159

Primarica, 158
Procter & Gamble, 63, 157, 159, 161,
        168, 170, 264, 384
Prowler International, 237
Public Service Enterprises, 181, 384
Putnam Intermediate Govt Income
        Trust, 13, 97
Putnam Master Income Trust, 119
Putnam Premier Income Trust, 345

Quaker Oats, 8, 64
QVC Network, 178

Ralston Purina, 8
Raymond James, 165, 368
Raytheon Co., 8, 165, 263, 368
Reader's Digest, 264, 286
Reebok, 158, 264, 286
Reliance Group, 165, 368
Reynolds & Reynolds, 166
Roadway Service, 384
ROC Taiwan Fund, 212
Rochester Telephone, 159
Rockwell International, 264
Rohm & Haas, 166
Rohr Inc., 237
Rollins, Inc., 264
Royal Bank of Canada, 157
Royal Dutch Petroleum, 13, 157,
        169, 297, 343, 344
Rubbermaid, Inc., 9, 264
Ryder Systems, 384

San Diego Gas & Electric, 63, 183
Santa Fe Southern Pacific, 384
Sara Lee Corp., 157, 161
SCANA Corp., 10
SCEcorp, 159, 384
Schering-Plough, 343, 344
Sciex Corp., 210

Scott Paper, 264
Scudder New Asia Fund, 212
Sears, Roebuck & Co., 159, 263, 344,
        384
Shaw Industries, 166
Shell Canada, 157
Shell Oil, 13
Shell Transport (ADR), 208
Singapore Fund, 212
Smithkline Beecham plc (ADR), 208
Smucker (J.M.), 8, 264, 342, 365
Snapple Beverage, 339
South Jersey Industries, 159
Southern California Edison "K", 174
Southern California Water, 183
Southern Indiana Gas & Electric, 13,
        159
Southwest Airlines, 166, 384
Southwestern Bell, 9, 159, 170, 182,
        263, 297
Spain Fund, 212
Spartan Motors, 166
Swiss Helvetia Fund, 212
Sysco Corp., 340

Taiwan Fund, 212
Tambrands, Inc., 157
TECO Energy, 10, 159
Telefonos de Chile, 209
Temple-Inland, 170
Templeton Emerging Markets, 212
Texaco Inc., 13, 63, 157, 344, 384
Texas Utilities, 263
Thai Fund, 212
Thomas & Betts, 159, 166
Tootsie Roll Industries, 158, 365
Toyota Motor (ADR), 157
Turkish Investors Fund, 212

UAL Corp., 384

Unilever (ADR), 157, 208
Union Carbide, 344, 384
Union Electric, 181, 183
Union Pacific, 157, 384
United Technologies, 384
United Water Resources, 183, 263
Universal Foods, 263
Upjohn, 169, 264
U.S. Air Group, 384
U.S. West, 182

Valspar Corp., 8
Virginia Electric & Power, 13
Virginia Electric "H", 174

Warner-Lambert, 13
Washington Energy, 181
Washington Post, 157
Washington REIT, 157
Waste Management, 161
Weiss Markets, 157, 173
Wells Fargo, 263
Western Publishing, 178
Westinghouse Electric, 344, 384
Williams Co., 181
Winn-Dixie Stores, 157, 264
Wisconsin Energy, 63, 170, 183
Witco Corp., 166
WMX Technology, 341, 342
Woolworth (F.W.), 384
Worthington Industries, 8, 170
WPL Holdings, 159, 263, 297
Wrigley (WM) Jr., 158, 168, 173, 264,
        286, 341, 342

Xerox Corp., 263, 264
XTRA Corp., 384

Zweig Fund, 98

MUTUAL FUNDS

AIM Constellation, 86
AIM Convertible Securities, 133
AIM Weingarten, 86
Alger Fund, 31
Alliance Quasar Fund, 202
Alliance Short-Term Multi Market, 214
American Capital Emerging Growth, 178, 202
American Capital Harbor, 133
American Capital High Yield, 148
American Capital Tax-exempt Insured, 140
American Fund's New Perspective, 211

Benham Adjustable Rate Government Securities, 279
Benham Target Maturities, 84
Benham Treasury Note, 83
Berger Funds, 286
Berger One Hundred, 83
Berger One Hundred & One, 83
Blanchard Flexible Income Fund, 12
Blanchard Short-Term Global Income, 214
Bull & Bear Gold Investors, 225

CGM Capital Development, 84
CGM Mutual, 83, 296
Calamos Convertible Income, 133
Calvert Money Market Fund, 86
Calvert Social Investment, 86
Calvert Tax-free Long Term, 141
Calvert Tax-free Reserves, 34
Capital Preservation Fund, 34
Colonial Utilities, 182
Columbia Special, 84

Dean Witter Value-Added Equity, 88
Dodge & Cox Stock, 83
Dreyfus Insured Tax-exempt Bond Fund, 140
Dreyfus Intermediate Tax-exempt Bond Fund, 141
Dreyfus Liquid Assets, 31
Dreyfus Tax-exempt Money Market, 34
Dreyfus Third Century, 86

Dreyfus US Govt Intermediate, 83
Dreyfus Worldwide Dollar Fund, 31, 36

Evergreen Fund, 31, 84

Fasciano Small Cap, 235
Fidelity Aggressive Tax-free Portfolio, 148
Fidelity Balanced, 73
Fidelity Contrafund, 86
Fidelity Global Bond, 84, 213
Fidelity Govt Reserves, 34
Fidelity Growth & Income, 83
Fidelity Growth Company Fund, 202
Fidelity Insured Tax-free, 140
Fidelity Market Index, 84, 88
Fidelity Massachusetts Tax-free, 34
Fidelity Municipal Bond, 141
Fidelity OTC Portfolio, 178, 235
Fidelity Overseas Fund, 211
Fidelity Short-Term World Income, 214
Fidelity Spartan, 31
Fidelity Spartan Govt Income, 83
Fidelity Spartan High Income, 148
Fidelity: Technology, 84
Fidelity Utilities Income, 182
Fidelity US Treasury Money Market, 34
Financial Strategic European Portfolio, 211
Financial Tax-free Income, 141
Flex-Fund, 31, 36
Founders Frontier, 84
Franklin High Yield Tax-free Income, 148
Franklin Minnesota Insured, 138
Franklin Tax-exempt Money Fund, 34
Franklin Utilities, 182
Freedom Global Income, 84

G.T. Global Government Income Fund, 213
G.T. Global Pacific, 211

Harbor Int'l, 8, 84

Harkwell Emerging Growth, 202

IAI Regional, 296
IDEX, 86
IDS New Dimensions, 86
IDS Utilities Income, 182
Ivy International, 84

Janus Venture, 84

Kaufman, 84

Lexington Gold Fund, 225
Lexington Tax-free Money Market, 34
Lexington Worldwide Emerging Markets, 84
Lindner Dividend, 73

MFS Managed California, 138
MFS Managed West Virginia, 138
Merrill Lynch Muni Insured Portfolio, 140
Merrill Lynch Short-Term Global, 214
MIM Funds, 286

Neuberger & Berman Partners Fund, 340, 341
Neuberger & Berman Selected Sectors, 84
New Horizon Fund, 202
New York Muni Fund, 141
Nicholas II, 235

Oppenheimer High Yield, 148
Oregon Municipal Bond Fund, 138

PaineWebber Master Global Bond, 213
Parnassus Fund, 86
Pax World Fund, 86
Pennsylvania Mutual, 235
Peoples Index, 88
Peoples MidCap Index, 84, 88
Phoenix Convertible Fund, 133
Pioneer Cash Reserves, 86
Pioneer Fund, 86
Pioneer Tax-Free Money Fund, 86

405

Pioneer U.S. Govt, 86
Prudential-Bache High Yield Corporate, 148
Prudential-Bache New York Money Market, 34
Prudential-Bache Short-Term Global, 214
Putnam Convertible Income Growth, 133
Putnam New York, 138

Rushmore US Govt Intermediate, 84

Safeco Growth, 83
Safeco Muni Bond, 84
Schwab 1000, 84, 88
Scudder Global, 84
Scudder High Yield Tax-free, 84
Scudder International Bond, 84, 213
Scudder Managed Municipal, 141
Scudder Short-Term Bond Fund, 11, 84
Scudder Short-Term Global Income, 214
Seligman California Money Market, 34
SteinRoe High Yield Muni, 148
SteinRoe Intermediate Municipal, 141
SteinRoe International Bond, 84
Stratton Monthly Dividend, 182

T. Rowe Price Adjustable Rate US Government, 279
T. Rowe Price European Stock Fund, 211
T. Rowe Price Growth & Income, 297
T. Rowe Price High Yield, 148
T. Rowe Price International Bond, 84, 213
T. Rowe Price International Discovery, 211
T. Rowe Price New American Growth, 84
T. Rowe Price OTC, 178
T. Rowe Price Spectrum Income, 12
T. Rowe Price Tax-free High Yield, 148
T. Rowe Price Tax-free Intermediate, 141
Templeton Income, 213
Twentieth Century Balanced, 83
Twentieth Century Ultra, 84, 202

United Services Govt Securities Savings Fund, 11
USAA Mutual Income, 297
USAA Tax-Exempt Money Market, 34
US Gold Shares, 225
US World Gold, 225

Value Line Convertible Fund, 133
Value Line Income, 83
Value Line Tax-exempt Fund, 141

Vanguard Energy, 84
Vanguard Equity Fund: Int'l, 8, 211
Vanguard Explorer Fund, 202
Vanguard High-Yield Muni, 84
Vanguard Index Trust Extended Market, 84, 88
Vanguard Index Trust 500, 88
Vanguard Investment Grade Bond, 84
Vanguard Long-Term Municipal, 141
Vanguard Muni Bond Insured Long Term, 140
Vanguard Muni Bond Intermediate Term, 12
Vanguard Muni Bond Limited Term, 11
Vanguard Preferred Stock, 297
Vanguard Prime Portfolio, 31
Vanguard Special Portfolio: Gold, 225
Vanguard Utilities Income, 182
Vanguard US Treasury Money Market, 34
Vanguard Wellington, 73, 84, 296, 297

Wellington (see Vanguard)
Winthrop-Focus Aggressive Growth, 235
Working Assets Money Fund, 86

ABOUT THE AUTHOR

NANCY DUNNAN is one of the nation's most respected financial advisers. She is the host of a regular call-in program on WNYC public radio in New York and writes a monthly column for *Your Money* magazine. She is the author of numerous books, including *How to Invest $50–$5,000, Financial Savvy for Singles, Your First Financial Steps* and the forthcoming *How to Make Money Investing Abroad.*

In 1991, Ms. Dunnan was awarded the Distinguished Service Award in Investment Education from the Investment Education Institute, an affiliate of the National Association of Investors Corporation.

A native of Fort Dodge, Iowa, Dunnan lives in Manhattan.